READING AND
WRITING
ABOUT
SHORT FICTION

READING AND WRITING ABOUT SHORT FICTION

EDWARD PROFFITT
Manhattan College

Harcourt Brace College Publishers
Fort Worth   Philadelphia   San Diego
New York   Orlando   Austin   San Antonio
Toronto   Montreal   London   Sydney   Tokyo

for Christopher
and Elizabeth
". . . more precious than rubies."

Cover: *Storm, Provincetown,* Joel Meyerowitz

ISBN: 0-15-575520-X
Library of Congress Catalog Card Number: 87-81873
Printed in the United States of America

Preface

This book provides an introduction to writing, an introduction to fiction, and an anthology of eighty-six stories. Chapter 1 focuses on the principles and process of writing—of both the paragraph and the essay—using Cynthia Ozick's powerful short story "The Shawl" as a reference point. In the course of chapter 1, the student also encounters all of the elements of fiction—plot, character, and so forth. Chapters 2 through 7 then examine in depth the central idea of theme and the various elements of fiction, always with an emphasis on the student's writing as well as reading. From eleven to fifteen very short stories follow each chapter introduction, enough to exemplify the points central to the chapter. Chapter 8 consists of ten widely taught longer stories, each with questions and writing assignments aimed at helping students consolidate the understanding they have gained from the previous chapters.

The use of very short stories (all under six pages) in chapters 2–7 offers several benefits. Because in these stories one or another of the elements of fiction tends to dominate, the instructor can illustrate the workings of fiction with exceptional ease and clarity. The stories are well suited for writing assignments for the same reason: it is easier for students to keep a character or a theme, say, in focus when reading a five-page story than a twenty-page one, and thus easier for them to keep a character, theme, plot, or whatever in focus when they write. Then, too, whereas only a handful of longer works can be treated in a semester, a great many stories of the length found in chapters 2–7 can be assigned (perhaps in combination with a few longer stories from chapter 8 and/or a novel), thereby allowing students a better view of the variety that fiction offers and the many possibilities for writing that it affords.

There is a subtler benefit for student writers as well: the great variety of structures that students will encounter in a semester can heighten their sense of structure generally. Finally, the stories assigned can easily be read several times, resulting in students' increased appreciation for detail not only in literature but in their own writing.

Throughout, then, the purpose of this book is dual. One aim is to help students toward a greater understanding, and therefore enjoyment, of fiction. The other aim, no less important, is to instruct students in the writing process. Both the writing assignments in each chapter introduction and the questions and assignments after each story embody these two aims, offering practice in working with a given element of fiction and, simultaneously, with the various types and structures of expository prose. Students will find help with terminology in the "Glossary of Literary and Writing Terms" on pages 589–94. The "Alternate Groupings for Comparison: Theme and Mode," on pages 581–88, suggest some of the many connections, thematic and formal, that can be made among the stories for purposes of discussion and, especially, writing. The "Appendix: A Brief Guide to the Use and Documentation of Sources and Related Matters," pages 558–80, offers advice on quoting, paraphrasing, summarizing, and documenting sources; it adheres to the style adopted by the Modern Language Association of America (MLA) in 1984.

We who have the opportunity to introduce students to the joys of reading literature and the excitement of discovering its inner workings through writing about it are fortunate indeed. My hope is that my own love of these endeavors as transmitted in this book will prove contagious.

Acknowledgments

I owe thanks to Terrence Paré and June Dwyer for reading and criticizing various manuscript drafts, to George Freije for sharing his ideas on narration, and to Mary Ann O'Donnell for her advice on the documentation of sources. As always, I am in debt to my wife, Nancy, for her sensitive and probing criticism. I should also thank Raymond Roswell for bringing Ozick's "The Shawl" to my attention and, of course, the many students whose questions and insights inform this book. I owe particular thanks to Marie Duchon, librarian extraordinary, and to Tom Broadbent, my editor and friend. Finally, I wish to express my appreciation to Tom's colleagues at Harcourt Brace Jovanovich, especially Ellen Wynn, eastern region manager, and Catherine Fauver, Diane Pella, Kim Turner, and Sharon Weldy, who were responsible for the book's production.

E. P.

Contents

4   CHARACTERIZATION   154

8 SOME LONGER STORIES FOR FURTHER READING

APPENDIX: A Brief Guide to the Use and Documentation of Sources and Related Matters

· 1 ·

READING AND WRITING

"HOW can I know what I think till I see what I say," says a character in an E. M. Forster novel. Exactly so. In large part we write in order to know, especially to know ourselves. Of course, we write as well to let others know what we think; and as writers we must never forget the audience whom we are addressing. Still, the most wonderful potential of writing is that it can show us ourselves.

For the purposes of writing, however, you might wonder why you should read fiction. After all, you are unlikely to be called upon to write a story outside of your English class, though you might choose to do so for your own reasons. One answer is that reading anything worth reading enlarges the reader's capacity for handling language. As to fiction specifically, because so many great writers have written fiction, reading fiction is one of the best ways of coming to understand the possibilities of sentence structure, for instance, or prose style. Moreover, to put it simply, fiction is fun. Everybody likes stories, so the reading of fiction in connection with writing combines instruction with pleasure.

As a subject to write about, fiction offers further advantages. Even the shortest story provides an abundance of materials to write on. Granted, the same is true of other types of writing (for example, the essay). Fiction's edge lies in its giving us something concrete to hold on to—plots, characters, narrators, and so forth. That is, while it stimulates ideas and thus gives the

1

reader something to write about, it also limits what can be said and so helps to organize the ideas it stimulates.

READING FICTION

Before we move to a more detailed discussion of fiction and the writing process, a few comments on reading fiction might prove helpful. These summary comments will be fleshed out in the chapters that follow. First, then, fiction asks you to be active as you read: to bring to your reading your experience of the world and also to open yourself to new experience as you actively construct in your mind scenes, actions, characters. As you read, bring to bear what you already know about people and the ways people behave; try to participate even when you come to stories whose characters seem alien, with values different from yours. All fiction asks is that you understand, not that you believe. Fiction is the reverse of propaganda, which seeks to close the mind to everything except the values its creators would have us accept. By asking us actively to participate in its unfolding design, fiction aims to expand our understanding of others and deepen our knowledge of ourselves.

"To participate in its unfolding design"—this phrase brings us to a central point about active reading. Part of coming to terms with a story is looking to see how it is constructed: which of the elements of fiction the author is working with and how. Somewhere along the line, active readers ask of stories questions like those that follow.

Of plot: What happens in the story? How are its incidents linked? What is the significance of what happens?

Of character: What kind of people does the story present? How are they drawn? What makes them do what they do? Is there anything to be learned from them?

Of narrators and narration: Who tells the story? Is the narrator one of its characters? Can the narrator be trusted? What is the narrator's (or narrative) point of view? Does the narrator somehow shed light on the story's meaning?

Of mood: What does the story make me feel? Why this mood (for instance, comic, grim, nostalgic, tragic)? How does the story's mood help establish its meaning?

Of style: What kinds of sentence structure does the author use? What kinds of vocabulary? Is the story's language figurative or mainly literal? What is the effect of the story's style? Why?

Of setting: Where does the story take place? Is its setting merely backdrop or does it have some particular significance? If the latter, what?

Of symbol: Is there anything in the story—an object, perhaps, or a descriptive detail—that could have meaning beyond its literal function in the story? In the context of the story, what special significance might this object, detail, or whatever have?

Of theme: What is the general, or overall, meaning of the story—the "big idea" that the elements in combination serve to establish?

Read a story first for pleasure, for its effect. Let it sink in. Then question how the story is made, for the meaning of a story depends immediately on how that story is put together. Students often ask about the "intention" of an author. The answer is that we can never know the author's intention directly; so we speak of the "implied intention," implied by how a story is constructed. Because no author has to write a story in a set way, the choices made by an author allow us to infer intention and arrive at meaning. But first we must observe what choices were made, or, again, actively consider the elements from which a story is molded.

The word *infer* brings us to a final point: active reading means the drawing of inference. Like life, fiction requires that we draw a host of conclusions from the evidence available, the difference being that even the densest of fictions directs us toward the proper conclusions, which life never does. Because a story is under the control of a writer, who can include or exclude anything, fiction is always a good deal more coherent than life. But we must be alert to the implications of what is before us. Sean O'Faolain, two of whose stories appear in this book, writes that

> a short-story writer does not directly tell us things so much as let us guess or know them by implying them. The technical advantage is obvious. It takes a long time to tell anything directly and explicitly, it is a rather heavyhanded way of conveying information, and it does not arrest our imagination or hold our attention so firmly as when we get a subtle hint. Telling never dilates the mind with suggestions as implication does. (151)

Implication is the writer's way of involving the reader, of creating an effect *in* the reader rather than just conveying information. But the reader must be sensitive to implications and make the appropriate inferences. Much of this book is aimed at helping you do that.

READING FOR WRITING

After you have read a story once for its effect, read it again, jotting down any ideas or questions it brings to mind and noting whatever feelings it evokes in you. Then, with the story as a whole in mind, consider its elements by asking the kinds of questions we looked at earlier. Mull over your jotted ideas and questions, seeking answers to the latter, and test the aptness of your feelings and responses. You might even wish to read the story a third time to carry out this testing and checking. Finally, taking everything into account, try to articulate the meaning of the story overall. Write down a few sentences about its theme and indicate why you now interpret it as you do, perhaps noting details in the story that have led you to your conclusions. Because most of the stories in this book are very short, following through on the plan just outlined should not prove unduly taxing.

Moving step by step, these activities fall under the heading of "prewriting." By following through on them as you read a story, you should arrive at a conscious awareness of your feelings about the story, some tested ideas that you could use in your writing on the story, and perhaps even a sense of direction in which your thoughts and feelings might take you as you write. As you turn to Cynthia Ozick's "The Shawl," go through the steps just outlined. Then, follow me as I go through them myself.

The Shawl

Cynthia Ozick

Stella, cold, cold, the coldness of hell. How they walked on the roads together, Rosa with Magda curled up between sore breasts, Magda wound up in the shawl. Sometimes Stella carried Magda. But she was jealous of Magda. A thin girl of fourteen, too small, with thin breasts of her own, Stella wanted to be wrapped in a shawl, hidden away, asleep, rocked by the march, a baby, a round infant in arms. Magda took Rosa's nipple, and Rosa never stopped walking, a walking cradle. There was not enough milk; sometimes Magda sucked air; then she screamed. Stella was ravenous. Her knees were tumors on sticks, her elbows chicken bones.

Rosa did not feel hunger; she felt light, not like someone walking but like someone in a faint, in trance, arrested in a fit, someone who is already a floating angel, alert and seeing everything, but in the air, not there, not touching the road. As if teetering on the tips of her fingernails. She looked into Magda's face through a gap in the shawl: a squirrel in a nest, safe, no one could reach her inside the little house of the shawl's windings. The face, very round, a pocket mirror of a face: but it was not Rosa's bleak complexion, dark like cholera, it was another kind of face altogether, eyes blue as air, smooth feathers of hair nearly as yellow as the Star sewn into Rosa's coat. You could think she was one of *their* babies.

Rosa, floating, dreamed of giving Magda away in one of the villages. She could leave the line for a minute and push Magda into the hands of any woman on the side of the road. But if she moved out of line they might shoot. And even if she fled the line for half a second and pushed the shawl-bundle at a stranger, would the woman take it? She might be surprised, or afraid; she might drop the shawl, and Magda would fall out and strike her head and die. The little round head. Such a good child, she gave up screaming, and sucked now only for the taste of the drying nipple itself. The neat grip of the tiny gums. One mite of a tooth tip sticking up in the bottom gum, how shining, an elfin tombstone of white marble, gleaming there. Without complaining, Magda relinquished Rosa's teats, first the left, then the right; both were cracked, not a sniff of milk. The duct crevice extinct, a dead volcano, blind eye, chill hole, so Magda took the corner of the shawl and milked it instead. She sucked and sucked, flooding the threads with wetness. The shawl's good flavor, milk of linen.

It was a magic shawl, it could nourish an infant for three days and three nights. Magda did not die, she stayed alive, although very quiet. A peculiar smell, of cinnamon and almonds, lifted out of her mouth. She held her eyes open every moment, forgetting how to blink or nap, and Rosa and sometimes Stella studied their blueness. On the road they raised one burden of a leg after another and studied Magda's face. "Aryan," Stella said, in a voice grown as thin as a string; and Rosa thought how Stella gazed at Magda like a young cannibal. And the time that Stella said "Aryan," it sounded to Rosa as if Stella had really said "Let us devour her."

But Magda lived to walk. She lived that long, but she did not walk very well, partly because she was only fifteen months old, and partly because the spindles of her legs could not hold up her fat belly. It was fat with air, full and round. Rosa gave almost all her food to Magda, Stella gave nothing; Stella was ravenous, a growing child herself, but not growing much. Stella did not menstruate. Rosa did not menstruate. Rosa was ravenous, but also not; she learned from Magda how to drink the taste of a finger in one's mouth. They were in a place without pity, all pity was annihilated in Rosa, she looked at Stella's bones without pity. She was sure that Stella was waiting for Magda to die so she could put her teeth into the little thighs.

Rosa knew Magda was going to die very soon; she should have been dead already, but she had been buried away deep inside the magic shawl, mistaken there for the shivering mound of Rosa's breasts; Rosa clung to the shawl as if it covered only herself. No one took it away from her. Magda was mute. She never cried.

Rosa hid her in the barracks, under the shawl, but she knew that one day someone would inform; or one day someone, not even Stella, would steal Magda to eat her. When Magda began to walk Rosa knew that Magda was going to die very soon, something would happen. She was afraid to fall asleep; she slept with the weight of her thigh on Magda's body; she was afraid she would smother Magda under her thigh. The weight of Rosa was becoming less and less; Rosa and Stella were slowly turning into air.

Magda was quiet, but her eyes were horribly alive, like blue tigers. She watched. Sometimes she laughed—it seemed a laugh, but how could it be? Magda had never seen anyone laugh. Still, Magda laughed at her shawl when the wind blew its corners, the bad wind with pieces of black in it, that made Stella's and Rosa's eyes tear. Magda's eyes were always clear and tearless. She watched like a tiger. She guarded her shawl. No one could touch it; only Rosa could touch it. Stella was not allowed. The shawl was Magda's own baby, her pet, her little sister. She tangled herself up in it and sucked on one of the corners when she wanted to be very still.

Then Stella took the shawl away and made Magda die.

Afterward Stella said: "I was cold."

And afterward she was always cold, always. The cold went into her heart: Rosa saw that Stella's heart was cold. Magda flopped onward with her little pencil legs scribbling this way and that, in search of the shawl; the pencils faltered at the barracks opening, where the light began. Rosa saw and pursued. But already Magda was in the square outside the barracks, in the jolly light. It was the roll-call arena. Every morning Rosa had to conceal Magda under the shawl against a wall of the barracks and go out and stand in the arena with Stella and hundreds of others, sometimes for hours, and Magda, deserted, was quiet under the shawl, sucking on her corner. Every day Magda was silent, and so she did not die. Rosa saw that today Magda was going to die, and at the same time a fearful joy ran in Rosa's two palms, her fingers were on fire, she was astonished, febrile: Magda, in the sunlight, swaying on her pencil legs, was howling. Ever since the drying up of Rosa's nipples, ever since Magda's last scream on the road, Magda had been devoid of any syllable; Magda was a mute. Rosa believed that something had gone wrong with her vocal cords, with her windpipe, with the cave of her larynx; Magda was defective, without a voice; perhaps she was deaf; there might be something amiss with her intelligence; Magda was dumb. Even the laugh that came when the ash-stippled wind made a clown out of Magda's shawl was only the air-blown showing of her teeth. Even when the lice, head lice and body lice, crazed her so that she became as wild as one of the big rats that plundered the barracks at daybreak looking for carrion, she rubbed and scratched and kicked and bit and rolled without a whimper. But now Magda's mouth was spilling a long viscous rope of clamor.

"Maaaa—"

It was the first noise Magda had ever sent out from her throat since the drying up of Rosa's nipples.

"Maaaa . . . aaa!"

Again! Magda was wavering in the perilous sunlight of the arena, scribbling on such pitiful little bent shins. Rosa saw. She saw that Magda was grieving for the loss of her shawl, she saw that Magda was going to die. A tide of commands hammered in Rosa's nipples: Fetch, get, bring! But she did not know which to go after first, Magda or the shawl. If she jumped out into the arena to snatch Magda up, the howling would not stop, because Magda would still not have the shawl; but if she ran back into the barracks to find the shawl, and if she found it, and if she came after Magda holding it and shaking it, then she would get Magda back, Magda would put the shawl in her mouth and turn dumb again.

Rosa entered the dark. It was easy to discover the shawl. Stella was heaped under it, asleep in her thin bones. Rosa tore the shawl free and flew—she could fly, she was only air—into the arena. The sunheat murmured of another life, of butterflies in summer. The light was placid, mellow. On the other side of the steel fence, far away, there were green meadows speckled with dandelions and deep-colored violets; beyond them, even farther, innocent tiger lilies, tall, lifting their orange bonnets. In the barracks they spoke of "flowers," of "rain": excrement, thick turd-braids, and the slow stinking maroon waterfall that slunk down from the upper bunks, the stink mixed with a bitter fatty floating smoke that greased Rosa's skin. She stood for an instant at the margin of the arena. Sometimes the electricity inside the fence would seem to hum; even Stella said it was only an imagining, but Rosa heard real sounds in the wire: grainy sad voices. The farther she was from the fence, the more clearly the voices crowded at her. The lamenting voices strummed so convincingly, so passionately, it was impossible to suspect them of being phantoms. The voices told her to hold up the shawl, high; the voices told her to shake it, to whip with it, to unfurl it like a flag. Rosa lifted, shook, whipped, unfurled. Far off, very far, Magda leaned across her air-fed belly, reaching out with the rods of her arms. She was high up, elevated, riding someone's shoulder. But the shoulder that carried Magda was not coming toward Rosa and the shawl, it was drifting away, the speck of Magda was moving more and more into the smoky distance. Above the shoulder a helmet glinted. The light tapped the helmet and sparkled it into a goblet. Below the helmet a black body like a domino and a pair of black boots hurled themselves in the direction of the electrified fence. The electric voices began to chatter wildly. "Maamaa, maaamaaa," they all hummed together. How far Magda was from Rosa now, across the whole square, past a dozen barracks, all the way on the other side! She was no bigger than a moth.

All at once Magda was swimming through the air. The whole of Magda traveled through loftiness. She looked like a butterfly touching a silver vine. And the moment Magda's feathered round head and her pencil legs and balloonish belly and zigzag arms splashed against the fence, the steel voices went mad in their growling, urging Rosa to run and run to the spot where Magda had fallen from her flight against the electrified fence; but of course Rosa did not obey them. She only stood, because if she ran they would shoot, and if she tried to pick up the sticks of Magda's body they would shoot, and if she let the wolf's screech ascending now through the ladder of her skeleton break out, they would shoot; so she took Magda's shawl and filled her own mouth with it, stuffed it in and stuffed it in, until she was swallowing up the wolf's screech and tasting the cinnamon and almond depth of Magda's saliva; and Rosa drank Magda's shawl until it dried.

[1980–U.S.A.]

First reading: What a story! I'm left with a host of feelings: pity, tenderness (for Rosa), outrage (for her guards), anxiety and fear (the fear of helplessness), and a sense of vertigo, my mind in a whirl from the rapidity of events.

Second reading: Having read the story a second time, I see that characterization and plot are prominent elements in it, and, because of my questions, that setting, narration, and style figure in as well. That is, all go into the making of how I feel and what I am made to see. The questions I've jotted down are these:

1. Where is the story set and why is the setting not spelled out?
2. Why the title "The Shawl"?
3. Why is the shawl called "magic"? To whom is it so? Why is the title not "The Magic Shawl"?
4. Why the deadpan narration? (Note that the narrator makes no direct comment nor expresses indignity or horror. And the description is understated, with most of the dreadful details—such as the state of the barracks—played down.)
5. Why the odd coupling of highly poetic imagery (for example, "She looked like a butterfly touching a silver vine") and savagery?

As to ideas, in general "The Shawl" makes me think of "what man has made of man" (Wordsworth). But the story is specific, making me engage myself fully with the plight of individuals. Focusing on Rosa, I am led to think about personal heroism and human endurance. I also see that Ozick touches on the fate of the individual in a world in which individuals do not count.

In looking over "The Shawl" again, I find that my initial feelings still hold: I respond in the same way, though the sense of helplessness seems even stronger to me now than on first reading. My initial ideas seem on the mark as well, but I feel that I haven't yet found adequate expression for my perception of the story overall. My statements are all too general and miss the power of this wrenching tale. By answering my questions I can perhaps come closer to an adequate statement.

1. Where is the story set and why is the setting not spelled out?

The reference to "the Star sewn into Rosa's coat" and the use of the word "Aryan"—details that might be overlooked on first reading—locate the story in Nazi Europe. That its location is not fully clarified, however, suggests that the story is not concerned with one historical moment only, but with a perpetual human possibility: that, alas, the Nazi atrocity is not the only such aberration perpetuated by humankind, but one of many. Also, the setting's not being specified adds to the sense of dislocation underscored by the march, seemingly from and to nowhere, described at the beginning of the story.

2. Why the title?

The title is apt because the shawl is a focal point and, indeed, the cause of the story's central action (a matter of plot). More, it helps us to feel Stella's need and Rosa's concern and deterioration (both matters of characterization). There's something wonderfully, horribly ironic about the title, too. What is a shawl?—something one wraps oneself in for protection. But it is exactly this—protection—that Ozick's characters lack. They are totally and horribly exposed, unprotected and helpless.

3. Why "magic"? To whom? Why not "The Magic Shawl"?

That the shawl offers any protection in this environment, as it seems to with respect to Magda, could almost make us believe in magic. But the title as it stands tell us otherwise. The shawl has the magic only of a security blanket. That it is believed to be magical by Rosa and Stella, however, tells us a great deal. Because of it we understand what has happened to Stella— her reversion to infancy, betokened as well by her fierce feelings of sibling rivalry. A belief in magic is a mark of early childhood. It is also a mark of mental degeneration. From the moment she begins to think of the shawl as magical, Rosa's deterioration is marked. That deterioration is complete, of course, at the end of the story, when Rosa herself becomes like her infant. What other response is possible? For here is true helplessness, its meaning laid bare. Nothing except magic could alter the situation.

4. Why the deadpan narration?

How many times has one been overwhelmed by pictures of the Holocaust or detailed descriptions of its horrors? And that's it—one is "overwhelmed." One can hardly grasp the larger picture because of the horrific details. By using a dispassionate narrator, who tells the story through Rosa's eyes yet uses descriptive detail sparingly and characteristically understates (both are aspects of the story's style), Ozick gains tremendous force. The disparity between statement and fact lends tension and irony, and gives all the more weight, finally, to the plight of the story's characters. At least, nothing else that I've read about imprisonment in a concentration camp has quite the impact of "The Shawl."

5. Why the coupling of poetic imagery and savagery?

The very beauty of some of Ozick's images underscores by way of contrast the hideous brutality inflicted on her characters. More, because we are seeing through Rosa's eyes as we read, the poetic quality of much of Ozick's imagery serves to portray Rosa as a gentle being yet also to reinforce our growing awareness of her deterioration. In context, the imagery in question a surreal quality (dreamlike, wild, crazed) about it, a quality that makes the world of the story seem mad. And indeed it is. Rosa's madness at the end is a token of the madness of her world. In such a world it is insane not to be insane. No wonder the sense of vertigo at the end of the story. It's as though we were falling helplessly, with no prop or stay, nothing for support and nothing to protect us.

My answers help me clarify to myself how "The Shawl" gains its effect. Narration, style, setting, and plot all move toward the same end. The functions of the first three I've already suggested. Plot is the story's driving force, leading to Rosa's disintegration incident by incident. But character is its focal element: the story concerns Rosa primarily and what happens in her. Now, perhaps, I'm in a position to express the story's meaning more adequately. Something I observe in my answers is the recurrence of the words "helpless" and "powerless." So noticing, I realize that what the story communicates most to me is the full import of what it is to be without even a modicum of control over one's own life. In a world in which power rather than pity is the ruling force, how truly terrible it is to be at the mercy of the whims of others. From the sense of dislocation at its beginning to the vertigo toward its end, Ozick's story details with extraordinary concreteness the effect of powerlessness on the human spirit.

FROM READING TO WRITING

Topic and Thesis

What, now, does "The Shawl" say to you? What do you have to write about? In deciding, first look to yourself. What do you want to write? What most moves you or stimulates you or delights you? Decent writing demands personal commitment. Then, what you choose must be feasible with respect to the length of what it is you are going to write: that is, just as your idea cannot be so narrow that you are left nothing to write, it must not be so broad as to require you to write a book (unless you are writing a book). For instance, "'The Shawl' is laid in a concentration camp" is too narrow; "man's inhumanity to man" is too broad. Though the phrase might serve as a title, it needs to be limited to, say, "Ozick shows in 'The Shawl' how truly barbarous humans can be." So stated, the idea could generate either a paragraph or a paper. The difference between the two is not a matter of thesis but of the number of details brought to bear for exemplification and the depth of discussion of, in the case of a story, its structure and impact.

But let's pause for a moment over the word "thesis." You might be asking, "What is a thesis? It is the same thing as the topic of a paper?" No, it is not, and the distinction is important. A topic is the general area from which a thesis is drawn. Consider the following examples of topics: "Character in 'The Shawl'"; "Powerlessness in Ozick's 'The Shawl'"; "Rosa's Psychosis"; "Power without Pity." I've deliberately written these phrases to look like titles because each could be a title. In fact, titles often indicate topic areas, stimulating in the reader thereby the question, "What about it?" Having a topic in mind, the writer needs to ask the same question. "Character in 'The Shawl'"—what about it? My answer is: "The central element of fiction in 'The Shawl' is character, for the story traces the breakdown of the human personality under such extreme conditions as Ozick describes." Here is my thesis, stated in a complete sentence (a thesis should be stated in at least one full sentence) that suggests how I might proceed—in this case, from exemplification of the extreme conditions in which we find Rosa to a consideration of her progressive breakdown under these conditions to a conclusion arguing that the story focuses on character because thematically the story is about character. The whole projected paper, notice, flows from the thesis statement, broad enough to leave something to say yet narrow enough to keep what is said specific and directed toward a specific end.

In sum, in deciding what to write, let your feelings guide you toward a topic. Then decide what it is *about the topic* you have to say. Write down your answer in at least one complete sentence. Then judge what you have written: is your statement still too broad, or is it now too narrow to be of any help to you or your reader? If either is the case, ask "What about it?" of your topic again and come up with another answer. Once you are satisfied that your statement is both one you feel committed to and one that will serve as a jumping-off point for the work to come, you are ready to write. Before we get to the writing stage, however, there are a few considerations that you should have in mind as you begin. The most important is the nature of your audience.

Considering Your Audience

Though what was said at the beginning of this chapter about writing as a tool of self-discovery is true, one usually writes for other people as well as oneself, and the written assignments you do in college will definitely have an audience. Because many judgments that one has to make when writing depend on whom one is writing for, it is important to judge one's audience at the outset and to keep that audience in mind when writing. To take an analogy, suppose you have to give a speech on some technical matter that you know thoroughly to a high school audience that knows nothing about your subject area. You would realize, no doubt, that you would have to simplify your presentation and define all terms. If you didn't, your audience would probably boo you off the stage. But if you were giving the speech to a group of experts in the same field, you could rely on their knowing your terms and being able to deal with the subject matter in its complexity. This second audience wouldn't know your approach (if they did, there would be no point in giving the speech), but they would have detailed knowledge of the subject area. In framing your speech, therefore, you would know what you could assume, or need not say, as well as what you must say to communicate your ideas.

The same is true of writing in general. Again, the audience must be judged and kept in mind. But how is the student's audience to be judged? To some extent, that depends on the type of course and the nature of the material, though what I'm going to say about writing done for a course in English applies generally to other courses as well. As to writing on fiction specifically, it is best to assume a knowledgeable audience, one that is familiar with your topic area and with literary analysis in general but not with your approach or the arguments you will bring to bear in backing up your ideas. In other words, you can assume that your audience knows about the technical aspects of fiction and has read the story that you intend to discuss. You need not define terms, therefore, or summarize a plot just for the purpose of filling your reader in. Rather, use your limited space to exemplify and argue your thesis. This is where your focus should be. By keeping your audience in view, you should find that the problem of deciding what need not be said and what absolutely must be said is greatly reduced. As a result, the writing process you go through should be facilitated.

Expository Prose

We shall return to this process shortly and consider the stages of composing expository prose—the kind of prose you are reading now and the kind college students are normally called upon to write. Before we move on, though, we should take a look at what exposition (or expository prose) is, both its functions and its types. As to function, exposition is prose designed to "expose," that is, to set forth facts, ideas, and opinions in an orderly fashion so as to come to a fuller understanding of some aspect of a topic oneself and to communicate that understanding to the intended audience. "In an orderly fashion" is a key phrase here. Because exposition has understanding as its goal, its greatest asset is clarity, and clarity demands that facts, ideas, and opinions be set forth point by point, with each clearly related to the next and with some plan of movement from point to point clearly followed. Perhaps this seems forbidding. But the more one writes, the less difficult writing becomes, just as the more time one puts in practicing a sport, the less difficult the sport becomes and the greater one's facility. One must know the ground rules to begin with, of course, as well as the purposes and ways of handling whatever equipment the sport entails. The same is true of writing. To continue the analogy, this whole chapter is aimed at acquainting you with the ground rules of exposition. As to equipment, we have the types of exposition, each type being a different piece of equipment that you need to learn how to handle. Again, expository prose is prose designed to set forth facts, ideas, opinions in an orderly fashion. Accordingly, there are three fundamental types of exposition, any of which a college student might encounter on assignments: informational, analytic, persuasive.

Informational. As its name implies, informational prose delivers information. If, for instance, you became interested in Cynthia Ozick, you might do some research on her life and write up what you've found. Or you might write an essay about the background of "The Shawl"—the anti-Semitism of the Nazis, the ghettos, the "final solution." Informational prose places two demands on the writer: first, it must be factual; second, like all expository prose, it must proceed in an orderly fashion. Some way of organizing must be chosen consciously according to the nature of the material and followed through.

Analytic.   From the Greek meaning "to break up," analysis entails first the breaking up of a subject into its component parts and then detailed discussion part by part. If asked to write on "The Shawl," I might select Stella for a psychological analysis: my thesis would be that she regresses to an infantile state marked by her narcissism, her attachment to the shawl, and her extreme feelings of sibling rivalry. Each step here would be taken up in turn in order to demonstrate the thesis. Or I might write on the effects of powerlessness as made manifest in "The Shawl," especially through Rosa's fantasies, her reaction to Stella, and her final breakdown. Here, too, I have thought into my material and thereby broken it into some of its constituents. What is left is to discuss each in its relationship to the general thesis (the effects of powerlessness as made manifest in "The Shawl") according to some plan of organization, with details from the text providing the tools of analysis. Analytic prose, note, can incorporate informational prose. In my suggested essays, for instance, I might want to give some background on Nazi Germany. But analytic prose is different in purpose from straight informational prose. Its purpose is not to set forth fact but to use fact to uncover and clarify meaning. For this reason, analytic prose is more complex than informational. Of the three broad types of exposition, it is analytic prose that you will most often be called upon to write in college. This is so because the ability to analyze in general is one of the main marks of an educated mind.

Persuasive.   Analytic prose overlaps with persuasive in that when writing an analysis one wishes the reader to accept one's ideas and when trying to persuade a reader one must be able to analyze in detail the reasons for the position one would persuade the reader to accept. And both analytic and persuasive prose can incorporate information. Yet persuasive prose is a category unto itself, for it is not so much ideas as judgments, feelings, and opinions that the writer of such prose hopes to make the reader accept. For instance, should your thesis be that "The Shawl" is a great work of art or, conversely, that it somehow fails to rise to its occasion, then you would be engaged in persuasion. You would be writing criticism in the purest sense of the word. Book reviews are of this order. Aimed at convincing the reader of a book's merit or lack of merit, a review proceeds to analyze why the reviewer concludes that the book is or is not worth reading. Analysis comes into play, but the goal is persuasion. Indeed, the difference between all three types of exposition can be defined in terms of goal: setting forth of straight fact (informational), delving into ideas stimulated by fact (analytic), defending opinions aroused by those ideas (persuasive).

WRITING THE COLLEGE ESSAY

Whatever one writes in whatever kind of format, it is useful to divide the work into stages and to proceed step by step. To exemplify, I'll use my own experience of writing and tell you what I do. After I have done all of the preparations I'm going to do, thought out all that I can beforehand, finished, in other words, the prewriting stage, I wind up with a good many notes, one note per slip of paper. Sitting down to my typewriter, I look through these notes carefully, dividing them into categories and trying to pull out something for a beginning and something for an end. With some plan of organization in mind, I begin to write. Generally, my notes help me to organize my thoughts and to stay on target more or less. But I don't restrain myself too much as I write my first draft. I let things flow as much as they will. Then, however, I become a critic; I look critically at what I've written and usually feel a moment of despair. It passes as I get down to the real work of writing, which is rewriting. I pinpoint what doesn't flow easily, where more support is necessary, where I have digressed from my topic or included material that is redundant. Next, I do a second draft, rearranging material and providing transitions when necessary, adding the supports that seem needed, and deleting what seems digressive or repetitive. I am usually left with a draft that can be checked for grammar, spelling, and the nuances of style. After checking and correcting, I am ready to type the final draft. Such is my writing process, which proceeds in steps because the mind cannot do everything at once. Note that what is crucial in the whole process is the matter of organization. Comprehensible organization is of primary importance if communication is to take place. So we shall go into the business of organization in some detail.

When you sit down to write, you probably have a number of things to say. How can they be brought together in an organized way? Everyone has this difficulty, and there are no rules to go by. But there are guidelines that can help in organizing, guidelines perhaps best exemplified by the one-paragraph essay (a form often required, incidentally, on examinations). The one-paragraph essay—hereafter called the discrete paragraph—is in its organization a model of the multiparagraph essay. To master the structure of the discrete paragraph, therefore, is to go far toward mastering the structure of the essay proper.

The Discrete Paragraph

Like the larger essay, the discrete paragraph has a beginning, a middle, and an end. The thesis statement—usually a sentence, though sometimes two sentences or even three—normally comes at the beginning. A thesis statement is necessary so that your reader will know what you will be talking about and so that you will too. When the writing of my own students goes wrong, it usually does so because there is no thesis statement to guide them as writers and me as the reader. So their work rambles on, making unrelated points and not conveying anything in particular. Getting a clear thesis statement and keeping it in mind is half the battle in writing. What follows the thesis statement (the middle) is a series of sentences designed to support that statement: to lend it credence, to develop its implications, to expand upon its meaning, to fill in the details. And the last sentence (the end) serves to conclude, ideally lending the paragraph a sense of wholeness and completion. Staying with "The Shawl" as our topic area, let us take a sample paragraph as example.

The Meaning of Powerlessness

Thesis

    The terrible effect of powerlessness on the human mind and spirit can be seen dramatically in Cynthia Ozick's "The Shawl" through the deterioration of Rosa, its central character.

Support

When we first meet Rosa, on the march, she has become physically decrepit, but her mind is still intact. She is still capable of rational choice (witness her decision, or her reasons for that decision, not to give Magda away).

Support

Soon after this, however, she starts to believe the shawl to be magic. Of course, it isn't—suggested by the story's title and more by the fact that it doesn't finally protect Magda but instead is the cause of her being discovered. That Rosa thinks of the

	shawl as magic, therefore, is our first
	indication of mental deterioration. Her way
Support	of seeing as the story progresses, that way
	communicated by some of the story's images,
	is a further indication. There is a sense of
	madness, for instance, when Rosa sees her
	baby thrown against an electric fence as "a
	butterfly touching a silver vine." At the
Support	end of the story her deterioration is
	complete: she has herself become an infant,
	a mad infant sucking on and trying to devour
	Magda's blanket. How truly terrible
Conclusion	powerlessness is, especially in a world in
	which power and not pity is the dominant
	force.

Notice that the first support statement sets up a contrast, for sanity must be established before one can speak of deterioration. The rest of the supports proceed straightforwardly. Note, too, that except for the last, each support can be divided into major support and minor support, the minor support serving to back up the major support, which in turn demonstrates, clarifies, or whatever the thesis. For instance, the third major support—that Rosa's way of seeing indicates her deterioration— is followed by an example, which could be called minor support. Finally, observe how the conclusion refers back to the thesis statement while taking that statement a bit further by generalizing it. This kind of conclusion is typical not only of the discrete paragraph but of the essay as well.

But what is most important to grasp about the sample paragraph is how the support material proceeds. The main writing problem posed by the discrete paragraph and by the essay alike is that of arrangement of supports. What should come first, what second, what third, and so on? To decide, the writer must think into the material at hand and see what kind of plan it suggests. Then the writer must consciously follow through. It would not be possible here to specify all the many ways material can be organized, nor would it probably be desirable. The most common ways should be mastered first, and those are:

Chronology.   Whenever something occurs in time, it can be written about in chronological sequence. Following the sequence of "The Shawl," for instance, the sample paragraph proceeds in chronological steps: from our first meeting of Rosa, when she seems sane, to the first sign of her deterioration, to the next, to the last. The markers of this movement, called *transitions* (we'll return to the subject to transition later), are: "When we first," "Soon after," "as the story progresses," and "At the end." Chronological arrangement is not difficult once its possibility is recognized. All one must do is follow the sequence of events as given, making sure the sequence is clear.

Spatial Sequence.   Whenever something exists in space or can be thought of in terms of space, spatial sequence can come into play: left to right or right to left, upward or downward, inward or outward, far to near, near to far, and so forth. For instance, in portraying Rosa one might begin with an overall physical description of how she appears from a few yards away and then focus in on her face, narrowing finally to her "bleak complexion." From externals, the writer might then move to the internal, or what we often refer to as the "inner space" occupied by our mental lives, and to Rosa's state of being. Because Rosa's inner life is what is most important, it comes last. Although spatial sequence governs this arrangement, note that order of climax (see page 20) is at work here, too. As with chronological arrangement, a spatial sequence must be clear to you when writing no less than to your reader when reading.

Comparison and Contrast.   Comparison and contrast is a prime way of understanding: in everyday life we frequently come to grasp something by seeing how it is like and how unlike something else. No less is true when we write. For the writer, comparison and contrast is a tool of analysis that also suggests ways in which the presentation can be organized. Technically, comparison emphasizes similarity and contrast emphasizes difference. The distinction, however, is not really helpful, for comparison involves contrast and contrast involves comparison. This is so because what makes a comparison meaningful is that the like things being compared actually have some significant difference, and what makes a contrast striking is that the unlike things being contrasted actually share some fundamental likeness. One could compare Magda and Stella, for instance. Both are infantile in their needs, behavior, and feelings. But what makes the comparison significant is the difference in their ages. It is this difference that makes the portrait of Stella meaningful given the context we find her in. Conversely, one could contrast Stella and Rosa, Stella's self-centeredness as against Rosa's selflessness, Stella's taking in contrast with Rosa's giving. Though different in their ages, they could be seen as two human types, their opposite responses to the same circumstance being typical of these types. Yet they both suffer massive regression by the end of the story. This is the point of the contrast: neither can finally cope with the unimaginable circumstance of the concentration camp.

As to organization, comparisons and contrasts can be arranged in several ways. What is important is to choose a way that will work for you and to follow through. For instance, both examples from "The Shawl" used above could proceed point by point: A/B, A/B, A/B (Magda/Stella, Magda/Stella, Magda/Stella or Stella/Rosa, Stella/Rosa, Stella/Rosa); or both could move in blocks: all of A and then all of B, with the comparison or contrast drawn in the B block (everything about Magda first, then everything about Stella in comparison with Magda; or everything about Stella first, then everything about Rosa in contrast with Stella—and then, whichever the mode of organization, the crucial point of difference or similarity and its meaning). Or you may find that some combination of these two types of arrangement is best on a given assignment, or that another type of arrangement entirely will serve you best (one could group material according to topics, say, and proceed topic by topic). Make your judgement according to the effect you desire and the length of the paper you have to write. If you wish your pace to be quick, use the point-by-point type of arrangement; if you wish it to be more leisurely, use the block type. If you're writing a long paper, it might be best to move point by point, each paragraph perhaps concerning one point of comparison or contrast (a block organization in a longer paper runs the risk that readers will forget some of what is in block A by the time they get into block B); if the paper you're doing is short, then blocking might be ideal. Whatever the case, what should come before what is a final decision that must be made. That is, let's say you've decided to move point by point: A/B, A/B, A/B. But which A/B to put first, which second, and which third? Here you should consider enumeration and especially order of climax.

Enumeration.　In enumeration, the writer usually lists in a thesis statement the points to be made in the paragraph or paper to follow, or at least suggests that a certain number of points will be taken up, and then goes on to develop them one by one. For example, one might state the thesis of a piece involving a psychological analysis of Stella as follows: "From the moment we meet her, we realize that Stella has regressed to infancy. Three major aspects of 'The Shawl' as it relates to Stella reveal her regression." "Three"—this is the key. The paragraph lays itself out: first her evident narcissism, then her attachment to the shawl, and finally her feelings of sibling rivalry. In arranging the parts in an enumerative structure, of course, the writer must have some reason for placing the first item first, the second second, and so forth. With respect to the essay on Stella, one could simply follow the story once more (chronology): "The first thing we notice about Stella is. . . . Next in the story we are told. . . . Finally, . . ." Or the parts could be arranged so as to build to the most important item (order of climax), which for me would be Stella's sibling rivalry. Whatever the choice, the principle is the same: the parts must be recognized, delineated, and ordered according to some thought-out plan.

Order of Climax.   I have saved order of climax—building to the most important item—for last because of its special importance. Climactic arrangement is of particular importance because it has application to all of the other ways of organizing. Notice, for instance, that while the sample discrete paragraph follows a chronological arrangement, it also reflects order of climax: it ends with its most dramatic example. To bring up the story's final scene in any position other than the last would be to fall into anticlimax, for that scene is the single most powerful proof of Rosa's deterioration, and so anything added after would seem irrelevant in comparison. At any rate, if your material suggests no other kind of arrangement, order of climax is always a possibility; decide what is more important and what less, then arrange your parts from the least important to the most. Even if you are working with some other kind of pattern, order of climax should never be out of mind. While exhibiting spatial sequence, the projected portrait of Rosa, for example, also moves by order of climax, from general appearance to state of being. And enumeration almost always calls for climactic arrangement, as does comparison and contrast. Order of climax, therefore, should always be considered when you come to arrange the parts of a paragraph and the paragraphs themselves into an essay.

WRITING ASSIGNMENT: A PARAGRAPH

Write a discrete paragraph of your own, perhaps using as a model the one that appears a few pages back. Take your thesis from some topic area related to "The Shawl" that interests you. State your thesis clearly so that you understand it; then gather your support materials, arrange them in some sensible way (remember to consider order of climax especially), and conclude. Try to make the paragraph coherent: that is, as you move from support to support, try to leave no gaps. The reader should always know the relationship of supports to each other and to the overriding thesis. Follow this diagram:

Title

Thesis Statement _____

Major Support _____

    minor supports _____

      (if any)

Major Support _____

    minor supports _____

      (if any)

Major Support _____

    minor supports _____

      (if any)

Conclusion _____

The Essay

Like the discrete paragraph, the full essay (of any length) has a beginning, a middle, and an end. And, again, the beginning usually entails the statement of the thesis, the middle involves support and demonstration, and the end serves to conclude. As we look at each in turn, keep in mind this brief outline of the functions of beginning, middle, and end. For the shape each of these takes depends upon its function.

The Beginning. The beginning of any essay is special—and especially difficult to write. The problem the beginning poses is how to present or lead in to the thesis statement. Simply to state the thesis in the first sentence would usually seem too abrupt. Most often, it is better to lead readers gently from wherever they are mentally to where one wants them to be. For this reason, a particularly useful kind of beginning is "the funnel," which very naturally leads the reader into the thesis statement. Also, of the many ways to begin, the funnel has the advantage of being the only kind of beginning that will *always* work.

The funnel can narrow down to a thesis statement in various ways: you may lead to your thesis by way of analogy, for instance, or some striking comparison that touches on some aspect of your thesis and so can lead to its explicit statement. For a thesis that is likely to be new to your reader, a way to set up a funnel beginning is to start with some aspect of the thesis that you know is familiar to your reader and then move toward the full statement of your thesis. Contrast, too, is a fine way to move, perhaps from something you consider wrong to a statement of what you are going to argue is right (your thesis), or from a negative to a positive way of viewing something. And many writers move from the general to the particular: from a generalization related to the thesis to the specific thesis itself. Whatever particular strategy you choose, the funnel beginning draws the reader naturally and smoothly to the thesis statement. The funnel also allows the writer to move smoothly into the material at hand because the thesis comes immediately before the first support paragraph. Thus, the funnel provides a jumping-off point for the essay as a whole.

A sample should help clarify. Notice that the writer begins with material related to the thesis but not with the thesis itself; moving from the general to the particular, the paragraph builds down to the particular thesis stated at the end. Observe, too, how the structure of the paragraph more or less lays out the structure of the entire essay that it would head.

        Adult behavior can sometimes be illuminated by a
    knowledge of the characteristics of the infant mind.
    The hallmark of infancy is the need for security. Born
    into a condition of helplessness, the infant must learn
    to devise strategies to feel secure——thus the famous
    "security blanket." Infantile narcissism is another
    kind of security blanket, protecting the unformed self
    by making it an enclosed world unto itself. The infant's
    self—centeredness finds expression in many ways, notably
    in sibling rivalry if there is a sibling in the family.
    In Cynthia Ozick's "The Shawl," Stella, though not an
    infant, exhibits all of these traits, her regression to

`infancy being the result of her enforced condition of`
`helplessness.`

Now the paper to follow should not be so hard to write: subsequent paragraphs or clusters of paragraphs would concern Stella's attachment to the shawl, her evident narcissism, and her feelings of sibling rivalry, all discussed in light of "her enforced condition of helplessness" and the effects of helplessness on the human mind and spirit. Much of the work of writing lies in writing a strong beginning, whenever it is written.

Note this last phrase. There is no rule that the beginning must be written first. To be sure, there are certain advantages of writing it up front: a good beginning, as we've noted, can guide the writer through the middle paragraphs; and because it leads to a clear thesis statement, a funnel beginning can help the writer stay on track. Nevertheless, as long as you have a fairly clear thesis in mind, you may find that it is best to write the middle first, or even the end, and then to work on the beginning. People work in different ways, and even people who customarily start with the beginning may need to proceed in some other way on a given assignment. A well-constructed beginning makes what follows seem natural to the reader and satisfying. But because when the beginning was written is irrelevant to any audience, it should not be of concern to the writer. What is important is that the beginning as finally written be well constructed. Then it will accomplish its task: to engage the reader, to inform the reader as to what the writer is going to do, and to make the reader wish to read on.

Middle Paragraphs.   Middle paragraphs contain the meat of an essay. Here is where the thesis is exemplified, argued, demonstrated, or whatever. With the exception of paragraphs whose purpose is to provide transition only, each middle paragraph comes from and is somehow related to the thesis. That is, each develops some central idea (one per paragraph) that backs up, demonstrates, exemplifies, or otherwise expands upon the thesis statement of the essay. The central idea of each middle paragraph is usually stated in a single sentence, often called a "topic sentence," which, though it may be found anywhere in the paragraph, is most commonly found at its beginning.

Like the discrete paragraph, each middle paragraph must be organized internally according to an appropriate plan—the ways of organizing discussed previously all apply to middle paragraphs. In addition, like individual sentences in a paragraph, the individual paragraphs in a paper must be arranged into some comprehensible sequence. Just as one must decide what to put first, what second, and so on within a single paragraph, one must do so with the middle paragraphs in the essay as a whole. Should you be writing on the plot of a story, chronology might serve, or a spatial sequence if your concern is the setting; if your thesis entails comparison and contrast, then that may be your governing strategy; or perhaps enumeration is what is called for because your thesis involves a list of steps. And, of course, order of climax is always to be considered, now with respect to the arrangement of paragraphs as they move one to the other.

Having a suitable design in the first place and following through on it will provide a coherent foundation for whatever paper you write. But transitional links between middle paragraphs are often needed, just as they are within paragraphs. Whenever a particular progression or relationship is not clear—even when the overall structure of the paper is apparent— some phrase, sentence, or even a whole transitional paragraph must be supplied to make the relationship clear and the movement fluid. In the sample essay that follows on page 25, note how the paragraphs are linked by phrases transitional in design and how, because of these transitions as well as the overall chronological design, the paragraphs move easily one to the next.

The Conclusion.   Like beginning, concluding demands some type of stratagem. Now, what can be done to tie things up and give a sense of completion? A summary is one possibility. The summary has the advantage of pulling everything together and of reminding readers of the main points made in an essay, some of which they may have lost sight of. Especially when writing a long paper, consider the summary as a possible way of ending. It is not generally as well suited to the short essay, however, for readers can be counted on to retain the points of an argument through five or six paragraphs. Another way of ending, suitable for the long and short paper alike, is to restate the thesis in such a way that it now applies not only to one's specific topic but to a wider area of things or number of people. This movement is from the particular to the general. Or one can ask a question of some central point made in the middle and come to a conclusion by answering it. This is the pattern of the following sample concluding paragraph, which also makes reference to the governing thesis as it fans out to the generalization of its last sentence.

       But why does Stella regress in these ways? The
    answer "The Shawl" points to is, clearly, her enforced
    condition of helplessness. With no control whatever
    over her life in the external world, she falls back upon
    the strategies of the infant for a fantasy sense of

```
control. It might be noted that much the same is true of
Rosa herself at the end of "The Shawl." Through Stella
and, at the last, through Rosa, Ozick brings home with
great force what it means to be a victim: it is to be a
child with no possible place of refuge except one's own
mind.
```

Two things in particular should be noted about this paragraph. First, through the phrases "her enforced condition of helplessness" and "strategies of the infant," it refers back to the thesis as stated at the end of the sample thesis paragraph (page 22). This referring back helps give an essay a sense of roundness and thus closure. Second, proceeding from question to answer, the sample concluding paragraph achieves final resolution in a generalized conclusion. This structure, "the reverse funnel," opens out to suggest wider applicability.

As I said when describing my own process of writing, I try to put aside something for my ending as I go through my notes. And if I have nothing at that point, I keep thinking about the end as I am writing and jotting down any ideas that come. Endings are hard, but they are important and so must be given due consideration. They're important because they're what readers are left with, the last word, the final chance the writer has to make the point. So don't slight the ending. Try to build to a climax at the end and to leave your reader with a sense of completion. Left thus, the reader will be more likely to remember and ponder the rest of your essay.

Sample Essay. Let us now draw the whole thing together, beginning, middle, and end. An expansion of the discrete paragraph found on page 16, the sample essay that follows sums up in its structure the various points about organization and coherence made so far. Observe where the thesis statement comes and how it is led to; notice how the middle paragraphs are related to it and to each other, as well as internally organized and arranged; mark how the last paragraph moves from the particular to a conclusion general in scope (the reverse funnel). Then try your hand at a like essay of your own.

```
                    The Meaning of Powerlessness
```

```
\  Funnel    /         For human beings to retain a sense of
 \ beginning/
  \        /      integrity and, indeed, even keep our sanity,
   \      /
    \    /        we need some degree of personal freedom.
     \  /
      \/          Stripped of autonomy entirely, we wither.
      ↓     ↓
```

Thesis

The self literally ceases to be itself
because it can have no effect in the
external world. Forced into a condition like
that of childhood, we tend to revert to
childish modes of thought and feeling. This
terrible effect of powerlessness on the
human mind and spirit can be seen
dramatically in Cynthia Ozick's "The Shawl"
through the deterioration of Rosa, its
central character.

Topic
sentence

Support

When we first meet Rosa, on the march,
she has become physically decrepit, but her
mind is still intact. Despite the
dislocating effect of the march itself and
the foul treatment received on it, she is
still capable of logical thought and
rational choice. Thus, she conceives a plan
to give Magda away to someone at the side of
the road; thinking the plan through,
however, she realizes its impossibility and
so rejects it. Here we have the operation
of a rational mind. How different from this

Transition

Rosa is the Rosa we leave at the end of the
story. Her deterioration proceeds subtly
but inevitably.

Support

The first mark of that deterioration
occurs soon after the incident above.
Suddenly we are told that "It was a magic
shawl," and this idea is pursued. Because

Support

Ozick's narrator makes us see through Rosa's
eyes, we know that it is Rosa who has started
to believe in magic. That the shawl is not

Support | magic, of course, is suggested by the story's title: the shawl is merely a shawl.

Support | Even more, the fact that it doesn't finally protect Magda but instead is the cause of her being discovered evidences its lack of magic properties.

Support | But that Rosa should come to feel the shawl to be magic quietly reveals her deterioration, or the start thereof.

Topic sentence | Resorting to a childish belief in magic, she is slowly receding into the confines of her own mind.

Topic sentence | Rosa's way of seeing as communicated by some of the story's images, especially at the end, is further indication that she is receding into herself.

Support | In the context of the prison camp as described, images like "Jolly light," "a clown out of Magda's shawl," "light tapped the helmet and sparkled it into a goblet," and, most pointedly, "a butterfly touching a silver vine" suggest a mind projecting itself onto the world in order thus to change reality.

Support | There is a surreal quality to these images in context, a quality that imparts a growing sense of madness.

Topic sentences | And Rosa does go mad. At the end of the story her deterioration is complete: she has herself become an infant sucking on and trying to devour Magda's blanket.

Support | With no choice possible as to external action, she retreats into herself entirely.

Support | But nothing I can say could communicate the final stage

of her deterioration as well as the last
lines of the story itself:

> so she took Magda's shawl and
> filled her own mouth with it,
> stuffed it in and stuffed it in,
> until she was swallowing up the
> wolf's screech and tasting the
> cinnamon and almond depth of
> Magda's saliva: and Rosa drank
> Magda's shawl until it dried.

Rosa's steady deterioration to this
point, portrayed subtly and in depth,
communicates vividly the effects of
powerlessness on the mind and spirit. Every
human being needs a sense of control,
however minimal, over his or her own life.
Robbed of this sense, the mind and spirit
wither. Stripped of autonomy, what can the
self do but, like Rosa, fall into fantasy
and then madness? How truly terrible
powerlessness is, but especially in a world
in which power and not pity is the dominant
force.

Reverse
funnel
conclusion

WRITING ASSIGNMENT: AN ESSAY

Using the essay you've just read as a model for structure, write a full essay of
your own. If you wish, take the discrete paragraph you wrote for the last assignment
(page 16) and develop it into an essay, as was done with respect to the essay we've
just looked at. Or get a new topic and thesis entirely if you would rather start afresh.
I suggest that you read the next section before writing or at least before rewriting. It
should help to clarify the nature of and need for transitional material.

WRITING TO REWRITING

Writing is difficult, so don't think that there's something wrong with you if you have difficulty doing it. Everyone does. What helps is to understand that, because the mind can't do everything at once, writing must proceed in stages, as I suggested when discussing the writing process: first a few jottings; then some thought about how to structure ideas; then a rough draft; then, usually, extensive revision; and finally proofreading and final typing. We will now turn to revision, or rewriting, which many writers consider to be the crucial stage of the writing process.

Revision, too, entails a number of steps. First of all, check what you have written, paragraph by paragraph, against your thesis statement. Should you find that you've wandered away from the point, then either bring the suspect passage into line or cut it out. You may even find that most of a paper doesn't go with the thesis as stated. One solution here would be to change the thesis. Because writing is a dynamic process, one never truly knows what one has to say until it is said. It is not surprising, therefore, that writers sometimes discover somewhere along the way that they actually have something other to say than what they initially thought they were going to say. Second, check the arrangement of your paragraphs to make sure that they move easily one to the next. You might find that some paragraphs should be repositioned. So reposition, making sure to change any transitional words or phrases as necessary. Third, check each paragraph internally for unity and coherence (see below), and check that you have provided whatever transitions are necessary between paragraphs. Finally, every time you look over what you have written, keep an eye out for what can be polished—a better word here, a more felicitous expression there—and polish as you go along.

Unity and Coherence

The main business of rewriting is to make sure that everything is to the point and follows as logically and gracefully as possible. These are the marks of readable prose. Prose that does not show unity and coherence is like the rambling of one of those radio talk-show callers who go on and on aimlessly. They are painful to listen to. Readers, too, want the writer to make a point and to stick to it (this is what "unity" means), as well as to relate all secondary ideas to it and to each other (coherence). Unity and coherence, therefore, should be checked and rechecked as you go through the process of rewriting.

Unity and coherence can be gained in a number of ways. Simple deletion, for instance, is a ready way of improving unity. If some sentence seems irrelevant, drop it. However, you may want to keep some of the information expressed in the sentence. Here, subordination will solve the problem: put the information in a subordinate clause or a phrase of some sort and combine the phrase or clause with a sentence with which it makes sense. Subordination is a technique of coherence as well as of unity. When sentences do not follow readily, the problem can often be solved by subordinating one idea to another, thereby expressing the relationship of ideas grammatically. Coherence can be gained as well by overt explanation of how a support relates to the thesis or to another support if the relationship is not clear. And, as we've seen, coherence is gained by the use of transitions, the sole purpose of which is to spell out the kind of relationship that exists between sentences and paragraphs when that relationship is not self-evident. An example should underscore the difference between writing that seems aimless because it lacks unity and coherence and writing that, because it is unified and coherent, stays to a point and makes it. Compare the sets of paragraphs that follow to see how the first set has been made readable by deletion, subordination, and the introduction of transitions when called for.

1.   Cynthia Ozick is a very fine writer. Her story "The Shawl" is laid in Nazi Germany. Six million Jews were killed by Germans. My grandfather took part in World War Two. He told me how horrible the death camps were where Jews were systematically slaughtered. They were forced into the camps. It must be a terrible thing to be deprived of liberty and put into a stinking hole. Many people went mad in the death camps.

   Rosa is a good woman, unselfish and caring. She reasons with herself whether or not to give her baby away. Magda is a poor, pathetic creature who is slowly starving to death. Rosa decides not to give her away because of the danger. She is rational.

Her physical condition is bad. She goes
mad. We see her sucking the shawl at the
end of the story.

2.

Deletion and Subordination

Subordination Deletion

[Polishing]

Cynthia Ozick depicts in her story
"The Shawl" the time when six million Jews
were killed by the Nazis. Forced into death
camps, they were systematically
slaughtered. It must surely be terrible to
be deprived of liberty and placed in a
stinking hole. No wonder many people went
mad in these so-called "camps."

Subordination Transition between paragraphs

Transition Subordination

Subordination

Transition

Transition and Subordination

A good woman, unselfish and caring,
Rosa is an example of how systematic
dehumanization can drive a person mad. At
first, she is clearly sane, evidenced by her
reasoning with herself whether or not to
give away Magda, a poor, pathetic creature
who is slowly starving to death. That Rosa
decides not to give away her baby because of
the danger demonstrates her sanity despite
her physical condition. But over the course
of the story she goes mad. At the end, when
we leave her sucking Magda's shawl, we
realize fully the effects on the mind that
dehumanization can have.

The first set of paragraphs lacks both unity and coherence from the first sentence on. In the revision, the first sentence has been deleted because, although it may be true, it really has nothing to do with the business at hand. The second sentence is not strictly true and it relates to nothing around it as stated. In fact, none of the first four sentences shows anything like a clear relationship; the reader is left to decipher what possible connections there could be. Few readers would even try. Read the first four sentences again quickly. When I do, I'm tempted to add, "and how's your grandmother?" Everything seems to come from left field. To be sure, except for the first, each sentence relates to World War Two. But how do they relate to each other? That's the question. And the answer is that as stated they don't. Look now at the first revised paragraph. To gain unity, the first and fourth sentences have been dropped, and the second and third sentences have been combined by subordination for the sake of coherence, as have been the fifth and sixth. The last two sentences have been retained but polished. Because similar problems mark the second paragraph of the original and similar solutions are found in its revised counterpart, you should be able to spot both problems and solutions yourself. Notice, though, the transition supplied between the two revised paragraphs and how it makes the relationship clear and meaningful. This is the sort of thing that rewriting entails. Almost any piece of writing can be made to be unified and coherent. But the writer must spot the changes needed to effect unity and coherence and then go about making them.

Proofreading and Titling

After you have gone through all of the steps outlined thus far in this section and have revised accordingly, you should have a final draft in hand. You're close to the end. What's left is careful proofreading. Because, once more, the mind cannot do everything at once, proofreading should also be done in steps. As I always suggest to my own students (and this is my own practice), read your final draft checking for subject-verb agreement only. Then read it again checking only for pronoun reference and agreement. These are potential problem spots of our language and therefore they require careful attention. Next, read your paper for spelling, punctuation, and other matters of mechanics, preferably aloud so that you can also check the sound of your prose. Watch especially for errors that you know you are prone to make.

After you have finished with these steps, give your paper a title. To be sure, you may have a tentative title in mind from the beginning. But it is best to wait until the last to make a final decision about the title, for one cannot be sure of what one has to say until it is said. A good title, note, should point to the thesis without stating it: for example, the title "Power without Pity" for a paper on "The Shawl" would point directly to a thesis about the terrible effects of helplessness on the story's characters. A title—the first thing a reader sees—is a tool for focusing the reader's attention and drawing the reader into the writer's discourse. Having decided on a title, you are now ready for the final typing, after which you should check your work one last time for typographical errors.

We come back to where we began. As you read the stories in this book, read with an eye toward writing. The reading should help stimulate ideas; the writing will help concretize those ideas and thus help you better understand both the story under consideration and yourself in relationship to it. Reading and writing alike should bring both the world and the self into play. "Into play"—the phrase leads me to my final point. Don't forget that reading, certainly, and even writing can be wonderful fun. The play of mind is full of delight when the mind allows itself the freedom to play.

·2·

FICTION/THEME

THE REALM OF FICTION

We all respond to fiction. How many of us did not like to be read stories by our parents or teachers when we were children? How many of us do not go to the movies from time to time or watch television, the fare of which is primarily fiction? And we devise our own fictions every night when we dream. Probably because of the structure of the brain itself, fiction continues to have power both to move us and to expand our understanding. But what is fiction?

Because dreams are fictions, we can move to an answer by way of dreams. Think of a dream you've had that seemed of some particular significance when you awoke. Of what was the dream composed? Surely it entailed some people in some locale doing something, as well as an "author" (you as dreamer) and feelings of some sort. Although both people and locale were most likely drawn from the external or "real" world, the dream created its own world. When you awoke, you might have wondered about the meaning of the dream and even tried to interpret it in light of its details and the way it made you feel. Your dream, then, became a text and you its reader. If you went further and told your dream to someone else, then you became a narrator with respect to the material of the dream.

Like dreams, formal works of fiction present characters located somewhere, engaged in something; formal works of fiction, too, involve feelings—the feelings of characters within the fiction and the feelings aroused in the reader. Also, although the people and locales in formal fiction may be drawn from the external world, every piece of fiction creates its own world. And in no formal fiction of any complexity does anyone simply tell us the meaning. We must interpret meaning for ourselves, just as we must interpret our own dreams. Fictions of whatever sort are dramatic rather than discursive: that is, they speak through action, mood, symbol rather than by logical proposition. In the words of Flannery O'Connor, a fine contemporary writer represented in this book, "The fiction writer doesn't state, he shows, renders." Finally, our interpretations of formal fictions, as of dreams, are always in some sense incomplete: an interpretation is like a map, always simpler than the region it is meant to guide the traveler through. In sum, just as a dream is a means of communication from one part of the self to another, formal fiction is a means of communication from one self to another. Indeed, fiction is one of the chief devices by which human beings communicate in *concrete terms* their understandings of the world, the self, and the human situation.

Fact and Fiction

"Why bother with fiction, which means 'untrue,' doesn't it?" This double question, which might be nagging at you, is indirectly answered by what has been said in the preceding paragraphs. The direct answer lies in what we go to fiction for. Granted, every piece of fiction is a story that to some extent is made up and so is untrue in the limited sense that it is not restricted to the merely factual. This is not to say that fictions do not contain facts, but only that we read fiction for something other than fact. The truth of fiction is not the truth of history or of science, but the more personal truth of human feeling and disposition, communicated best when that substantial part of ourselves that understands primarily through the senses and the emotions is touched. In other words, for a recounting of fact we go to history books, biographies, science texts, and so forth. We go to fiction for exactly what history and science cannot deliver: an intimate sense of the inner lives of people, their deepest feelings, their conflicts and confusions, their most secret joys and fears—all of which can only be imagined and which can be communicated only through concrete depictions of characters and their thoughts and actions. We go to fiction to understand life not in the abstract, but in the flesh. The beauty of fiction is that because it is fictional it can be constructed to reveal what can be revealed in no other way.

We have seen as much when looking at Cynthia Ozick's "The Shawl" in chapter 1. What we saw, recall, was how the story's elements work to communicate fully, through concrete depiction, the meaning of powerlessness—an abstraction embodied and made real by the story's characters. Though its setting and incidents are generally factual, what is important is the inner life of those characters. This is the realm of fiction, its nature and its kind of truth.

Fiction and the Written Word

Because fiction is made out of words, let us consider it briefly within the world of other things made of words, such as news reports and human interest stories. Think of the typical news story first. Reporters, we're told, ask five questions: who? what? when? where? and why?—that is, who did what at what time, in what place, and for what reason? So a brief report of a fatal accident might read:

> On Saturday morning Harold Taylor, 52, of 57 Acre Lane, Sloatsburg, New York, was fatally injured when his car went out of control at the corner of Broadway and Main. Evidently Mr. Taylor, who was proceeding west on Main, hit a patch of ice as he tried to make it through the intersection on a yellow light. According to Alice Miller, who witnessed the incident, before Mr. Taylor could regain control, his car was struck by a dump truck, which skidded through the intersection as it attempted to slow for the red light. The driver of the truck was treated for minor injuries at Mercy Hospital and released. Coincidentally, Mr. Taylor's wife had died of a heart attack the morning before.

There are the facts, analogous to some of the facts of fiction—characters, an occurrence or situation, a setting. But the facts never tell all.

Newspapers, of course, also contain human interest stories, in which the reporter tries to fill in what's missing from the straight report: the backgrounds of the people involved, their states of mind if such can be determined, their feelings about what has occurred. Here we are moving closer to fiction. The reporter, however, is still strictly held to what can be thought of as fact: to circumstantial evidence as reported by eyewitnesses, to whatever is unearthed by field investigation, to what the people involved say of their motivation. That is, even in a human interest story, nothing not a matter of fact or of well-grounded supposition can be included.

In contrast, fiction is not limited to circumstantial fact, and so it can take us into occurrences, situations, and minds to a degree that no news report or human interest story could. While fiction portrays particular characters and events, it also goes beyond the particular to a concern with the general, with revealing something about the nature of human beings and human life. But the fiction writer doesn't tell us anything directly except a story, which is designed to probe into human life via dramatic presentation of incident and character. This combination of the particular and the general, with the general *embodied in* the particular, is the hallmark not only of fiction but of every kind of literature, and is the source of its impact. Because literature is fashioned to have the effect of immediate experience, it involves the reader personally.

Thus, like the other types of literature, fiction is double in nature: it asks us to focus on the particular (on details of plot, for instance, or character) yet to feel in the particular something of general consequence. That is, it asks us to see, through its unique happenings and characters, something generally true of human beings and the human condition. Every literary artist—the poet, for instance, no less than the writer of prose fiction—has the same aim: to embody in words some significant perception of human life. What distinguishes the various types of literature is not the end striven for but the means used to attain that end. The tools with which the writer of prose fiction works are the elements that we have already considered in passing and will study more thoroughly in succeeding chapters: plot, characterization, narration, mood, style, setting, and symbol. In some combination or other (every piece of fiction does not necessarily contain all of the elements), these constitute the means of fiction. Again, the more fully we understand these means, the more readily we can move to interpretation and grasp what a given story is about—its theme.

WHAT'S THE BIG IDEA?

When we speak of theme, we're referring to a story's general significance, which can be thought of as attitude, insight, or point. It is valid to think of theme in terms of the author's attitude as communicated by the story as a whole. Or we could conceive of theme as the general insight of an author into people or ideas established, again, by all of the particulars of a story. Or we might think of theme simply as the point, the meaning in general terms that gives a story focus. If we're careful not to limit the meaning of the word "idea" too much, we might even say that theme is the big idea, the perception that unifies all of the details in a story and accounts for why a story is structured as it is. Much of the pleasure of reading fiction lies in our pursuit of the general or big idea, that is, in our effort to arrive at the richest possible interpretation.

One important caution: never jump to interpretation. Themes, which must be inferred from the gathering particulars of stories, take shape gradually. Postpone the consideration of overall meaning until you've lived with a story long enough to have mastered its construction, to have understood the elements that go into its making. Remember that, as we saw in chapter 1, theme is not an element of fiction but an end that accounts for all of the means employed. To get to that end ourselves, we must first take up and examine the means that lead to it.

Bear in mind, however, that the theme is not the story. Even though you may feel that you have formulated a theme as fully and clearly as possible, the story cannot be put aside and forgotten as if it were a container from which you have poured out the meaning. The truths of fiction cannot be separated from their embodiment, just as the truths of human experience cannot be separated from that experience. Even the best formulation of a theme on the reader's part is never complete; the story retains its integrity. Think once more of a map: a map is a guide to a region but no substitute for traveling in it. Missing are the specific features of the region the map defines—the rocks and crags, paths and bypaths, springs and rivulets, not to mention sounds, odors, the variety of coloration: in a word, all that makes the place unique. So, too, theme or its articulation is no substitute for the experience of a story itself.

Still, articulating a story's theme is an essential step to understanding. I don't mean to suggest, however, that themes should be stated like philosophical postulates or that the theme of every story must be or can be formulated in a declarative statement. Many a story resolves itself only into a question or a hint at some direction of thought to be taken up by the reader. The question or direction is the theme. And in a great many stories the revelation that comes from insight into a character is the theme. Indeed, probing of human motivation and of the uncertain relation between what people feel, think, and believe is fundamental to first-rate fiction, which digs under the surface and attempts to uncover what goes on deep inside of people. Its themes, therefore, are complex and worked out with subtlety; they often cannot be stated simply.

Perhaps an example will help tie together the various points we've considered so far. Recall the news report we looked at earlier (page 36). Though it has no theme, the report contains ample material for a story. It is especially the last sentence of the report that catches my eye: "Coincidentally, Mr. Taylor's wife had died of a heart attack the morning before." In the news report, this is merely a matter of coincidence, but the fact of the wife's death could be of particular importance from the fiction writer's point of view. Conceivably, Mr. Taylor had had little sleep the night before his accident because he had to inform relatives, make the necessary arrangements, and so on. His shock and grief probably kept him awake in any case and greatly affected his judgment. Conceivably, too, he was distracted for just a moment as he headed into the intersection by the female witness, who may have reminded him of his dead wife. Possibly that, as much as icy conditions, made him lose control of his car. Reading the news report alone, we would have to settle for an explanation of the accident as having resulted from bad judgment, ice, and a skidding truck; a jury would have to come to such a conclusion. But deep down we know better. We know, for instance, that people often have accidents when they're emotionally disturbed. Someone writing a work of fiction based on incidents such as those in the report would look beneath the circumstantial evidence and explore the state of Mr. Taylor's mind just before the accident. Perhaps there was what psychologists call a "death wish" lurking under the surface, the accident's having been no accident at all, strictly speaking. There, then, could be our theme, nowhere stated in our hypothetical story but everywhere felt once the details (factual or imagined) chosen by the writer are seen clearly.

Theme Versus Moral

From all that has been said, it should be clear that a theme is different from a "moral" or a "message." But so many beginning students still look for "the moral," or at least speak in terms of "the moral of the story," that the distinction needs clarification. What "moral" or "message" means in this context, I suppose, is a statement about how people should behave. This is an important concern, but not directly a concern of fiction, at least over the past few hundred years. The fiction writer does not seek to tell us how to behave according to some abstract code of behaviour but rather to shed light on how we do behave. By so doing, fiction can show us ourselves, which seems to me to be more than enough.

There was a time, however, when fiction was aimed at specific moral instruction. In fact, from ancient days right on down to sometime in the eighteenth century, cautionary tales, fables, parables, and the like flourished, and they are still widely retold. Consider, for instance, the following version of Aesop's fable "The Ant and the Grasshopper."

> There once was an ant who was, like all ants, a paragon of industry. All summer long he worked from morning to night stocking his stores with food and fuel for the winter. Many a time his neighbor, the grasshopper, would deride his efforts, but the ant was undaunted. All he said was, "Wait until winter," and went about his work as the grasshopper, frivolous as ever, hopped hither and yon, paying no heed to the ant's warning. Summer faded into fall, and the ant worked on as the grasshopper chirped his songs and played the day

away. Then came the first snowfall. Warm and cozy at his hearth, the ant heard a knock at the door. There was the grasshopper, shivering in the cold and starving. "Please, oh please, let me in," he said. "Not on your life," replied the ready ant, "you who frittered the summer and fall away and gave no heed to my warning." The ant slammed the door and went back to the fireside. The grasshopper hopped sadly away, realizing too late his folly. He died that very night.

Moral: Work hard and save for a rainy (or snowy) day.

Like Aesop's other fables, and many cautionary tales, fables, and parables by others, "The Ant and the Grasshopper" still has a certain charm. But its moral, or what I call "moral tag," seems merely conventional and not very instructive at that. Because of the nature of the modern world, with its megacities and massive bureaucratic governments (not to mention credit cards), our realities are far too intricate to be caught in moral tags like this. Our fiction reflects our world by being structured to embody themes in their complexity instead of designed to communicate simple messages.

To be sure, modern fiction (especially short fiction) has its roots in older forms of literature like the fable. The two tales by James Thurber placed first among the stories that follow (pages 45 and 47) suggest the relationship. But, the ancestry acknowledged, what is notable is the difference between Thurber's fables and those like Aesop's. Look at the "moral" of "The Owl Who Was God": "You can fool too many of the people too much of the time." This is substantially different in character from any conventional moral or tag. If anything, Thurber is poking fun at conventional moral tags and (this is his theme) suggesting how irrelevant they are to the complexities of modern life. (The title of the book from which the story is taken suggests as much: *Fables for Our Time*.) Thurber's theme, then, is of much greater complexity than his bogus moral, and the same is true of modern themes in general. No piece of fiction of substance resolves itself into a moral, so no moral tag will do as a statement of theme. One must phrase things more subtly, more in line with the character of what is being articulated as well as with the realities of our lives.

Articulating Fiction's Themes

Details come first. Before even thinking of interpretation, clarify the details of a story to yourself—its plot, its setting, the characteristics of the people it presents, and so on. Remember that the best interpretation accounts for the details and suggests how they are related. Also, look at titles: a title will often point to the heart of a story. Finally, as you read, keep an eye out for anything that is repeated or elaborated upon. Repetition and elaboration are likely to signal significance. Once you have come to see a story clearly, the question then is how to articulate its meaning. Here is a list of suggestions aimed at summarizing how one goes about discovering and expressing a theme.

SUMMARY SUGGESTIONS: UNDERSTANDING THEME

1. Though no statement of the theme of a work of fiction will exhaust its meaning, some statements are both richer and fuller than others. Stretching yourself, perhaps, try to express your understanding in language that does justice to that understanding as well as to the story's complexity.

2. Always check your statement of theme against the particulars of a story. What you say must not be at odds with any important detail. More, test that your statement accounts for major details: that is, your statement should implicitly make clear why an author chose, for instance, to develop one character instead of another or to emphasize setting instead of narration.

3. Be careful to distinguish between a theme and a moral. Because the themes of most stories are complex, they require more than a brief sentence to express. In fact, the themes of most stories cannot be stated adequately in one sentence alone.

4. In stating a theme, don't summarize a plot or refer to specific characters in your statement. Theme, don't forget, is the generalized meaning of a story.

5. On the other hand, fiction by its nature should keep us from blanket generalizations, for it confronts us at every turn with particulars—specific locales, a few detailed characters, definite events. Consequently, we can generalize only so far. In stating a theme, then, be a little guarded. For example, the theme of the hypothetical fiction that we constructed from the incidents in the news report should not be stated: "If the facts are known, accidents result from a death wish." A statement like the following is both more accurate and more meaningful: "Often, the causes of an accident are not exactly what they appear to be. Some accidents, at least, may result from inner turmoil as much as from external conditions. At certain points in their lives, people may even have a death wish, though they might not know that they do."

WRITING ON THEME

In some ways, writing on theme is easier than writing on any other aspect of fiction. To be sure, to articulate a theme fully, without reducing a story to some trite observation, is difficult. One must understand a story and how it is constructed first; then one must find the right words to capture its subtlety and account for its details. But once you come to the point of adequate articulation, you are home free: you have in hand both a thesis for your paper and materials to support your thesis.

That is, your articulation of a story's theme can be your thesis. Your job is now clear: you must show why you interpret the story as you do, or why you feel its theme to be what you say it is (your thesis). State the theme as you see it and then move on step by step to back up your statement. Your support materials, of course, are immediately available for you in the story you're writing on. You will, naturally, have to decide which materials to select and what order to present them in. To establish the validity of your thesis, be sure to account for and include the major facts of the story. The title, too, is often of particular significance. In writing a longer paper, you would probably want to include minor details as well. Keep your statement of theme (your thesis) in mind at all times and be sure that everything you write is related to it.

Turn back to the sample essay in chapter 1 (page 25) as an example of what writing on theme entails. The theme it proposes for Ozick's "The Shawl" is the "terrible effect of powerlessness on the human mind and spirit." Rosa is singled out as the character whose experience embodies this theme, and so Rosa's experience as related in the story becomes the focal point of the essay as it proceeds. Detail by detail, the essay builds support for the statement of theme (the writer's thesis). By the end, the reader feels that, although the story may concern other matters as well or its theme may be stated in some other way, the writer has touched something significant in it. The reader now understands the story a little better. This is the task of analysis—to shed light, to increase understanding. If your articulation of theme is adequate and your marshaling of support material cogent, you will achieve your goal: to broaden your own understanding and that of your reader.

To be sure, you may wish to write on or be asked to write on something other than a story's theme—on a character, perhaps, or on a story's mood. In this context you must still be concerned with theme as it relates to your topic. A paragraph might be devoted to a statement of theme followed by a discussion of how that theme relates to, sheds light on, or emerges from character, mood, or whatever it is you are writing on. For instance, if you were writing a paper on Stella's regression to infancy and how that regression is communicated, you might bring up its cause: her utter helplessness and dependency. Stella, no less than Rosa, embodies the story's theme, so in writing on her it would be a good idea to discuss how she contributes to the development of the theme overall or, conversely, what the theme of the story leads us to understand about her.

Or you could use a statement of theme for your conclusion, leaving your reader with a sense of the wider significance of your topic. That is, having gone into some aspect of a story in detail, you could move at the end to a discussion of the story's general meaning: to how what you have considered both relates to and helps establish the story's theme. To take Stella again, one could write a paper on her regression by discussing first what we know about human regression generally and then by applying that knowledge to an examination of Stella herself and the stages of her fall back to infancy. "But what is the cause of Stella's slide into infantile desires and feelings?" your conclusion could begin. Then you would specify helplessness because of her situation, and that would take you to a statement of theme, which could bring the paper to a satisfying close.

In sum, theme may be written on directly or used for support or in a conclusion. Whatever you write on, however, you probably will need to relate it to a story's theme. For theme is the end for which the elements are means; because means cannot be understood without an understanding of the end they serve, the elements of a story cannot be fully grasped in isolation from the theme that together they create. When you write on fiction, the full articulation of theme must come first.

GENERAL WRITING ASSIGNMENTS

1. (a) Write up a dream you've had that seems of some particular significance to you. Don't interpret it; just present the details of the dream as vividly as possible so as to capture its mood. You might give a title to your piece that suggests an interpretation, but write the dream as though you were having it instead of talking about it. If you cannot recall a dream, make one up. It will nevertheless reflect your concerns and feelings.

(b) Now write a paragraph in which you state what you think the dream means and give your reasons for your interpretation. You might bring to bear things external to the dream (for example, what you did during the day that conceivably gave rise to it), but be sure to discuss the details of the dream itself as you move along. They should support your general interpretation of the meaning (theme) of your dream; conversely, your general interpretation should account for the details enumerated.

2. Define "fiction" as you now understand the meaning of the word. Argue the validity of your definition and give examples from any source you like (for instance, the movies). You could conclude with a statement as to why most people enjoy fiction and what they get out of it.

3. Television fare consists mainly of fiction, some good and some awful. Compare and contrast a program you judge good and one you loathe. State your criteria of judgment and apply those criteria to the programs in question.

4. We have spoken of the word "theme" in connection with literary fiction. In what other contexts is the word used? Give examples (the theme song of a movie, say, or the theme of a movement from a symphony). Are these uses alike? How so? How, for instance, is the theme song of a movie like the theme of a story? If you detect any differences in meaning between the various uses of the word, discuss those differences as well. Conclude, if possible, with a definition of "theme" that covers all of the uses you have specified.

The Owl Who Was God

James Thurber

Once upon a starless midnight there was an owl who sat on the branch of an oak tree. Two ground moles tried to slip quietly by, unnoticed. "You!" said the owl. "Who?" they quavered, in fear and astonishment, for they could not believe it was possible for anyone to see them in that thick darkness. "You two!" said the owl. The moles hurried away and told the other creatures of the field and forest that the owl was the greatest and wisest of all animals because he could see in the dark and because he could answer any question. "I'll see about that," said a secretary bird, and he called on the owl one night when it was again very dark. "How many claws am I holding up?" said the secretary bird. "Two," said the owl, and that was right. "Can you give me another expression for 'that is to say' or 'namely'?" asked the secretary bird. "To wit," said the owl. "Why does a lover call on his love?" asked the secretary bird. "To woo," said the owl.

The secretary bird hastened back to the other creatures and reported that the owl was indeed the greatest and wisest animal in the world because he could see in the dark and because he could answer any question. "Can he see in the daytime, too?" asked a red fox. "Yes," echoed a dormouse and a French poodle. "Can he see in the daytime, too?" All the other creatures laughed loudly at this silly question, and they set upon the red fox and his friends and drove them out of the region. Then they sent a messenger to the owl and asked him to be their leader.

When the owl appeared among the animals it was high noon and the sun was shining brightly. He walked very slowly, which gave him an appearance of great dignity, and he peered about him with large, staring eyes, which gave him an air of tremendous importance. "He's God!" screamed a Plymouth Rock hen. And the others took up the cry "He's God!" So they followed him wherever he went and when he began to bump into things they began to bump into things, too. Finally he came to a concrete highway and he started up the middle of it and all the other creatures followed him. Presently a hawk, who was acting as outrider, observed a truck coming toward them at fifty miles an hour, and he reported to the secretary bird and the secretary bird reported to the owl. "There's danger ahead," said the secretary bird. "To wit?" said the owl. The secretary bird told him. "Aren't you afraid?" he asked. "Who?" said the owl calmly, for he could not see the truck. "He's God!" cried all the creatures again, and they were still crying "He's God!" when the truck hit them and ran them down. Some of the animals were merely injured, but most of them, including the owl, were killed.

Moral: You can fool too many of the people too much of the time.

[1939—U.S.A.]

QUESTIONS

1. Thurber backs up his "moral" by his depiction of the behavior of his chosen animals. Why are they so readily taken in?
2. The appended "moral" here seems quite different from that of a traditional fable (like Aesop's "The Fox and the Grapes" or "The Ant and the Grasshopper"). In what ways do they differ? What does the difference say about our world? Formulate the story's theme in terms of this difference.
3. Published in 1939, on the eve of World War II, the story could be seen to have political significance. How so?

WRITING SUGGESTIONS

1. In a paragraph, compare and contrast Thurber's story with a traditional fable. What are their similarities? How do they differ? What theme does the difference suggest?
2. In a paragraph or two, discuss the owl as fascist dictator (Mussolini, for example). How is the owl described so as to make us think of such a leader? What is the point of the allusion?
3. Write an informational paragraph on the political situation of Europe in the 1930s. (You might have to do some research here.) Then, in a separate paragraph, relate your information to "The Owl Who Was God."

The Unicorn in the Garden

James Thurber

Once upon a sunny morning a man who sat in a breakfast nook looked up from his scrambled eggs to see a white unicorn with a golden horn quietly cropping roses in the garden. The man went up to the bedroom where his wife was still asleep and woke her. "There's a unicorn in the garden," he said. "Eating roses." She opened one unfriendly eye and looked at him. "The unicorn is a mythical beast," she said, and turned her back on him. The man walked slowly downstairs and out into the garden. The unicorn was still there; he was now browsing among the tulips. "Here, unicorn," said the man, and he pulled up a lily and gave it to him. The unicorn ate it gravely. With a high heart, because there was a unicorn in his garden, the man went upstairs and roused his wife again. "The unicorn ate a lily," he said. His wife sat up in bed and looked at him coldly. "You are a booby," she said, "and I am going to have you put in the booby hatch." The man, who had never liked the words "booby" and "booby hatch," and who liked them even less on a shining morning when there was a unicorn in the garden, thought for a moment. "We'll see about that," he said. He walked over to the door. "He has a golden horn in the middle of his forehead," he told her. Then he went back to the garden to watch the unicorn, but the unicorn had gone away. The man sat down among the roses and went to sleep.

As soon as the husband had gone out of the house, the wife got up and dressed as fast as she could. She was very excited and there was a gloat in her eye. She telephoned the police and she telephoned a psychiatrist; she told them to hurry to her house and bring a strait jacket. When the police and the psychiatrist arrived, they sat down in chairs and looked at her with

47

great interest. "My husband," she said, "saw a unicorn this morning." The police looked at the psychiatrist and the psychiatrist looked at the police. "He told me it ate a lily," she said. The psychiatrist looked at the police and the police looked at the psychiatrist. "He told me it had a golden horn in the middle of its forehead," she said. At a solemn signal from the psychiatrist, the police leaped from their chairs and seized the wife. They had a hard time subduing her, for she put up a terrific struggle, but they finally subdued her. Just as they got her into the strait jacket, her husband came back into the house. "Did you tell your wife you saw a unicorn?" asked the psychiatrist. "Of course not," said the husband. "The unicorn is a mythical beast." "That's all I wanted to know," said the psychiatrist. "Take her away. I'm sorry, sir, but your wife is as crazy as a jay bird." So they took her away, cursing and screaming, and shut her up in an institution. The husband lived happily ever after.

Moral: Don't count your boobies until they are hatched.

[1939–U.S.A.]

QUESTIONS

1. Contrast the husband and wife.
2. How does Thurber keep us from sympathizing with the wife, whose mood at the end of the story is certainly different from the mood induced in the reader?
3. Why are the characters not named?
4. The "moral" appended here is clearly bogus. What, then, is the story's theme? What general point does it comically make regarding the sexes and especially marriage?

WRITING SUGGESTIONS

1. Write a paragraph in which you contrast Thurber's husband and wife. How do they differ? How does how they differ make their conflict seem inevitable? How does Thurber turn all of this to comedy?
2. In a paragraph, state and discuss the theme of "The Unicorn in the Garden." Is it dated, or does the story still have something to say about the tensions of marriage? Defend your judgment.

The Ones Who Walk Away from Omelas

(*Variations on a theme by William James*)*

Ursula K. Le Guin

With a clamor of bells that set the swallows soaring, the Festival of Summer came to the city Omelas, bright-towered by the sea. The rigging of the boats in harbor sparkled with flags. In the streets between houses with red roofs and painted walls, between old moss-grown gardens and under avenues of trees, past great parks and public buildings, processions moved. Some were decorous: old people in long stiff robes of mauve and grey, grave master workmen, quiet, merry women carrying their babies and chatting as they walked. In other streets the music beat faster, a shimmering of gong and tambourine, and the people went dancing, the procession was a dance. Children dodged in and out, their high calls rising like the swallows' crossing flights over the music and the singing. All the processions wound towards the north side of the city, where on the great water-meadow called the Green Fields boys and girls, naked in the bright air, with mud-stained feet and ankles and long, lithe arms, exercised their restive horses, before the race. The horses wore no gear at all but a halter without bit. Their manes were braided with streamers of silver, gold, and green. They flared their nostrils and pranced and boasted to one another;

---

* The theme from William James, American philosopher and psychologist, is from "The Moral Philosopher and the Moral Life":

> Or if the hypothesis were offered us of a world in which . . . utopias should all be outdone, and millions kept permanently happy on the one simple condition that a certain lost soul on the far-off edge of things should lead a life of lonely torment, what except a specific and independent sort of emotion can it be which would make us immediately feel, even though an impulse arose within us to clutch at the happiness so offered, how hideous a thing would be its enjoyment when deliberately accepted as the fruit of such a bargain?

they were vastly excited, the horse being the only animal who has adopted our ceremonies as his own. Far off to the north and west the mountains stood up half encircling Omelas on her bay. The air of morning was so clear that the snow still crowning the Eighteen Peaks burned with white-gold fire across the miles of sunlit air, under the dark blue of the sky. There was just enough wind to make the banners that marked the racecourse snap and flutter now and then. In the silence of the broad green meadows one could hear the music winding through the city streets, farther and nearer and ever approaching, a cheerful faint sweetness of the air that from time to time trembled and gathered together and broke out into the great joyous clanging of the bells.

Joyous! How is one to tell about joy? How describe the citizens of Omelas?

They were not simple folk, you see, though they were happy. But we do not say the words of cheer much any more. All smiles have become archaic. Given a description such as this one tends to make certain assumptions. Given a description such as this one tends to look next for the King, mounted on a splendid stallion and surrounded by his noble knights, or perhaps in a golden litter borne by great-muscled slaves. But there was no king. They did not use swords, or keep slaves. They were not barbarians. I do not know the rules and laws of their society, but I suspect that they were singularly few. As they did without monarchy and slavery, so they also got on without the stock exchange, the advertisement, the secret police, and the bomb. Yet I repeat that these were not simple folk, not dulcet shepherds, noble savages, bland utopians. They were not less complex than us. The trouble is that we have a bad habit, encouraged by pedants and sophisticates, of considering happiness as something rather stupid. Only pain is intellectual, only evil interesting. This is the treason of the artist: a refusal to admit the banality of evil and the terrible boredom of pain. If you can't lick 'em, join 'em. If it hurts, repeat it. But to praise despair is to condemn delight, to embrace violence is to lose hold of everything else. We have almost lost hold; we can no longer describe a happy man, nor make any celebration of joy. How can I tell you about the people of Omelas? They were not naïve and happy children—though their children were, in fact, happy. They were mature, intelligent, passionate adults whose lives were not wretched. O miracle! but I wish I could describe it better. I wish I could convince you. Omelas sounds in my words like a city in a fairy tale, long ago and far away, once upon a time. Perhaps it would be best if you imagined it as your own fancy bids, assuming it will rise to the occasion, for certainly I cannot suit you all. For instance, how about technology? I think that there would be no cars or helicopters in and above the streets; this follows from the fact that the people of Omelas are happy people. Happiness is based on a just discrimination of what is necessary, what is neither necessary nor destructive, and what is destructive. In the middle category, however—that of the unnecessary but undestructive, that of comfort, luxury, exuberance, etc.—they could perfectly well have central heating, subway trains, washing machines, and all kinds of marvelous devices not yet invented here, floating light-sources, fuelless power, a cure for the common cold. Or they could have none of that: it doesn't matter. As you like it. I incline to think that people from towns up and down the coast have been coming in to Omelas during the last days before the Festival on very fast little trains and double-decked trams, and that the train station of Omelas is actually the handsomest building in town, though plainer than the magnificent Farmers' Market. But even granted trains, I fear that Omelas so far strikes some of you as goody-goody. Smiles, bells, parades, horses, bleh. If so, please add an orgy. If an orgy would help, don't hesitate. Let us not, however, have temples from which issue beautiful nude priests and priestesses already half in ecstasy and ready to copulate with any man or woman, lover or stranger, who desires union with the deep godhead of the blood, although that was my first idea. But really it would be better not to have any temples in Omelas—at least, not manned temples. Religion yes, clergy no. Surely the beautiful nudes can just wander about, offering themselves like divine soufflés to the hunger of the needy and the rapture of the flesh. Let them join the processions. Let tambourines be struck above the copulations, and the glory of desire be proclaimed upon the gongs, and (a not unimportant point) let the offspring of these delightful rituals be beloved and looked after by all. One thing I know there is none of in Omelas is guilt. But what else should there be? I thought at first there were no drugs, but that is puritanical. For those who like it, the faint insistent sweetness of *drooz* may perfume the ways of the city, *drooz* which first brings a great lightness and brilliance to the mind and limbs, and then after some hours a dreamy languor, and wonderful visions at last of the very arcana and inmost secrets of the Universe, as well as exciting the pleasure of sex beyond all belief; and it is not habit-forming. For more modest tastes I think there ought to be beer. What else, what else belongs in the joyous city? The sense of victory, surely, the celebration of courage. But as we did without clergy, let us do without soldiers. The joy built upon successful slaughter is not the right kind of joy; it will not do; it is fearful and it is trivial. A boundless and generous contentment, a magnanimous triumph felt not against some outer enemy but in communion with the finest and fairest in the souls of all men everywhere and the splendor of the world's summer: this is what swells the hearts of the people of Omelas, and the victory they celebrate is that of life. I really don't think many of them need to take *drooz*.

Most of the processions have reached the Green Fields by now. A marvelous smell of cooking goes forth from the red and blue tents of the provisioners. The faces of small children are amiably sticky; in the benign grey beard of a man a couple of crumbs of rich pastry are entangled. The youths and girls have mounted their horses and are beginning to group around the starting line of the course. An old woman, small, fat, and laughing, is passing out flowers from a basket, and tall young men wear her flowers in their shining hair. A child of nine or ten sits at the edge of the crowd, alone, playing on a wooden flute. People pause to listen, and they smile, but they do not speak to him, for he never ceases playing and never sees them, his dark eyes wholly rapt in the sweet, thin magic of the tune.

He finishes, and slowly lowers his hands holding the wooden flute.

As if that little private silence were the signal, all at once a trumpet sounds from the pavilion near the starting line: imperious, melancholy, piercing. The horses rear on their slender legs, and some of them neigh in answer. Sober-faced, the young riders stroke the horses' necks and soothe them, whispering, "Quiet, quiet, there my beauty, my hope . . ." They begin to form in rank along the starting line. The crowds along the racecourse are like a field of grass and flowers in the wind. The Festival of Summer has begun.

Do you believe? Do you accept the festival, the city, the joy? No? Then let me describe one more thing.

In a basement under one of the beautiful public buildings of Omelas, or perhaps in the cellar of one of its spacious private homes, there is a room. It has one locked door, and no window. A little light seeps in dustily between cracks in the boards, secondhand from a cobwebbed window somewhere across the cellar. In one corner of the little room a couple of mops, with stiff, clotted, foul-smelling heads, stand near a rusty bucket. The floor is dirt, a little damp to the touch, as cellar dirt usually is. The room is about three paces long and two wide: a mere broom closet or disused tool room. In the room a child is sitting. It could be a boy or a girl. It looks about six, but actually is nearly ten. It is feebleminded. Perhaps it was born defective, or perhaps it has become imbecile through fear, malnutrition, and neglect. It picks its nose and occasionally fumbles vaguely with its toes or genitals, as it sits hunched in the corner farthest from the bucket and the two mops. It is afraid of the mops. It finds them horrible. It shuts its eyes, but it knows the mops are still standing there; and the door is locked; and nobody will come. The door is always locked; and nobody ever comes, except that sometimes—the child has no understanding of time or interval—sometimes the door rattles terribly and opens, and a person, or several people, are there. One of them may come in and kick the child to make it stand up. The others never come close, but peer in at it with frightened, disgusted eyes. The food bowl and the water jug are hastily filled, the door is locked, the eyes disappear. The people at the door never say anything, but the child, who has not always lived in the tool room, and can remember sunlight and its mother's voice, sometimes speaks. "I will be good," it says. "Please let me out. I will be good!" They never answer. The child used to scream for help at night, and cry a good deal, but now it only makes a kind of whining, "eh-haa, eh-haa," and it speaks less and less often. It is so thin there are no calves to its legs; its belly protrudes; it lives on a half-bowl of corn meal and grease a day. It is naked . Its buttocks and thighs are a mess of festered sores, as it sits in its own excrement continually.

They all know it is there, all the people of Omelas. Some of them have come to see it, others are content merely to know it is there. They all know that it has to be there. Some of them understand why, and some do not, but they all understand that their happiness, the beauty of their city, the tenderness of their friendships, the health of their children, the wisdom of their scholars, the skill of their makers, even the abundance of their harvest and the kindly weathers of their skies, depend wholly on this child's abominable misery.

This is usually explained to children when they are between eight and twelve, whenever they seem capable of understanding; and most of those who come to see the child are young people, though often enough an adult comes, or comes back, to see the child. No matter how well the matter has been explained to them, these young spectators are always shocked and sickened at the sight. They feel disgust, which they had thought themselves superior to. They feel anger, outrage, impotence, despite all the explanations. They would like to do something for the child. But there is nothing they can do. If the child were brought up into the sunlight out of the vile place, if it were cleaned and fed and comforted, that would be a good thing, indeed; but if it were done, in that day and hour all the prosperity and beauty and delight of Omelas would wither and be destroyed. Those are the terms. To exchange all the goodness and grace of every life in Omelas for that single, small improvement: to throw away the happiness of thousands for the chance of the happiness of one: that would be to let guilt within the walls indeed.

The terms are strict and absolute; there may not even be a kind word spoken to the child.

Often the young people go home in tears, or in a tearless rage, when they have seen the child and faced this terrible paradox. They may brood over it for weeks or years. But as time goes on they begin to realize that even if the child could be released, it would not get much good of its freedom: a little vague pleasure of warmth and food, no doubt, but little more. It is too degraded and imbecile to know any real joy. It has been afraid too long ever to be free of fear. Its habits are too uncouth for it to respond to humane treatment. Indeed, after so long it would probably be wretched without walls about it to protect it, and darkness for its eyes, and its own excrement to sit in. Their tears at the bitter injustice dry when they begin to perceive the terrible justice of reality, and to accept it. Yet it is their tears and anger, the trying of their generosity and the acceptance of their helplessness, which are perhaps the true source of the splendor of their lives. Theirs is no vapid, irresponsible happiness. They know that they, like the child, are not free. They know compassion. It is the existence of the child, and their knowledge of its existence, that makes possible the nobility of their architecture, the poignancy of their music, the profundity of their science. It is because of the child that they are so gentle with children. They know that if the wretched one were not there snivelling in the dark, the other one, the flute-player, could make no joyful music as the young riders line up in their beauty for the race in the sunlight of the first morning of summer.

Now do you believe in them? Are they not more credible? But there is one more thing to tell, and this is quite incredible.

At times one of the adolescent girls or boys who go to see the child does not go home to weep or rage, does not, in fact, go home at all. Sometimes also a man or woman much older falls silent for a day or two, and then leaves home. These people go out into the street, and walk down the street alone. They keep walking, and walk straight out of the city of Omelas, through the beautiful gates. They keep walking across the farmlands of Omelas. Each one goes alone, youth or girl, man or woman. Night falls; the traveler must pass down village streets, between the houses with yellow-lit windows, and on out into the darkness of the fields. Each alone, they go west or north, towards the mountains. They go on. They leave Omelas, they walk ahead into the darkness, and they do not come back. The place they go towards is a place even less imaginable to most of us than the city of happiness. I cannot describe it at all. It is possible that it does not exist. But they seem to know where they are going, the ones who walk away from Omelas.

[1973–U.S.A.]

QUESTIONS

1. What do we learn about Le Guin's narrator, who is not to be identified with Le Guin herself (the distinction between narrator and author will be discussed in detail later in the book)? "And this is quite incredible," the narrator says when about to discuss "the ones who walk away." What, then, is the narrator's view of Omelas?
2. What attitude would Le Guin have us take toward her narrator? What view does the title, repeated in the story's last sentence, suggest we are meant to take of Omelas?
3. Do the people of Omelas really "know compassion," as the narrator asserts? If so, how have they learned it? What is wrong with their reasoning as reported in the third to last paragraph (that is, their reasoning about the child's remaining in the basement)?
4. Which is this tale closer to, a fable or a story? Or is it a hybrid of the two? What, finally, is its moral and/or theme? What criticism does it make of contemporary American society?

WRITING SUGGESTIONS

1. In a paragraph, argue that the well-being of many is more important than the happiness of one. Draw on "The Ones Who Walk Away from Omelas" for examples.
2. Conversely, write a paragraph in which you argue that the well-being of society as a whole depends on that of each and every individual. Again, use Le Guin's tale for exemplification.
3. Which of the two positions just stated seems closer to Le Guin's? Write an interpretative paragraph on her tale using textual details to support the position you take. Conclude with a statement as to whether "The Ones Who Walk Away from Omelas" is more like a traditional fable or a modern short story.

The Doctor's Heroism*
Villiers de L'Isle-Adam

To kill in order to cure!
—Official Motto of the Broussais Hospital

The extraordinary case of Doctor Hallidonhill is soon to be tried in London. The facts in the matter are these:

On the 20th of last May, the two great waiting rooms of the illustrious specialist were thronged with patients, holding their tickets in their hands.

At the entrance stood the cashier, wearing a long black frock coat; he took the indispensible fee of two guineas from each patient, tested the gold with a sharp tap of the hammer, and cried automatically, "All right."

In his glassed-in office, around which were ranged great tropical shrubs, each growing in a huge Japanese pot, sat the stiff little Doctor Hallidonhill. Beside him, at a little round table, his secretary kept writing out brief prescriptions. At the swinging doors, covered with red velvet studded with gold-headed nails, stood a giant valet whose duty it was to carry the feeble consumptives to the lobby whence they were lowered in a luxurious elevator as soon as the official signal, "Next!" had been given.

The patients entered with dim and glassy eyes, stripped to the waist, with their clothes thrown over their arms. As soon as they entered they received the application of the plessimeter and the tube on back and chest.

"Tick! tick! plaff! Breathe now! . . . Plaff . . . Good . . ."

Then followed a prescription dictated in a second or two; then the well-known "Next!"

Every morning for three years, between nine o'clock and noon, this procession of sufferers filed past.

* Translated by Roger B. Goodman.

On this particular day, May 20th, just at the stroke of nine, a sort of long skeleton, with wild, wandering eyes, cavernous cheeks, and nude torso that looked like a parchment-covered cage lifted occasionally by a racking cough—in short a being so wasted that it seemed impossible for him to live—came in with a blue-fox skin mantle thrown over his arm, and tried to keep himself from falling by catching at the long leaves of the shrubs.

"Tick, tick, plaff! Oh, the devil! Can't do anything for you!" grumbled Doctor Hallidonhill. "What do you think I am—a coroner? In less than a week you will spit up the last cell of this left lung—the right is already riddled like a sieve! Next!"

The valet was just about to carry out the client, when the eminent therapeutist suddenly slapped himself on the forehead, and brusquely asked, with a dubious smile:

"Are you rich?"

"I'm a millionaire—much more than a millionaire," sobbed the unhappy being whom Hallidonhill thus peremptorily had dismissed from the world of the living.

"Very well, then. Go at once to Victoria Station. Take the eleven-o'clock express for Dover! Then the steamer for Calais. Then take the train from Calais to Marseilles—secure a sleeping car with steam in it! And then to Nice. There try to live on watercress for six months—nothing but watercress—no bread, no fruit, no wine, nor meats of any kind. One teaspoonful of iodized rainwater every two days. And watercress, watercress, watercress—pounded and brayed in its own juice . . . that is your only chance—and still, let me tell you this: this supposed cure I know of only through hearsay; it is being dinned into my ears all the time; I don't believe in it the least bit. I suggest it only because yours seems to be a hopeless case, yet I think it is worse than absurd. Still, anything is possible. . . . Next!"

The consumptive Croesus was carefully deposited in the cushioned car of the elevator; and the regular procession commenced through the office.

Six months later, the 3rd of November, just at the stroke of nine o'clock, a sort of giant, with a terrifying yet jovial voice whose tones shook every pane of glass in the doctor's office and set all the leaves of all the tropical plants a-tremble, a great chubby-cheeked colossus, clothed in rich furs—burst like a human bombshell through the sorrowful ranks of Doctor Hallidonhill's clients, and rushed, without ticket, into the sanctum of the Prince of Science, who had just come to sit down before his desk. He seized him round the body, and, bathing the wan and worn cheeks of the doctor in tears, kissed him noisily again and again. Then he set him down in his green armchair in an almost suffocated state.

"Two million francs—if you want," shouted the giant. "Or three million. I owe my breath to you—the sun, resistless passions, life— everything. Ask me for anything—anything at all."

"Who is this madman? Put him out of here," feebly protested the doctor, after a moment's prostration.

"Oh, no you don't," growled the giant, with a glance at the valet that made him recoil as from a blow. "The fact is," he continued, "I understand now, that even you, you my savior, cannot recognize me. I am the watercress man, the hopeless skeleton, the helpless patient. Nice. Watercress, watercress, watercress! Well, I've done my six months of watercress diet—look at your work now! See here—listen to that!"

And he began to drum upon his chest with two huge fists solid enough to shatter the skull of an ox.

"What!" cried the doctor, leaping to his feet, "you are—my gracious, are you the dying man whom I . . ."

"Yes, yes, a thousand times yes!" yelled the giant. "I am the very man. The moment I landed yesterday evening I ordered a bronze statue of you; and I will secure you a monument in Westminster when you die."

Then dropping himself upon an immense sofa, whose springs creaked and groaned beneath his weight, he continued with a sigh of delight, and a beatific smile:

"Ah, what a good thing life is!"

The doctor said something in a whisper, and the secretary and the valet left the room. Once alone with his resuscitated patient, Hallidonhill, stiff, wan and glacial as ever, stared at the giant's face in silence for a minute or two. Then, suddenly:

"Allow me, if you please, to take that fly off your forehead!"

And rushing forward as he spoke, the doctor pulled a short "Bulldog revolver" from his pocket, and quick as a flash fired into the left temple of the visitor.

The giant fell with his skull shattered, scattering his grateful brains over the carpet of the room. His hands thrashed automatically for a few moments.

In ten cuts of the doctor's scissors, through cloak, garments, and underwear, the dead man's breast was laid bare. The grave surgeon cut open the chest lengthwise, with a single stroke of his broad scalpel.

When, about a quarter of an hour later, a policeman entered the office to request Doctor Hallidonhill to go with him, he found him sitting calmly at his bloody desk, examining with a strong magnifying glass, an enormous pair of lungs that lay spread out before him. The Genius of

Science was trying to find, from the case of the deceased, some satisfactory explanation of the more than miraculous action of watercress.

"Constable," he said as he rose to his feet, "I felt it necessary to kill that man, as an immediate autopsy of his case might, I thought, reveal to me a secret of the gravest importance, regarding the now degenerating vitality of the human species. That is why I did not hesitate, let me confess, *to sacrifice my conscience to my duty*."

Needless to add that the illustrious doctor was almost immediately released upon a nominal bond, his liberty being of far more importance than his detention. This strange case, as I have said, is shortly to come up before the British Assizes.

We believe that this sublime crime will not bring its hero to the gallows; for the English, as well as ourselves, are fully able to comprehend *that the exclusive love of the Humanity of the Future without any regard for the individual of the Present is, in our own time, the one sole motive that ought to justify the acquittal under any circumstances, of the magnanimous Extremists of Science.*

[1890—France]

QUESTIONS

1. Though written by a Frenchman, the story is laid in England. Why?
2. Doctor Hallidonhill's motivation is not narrowly selfish, for he stands to gain much from his living client. Is his motivation truly humanitarian, however? Are duty and conscience really at odds? Does the way in which the doctor is depicted help sway us toward an answer?
3. The theme of the story entails the values of science and scientists. Does it expose some flaw in scientific valuation?
4. Does the attitude of the narrator in the final paragraph coincide with that implied by the story as a whole? Why or why not?

WRITING SUGGESTIONS

1. Modern medicine is scientific. But does that mean that it is good medicine? Could humanity and science be at odds? Taking the present story as example, write a paragraph on how modern scientific medicine does not always meet the needs of individual patients.
2. Discuss the theme of this story as it relates to contemporary science generally. In its quest for knowledge, has our science possibly forgotten the purpose of rational inquiry? Give examples both from the story and from the contemporary world of how this might be so.

The First Death of Her Life
Elizabeth Taylor

Suddenly, tears poured from Lucy's eyes. She rested her forehead against her mother's hand and let the tears soak into the counterpane.

Dear Mr. Wilcox, she began, for her mind was always composing letters, I shall not be at the shop for the next four days, as my mother has passed away and I shall not be available until after the funeral. My mother passed away very peacefully . . . .

The nurse came in. She took her patient's wrist for a moment, replaced it on the bed, removed a jar of white lilac from the table, as if this were no longer necessary, and went out again.

The girl kneeling by the bed had looked up, but Dear Mr. Wilcox, she resumed, her eyes returning to the counterpane, My mother has died. I shall come back to work the day after tomorrow. Yours sincerely, Lucy Mayhew.

Her father was late. She imagined him hurrying from work, bicycling through the darkening streets, dogged, hunched up, slush thrown up by his wheels. Her mother did not move. Lucy stroked her mother's hand, with its loose gold ring, the calloused palm, the fine, long fingers. Then she stood up stiffly, her knees bruised from the waxed floor, and went to the window.

Snowflakes turned idly, drifting down over the hospital gardens. It was four o'clock in the afternoon and already the day seemed over. So few sounds came from this muffled and discolored world. In the hospital itself, there was a deep silence.

Her thoughts came to her in words, as if her mind spoke them first, understood them later. She tried to think of her childhood—little scenes she selected to prove how she and her mother had loved one another. Other scenes, especially last week's quarrel, she chose to forget, not knowing that in this moment she sent them away forever. Only loving-kindness remained. But, all the same, intolerable pictures broke through—her mother at the sink; her mother ironing; her mother standing between the lace curtains, staring out at the dreary street with a wounded look in her eyes; her mother tying the same lace curtains with yellow ribbons; attempts at lightness, gaiety, which came to nothing; her mother gathering her huge black cat to her, burying her face in its fur while a great, shivering sigh—of despair, of boredom—escaped her.

Her mother no longer sighed. She lay very still and sometimes took a little sip of air. Her arms were neatly at her side. Her eyes, which all day long had been turned to the white lilacs, were closed. Her cheekbones rose sharply from her bruised, exhausted face. She smelled faintly of wine. A small lilac flower floated on a glass of champagne, now discarded on the table at her side.

The champagne, with which they hoped to stretch out the thread of her life minute by minute, the lilac, the room of her own, all came to her at the end of a life of drabness and denial, just as, all along the mean street of the small English town where they lived, the dying and the dead were able to claim a lifetime's savings from the bereaved.

She is no longer there, Lucy thought, standing beside the bed. All day, her mother had stared at the white lilac; now she had sunk away. Outside, beyond the hospital gardens, mist settled over the town, blurred the street lamps.

The nurse returned with the matron. Lucy tautened, ready to be on her best behavior. In her heart, she trusted her mother to die without frightening her, and when the matron, deftly drawing Lucy's head to rest on her own shoulder, said in her calm voice, "She has gone," Lucy felt she had met this happening halfway.

A little bustle began, quick footsteps along the empty passages, and for a moment she was left alone with her dead mother. She laid her hand timidly on the soft, dark hair, so often touched, played with, when she was a child, standing on a stool behind her mother's chair while she sewed.

There were still the smell of wine and the hospital smell. It was growing dark in the room. She went to the dressing table and took her mother's handbag, very worn and shiny, and a book, a library book that she had chosen carefully, believing her mother would read it. Then she had a quick sip from the glass on the table, a mouthful of champagne, which she had never tasted before, and, looking wounded and aloof, walked down the middle of the corridor, feeling nurses falling away to left and right.

Opening the glass doors onto the snowy gardens, she thought that it was like the end of a film. But no music rose up and engulfed her. Instead, there was her father turning in at the gates. He propped his bicycle against the wall and began to run clumsily across the wet gravel.

[1949–Great Britain]

QUESTIONS

1. This story is constructed on contrasts, beginning with the contrast between the two letters composed by Lucy in her head (paragraphs two and four). What is the difference between the letters?
2. Though short, the story conveys much information about mother, father, and daughter. What have their lives been like? The words "staring," "bruised," and "wounded" appear twice each, thus calling some degree of attention to themselves. Why? In this context, "champagne" and "lilac" serve to heighten our impression by way of contrast. How so?
3. What does the statement "Her mind was always composing letters" tell us about Lucy? What does the title tell us?
4. "... in this moment she sent them [troublesome thoughts about her mother] away forever. Only loving-kindness remained. But all the same, intolerable pictures broke through. ..." Here is another contrast. What is being contrasted with what?
5. The last four sentences of the story contain its final contrast. What is that contrast? Relating this final contrast to the other contrasts mentioned above, formulate the story's theme.

WRITING SUGGESTIONS

1. In a paragraph, describe the lives of Taylor's three characters. Discuss their usual physical environment along with their emotional lives, relating the two as you go. Conclude by suggesting what it is about the lives of these people that makes Lucy the way she is.
2. Starting with the two letters referred to in the first question above, discuss the contrasts that run through "The First Death of Her Life." Give examples and end with a conclusion as to the story's theme as expressed by these contrasts.
3. Have you experienced a death of someone you loved? If so, write on your feelings in relation to Elizabeth Taylor's story. Does the story touch anything you felt? If not, what is the difference between what you felt and what Lucy feels? In either case, judge the story in terms of your own experience of death.

The Snake

Stephen Crane

Where the path wended across the ridge, the bushes of huckleberry and sweet fern swarmed at it in two curling waves until it was a mere winding line traced through a tangle. There was no interference by clouds, and as the rays of the sun fell full upon the ridge, they called into voice innumerable insects which chanted the heat of the summer day in steady, throbbing, unending chorus.

A man and a dog came from the laurel thickets of the valley where the white brook brawled with the rocks. They followed the deep line of the path across the ridge. The dog—a large lemon-and-white setter—walked, tranquilly meditative, at his master's heels.

Suddenly from some unknown and yet near place in advance there came a dry, shrill, whistling rattle that smote motion instantly from the limbs of the man and the dog. Like the fingers of a sudden death, this sound seemed to touch the man at the nape of the neck, at the top of the spine, and change him, as swift as thought, to a statute of listening horror, surprise, rage. The dog, too—the same icy hand was laid upon him, and he stood crouched and quivering, his jaw dropping, the froth of terror upon his lips, the light of hatred in his eyes.

Slowly the man moved his hands toward the bushes, but his glance did not turn from the place made sinister by the warning rattle. His fingers, unguided, sought for a stick of weight and strength. Presently they closed about one that seemed adequate, and holding this weapon poised before him, the man moved slowly forward, glaring. The dog, with his nervous nostrils fairly fluttering, moved warily, one foot at a time, after his master.

But when the man came upon the snake, his body underwent a shock as if from a revelation, as if after all he had been ambushed. With a blanched face, he sprang forward, and his breath came in strained gasps, his chest heaving as if he were in the performance of an extraordinary muscular trial. His arm with the stick made a spasmodic, defensive gesture.

The snake had apparently been crossing the path in some mystic travel when to his sense there came the knowledge of the coming of his foes. The dull vibration perhaps informed him, and he flung his body to face the danger. He had no knowledge of paths; he had no wit to tell him to slink noiselessly into the bushes. He knew that his implacable enemies were approaching; no doubt they were seeking him, hunting him. And so he cried his cry, an incredibly swift jangle of tiny bells, as burdened with pathos as the hammering upon quaint cymbals by the Chinese at war—for, indeed, it was usually his death music.

"Beware! Beware! Beware!"

The man and the snake confronted each other. In the man's eyes were hatred and fear. In the snake's were hatred and fear. These enemies maneuvered, each preparing to kill. It was to be a battle without mercy. Neither knew of mercy for such a situation. In the man was all the wild strength of the terror of his ancestors, of his race, of his kind. A deadly repulsion had been handed from man to man through long dim centuries. This was another detail of a war that had begun evidently when first there were men and snakes. Individuals who do not participate in this strife incur the investigations of scientists. Once there was a man and a snake who were friends, and at the end, the man lay dead with the marks of the snake's caress just over his East Indian heart. In the formation of devices, hideous and horrible, Nature reached her supreme point in the making of the snake, so that priests who really paint hell well fill it with snakes instead of fire. These curving forms, these scintillant colorings create at once, upon sight, more relentless animosities than do shake barbaric tribes. To be born a snake is to be thrust into a place aswarm with formidable foes. To gain an appreciation of it, view hell as pictured by priests who are really skillful.

As for this snake in the pathway, there was a double curve some inches back of its head, which merely by the potency of its lines, made the man feel with tenfold eloquence the touch of the death-fingers at the nape of his neck. The reptile's head was waving slowly from side to side and its hot eyes flashed like little murder-lights. Always in the air was the dry, shrill whistling of the rattles.

"Beware! Beware! Beware!"

The man made a preliminary feint with his stick. Instantly the snake's heavy head and neck were bent back on the double curve and instantly the snake's body shot forward in a low, straight, hard spring. The man jumped with a convulsive chatter and swung his stick. The blind, sweeping blow fell upon the snake's head and hurled him so that steelcolored plates were for a moment uppermost. But he rallied swiftly, agilely, and again the head and neck bent back to the double curve, and the steaming, wide-open mouth made its desperate effort to reach its enemy. This attack, it could be seen, was despairing, but it was nevertheless impetuous, gallant, ferocious, of the same quality as the charge of the lone chief when the walls of white faces close upon him in the mountains. The stick swung unerringly again, and the snake, mutilated, torn, whirled himself into the last coil.

And now the man went sheer raving mad from the emotions of his forefathers and from his own. He came to close quarters. He gripped the stick with his two hands and made it speed like a flail. The snake, tumbling in the anguish of final despair, fought, bit, flung itself upon this stick which was taking its life.

At the end, the man clutched his stick and stood watching in silence. The dog came slowly, and with infinite caution stretched his nose forward, sniffing. The hair upon his neck and back moved and ruffled as if a sharp wind was blowing. The last muscular quivers of the snake were causing the rattles to still sound their treble cry, the shrill, ringing war chant and hymn of the grave of the thing that faces foes at once countless, implacable, and superior.

"Well, Rover," said the man, turning to the dog with a grin of victory, "we'll carry Mr. Snake home to show the girls."

His hands still trembled from the strain of the encounter, but he pried with his stick under the body of the snake and hoisted the limp thing upon it. He resumed his march along the path, and the dog walked, tranquilly meditative, at his master's heels.

[1896–U.S.A.]

QUESTIONS

1. What is suggested by the description in the first paragraph of the path's having become a "tangle"?
2. The unnamed man here, who seems representative of the whole human race, could take the snake's warning and back off. Why doesn't he?
3. Most human beings do "hate and fear" snakes, poisonous or not. In Crane's story, what might be the significance of this antipathy?

4. Beginnings and endings are of special importance. Toward the beginning of "The Snake," a dog is introduced; and the story concludes with reference to the dog. Why?

5. The man proves to be the true aggressor. How does this fact point toward the theme?

WRITING SUGGESTIONS

1. Compare "The First Death of Her Life" and "The Snake." Though vastly different, both stories touch on a like aspect of the human condition. Define what that "aspect" is and discuss it so as to shed light on the man in Crane's story.

2. Formulate the theme of "The Snake," taking into account the contrast between snake and dog as they relate to man. How do snake and dog differ? What does the difference, or the difference in attitude toward each on the part of humans, say about human beings? Then deepen your formulation by considering the aggressive nature of the man in the story.

On the Road

Langston Hughes

He was not interested in the snow. When he got off the freight, one early evening during the depression, Sargeant never even noticed the snow. But he must have felt it seeping down his neck, cold, wet, sopping in his shoes. But if you had asked him, he wouldn't have known it was snowing. Sargeant didn't see the snow, not even under the bright lights of the main street, falling white and flaky against the night. He was too hungry, too sleepy, too tired.

The Reverend Mr. Dorset, however, saw the snow when he switched on his porch light, opened the front door of his parsonage, and found standing there before him a big black man with snow on his face, a human piece of night with snow on his face—obviously unemployed.

Said the Reverend Mr. Dorset before Sargeant even realized he'd opened his mouth: "I'm sorry. No! Go right on down this street four blocks and turn to your left, walk up seven and you'll see the Relief Shelter. I'm sorry. No!" He shut the door.

Sargeant wanted to tell the holy man that he had already been to the Relief Shelter, been to hundreds of relief shelters during the depression years, the beds were always gone and supper was over, the place was full, and they drew the color line anyhow. But the minister said, "No," and shut the door. Evidently he didn't want to hear about it. And he *had* a door to shut.

The big black man turned away. And even yet he didn't see the snow, walking right into it. Maybe he sensed it, cold, wet, sticking to his jaws, wet on his black hands, sopping in his shoes. He stopped and stood on the sidewalk hunched over—hungry, sleepy, cold—looking up and down.

67

Then he looked right where he was—in front of a church. Of course! A church! Sure, right next to a parsonage, certainly a church.

It had *two* doors.

Broad white steps in the night all snowy white. Two high arched doors with slender stone pillars on either side. And way up, a round lacy window with a stone crucifix in the middle and Christ on the crucifix in stone. All this was pale in the street lights, solid and stony pale in the snow.

Sargeant blinked. When he looked up, the snow fell into his eyes. For the first time that night he *saw* the snow. He shook his head. He shook the snow from his coat sleeves, felt hungry, felt lost, felt not lost, felt cold. He walked up the steps of the church. He knocked at the door. No answer. He tried the handle. Locked. He put his shoulder against the door and his long black body slanted like a ramrod. He pushed. With loud rhythmic grunts, like the grunts in a chain-gang song, he pushed against the door.

"I'm tired . . . Huh! . . . Hongry . . . Uh! . . . I'm sleepy . . . Huh! I'm cold . . . I got to sleep somewheres," Sargeant said. "This here is a church, ain't it? Well, uh!"

He pushed against the door.

Suddenly, with an undue cracking and screaking, the door began to give way to the tall black Negro who pushed ferociously against it.

By now two or three white people had stopped in the street, and Sargeant was vaguely aware of some of them yelling at him concerning the door. Three or four more came running, yelling at him.

"Hey!" they said. "Hey!"

"Uh-huh," answered the big tall Negro, "I know it's a white folks' church, but I got to sleep somewhere." He gave another lunge at the door. "Huh!"

And the door broke open.

But just when the door gave way, two white cops arrived in a car, ran up the steps with their clubs, and grabbed Sargeant. But Sargeant for once had no intention to being pulled or pushed away from the door.

Sargeant grabbed, but not for anything so weak as a broken door. He grabbed for one of the tall stone pillars beside the door, grabbed at it and caught it. And held it. The Cops pulled and Sargeant pulled. Most of the people in the street got behind the cops and helped them pull.

"A big black unemployed Negro holding onto our church!" thought the people. "The idea!"

The cops began to beat Sargeant over the head, and nobody protested. But he held on.

And then the church fell down.

Gradually, the big stone front of the church fell down, the walls and the rafters, the crucifix and the Christ. Then the whole thing fell down, covering the cops and the people with bricks and stones and debris. The whole church fell down in the snow.

Sargeant got out from under the church and went walking on up the street with the stone pillar on his shoulder. He was under the impression that he had buried the parsonage and the Reverend Mr. Dorset who said, "No!" So he laughed, and threw the pillar six blocks up the street and went on.

Sargeant thought he was alone, but listening to the *crunch, crunch, crunch* on the snow of his own footsteps, he heard other footsteps, too, doubling his own. He looked around, and there was Christ walking along beside him, the same Christ that had been on the cross on the church—still stone with a rough stone surface, walking along beside him just like he was broken off the cross when the church fell down.

"Well, I'll be dogged," said Sargeant. "This here's the first time I ever seed you off the cross."

"Yes," said Christ, crunching his feet in the snow. "You had to pull the church down to get me off the cross."

"You glad?" said Sargeant.

"I sure am," said Christ.

They both laughed.

"I'm a hell of a fellow, ain't I?" said Sargeant. "Done pulled the church down!"

"You did a good job," said Christ. "They have kept me nailed on a cross for nearly two thousand years."

"Whee-ee-e!" said Sargeant. "I know you are glad to get off."

"I sure am," said Christ.

They walked on in the snow. Sargeant looked at the man of stone.

"And you have been up there two thousand years?"

"I sure have," Christ said.

"Well, if I had a little cash," said Sargeant, "I'd show you around a bit."

"I been around," said Christ.

"Yeah, but that was a long time ago."

"All the same," said Christ, "I've been around."

They walked on in the snow until they came to the railroad yards. Sargeant was tired, sweating and tired.

"Where you goin'?" Sargeant said, stopping by the tracks. He looked at Christ. Sargeant said, "I'm just a bum on the road. How about you? Where you goin'?"

"God knows," Christ said "but I'm leavin' here."

They saw the red and green lights of the railroad yard half veiled by the snow that fell out of the night. Away down the track they saw a fire in a hobo jungle.

"I can go there and sleep," Sargeant said.

"You can?"

"Sure," said Sargeant. "That place ain't got no doors."

Outside the town, along the tracks, there were barren trees and bushes below the embankment, snow-gray in the dark. And down among the trees and bushes there were makeshift houses made out of boxes and tin and old pieces of wood and canvas. You couldn't see them in the dark, but you knew they were there if you'd ever been on the road, if you had ever lived with the homeless and hungry in a depression.

"I'm side-tracking," Sargeant said. "I'm tired."

"I'm gonna make it on to Kansas City," said Christ.

"O.K.," Sargeant said. "So long!"

He went down into the hobo jungle and found himself a place to sleep. He never did see Christ no more. About 6:00 A.M. a freight came by. Sargeant scrambled out of the jungle with a dozen or so more hobos and ran along the track, grabbing at the freight. It was dawn, early dawn, cold and gray.

"Wonder where Christ is by now?" Sargeant thought. "He musta gone on way on down the road. He didn't sleep in this jungle."

Sargeant grabbed the train and started to pull himself up into a moving coal car, over the edge of a wheeling coal car. But strangely enough, the car was full of cops. The nearest cop rapped Sargeant soundly across the knuckles with his night stick. Wham! Rapped his big black hands for clinging to the top of the car. Wham! but Sargeant did not turn loose. He clung on and tried to pull himself into the car. He hollered at the top of his voice, "Damn it, lemme in this car!"

"Shut up," barked the cop. "You crazy coon!" He rapped Sargeant across the knuckles and punched him in the stomach. "You ain't out in no jungle now. This ain't no train. You in jail."

Wham! across his bare black fingers clinging to the bars of his cell. Wham! between the steel bars low down against his shins.

Suddenly Sargeant realized that he really was in jail. He wasn't on no train. The blood of the night before had dried on his face, his head hurt terribly, and a cop outside in the corridor was hitting him across the knuckles for holding onto the door, yelling and shaking the cell door.

"They musta took me to jail for breaking down the door last night," Sargeant thought, "that church door."

Sargeant went over and sat on a wooden bench against the cold stone wall. He was emptier than ever. His clothes were wet, clammy cold wet, and shoes sloppy with snow water. It was just about dawn. There he was, locked up behind a cell door, nursing his bruised fingers.

The bruised fingers were his, but not the *door.*

Not the *club,* but the fingers.

"You wait," mumbled Sargeant, black against the jail wall. "I'm gonna break down this door, too."

"Shut up—or I'll paste you one," said the cop.

"I'm gonna break down this door," yelled Sargeant as he stood up in his cell.

Then he must have been talking to himself because he said, "I wonder where Christ's gone? I wonder if he's gone to Kansas City?"

[1935–U.S.A.]

QUESTIONS

1. What does Hughes's title make you think of? In what way does it apply to Christ?
2. What biblical hero does Sargeant become in his fantasy? Who, then, must the townspeople be? What comment does Sargeant's fantasy make on the town and its people?
3. What is the significance of what happens to Christ in Sargeant's fantasy? Why does Christ intend to leave town?
4. Sargeant's question as to "where Christ's gone" summarizes in brief the thematic content of "On the Road." How so? How would you articulate its theme?

WRITING SUGGESTIONS

1. Do some research into the social conditions of blacks in this country in the 1930s. Then write an informational paragraph aimed at providing background for and thereby shedding light on Hughes's story.
2. Read Judges 16 in the Old Testament. Then write a paragraph addressing question 2 above. Point out specifically how Hughes draws the parallel between Sargeant and the biblical hero in question. Go on to discuss the significance of the whole biblical account to what Hughes is saying about the town in his story and generally about American life in his day.

What Good Are Relatives?*

Mikhail Zoshchenko

For two days Timofei Vasil'evich had been looking for his nephew, Serega Vlasov. On the third day, just before leaving town, he found him. He met him in a trolley car.

Timofei Vasil'evich boarded the trolley, took out a coin, and was about to give it to the conductor, only he looked—who could it be? The conductor's face seemed very familiar. Timofei Vasil'evich stared—yes! That's who it was—Serega Vlasov, his very own self, working as a trolley conductor.

"Well!" exclaimed Timofei Vasil'evich. "Serega! Is it really you, my fine friend?"

The conductor seemed embarrassed, checked his roll of tickets without any apparent need to do so, and said:"Just a moment, uncle . . . let me give out the tickets."

"O.K.! Go right ahead," his uncle said happily. "I'll wait."

Timofei Vasil'evich smiled and began to explain to the passengers: "He's a blood relative of mine, Serega Vlasov. My brother Peter's son . . . I haven't seen him for seven years . . ."

Timofei Vasil'evich looked with joy on his nephew and shouted to him: "Serega, my fine friend, I've been looking for you two days. All over town. And look where you are! A conductor . . . And I went to your address. On Raznochin Street. Not here, they answer. He went away, left this place. Where, says I, did he go, answer me, says I. I'm his blood uncle. We don't know, says they . . . And there you are—a conductor, aren't you?"

* Translated by Sidney Monas.

"A conductor," the nephew answered cautiously.

The passengers began to stare with curiosity at the relative. The uncle laughed happily and looked lovingly at his nephew, but the nephew was obviously embarrassed and, feeling that he was after all on duty, did not know what to say to his uncle or how to behave in his presence.

"So," the uncle said again, "you're a conductor on the trolley line?"

"A conductor . . ."

"Say, isn't that a coincidence! And I, Serega, my fine friend, I was just looking into the trolley—and what's that? The face on that conductor looks very familiar. And it turned out to be you. Ah, there's luck for you! Well, I'm so glad. I'm so pleased, really . . ."

For a moment the conductor shifted from foot to foot, and then suddenly he said:"You've got to pay, uncle. To get a ticket . . . Are you going far?"

The uncle laughed happily and slapped him across the change purse.

"I would have to paid! I swear to God! If I'd gotten on another car, or if I'd missed this one—O.K.—I would have paid. I would have paid my good money. Ah, there's luck for you! . . . I'm going to the railroad station, Serega, my fine friend."

"Two stops," said the conductor wearily, looking to the side.

"No, you don't mean it?" Timofei Vasil'evich seemed surprised. "You don't mean it? You're kidding?"

"You must pay, uncle," the conductor said softly. "Two stops. Because you can't travel for nothing and without a ticket."

Timofei Vasil'evich, offended, pressed his lips together and looked sternly at his nephew.

"Is this the way you treat your blood uncle? You rob your uncle?"

The conductor stared gloomily out of the window.

"That's piracy!" the uncle said angrily. "I haven't seen you, you son of a bitch, for seven years, and what do you do? You ask money for a trip. From your blood uncle? Don't you wave your hands at me. You may be my blood relative, but I'm not scared of your hands. Don't wave, you'll give the passengers a chill."

Timofei Vasil'evich turned the coin over in his hand and put it back in his pocket.

"What do you think of the likes of him, brothers?" Timofei Vasil'evich appealed to the public. "From his blood uncle he asks. Two stops, he says . . . Eh?"

"You must pay," said the nephew, almost in tears. "Please don't be angry, comrade uncle. Because this isn't my trolley. It's a state trolley. It belongs to the people."

"To the people," said the uncle, "that's not my business. You could show a little respect for your blood uncle. You could say, 'Uncle, put away your hard-earned ten kopecks. Travel free.' Your trolley wouldn't fall apart on account of that. I was riding in a train the other day . . . The conductor was no relation, but still he said: 'Please, Timofei Vasil'evich,' says he, 'why bring up such a thing . . . just sit . . .' And he took me along . . . And he's no relation . . . Just an old village friend. And you do this to your blood uncle . . . You'll get no money from me."

The conductor wiped his forehead with his hands and suddenly rang the bell.

"Get off, comrade uncle," said the nephew officially.

Seeing the matter was taking a serious turn, Timofei Vasil'evich wrung his hands, took out his ten-kopeck piece again, and then again put it back.

"No," he said, "I can't! Pay you, you snot, I can't. Better let me get off."

Timofei Vasil'evich arose solemnly and indignantly and made his way to the exit. Then he turned.

"Driving out your uncle . . . Your blood uncle," Timofei Vasil'evich said in a fury, "Why, you snot . . . I can have you shot for this."

Timofei Vasil'evich threw a withering glance at his nephew and got off the trolley.

[1923–U.S.S.R.]

QUESTIONS

1. Values and modes of social organization change with the times. People, however, do not always change accordingly. Compare and contrast the uncle and the nephew on this score.
2. The uncle says that he would have paid had he not found his nephew as conductor. Why does the fact that his nephew is the conductor make him so adamant against paying?
3. This story presents two opposing mentalities—those of the uncle and nephew—rooted in differing historical moments. Does the story sway us to prefer one over the other? What is the theme of this quietly satirical piece?

WRITING SUGGESTIONS

1. In an essay, first write character sketches of the uncle and nephew in which you contrast their mentalities. Then move on to contrast the social worlds they come from. Conclude by considering what these contrasts say about the modern world.

2. In that its theme could not possibly be reduced to a phrase, "What Good Are Relatives?" clearly demonstrates the difference between a theme and a moral. Using the story as example, discuss the difference between the two. To do so you will have to state the story's theme with as much subtlety as you can muster.
3. Argue that the uncle or that the nephew is in the right. How so? Or is neither right? If that is your conclusion, argue your case with reference to the limitations of the world view of each.

Swaddling Clothes*
Yukio Mishima

He was always busy, Toshiko's husband. Even tonight he had to dash off to an appointment, leaving her to go home alone by taxi. But what else could a woman expect when she married an actor—an attractive one? No doubt she had been foolish to hope that he would spend the evening with her. And yet he must have known how she dreaded going back to their house, unhomely with its Western-style furniture and with the bloodstains still showing on the floor.

Toshiko had been oversensitive since girlhood: that was her nature. As the result of constant worrying she never put on weight, and now, an adult woman, she looked more like a transparent picture than a creature of flesh and blood. Her delicacy of spirit was evident to her most casual acquaintance.

Earlier that evening, when she had joined her husband at a night club, she had been shocked to find him entertaining friends with an account of "the incident." Sitting there in his American-style suit, puffing at a cigarette, he had seemed to her almost a stranger.

"It's a fantastic story," he was saying, gesturing flamboyantly as if in an attempt to outweigh the attractions of the dance band. "Here this new nurse for our baby arrives from the employment agency, and the very first thing I notice about her is her stomach. It's enormous—as if she had a pillow stuck under her kimono! No wonder, I thought, for I soon saw that she could eat more than the rest of us put together. She polished off the contents of our rice bin like that. . . ." He snapped his fingers. " 'Gastric

* Translated by Ivan Morris.

dilation'—that's how she explained her girth and her appetite. Well, the day before yesterday we heard groans and moans coming from the nursery. We rushed in and found her squatting on the floor, holding her stomach in her two hands, and moaning like a cow. Next to her our baby lay in his cot, scared out of his wits and crying at the top of his lungs. A pretty scene, I can tell you!"

"So the cat was out of the bag?" suggested one of their friends, a film actor like Toshiko's husband.

"Indeed it was! And it gave me the shock of my life. You see, I'd completely swallowed that story about 'gastric dilation.' Well, I didn't waste any time. I rescued our good rug from the floor and spread a blanket for her to lie on. The whole time the girl was yelling like a stuck pig. By the time the doctor from the maternity clinic arrived, the baby had already been born. But our sitting room was a pretty shambles!"

"Oh, that I'm sure of!" said another of their friends, and the whole company burst into laughter.

Toshiko was dumbfounded to hear her husband discussing the horrifying happening as though it were no more than an amusing incident which they chanced to have witnessed. She shut her eyes for a moment and all at once she saw the newborn baby lying before her: on the parquet floor the infant lay, and his frail body was wrapped in bloodstained newspapers.

Toshiko was sure that the doctor had done the whole thing out of spite. As if to emphasize his scorn for this mother who had given birth to a bastard under such sordid conditions, he had told his assistant to wrap the baby in some loose newspapers, rather than proper swaddling. This callous treatment of the newborn child had offended Toshiko. Overcoming her disgust at the entire scene, she had fetched a brand-new piece of flannel from her cupboard and, having swaddled the baby in it, had laid him carefully in an armchair.

This all had taken place in the evening after her husband had left the house. Toshiko had told him nothing of it, fearing that he would think her oversoft, oversentimental; yet the scene had engraved itself deeply in her mind. Tonight she sat silently thinking back on it, while the jazz orchestra brayed and her husband chatted cheerfully with his friends. She knew that she would never forget the sight of the baby, wrapped in stained newspapers and lying on the floor—it was a scene fit for a butchershop. Toshiko, whose own life had been spent in solid comfort, poignantly felt the wretchedness of the illegitimate baby.

I am the only person to have witnessed its shame, the thought occurred to her. The mother never saw her child lying there in its newspaper wrappings, and the baby itself of course didn't know. I alone shall have to preserve that terrible scene in my memory. When the baby grows up and wants to find out about his birth, there will be no one to tell him, so long as I preserve silence. How strange that I should have this feeling of guilt! After all, it was I who took him up from the floor, swathed him properly in flannel, and laid him down to sleep in the armchair.

They left the night club and Toshiko stepped into the taxi that her husband had called for her. "Take this lady to Ushigomé," he told the driver and shut the door from the outside. Toshiko gazed through the window at her husband's smiling face and noticed his strong, white teeth. Then she leaned back in the seat, oppressed by the knowledge that their life together was in some way too easy, too painless. It would have been difficult for her to put her thoughts into words. Through the rear window of the taxi she took a last look at her husband. He was striding along the street toward his Nash car, and soon the back of his rather garish tweed coat had blended with the figures of the passers-by.

The taxi drove off, passed down a street dotted with bars and then by a theatre, in front of which the throngs of people jostled each other on the pavement. Although the performance had only just ended, the lights had already been turned out and in the half dark outside it was depressingly obvious that the cherry blossoms decorating the front of the theatre were merely scraps of white paper.

Even if that baby should grow up in ignorance of the secret of his birth, he can never become a respectable citizen, reflected Toshiko, pursuing the same train of thoughts. Those soiled newspaper swaddling clothes will be the symbol of his entire life. But why should I keep worrying about him so much? Is it because I feel uneasy about the future of my own child? Say twenty years from now, when our boy will have grown up into a fine, carefully educated young man, one day by a quirk of fate he meets that other boy, who then will also have turned twenty. And say that the other boy, who has been sinned against, savagely stabs him with a knife. . . .

It was a warm, overcast April night, but thoughts of the future made Toshiko feel cold and miserable. She shivered on the back seat of the car.

No, when the time comes I shall take my son's place, she told herself suddenly. Twenty years from now I shall be forty-three. I shall go to that young man and tell him straight out about everything—about his newspaper swaddling clothes, and about how I went and wrapped him in flannel.

The taxi ran along the dark wide road that was bordered by the park and by the Imperial Palace moat. In the distance Toshiko noticed the pinpricks of light which came from the block of tall office buildings.

Twenty years from now that wretched child will be in utter misery. He will be living a desolate, hopeless, poverty-stricken existence—a lonely rat. What else could happen to a baby who has had such a birth? He'll be wandering through the streets by himself, cursing his father, loathing his mother.

No doubt Toshiko derived a certain satisfaction from her somber thoughts: she tortured herself with them without cease. The taxi approached Hanzomon and drove past the compound of the British Embassy. At that point the famous rows of cherry trees were spread out before Toshiko in all their purity. On the spur of the moment she decided to go and view the blossoms by herself in the dark night. It was a strange decision for a timid and unadventurous young woman, but then she was in a strange state of mind and she dreaded the return home. That evening all sorts of unsettling fancies had burst open in her mind.

She crossed the wide street—a slim, solitary figure in the darkness. As a rule when she walked in the traffic Toshiko used to cling fearfully to her companion, but tonight she darted alone between the cars and a moment later had reached the long narrow park that borders the Palace moat. Chidorigafuchi, it is called—the Abyss of the Thousand Birds.

Tonight the whole park had become a grove of blossoming cherry trees. Under the calm cloudy sky the blossoms formed a mass of solid whiteness. The paper lanterns that hung from wires between the trees had been put out; in their place electric light bulbs, red, yellow, and green, shone dully beneath the blossoms. It was well past ten o'clock and most of the flower-viewers had gone home. As the occasional passers-by strolled through the park, they would automatically kick aside the empty bottles or crush the waste paper beneath their feet.

Newspapers, thought Toshiko, her mind going back once again to those happenings. Bloodstained newspapers. If a man were ever to hear of that piteous birth and know that it was he who had lain there, it would ruin his entire life. To think that I, a perfect stranger, should from now on have to keep such a secret—the secret of a man's whole existence . . . .

Lost in these thoughts, Toshiko walked on through the park. Most of the people still remaining there were quiet couples; no one paid her any attention. She noticed two people sitting on a stone bench beside the moat, not looking at the blossoms, but gazing silently at the water. Pitch black it was, and swathed in heavy shadows. Beyond the moat the somber forest of the Imperial Palace blocked her view. The trees reached up, to form a solid dark mass against the night sky. Toshiko walked slowly along the path beneath the blossoms hanging heavily overhead.

On a stone bench, slightly apart from the others, she noticed a pale object—not, as she had at first imagined, a pile of cherry blossoms, nor a garment forgotten by one of the visitors to the park. Only when she came closer did she see that it was a human form lying on the bench. Was it, she wondered, one of those miserable drunks often to be seen sleeping in public places? Obviously not, for the body had been systematically covered with newspapers, and it was the whiteness of those papers that had attracted Toshiko's attention. Standing by the bench, she gazed down at the sleeping figure.

It was a man in a brown jersey who lay there, curled up on layers of newspapers, other newspapers covering him. No doubt this had become his normal night residence now that spring had arrived. Toshiko gazed down at the man's dirty, unkempt hair, which in places had become hopelessly matted. As she observed the sleeping figure wrapped in its newspapers, she was inevitably reminded of the baby who had lain on the floor in its wretched swaddling clothes. The shoulder of the man's jersey rose and fell in the darkness in time with his heavy breathing.

It seemed to Toshiko that all her fears and premonitions had suddenly taken concrete form. In the darkness the man's pale forehead stood out, and it was a young forehead, though carved with the wrinkles of long poverty and hardship. His khaki trousers had been slightly pulled up; on his sockless feet he wore a pair of battered gym shoes. She could not see his face and suddenly had an overmastering desire to get one glimpse of it.

She walked to the head of the bench and looked down. The man's head was half buried in his arms, but Toshiko could see that he was surprisingly young. She noticed the thick eyebrows and the fine bridge of his nose. His slightly open mouth was alive with youth.

But Toshiko had approached too close. In the silent night the newspaper bedding rustled, and abruptly the man opened his eyes. Seeing the young woman standing directly beside him, he raised himself with a jerk, and his eyes lit up. A second later a powerful hand reached out and seized Toshiko by her slender wrist.

She did not feel in the least afraid and made no effort to free herself. In a flash the thought had struck her, Ah, so the twenty years have already gone by! The forest of the Imperial Palace was pitch dark and utterly silent.

[1966–Japan]

QUESTIONS

1. What is the import of the many references to the West: for example, "Western-style furniture," "his American-style suit," "blocks of tall office buildings," "the British Embassy"? In what way is the fact that Toshiko's husband is a "film actor" significant?
2. What does Toshiko's finding the incident with the baby a "horrifying happening" but her husband's finding it "no more than an amusing incident" reveal about each? What does the implied difference in their feelings about their furniture reveal? What values or ways of seeing, then, does each represent?
3. Why is Toshiko so moved and upset by the baby's being wrapped in newspaper? What is the origin of her guilt? Why should her "somber thoughts" give her "a certain satisfaction"?
4. With its cherry trees and proximity to the "Palace moat" and "somber forest of the Imperial Palace," what does the park represent to Toshiko? Why does she come here? Might she have some unconscious motive?
5. The end of "Swaddling Clothes" could be read as realistic or as surrealistic. How so? In either case, it is also symbolic, as is the story as a whole. What symbolic statement does "Swaddling Clothes" make? What is its general theme?

WRITING SUGGESTIONS

1. Write a discrete paragraph in which you contrast Toshiko and her husband. Establish the contrast with reference to the story's details (see the first and second questions above); then conclude with a consideration of what each represents in the world of Mishima's story.
2. To a greater or lesser extent, we are all culture-bound. In a short analytic essay, consider how we humans define ourselves in accordance with the culture each of us is born into. As you conclude, suggest to what extent we are free agents and to what we are tied to the definitions, biases, and so forth of our cultural backgrounds.
3. And what of you in this regard? Write a paragraph about your own cultural background and how it has shaped the person you are.

Just Lather, That's All*

Hernando Tellez

He said nothing when he entered. I was passing the best of my razors back and forth on a strop. When I recognized him I started to tremble. But he didn't notice. Hoping to conceal my emotion, I continued sharpening the razor. I tested it on the meat of my thumb, and then held it up to the light. At that moment he took off the bullet-studded belt that his gun holster dangled from. He hung it up on a wall hook and placed his military cap over it. Then he turned to me, loosening the knot of his tie, and said, "It's hot as hell. Give me a shave." He sat in the chair.

I estimated he had a four-day beard. The four days taken up by the latest expedition in search of our troops. His face seemed reddened, burned by the sun. Carefully, I began to prepare the soap. I cut off a few slices, dropped them into the cup, mixed in a bit of warm water, and began to stir with the brush. Immediately the foam began to rise. "The other boys in the group should have this much beard, too." I continued stirring the lather.

"But we did all right, you know. We got the main ones. We brought back some dead, and we've got some others still alive. But pretty soon they'll all be dead."

"How many did you catch?" I asked.

"Fourteen. We had to go pretty deep into the woods to find them. But we'll get even. Not one of them comes out of this alive, not one."

He leaned back on the chair when he saw me with the lather-covered brush in my hand. I still had to put the sheet on him. No doubt about it, I

* Translated by Angel Flores.

82

was upset. I took a sheet out of a drawer and knotted it around my customer's neck. He wouldn't stop talking. He probably thought I was in sympathy with his party.

"The town must have learned a lesson from what we did the other day," he said.

"Yes," I replied, securing the knot at the base of his dark, sweaty neck.

"That was a fine show, eh?"

"Very good," I answered, turning back for the brush. The man closed his eyes with a gesture of fatigue and sat waiting for the cool caress of the soap. I had never had him so close to me. The day he ordered the whole town to file into the patio of the school to see the four rebels hanging there, I came face to face with him for an instant. But the sight of the mutilated bodies kept me from noticing the face of the man who had directed it all, the face I was now about to take into my hands. It was not an unpleasant face, certainly. And the beard, which made him seem a bit older than he was, didn't suit him badly at all. His name was Torres. Captain Torres. A man of imagination, because who else would have thought of hanging the naked rebels and then holding target practice on certain parts of their bodies? I began to apply the first layer of soap. With his eyes closed, he continued. "Without any effort I could go straight to sleep," he said, "but there's plenty to do this afternoon." I stopped the lathering and asked with a feigned lack of interest: "A firing squad?" "Something like that, but a little slower." I got on with the job of lathering his beard. My hands started trembling again. The man could not possibly realize it, and this was in my favor. But I would have preferred that he hadn't come. It was likely that many of our faction had seen him enter. And an enemy under one's roof imposes certain conditions. I would be obliged to shave that beard like any other one, carefully, gently, like that of any customer, taking pains to see that no single pore emitted a drop of blood. Being careful to see that the little tufts of hair did not lead the blade astray. Seeing that his skin ended up clean, soft, and healthy, so that passing the back of my hand over it I couldn't feel a hair. Yes, I was secretly a rebel, but I was also a conscientious barber, and proud of the preciseness of my profession. And this four-days' growth of beard was a fitting challenge.

I took the razor, opened up the two protective arms, exposed the blade and began the job, from one of the sideburns downward. The razor responded beautifully. His beard was inflexible and hard, not too long, but thick. Bit by bit the skin emerged. The razor rasped along, making its customary sound as fluffs of lather mixed with bits of hair gathered along the blade. I paused a moment to clean it, then took up the strop again to sharpen the razor, because I'm a barber who does things properly. The man, who had kept his eyes closed, opened them now, removed one of his hands from under the sheet, felt the spot on his face where the soap had been cleared off, and said, "Come to the school today at six o'clock." "The same thing as the other day?" I asked horrified. "It could be better," he replied. "What do you plan to do?" "I don't know yet. But we'll amuse ourselves." Once more he leaned back and closed his eyes. I approached him with the razor poised. "Do you plan to punish them all?" I ventured timidly. "All." The soap was drying on his face. I had to hurry. In the mirror I looked toward the street. It was the same as ever: the grocery store with two or three customers in it. Then I glanced at the clock: two-twenty in the afternoon. The razor continued on its downward stroke. Now from the other sideburn down. A thick, blue beard. He should have let it grow like some poets or priests do. It would suit him well. A lot of people wouldn't recognize him. Much to his benefit, I thought, as I attempted to cover the neck area smoothly. There, for sure, the razor had to be handled masterfully, since the hair, although softer, grew into little swirls. A curly beard. One of the tiny pores could be opened up and issue forth its pearl of blood. A good barber such as I prides himself on never allowing this to happen to a client. And this was a first-class client. How many of us had he ordered shot? How many of us had he ordered mutilated? It was better not to think about it. Torres did not know that I was his enemy. He did not know it nor did the rest. It was a secret shared by very few, precisely so that I could inform the revolutionaries of what Torres was doing in the town and of what he was planning each time he undertook a rebel-hunting excursion. So it was going to be very difficult to explain that I had him right in my hands and let him go peacefully—alive and shaved.

The beard was now almost completely gone. He seemed younger, less burdened by years than when he had arrived. I suppose this always happens with men who visit barber shops. Under the stroke of my razor Torres was being rejuvenated—rejuvenated because I am a good barber, the best in the town, if I may say so. A little more lather here, under his chin, on his Adam's apple, on this big vein. How hot it is getting! Torres must be sweating as much as I. But he is not afraid. He is a calm man, who is not even thinking about what he is going to do with the prisoners this afternoon. On the other hand I, with this razor in my hands, stroking and restroking this skin, trying to keep blood from oozing from these pores, can't even think clearly. Damn him for coming, because I'm a revolutionary and not a murderer. And how easy it would be to kill him. And he deserves it. Does he? No! What the devil! No one deserves to have someone else make the sacrifice of becoming a murderer. What do you gain by it? Nothing. Others come along and still others, and the first ones kill the second ones and they the next ones and it goes on like this until everything is a sea of blood. I could cut this throat just so, zip! zip! I wouldn't give him time to complain and since he has his eyes closed he wouldn't see the glistening knife blade or my glistening eyes. But I'm trembling like a real murderer. Out of his neck a gush of blood would spout onto the sheet, on the chair, on my hands, on the floor. I would have to close the door. And the blood would keep inching along the floor, warm, ineradicable, uncontainable, until it reached the street, like a little scarlet stream. I'm sure that one solid stroke, one deep incision, would prevent any pain. He wouldn't suffer. But what would I do with the body? Where would I hide it? I would have to flee, leaving all I have behind, and take refuge far away, far, far away. But they would follow until they found me. "Captain Torres' murderer. He slit his throat while he was shaving him—a coward." And then on the other side. "The avenger of us all. A name to remember. (And here they would mention my name.) He was the town barber. No one knew he was defending our cause."

And what of all this? Murderer or hero? My destiny depends on the edge of this blade. I can turn my hand a bit more, press a little harder on the razor, and sink it in. The skin would give way like silk, like rubber, like the strop. There is nothing more tender than human skin and the blood is always there, ready to pour forth. A blade like this doesn't fail. It is my best. But I don't want to be a murderer, no sir. You come to me for a shave. And I perform my work honorably . . . . I don't want blood on my hands. Just lather, that's all. You are an executioner and I am only a barber. Each person has his own place in the scheme of things. That's right. His own place.

Now his chin had been stroked clean and smooth. The man sat up and looked into the mirror. He rubbed his hands over his skin and felt it fresh, like new.

"Thanks," he said. He went to the hanger for his belt, pistol and cap. I must have been very pale; my shirt felt soaked. Torres finished adjusting the buckle, straightened his pistol in the holster and after automatically smoothing down his hair, he put on the cap. From his pants pocket he took out several coins to pay me for my services. And he began to head toward the door. In the doorway he paused for a moment, and turning to me he said:

"They told me that you'd kill me. I came to find out. But killing isn't easy. You can take my word for it." And he headed on down the street.

[1950–Colombia]

QUESTIONS

1. Is it meaningful that we are not told where (that is, in what country) the story takes place or what the political issues are and what has caused the revolution? How so?
2. The conflict and drama here are entirely internal. What obligations are at odds within the barber?
3. Though true, the facts that the barber would lose his cover if he killed his customer and that nothing much would be accomplished anyway because another would only come to take the place of Captain Torres are rationalizations. What are the barber's true reasons for not murdering the Captain?
4. The last sentence of the story suggests that the Captain thinks the barber to be a coward. Is he?
5. What does the barber come to realize during the course of "Just Lather, That's All"? What, finally, is the theme of the story?

WRITING SUGGESTIONS

1. In a paragraph, argue that the barber is wrong and that he should kill Captain Torres. Why should he? Specify possible benefits that could come to the revolutionaries from the killing. In not killing the Captain, is the barber selfish? In another paragraph, argue that he is and that in choosing private integrity he sacrifices public good.
2. But can public good ever really result from the sacrifice of individual integrity? In a short essay, argue the opposite case: that the barber is right, not only with respect to himself but indeed with respect to the revolutionary cause he has served.
3. Which of the two views just proposed seems better to describe the attitude conveyed by "Just Lather, That's All"? Write an essay in which you consider both views and defend your choice with specifics drawn from the story.

Theme of the Traitor and Hero*

Jorge Luis Borges

So the Platonic Year
Whirls out new right and wrong,
Whirls in the old instead;
All men are dancers and their tread
Goes to the barbarous clangour of a gong.
—W. B. Yeats, The Tower

Under the influence of the flagrant Chesterton (contriver and embellisher of elegant mysteries) and of the court counsellor Leibnitz (who invented pre-established harmony), I have imagined the following argument, which I shall doubtless develop (and which already justifies me in some way), on profitless afternoons. Details, revisions, adjustments are lacking; there are areas of this history which are not yet revealed to me; today, the third of January of 1944, I dimly perceive it thus:

The action transpires in some oppressed and stubborn country: Poland, Ireland, the Republic of Venice, some state in South America or the Balkans. . . . *Has transpired*, we should say, for although the narrator is contemporary, the narrative related by him occurred toward the middle or beginnings of the nineteenth century. Let us say, for purposes of narration, that it was in Ireland, in 1824. The narrator is named Ryan; he is a great-grandson of the young, heroic, handsome, assassinated Fergus Kilpatrick, whose sepulchre was mysteriously violated, whose name embellishes the verse of Browning and Hugo, whose statue presides over a gray hill amidst red moors.

Kilpatrick was a conspirator, a secret and glorious captain of conspirators; he was like Moses in that, from the land of Moab, he described the Promised Land but would not ever set foot there, for he perished on the eve of the victorious rebellion which he had premeditated and conjured. The date of the first centenary of his death draws near; the circumstances of the crime are enigmatic; Ryan, engaged in compiling a biography of the hero, discovers that the enigma goes beyond the purely criminal. Kilpatrick was

* Translated by Anthony Kerrigan.

assassinated in a theater; the English police could find no trace of the killer; historians declare that the failure of the police does not in any way impugn their good intentions, for he was no doubt killed by order of this same police. Other phases of the enigma disquiet Ryan. These facets are of cyclic character: they seem to repeat or combine phenomena from remote regions, from remote ages. Thus, there is no one who does not know that the bailiffs who examined the hero's cadaver discovered a sealed letter which warned him of the risk of going to the theater on that particular night: Julius Caesar, too, as he walked toward the place where the knives of his friends awaited him, was handed a message, which he never got to the point of reading, in which the treason was declared, and the names of the traitors given. In her dreams, Caesar's wife, Calpurnia, saw a tower, which the Senate had dedicated to her husband, fallen to the ground; false and anonymous rumors throughout the land were occasioned, on the eve of Kilpatrick's death, by the burning of the round tower of Kilgarvan—an event which might have seemed an omen, since Kilpatrick had been born at Kilgarvan. These parallels (and others) in the history of Caesar and the history of an Irish conspirator induce Ryan to assume a secret pattern in time, a drawing in which the lines repeat themselves. He ponders the decimal history imagined by Condorcet; the morphologies proposed by Hegel, Spengler, and Vico; the characters of Hesiod, who degenerate from gold to iron. He considers the transmigration of souls, a doctrine which horrifies Celtic belles-lettres and which the very same Caesar attributed to the Britannic Druids; he thinks that before the hero was Fergus Kilpatrick, Fergus Kilpatrick was Julius Caesar. From these circular labyrinths he is saved by a curious species of proof which immediately plunges him into other labyrinths even more inextricable and heterogeneous: certain words spoken by a mendicant who conversed with Fergus Kilpatrick on the day of his death were prefigured in the tragedy of Macbeth. That history should have imitated history was already sufficiently marvelous; that history should imitate literature is inconceivable. . . .

Ryan discovers that in 1814, James Alexander Nolan, the oldest of the hero's comrades, had translated into Gaelic the principal dramas of Shakespeare, among them *Julius Caesar*. In the archives he also finds a manuscript article by Nolan on *Festspiele* of Switzerland: vast and roving theatrical representations these, which require thousands of actors and which reiterate historic episodes in the same cities and mountains where they occurred. Still another unpublished document reveals that a few days before the end, Kilpatrick, presiding over his last conclave, had signed the death sentence of a traitor, whose name has been blotted out. This sentence scarcely harmonizes with Kilpatrick's pious attitude. Ryan goes deeper into the matter (the investigation covers one of the hiatuses in the argument) and he succeeds in solving the enigma.

Kilpatrick was brought to his end in a theater, but he made of the entire city a theater, too, and the actors were legion. And the drama which was climaxed by his death embraced many days and many nights. Here is what happened:

On the second of August of 1824, the conspirators gathered. The country was ripe for rebellion. But somehow every attempt always failed: there was a traitor in the group. Fergus Kilpatrick ordered James Nolan to uncover this traitor. Nolan carried out his orders: before the gathering as a whole, he announced that the traitor was Kilpatrick himself. He demonstrated the truth of his accusation with irrefutable proofs; the conspirators condemned their president to death. The latter signed his own death sentence; but he implored that his condemnation not be allowed to hurt the fatherland.

Nolan thereupon conceived his strange project. Ireland idolized Kilpatrick; the most tenuous suspicion of his disgrace would have compromised the rebellion; Nolan proposed a plan which would make Kilpatrick's execution an instrument for the liberation of the fatherland. He suggested the condemned man die at the hands of an unknown assassin, in circumstances deliberately dramatic, which would engrave themselves upon the popular imagination and which would speed the revolt. Kilpatrick swore to collaborate in a project which allowed him the opportunity to redeem himself and which would add a flourish to his death.

Pressed for time, Nolan was unable to integrate the circumstances he invented for the complex execution; he was forced to plagiarize another dramatist, the enemy-Englishman William Shakespeare. He repeated scenes from *Macbeth*, and from *Julius Caesar*. The public—and the secret—presentation took several days. The condemned man entered Dublin, discussed, worked, prayed, reproved, spoke words which seemed (later) to be pathetic—and each one of these acts, which would eventually be glorious, had been foreordained by Nolan. Hundreds of actors collaborated with the protagonist; the role of some was stellar, that of others ephemeral. What they said and did remains in the books of history, in the impassioned memory of Ireland. Kilpatrick, carried away by the minutely scrupulous destiny which redeemed and condemned him, more than once enriched the text (Nolan's text) with words and deeds of his own improvisation. And thus did the popular drama unfold in Time, until, on the sixth of August of 1824, in a theater box hung with funereal curtains, which foreshadowed Abraham Lincoln's, the anticipated pistol-shot entered the breast of the traitor and hero, who could scarcely articulate, between two effusions of violent blood, some prearranged words.

In Nolan's work, the passages imitated from Shakespeare are the *least* dramatic; Ryan suspects that the author interpolated them so that one person, in the future, might realize the truth. He understands that he, too, forms part of Nolan's plan. . . . At the end of some tenacious caviling, he resolves to keep silent his discovery. He publishes a book dedicated to the glory of the hero; this, too, no doubt was foreseen.

[1944–Argentina]

QUESTIONS

1. The title announces the story's theme. For the moment, consider only the story of Kilpatrick as unearthed by his fictional biographer, Ryan. Is Kilpatrick a traitor now all is known, or is he a hero because he furthered the revolution by doing a grand job of acting the part devised for him by Nolan?
2. And what of Nolan, stage manager and assassin, and Ryan, idealistic falsifier of the facts, if facts they be? Are these men traitors or heroes?
3. What is a traitor, what a hero? It depends, doesn't it, on what historians have chosen to record? Certainly, we've seen many reputations altered and then altered again as a result of historical revisionism. Is history, then, fictional?
4. What do you make of the initial premise of the story—that the whole thing is not a story but only an idea for a piece of fiction inspired by Chesterton (a mystery writer) and Leibnitz (a philosopher)? (That the philosophy of history is a concern of the story, incidentally, is suggested by the references to Condorcet, Hegel, Spengler, and Vico, all philosophers of history.) The nature of fiction and its relationship to history as well as to other realms of human endeavor, including works of literature, is Borges's deeper theme (thus the story's references to Lincoln and Moses, Yeats, Browning, and Hugo). What does the story suggest about fiction in this regard? What does it suggest about history and other types of written texts?

WRITING SUGGESTIONS

1. Might Ryan be mad? In a paragraph, define madness and then make a case for his being a good example. Alternatively, define sanity and make a case in light of your definition that he is perfectly sane.
2. In a short essay, compare and contrast "Theme of the Traitor and Hero" with any other story in this book. Show what makes Borges's story remarkably different.

3. Write a paragraph in answer to question 1 above. State your answer and defend it. Note, however, that whatever your answer, the story itself is not clear-cut. As you move to conclude, consider the implications of the story's ambiguity, especially as to history as we read of it in books.

4. Certain contemporary French and American critics argue that *all* texts are fictional. If this is so, as Borges might agree, then the truth-value of fiction is perhaps greater than that of other types of writing simply because fiction is known to be fiction. Write an essay defending this proposition.

· 3 ·
PLOT/SITUATION

PLOT AS CAUSAL SEQUENCE

Plot entails action. It also entails causality, or a sense of what it is that brought about an action and, thus, what the meaning of that action is. As E. M. Forster observes, the sentence "The queen died; then the king died" does not exhibit a plot; the sentence "The queen died; therefore, the king died" does (86). Plot, then, is a structural element, always pointing to the springs of action, to the relationship of cause and effect. So instead of "plot," people sometimes speak of "the *course* of events" or "the story *line*" of a work of fiction. Both the word "course" and the word "line" suggest that a plot is more than a simple description of events. It is, rather, the construction of events into a coherent sequence, with the sequence shedding light on the events that compose it.

But you know all of this already. The last time you told someone about a movie you had seen, you probably summarized its plot: this happened and so that happened and then the other thing happened because this and that happened. And if something happened in the movie that was not causally related to the action overall, violating your sense of its inner logic, you probably criticized the movie for "not holding together." You also know that a plot does not have to proceed chronologically, which alone suggests that it is different from a simple narrative report. Many works of fiction, like many movies, begin in the middle of things (critics say "*in medias res*") or even at the end, and many show earlier events in flashbacks, in which, for example, we are taken back to scenes from a character's childhood to help explain his or her actions in the present. Once again, it is the establishing of the relationship of cause and effect that turns what otherwise would be a simple narrative report of events into a plot.

MEANS AND ENDS

Because it is the easiest element to summarize, plot—the sequenced events or occurrences in a story—is what beginning students inevitably speak of when asked what a story is about: "This story is about a man who does such and such, and as a result so and so happens, and therefore it turns out that he shouldn't have done such and such in the first place." But no story is *about* its plot. Plot can point to theme (what a story *is* about) in many ways, but the plot itself is not the meaning. It is not an end in itself but a means. Granted, some modes of fiction depend heavily on plot: mysteries, for example, and often comedies gain their effects by the twists and turns of an intricately plotted story line. Even here, however, plot is a means to an end—specifically, to the creation of suspense or the provocation of laughter. However elaborate the plot, then, it functions as a means and must be taken as such.

But plots don't have to be elaborate to function. Though first-rate fiction can be intricately plotted, suspenseful, and charged with physical action, many fine stories have none of these traits. Some have plots— and their plots are important—that are relatively slender, straightforward, and quiet. Other stories have so little plot, if any, that there is no point in speaking of their plot at all. In this kind of fiction nothing much happens in terms of external action: there are no events, no occurrences, no happenings of any consequence, and so no plot. In such stories we attend, rather, to internal states of feeling or to the nuances of personality. Two stories in chapter 2 are of this sort: "The First Death of Her Life" and "Just Lather, That's All." In both, the drama is purely internal. We find the central character (or protagonist) of each in a situation and attend not to what either of them does but to what they feel as a result of the situation each is in. A situation can serve just as well as a plot to anchor a story in the world and to lead to character revelation, for instance, or to mood.

PLOT AND THE OTHER ELEMENTS OF FICTION

Each a means rather than an end, all of the elements that compose a story work together toward the embodiment of some significant perception of human life. (Remember, incidentally, that in a given work some elements will be more prominent than others, and some might not figure in at all.) And always, the elements that are present are interlinked, one helping to establish another. How plot goes into the making of mood, for example, can be seen in Thurber's "The Night the Bed Fell" (pages 130–33). Here the sequence of actions—the plot—is humorous; the mood of the story, therefore, is comic. Plot in this case creates mood, which shapes our attitude toward the material of the story and so moves us toward an understanding of theme. To give another example, plot is usually an agent of characterization. Just as what a person does in real life reveals something about that person, so what a character does in a story shows us something important about that character. Here again plot leads us toward theme, for character is usually a prime element in establishing theme and in many stories what is revealed about character *is* the theme.

CONFLICT AND HAPPY ENDINGS

In one way or another, the plots of most works of fiction involve conflict: between characters and the world (natural or social), between one character and another, or between opposing sides within a single character. Conflict in first-rate fiction, whether established by plot or situation, is usually subtle and complex; as in life, there are no simple rights and wrongs, judgments are hard to come by, and resolutions are seldom clear-cut. And because resolutions are seldom clear-cut, few stories that are worth the reader's effort have happy endings. "And they lived happily ever after," most fairy tales tell us. But no one's life is altogether happy and no one lives *ever* after; even if our lives were conflict free, which seems all but impossible to imagine, we would still have to face growing old and dying. In good fiction—whether plotted or situational—such realities are never out of mind; thus, we are most often left to ponder an ironic or indeterminate end, one that smacks of the realities of life rather than the wishes of fairy tales.

As we saw in chapter 1, worthwhile fiction involves us actively as readers in probing the complexity of human beings and human life. Though perhaps satisfying on a certain level, fiction that casts opposing forces in simple terms of right and wrong, and whose plot builds to a happy ending with the triumph of right, leaves little to think about. There's nothing like irony, or inconclusiveness, or the sting of a tragic end, to spur the mind into action of its own, to involve us immediately, that is, and to lead us to probe more deeply into the nature of things. Marked by subtle conflict and plots (or situations) that do not necessarily resolve themselves, at least in any simplistic way, fiction can do just that.

SUMMARY SUGGESTIONS: UNDERSTANDING PLOT/SITUATION

1. When you are reading a story, put aside the question of what will happen next and ask instead why what is happening is happening. It is the why and not the what that will lead you to comprehension.

2. Decide whether a given story presents a plot or a situation. If the latter, then there is nothing more to be concerned with along the lines of plot, though, like plot, a situation must be considered in relation to a story's other elements.

3. If the story contains a plot, clarify to yourself how the plot moves by determining the causal relationship between events. Then judge whether or not the relationship between events within the world of the story is consistent in light of the type of world created by the story. This world may be very different from your own, but still you can judge as to whether its causal relationships make sense. If they don't, either you have missed something in the story or its plot is inept or dishonest, contrived by the writer merely to produce an effect. You must be the judge as to which is the case.

4. Look to see how the plot (or situation if the story has no plot) functions with respect to the other elements from which the story is constructed. Does the plot (or situation) help to create mood? Is plot an agent of characterization? Does it produce irony? What other functions does it serve? By considering how the plot functions, you will be moving toward theme.

WRITING ON PLOT/SITUATION

Good writing on plot (or situation) always involves far more than summarizing, but at times a summary may be useful or even essential. For instance, take a movie review or the review of a novel. Though reviews do not confine themselves to mere summaries of plots, most contain summaries somewhere along the line, usually toward the beginning. Similarly, an essay on a story might easily call for a plot summary as support material. Should a summary help to support your argument, you have good reason to incorporate it.

Further, following the plot can often help provide the structure for an essay although the plot is not summarized anywhere in the essay. Both the sample paragraph and the sample essay in chapter 1 (pages 16 and 25 respectively) are structured in this way (by reference to the plot of "The Shawl"). By following the movements of Ozick's plot, both gain coherence as well as a certain forward momentum. When writing on a story, you can often gain coherence in this way: by following the movement of the story itself as you move from point to point.

Plot can also be the central focus of paragraph or essay. For instance, you could write an analysis of a plot (in which case you would probably want to summarize it at the start). Plot analysis involves the consideration of the inner logic of a story: not just what happens first and then what happens next, but the causal relationship of events—*why* one event leads to another, the *meaning* of their interaction. For example, in analyzing the plot of "The Shawl," the writer would want to discuss *how* the stealing of the shawl gives rise to Magda's death and *how*, therefore, Magda's death results from Stella's sibling rivalry. Another kind of paper focusing centrally on plot would be one that examines how plot functions with respect to one or more of the other elements in a given piece of fiction. In either kind of paper, of course, what is finally important is the function of plot in the fiction as a whole. For instance, as we've noted, a plot might help create a story's mood, which, because it shapes our attitude, moves us toward theme. Thurber's "The Night the Bed Fell," which appears later in this chapter, provides a good example. In arriving at a statement of the theme of the story, you would surely want to think out the relation between its plot and its mood. In writing a paper on the story thereafter, you might bring up the relationship between the story's plot and mood in order to argue whatever you have to say about its theme. Or a story's situation might give rise to irony, which in turn points toward theme. Such is the case in Chekhov's "The Lottery Ticket," also found in this chapter. One of many things that could be written on the story is an analysis of its situation and resultant irony. Such a paper could conclude with a statement of theme as it springs from the irony of the story overall.

There is much, then, that can be done with plot (or situation) when one comes to writing on fiction. Plot can be summarized to serve as support or used to structure an essay. It can also be made the subject of an essay, analyzed either in and of itself or in its relationship to the other elements of a story. In any case, the purpose is always to shed light in one way or another on the full meaning of the story. Whatever you choose to do, remember that a simple summary, standing alone, will not satisfy your reader. Your reader will want to learn more than the plot; your reader will want to see how plot (or situation) functions in the story in relation to the theme.

GENERAL WRITING ASSIGNMENTS

1. Keep a journal for one week during the present month. Many of the events of the week will prove discrete (that is, they will bear no relationship to other events). Others, however, will prove to be causally related, sometimes in surprising ways. Pick and choose events from your journal that are related and write them in sequence, introducing fictional details if you wish. Then compare what you have written with the jottings in your journal. The journal will be only a record of events; in contrast, what you have abstracted from it should have a plot. It might even have a theme, in which case you will have written a story.

2. Take a straight news report from your local paper: for example, a report of a fire or of a local scandal or even nothing more than a piece on a meeting of the zoning board at town hall. Now turn your material into a story of sorts by rewriting it in such a way as to suggest interesting causes for the events or the behavior of those involved.

3. Discuss a murder mystery you've read or seen and liked (here a plot summary at the start may be in order). What effects did its plot create? How did its plot bring these effects about? What was it about the plot that made the book or movie pleasurable?

4. Choose a movie, television show, book, or story whose plot seemed flawed to you. Discuss in what way or ways it was flawed and the effect on the audience (you) of its being flawed. You could conclude with a statement about plot in general derived from your observations.

5. Write a review of a book or movie. To do so, you may wish to give a plot summary up front. But if you do, remember that that summary is not an end in itself. It should serve as a springboard to your discussion of whether the book or movie succeeds or fails. This is the point of a review. State your opinion and then back it up, telling why you judge the book or movie as you do.

The Lottery Ticket*

Anton Chekhov

Ivan Dmitritch, a middle-class man who lived with his family on an income of twelve hundred a year and was very well satisfied with his lot, sat down on the sofa after supper and began reading the newspaper.

"I forgot to look at the newspaper today," his wife said to him as she cleared the table. "Look and see whether the list of drawings is there."

"Yes, it is," said Ivan Dmitritch; "but hasn't your ticket lapsed?"

"No; I took the interest on Tuesday."

"What is the number?"

"Series 9,499, number 26."

"All right . . . we will look . . . 9,499 and 26."

Ivan Dmitritch had no faith in lottery luck, and would not, as a rule, have consented to look at the lists of winning numbers, but now, as he had nothing else to do and as the newspaper was before his eyes, he passed his finger downwards along the column of numbers. And immediately, as though in mockery of his scepticism, no further than the second line from the top, his eye was caught by the figure 9,499! Unable to believe his eyes, he hurriedly dropped the paper on his knees without looking to see the number of the ticket, and, just as though some one had given him a douche of cold water, he felt an agreeable chill in the pit of the stomach; tingling and terrible and sweet!

"Masha, 9,499 is there!" he said in a hollow voice.

His wife looked at his astonished and panic-stricken face, and realized that he was not joking.

* Translated by Constance Garnett.

"9,499?" she asked, turning pale and dropping the folded tabecloth on the table.

"Yes, yes . . . it really is there!"

"And the number of the ticket?"

"Oh, yes! There's the number of the ticket too. But stay . . . wait! No, I say! Anyway, the number of our series is there! Anyway, you understand. . . ."

Looking at his wife, Ivan Dmitritch gave a broad, senseless smile, like a baby when a bright object is shown it. His wife smiled too; it was as pleasant to her as to him that he only mentioned the series, and did not try to find out the number of the winning ticket. To torment and tantalize oneself with hopes of possible fortune is so sweet, so thrilling!

"It is our series," said Ivan Dmitritch, after a long silence. "So there is a probability that we have won. It's only a probability, but there it is!"

"Well, now look!"

"Wait a little. We have plenty of time to be disappointed. It's on the second line from the top, so the prize is seventy-five thousand. That's not money, but power, capital! And in a minute I shall look at the list, and there—26! Eh? I say, what if we really have won?"

The husband and wife began laughing and staring at one another in silence. The possibility of winning bewildered them; they could not have said, could not have dreamed, what they both needed that seventy-five thousand for, what they would buy, where they would go. They thought only of the figures 9,499 and 75,000 and pictured them in their imagination, while somehow they could not think of the happiness itself which was so possible.

Ivan Dmitritch, holding the paper in his hand, walked several times from corner to corner, and only when he had recovered from the first impression began dreaming a little.

"And if we have won," he said—"why, it will be a new life, it will be a transformation! The ticket is yours, but if it were mine I should, first of all, of course, spend twenty-five thousand on real property in the shape of an estate; ten thousand on immediate expenses, new furnishing . . . travelling . . . paying debts, and so on. . . . The other forty thousand I would put in the bank and get interest on it."

"Yes, an estate, that would be nice," said his wife, sitting down and dropping her hands in her lap.

"Somewhere in the Tula or Oryol provinces. . . . In the first place we shouldn't need a summer villa, and besides, it would always bring in an income."

And pictures came crowding on his imagination, each more gracious and poetical than the last. And in all these pictures he saw himself well-fed, serene, healthy, felt warm, even hot! Here, after eating a summer soup, cold as ice, he lay on his back on the burning sand close to a stream or in the garden under a lime-tree. . . . It is hot. . . . His little boy and girl are crawling about near him, digging in the sand or catching ladybirds in the grass. He dozes sweetly, thinking of nothing, and feeling all over that he need not go to the office today, tomorrow, or the day after. Or, tired of lying still, he goes to the hayfield, or to the forest for mushrooms, or watches the peasants catching fish with a net. When the sun sets he takes a towel and soap and saunters to the bathing shed, where he undresses at his leisure, slowly rubs his bare chest with his hands, and goes into the water. And in the water, near the opaque soapy circles, little fish flit to and fro and green water-weeds nod their heads. After bathing there is tea with cream and milk rolls. . . . In the evening a walk or *vint* with the neighbors.

"Yes, it would be nice to buy an estate," said his wife, also dreaming, and from her face it was evident that she was enchanted by her thoughts.

Ivan Dmitritch pictured to himself autumn with its rains, its cold evenings, and its St. Martin's summer. At that season he would have to take longer walks about the garden and beside the river, so as to get thoroughly chilled, and then drink a big glass of vodka and eat a salted mushroom or a soused cucumber, and then—drink another. . . . The children would come running from the kitchen-garden, bringing a carrot and a radish smelling of fresh earth. . . . And then, he would lie stretched full length on the sofa, and in leisurely fashion turn over the pages of some illustrated magazine, or, covering his face with it and unbuttoning his waistcoat, give himself up to slumber.

The St. Martin's summer is followed by cloudy, gloomy weather. It rains day and night, the bare trees weep, the wind is damp and cold. The dogs, the horses, the fowls—all are wet, depressed, downcast. There is nowhere to walk; one can't go out for days together; one has to pace up and down the room, looking despondently at the grey window. It is dreary!

Ivan Dmitritch stopped and looked at his wife.

"I should go abroad, you know, Masha," he said.

And he began thinking how nice it would be in late autumn to go abroad somewhere to the South of France . . . to Italy . . . to India!

"I should certainly go abroad too," his wife said. "But look at the number of the ticket!"

"Wait, wait! . . ."

He walked about the room and went on thinking. It occurred to him: what if his wife really did go abroad? It is pleasant to travel alone, or in the society of light, careless women who live in the present, and not such as think and talk all the journey about nothing but their children, sigh, and tremble with dismay over every farthing. Ivan Dmitritch imagined his wife in the train with a multitude of parcels, baskets, and bags; she would be sighing over something, complaining that the train made her head ache, that she had spent so much money. . . . At the stations he would continually be having to run for boiling water, bread and butter. . . . She wouldn't have dinner because of its being too dear. . . .

"She would begrudge me every farthing," he thought, with a glance at his wife. "The lottery ticket is hers, not mine! Besides, what is the use of her going abroad? What does she want there? She would shut herself up in the hotel, and not let me out of her sight. . . I know!"

And for the first time in his life his mind dwelt on the fact that his wife had grown elderly and plain, and that she was saturated through and through with the smell of cooking, while he was still young, fresh, and healthy, and might well have got married again.

"Of course, all that is silly nonsense," he thought; "but . . . why should she go abroad? What would she make of it? And yet she would go, of course. . . . I can fancy. . . . In reality it is all one to her, whether it is Naples or Klin. She would only be in my way. I should be dependent upon her. I can fancy how, like a regular woman, she will lock the money up as soon as she gets it. . . . She will look after her relations and grudge me every farthing."

Ivan Dmitritch thought of her relations. All those wretched brothers and sisters and aunts and uncles would come crawling about as soon as they heard of the winning ticket, would begin whining like beggars, and fawning upon them with oily, hypocritical smiles. Wretched, detestable people! If they were given anything, they would ask for more; while if they were refused, they would swear at them, slander them, and wish them every kind of misfortune.

Ivan Dmitritch remembered his own relations, and their faces, at which he had looked impartially in the past, struck him now as repulsive and hateful.

"They are such reptiles!" he thought.

And his wife's face, too, struck him as repulsive and hateful. Anger surged up in his heart against her, and he thought malignantly:

"She knows nothing about money, and so she is stingy. If she won it she would give me a hundred roubles, and put the rest away under lock and key."

And he looked at his wife, not with a smile now, but with hatred. She glanced at him too, and also with hatred and anger. She had her own daydreams, her own plans, her own reflections; she understood perfectly well what her husband's dreams were. She knew who would be the first to try to grab her winnings.

"It's very nice making daydreams at other people's expense!" is what her eyes expressed. "No, don't you dare!"

Her husband understood her look, hatred began stirring again in his breast, and in order to annoy his wife he glanced quickly, to spite her at the fourth page on the newspaper and read out triumphantly:

"Series 9,499, number 46! Not 26!"

Hatred and hope both disappeared at once, and it began immediately to seem to Ivan Dmitritch and his wife that their rooms were dark and small and low-pitched, that the supper they had been eating was not doing them good, but lying heavy on their stomachs, that the evenings were long and wearisome. . . .

"What the devil's the meaning of it?" said Ivan Dmitritch, beginning to be ill-humored. "Wherever one steps there are bits of paper under one's feet, crumbs, husks. The rooms are never swept! One is simply forced to go out. Damnation take my soul entirely! I shall go and hang myself on the first aspen-tree!"

[1886–Russia]

QUESTIONS

1. Does Chekhov's story present us with a plot or a situation?
2. The story is narrated from Ivan's point of view. Why didn't Chekhov simply have Ivan tell of the incident in the first person?
3. By the end of the story we know that Ivan is thoroughly discontented with his lot. Why, then, are we told at the beginning that he is "very well satisfied"? What do we call this kind of discrepancy?
4. Is it plausible that Ivan should come to feel what he does "for the first time in his life"?
5. The drama of this story is internal, the drama of developing self-knowledge. The knowledge that Ivan and his wife gain will surely prevent them from continuing as though nothing had happened. What are the likely consequences of their new self-knowledge? What might be Chekhov's theme with respect to self-knowledge?

WRITING SUGGESTIONS

1. Write a paragraph in which you describe Ivan as you imagine him just before the story takes place. What did he think of his life? Did he think much at all? Given that it takes only a trivial circumstance to raise up in him a wealth of

discontent, what must he really have felt without allowing his feelings to surface? What conclusion can be drawn from all of this?

2. (a) In a paragraph, explain how the situation of "The Lottery Ticket" contributes to both mood and characterization.

   (b) In a separate paragraph, state your response to the story and explain why you respond as you do. Be specific.

3. We tend to believe that knowledge is an absolute good—always desirable. Write an essay on how "The Lottery Ticket" calls this assumption into question.

A String of Beads

Somerset Maugham

"What a bit of luck that I'm placed next to you," said Laura, as we sat down to dinner.

"For me," I replied politely.

"That remains to be seen. I particularly wanted to have the chance of talking to you. I've got a story to tell you."

At this my heart sank a little.

"I'd sooner you talked about yourself," I answered. "Or even about me."

"Oh, but I must tell you the story. I think you'll be able to use it."

"If you must, you must. But let's look at the menu first."

"Don't you want me to?" she said, somewhat aggrieved. "I thought you'd be pleased."

"I am. You might have written a play and wanted to read me that."

"It happened to some friends of mine. It's perfectly true."

"That's no recommendation. A true story is never quite so true as an invented one."

"What does that mean?"

"Nothing very much," I admitted. "But I thought it sounded well."

"I wish you'd let me get on with it."

"I'm all attention. I'm not going to eat the soup. It's fattening."

She gave me a pinched look and then glanced at the menu. She uttered a little sigh.

"Oh, well, if you're going to deny yourself I suppose I must too. Heaven knows, I can't afford to take liberties with my figure."

"And yet is there any soup more heavenly than the sort of soup in which you put a great dollop of cream?"

"Borsht," she sighed. "It's the only soup I really like."

"Never mind. Tell me your story and we'll forget about food till the fish comes."

"Well, I was actually there when it happened. I was dining with the Livingstones. Do you know the Livingstones?"

"No, I don't think I do."

"Well, you can ask them and they'll confirm every word I say. They'd asked their governess to come in to dinner because some woman had thrown them over at the last moment—you know how inconsiderate people are—and they would have been thirteen at table. Their governess was a Miss Robinson, quite a nice girl, young, you know, twenty or twenty-one, and rather pretty. Personally I would never engage a governess who was young and pretty. One never knows."

"But one hopes for the best."

Laura paid no attention to my remark.

"The chances are that she'll be thinking of young men instead of attending to her duties and then, just when she's got used to your ways, she'll want to go and get married. But Miss Robinson had excellent references, and I must allow that she was a very nice, respectable person. I believe in point of fact she was a clergyman's daughter.

"There was a man at dinner whom I don't suppose you've ever heard of, but who's quite a celebrity in his way. He's a Count Borselli and he knows more about precious stones than anyone in the world. He was sitting next to Mary Lyngate, who rather fancies herself on her pearls, and in the course of conversation she asked him what he thought of the string she was wearing. He said it was very pretty. She was rather piqued at this and told him it was valued at eight thousand pounds.

"'Yes, it's worth that,'" he said.

"Miss Robinson was sitting opposite to him. She was looking rather nice that evening. Of course I recognized her dress, it was one of Sophie's old ones; but if you hadn't known Miss Robinson was the governess you would never have suspected it.

"'That's a very beautiful necklace that young lady has on,' said Borselli.

"'Oh, but that's Mrs. Livingstone's governess,' said Mary Lyngate.

"'I can't help that,' he said. 'She's wearing one of the finest strings of pearls for its size that I've ever seen in my life. It must be worth fifty thousand pounds.'

"'Nonsense.'

"'I give you my word it is.'

"Mary Lyngate leant over. She has rather a shrill voice.

"'Miss Robinson, do you know what Count Borselli says?' she exclaimed. 'He says that string of pearls you're wearing is worth fifty thousand pounds.'

"Just at that moment there was a sort of pause in the conversation so that everybody heard. We all turned and looked at Miss Robinson. She flushed a little and laughed.

"'Well, I made a very good bargain,' she said, 'because I paid fifteen shillings for it.'

"'You certainly did.'

"We all laughed. It was of course absurd. We've all heard of wives palming off on their husbands as false a string of pearls that was real and expensive. That story is as old as the hills."

"Thank you," I said, thinking of a little narrative of my own.

"But it was too ridiculous to suppose that a governess would remain a governess if she owned a string of pearls worth fifty thousand pounds. It was obvious that the Count had made a bloomer. Then an extraordinary thing happened. The long arm of coincidence came in."

"It shouldn't," I retorted. "It's had too much exercise. Haven't you seen that charming book called A *Dictionary of English Usage?*"

"I wish you wouldn't interrupt just when I'm really getting to the exciting point."

But I had to do so again, for just then a young grilled salmon was insinuated round my left elbow.

"Mrs. Livingstone is giving us a heavenly dinner," I said.

"Is salmon fattening?" asked Laura.

"Very," I answered as I took a large helping.

"Bunk," she said.

"Go on," I begged her. "The long arm of coincidence was about to make a gesture."

"Well, at that very moment the butler bent over Miss Robinson and whispered something in her ear. I thought she turned a trifle pale. It's such a mistake not to wear rouge; you never know what tricks nature will play on you. She certainly looked startled. She leant forwards.

"'Mrs. Livingstone, Dawson says there are two men in the hall who want to speak to me at once.'

"'Well, you'd better go,' said Sophie Livingstone.

"Miss Robinson got up and left the room. Of course the same thought flashed through all our minds, but I said it first.

"'I hope they haven't come to arrest her,' I said to Sophie. 'It would be too dreadful for you, my dear.'

"'Are you sure it was a real necklace, Borselli?' she asked.

"'Oh, quite.'

"'She could hardly have had the nerve to wear it tonight if it were stolen,' I said.

"Sophie Livingstone turned as pale as death under her makeup, and I saw she was wondering if everything was all right in her jewel case. I only had on a little chain of diamonds, but instinctively I put my hand up to my neck to feel if it was still there.

"'Don't talk nonsense,' said Mr. Livingstone. 'How on earth would Miss Robinson have had the chance of sneaking a valuable string of pearls?'

"'She may be a receiver,' I said.

"'Oh, but she had such wonderful references,' said Sophie.

"'They always do,' I said."

I was positively forced to interrupt Laura once more.

"You don't seem to have been determined to take a very bright view of the case," I remarked.

"Of course I knew nothing against Miss Robinson, and I had every reason to think her a very nice girl, but it would have been rather thrilling to find out that she was a notorious thief and a well-known member of a gang of international crooks."

"Just like a film. I'm dreadfully afraid that it's only in films that exciting things like that happen."

"Well, we waited in breathless suspense. There was not a sound. I expected to hear a scuffle in the hall or at least a smothered shriek. I thought the silence very ominous. Then the door opened and Miss Robinson walked in. I noticed at once that the necklace was gone. I could see that she was pale and excited. She came back to the table, sat down and with a smile threw on it . . ."

"On what?"

"On the table, you fool. A string of pearls."

"'There's my necklace,' she said.

"Count Borselli leant forwards.

"'Oh, but those are false,' he said.

"'I told you they were,' she laughed.

"'That's not the same string that you had on a few moments ago,' he said.

"She shook her head and smiled mysteriously. We were all intrigued. I don't know that Sophie Livingstone was so very much pleased at her governess making herself the centre of interest like that and I thought there was a suspicion of tartness in her manner when she suggested that Miss

Robinson had better explain. Well, Miss Robinson said that when she went into the hall she found two men who said they'd come from Jarrot's Stores. She'd bought her string there, as she said, for fifteen shillings, and she'd taken it back because the clasp was loose and had only fetched it that afternoon. The men said they had given her the wrong string. Someone had left a string of real pearls to be re-strung and the assistant had made a mistake. Of course I can't understand how anyone could be so stupid as to take a really valuable string to Jarrot's, they aren't used to dealing with that sort of thing, and they wouldn't know real pearls from false; but you know what fools some women are. Anyhow, it was the string Miss Robinson was wearing, and it was valued at fifty thousand pounds. She naturally gave it back to them—she couldn't do anything else, I suppose, though it must have been a wrench—and they returned her own string to her; then they said that although of course they were under no obligation—you know the silly, pompous way men talk when they're trying to be businesslike—they were instructed, as a solatium or whatever you call it, to offer her a cheque for three hundred pounds. Miss Robinson actually showed it to us. She was as pleased as Punch."

"Well, it was a piece of luck, wasn't it?"

"You'd have thought so. As it turned out it was the ruin of her."

"Oh, how was that?"

"Well, when the time came for her to go on her holiday she told Sophie Livingstone that she'd made up her mind to go to Deauville for a month and blow the whole three hundred pounds. Of course Sophie tried to dissuade her, and begged her to put the money in the savings bank, but she wouldn't hear of it. She said she'd never had such a chance before and would never have it again and she meant for at least four weeks to live like a duchess. Sophie couldn't really do anything and so she gave way. She sold Miss Robinson a lot of clothes that she didn't want; she'd been wearing them all through the season and was sick to death of them; she says she gave them to her, but I don't suppose she quite did that—I dare say she sold them very cheap—and Miss Robinson started off, entirely alone, for Deauville. What do you think happened then?"

"I haven't a notion," I replied. "I hope she had the time of her life."

"Well, a week before she was due to come back she wrote to Sophie and said that she'd changed her plans and had entered another profession, and hoped that Mrs. Livingstone would forgive her if she didn't return. Of course poor Sophie was furious. What had actually happened was that Miss Robinson had picked up a rich Argentine in Deauville and had gone off to Paris with him. She's been in Paris ever since. I've seen her myself at Florence's, with bracelets right up to her elbow and ropes of pearls round her neck. Of course I cut her dead. They say she has a house in the Bois de Boulogne and I know she has a Rolls. She threw over the Argentine in a few months and then got hold of a Greek; I don't know who she's with now, but the long and short of it is that she's far and away the smartest cocotte in Paris."

"When you say she was ruined you use the word in a purely technical sense, I conclude," said I.

"I don't know what you mean by that," said Laura. "But don't you think you could make a story out of it?"

"Unfortunately I've already written a story about a pearl necklace. One can't go on writing stories about pearl necklaces."

"I've got half a mind to write it myself. Only, of course, I should change the end."

"Oh, how would you end it?"

"Well, I should have had her engaged to a bank clerk who had been badly knocked about in the war, with only one leg, say, or half his face shot away; and they'd be dreadfully poor and there would be no prospect of their marriage for years, and he would be putting all his savings into buying a little house in the suburbs, and they'd have arranged to marry when he had saved the last installment. And then she takes him the three hundred pounds and they can hardly believe it, they're so happy, and he cries on her shoulder. He just cries like a child. And they get the little house in the suburbs and they marry, and they have his old mother to live with them, and he goes to the bank every day, and if she's careful not to have babies she can still go out as a daily governess, and he's often ill—with his wound, you know—and she nurses him, and it's all very pathetic and sweet and lovely."

"It sounds rather dull to me," I ventured.

"Yes, but moral," said Laura.

[1936–Great Britain]

QUESTIONS

1. Maugham's story presents us with both a situation—the circumstance in which Laura tells her story—and a plot. Summarize both.
2. What is Laura's dinner companion (the writer) getting at with the question, "When you say she was ruined you use the word in a purely technical sense, I conclude"? What might "technical sense" mean here?
3. Compare and contrast the story's two narrators—Laura, who tells the pearl story, and the writer to whom she tells her story and who, presumably, is telling

us the story of Laura's telling of the pearl story. Which of the two do you prefer? Why?

4. Why didn't Maugham just tell the pearl story? Why the framework of a dinner conversation?

5. In light of its somewhat elaborate framework, what is the story as a whole about? In answering this question, consider the personality differences between Laura and her dinner companion and their differing views as to the function of storytelling. Toward which view would the story sway us?

WRITING SUGGESTIONS

1. Write an essay that is based on the comparison called for in question 3 above and moves to a consideration of which of the two characters the story would sway the reader to prefer.

2. In a paragraph, explain how the situation of the story shifts the focus away from Laura's plotty tale and onto Laura herself, and what the purpose of this shift is.

3. Write an essay arguing that "A String of Beads" is about two types of fiction and hence two types of reader.

The Tell-Tale Heart

Edgar Allan Poe

True!—nervous—very, very dreadfully nervous I had been and am; but why *will* you say that I am mad? The disease had sharpened my senses—not destroyed—not dulled them. Above all was the sense of hearing acute. I heard all things in the heaven and in the earth. I heard many things in hell. How, then, am I mad? Hearken! and observe how healthy—how calmly I can tell the whole story.

It is impossible to say how first the idea entered my brain; but once conceived, it haunted me day and night. Object there was none. Passion there was none. I loved the old man. He had never wronged me. He had never given me insult. For his gold I had no desire. I think it was his eye! yes, it was this! He had the eye of a vulture—a pale blue eye, with a film over it. Whenever it fell upon me, my blood ran cold; and so by degrees—very gradually—I made up my mind to take the life of the old man, and thus rid myself of the eye for ever.

Now this is the point. You fancy me mad. Madmen know nothing. But you should have seen *me*. You should have seen how wisely I proceeded—with what caution—with what foresight—with what dissimulation I went to work! I was never kinder to the old man than during the whole week before I killed him. And every night, about midnight, I turned the latch of his door and opened it—oh so gently! And then, when I had made an opening sufficient for my head, I put in a dark lantern, all closed, closed, so that no light shone out, and then I thrust in my head. Oh, you would have laughed to see how cunningly I thrust it in! I moved it slowly—very, very slowly, so that I might not disturb the old man's sleep. It took me an hour to place my whole head within the opening so far that I could see him as he lay upon his bed. Ha!—would a madman have been so wise as this? And then, when my head was well in the room, I undid the lantern cautiously—oh, so cautiously—cautiously (for the hinges creaked)—I undid it just so much that a single thin ray fell upon the vulture eye. And this I did for seven long nights—every night just at midnight—but I found the eye always closed; and so it was impossible to do the work; for it was not the old man who vexed me, but his Evil Eye. And every morning, when the day broke, I went boldly into the chamber, and spoke courageously to him, calling him by name in a hearty tone, and inquiring how he had passed the night. So you see he would have been a very profound old man, indeed, to suspect that every night, just at twelve, I looked in upon him while he slept.

Upon the eighth night I was more than usually cautious in opening the door. A watch's minute hand moves more quickly than did mine. Never before that night, had I *felt* the extent of my own powers—of my sagacity. I could scarcely contain my feelings of triumph. To think that there I was, opening the door, little by little, and he not even to dream of my secret deeds or thoughts. I fairly chuckled at the idea; and perhaps he heard me; for he moved on the bed suddenly, as if startled. Now you may think that I drew back—but no. His room was as black as pitch with the thick darkness (for the shutters were close fastened, through fear of robbers), and so I knew that he could not see the opening of the door, and I kept pushing it on steadily, steadily.

I had my head in, and was about to open the lantern, when my thumb slipped upon the tin fastening, and the old man sprang up in bed, crying out—"Who's there?"

I kept quite still and said nothing. For a whole hour I did not move a muscle, and in the meantime I did not hear him lie down. He was still sitting up in bed, listening;—just as I have done, night after night, hearkening to the death watches in the wall.

Presently I heard a slight groan, and I knew it was the groan of mortal terror. It was not a groan of pain or of grief—oh, no!—it was the low stifled sound that arises from the bottom of the soul when overcharged with awe. I knew the sound well. Many a night, just at midnight, when all the world slept, it has welled up from my own bosom, deepening, with its dreadful echo, the terrors that distracted me. I say I knew it well. I knew what the old man felt, and pitied him, although I chuckled at heart. I knew that he had been lying awake ever since the first slight noise, when he had turned in the bed. His fears had been ever since growing upon him. He had been trying to fancy them causeless, but could not. He had been saying to himself—"It is nothing but the wind in the chimney—it is only a mouse crossing the floor," or "it is merely a cricket which has made a single chirp." Yes, he had been trying to comfort himself with these suppositions: but he had found all in vain. *All in vain*; because Death, in approaching him, had stalked with his black shadow before him, and enveloped the victim. And it was the mournful influence of the unperceived shadow that caused him to feel—although he neither saw nor heard—to *feel* the presence of my head within the room.

When I had waited a long time, very patiently, without hearing him lie down, I resolved to open a little—a very, very little crevice in the lantern. So I opened it—you cannot imagine how stealthily, stealthily—until, at length, a single dim ray, like the thread of the spider, shot from out the crevice and fell full upon the vulture eye.

It was open—wide, wide open—and I grew furious as I gazed upon it. I saw it with perfect distinctness—all a dull blue, with a hideous veil over it that chilled the very marrow in my bones; but I could see nothing else of the old man's face or person: for I had directed the ray as if by instinct, precisely upon the damned spot.

And now have I not told you that what you mistake for madness is but over acuteness of the senses?—now, I say, there came to my ears a low, dull, quick sound, such as a watch makes when enveloped in cotton. I knew *that* sound well, too. It was the beating of the old man's heart. It increased my fury, as the beating of a drum stimulates the soldier into courage.

But even yet I refrained and kept still. I scarcely breathed. I held the lantern motionless. I tried how steadily I could maintain the ray upon the eye. Meantime the hellish tattoo of the heart increased. It grew quicker and quicker, and louder and louder every instant. The old man's terror *must* have been extreme! It grew louder, I say, louder every moment!—do you mark me well? I have told you that I am nervous: so I am. And now at the dead hour of the night, amid the dreadful silence of that old house, so strange a noise as this excited me to uncontrollable terror. Yet, for some minutes longer I refrained and stood still. But the beatings grew louder, louder! I thought the heart must burst. And now a new anxiety seized me—the sound would be heard by a neighbor! The old man's hour had come! With a loud yell, I threw open the lantern and leaped into the room. He shrieked once—once only. In an instant I dragged him to the floor, and pulled the heavy bed over him. I then smiled gaily, to find the deed so far done. But, for many minutes, the heart beat on with a muffled sound. This, however, did not vex me; it would not be heard through the wall. At length it ceased. The old man was dead. I removed the bed and examined the corpse. Yes, he was stone, stone dead. I placed my hand upon the heart and held it there many minutes. There was no pulsation. He was stone dead. His eye would trouble me no more.

If still you think me mad, you will think so no longer when I describe the wise precautions I took for the concealment of the body. The night waned, and I worked hastily, but in silence. First of all I dismembered the corpse. I cut off the head and the arms and the legs.

I then took up three planks from the flooring of the chamber, and deposited all between the scantlings. I then replaced the boards so cleverly, so cunningly, that no human eye—not even *his*—could have detected any thing wrong. There was nothing to wash out—no stain of any kind—no bloodspot whatever. I had been too wary for that. A tub had caught all—ha! ha!

When I had made an end of these labors, it was four o'clock—still dark as midnight. As the bell sounded the hour, there came a knocking at the street door. I went down to open it with a light heart,—for what had I *now* to fear? There entered three men, who introduced themselves, with perfect suavity, as officers of the police. A shriek had been heard by a neighbor during the night; suspicion of foul play had been aroused; information had been lodged at the police office, and they (the officers) had been deputed to search the premises.

I smiled,—for *what* had I to fear? I bade the gentlemen welcome. The shriek, I said, was my own in a dream. The old man, I mentioned, was absent in the country. I took my visitors all over the house. I bade them search—search *well.* I led them, at length to *his* chamber. I showed them his treasures, secure, undisturbed. In the enthusiasm of my confidence, I brought chairs into the room, and desired them *here* to rest from their fatigues, while I myself, in the wild audacity of my perfect triumph, placed my own seat upon the very spot beneath which reposed the corpse of the victim.

The officers were satisfied. My *manner* had convinced them. I was singularly at ease. They sat, and while I answered cheerily, they chatted of familiar things. But, ere long, I felt myself getting pale and wished them gone. My head ached, and I fancied a ringing in my ears; but still they sat and still chatted. The ringing became more distinct:—I talked more freely to get rid of the feeling: but it continued and gained definiteness—until, at length, I found that the noise was *not* within my ears.

No doubt I now grew *very pale;*—but I talked more fluently, and with a heightened voice. Yet the sound increased—and what could I do? It was *a low, dull, quick sound—much such a sound as a watch makes when enveloped in cotton.* I gasped for breath—and yet the officers heard it not. I talked more quickly—more vehemently; but the noise steadily increased. I arose and argued about trifles, in a high key and with violent gesticulations; but the noise steadily increased. Why *would* they not be gone? I paced the floor to and fro with heavy strides, as if excited to fury by the observations of the men—but the noise steadily increased. Oh, God! what *could* I do? I foamed—I raved—I swore! I swung the chair upon which I had been sitting, and grated it upon the boards, but the noise arose over all and continually increased. It grew louder—louder—*louder!* And still the men chatted pleasantly and smiled. Was it possible they heard not? Almighty God!—no, no! They heard!—they suspected!—they *knew!*—they were making a mockery of my horror!—this I thought, and this I think. But anything was better than this agony! Anything was more tolerable than this derision! I could bear those hypocritical smiles no longer! I felt that I must scream or die!—and now—again!—hark! louder! louder! louder! *louder!*—

"Villains—" I shrieked, "dissemble no more! I admit the deed!—tear up the planks—here, here!—it is the beating of his hideous heart!"

[1850–U.S.A.]

Questions

1. Can we believe everything Poe's narrator tells us? Can we believe anything?
2. Is the beating heart—heard by the speaker, though by no one else—merely a bit of horror-story machinery, or is there possibly a realistic explanation for what the murderer hears?
3. The story explores profound issues. What are they? Why is the story as chilling as it is?
4. Summarize the plot of Poe's tale. In what way does the plot function with respect to the story's theme?

Writing Suggestions

1. (a) Whether we believe him or not, Poe's narrator is clearly mad by any definition. Write a paragraph giving examples to show this.

   (b) In a separate paragraph, state your response to the story and give your reasons for responding thus.
2. Write a paragraph explaining how the story's plot helps shape the reader's attitude toward the narrator.
3. Write an essay explaining how the plot of "The Tell-Tale Heart" helps to establish the mood and how both plot and mood are related to the theme.

After the Fair

Dylan Thomas

The fair was over, the lights in the cocoanut stalls were put out, and the wooden horses stood still in the darkness, waiting for the music and the hum of the machines that would set them trotting forward. One by one, in every booth, the naphtha jets were turned down and the canvases pulled over the little gambling tables. The crowd went home, and there were lights in the windows of the caravans.

Nobody had noticed the girl. In her black clothes she stood against the side of the roundabouts, hearing the last feet tread upon the sawdust and the last voices die into the distance. Then, all alone on the deserted ground, surrounded by the shapes of wooden horses and cheap fairy boats, she looked for a place to sleep. Now here and now there, she raised the canvas that shrouded the cocoanut stalls and peered into the warm darkness. She was frightened to step inside, and as a mouse scampered across the littered shavings on the floor, or as the canvas creaked and a rush of wind set it dancing, she ran away and hid again near the roundabouts. Once she stepped on the boards; the bells round a horse's throat jingled and were still; she did not dare breathe until all was quiet again and the darkness had forgotten the noise of the bells. Then here and there she went peeping for a bed, into each gondola, under each tent. But there was nowhere, nowhere in all the fair for her to sleep. One place was too silent, and in another was the noise of mice. There was straw in the corner of the Astrologer's tent, but it moved as she touched it; she knelt by its side and put out her hand; she felt a baby's hand upon her own.

Now there was nowhere; so slowly she turned towards the caravans, and reaching them where they stood on the outskirts of the field, found all but two to be unlit. She stood, clutching her empty bag, and wondering which caravan she should disturb. At last she decided to knock upon the window of the little, shabby one near her and standing on tiptoe, she looked in. The fattest man she had ever seen was sitting in front of the stove, toasting a piece of bread. She tapped three times on the glass, then hid in the shadows. She heard him come to the top of the steps and call out Who? Who? but she dared not answer. Who? Who? he called again; she laughed at his voice which was as thin as he was fat. He heard her laughter and turned to where the darkness concealed her. First you tap, he said. Then you hide, then, by jingo, you laugh. She stepped into the circle of light, knowing she need no longer hide herself. A girl, he said, Come in and wipe your feet. He did not wait but retreated into his caravan, and she could do nothing but follow him up the steps and into the crowded room. He was seated again, and toasting the same piece of bread. Have you come in? he said, for his back was towards her. Shall I close the door? she asked, and closed it before he replied.

She sat on the bed and watched him toasting the bread until it burnt. I can toast better than you, she said. I don't doubt it, said the Fat Man. She watched him put down the charred toast upon a plate by his side, take another round of bread and hold that, too, in front of the stove. It burnt very quickly. Let me toast it for you, she said. Ungraciously he handed her the fork and the loaf. Cut it, he said, Toast it, and eat it, by jingo. She sat on the chair. See the dent you've made on my bed, said the Fat Man. Who are you to come in and dent my bed? My name is Annie, she told him. Soon all the bread was toasted and buttered, so she put it in the centre of the table and arranged two chairs. I'll have mine on the bed, said the Fat Man. You'll have it here.

When they had finished their supper, he pushed back his chair and stared at her across the table. I am the Fat Man, he said. My home is Treorchy; the Fortune Teller next door is Aberdare. I am nothing to do with the fair—I am Cardiff, she said. There's a town, agreed the Fat Man. He asked her why she had come away. Money, said Annie. I have one and three, said the Fat Man. I have nothing, said Annie.

Then he told her about the fair and the places he had been to and the people he had met. He told her his age and his weight and the names of his brothers and what he would call his son. He showed her a picture of Boston Harbour and the photograph of his mother who lifted weights. He told her how summer looked in Ireland. I've always been a fat man, he said. And now I'm *the* Fat Man; there's nobody to touch me for fatness. He told her of a heat wave in Sicily and of the Mediterranean Sea and of the wonders of the South stars. She told him of the baby in the Astrologer's tent.

That's the stars again, by jingo; looking at the stars doesn't do anybody any good.

The baby'll die, said Annie. He opened the door and walked out into the darkness. She looked about her but did not move, wondering if he had gone to fetch a policeman. It would never do to be caught by the policeman again. She stared through the open door into the inhospitable night and drew her chair closer to the stove. Better to be caught in the warmth, she said. But she trembled at the sound of the Fat Man approaching, and pressed her hands upon her thin breast, as he climbed up the steps like a walking mountain. She could see him smile in the darkness. See what the stars have done, he said, and brought in the Astrologer's baby in his arms.

After she had nursed it against her and it had cried on the bosom of her dress, she told him how she had feared his going. What should I be doing with a policeman? She told him that the policeman wanted her. What have you done for a policeman to be wanting you? She did not answer but took the child nearer again to her wasted breast. If it was money, I could have given you one and three, he said. Then he understood her and begged her pardon. I'm not quick, he told her. I'm just fat; sometimes I think I'm almost too fat. She was feeding the child; he saw her thinness. You must eat, Cardiff, he said.

Then the child began to cry. From a little wail its crying rose into a tempest of despair. The girl rocked it to and fro on her lap, but nothing soothed it. All the woe of a child's world flooded its tiny voice. Stop it, stop it, said the Fat Man, and the tears increased. Annie smothered it in kisses, but its wild cry broke on her lips like water upon rocks. We must do something, she said. Sing it a lullabee. She sang, but the child did not like her singing.

There's only one thing, said Annie, we must take it on the roundabouts. With the child's arm around her neck, she stumbled down the steps and ran towards the deserted fair, the Fat Man panting behind her. She found her way through the tents and stalls into the centre of the ground where the wooden horses stood waiting, and clambered up on to a saddle. Start the engine, she called out. In the distance the Fat Man could be heard cranking up the antique machine that drove the horses all the day into a wooden gallop. She heard the sudden spasmodic humming of the engine; the boards rattled under the horses' feet. She saw the Fat Man clamber up by her side, pull the central lever and climb on to the saddle of the smallest horse of all. As the roundabout started, slowly at first and slowly gaining speed, the child at the girl's breast stopped crying, clutched its hands together, and crowed with joy. The night wind tore through its hair, the music jangled in its ears. Round and round the wooden horses sped, drowning the cries of the wind with the beating of their wooden hooves.

And so the men from the caravans found them, the Fat Man and the girl in black with a baby in her arms, racing round and round on their mechanical steeds to the ever-increasing music of the organ.

[1939–Great Britain]

QUESTIONS

1. Summarize the plot of this highly poetic story. What is the primary incident that the plot turns on? In what ways does this incident set into motion what follows?
2. The protagonists of "After the Fair" are outsiders, misfits. Yet at the end of the story, we come to feel their humanity by seeing the common ground we share with this "family" of derelicts. How does the plot contribute to this effect?
3. What, then, is the theme of this story, and how does the plot help to establish it?

WRITING SUGGESTIONS

1. In a paragraph, describe the effect of the image with which we are left at the end of the story. In the same or in a second paragraph, relate this effect to the story's theme.
2. Though relatively slight, the plot of "After the Fair" is crucial. Write an essay showing how the events form a chain leading to the story's conclusion and thus serve as an agent of theme.

Sportmanship

John O'Hara

Jerry straightened his tie and brushed the sleeves of his coat, and went down the stairway where it said "The Subway Arcade." The sign was misleading only to strangers to that neighborhood; there was no subway anywhere near, and it was no arcade.

It was early in the afternoon and there were not many people in the place. Jerry walked over to where a man with glasses, and a cigar in an imitation amber holder, was sitting quietly with a thin man, who also had a cigar.

"Hyuh, Frank," said Jerry.

"Hyuh," said the man with glasses.

"Well, how's every little thing?" said Jerry.

Frank looked around the place, a little too carefully and slowly. "Why," he said finally, "it looks like every little thing is fine. How about it, Tom? Would you say every little thing was O.K.?"

"Me?" said Tom. "Yes, I guess so. I guess every little thing is—No. No. I think I smell sumpn. Do you smell sumpn, Frank? I think I do."

"Aw, you guys. I get it," said Jerry. "Still sore. I don't blame you."

"Who? Me? Me sore?" said Frank. "Why, no. Would you say I was sore, Tom? This stranger here says I'm sore. Oh, no, stranger. That's my usual way of looking. Of course you wouldn't have no way of knowing that, being a stranger. It's funny, though, speaking of looks. You look the dead spit of a guy I used to know, to my sorrow. A rat by the name of Jerry. Jerry—Jerry, uh, Daley. You remember that Jerry Daley rat I told you about one time? Remember him, Tom?"

"Oh, yes. Come to think of it," said Tom, "I recall now I did hear you speak of a heel by that name. I recall it now. I would of forgot all about the rat if you wouldn't of reminded me. What ever did happen to him? I heard he was drowned out City Island."

"Oh, no," said Frank. "They sent him to Riker's Island, the party I mean."

"All right. I get it. Still sore. Well, if that's the way you feel about it," said Jerry. He lit a cigarette and turned away. "I only come back to tell you, Frank, I wanted to tell you I'd be satisfied to work out the dough I owe you if you leave me have a job."

"Hmm," said Frank, taking the cigar out of his mouth. "Hear that, Tom? The stranger is looking for work. Wants a job."

"Well, waddia know about that? Wants a job. What doing, I wonder," said Tom.

"Yeah. What doing? Cashier?" said Frank.

"Aw, what the hell's the use trying to talk to you guys? I came here with the best intention, but if that's your attitude, *so long.*"

"Guess he's not satisfied with the salary you offered, Frank," said Tom.

Jerry was back on the stairway when Frank called him. "Wait a minute." Jerry returned. "What's your proposition?" said Frank. Tom looked surprised.

"Give me the job as house man. Twenty-five a week. Take out ten a week for what I owe you. I'll come here in the mornings and clean up, and practice up my game, and then when I get my eye back, I'll shoot for the house—"

"Using house money, of course," said Tom.

"Let him talk, Tom," said Frank.

"Using house money. What else? And the house and I split what I make." Jerry finished his proposition and his cigarette.

"How long it take you to get shooting good again?" said Frank.

"That's pretty hard to say. Two weeks at least," said Jerry.

Frank thought a minute while Tom watched him incredulously. Then he said, "Well, I might take a chance on you, Daley. Tell you what I'll do. You're on the nut. All right. Here's my proposition: the next two weeks, you can sleep here and I'll give you money to eat on, but no pay. You practice up, and in two weeks I'll play you, say, a hundred points. If you're any good, I'll give you thirty bucks cash and credit you with twenty bucks against what you're in me for. Then you can use your thirty to play with. That oughta be enough to start on, if you're any good. I seen you go into many a game when you were shooting on your nerve and come out the winner, so thirty bucks oughta be plenty. *But* if you're no good at the end of two weeks, then I'll have to leave you go. I'll charge up twenty bucks against what you owe me, and you can go out in the wide, wide world and look for adventure, the way you did once before. Is that a deal?"

"Sure. What can I lose?" said Jerry.

"Sure, what can you lose? How long since you ate last?"

In two weeks Jerry had lost the tan color of his face, and his hands were almost white again, but he looked healthier. Eating regularly was more important than the sun. The regulars who had known Jerry before he stole the hundred and forty dollars from Frank were glad to see him and made no cracks. They may have figured Frank for a real sucker, some of them, but some of the others said there were a lot of angles in a thing like that; nobody knew the whole story in a thing of that kind, and besides, Frank was no dope. It didn't look like it. Jerry was brushing off the tables, putting the cues in their right bins—the twenty-ounce cues into bins marked 20, the nineteen-ouncers in the 19 bins, and so on—and retipping cues, and cleaning garboons and filling them with water, and dusting everywhere. He caught on soon about the new regulars, who wanted what table, and what they usually played. For instance, every afternoon at three o'clock two guys in Tuxedos would come in and play two fifty-point games, and the rest of the afternoon, before they had to go and play in an orchestra, they would play rotation. Well, you had to keep an eye on them. They paid by the hour, of course, but if you didn't watch them, they would use the ivory cue ball to break with in the games of rotation, instead of using the composition ball, which did not cost as much as the ivory ball and stood the hard usage better. The ivory ball cost Frank around twenty bucks, and you can't afford to have an ivory ball slammed around on the break in a game of rotation. Things like that, little things—that was where an experienced house man like Jerry could save Frank money.

Meanwhile he practiced up and his game came back to him, so that at the end of the two weeks he could even do massé shots almost to his own satisfaction. He hardly ever left except to go out to a place, a Coffee Pot on Fordham Road, for his meals. Frank gave him a "sayfitty" razor and a tube of no-brush-needed cream. He slept on the leather couch in front of the cigar counter.

He also observed that Frank was shooting just about the same kind of game he always shot—no better, and no worse. Jerry therefore was confident of beating Frank, and when the day came that ended the two weeks agreed upon, he reminded Frank of the date, and Frank said he would be in at noon the next day to play the hundred points.

Next day, Frank arrived a little after twelve. "I brought my own referee," said Frank. "Shake hands with Jerry Daley," he said, and did not add the name of the burly man, who might have been Italian, or even an octoroon. The man was dressed quietly, except for a fancy plaid cap. Frank addressed him as Doc, Jerry first thought, but then he realized that Frank, who was originally from Worcester Massachusetts, was calling the man Dark.

Dark sat down on one of the high benches, and did not seem much interested in the game. He sat there smoking cigarettes, wetting them almost halfway down their length with his thick lips. He hardly looked at the game, and with two players like Frank and Jerry there wasn't much use for a referee. Jerry had Frank forty-four to twenty before Dark even looked up at the marker. "Geez," he said. "Forty-four to twenty. This kid's good, eh?"

"Oh, yeah," said Frank. "I told you one of us was gonna get a good beating."

"Maybe the both of you, huh?" said Dark, and showed that he could laugh. Then Jerry knew there was something wrong. He missed the next two times up, on purpose. "There they are, Frank," said Dark. Frank ran six or seven. "Got a mistake in the score, there," said Dark. He got up and took a twenty-two-ounce cue out of the bin, and reached up and slid the markers over so that the score was even.

"Hey," said Jerry. "What is it?"

"That's the right score, ain't it?" said Dark. "Frank just run twenty-four balls. I seen him, and I'm the referee. Neutral referee."

"What is it, Frank? The works or something?" said Jerry.

"He's the referee,'" said Frank. "Gotta abide by his decision in all matters. Specially the scoring. You have to abide by the referee, specially on matters of scoring. You know that."

"So it's the works," said Jerry. "O.K. I get it. Pick up the marbles." He laid down his cue. "What a sap I been. I thought this was on the up-and-up."

"I hereby declare this game is forfeited. Frank wins the match. Congratulate the winner, why don't you, kid?"

"This means I'm out, I guess, eh, Frank?" said Jerry.

"Well, you know our agreement," said Frank. "We gotta abide by the decision of the referee, and he says you forfeited, so I guess you don't work here any more."

"Congratulate the winner," said Dark. "Where's your sportmanship, huh? Where's your sportmanship?"

"Don't look like he has any," said Frank, very sadly. "Well, that's the way it goes."

"Maybe we better teach him a little sportmanship," said Dark.

"All right by me," said Frank. "One thing I thought about Mr. Daley, I thought he'd be a good loser, but it don't look that way. It don't look that way one bit, so maybe you better teach him a little sportmanship. Only a little, though. Just give him a little bit of a lesson."

Jerry reached for the cue that he had laid on the table, but as he did, Dark brought his own cue down on Jerry's hands. "Shouldn't do that," said Dark. "You oughtn't to scream, either. Cops might hear you, and you don't want any cops. You don't want any part of the cops, wise guy."

"You broke me hands, you broke me hands!" Jerry screamed. The pain was awful, and he was crying.

"Keep them out of other people's pockets," said Frank. "Beat it."

[1934–U.S.A.]

QUESTIONS

1. "After the Fair" seems to ask us to sympathize with and at the end even identify with its characters; "Sportmanship" does not. Its low-life characters, realistically drawn, are hardly people we would wish to know. Still, they reveal something about us, or at least about human communities. What?
2. Describe Frank's dark scheme, which provides the plot of the story. Why doesn't Frank take his revenge right away? If he did, of course, there wouldn't be much of a story. But aside from that, what does the two-week delay tell us about Frank and his world? Why, incidentally, doesn't Frank simply turn Jerry over to the police?
3. In part the title is ironic. Yet Frank, Tom, Dark, and the patrons of "The Subway Arcade" do have a sense of "sportmanship," however crude. Certainly, they understand the concept of justice, if not mercy. How does Frank's scheme reveal this?
4. Taking the social group portrayed here as a model in miniature of social groups generally and their codes of behavior, try to state the theme of this story.

WRITING SUGGESTIONS

1. Central to the story's plot, the two-week delay tells us a great deal about Frank and his world. Write a paragraph explaining what Frank's scheme also suggests about the outside world and its concepts of justice.
2. Write an essay comparing and contrasting "Sportmanship" and "After the Fair." Consider the type of characters each presents and their worlds, as well as the attitudes toward its characters that each story conveys.

Book of Harlem

Zora Neale Hurston

1. A *pestilence visiteth the land of Hokum, and the people cry out. 4. Toothsome, a son of Georgia returns from Babylon, and stirreth up the Hamites. 10. Mandolin heareth him and resolveth to see Babylon. 11. He convinceth his father and departs for Babylon. 21. A red-cap toteth his bag, and uttereth blasphemy against Mandolin. 26. He lodgeth with Toothsome, and trieth to make the females of Harlem, but is scorned by them. 28. One frail biddeth him sit upon a tack. 29. He taketh council with Toothsome and is comforted. 33. He goeth to an hall of dancing, and meeting a damsel there, shaketh vehemently with her. 42. He discloseth himself to her and she telleth him what to read. 49. He becometh Panic. 50. The Book of Harlem.*

1. And in those days when King Volstead sat upon the throne in Hokum, then came a mighty drought upon the land, many cried out in agony thereof.

2. Then did the throat parch and the tongue was thrust into the cheek of many voters.

3. And men grew restless and went up and down in the land saying, "We are verily the dry-bones of which the prophet Ezekiel prophesied."

4. Then returned one called Toothsome unto his town of Standard Bottom, which is in the province of Georgia. And he was of the tribe of Ham.

5. And his raiment was very glad, for he had sojourned in the city of Babylon, which is ruled by the tribe of Tammany. And his garments

putteth out the street lamps, and the vaseline upon his head, yea verily the slickness thereof did outshine the sun at noonday.

6. And the maidens looked upon him and were glad, but the men gnasheth together their bridgework at sight of him. But they drew near unto him and listened to his accounts of the doings of Babylon, for they all yearned unto that city.

7. And the mouth of Toothsome flapped loudly and fluently in the marketplace, and the envy of his hearers increased an hundredfold.

8. Then stood one youth before him, and his name was called Mandolin. And he questioned Toothsome eagerly, asking 'how come' and 'wherefore' many times.

9. And Toothsome answered him according to his wit. Moreover he said unto the youth, "Come thou also to the city as unto the ant, and consider her ways and be wise."

10. And the heart of Mandolin was inflamed, and he stood before his father and said, "I beseech thee now, papa, to give unto me now my portion that I may go hence to great Babylon and see life."

11. But his father's heart yearned towards him, and he said, "Nay, my son, for Babylon is full of wickedness, and thou art but a youth."

12. But Mandolin answered him saying, "I crave to gaze upon its sins. What do you think I go to see, a prayer-meeting?"

13. But his father strove with him and said, "Why dost thou crave Babylon when Gussie Smith, the daughter of our neighbor, will make thee a good wife? Tarry now and take her to wife, for verily she is a mightly biscuit cooker before the Lord."

14. Then snorted Mandolin with scorn and he said, "What care I for biscuit-cookers when there be Shebas of high voltage on every street in Harlem? For verily man liveth not by bread alone, but by every drop of banana oil that drippeth from the tongue of the lovely."

15. Then strove they together all night. But at daybreak did Mandolin touch the old man upon the hip, yea verily upon the pocket-bearing joint, and triumphed.

16. So the father gave him his blessing, and he departed out of Standard Bottom on his journey to Babylon.

17. And he carried with him of dreams forty-and-four thousands, and of wishes ten thousands, and of hopes ten thousands.

18. But of tears or sorrows carried he none out of all that land. Neither bore he any fears away with him.

19. And journeyed he many days upon the caravan of steel, and came at last unto the city of Babylon, and got him down within the place.

20. Then rushed there many upon him who wore scarlet caps upon the head, saying "Porter? Shall I tote thy bags for thee?"

21. And he marvelled greatly within himself, saying, "How charitably are the Babylons, seeing they permit no stranger to tote his own bag! With what great kindness am I met!"

22. And he suffered one to prevail and tote his bag for him. Moreover he questioned him concerning the way to Harlem which is a city of Ham in Babylonia.

23. And when he of the scarlet cap had conducted Mandolin unto a bus, then did Mandolin shake hands with him and thank him greatly for his kindness, and stepped upon the chariot as it rolled away, and took his way unto Harlem.

24. Then did the bag-toter blaspheme greatly, saying, "Oh, the cock-eyed son of a wood louse! Oh, the hawg! Oh, the sea-buzzard! Oh, the splay-footed son of a doodle bug and cockroach! What does he take me for? The mule's daddy! The clod-hopper! If only I might lay my hands upon him, verily would I smite him, yea, until he smelt like onions!"

25. But Mandolin journeyed on to Harlem, knowing none of these things.

26. And when he had come unto the place, he lodged himself with Toothsome, and was glad.

27. And each evening stood he before the Lafayette theatre and a-hemmed at the knees that passed, but none took notice of him.

28. Moreover one frail of exceeding sassiness bade him go to and cook an radish, and seat himself upon a tack, which being interpreted is slander.

29. Then went he unto his roommate and saith, "How now doth the damsel think me? Have I not a smiling countenance, and coin in my jeans? My heart is heavy for I have sojourned in Harlem for many weeks, but as yet I have spoken to no female."

30. Then spoke Toothsome, and answered him saying, "Seek not swell Shebas in mail-order britches. Go thou into the marketplace and get thee Oxford bags and jacket thyself likewise. Procure thee shoes and socks. Yea, anoint thy head with oil until it runneth over so that thou dare not hurl thyself into bed unless thou wear Weed chains upon the head, lest thou skid out again."

31. "Moreover lubricate thy tongue with banana oil, for from the oily lips proceedeth the breath of love."

32. And Mandolin hastened to do all that his counsellor bade him.

33. Then hied him to the hall of dancing where many leaped with the cymbal, and shook with the drums.

34. And his belly was moved, for he saw young men seize upon damsels and they stood upon the floor and 'messed around' meanly. Moreover many 'bumped' them vehemently. Yea, there were those among them who shook with many shakings.

35. And when he saw all these things, Mandolin yearned within his heart to do likewise, but as yet he had spoken to no maiden.

36. But one damsel of scarlet lips smiled broadly upon him, and encouraged him with her eyes, and the water of his knees turned to bone, and he drew nigh unto her.

37. And his mouth flew open and he said, "See now how the others do dance with the cymbal and harp, yea, even the saxophone? Come thou and let us do likewise."

38. And he drew her and they stood upon the floor. Now this maiden was a mighty dancer before the Lord; yea, of the mightiest of all the tribe of Ham. And the shakings of the others was as one stricken with paralysis beside a bowl of gelatine. And the heart of the youth leaped for joy.

39. And he was emboldened, and his mouth flew open and the banana oil did drip from his lips, yea even down to the floor, and the maiden was moved.

40. And he said, "Thou sure art propaganda! Yea, verily thou shakest a wicked ankle."

41. And she being pleased, answered him, "Thou art some sheik thyself. I do shoot a little pizen to de ankle if I do say so myself. Where has thou been all my life that I have not seen thee?"

42. Then did his mouth fly open, and he told her everything of Standard Bottom, Georgia, and of Babylon, and of all those things which touched him.

43. And her heart yearned towards him, and she resolved to take him unto herself and to make him wise.

44. And she said unto him, "Go thou and buy the books and writings of certain scribes and Pharisees which I shall name unto you, and thou shalt learn everything of good and of evil. Yea, thou shalt know as much as the Chief of the Niggerati, who is called Carl Van Vechten."

45. And Mandolin diligently sought all these books and writings that he was bidden, and read them.

46. Then was he sought for all feasts, and stomps, and shakings, and none was complete without him. Both on 139th street and on Lenox avenue was he sought, and his fame was great.

47. And his name became Panic, for they asked one of the other, "Is he not a riot in all that he doeth?"

48. Then did he devise poetry, and played it upon the piano, saying:

Skirt by skirt on every flirt
They're getting higher and higher
Day by day in every way
There's more to admire
Sock by sock and knee by knee
The more they show, the more we see
The skirts run up, the socks run down
Jingling bells run round and round
Oh week by week, and day by day
Let's hope that things keep on this way
Let's kneel right down and pray.

49. And the women all sought him, and damsels and the matrons and the grandmothers and all those who wear the skirt, and with them his name was continually Panic.

50. Of his doings and success after that, is it not written in The Book of Harlem?

[1927–U.S.A.]

QUESTIONS

1. Look up in an encyclopedia the following: Volstead Act, Tammany Hall, Carl Van Vechten, Harlem Renaissance. Be ready in class to discuss how a knowledge of these references sheds light on Hurston's story.
2. What is the effect of Hurston's combination of a biblical structure and biblical language with a mundane, everyday plot?
3. That plot is the central element of the present story is highlighted by the Bible-like summary of plot at the beginning. In what way does the theme of "Book of Harlem" make the emphasis on plot inevitable.

WRITING SUGGESTIONS

1. Write an essay on the story's humor and how it functions. That is, after establishing in what ways the story is funny, relate its comic mood to its theme.
2. Write a paragraph or more suggesting how the story's plot and its general high-spiritedness reflect the mood of Harlem in the 1920s. You will probably have to do some research before you begin writing. Start by looking up the references cited in question 1 above if you have not already done so.

The Night the Bed Fell

James Thurber

I suppose that the high-water mark of my youth in Columbus, Ohio, was the night the bed fell on my father. It makes a better recitation (unless, as some friends of mine have said, one has heard it five or six times) than it does a piece of writing, for it is almost necessary to throw furniture around, shake doors, and bark like a dog, to lend the proper atmosphere and verisimilitude to what is admittedly a somewhat incredible tale. Still, it did take place.

It happened, then, that my father had decided to sleep in the attic one night, to be away where he could think. My mother opposed the notion strongly because, she said, the old wooden bed up there was unsafe: it was wobbly and the heavy headboard would crash down on father's head in case the bed fell, and kill him. There was no dissuading him, however, and at a quarter past ten he closed the attic door behind him and went up the narrow twisting stairs. We later heard ominous creakings as he crawled into bed. Grandfather, who usually slept in the attic bed when he was with us, had disappeared some days before. (On these occasions he was usually gone six or eight days and returned growling and out of temper, with the news that the federal Union was run by a passel of blockheads and that the Army of the Potomac didn't have any more chance than a fiddler's bitch.)

We had visiting us at this time a nervous first cousin of mine named Briggs Beall, who believed that he was likely to cease breathing when he was asleep. It was his feeling that if he were not awakened every hour during the night, he might die of suffocation. He had been accustomed to setting an alarm clock to ring at intervals until morning, but I persuaded him to abandon this. He slept in my room and I told him that I was such a light sleeper that if anybody quit breathing in the same room with me, I would wake instantly. He tested me the first night—which I had suspected he would—by holding his breath after my regular breathing had convinced him I was asleep. I was not asleep, however, and called to him. This seemed to allay his fears a little, but he took the precaution of putting a glass of spirits of camphor on a little table at the head of his bed. In case I didn't arouse him until he was almost gone, he said, he would sniff the camphor, a powerful reviver. Briggs was not the only member of his family who had his crotchets. Old Aunt Melissa Beall (who could whistle like a man, with two fingers in her mouth) suffered under the premonition that she was destined to die on South High Street, because she had been born on South High Street and married on South High Street. Then there was Aunt Sarah Shoaf, who never went to bed at night without the fear that a burglar was going to get in and blow chloroform under her door through a tube. To avert this calamity—for she was in greater dread of anesthetics than of losing her household goods—she always piled her money, silverware, and other valuables in a neat stack just outside her bedroom, with a note reading: "This is all I have. Please take it and do not use your chloroform, as this is all I have." Aunt Gracie Shoaf also had a burglar phobia, but she met it with more fortitude. She was confident that burglars had been getting into her house every night for forty years. The fact that she never missed anything was to her no proof to the contrary. She always claimed that she scared them off before they could take anything, by throwing shoes down the hallway. When she went to bed she piled, where she could get at them handily, all the shoes there were about her house. Five minutes after she had turned off the light, she would sit up in bed and say "Hark!" Her husband, who had learned to ignore the whole situation as long ago as 1903, would either be sound asleep or pretend to be sound asleep. In either case he would not respond to her tugging and pulling, so that presently she would arise, tiptoe to the door, open it slightly and heave a shoe down the hall in one direction and its mate down the hall in the other direction. Some nights she threw them all, some nights only a couple of pair.

But I am straying from the remarkable incidents that took place during the night that the bed fell on father. By midnight we were all in bed. The layout of the rooms and the disposition of their occupants is important to an understanding of what later occurred. In the front room upstairs (just under father's attic bedroom) were my mother and my brother Herman, who sometimes sang in his sleep, usually "Marching Through Georgia" or "Onward, Christian Soldiers." Briggs Beall and myself were in a room adjoining this one. My brother Roy was in a room across the hall from ours. Our bull terrier, Rex, slept in the hall.

My bed was an army cot, one of those affairs which are made wide enough to sleep on comfortably only by putting up, flat with the middle section, the two sides which ordinarily hang down like the sideboards of a drop-leaf table. When these sides are up, it is perilous to roll too far toward the edge, for then the cot is likely to tip completely over, bringing the whole bed down on top of one with a tremendous banging crash. This, in fact, is precisely what happened, about two o'clock in the morning. (It was my mother who, in recalling the scene later, first referred to it as "the night the bed fell on your father.")

Always a deep sleeper, slow to arouse (I had lied to Briggs), I was at first unconscious of what had happened when the iron cot rolled me onto the floor and toppled over on me. It left me still warmly bundled up and unhurt, for the bed rested above me like a canopy. Hence I did not wake up, only reached the edge of consciousness and went back. The racket, however, instantly awakened my mother, in the next room, who came to the immediate conclusion that her worst dread was realized: the big wooden bed upstairs had fallen on father. She therefore screamed, "Let's go to your poor father!" It was this shout, rather than the noise of my cot falling, that awakened my brother Herman, in the same room with her. He thought that mother had become, for no apparent reason, hysterical. "You're all right, mamma!" he shouted, trying to calm her. They exchanged shout for shout perhaps ten seconds: "Let's go to your poor father!" and "You're all right!" That woke up Briggs. By this time I was conscious of what was going on, in a vague way, but did not yet realize that I was under my bed instead of on it. Briggs, awakening in the midst of loud shouts of fear and apprehension, came to the quick conclusion that he was suffocating and that we were all trying to "bring him out." With a low moan, he grasped the glass of camphor at the head of his bed and instead of sniffing it poured it over himself. The room reeked of camphor. "Ugf, ahfg!" choked Briggs, like a drowning man, for he had almost succeeded in stopping his breath under the deluge of pungent spirits. He leaped out of bed and groped toward the open window, but he came up against one that was closed. With his hand, he beat out the glass, and I could hear it crash and tinkle in the alleyway below. It was at this juncture that I, in trying to get up, had the uncanny sensation of feeling my bed above me! Foggy with sleep, I now suspected, in my turn, that the whole uproar was being made in a frantic endeavor to extricate me from what must be an unheard-of and perilous situation. "Get me out of this!" I bawled. "Get me out!" I think I had the nightmarish belief that I was entombed in a mine. "Gugh!" gasped Briggs, floundering in his camphor.

By this time my mother, still shouting, pursued by Herman, still shouting, was trying to open the door to the attic, in order to go up and get my father's body out of the wreckage. The door was stuck, however, and wouldn't yield. Her frantic pulls on it only added to the general banging and confusion. Roy and the dog were now up, the one shouting questions, the other barking.

Father, farthest away and soundest sleeper of all, had by this time been awakened by the battering on the attic door. He decided that the house was on fire. "I'm coming, I'm coming!" he wailed in a slow, sleepy voice—it took him many minutes to regain full consciousness. My mother, still believing he was caught under the bed, detected in his "I'm coming!" the mournful, resigned note of one who is preparing to meet his Maker. "He's dying!" she shouted.

"I'm all right!" Briggs yelled, to reassure her. "I'm all right!" He still believed that it was his own closeness to death that was worrying mother. I found at last the light switch in my room, unlocked the door, and Briggs and I joined the others at the attic door. The dog, who never did like Briggs, jumped for him—assuming that he was the culprit in whatever was going on—and Roy had to throw Rex and hold him. We could hear father crawling out of bed upstairs. Roy pulled the attic door open, with a mighty jerk, and father came down the stairs, sleepy and irritable but safe and sound. My mother began to weep when she saw him. Rex began to howl. "What in the name of God is going on here?" asked father.

The situation was finally put together like a gigantic jigsaw puzzle. Father caught a cold from prowling around in his bare feet but there were no other bad results. "I'm glad," said mother, who always looked on the bright side of things, "that your grandfather wasn't here."

[1933–U.S.A.]

QUESTIONS

1. Are Thurber's characters at all realistic? What is it about them that helps make the story comic? Why did Thurber include Aunt Beall and the Shoaf aunts, who have nothing to do with the action of the story?
2. How does Thurber, even while creating suspense, keep the reader from fearing the worst, thus freeing the reader to laugh?
3. How does Thurber make us believe in the story, however improbable and outrageous his characters and their actions may be? Consider in this regard the time when the story takes place and its narrator's tone in general.
4. How does the story's plot contribute to its comic mood?
5. Thematically, the story conveys a sense of what might be called "jumping to delusions." What light does it shed in this regard on human behavior generally? What attitude would Thurber have us take toward our quirkiness? What

kind of laughter, then, does the story evoke—derisive, affectionate, appalled, liberating?

WRITING SUGGESTIONS

1. The intricacy of cause and effect is a prime source of this story's humor. Write a paragraph detailing this intricacy and pointing out how it gives rise to laughter.
2. Under the right circumstances, most of us can act in a ludicrous way. Narrate an incident in your life that could be seen as farcical. Try to make the incident seem as funny to the reader as it does to you.
3. Write a brief review of Thurber's story for a reader who has not read it. Does the story succeed or fail in your judgment? Explain why you judge it as you do.

A Conversation with My Father

Grace Paley

My father is eighty-six years old and in bed. His heart, that bloody motor, is equally old and will not do certain jobs any more. It still floods his head with brainy light. But it won't let his legs carry the weight of his body around the house. Despite my metaphors, this muscle failure is not due to his old heart, he says, but to a potassium shortage. Sitting on one pillow, leaning on three, he offers last-minute advice and makes a request.

"I would like you to write a simple story just once more," he says, "the kind de Maupassant wrote, or Chekhov, the kind you used to write. Just recognizable people and then write down what happened to them next."

I say, "Yes, why not? That's possible." I want to please him, though I don't remember writing that way. I *would* like to try to tell such a story, if he means the kind that begins: "There was a woman . . ." followed by plot, the absolute line between two points which I've always despised. Not for literary reasons, but because it takes all hope away. Everyone, real or invented, deserves the open destiny of life.

Finally I thought of a story that had been happening for a couple of years right across the street. I wrote it down, then read it aloud. "Pa, I said, "how about this? Do you mean something like this?"

Once in my time there was a woman and she had a son. They lived nicely, in a small apartment in Manhattan. This boy at about fifteen became a junkie, which is not unusual in our neighborhood. In order to maintain her close friendship with him, she became a junkie too. She said it was part of the youth culture, with which she felt very much at home. After a while, for a number of reasons, the boy gave it all up and left the city and his mother in disgust. Hopeless and alone, she grieved. We all visit her.

"O.K., Pa, that's it," I said, "an unadorned and miserable tale."

"But that's not what I mean," my father said. "You misunderstood me on purpose. You know there's a lot more to it. You know that. You left everything out. Turgenev wouldn't do that. Chekhov wouldn't do that. There are in fact Russian writers you never heard of, you don't have an inkling of, as good as anyone, who can write a plain ordinary story, who would not leave out what you have left out. I object not to facts but to people sitting in trees talking senselessly, voices from who knows where . . ."

"Forget that one, Pa, what have I left out now? In this one?"

"Her looks, for instance."

"Oh. Quite handsome, I think. Yes."

"Her hair?"

"Dark, with heavy braids, as though she were a girl or a foreigner."

"What were her parents like, her stock? That she became such a person. It's interesting, you know."

"From out of town. Professional people. The first to be divorced in their county. How's that? Enough?" I asked.

"With you, it's all a joke," he said. "What about the boy's father? Why didn't you mention him? Who was he? Or was the boy born out of wedlock?"

"Yes," I said. "He was born out of wedlock."

"For Godsakes, doesn't anyone in your stories get married? Doesn't anyone have the time to run down to City Hall before they jump into bed?"

"No," I said. "In real life, yes. But in my stories, no."

"Why do you answer me like that?"

"Oh, Pa, this is a simple story about a smart woman who came to N.Y.C. full of interest love trust excitement very up to date, and about her son, what a hard time she had in this world. Married or not, it's of small consequence."

"It is of great consequence," he said.

"O.K.," I said.

"O.K. O.K. yourself," he said, "but listen. I believe you that she's good-looking but I don't think she was so smart."

"That's true," I said. "Actually that's the trouble with stories. People start out fantastic. You think they're extraordinary, but it turns out as the work goes along, they're just average with a good education. Sometimes the other way around, the person's a kind of dumb innocent, but he outwits you and you can't even think of an ending good enough."

"What do you do then?" he asked. He had been a doctor for a couple of decades and then an artist for a couple of decades and he's still interested in details, craft, technique.

"Well, you just have to let the story lie around till some agreement can be reached between you and the stubborn hero."

"Aren't you talking silly, now?" he asked. "Start again," he said. "It so happens I'm not going out this evening. Tell the story again. See what you can do this time."

"O.K.," I said. "But it's not a five-minute job." Second attempt:

Once, across the street from us, there was a fine handsome woman, our neighbor. She had a son whom she loved because she'd known him since birth (in helpless chubby infancy, and in the wrestling, hugging ages, seven to ten, as well as earlier and later). This boy, when he fell into the fist of adolescence, became a junkie. He was not a hopeless one. He was in fact hopeful, an ideologue and successful converter. With his busy brilliance, he wrote persuasive articles for his high-school newspaper. Seeking a wider audience, using important connections, he drummed into Lower Manhattan newsstand distribution a periodical called *Oh! Golden Horse!*

In order to keep him from feeling guilty (because guilt is the stony heart of nine tenths of all clinically diagnosed cancers in America today, she said), and because she had always believed in giving bad habits room at home where one could keep an eye on them, she too became a junkie. Her kitchen was famous for a while —a center for intellectual addicts who knew what they were doing. A few felt artistic like Coleridge and others were scientific and revolutionary like Leary. Although she was often high herself, certain good mothering reflexes remained, and she saw to it that there was lots of orange juice around and honey and milk and vitamin pills. However, she never cooked anything but chili, and that no more than once a week. She explained, when we talked to her, seriously, with neighborly concern, that it was her part in the youth culture and she would rather be with the young, it was an honor, than with her own generation.

One week, while nodding through an Antonioni film, this boy was severely jabbed by the elbow of a stern and proselytizing girl, sitting beside him. She offered immediate apricots and nuts for his sugar level, spoke to him sharply, and took him home.

She had heard of him and his work and she herself published, edited, and wrote a competitive journal called *Man Does Live By Bread Alone*. In the organic heat of her continuous presence he could not help but become interested once more in his muscles, his arteries, and nerve connections. In fact he began to love them, treasure them, praise them with funny little songs in *Man Does Live* . . .

> the fingers of my flesh transcend
> my transcendental soul
> the tightness in my shoulders end
> my teeth have made me whole

To the mouth of his head (glory of will and determination) he brought hard apples, nuts, wheat germ, and soy-bean oil. He said to his old friends, From now on, I guess I'll keep my wits about me. I'm going on the natch. He said he was about to begin a spiritual deep-breathing journey. How about you too, Mom? he asked kindly.

His conversion was so radiant, splendid, that neighborhood kids his age began to say that he had never been a real addict at all, only a journalist along for the smell of the story. The mother tried several times to give up what had become without her son and his friends a lonely habit. This effort only brought it to supportable levels. The boy and his girl took their electronic mimeograph and moved to the bushy edge of another borough. They were very strict. They said they would not see her again until she had been off drugs for sixty days.

At home alone in the evening, weeping, the mother read and reread the seven issues of *Oh! Golden Horse!* They seemed to her as truthful as ever. We often crossed the street to visit and console. But if we mentioned any of our children who were at college or in the hospital or dropouts at home, she would cry out, My baby! My baby! and burst into terrible, face-scarring, time-consuming tears. The End.

First my father was silent, then he said, "Number One: You have a nice sense of humor. Number Two: I see you can't tell a plain story. So don't waste time." Then he said sadly, "Number Three: I suppose that means she was alone, she was left like that, his mother. Alone. Probably sick?"

I said, "Yes."

"Poor woman. Poor girl, to be born in a time of fools, to live among fools. The end. The end. You were right to put that down. The end."

I didn't want to argue, but I had to say, "Well, it is not necessarily the end, Pa."

"Yes," he said, "what a tragedy. The end of a person."

"No, Pa," I begged him. "It doesn't have to be. She's only about forty. She could be a hundred different things in this world as time goes on. A teacher or a social worker. An ex-junkie! Sometimes it's better than having a master's in education."

"Jokes," he said. "As a writer that's your main trouble. You don't want to recognize it. Tragedy! Plain tragedy! Historical tragedy! No hope. The end."

"Oh, Pa," I said. "She could change."

"In your own life, too, you have to look it in the face." He took a couple of nitroglycerin. "Turn to five," he said, pointing to the dial on the oxygen tank. He inserted the tubes into his nostrils and breathed deep. He closed his eyes and said, "No."

I had promised the family to always let him have the last word when arguing, but in this case I had a different responsibility. That woman lives across the street. She's my knowledge and my invention. I'm sorry for her. I'm not going to leave her there in that house crying. (Actually neither would Life, which unlike me has no pity.)

Therefore: She did change. Of course her son never came home again. But right now, she's the receptionist in a storefront community clinic in the East Village. Most of the customers are young people, some old friends. The head doctor has said to her, "If we only had three people in this clinic with your experiences . . ."

"The doctor said that?" My father took the oxygen tubes out of his nostrils and said, "Jokes. Jokes again."

"No, Pa, it could really happen that way, it's a funny world nowadays."

"No." he said. "Truth first. She will slide back. A person must have character. She does not."

"No, Pa," I said. "That's it. She's got a job. Forget it. She's in that storefront working."

"How long will it be?" he asked. "Tragedy! You too. When will you look it in the face?"

[1972–U.S.A.]

QUESTIONS

1. Why does the father dislike his daughter's stories? What does he feel she leaves out? In what way does what she leaves out amount to an avoidance, at least in his eyes, not just in her fiction but in her life?
2. How does the narrator define "plot" and why does she dislike it? Father and daughter seem to agree on the relation of plot to life. How so?
3. The father believes that stories should concern "recognizable people," which he

does not find in his daughter's stories. Why might the daughter dislike character as well as plot?

4. Does the second version of the daughter's story have a greater sense of plot than the first? Does the second version have a plot according to the daughter's definition of the word?

5. In what way, if any, is the father's final judgment of his daughter (see the story's last sentence) not a judgment of Grace Paley herself as author?

WRITING SUGGESTIONS

1. In a short essay compare and contrast the two versions of the story told by Paley's narrator. Conclude by considering whether their likenesses or their differences are more significant in terms of the story as a whole.

2. Write a paper pinpointing the differences between the narrator's story (in both versions) and the "conversation" in which she is one of the characters. What theme do these differences suggest?

3. Read Grace Paley's "Wants" (pages 178–80). Then write a paragraph or short paper on it from the point of view of the father in "Conversation with My Father." What would be his criteria of judgment? Does "Wants" fulfill those criteria? Would the story satisfy him finally?

Continuity of Parks*

Julio Cortázar

He had begun to read the novel a few days before. He had put it down because of some urgent business conferences, opened it again on his way back to the estate by train; he permitted himself a slowly growing interest in the plot, in the characterizations. That afternoon, after writing a letter giving his power of attorney and discussing a matter of joint ownership with the manager of his estate, he returned to the book in the tranquillity of his study which looked out upon the park with its oaks. Sprawled in his favorite armchair, its back toward the door—even the possibility of an intrusion would have irritated him, had he thought of it—he let his left hand caress repeatedly the green velvet upholstery and set to reading the final chapters. He remembered effortlessly the names and his mental images of the characters; the novel spread its glamour over him almost at once. He tasted the almost perverse pleasure of disengaging himself line by line from the things around him, and at the same time feeling his head rest comfortably on the green velvet of the chair with its high back, sensing that the cigarettes rested within reach of his hand, that beyond the great windows the air of afternoon danced under the oak trees in the park. Word by word, licked up by the sordid dilemma of the hero and heroine, letting himself be absorbed to the point where the images settled down and took on color and movement, he was witness to the final encounter in the mountain cabin. The woman arrived first, apprehensive; now the lover

* Translated by Paul Blackburn.

141

came in, his face cut by the backlash of a branch. Admirably, she stanched the blood with her kisses, but he rebuffed her caresses, he had not come to perform again the ceremonies of a secret passion, protected by a world of dry leaves and furtive paths through the forest. The dagger warmed itself against his chest, and underneath liberty pounded, hidden close. A lustful, panting dialogue raced down the pages like a rivulet of snakes, and one felt it had all been decided from eternity. Even to those caresses which writhed about the lover's body, as though wishing to keep him there, to dissuade him from it; they sketched abominably the frame of that other body it was necessary to destroy. Nothing had been forgotten: alibis, unforeseen hazards, possible mistakes. From this hour on, each instant had its use minutely assigned. The cold-blooded, twice-gone-over re-examination of the details was barely broken off so that a hand could caress a cheek. It was beginning to get dark.

Not looking at one another now, rigidly fixed upon the task which awaited them, they separated at the cabin door. She was to follow the trail that led north. On the path leading in the opposite direction, he turned for a moment to watch her running, her hair loosened and flying. He ran in turn, crouching among the trees and hedges until, in the yellowish fog of dusk, he could distinguish the avenue of trees which led up to the house. The dogs were not supposed to bark, they did not bark. The estate manager would not be there at this hour, and he was not there. He went up the three porch steps and entered. The woman's words reached him over the thudding of blood in his ears: first a blue chamber, then a hall, then a carpeted stairway. At the top, two doors. No one in the first room, no one in the second. The door of the salon, and then, the knife in hand, the light from the great windows, the high back of an armchair covered in green velvet, the head of the man in the chair reading a novel.

[1963–Argentina]

QUESTIONS

1. Summarize what we know of the plot of the novel being read in the story. Now summarize the plot of the story.
2. Are we to believe that what the man reads about in the novel actually happens to him, or is it that he is totally absorbed in the novel imaginatively?
3. How is your own relation to Cortázar's story like or unlike the relation between the reader and the novel in the story?

4. In what way or ways might "Continuity of Parks" be about the relation between language and reality?

WRITING SUGGESTIONS

1. Write a paragraph or two explaining how the plot of the novel being read in the story and the plot of the story itself coincide and what this coincidence suggests about the relation of language and reality.
2. In a short essay, compare the reader of the novel in "Continuity of Parks" and yourself as reader of the story, and consider the theme of the story in light of this comparison.

Bitterness for Three Sleepwalkers*

Gabriel García Márquez

Now we had her there, abandoned in a corner of the house. Someone had told us, before we brought her things—her clothes which smelled of newly cut wood, her weightless shoes for the mud—that she would be unable to get used to that slow life, with no sweet tastes, no attraction except that harsh, wattled solitude, always pressing on her back. Someone told us—and a lot of time had passed before we remembered it—that she had also had a childhood. Maybe we didn't believe it then. But now, seeing her sitting in the corner with her frightened eyes and a finger placed on her lips, maybe we accepted the fact that she'd had a childhood once, that once she'd had a touch that was sensitive to the anticipatory coolness of the rain, and that she always carried an unexpected shadow in profile to her body.

All this—and much more—we believed that afternoon when we realized that above her fearsome subworld she was completely human. We found it out suddenly, as if a glass had been broken inside, when she began to give off anguished shouts; she began to call each one of us by name, speaking amidst tears until we sat down beside her; we began to sing and clap hands as if our shouting could put the scattered pieces of glass back together. Only then were we able to believe that at one time she had had a childhood. It was as if her shouts were like a revelation somehow; as if they had a lot of remembered tree and deep river about them. When she got up,

* Translated by Gregory Rabassa.

144

she leaned over a little and, still without covering her face with her apron, still without blowing her nose, and still with tears, she told us:

"I'll never smile again."

We went out into the courtyard, the three of us, not talking; maybe we thought we carried common thoughts. Maybe we thought it would be best not to turn on the lights in the house. She wanted to be alone—maybe—sitting in the dark corner, weaving the final braid which seemed to be the only thing that would survive her passage toward the beast.

Outside, in the courtyard, sunk in the deep vapor of the insects, we sat down to think about her. We'd done it so many times before. We might have said that we were doing what we'd been doing every day of our lives.

Yet it was different that night: she'd said that she would never smile again, and we, who knew her so well, were certain that the nightmare had become the truth. Sitting in a triangle, we imagined her there inside, abstract, incapacitated, unable even to hear the innumerable clocks that measured the marked and minute rhythm with which she was changing into dust. "If we only had the courage at least to wish for her death," we thought in a chorus. But we wanted her like that: ugly and glacial, like a mean contribution to our hidden defects.

We'd been adults since before, since a long time back. She, however, was the oldest in the house. That same night she had been able to be there, sitting with us, feeling the measured throbbing of the stars, surrounded by healthy sons. She would have been the respectable lady of the house if she had been the wife of a solid citizen or the concubine of a punctual man. But she became accustomed to living in only one dimension, like a straight line, perhaps because her vices or her virtues could not be seen in profile. We'd known that for many years now. We weren't even surprised one morning, after getting up, when we found her face down in the courtyard, biting the earth in a hard, ecstatic way. Then she smiled, looked at us again; she had fallen out of the second-story window onto the hard clay of the courtyard and had remained there, stiff and concrete, face down on the damp clay. But later we learned that the only thing she had kept intact was her fear of distances, a natural fright upon facing space. We lifted her up by the shoulders. She wasn't as hard as she had seemed to us at first. On the contrary, her organs were loose, detached from her will, like a lukewarm corpse that hadn't begun to stiffen.

Her eyes were open, her mouth was dirty with that earth that already must have had a taste of sepulchral sediment for her when we turned her face up to the sun, and it was as if we had placed her in front of a mirror. She looked at us all with a dull, sexless expression that gave us—holding her in my arms now—the measure of her absence. Someone told us she was dead; and afterward she remained smiling with that cold and quiet smile that she wore at night when she moved about the house awake. She said she didn't know how she got to the courtyard. She said that she'd felt quite warm, that she'd been listening to a cricket, penetrating, sharp, which seemed—so she said—about to knock down the wall of her room, and that she had set herself to remembering Sunday's prayers, with her cheek tight against the cement floor.

We knew, however, that she couldn't remember any prayer, for we discovered later that she'd lost the notion of time when she said she'd fallen asleep holding up the inside of the wall that the cricket was pushing on from outside and that she was fast asleep when somone, taking her by the shoulders, moved the wall aside and laid her down with her face to the sun.

That night we knew, sitting in the courtyard, that she would never smile again. Perhaps her inexpressive seriousness pained us in anticipation, her dark and willful living in a corner. It pained us deeply, as we were pained the day we saw her sit down in the corner where she was now; and we heard her say that she wasn't going to wander through the house any more. At first we couldn't believe her. We'd seen her for months on end going through the rooms at all hours, her head hard and her shoulders drooping, never stopping, never growing tired. At night we would hear her thick body noise moving between two darknesses, and we would lie awake in bed many times hearing her stealthy walking, following her all through the house with our ears. Once she told us that she had seen the cricket inside the mirror glass, sunken, submerged in the solid transparency, and that it had crossed through the glass surface to reach her. We really didn't know what she was trying to tell us, but we could all see that her clothes were wet, sticking to her body, as if she had just come out of a cistern. Without trying to explain the phenomenon, we decided to do away with the insects in the house: destroy the objects that obsessed her.

We had the walls cleaned; we ordered them to chop down the plants in the courtyard and it was as if we had cleansed the silence of the night of bits of trash. But we no longer heard her walking, nor did we hear her talk about crickets any more, until the day when, after the last meal, she remained looking at us, she sat down on the cement floor, still looking at us, and said:"I'm going to stay here, sitting down," and we shuddered, because we could see that she begun to look like something already almost completely like death.

That had been a long time ago and we had even grown used to seeing her there, sitting, her braid always half wound, as if she had become dissolved in her solitude and, even though she was there to be seen, had lost her natural faculty of being present. That's why we now knew that she would never smile again; because she had said so in the same convinced and certain way in which she had told us once that she would never walk again. It was as if we were certain that she would tell us later: "I'll never see again," or maybe "I'll never hear again," and we knew that she was sufficiently human to go along willing the elimination of her vital functions and that spontaneously she would go about ending herself, sense by sense, until one day we would find her leaning against the wall, as if she had fallen asleep for the first time in her life. Perhaps there was still a lot of time left for that, but the three of us, sitting in courtyard, would have liked to hear her sharp and sudden broken-glass weeping that night, at least to give us the illusion that a baby . . . a girl baby had been born in the house. In order to believe that she had been born renewed.

[1949–Colombia]

QUESTIONS

1. What has caused the "she" of this story to be stripped progressively of sensual gratification and mobility, so that she lives "in only one dimension"? Why will she "never smile again"?
2. Is there any evidence that her three sons, who speak collectively through the narrator, love the old woman? Why are they surprised when they are reminded that she, too, had had a childhood? Why, if they love her, does the narrator seem rather distanced from the woman?
3. Several incidents are recorded in the story. Summarize them. How are they linked to provide something like a plot? What initiates the sequence of incidents described?
4. "We realized that above her fearsome subworld she was completely human," the narrator says. Taking into account this statement, together with the title of the story, express the theme as fully as you can.

WRITING SUGGESTIONS

1. In a paragraph or two, summarize the plot of "Bitterness for Three Sleep-walkers" as best you can and discuss the effect of the way plot is treated here.
2. If you have ever known someone dying of Alzheimer's disease, say, or some form of cancer, then you should have special insight into the old woman of the present story and perhaps into her sons as well. Write an essay about García Márquez's strange but moving story in which you bring to bear your firsthand knowledge of the effects of such a disease on both the dying person and the loved ones around. That is, interpret the story in light of your experience.

Smile

D. H. Lawrence

He had decided to sit up all night, as a kind of penance. The telegram had simply said: "Ophelia's condition critical." He felt, under the circumstances, that to go to bed in the *wagon-lit* would be frivolous. So he sat wearily in the first-class compartment as night fell over France.

He ought, of course, to be sitting by Ophelia's bedside. But Ophelia didn't want him. So he sat up in the train.

Deep inside him was a black and ponderous weight: like some tumour filled with sheer gloom, weighing down his vitals. He had always taken life seriously. Seriousness now overwhelmed him. His dark, handsome, clean-shaven face would have done for Christ on the Cross, with the thick black eyebrows tilted in the dazed agony.

The night in the train was like an inferno: nothing was real. Two elderly Englishwomen opposite him had died long ago, perhaps even before he had. Because, of course, he was dead himself.

Slow, grey dawn came in the mountains of the frontier, and he watched it with unseeing eyes. But his mind repeated:

> "And when the dawn came, dim and sad
> And chill with early showers,
> Her quiet eyelids closed: she had
> Another morn than ours."

And his monk's changeless, tormented face showed no trace of the contempt he felt, even self-contempt, for this bathos, as his critical mind judged it.

He was in Italy: he looked at the country with faint aversion. Not capable of much feeling any more, he had only a tinge of aversion as he saw the olives and the sea. A sort of poetic swindle.

It was night again when he reached the home of the Blue Sisters, where Ophelia had chosen to retreat. He was ushered into the Mother Superior's room, in the palace. She rose and bowed to him in silence, looking at him along her nose. Then she said in French:

"It pains me to tell you. She died this afternoon."

He stood stupefied, not feeling much, anyhow, but gazing at nothingness from his handsome, strong-featured monk's face.

The Mother Superior softly put her white, handsome hand on his arm and gazed up into his face, leaning to him.

"Courage!" she said softly. "Courage, no?"

He stepped back. He was always scared when a woman leaned at him like that. In her voluminous skirts, the Mother Superior was very womanly.

"Quite!" he replied in English. "Can I see her?"

The Mother Superior rang a bell, and a young sister appeared. She was rather pale, but there was something naive and mischievous in her hazel eyes. The elder woman murmured an introduction, the young woman demurely made a slight reverence. But Matthew held out his hand, like a man reaching for the last straw. The young nun unfolded her white hands and shyly slid one into his, passive as a sleeping bird.

And out of the fathomless Hades of his gloom he thought: "What a nice hand!"

"They went along a handsome but cold corridor, and tapped at a door. Matthew, walking in far-off Hades, still was aware of the soft, fine voluminousness of the women's black skirts, moving with soft, fluttered haste in front of him.

He was terrified when the door opened, and he saw the candles burning round the white bed, in the lofty, noble room. A sister sat beside the candles, her face dark and primitive, in the white coif, as she looked up from her breviary. Then she rose, a sturdy woman, and made a little bow, and Matthew was aware of creamy-dusky hands twisting a black rosary, against the rich, blue silk of her bosom.

The three sisters flocked silent, yet fluttered and very feminine, in their volumes of silky black skirts, to the bed-head. The Mother Superior leaned, and with utmost delicacy lifted the veil of white lawn from the dead face.

Matthew saw the dead, beautiful composure of his wife's face, and instantly, something leaped like laughter in the depths of him, he gave a little grunt, and an extraordinary smile came over his face.

The three nuns, in the candle glow that quivered warm and quick like a Christmas tree, were looking at him with heavily compassionate eyes, from under their coif-bands. They were like a mirror. Six eyes suddenly started with a little fear, then changed, puzzled, into wonder. And over the three nuns' faces, helplessly facing him in the candle-glow, a strange, involuntary smile began to come. In the three faces, the same smile growing so differently, like three subtle flowers opening. In the pale young nun, it was almost pain, with a touch of mischievous ecstasy. But the dark Ligurian face of the watching sister, a mature level-browed woman, curled with a pagan smile, slow, infinitely subtle in its archaic humour. It was the Etruscan smile, subtle and unabashed and unanswerable.

The Mother Superior, who had a large-featured face something like Matthew's own, tried hard not to smile. But he kept his humorous, malevolent chin uplifted at her, and she lowered her face as the smile grew, grew and grew over her face.

The young, pale sister suddenly covered her face with her sleeve, her body shaking. The Mother Superior put her arm over the girl's shoulder, murmuring with Italian emotion: "Poor little thing! Weep, then, poor little thing!" But the chuckle was still there, under the emotion. The sturdy dark sister stood unchanging, clutching the black beads, but the noiseless smile immovable.

Matthew suddenly turned to the bed, to see if his dead wife had observed him. It was a movement of fear.

Ophelia lay so pretty and so touching, with her peaked, dead little nose sticking up, and her face of an obstinate child fixed in the final obstinacy. The smile went away from Matthew, and the look of super-martyrdom took its place. He did not weep: he just gazed without meaning. Only, on his face deepened the look: I knew this martyrdom was in store for me!

She was so pretty, so childlike, so clever, so obstinate, so worn—and so dead! He felt so blank about it all.

They had been married ten years. He himself had not been perfect—no, no, not by any means! But Ophelia had always wanted her own will. She had loved him, and grown obstinate, and left him, and grown wistful, or contemptuous, or angry, a dozen times, and a dozen times come back to him.

They had no children. And he, sentimentally, had always wanted children. He felt very largely sad.

Now she would never come back to him. This was the thirteenth time, and she was gone for ever.

But was she? Even as he thought it, he felt her nudging him somewhere in the ribs, to make him smile. He writhed a little, and an angry frown came on his brow. He was not *going* to smile! He set his square, naked jaw, and bared his big teeth, as he looked down at the infinitely provoking dead woman. "At it again!"—he wanted to say to her, like the man in Dickens.

He himself had not been perfect. He was going to dwell on his own imperfections.

He turned suddenly to the three women, who had faded backwards beyond the candles, and now hovered, in the white frames of their coifs, between him and nowhere. His eyes glared, and he bared his teeth.

"*Mea culpa! Mea culpa!*" he snarled.

"*Macchè!*" exclaimed the daunted Mother Superior, and her two hands flew apart, then together again, in the density of the sleeves, like birds nesting in couples.

Matthew ducked his head and peered round, prepared to bolt. The Mother Superior, in the background, softly intoned a Pater Noster, and her beads dangled. The pale young sister faded farther back. But the black eyes of the sturdy, black-avised sister twinkled like eternally humorous stars upon him, and he felt the smile digging him in the ribs again.

"Look here!" he said to the women, in expostulation, "I'm awfully upset. I'd better go."

They hovered in fascinating bewilderment. He ducked for the door. But even as he went, the smile began to come on his face, caught by the tail of the sturdy sister's black eye, with its everlasting twinkle. And, he was secretly thinking, he wished he could hold both her creamy-dusky hands, that were folded like mating birds, voluptuously.

But he insisted on dwelling upon his own imperfections. *Mea culpa!* he howled at himself. And even as he howled it, he felt something nudge him in the ribs, saying to him: *Smile!*

The three women left behind in the lofty room looked at one another, and their hands flew up for a moment, like six birds flying suddenly out of the foliage, then settling again.

"Poor thing!" said the Mother Superior, compassionately.

"Yes! Yes! Poor thing!" cried the young sister, with naive, shrill impulsiveness.

"Già" said the dark-avised sister.

The Mother Superior noiselessly moved to the bed, and leaned over the dead face.

"She seems to know, poor soul!" she murmured. "Don't you think so?"

The three coifed heads leaned together. And for the first time they saw the faint ironical curl at the corners of Ophelia's mouth. They looked in fluttering wonder.

"She has seen him!" whispered the thrilling young sister.

The Mother Superior delicately laid the fine-worked veil over the cold face. Then they murmured a prayer for the anima, fingering their beads. Then the Mother Superior set two of the candles straight upon their spikes, clenching the thick candle with firm, soft grip, and pressing it down.

The dark-faced, sturdy sister sat down again with her little holy book. The other two rustled softly to the door, and out into the great white corridor. There softly, noiselessly sailing in all their dark drapery, like dark swans down a river, they suddenly hesitated. Together they had seen a forlorn man's figure, in a melancholy overcoat, loitering in the cold distance at the corridor's end. The Mother Superior suddenly pressed her pace into an appearance of speed.

Matthew saw them bearing down on him, these voluminous figures with framed faces and lost hands. The young sister trailed a little behind.

"*Pardon, ma Mère!*" he said, as if in the street. "I left my hat somewhere . . . ."

He made a desperate, moving sweep with his arm, and never was man more utterly smileless.

[1926–Great Britain]

QUESTIONS

1. In terms of what we see directly, this story presents us with a situation rather than a plot. A plot, however, is intimated. How so?
2. Many readers enjoy speculating about what might happen to this or that character after a story or novel concludes. Lawrence reverses the process: he gives us the end and makes us wonder about the beginning. Construct a past for the former husband and wife which explains why they separated and why he became a monk and she a nun, and which accounts for his smile and hers as well as for his final smilelessness.
3. Why does Lawrence leave the reader to fill in the crucial background? What is the theme of the story?

WRITING SUGGESTIONS

1. Write a paragraph or more addressed to question 2 above. The plot you construct must fall into sequence with the story Lawrence wrote.
2. In a short essay explore the ways in which Lawrence's giving the end of the story and not the beginning involves the reader, and explain what the nature of that involvement implies.
3. Write a paper in which you compare and contrast "The Smile," Cortázar's "Continuity of Parks," and García Márquez's "Bitterness for Three Sleepwalkers" as to the treatment and consequent effects of plot in each. What can be concluded about plot from the three stories taken together?

·*4*·

CHARACTERIZATION

FICTION'S PEOPLE

Almost anything in a story can serve to establish and delineate its characters—to dramatize their motivations, their emotions, their natures. As we've seen, for example, plot can be an agent of characterization: we see who people are by observing what they do. In turn, like the other elements of fiction, characterization helps lead to theme, and in some stories what is revealed about characters is the theme. People are interested in people. In fact, most of us are more interested in people than in anything else. Whatever it is that makes human beings tick is theme enough.

This does not mean, however, that we must recognize ourselves in every character we encounter. Fiction does not ask us to identify in that way with its people. If it did, then no one could be moved by more than a handful of stories; most would leave us cold. It asks instead for imaginative participation in the circumstances and lives of people often of vastly different backgrounds, values, potentials, and understanding from ourselves. If a character does strike home, fine; but many will not. Certainly, fiction contains a good number of unsavory characters, with whom we would not want to identify in any way. Still, such characters can be fascinating. One of the beauties of fiction is that it offers us a world of people to observe. By observing closely, we can come to participate in their imagined lives and thereby come to new insights.

In real life we can never truly get inside another person's skin. Our insights into people's behaviour must be fragmentary, incomplete at best.

Fictional characters, just because they are fictional, offer us a unique opportunity to penetrate into human complexity. We can look at a character from every side, ponder the details that go into the making of that character, then come back and look at the character again. Fiction allows us to hold life in crystal, so to speak, and see into the mystery of human personality. By so doing, it can lead to a heightened compassion for all kinds of people—all human, all caught with us in this mortal condition, but different from us with respect to the particulars of their lives.

MODES OF CHARACTERIZATION

But how do we come an to understanding of a character in a story? How can the intangibles of personality be captured in words? One way is for the narrator simply to tell everything an author wants us to know about a character: "Miss Jones was a vain young woman, always primping and fussing, little concerned with the feelings of others." And narrators sometimes do tell us things of this sort. The experienced reader, however, understands that narrators are not always to be trusted (we'll return to this matter in the next chapter). Of greater immediate importance, telling does not involve us: we want to be shown. We want to observe for ourselves the qualities that make up a character. Even if I am told that Miss Jones is vain, I want to see her vanity concretely: I want to look into her wardrobe, catch her in front of a mirror, watch how she interacts with others. From all of this I can then infer her vanity with conviction.

Inference of this sort is the key to understanding literary characters as it is to understanding people in everyday life. Only the most naive of us simply takes people at their own word. For some will be dishonest and even those who are totally honest can be self-deceived. In determining people's character, we know that we must be somewhat wary and base our judgment on observation of what they do and how they respond to the situations we find them in. In fiction, plot or situation usually exposes some aspect of the nature of a character, which we observe and at least in part base our judgment of the character on. We also infer much about people from their appearance and possessions. The same is true of the appearance and possessions of literary characters: both become symbolic, telling us something about the intangible qualities of personality as revealed by their tangible manifestations. Setting, too—the time and place in which we find characters—can suggest something about them. Also important is how they speak—not just what they say, but how they say it. Though what people say is important, it must be weighed against our perception of them generally, for we know that we cannot necessarily believe everything we're told. On the other hand, how people speak in a conversation can be immediately revealing. An author might have a character speak in short, incomplete sentences to convey the character's excitement; a character who speaks in long, complex sentences, in contrast, will convey something quite different.

Most important, in coming to conclusions about people we watch how they interact; we compare one person with another and listen to what they say to and about each other. Of course, we generally heed only those who have proven themselves to be reliable. As we read a story we must be sure to determine each character's reliability—truthfulness, knowledge, and so forth. Then, if a character whom we have judged to be reliable says something about another, we know that what is said is prime information. Even if limited in point of view, what is said about one character by others can show us different sides of that character. In some stories, though, we learn everything about the story's characters from interaction alone; we are told nothing directly. One story in the last chapter—Somerset Maugham's "A String of Beads"—is an excellent example. What we learn about the male speaker engaged in a dialogue with a rather garrulous female as well as what we learn about her comes entirely from comparing the two as they intereact. Our assessments, note, are based on inference, but valid inference, derived from the textual facts available.

TYPES OF CHARACTER

Many stories do not present us with highly developed characters, and even those that do usually treat only a few characters in any depth. Accordingly, in analyzing fiction we can divide characters into two broad categories: flat and round. Round characters are the sort we've been speaking of, characters treated in some depth, constructed by the reader by way of inference from plot, situation, setting, style, character contrast, and so on. As we watch them acting and responding, hear them speaking and interacting, and observe them undergoing internal change, we come to know them well. In contrast, we know flat characters only by a few prevailing characteristics, which most often remain constant over the course of a work. This is not to say that flat characters are unrealistic. In a sense, they are probably more true to life than round ones in that most people we come in contact with every day are flat to us, seen in one limited role only. And we seldom if ever see into another human being as thoroughly as we can a round character in fiction. As readers we tend to prefer round characters, but we should realize that fiction couldn't do without flat characters as well. It's a matter of both space and focus. There simply isn't enough space even in the longest novel to develop every character fully, and even if there were, to do so would not be desirable because then there would be no focus. We can focus on only so much at a time, after all. In some stories, too, character is not really significant. These stories have their focus elsewhere, so it would be erroneous for the reader to look for developed characters. We as readers must determine the kind of characters we're presented with and adapt ourselves accordingly.

Finally, a word should be said about a particular type of flat character: the stock or type character—the mad scientist, the absent-minded professor, the strong but silent lawman. Even flatter than the usual flat character, stock characters are easily recognizable because the stereotypes they're based on are widespread in the culture. Stock characters are the stuff of propaganda on the one hand and of second-rate fiction on the other. However, we also find them in certain types of the best fiction, though in the hands of a topflight writer stock characters have a way of becoming particularized and memorable. Such characters are especially suitable to comedy and satire, for the less we see into a character the more likely we are to laugh at that character. This is why Dickens is full of stock characters. To be sure, there are many wonderfully round characters in Dickens (Nicholas Nickleby and his friend Smike, David Copperfield, and even old Scrooge, perhaps) as well as many memorable flat characters (Bob Cratchit and Tiny Tim). But it is the parade of stock characters, each lovingly particularized by some trait or manner, that one associates most with Dickens—the cousins, the uncles, the aunts; the beggars and street people; the fops; and all manner of lost souls. All are stock characters, yet all are made to come to life if only for an instant.

CHARACTER AND THEME

Fictional characters of any sort result from the human desire both to individualize and to typify. Thus, even the roundest of characters typifies one or another human possibility, and even a purely stock character, if handled by a competent writer, will have marks of individuality. We're back again to the business of the particular and the general. Particularization gives a story life; generalization gives it meaning. Therefore, while appearing as individuals, characters in fiction tend to raise general questions. Conversely, because ideas in fiction are seen in connection with people, we're made to feel concretely what otherwise would be impersonal abstraction.

For example, take Cynthia Ozick's "The Shawl" once more. The story concerns powerlessness, as we've seen. But powerlessness is only an idea. In "The Shawl" it is made to live by way of Magda, Stella, and especially Rosa, as round a character as is possible in three pages or so. In coming to see what happens to Rosa as she deteriorates, we see what powerlessness means in the flesh. Because the theme of the story concerns the effect of powerlessness on the human spirit, the story necessarily centers on character. There are stories, however, whose themes are more philosophical (as opposed to psychological). In stories of this sort, character and characterization are often secondary, while some other element (symbolism, for example) becomes controlling. The themes of those stories that focus on the human psyche or soul might be thought of as "internal," whereas the themes of stories whose focus is elsewhere might be thought of as "external." In any case, no story can do without some degree of characterization, and in many stories character is a prime element.

SUMMARY SUGGESTIONS: UNDERSTANDING CHARACTERS

1. As you read a story determine the prime elements that go into its making. By determining what elements are prime and what are secondary, one can start to perceive where the focus of a story lies and so begin to think about theme. And if character is prime, then character or character revelation may be theme.

2. Evaluate the types of character used in a story—round, flat, stock. If all of the characters seem flat or stock, then character revelation is probably not the point. Your attention should be elsewhere.

3. If a character starts to seem round, however, or seems important for some other reason, then attend to the matters of characterization that we've discussed. What elements help to establish or reveal character (such as plot, setting) and how? How is the character like or unlike other characters in the story? What do we learn from other characters about the character in question? What can be infered from these and other of the story's details about the character?

4. You might also check for character consistency. Ask questions like "Are a character's actions and motives consistent with what we know about the character? Does the character undergo any change? If so, how?"

5. Finally, determine the trustworthiness of characters. If they prove trustworthy, you may take their judgements as evidence. If they are untrustworthy, there is a reason, and that reason is significant and should be taken into account.

WRITING ON CHARACTERS

Almost any character in fiction might be made the subject of an interesting paper. This is especially true of those stories in which the revelation of character is thematically central. Here you might explore, for example, how plot or situation helps us to understand a character; what the setting suggests; what the character's manner of speech reveals; what we learn from what other characters say and from character interaction; and so forth. In the case of a story focused on character, your thesis would probably be a statement of your assessment of the character central to the story; your support would be a step-by-step consideration of what in the story validates the judgment that is your thesis.

Even minor characters, flat or stock, may be worth looking at. Consider, for instance, Stella in Ozick's "The Shawl." One could easily write an essay on her, as we saw in chapter 1 (pages 22–25). To do so, one could make a statement about her regression to infantile behavior, exemplify it, and then suggest why she has regressed. Her stealing of the shawl—a matter of plot—certainly marks this regression, which is also displayed in various ways by her interactions with both Magda and Rosa. What has caused her regression, of course, is her circumstance; here the setting—in both place and time—comes into play. When you are writing on any kind of character in any kind of story, remember that you must support your thesis with the particulars of the story itself if your paper is to be convincing.

Another possible focus for a paper on characters is consistency or the lack of it. If a character seems inconsistent, you have an immediate thesis: in such and such a story so and so is inconsistent. Now, how so and why? Your first task is to analyze and demonstrate the inconsistency; your second is to draw a conclusion as to why. If you can discern no valid reason, then perhaps the writer is inept or manipulative. Such would be your conclusion. Remember, however, that sometimes character inconsistency can be well motivated (we all can act "out of character" when given the right circumstance). If this is the case, then the inconsistency is crucial information, telling us even more than we knew before about the character at hand. And remember that, like real people, characters in fiction can change. Indeed, to detail how and why a character grows or perhaps deteriorates is a fine thing to do. If you perceive change, then you have a ready-made thesis and support material that should be immediately apparent.

Even when you write on something other than character, you may find it useful to discuss character somewhere along the way. For example, if you were writing on the meaning of a story's setting, you would probably get into characterization because, at least in part, the setting would probably be an agent of characterization. Still, you would be writing on setting and not characterization. The latter would be secondary in this case, support rather than thesis.

A final word. When reading about and writing on characters, bring everything you know about people, including yourself, to bear. You already have a wide experience of life. Don't leave it at the door when it comes to reading and writing. You know much about people—how we act or respond in one or another circumstance; how we can fool others and ourselves; how we relate to one another and how we don't. Carry all of this with you when it comes to dealing with fiction's people. In turn, let your reading and then your writing broaden your experience. There is much to be learned from fiction, especially about people and their interactions.

GENERAL WRITING ASSIGNMENTS

1. (a) Portray a person whom you know or have invented in such a way that some personality trait is revealed even though not stated explicitly. That is, *don't* simply tell what the trait is; reveal it dramatically. Make your reader respond to your person as people respond to others in real life. To bring out the character trait you have in mind, you might put your character in an action or a situation; or you might make something in the setting speak; or you might introduce another character with whom your primary character interacts. Your goal, don't forget, is character revelation through dramatic presentation.

   (b) In a separate discrete paragraph, analyze your characterization. State what the trait revealed is and then discuss how the revelation is accomplished (that is, what elements of fiction in your piece are the agents of characterization). Do you feel your sketch is successful or not? Why?

2. (a) Take a favorite character of yours from a book, a movie, or a television show and explain why you like him or her. What makes the character believable? What light, if any, does the character shed on human beings generally?

   (b) Take the same character and analyze how he or she is characterized. What elements of book, movie, or television show lead you to understand the character? Is action important, or perhaps character interaction? Exemplify.

3. We all know people who are called "characters" (as in the phrase "Boy, that guy's a character"). Briefly describe such a person, and then argue that the

person really *is* like a stock character in fiction (I know people who do seem such) or that when called "a character" the person is being seen from only one side. In either case, conclude with a consideration of what all of this tells you about the relationship of life and fiction.

4. We do not always act consistently, though anything we do in real life tells something about us. Write a paragraph detailing some act of yours that was out of character. What led you to it? What was your motivation? What does the act reveal about you?

Chaos, Disorder and the Late Show

Warren Miller

I am a certified public accountant and a rational man. More exactly, and putting things in their proper order, I am a rational man first and an accountant second. I insist on order; I like the symbols of order—a blunt, hardy plus sign or a forthright minus delights me. I make lists, I am always punctual, I wear a hat. Maltz believes this has caused my hairline to recede. Maltz is one of my associates at the office. He married too young and he regrets it.

In fact, there is no scientific foundation for his view that wearing a hat causes the hairline to recede. Such things are largely a matter of heredity, although my father has a luxuriant head of hair. But what of my grandfathers? I have no doubt that one of them accounts for my high forehead. Talent, I believe I have read somewhere, often skips a generation or jumps from uncle to nephew. Studies have been made. Naturally there are exceptions. But it provides one with the beginning of an explanation. The notion of having been an adopted child is a fancy I have never indulged. I have never doubted that my parents are my true parents. But I sometimes suspect they think I am not their true son.

Let me say just this about my father: He is a high-school history teacher, and every summer for twenty-five years he has had a three-month vacation. Not once has he ever put this time to any real use. He could have been a counselor at a camp, taught the summer session, clerked at a department store or . . . any number of things. I recall that he spent one entire summer lying on the sofa, reading. Some years he goes to the beach. Once he went to Mexico. His income is, to be sure, adequate, but I am certain that one major illness would wipe out his savings. I have tried to speak to him about preplanning; he listens, but he does not seem to hear.

162

My mother—I think this one example will suffice—my mother believes that Leslie Howard, who was a Hollywood actor killed in the war, is still alive. My father merely smiles when she speaks of Leslie Howard—I believe he actually enjoys it—but I have brought home almanacs and circled references in *Harper's* and other magazines attesting to the fact that Leslie Howard is, in fact and in truth, dead. Definitive proof.

Not that I care; not that I care very deeply. It is a harmless-enough delusion; but it is sloppy. I believe that the world tends naturally to chaos and that we all have to make our daily—even hourly—contribution toward order. My parents, in my opinion, are unwilling to shoulder their share of this responsibility.

I have, once or twice, discussed the matter with Maltz, whose wife has proved to be unreliable in some ways and who has a sympathy in matters of this kind. Maltz agrees that my father is mistaken in his indulgent attitude; on the other hand, he believes it would, perhaps, be better psychologically if I ignored my mother's pitiful little delusion—as he called it.

But it is like a pebble in my shoe or loose hair under my shirt collar. Choas and disorder in the world, in the natural scheme of things, is bad enough; one does not want to put up with it at home too. The subways are dirty and unreliable; the crosstown buses are not properly spaced; clerks in stores never know where their stock is.

The extent of the breakdown is incredible. Every year at this time I rent an empty store on upper Broadway and help people with their income-tax returns. These people keep no records! They have no receipts! They lose their canceled checks! They guess! The year just past is, to them, a fast-fading and already incomplete collection of snapshots. It was full of medical and business expenses and deductions for entertaining, yet they remember nothing. Believe me, the chaos of subways and crosstown buses and our traffic problems is as nothing compared to the disorder in the heads of *people*. Every year I am struck with this anew.

This extra-time work continues for three months and becomes more intense as deadline time draws near. It is amazing how many people wait until the last possible moment. Often I am there until nearly midnight.

At the beginning of March I hire Maltz and pay him by the head. He is not as fast as I would like, but he is reliable and, because of his wife and her extravagances, he needs the money. "It would embarrass me," he says, "if I had to tell you how much she spends every week on magazines alone." Poor guy.

I live with my parents. The store I rent is near their apartment, a matter of three blocks, walking distance. It is a neighborhood of small shops and large supermarkets which once were movie houses; their marquees now advertise turkeys and hams. Maltz occasionally will walk me to my door.

That night, the night of the incident, it was snowing. It had been snowing all day. No one had cleaned his sidewalk, and it made walking treacherous. I almost slipped twice.

"Isn't there a city ordinance about people cleaning their sidewalks? Isn't it mandatory?" I asked.

Maltz said, "There is such an ordinance, Norman, but it is more honored in the breach than in the practice."

The sadness of his marriage has given Maltz a kind of wisdom. The next time he slipped I took his arm, and I thought, Here is a man who might one day be my friend. The loneliness of the mismated is a terrible thing to see. It touches me. I believe I understand it. At the door of my building I said good night and I watched for a moment as Maltz proceeded reluctantly toward home.

The elevator was out of order again. When a breakdown occurs, tenants must use the freight elevator at the rear of the lobby. I had to ring for it three times and wait more than five minutes; then I had to ride up with two open garbage cans. It was not very pleasant. The elevator man said, "How's business, Mr. Whitehead?"

"Very good, thank you, Oscar," I said.

"I'll be in to see you real soon, Mr. Whitehead."

I nodded. I knew he'd wait, as he did last year, until the last possible moment. I tried to shrug it off. It's no good trying to carry the next man's share on your own shoulders, I told myself. Forget it, I thought.

Because I had come up in the freight elevator, I therefore entered our apartment by way of the kitchen. I took off my rubbers and carried them in with me, my briefcase in the other hand. As a result the door slammed shut, since I had no free hand to close it slowly.

"Is it you?" my mother called.

She was at the kitchen table having her midnight cup of tea; she said it calmed her and made sleeping easier to have tea before bed. I have tried to explain to her that tea has a higher percentage of caffine than coffee, but she continues to drink it.

She was smiling.

"What is it?" I said.

"Mr. Know-it-all, come here and I would like to show you something."

She had a newspaper on the table. I did not move. "What is it?" I asked.

"Come here and I will show you, Norman," she said, still smiling.

At this point my father shouted something unintelligible from their bedroom.

"What did you say, dear? What?"

"Bette Davis on the late show. *Dark Victory!*"

My mother put her hand to her heart. "I remember the day I saw it," she said. "At the Rivoli, with Millie Brandon." She sat there, staring at nothing; she had forgotten all about me.

"What was it you wanted, Mother?" I said.

"Twenty-five cents if you got there before noon, would you believe it," she said.

I looked at the newspaper. I was astonished to see that she had brought such a newspaper into the house. There it was, beside her teacup, one of those weekly papers that always has headlines such as: MOTHER POISONS HER FIVE BABIES or TAB HUNTER SAYS "I AM LONELY." The inside pages, I have been told, are devoted to racing news.

"Mr. Know-it-all," she said and began to smile again.

"What are you doing with *that* paper, Mother?"

"Millie called me this afternoon and I ran out and bought it. Look!" she cried, and with an all-too-typical dramatic flourish she unfolded it and showed me the front page. The headline read: LESLIE HOWARD STILL ALIVE.

"So much for your almanacs and your definitive proof," she said. "Now what have you got to say, my dear?"

"Two minutes, dear," my father called in on her. "Commercial on now."

"Coming," she called back.

"Mother," I said, "you know very well what kind of paper this is."

"Why should they pick this subject?" she said, tapping the headline with her fingernail. "Why should they pick this particular subject right out of the blue? I would like to ask you that."

"Did you read the article itself, Mother? Is there one iota of hard fact in it?"

"There are facts, and there are facts, my dear boy."

I was very patient with her. "Mother," I said, "he is dead. It is well known that he is dead. He went down at sea in a transport plane . . ."

"First of all, Mr. Smart One, it was not a transport. It was a Spitfire. He always flew Spitfires. He and David Niven."

"Well, then, Mother, just tell me this," I said. "If he's alive, where is he? Where is he?"

"It's starting, dear," my father called.

"The loveliest man who ever walked this earth," she said.

"I have never had the pleasure of seeing him, Mother."

"Steel-rimmed glasses. A pipe. Tweed jackets."

"Well, where is he, Mother?"

"So gentle. Gentle, yet dashing. If everybody was like Leslie Howard, wouldn't this be one beautiful world. Oh, what a beautiful world it would be!"

"Under no circumstances would I trust that particular newspaper," I said.

"This newspaper, my dear boy, is like every other newspaper. It is sometimes right."

I put my rubbers under the sink.

"The year you were born I saw him in *Intermezzo*, Ingrid Bergman's first American movie. Produced by Selznick, who was then still married, I believe, to Louis B. Mayer's daughter Irene." She sipped her tea and looked at the headline. She said, "These days they don't even name boys Leslie anymore. *Girls* are now named Leslie. Before the war people had such lovely names. Leslie, Cary, Myrna, Fay, Claudette. What has happened?"

She looked at me as if it were all my fault. "I don't know what's happened, Mother," I said, perhaps a little testily.

"It's your world, my dear; therefore you should know," she said. "Nowadays they even name them after the days of the week."

"I have named no one after any day of the week, Mother," I said, but she was not listening.

"You could always find a parking place. People were polite. Self-service was unheard of. Frozen food was something to be avoided at all costs."

"I can put no confidence at all in that particular newspaper," I said. "Absolutely none."

"Then I am sorry for you and I pity you," she said in a manner that I thought entirely uncalled for.

"Why? Why should you be sorry for me and pity me?" I asked.

I waited for her to answer, but she went back to sipping her tea and reading the headline.

"I have a good job," I said, "and I am doing the work I like."

"Nevertheless, Norman, I feel sorry for you."

I had not even taken off my overcoat, and I was forced to put up with an attack of this nature! I was struck by the unfairness of it. I said, "You *know* what a silly newspaper that is, Mother. What is the matter with you? You know he is dead. I know you know it. Everybody knows that he is dead."

She banged down her cup. "He is not!" she said. "He is not dead! He is not!"

"What's going on in there?" my father called.

"He is alive!"

"Then where is he?" I demanded, and I raised my voice, too; I admit that I raised my voice. "Where is he?"

"Oh," she said as if she were completely disgusted with me. "Oh, Mr. Born Too Late, I'll tell you where he is," she said, getting up from her chair, the newspaper in her hand. And she began to hit me on the head with it. She hit me on the head with it. Every time she mentioned a name she hit me. "I'll tell you where he is, I'll tell you where he is. He is with Carole Lombard and Glenn Miller and Will Rogers and Franklin . . ."

I ran out of the room. Why argue? She has a harmless delusion. From now on I will try to ignore her when she gets on this particular subject. Maltz may be right about this. I hung up my coat. Fortunately it is only when I stand at my closet door that I can hear the sound of their television set, which often goes on until three in the morning. Once I shut that door, however, my room is perfectly silent.

[1963–U.S.A.]

QUESTIONS

1. Does this story presents us with a plot or a situation? Why is the one or the other appropriate to its content?
2. Contrast Norman with his mother and father. What type of character is each (round, flat, stock)? What do we learn about Norman by these contrasts? Of the three, whom do you sympathize with and why?
3. What can we tell about Norman from his general reaction to things, from his manner of dress, from his "perfectly silent" room? Is Norman truly a rational man?
4. *Dark Victory*, a movie of much emotional turmoil which Norman has never seen, hovers in the background of this story. What does reference to it serve to do there?
5. Would the world according to Norman (that is, the world as he would like it to be) be better or worse than it is now? How so?

WRITING SUGGESTIONS

1. In a few paragraphs compare and contrast Norman with his mother and father. Be specific, providing examples to support what you say about each character.
2. Write an essay on how Norman is characterized. What elements of the story go into his making and help to condition the reader's response to him? In light of the response the story directs us toward, what might be its theme?

Like It Is

Edward Proffitt

Ahh, this job's not bad. Better than last summer. I worked for old doc
Keenan, . . . you know, the vet. Lab Assistant, though all I did was clean
up. But it impressed the hell out of my mother.

He's all right, I guess. Only, he treated me like a kid. Wanted to
"disabuse" me—that's what he said—of my "childish illusions." Ahh, I
let him go on. Always talking about reality and how people can't stand
much of it. What crap! This job, at least, you don't have to hear
somebody talking all the time.

Sure I could a gone back this summer. But with the talking and all.
And something else. I couldn't stomach something he did.

This old lady comes walking in with this bird cage. Says her bird won't
eat. Keenan takes the cover off and there's this fat lump on the bird's back.
"Tumor," he says. "Must be put away." The old lady starts crying. "I know
how this must upset you," he says, real sympathetic like. "Believe me, it
will be completely painless. We use a tiny needle in the bottom of a claw.
He'll simply fall asleep. Then my assistant will put him in a little box and
bury him in our Bird Cemetery." "Oh, doctor," she says, "he means so
much to me. Thank you." So she pays her twenty-five bucks and even
leaves the cage, not that it was worth much.

Anyway, as soon as she's gone, he reaches into the cage, takes out the
bird, and just like that snaps its head off. Bird never felt anything, I guess.
Still, I felt real sorry for it. Then he throws it into the garbage. There
wasn't any cemetery at all!

Well, I don't see why he didn't use the needle he said he was gonna.
He wasn't telling it like it is. That's what I couldn't stand. And all the time

168

the old lady thinking her bird was in some bird cemetery. Piss. I'd rather haul bricks any day.

[1975–U.S.A.]

QUESTIONS

1. Contrast the narrator of "Like It Is" with the veterinarian. How do the two characters help to define one another?
2. Which of the two characters do you prefer? Why?
3. Toward whose view would the story sway us, the narrator's or the veterinarian's? Or would it sway us toward neither? Incorporate your answer in stating the story's theme.

WRITING SUGGESTIONS

1. In a paragraph argue that the veterinarian is simply realistic and the narrator is merely sentimental. In a separate paragraph argue that the veterinarian is crass and self-serving and that the narrator is endearingly idealistic.
2. In a paragraph write a character sketch of the narrator of "Like It Is." What can be inferred about him from situation, character contrast, style, and so forth? Exemplify as you go.

Miss Brill

Katherine Mansfield

Although it was so brilliantly fine—the blue sky powdered with gold and great spots of light like white wine splashed over the Jardins Publiques—Miss Brill was glad that she had decided on her fur. The air was motionless, but when you opened your mouth there was just a faint chill, like a chill from a glass of iced water before you sip, and now and again a leaf came drifting—from nowhere, from the sky. Miss Brill put up her hand and touched her fur. Dear little thing! It was nice to feel it again. She had taken it out of its box that afternoon, shaken out the moth-powder, given it a good brush, and rubbed the life back into the dim little eyes. "What has been happening to me?" said the sad little eyes. Oh, how sweet it was to see them snap at her again from the red eiderdown! . . . But the nose, which was of some black composition, wasn't at all firm. It must have had a knock, somehow. Never mind—a little dab of black sealing-wax when the time came—when it was absolutely necessary. . . . Little rogue! Yes, she really felt like that about it. Little rogue biting its tail just by her left ear. She could have taken it off and laid it on her lap and stroked it. She felt a tingling in her hands and arms, but that came from walking, she supposed. And when she breathed, something light and sad—no, not sad, exactly—something gentle seemed to move in her bosom.

There were a number of people out this afternoon, far more than last Sunday. And the band sounded louder and gayer. That was because the Season had begun. For although the band played all the year round on Sundays, out of season it was never the same. It was like some one playing with only the family to listen; it didn't care how it played if there weren't any strangers present. Wasn't the conductor wearing a new coat, too? She was sure it was new. He scraped with his foot and flapped his arms like a rooster about to crow, and the bandsmen sitting in the green rotunda blew out their cheeks and glared at the music. Now there came a little "flutey" bit—very pretty!—a little chain of bright drops. She was sure it would be repeated. It was; she lifted her head and smiled.

Only two people shared her "special" seat: a fine old man in a velvet coat, his hands clasped over a huge carved walking-stick, and a big old woman, sitting upright, with a roll of knitting on her embroidered apron. They did not speak. This was disappointing, for Miss Brill always looked forward to the conversation. She had become really quite expert, she thought, at listening as though she didn't listen, at sitting in other people's lives just for a minute while they talked round her.

She glanced, sideways, at the old couple. Perhaps they would go soon. Last Sunday, too, hadn't been as interesting as usual. An Englishman and his wife, he wearing a dreadful Panama hat and she button boots. And she'd gone on the whole time about how she ought to wear spectacles; she knew she needed them, but that it was no good getting any; they'd be sure to break and they'd never keep on. And he'd been so patient. He'd suggested everything—gold rims, the kind that curved round your ears, little pads inside the bridge. No, nothing would please her. "They'll always be sliding down my nose!" Miss Brill had wanted to shake her.

The old people sat on the bench, still as statues. Never mind, there was always the crowd to watch. To and fro, in front of the flower-beds and the band rotunda, the couples and groups paraded, stopped to talk, to greet, to buy a handful of flowers from the old beggar who had his tray fixed to the railings. Little children ran among them, swooping and laughing; little boys with big white silk bows under their chins, little girls, little French dolls, dressed up in velvet and lace. And sometimes a tiny staggerer came suddenly rocking into the open from under the trees, stopped, stared, as suddenly sat down "flop," until its small high-stepping mother, like a young hen, rushed scolding to its rescue. Other people sat on the benches and green chairs, but they were nearly always the same, Sunday after Sunday, and—Miss Brill had often noticed—there was something funny about nearly all of them. They were odd, silent, nearly all old, and from the way they stared they looked as though they'd just come from dark little rooms or even—even cupboards!

Behind the rotunda the slender trees with yellow leaves down drooping, and through them just a line of sea, and beyond the blue sky with gold-veined clouds.

Tum-tum-tum tiddle-um! tiddle-um! tum tiddley-um tum ta! blew the band.

Two young girls in red came by and two young soldiers in blue met them, and they laughed and paired and went off arm-in-arm. Two peasant women with funny straw hats passed, gravely, leading beautiful smoke-coloured donkeys. A cold, pale nun hurried by. A beautiful woman came along and dropped her bunch of violets, and a little boy ran after to hand them to her, and she took them and threw them away as if they'd been poisoned. Dear me! Miss Brill didn't know whether to admire that or not! And now an ermine toque and a gentleman in grey met just in front of her. He was tall, stiff, dignified, and she was wearing the ermine toque she'd bought when her hair was yellow. Now everything, her hair, her face, even her eyes, was the same colour as the shabby ermine, and her hand, in its cleaned glove, lifted to dab her lips, was a tiny yellowish paw. Oh, she was so pleased to see him—delighted! She rather thought they were going to meet that afternoon. She described where she'd been—everywhere, here, there, along by the sea. The day was so charming—didn't he agree? And wouldn't he, perhaps?... But he shook his head, lighted a cigarette, slowly breathed a great deep puff into her face, and even while she was still talking and laughing, flicked the match away and walked on. The ermine toque was alone; she smiled more brightly than ever. But even the band seemed to know what she was feeling and played more softly, played tenderly, and the drum beat, "The Brute! The Brute!" over and over. What would she do? What was going to happen now? But as Miss Brill wondered, the ermine toque turned, raised her hand as though she'd seen some one else, much nicer, just over there, and pattered away. And the band changed again and played more quickly, more gaily than ever, and the old couple on Miss Brill's seat got up and marched away, and such a funny old man with long whiskers hobbled along in time to the music and was nearly knocked over by four girls walking abreast.

Oh, how fascinating it was! How she enjoyed it! How she loved sitting here, watching it all! It was like a play. It was exactly like a play. Who could believe the sky at the back wasn't painted? But it wasn't till a little brown dog trotted on solemn and then slowly trotted off, like a little "theatre" dog, a little dog that had been drugged, that Miss Brill discovered what it was that made it so exciting. They were all on the stage. They weren't only the audience, not only looking on; they were acting. Even she had a part and came every Sunday. No doubt somebody would have noticed if she hadn't been there; she was part of the performance after all. How strange she'd never thought of it like that before! And yet it explained why she made such a point of starting from home at just the same time each week—so as not to be late for the performance—and it also explained why she had quite a queer, shy feeling at telling her English pupils how she spent her Sunday afternoons. No wonder! Miss Brill nearly laughed out loud. She was on the stage. She thought of the old invalid gentleman to whom she read the newspaper four afternoons a week while he slept in the garden. She had got quite used to the frail head on the cotton pillow, the hollowed eyes, the open mouth and the high pinched nose. If he'd been dead she mightn't have noticed for weeks; she wouldn't have minded. But suddenly he knew he was having the paper read to him by an actress! "An actress!" The old head lifted; two points of light quivered in the old eyes. "An actress—are ye?" And Miss Brill smoothed the newspaper as though it were the manuscript of her part and said gently: "Yes, I have been an actress for a long time."

The band had been having a rest. Now they started again. And what they played was warm, sunny, yet there was just a faint chill—a something, what was it?—not sadness—no, not sadness—a something that made you want to sing. The tune lifted, lifted, the light shone; and it seemed to Miss Brill that in another moment all of them, all the whole company, would begin singing. The young ones, the laughing ones who were moving together, they would begin, and the men's voices, very resolute and brave, would join them. And then she too, she too, and the others on the benches—they would come in with a kind of accompaniment—something low, that scarcely rose or fell, something so beautiful—moving. . . . And Miss Brill's eyes filled with tears and she looked smiling at all the other members of the company. Yes, we understand, we understand, she thought—though what they understood she didn't know.

Just at that moment a boy and a girl came and sat down where the old couple had been. They were beautifully dressed; they were in love. The hero and heroine, of course, just arrived from his father's yacht. And still soundlessly singing, still with that trembling smile, Miss Brill prepared to listen.

"No, not now," said the girl. "Not here, I can't."

"But why? Because of that stupid old thing at the end there?" asked the boy. "Why does she come here at all—who wants her? Why doesn't she keep her silly old mug at home?"

"It's her fu-fur which is so funny," giggled the girl. "It's exactly like a fried whiting."

"Ah, be off with you!" said the boy in an angry whisper. Then: "Tell me, ma petite chère—"

"No, not here," said the girl. "Not *yet*."

On her way home she usually bought a slice of honey-cake at the baker's. It was her Sunday treat. Sometimes there was an almond in her slice, sometimes not. It made a great difference. If there was an almond it was like carrying home a tiny present—a surprise—something that might very well not have been there. She hurried on the almond Sundays and struck the match for the kettle in quite a dashing way.

But to-day she passed the baker's by, climbed the stairs, went into the little dark room—her room like a cupboard—and sat down on the red eiderdown. She sat there for a long time. The box that the fur came out of was on the bed. She unclasped the necklet quickly; quickly, without looking, laid it inside. But when she put the lid on she thought she heard something crying.

[1922–Great Britain]

QUESTIONS

1. Is Miss Brill a round, flat, or stock character? Does the conclusion of the story round her out in any way?
2. In what season is "Miss Brill" set? Does this particular setting tell us anything about Miss Brill herself?
3. "All the world's a stage," wrote Shakespeare, and Miss Brill would agree. Pinpoint some of the many references in the story to the theatre. Why would Miss Brill wish to see the world as a stage and all the men and women, herself included, as players?
4. The story skillfully suggests that until its end Miss Brill has a distorted view of things. In what way does she mentally alter what she sees? Comment on her shifting reception of the music she hears and on her feeling that "in another moment all of them, all the whole company, would begin singing."
5. Miss Brill changes during the course of her story. How does her fur piece as described at the beginning and the end help to reinforce the reader's sense of that change?
6. With the introduction of the "hero and heroine," the story suddenly takes a different direction. How so? What is its mood before and what after the appearance of the young man and woman?

WRITING SUGGESTIONS

1. (a) Write a paragraph showing two or three ways Miss Brill is characterized. What does each reveal about her?

   (b) What is your response to the story? In a separate paragraph, state your response and defend it.
2. In a paragraph or short paper, compare and contrast Norman ("Chaos, Disorder and the Late Show") with Miss Brill. Or write a dialogue between the two aimed at showing the differences yet also their fundamental similarity.
3. Write an essay on the change in Miss Brill that takes place in the story. How does she change? What in the story signals the change and symbolizes it? How is our perception of her altered? How does the change in Miss Brill lead to the story's theme?

Late at Night

Katherine Mansfield

(Virginia is seated by the fire. Her outdoor things are thrown on a chair; her boots are faintly steaming in the fender.)

VIRGINIA *(laying the letter down)*: I don't like this letter at all—not at all. I wonder if he means it to be so snubbing—or if it's just his way. *(Reads.)* "Many thanks for the socks. As I have had five pairs sent me lately, I am sure you will be pleased to hear I gave yours to a friend in my company." No; it can't be my fancy. He must have meant it; it is a dreadful snub.

Oh, I wish I hadn't sent him that letter telling him to take care of himself. I'd give anything to have that letter back. I wrote it on a Sunday evening, too—that was so fatal. I never ought to write letters on Sunday evenings—I always let myself go so. I can't think why Sunday evenings always have such a funny effect on me. I simply yearn to have someone to write to—or to love. Yes, that's it; they make me feel sad and full of love. Funny, isn't it!

I must start going to church again; it's fatal sitting in front of the fire and thinking. There are the hymns, too; one can let oneself go so safely in the hymns. *(She croons)* "And then for those our Dearest and our Best"—*(but her eye lights on the next sentence in the letter)*. "It was most kind of you to have knitted them yourself." Really! Really, that is too much! Men are abominably arrogant! He actually imagines that I knitted them myself. Why, I hardly know him; I've only spoken to him a few times. Why on earth should I knit him socks? He must think I am far gone to throw myself at his head like that. For it certainly is throwing oneself at a

175

man's head to knit him socks—if he's almost a stranger. Buying him an odd pair is a different matter altogether. No; I shan't write to him again—that's definite. And, besides, what would be the use? I might get really keen on him and he'd never care a straw for me. Men don't.

I wonder why it is that after a certain point I always seem to repel people. Funny, isn't it! They like me at first; they think me uncommon, or original; but then immediately I want to show them—even give them a hint—that I like them, they seem to get frightened and begin to disappear. I suppose I shall get embittered about it later on. Perhaps they know somehow that I've got so much to give. Perhaps it's that that frightens them. Oh, I feel I've got such boundless, boundless love to give to somebody—I would care for somebody so utterly and so completely— watch over them—keep everything horrible away—and make them feel that if ever they wanted anything done I lived to do it. If only I felt that somebody wanted me, that I was of use to somebody, I should become a different person. Yes; that is the secret of life for me—to feel loved, to feel wanted, to know that somebody leaned on me for everything absolutely— for ever. And I am strong, and far richer than most women. I am sure that most women don't have this tremendous yearning to—express themselves. I suppose that's it—to come into flower, almost. I'm all folded and shut away in the dark, and nobody cares. I suppose that is why I feel this tremendous tenderness for plants and sick animals and birds—it's one way of getting rid of this wealth, this burden of love. And then, of course, they are so helpless—that's another thing. But I have a feeling that if a man were really in love with you he'd be just as helpless, too. Yes, I am sure that men are very helpless. . . .

I don't know why, I feel inclined to cry to-night. Certainly not because of this letter; it isn't half important enough. But I keep wondering if things will ever change or if I shall go on like this until I am old—just wanting and wanting. I'm not as young as I was even now. I've got lines, and my skin isn't a bit what it used to be. I never was really pretty, not in the ordinary way, but I did have lovely skin and lovely hair—and I walked well. I only caught sight of myself in a glass to-day—stooping and shuffling along. . . . I looked dowdy and elderly. Well, no; perhaps not quite as bad as that; I always exaggerate about myself. But I'm faddy about things now—that's a sign of age, I'm sure. The wind—I can't bear being blown about in the wind now; and I hate having wet feet. I never used to care about those things—I used almost to revel in them—they made me feel so *one* with Nature in a way. But now I get cross and I want to cry and I yearn for something to make me forget. I suppose that's why women take to drink. Funny, isn't it!

The fire is going out. I'll burn this letter. What's it to me? Pooh! I don't care. What is it to me? The five other women can send him socks! And I don't suppose he was a bit what I imagined. I can just hear him saying, "It was most kind of you, to have knitted them yourself." He has a fascinating voice. I think it was his voice that attracted me to him—and his hands; they looked so strong—they were such man's hands. Oh, well, don't sentimentalize over it; burn it! . . . No, I can't now—the fire's gone out. I'll go to bed. I wonder if he really meant to be snubbing. Oh, I am tired. Often when I go to bed now I want to pull the clothes over my head—and just cry. Funny, isn't it!

[1917–Great Britain]

QUESTIONS

1. What do we learn about the story's speaker, Virginia? What kind of person is she? What in the story leads you to your assessment of her? In what way is character revelation its theme?
2. Is Virginia a stock, flat, or round character? Or does she exhibit traits of more than one type?
3. Are we meant to take Virginia at her word, or should we see more about her than she does herself? Why, for instance, does she frighten people off? She thinks it's because she has "so much to give." Is she right? What reason might those who drop her give for doing so?

WRITING SUGGESTIONS

1. In a paragraph or two, compare and contrast Virginia and Miss Brill. They seem alike in many ways; yet they differ markedly as to final effect. How do their differences make for the final difference in our response?
2. In a short paper, analyze Virginia's personality. What type of person is she? Why does she frighten other people off? In what ways is she blind to herself? How does this blindness itself reveal her character and suggest why she affects other people the way she does?

Wants

Grace Paley

I saw my ex-husband in the street. I was sitting on the steps of the new library.

Hello, my life, I said. We had once been married for twenty-seven years, so I felt justified.

He said, What? What life? No life of mine.

I said, O.K. I don't argue when there's real disagreement. I got up and went into the library to see how much I owed them.

The librarian said $32 even and you've owed it for eighteen years. I didn't deny anything. Because I don't understand how time passes. I have had those books. I have often thought of them. The library is only two blocks away.

My ex-husband followed me to the Books Returned desk. He interrupted the librarian, who had more to tell. In many ways, he said, as I look back, I attribute the dissolution of our marriage to the fact that you never invited the Bertrams to dinner.

That's possible, I said. But really, if you remember: first, my father was sick that Friday, then the children were born, then I had those Tuesday-night meetings, then the war began. Then we didn't seem to know them any more. But you're right. I should have had them to dinner.

I gave the librarian a check for $32. Immediately she trusted me, put my past behind her, wiped the record clean, which is just what most other municipal and/or state bureaucracies will *not* do.

178

I checked out the two Edith Wharton books I had just returned because I'd read them so long ago and they are more apropos now than ever. They were *The House of Mirth* and *The Children*, which is about how life in the United States in New York changed in twenty-seven years fifty years ago.

A nice thing I do remember is breakfast, my ex-husband said. I was surprised. All we ever had was coffee. Then I remembered there was a hole in the back of the kitchen closet which opened into the apartment next door. There, they always ate sugar-cured smoked bacon. It gave us a very grand feeling about breakfast, but we never got stuffed and sluggish.

That was when we were poor, I said.

When were we ever rich? he asked.

Oh, as time went on, as our responsibilities increased, we didn't go in need. You took adequate financial care, I reminded him. The children went to camp four weeks a year and in decent ponchos with sleeping bags and boots, just like everyone else. They looked very nice. Our place was warm in winter, and we had nice red pillows and things.

I wanted a sailboat, he said. But you didn't want anything.

Don't be bitter, I said. It's never too late.

No, he said with a great deal of bitterness. I may get a sailboat. As a matter of fact I have money down on an eighteen-foot two-rigger. I'm doing well this year and can look forward to better. But as for you, it's too late. You'll always want nothing.

He had had a habit throughout the twenty-seven years of making a narrow remark which, like a plumber's snake, could work its way through the ear down the throat, halfway to my heart. He would then disappear, leaving me choking with equipment. What I mean is, I sat down on the library steps and he went away.

I looked through *The House of Mirth*, but lost interest. I felt extremely accused. Now, it's true, I'm short of requests and absolute requirements. But I do want *something*.

I want, for instance, to be a different person. I want to be the woman who brings these two books back in two weeks. I want to be the effective citizen who changes the school system and addresses the Board of Estimate on the troubles of this dear urban center.

I *had* promised my children to end the war before they grew up.

I wanted to have been married forever to one person, my ex-husband or my present one. Either has enough character for a whole life, which as it turns out is really not such a long time. You couldn't exhaust either man's qualities or get under the rock of his reasons in one short life.

Just this morning I looked out the window to watch the street for a while and saw that the little sycamores the city had dreamily planted a couple of years before the kids were born had come that day to the prime of their lives.

Well! I decided to bring those two books back to the library. Which proves that when a person or an event comes along to jolt or appraise me I *can* take some appropriate action, although I am better known for my hospitable remarks.

[1971–U.S.A.]

QUESTIONS

1. What does Paley's narrator want? What does her ex-husband want? In what ways do their wants differ?
2. How else do the two differ? Why did they get divorced?
3. What kind of person is Paley's narrator? What in the story helps to characterize her?
4. What is the point of this story? In addressing this question, consider its title, "Wants."

WRITING SUGGESTIONS

1. Write a paragraph addressed to question 3 above. Give examples of how we learn about Paley's narrator.
2. In a paragraph or more, analyze the wants of Paley's narrator as contrasted with those of her ex-husband. What do their differing wants tell us about each of them? In what way does the difference in what each wants help to explain their divorce?
3. At one point or another in life, many people desire to change. Consider Paley's narrator in this regard. Write a short essay describing what kind of a person she is and what kind of a person she would like to be. Is there any evidence in the story that she is changing? Will she become the person she can imagine being?

Love

Jesse Stuart

Yesterday when the bright sun blazed down on the wilted corn my father and I walked around the edge of the new ground to plan a fence. The cows kept coming through the chestnut oaks on the cliff and running over the young corn. They bit off the tips of the corn and trampled down the stubble.

My father walked in the cornbalk. Bob, our Collie, walked in front of my father. We heard a ground squirrel whistle down over the bluff among the dead treetops at the clearing's edge. "Whoop, take him, Bob," said my father. He lifted up a young stalk of corn, with wilted dried roots, where the ground squirrel had dug it up for the sweet grain of corn left on its tender roots. This has been a dry spring and the corn has kept well in the earth where the grain has sprouted. The ground squirrels love this corn. They dig up rows of it and eat the sweet grains. The young corn stalks are killed and we have to replant the corn.

I can see my father keep sicking Bob after the ground squirrel. He jumped over the corn rows. He started to run toward the ground squirrel. I, too, started running toward the clearing's edge where Bob was jumping and barking. The dust flew in tiny swirls behind our feet. There was a cloud of dust behind us.

"It's a big bull blacksnake," said my father. "Kill him, Bob! Kill him, Bob!"

Bob was jumping and snapping at the snake so as to make it strike and throw itself off guard. Bob had killed twenty-eight copperheads this spring. He knows how to kill a snake. He doesn't rush to do it. He takes his time and does the job well.

181

"Let's don't kill the snake," I said. "A blacksnake is a harmless snake. It kills poison snakes. It kills the copperhead. It catches more mice from the fields than a cat."

I could see the snake didn't want to fight the dog. The snake wanted to get away. Bob wouldn't let it. I wondered why it was crawling toward a heap of black loamy earth at the bench of the hill. I wondered why it had come from the chestnut oak sprouts and the matted greenbriars on the cliff. I looked as the snake lifted its pretty head in response to one of Bob's jumps. "It's not a bull blacksnake," I said. "It's a she-snake. Look at the white on her throat."

"A snake is an enemy to me," my father snapped. "I hate a snake. Kill it, Bob. Go in there and get that snake and quit playing with it!"

Bob obeyed my father. I hated to see him take this snake by the throat. She was so beautifully poised in the sunlight. Bob grabbed the white patch on her throat. He cracked her long body like an ox whip in the wind. He cracked it against the wind only. The blood spurted from her fine-curved throat. Something hit against my legs like pellets. Bob threw the snake down. I looked to see what had struck my legs. It was snake eggs. Bob had slung them from her body. She was going to the sand heap to lay her eggs, where the sun is the setting-hen that warms them and hatches them.

Bob grabbed her body there on the earth where the red blood was running down on the gray-piled loam. Her body was still writhing in pain. She acted like a greenweed held over a new-ground fire. Bob slung her viciously many times. He cracked her limp body against the wind. She was now limber as a shoestring in the wind. Bob threw her riddled body back on the sand. She quivered like a leaf in the lazy wind, then her riddled body lay perfectly still. The blood colored the loamy earth around the snake.

"Look at the eggs, won't you?" said my father. We counted thirty-seven eggs. I picked an egg up and held it in my hand. Only a minute ago there was life in it. It was an immature seed. It would not hatch. Mother sun could not incubate it on the warm earth. The egg I held in my hand was almost the size of a quail's egg. The shell on it was thin and tough and the egg appeared under the surface to be a watery egg.

"Well, Bob, I guess you see now why this snake couldn't fight," I said. "It is life. Weaker devour the stronger even among human beings. Dog kills snake. Snake kills birds. Birds kill the butterflies. Man conquers all. Man, too, kills for sport."

Bob was panting. He walked ahead of us back to the house. His tongue was out of his mouth. He was tired. He was hot under his shaggy coat of hair. His tongue nearly touched the dry dirt and white flecks of foam dripped from it. We walked toward the house. Neither my father nor I spoke. I still thought about the dead snake. The sun was going down over the chestnut ridge. A lark was singing. It was late for a lark to sing. The red evening clouds floated above the pine trees on our pasture hill. My father stood beside the path. His black hair was moved by the wind. His face was red in the blue wind of day. His eyes looked toward the sinking sun.

"And my father hates a snake," I thought.

I thought about the agony women know of giving birth. I thought about how they will fight to save their children. Then, I thought of the snake. I thought it was silly for me to think such thoughts.

This morning my father and I got up with the chickens. He says one has to get up with the chickens to do a day's work. We got the posthole digger, ax, spud, measuring pole and the mattock. We started for the clearing's edge. Bob didn't go along.

The dew was on the corn. My father walked behind with the posthole digger across his shoulder. I walked in front. The wind was blowing. It was a good morning wind to breathe and a wind that makes one feel like he can get under the edge of a hill and heave the whole hill upside down.

I walked out the corn row where we had come yesterday afternoon. I looked in front of me. I saw something. I saw it move. It was moving like a huge black rope winds around a windlass. "Steady," I says to my father. "Here is the bull blacksnake." He took one step up beside me and stood. His eyes grew wide apart.

"What do you know about this," he said.

"You have seen the bull blacksnake now," I said. "Take a good look at him! He is lying beside his dead mate. He has come to her. He, perhaps, was on her trail yesterday."

The male snake had trailed her to her doom. He had come in the night, under the roof of stars, as the moon shed rays of light on the quivering clouds of green. He had found his lover dead. He was coiled beside her, and she was dead.

The bull blacksnake lifted his head and followed us as we walked around the dead snake. He would have fought us to his death. He would have fought Bob to his death. "Take a stick," said my father, "and throw him over the hill so Bob won't find him. Did you ever see anything to beat that? I've heard they'd do that. But this is my first time to see it." I took a stick and threw him over the bank into the dewy sprouts on the cliff.

[1940–U.S.A]

QUESTIONS

1. "A snake is an enemy to me," says the father. Why, then, does he save the bull blacksnake at the end?
2. Thinking of "the agony women know giving birth" and then of the snake, the boy who narrates "Love" adds: "I thought it was silly for me to think such thoughts." Was it? Or does this last thought reveal something important about the boy? What?
3. Both father and son change during the course of this story. That, indeed, is its point. In what ways does each of them change because of the incident narrated?

WRITING SUGGESTIONS

1. Consider question 3 and then write a paragraph or two in answer. Outline how each character changes and what in the story points to growth on the part of each.
2. In a short paper, compare and contrast "Love" and Crane's "The Snake" (pages 63–65). Taken together, what do the two stories suggest about the complexity of human experience?
3. Have you ever experienced a sense of life's grandeur, transcending all of your immediate cares and concerns? If so, write a short essay about the experience, relating it to what both father and son come to feel at the end of "Love."

After the Theatre*

Anton Chekhov

Nadya Zelenin and her mother had returned from a performance of
Eugene Onegin at the theatre. Going into her room, the girl swiftly threw
off her dress and let her hair down. Then she quickly sat at the table in her
petticoat and white bodice to write a letter like Tatyana's.

"I love you," she wrote, "but you don't love me, you don't love me!"
Having written this, she laughed.

She was only sixteen and had never loved anyone yet. She knew that
Gorny (an army officer) and Gruzdyov (a student) were both in love with
her, but now, after the opera, she wanted to doubt their love. To be
unloved and miserable: what an attractive idea! There was something
beautiful, touching and romantic about A loving B when B wasn't
interested in A. Onegin was attractive in not loving at all, while Tatyana
was enchanting because she loved greatly. Had they loved equally and
been happy they might have seemed boring.

"Do stop telling me you love me because I don't believe you," Nadya
wrote on, with Gorny, the officer, in mind. "You are highly intelligent,
well-educated and serious, you're a brilliant man—with a dazzling future,
perhaps—whereas I'm a dull girl, a nobody. As you're perfectly well
aware, I should only be a burden to you. Yes, you have taken a fancy to
me, I know, you thought you'd found your ideal woman. But that was a
mistake. You're already wondering frantically why you ever had to meet
such a girl and only your good nature prevents you admitting as much."

* Translated by Ronald Hingley.

Nadya began to feel sorry for herself, and burst into tears.

"I can't bear to leave my mother and brother," she went on, "or else I'd take the veil and go off into the blue, and you'd be free to love another. Oh, if only I were dead!"

Tears blurred what Nadya had written, while rainbow flashes shimmered on table, floor and ceiling, as if she was looking through a prism. Writing was impossible, so she lolled back in her arm-chair and began thinking of Gorny.

How attractive, ye gods, how seductive men were! Nadya remembered what a beautiful expression—pleading, guilty, gentle—Gorny wore whenever anyone discussed music with him and what efforts it cost him to keep a ring of enthusiasm out of his voice. In a society where coolness, hauteur and nonchalance are judged signs of breeding and good manners, one must hide one's passions. Hide them he does, but without success, and it's common knowledge that he's mad about music. Those endless arguments about music, the brash verdicts of ignoramuses . . . they keep him constantly on edge, making him scared, timid, taciturn. He plays the piano magnificently, like a professional pianist, and he might well have been a famous musician had he not been in the army.

Nadya's tears dried and she remembered Gorny declaring his love to her: at a symphony concert and then by the coat-hooks downstairs, with a draught blowing in all directions.

"I'm so glad you've met my student friend Gruzdyov at last," she wrote on. "He is very bright and you're sure to like him. He came to see us yesterday and stayed until two in the morning. We were all delighted and I was sorry you hadn't joined us. He made many remarkable observations."

Putting her hands on the table, Nadya leant her head on them, and her hair covered the letter. She remembered that Gruzdyov also loved her, that he had as much right to a letter as Gorny. Wouldn't it be better, actually, to write to Gruzdyov? Happiness stirred spontaneously in her breast. First it was small and rolled about like a rubber ball, then it swelled broader and bigger and surged on like a wave. Now Nadya had forgotten Gorny and Gruzdyov, her mind was muddled and ever greater grew her joy. It moved from breast to arms and legs, and she felt as if a light, cool breeze had fanned her head and stirred her hair. Her shoulders shook with silent laughter, the table and lamp-chimney trembled too, and her tears sprinkled the letter. Unable to stop laughing, she quickly thought of something funny to prove that she wasn't laughing about nothing.

"What a funny poodle!" she brought out, feeling as if she was choking with laughter. "How funny that poodle was!"

She had remembered Gruzdyov romping with Maxim, the family poodle, after tea yesterday and then telling a story about a very clever poodle chasing a raven in some yard. The raven had turned round and spoken: "Oh, you wretched little dog." Not knowing that it was involved with a talking raven, the poodle had been terribly embarrassed. It had retreated, baffled, and started barking.

"No, I'd rather love Gruzdyov," Nadya decided, tearing up the letter.

She began thinking of the student, of his love, of her love, but the upshot was that her head swam and she thought about everything at once: mother, street, pencil, piano.

She thought happily and found everything simply wonderful. And this was only the beginning, happiness whispered to her, before long things would be even better still. Soon spring would come, and summer. She and Mother would go to Gorbiki, Gorny would have leave and he would walk round the garden with her, dancing attendance. Gruzdyov would come too. They would play croquet and skittles together, and he would make funny or surprising remarks. Garden, darkness, clear skies, stars . . . she yearned for them passionately. Once more her shoulders shook with laughter and she seemed to smell wormwood in the room, seeemed to hear a bough slap the window.

She went and sat on her bed. Not knowing how to cope with the immense happiness which weighed her down, she gazed at the icon hanging at the head of her bed.

"Lord, how marvellous!" she said.

[1892–Russia]

QUESTIONS

1. The adolescent girl in this story experiences two quite different emotions after she returns from having seen Tchaikovsky's opera *Eugene Onegin*, a turbulent story of unrequited love. What exactly are her feelings?
2. Is Chekhov's portrait of the girl true to life? Do young people generally experience such feelings?
3. Have you ever been in an analogous situation? What were your feelings?

WRITING SUGGESTIONS

1. Write a critique of "After the Theatre" in which you analyze its protagonist in terms of what you know about the experience of adolescence. What are the confusions of this stage of life? In what ways does your knowledge of this phase of growing up relate to what Nadya feels?
2. Does this story ring true? In an essay, argue that it does or doesn't in light of your own experience when you were Nadya's age. Conclude with a statement as to the effectiveness of Chekhov's treatment of the emotions of a teenager, especially with respect to the opposite sex.

The Test

Angelica Gibbs

On the afternoon Marian took her second driver's test, Mrs. Ericson went with her. "It's probably better to have someone a little older with you," Mrs. Ericson said as Marian slipped into the driver's seat beside her. "Perhaps the last time your Cousin Bill made you nervous, talking too much on the way."

"Yes, Ma'am," Marian said in her soft unaccented voice. "They probably do like it better if a white person shows up with you."

"Oh, I don't think it's *that*," Mrs. Ericson began, and subsided after a glance at the girl's set profile. Marian drove the car slowly through the shady suburban streets. It was one of the first hot days in June, and when they reached the boulevard they found it crowded with cars headed for the beaches.

"Do you want me to drive?" Mrs. Ericson asked. "I'll be glad to if you're feeling jumpy." Marian shook her head. Mrs. Ericson watched her dark, competent hands and wondered for the thousandth time how the house had ever managed to get along without her, or how she had lived through those earlier years when her household had been presided over by a series of slatternly white girls who had considered housework demeaning and the care of children an added insult. "You drive beautifully, Marian," she said. "Now, don't think of the last time. Anybody would slide on a steep hill on a wet day like that."

"It takes four mistakes to flunk you," Marian said. "I don't remember doing all the things the inspector marked down on my blank."

"People say that they only want you to slip them a little something," Mrs. Ericson said doubtfully.

"No," Marian said. "That would only make it worse, Mrs. Ericson, I know."

The car turned right, at a traffic signal, into a side road and slid up to the curb at the rear of a short line of parked cars. The inspectors had not arrived yet.

"You have the papers?" Mrs. Ericson asked. Marian took them out of her bag: her learner's permit, the car registration, and her birth certificate. They settled down to the dreary business of waiting.

"It will be marvellous to have someone dependable to drive the children to school every day," Mrs. Ericson said.

Marian looked up from the list of driving requirements she had been studying. "It'll make things simpler at the house, won't it?" she said.

"Oh, Marian," Mrs. Ericson exclaimed, "if I could only pay you half of what you're worth!"

"Now, Mrs. Ericson," Marian said firmly. They looked at each other and smiled with affection.

Two cars with official insignia on their doors stopped across the street. The inspectors leaped out, very brisk and military in their neat uniforms. Marian's hands tightened on the wheel. "There's the one who flunked me last time," she whispered, pointing to a stocky, self-important man who had begun to shout directions at the driver at the head of the line. "Oh, Mrs. Ericson."

"Now, Marian," Mrs. Ericson said. They smiled at each other again, rather weakly.

The inspector who finally reached their car was not the stocky one but a genial, middle-aged man who grinned broadly as he thumbed over their papers. Mrs. Ericson started to get out of the car. "Don't you want to come along?" the inspector asked. "Mandy and I don't mind company."

Mrs. Ericson was bewildered for a moment. "No," she said, and stepped to the curb. "I might make Marian self-conscious. She's a fine driver, Inspector."

"Sure thing," the inspector said, winking at Mrs. Ericson. He slid into the seat beside Marian. "Turn right at the corner, Mandy-Lou."

From the curb, Mrs. Ericson watched the car move smoothly up the street.

The inspector made notations in a small black book. "Age?" he inquired presently, as they drove along.

"Twenty-seven."

He looked at Marian out of the corner of his eye. "Old enough to have quite a flock of pickaninnies, eh?"

Marian did not answer.

"Left at this corner," the inspector said, "and park between that truck and the green Buick."

The two cars were very close together, but Marian squeezed in between them without too much maneuvering. "Driven before, Mandy-Lou?" the inspector asked.

"Yes, sir. I had a license for three years in Pennsylvania."

"Why do you want to drive a car?"

"My employer needs me to take her children to and from school."

"Sure you don't really want to sneak out nights to meet some young blood?" the inspector asked. He laughed as Marian shook her head.

"Let's see you take a left at the corner and then turn around in the middle of the next block," the inspector said. He began to whistle "Swanee River." "Make you homesick?" he asked.

Marian put out her hand, swung around neatly in the street, and headed back in the direction from which they had come. "No," she said. "I was born in Scranton, Pennsylvania."

The inspector feigned astonishment. "You-all ain't Southern?" he said. "Well, dog my cats if I didn't think you-all came from down yondah."

"No, sir," Marian said.

"Turn onto Main Street and let's see how you-all does in heavier traffic."

They followed a line of cars along Main Street for several blocks until they came in sight of a concrete bridge which arched high over the railroad tracks.

"Read that sign at the end of the bridge," the inspector said.

" 'Proceed with caution. Dangerous in slippery weather,' " Marian said.

"You-all sho can read fine," the inspector exclaimed. "Where d'you learn to do that, Mandy?"

"I got my college degree last year," Marian said. Her voice was not quite steady.

As the car crept up the slope of the bridge the inspector burst out laughing. He laughed so hard he could scarcely give his next direction. "Stop here," he said, wiping his eyes, "then start'er up again. Mandy got her degree, did she? Dog my cats!"

Marian pulled up beside the curb. She put the car in neutral, pulled on the emergency, waited a moment, and then put the car into gear again. Her face was set. As she released the brake her foot slipped off the clutch pedal and the engine stalled.

"Now, Mistress Mandy," the inspector said, "remember your degree."

"*Damn* you!" Marian cried. She started the car with a jerk.

The inspector lost his joviality in an instant. "Return to the starting place, please," he said, and made four very black crosses at random in the squares on Marian's application blank.

Mrs. Ericson was waiting at the curb where they had left her. As Marian stopped the car, the inspector jumped out and brushed past her, his face purple. "What happened?" Mrs. Ericson asked, looking after him with alarm.

Marian stared down at the wheel and her lip trembled.

"Oh, Marian, *again?*" Mrs. Ericson said.

Marian nodded. "In a sort of different way," she said, and slid over to the right-hand side of the car.

[1940–U.S.A.]

QUESTIONS

1. What character type is Mrs. Ericson? Marian? The driving inspector? Characterize each of the three. In what way is the inspector's character type appropriate to the villian he is?

2. Why is Marian, a woman with a college degree, a maid? Why is her reaction to the inspector so long in coming and so relatively mild? Why is his final response to her so vindictive? Before answering, consider the social context of this realistic piece in light of its date of publication.

3. Mood, as will be discussed later in the book, is the feeling a story raises in a reader. What is the mood of "The Test"? In what way is its mood, established especially by character and plot, related to its theme?

4. Why the title? Why "the" instead of "a"? What are the wider implications of the story in light of its title?

WRITING SUGGESTIONS

1. An ill-tempered villain may be easier to cope with than a jocular one. Develop this idea in a paragraph, using Gibbs's driving inspector as a case in point. First characterize him; then consider why the particular way he vents his bigotry is particularly insidious.

2. With respect to the bigotry it depicts, is "The Test" still relevant today? Have things changed for blacks since the story was written, or are blacks still second-class citizens? Using what evidence you have, write an essay arguing one side or the other of this matter. Along the way, take note of the arguments on the opposite side.

My First Goose*

Isaac Babel

Savitsky, Commander of the VI Division, rose when he saw me, and I wondered at the beauty of his giant's body. He rose, the purple of his riding breeches and the crimson of his little tilted cap and the decorations stuck on his chest cleaving the hut as a standard cleaves the sky. A smell of scent and the sickly sweet freshness of soap emanated from him. His long legs were like girls sheathed to the neck in shining riding boots.

He smiled at me, struck his riding whip on the table, and drew toward him an order that the Chief of Staff had just finished dictating. It was an order for Ivan Chesnokov to advance on Chugunov-Dobryvodka with the regiment entrusted to him, to make contact with the enemy and destroy the same.

"For which destruction," the Commander began to write, smearing the whole sheet, "I make this same Chesnokov entirely responsible, up to and including the supreme penalty, and will if necessary strike him down on the spot; which you, Chesnokov, who have been working with me at the front for some months now, cannot doubt."

The Commander signed the order with a flourish, tossed it to his orderlies and turned upon me gray eyes that danced with merriment.

I handed him a paper with my appointment to the Staff of the Division.

"Put it down in the Order of the Day," said the Commander. "Put him down for every satisfaction save the front one. Can you read and write?"

* Translated by Walter Morison.

192

"Yes, I can read and write," I replied, envying the flower and iron of that youthfulness. "I graduated in law from St. Petersburg University."

"Oh, are you one of those grinds?" he laughed. "Specs on your nose, too! What a nasty little object! They've sent you along without making any enquiries; and this is a hot place for specs. Think you'll get on with us?"

"I'll get on all right," I answered, and went off to the village with the quartermaster to find a billet for the night.

The quartermaster carried my trunk on his shoulder. Before us stretched the village street. The dying sun, round and yellow as a pumpkin, was giving up its roseate ghost to the skies.

We went up to a hut painted over with garlands. The quartermaster stopped, and said suddenly, with a guilty smile:

"Nuisance with specs. Can't do anything to stop it, either. Not a life for the brainy type here. But you go and mess up a lady, and a good lady too, and you'll have the boys patting you on the back."

He hesitated, my little trunk on his shoulder; then he came quite close to me, only to dart away again despairingly and run to the nearest yard. Cossacks were sitting there, shaving one another.

"Here, you soldiers," said the quartermaster, setting my little trunk down on the ground. "Comrade Savitsky's orders are that you're to take this chap in your billets, so no nonsense about it, because the chap's been through a lot in the learning line."

The quartermaster, purple in the face, left us without looking back. I raised my hand to my cap and saluted the Cossacks. A lad with long straight flaxen hair and the handsome face of the Ryazan Cossacks went over to my little trunk and tossed it out at the gate. Then he turned his back on me and with remarkable skill emitted a series of shameful noises.

"To your guns—number double-zero!" an older Cossack shouted at him, and burst out laughing. "Running fire!"

His guileless art exhausted, the lad made off. Then, crawling over the ground, I began to gather together the manuscripts and tattered garments that had fallen out of the trunk. I gathered them up and carried them to the other end of the yard. Near the hut, on a brick stove, stood a cauldron in which pork was cooking. The steam that rose from it was like the far-off smoke of home in the village, and it mingled hunger with desperate loneliness in my head. Then I covered my little broken trunk with hay, turning it into a pillow, and lay down on the ground to read in *Pravda* Lenin's speech at the Second Congress of the Comintern. The sun fell upon me from behind the toothed hillocks, the Cossacks trod on my feet, the lad made fun of me untiringly, the beloved lines came toward me along a thorny path and could not reach me. Then I put aside the paper and went out to the landlady, who was spinning on the porch.

"Landlady," I said, "I've got to eat."

The old woman raised to me the diffused whites of her purblind eyes and lowered them again.

"Comrade," she said, after a pause, "what with all this going on, I want to go and hang myself."

"Christ!" I muttered, and pushed the old woman in the chest with my fist. "You don't suppose I'm going to go into explanations with you, do you?"

And turning around I saw somebody's sword lying within reach. A severe-looking goose was waddling about the yard, inoffensively preening its feathers. I overtook it and pressed it to the ground. Its head cracked beneath my boot, cracked and emptied itself. The white neck lay stretched out in the dung, the wings twitched.

"Christ!" I said, digging into the goose with my sword. "Go and cook it for me, landlady."

Her blind eyes and glasses glistening, the old woman picked up the slaughtered bird, wrapped it in her apron, and started to bear it off toward the kitchen.

"Comrade," she said to me, after a while, "I want to go and hang myself." And she closed the door behind her.

The Cossacks in the yard were already sitting around their cauldron. They sat motionless, stiff as heathen priests at a sacrifice, and had not looked at the goose.

"The lad's all right," one of them said, winking and scooping up the cabbage soup with his spoon.

The Cossacks commenced their supper with all the elegance and restraint of peasants who respect one another. And I wiped the sword with sand, went out at the gate, and came in again, depressed. Already the moon hung above the yard like a cheap earring.

"Hey, you," suddenly said Surovkov, an older Cossack. "Sit down and feed with us till your goose is done."

He produced a spare spoon from his boot and handed it to me. We supped up the cabbage soup they had made, and ate the pork.

"What's in the newspaper?" asked the flaxen-haired lad, making room for me.

"Lenin writes in the paper," I said, pulling out *Pravda*. "Lenin writes that there's a shortage of everything."

And loudly, like a triumphant man hard of hearing, I read Lenin's speech out to the Cossacks.

Evening wrapped about me the quickening moisture of its twilight sheets; evening laid a mother's hand upon my burning forehead. I read on and rejoiced, spying out exultingly the secret curve of Lenin's straight line.

"Truth tickles everyone's nostrils," said Surovkov, when I had come to the end. "The question is, how's it to be pulled from the heap. But he goes and strikes at it straight off like a hen pecking at a grain!"

This remark about Lenin was made by Surovkov, platoon commander of the Staff Squadron; after which we lay down to sleep in the hayloft. We slept, all six of us, beneath a wooden roof that let in the stars, warming one another, our legs intermingled. I dreamed: and in my dreams saw women. But my heart, stained with bloodshed, grated and brimmed over.

[1926–U.S.S.R.]

QUESTIONS

1. From the clues given in the story, describe the narrator's physical appearance.
2. Just as we sometimes think of other people in broad terms, as though they were stock characters, so the characters in "My First Goose" view the narrator. What kind of stock character do they see him as? Point to specifics that support your answer.
3. Describe the personality of the narrator. How do we come to see him as clearly as we do (consider such things as plot, character contrast, the narrator's personal effects, his style of speech, and so forth)?
4. "The lad's all right," says one Cossack after the narrator has brutally killed the goose and tormented the old woman. Why? In what way is the Cossack's reason related to something said earlier: "Not a life for the brainy type here. But you go and mess up a lady, and a good lady too, and you'll have the boys patting you on the back"?
5. The narrator needs to be, and indeed wants to be, accepted by his fellow soldiers. At what price to himself does he gain their acceptance? What in the story indicates that the change in the narrator brought about by his circumstances is for the worse?
6. What does the title suggest?

WRITING SUGGESTIONS

1. Write a paragraph describing the protagonist both physically and emotionally. What does his physical appearance tell us about him? In what way does the kind of person he is give rise to his admiration of Savitsky and the Cossacks?
2. Write a short essay on the theme of the present story as its theme relates to character revelation and change. How does its narrator change? The tale ends on a note of profound regret. What does this tell us about the change in the narrator and his own attitude toward that change? Generally, how does experience sometimes alter people for the worse?

The World War I
Los Angeles Airplane

Richard Brautigan

He was found lying dead near the television set on the front room floor of a small rented house in Los Angeles. My wife had gone to the store to get some ice cream. It was an early-in-the-night-just-a-few-blocks-away store. We were in an ice-cream mood. The telephone rang. It was her brother to say that her father had died that afternoon. He was seventy. I waited for her to come home with the ice cream. I tried to think of the best way to tell her that her father was dead with the least amount of pain but you cannot camouflage death with words. Always at the end of the words somebody is dead.

She was very happy when she came back from the store.

"What's wrong?" she said.

"Your brother just called from Los Angeles," I said.

"What happened?" she said.

"Your father died this afternoon."

That was in 1960 and now it's just a few weeks away from 1970. He has been dead for almost ten years and I've done a lot of thinking about what his death means to all of us.

1. He was born from German blood and raised on a farm in South Dakota. His grandfather was a terrible tyrant who completely destroyed his three grown sons by treating them exactly the way he treated them when they were children. They never grew up in his eyes and they never grew up in their own eyes. He made sure of that. They never left the farm. They of course got married but he handled all of their domestic matters except for the siring of his grandchildren. He never allowed them to discipline their

196

own children. He took care of that for them. Her father thought of his father as another brother who was always trying to escape the never-relenting wrath of their grandfather.

2. He was smart, so he became a schoolteacher when he was eighteen and he left the farm, which was an act of revolution against his grandfather who from that day forth considered him dead. He didn't want to end up like his father, hiding behind the barn. He taught school for three years in the Midwest and then he worked as an automobile salesman in the pioneer days of car selling.

3. There was an early marriage followed by an early divorce with feelings afterward that left the marriage hanging like a skeleton in her family's closet because he tried to keep it a secret. He probably had been very much in love.

4. There was a horrible automobile accident just before the First World War in which everybody was killed except him. It was one of those automobile accidents that leave deep spiritual scars like historical landmarks on the family and friends of the dead.

5. When America went into the First World War in 1917, he decided that he wanted to be a pilot, though he was in his late twenties. He was told that it would be impossible because he was too old but he projected so much energy into his desire to fly that he was accepted for pilot training and went to Florida and became a pilot.

In 1918 he went to France and flew a De Havilland and bombed a railroad station in France and one day he was flying over the German lines when little clouds began appearing around him and he thought that they were beautiful and flew for a long time before he realized that they were German antiaircraft guns trying to shoot him down.

Another time he was flying over France and a rainbow appeared behind the tail of his plane and every turn that the plane made, the rainbow also made the same turn and it followed after him through the skies of France for part of an afternoon in 1918.

6. When the war was over he got out a captain and he was traveling on a train through Texas when the middle-aged man sitting next to him and with whom he had been talking for about three hundred miles said, "If I was a young man like you and had a little extra cash, I'd go up to Idaho and start a bank. There's a good future in Idaho banking."

7. That's what her father did.

8. He went to Idaho and started a bank which soon led to three more banks and a large ranch. It was by now 1926 and everything was going all right.

9. He married a schoolteacher who was sixteen years his junior and for their honeymoon they took a train to Philadelphia and spent a week there.

10. When the stock market crashed in 1929 he was hit hard by it and had to give up his banks and a grocery store that he had picked up along the way, but he still had the ranch, though he had to put a mortgage on it.

11. He decided to go into sheep raising in 1931 and got a big flock and was very good to his sheepherders. He was so good to them that it was a subject of gossip in his part of Idaho. The sheep got some kind of horrible sheep disease and all died.

12. He got another big flock of sheep in 1933 and added more fuel to the gossip by continuing to be so good to his men. The sheep got some kind of horrible sheep disease and all died in 1934.

13. He gave his men a big bonus and went out of the sheep business.

14. He had just enough money left over after selling the ranch to pay off all his debts and buy a brand-new Chevrolet which he put his family into and he drove off to California to start all over again.

15. He was forty-four, had a twenty-eight-year-old wife and an infant daughter.

16. He didn't know anyone in California and it was the Depression.

17. His wife worked for a while in a prune shed and he parked cars at a lot in Hollywood.

18. He got a job as a bookkeeper for a small construction company.

19. His wife gave birth to a son.

20. In 1940 he went briefly into California real estate, but then decided not to pursue it any further and went back to work for the construction company as a bookkeeper.

21. His wife got a job as a checker in a grocery store where she worked for eight years and then an assistant manager quit and opened his own store and she went to work for him and she still works there.

22. She has worked twenty-three years now as a grocery checker for the same store.

23. She was very pretty until she was forty.

24. The construction company laid him off. They said he was too old to take care of the books. "It's time for you to go out to pasture," they joked. He was fifty-nine.

25. They rented the same house they lived in for twenty-five years, though they could have bought it at one time with no down payment and monthly payments of fifty dollars.

26. When his daughter was going to high school he was working there

as the school janitor. She saw him in the halls. His working as a janitor was a subject that was very seldom discussed at home.

27. Her mother would make lunches for both of them.

28. He retired when he was sixty-five and became a very careful sweet-wine alcoholic. He liked to drink whiskey but they couldn't afford to keep him in it. He stayed in the house most of the time and started drinking about ten o'clock, a few hours after his wife had gone off to work at the grocery store.

29. He would get quietly drunk during the course of the day. He always kept his wine bottles hidden in a kitchen cabinet and would secretly drink from them, though he was alone.

He very seldom made any bad scenes and the house was always clean when his wife got home from work. He did though after a while take on that meticulous manner of walking that alcoholics have when they are trying very carefully to act as if they aren't drunk.

30. He used sweet wine in place of life because he didn't have any more life to use.

31. He watched afternoon television.

32. Once he had been followed by a rainbow across the skies of France while flying a World War I airplane carrying bombs and machine guns.

33. "Your father died this afternoon."

[1963–U.S.A.]

QUESTIONS

1. Despite the abundance of facts presented about the narrator's father-in-law, he remains flat. Why? Might he be meant to be thought of as a representative figure rather than a person? What does he represent?

2. The father-in-law's life spanned our century, from the introduction of the automobile to the television. Yet does his story have a plot as we have defined the term? Did causality or chance govern this life? Given your answer, what is Brautigan's point?

3. Why the list structure? Why the repetition of item 5 (see 32)? Why the juxtaposition of items 32 and 33?

4. The narrator says that in the ten years since his father-in-law's death he has "done a lot of thinking about what his death means to all of us." Whom does he refer to by "all of us"? Has he found the meaning?

5. In what ways might the story's theme be fiction itself and its elements (plot, characterization, and so on)? What does it say about American life through its dramatized statements about fiction?

WRITING SUGGESTIONS

1. Because the story sets out to be a character study, its lack of significant characterization is itself significant. Write a paragraph on how absence here is presence, that is, on how the story's lack of characterization reflects a view of the collective American personality in the late twentieth century.
2. Taking note of all of the details we're given about him, argue in a paragraph or more that the father-in-law of the narrator is representative of our rootless culture. Or argue the reverse: that, although many of us may be like the father-in-law, traditional values still govern the nation at large.
3. Write an essay in which you present and assess both of the possibilities suggested in the previous writing suggestion. Which view of America seems more accurate to you? Give reasons for your judgment.

The Waiting*

Jorge Luis Borges

The cab left him at number four thousand four on that street in the northwest part of Buenos Aires. It was not yet nine in the morning; the man noted with approval the spotted plane trees, the square plot of earth at the foot of each, the respectable houses with their little balconies, the pharmacy alongside, the dull lozenges of the paint and hardware store. A long windowless hospital wall backed the sidewalk on the other side of the street; the sun reverberated, farther down, from some greenhouses. The man thought that these things (now arbitrary and accidental and in no special order, like the things one sees in dreams) would in time, if God willed, become invariable, necessary and familiar. In the pharmacy window porcelain letters spelled out the name "Breslauer"; the Jews were displacing the Italians, who had displaced the Creoles. It was better that way; the man preferred not to mingle with people of his kind.

The cabman helped him take down his trunk; a woman with a distracted or tired air finally opened the door. From his seat, the cabman returned one of the coins to him, a Uruguayan twenty-centavo piece which had been in his pocket since that night in the hotel at Melo. The man gave him forty centavos and immediately felt: "I must act so that everyone will forgive me. I have made two errors: I have used a foreign coin and I have shown that the mistake matters to me."

Led by the woman, he crossed the entrance hall and the first patio. The room they had reserved for him opened, happily, onto the second

---

* Translated by James E. Irby.

patio. The bed was of iron, deformed by the craftsman into fantastic curves representing branches and tendrils; there was also a tall pine wardrobe, a bedside table, a shelf with books at floor level, two odd chairs and a washstand with its basin, jar, soap dish and bottle of turbid glass. A map of the province of Buenos Aires and a crucifix adorned the walls; the wallpaper was crimson, with a pattern of huge spread-tailed peacocks. The only door opened onto the patio. It was necessary to change the placement of the chairs in order to get the trunk in. The roomer approved of everything; when the woman asked him his name, he said Villari, not as a secret challenge, not to mitigate the humiliation which actually he did not feel, but because that name troubled him, because it was impossible for him to think of any other. Certainly he was not seduced by the literary error of thinking that assumption of the enemy's name might be an astute maneuver.

Mr. Villari, at first, did not leave the house; after a few weeks, he took to going out for a while at sundown. One night he went into the movie theater three blocks away. He never went beyond the last row of seats; he always got up a little before the end of the feature. He would see tragic stories of the underworld; these stories, no doubt, contained errors; these stories, no doubt, contained images which were also those of his former life; Villari took no notice of them because the idea of a coincidence between art and reality was alien to him. He would submissively try to like the things; he wanted to anticipate the intention with which they were shown. Unlike people who read novels, he never saw himself as a character in a work of art.

No letters nor even a circular ever arrived for him, but with vague hope he would always read one of the sections of the newspaper. In the afternoons, he would put one of the chairs by the door and gravely make and drink his maté, his eyes fixed on the vine covering the wall of the several-storied building next door. Years of solitude had taught him that, in one's memory, all days tend to be the same, but that there is not a day, not even in jail or in the hospital, which does not bring surprises, which is not a translucent network of minimal surprises. In other confinements, he had given in to the temptation of counting the days and the hours, but this confinement was different, for it had no end—unless one morning the newspaper brought news of Alejandro Villari's death. It was also possible that Villari *had already died* and in that case this life was a dream. This possibility disturbed him, because he could never quite understand whether it seemed a relief or a misfortune; he told himself it was absurd and discounted it. In distant days, less distant because of the passage of time than because of two or three irrevocable acts, he had desired many things with an unscrupulous passion; this powerful will, which had moved the hatred of men and the love of some women, no longer wanted any particular thing: it only wanted to endure, not to come to an end. The taste of the maté, the taste of black tobacco, the growing line of shadows gradually covering the patio—these were sufficient incentives.

In the house there was a wolf-dog, now old. Villari made friends with him. He spoke to him in Spanish, in Italian, in the few words he still retained of the rustic dialect of his childhood. Villari tried to live in the simple present, with no memories or anticipation; the former mattered less to him than the latter. In an obscure way, he thought he could see that the past is the stuff time is made of; for that reason, time immediately turns into the past. His weariness, one day, was like a feeling of contentment; in moments like this, he was not much more complex than the dog.

One night he was left astonished and trembling by an intimate discharge of pain in the back of his mouth. This horrible miracle recurred in a few minutes and again towards dawn. Villari, the next day, sent for a cab which left him at a dentist's office in the Once section. There he had the tooth pulled. In this ordeal he was neither more cowardly nor more tranquil than other people.

Another night, returning from the movies, he felt that he was being pushed. With anger, with indignation, with secret relief, he faced the insolent person. He spat out a coarse insult; the other man, astonished, stammered an excuse. He was tall, young, with dark hair, accompanied by a German-looking woman; that night, Villari repeated to himself that he did not know them. Nevertheless, four or five days went by before he went out into the street.

Amongst the books on the shelf there was a copy of the *Divine Comedy*, with the old commentary by Abdreoli. Prompted less by curiosity than by a feeling of duty, Villari undertook the reading of this capital work; before dinner, he would read a canto and then, in rigorous order, the notes. He did not judge the punishments of hell to be unbelievable or excessive and did not think Dante would have condemned him to the last circle, where Ugolino's teeth endlessly gnaw Ruggieri's neck.

The peacocks on the crimson wallpaper seemed destined to be food for tenacious nightmares, but Mr. Villari never dreamed of a monstrous arbor inextricably woven of living birds. At dawn he would dream a dream whose substance was the same, with varying circumstances. Two men and Villari would enter the room with revolvers or they would attack him as he left the movie house or all three of them at once would be the stranger who had pushed him or they would sadly wait for him in the patio and seem not to recognize him. At the end of the dream, he would take his revolver from the drawer of the bedside table (and it was true he kept a revolver in that drawer) and open fire on the men. The noise of the weapon would wake him, but it was always a dream and in another dream the attack would be repeated and in another dream he would have to kill them again.

One murky morning in the month of July, the presence of strange people (not the noise of the door when they opened it) woke him. Tall in the shadows of the room, curiously simplified by those shadows (in the fearful dreams they had always been clearer), vigilant, motionless and patient, their eyes lowered as if weighted down by the heaviness of their weapons, Alejandro Villari and a stranger had overtaken him at last. With a gesture, he asked them to wait and turned his face to the wall, as if to resume his sleep. Did he do it to arouse the pity of those who killed him, or because it is less difficult to endure a frightful happening than to imagine it and endlessly await it, or—and this is perhaps most likely—so that the murderers would be a dream, as they had already been so many times, in the same place, at the same hour?

He was in this act of magic when the blast obliterated him.

[1949–Argentina]

QUESTIONS

1. Summarize all that we learn about the false Villari (for instance, where he comes from, what he used to do, what his present feelings about himself are). How does he differ now from what he was before his "irrevocable acts"? How do we learn what we do about him?
2. What is suggested by his having no name of his own? How does what is suggested tie in with the story's theme?
3. If ever there was a flat character, the false Villari is he. Often, indeed, he seems "not much more complex than the dog." Why? What might Borges's theme be with respect to time, memory, and human personality?
4. Keeping in mind your answer to the last question, how do you take Borges's title? How do you take the story's ending?

WRITING SUGGESTIONS

1. Draw up a list of everything that can be inferred about Borges's protagonist. Now, using the items on this list as support, write a short essay on inference itself. How do we go about making inferences? How do we know an inference to be valid? Why do writers in general, and clearly Borges in particular, prefer inference to direct statement?

2. Write a paragraph comparing the false Villari and the father-in-law in Brautigan's story just before this. Explain in what ways they are similar and how the similarity sheds light on both stories.
3. Consider living entirely in the present, with no past and no future. Would this be possible for human beings? Write an essay analyzing "The Waiting" with this question in mind. Cut off from past and future, what would we become? Define what being human means by way of contrast with the life as we see it of the false Villari.

NARRATION/POINT
OF VIEW

THE NARRATOR

Every story must somehow get told. The teller is "the narrator" and what the narrator says is called "the narration." What is most important to grasp about narrators from the start is that they should not be confused with authors. The writer of a piece of fiction stands outside of it, constructing its plot, shaping its characters, *and* manipulating its narrator to achieve the end desired. Authors are like puppeteers, invisibly pulling the strings of characters and narrators alike to produce the show as a whole. The writer's attitude is expressed through the story overall rather than through one or another of its components. As to narration, there are many ways in which stories can be told, and each affects meaning in its own way. Narration, therefore, is intimately related to theme: how we come to understand a piece of fiction depends in large measure on the way in which its narrator presents things. What the reader must understand about narration is that what we are told is not always meant to be taken at face value. Like real people, narrators can vary in reliability from complete trustworthiness to utter blindness. They may even be made to lie. Consequently, what is said (that is, the narration) must be questioned and evaluated according to our judgment of who says it (that is, the narrator). The discussion that follows should help clarify the nature of narrators and their points of view.

Before we move on, however, we should establish what is meant by "narrative point view." A narrative point of view is simply the perspective (or sometimes perspectives) devised by the author through which a story's characters, actions, setting, and so forth are presented to the reader. In this regard we might think of a narrator as a camera. Looking through a camera's eyepiece, one can, if the lens is clear, see a scene as though looking at it directly. However, the image seen through the camera's eye can be distorted because of poor focus or altered in various ways by different kinds of filters. Some narrators, too, seem all but invisible, like a clear lens. Most, however, filter what they present to one degree or another, and some are out of focus, distorting entirely what they report. Narrative point of view, thus, is dependent on the kind of narrator chosen by an author.

MODES OF NARRATION

It is possible to write a story without a narrator by confining it to dialogue between the characters—the mode of Dorothy Parker's "You Were Perfectly Fine" (pages 215–18). Turn to the story for a second and just look at it. You'll notice that even here there is a bit of narration (the first paragraph, for instance). But because what is narrated amounts to something like "stage directions," we can say that, like most plays, the story has no narrator. The advantage of this technique is that it lends the story a sense of immediacy, for it entails no mediating consciousness between reader and characters. Nevertheless, there are few stories composed entirely of dialogue. The reason why is that dialogue is all talk and no action. Whereas in a play we can see actors doing things while they talk, in a story we must be told what characters are doing, which means there must be a narrator.

How, then, can a story be told? Almost always, fiction is written either from the perspective of a character in the story telling it in the first person (I) or from the perspective of someone not involved in the story telling it in the third person (he, she, it, they). Whichever the case, there is always a narrative voice to be heard and consequently a tone of voice, which can be intimate, austere, kindly, urbane, harsh, and so forth, just like the tones of voice that we project every day when talking to others. Because first-person narrators are to be thought of as people, it is only natural that what they say should be heard as utterance exhibiting tone of voice. But third-person narrators, though not to be thought of as people, also betray various tones of voice. The point is that every story should be heard as spoken by a narrator and therefore, in one way or another, every story exhibits tone. With this in mind, let's now take up each narrative perspective in turn.

First-Person Narration

First-person narrators are always characters in the stories they narrate and always meant to be thought of as people. They might be protagonists, minor characters, or merely bystanders, but they are characters and must be treated accordingly. In other words, we must remember to question first-person narrators and to judge what they say according to our gradually developing awareness of who they are. Sometimes we can accept what they say; sometimes we can't. There are, consequently, two types of first-person narration.

First-Person Credible. "You don't know about me without you have read a book by the name of *The Adventures of Tom Sawyer*. That book was made by Mr. Mark Twain, and he told the truth, mainly"—so begins *The Adventures of Huckleberry Finn*, by Mark Twain. This is an example of first-person narration. But can we believe the narrator? That is the prime question that the first-person narrative point of view demands the reader ask. Having observed the narrator and compared his or her judgments with our own, we determine whether the narrator is credible. If so, we accept the narrator as a guide in forming our own attitudes and interpretation. Somerset Maugham's description of this kind of narrator is apt:

> There is one point I want to make about these stories. The reader will notice that many of my stories are written in the first person singular. That is a literary convention which is as old as the hills. It was used by Petronius Arbiter in the *Satyricon* and by many of the story-tellers in *The Thousand and One Nights*. Its object is of course to achieve credibility, for when someone tells you what he states happened to himself you are more likely to believe that he is telling the truth than when he tells you what happened to somebody else. It has besides the merit from the story-teller's point of view that he need only tell you what he knows for a fact and can leave to your imagination what he doesn't or couldn't know. Some of the older novelists who wrote in the first person were in this respect very careless. They would narrate long conversations that they couldn't possibly have heard and incidents which in the nature of things they couldn't possibly have witnessed. Thus they lost the great advantage of verisimilitude which writing in the first person singular offers. But the *I* who writes is just as much a character in the story as the other persons with whom it is concerned. He may be the hero or he may be an onlooker or a confidant. But he is a character. The writer who uses this device is writing fiction and if he makes the *I* of his story a little quicker on the uptake, a little more level-headed, a little shrewder, a little braver, a little more ingenious, a little wittier, a little wiser than he, the writer, really is, the

reader must show indulgence. He must remember that the author is not drawing a faithful portrait of himself, but creating a character for the particular purposes of his story. (Maugham 2:7)

Maugham's own "The Ant and the Grasshopper" (pages 288–91) is a perfect example: its narrator proves to be credible, and because he does, he becomes an agent directing us in our judgments of the other characters in the story and ultimately guiding us toward its theme.

First-Person Unreliable. Some narrators, however, are not to be trusted. If in our judgment a narrator is naive (a child as narrator, for instance) or biased, then the point of the story becomes something other than the narrator's point. But we must recognize the narrator to be unreliable. Unreliable narration can be tricky for the reader because we are ever inclined to believe narrators. Take Williams's "The Buffalos" (pages 256–59), a story that is usually missed by students because they take the narrator at his word. But here the narrator is unreliable. If we attend closely, we start to realize not only that the narrator contradicts himself (a sure sign of unreliability) but that, though he protests his love for the woman he discusses, he knows very little about her. Because we, through him, learn almost nothing about her, we can conclude that this terribly biased narrator is rather juvenile; he is in love with love and not with a particular person. Once we see this, the story suddenly turns around 180 degrees. Its point is the opposite of its narrator's, the revelation of whose character becomes the story's theme. Potentially, unreliable narration can have great impact. It also allows for all kinds of irony. We'll take up irony when we consider mood and style, but in anticipation you might look at Chekhov's "At Sea" (pages 252–54) with an eye to the fact that we know more than its naive narrator. Chekhov's story is another example of unreliable narration, its young narrator proving blind to the meaning of what he relates; therein lies the irony.

Third-Person Narration

A story narrated in the third person is one in which the narrator is not a character in the story and, indeed, is not to be thought of as person at all. Third-person narrators can be used by authors in several ways; that is, several narrative points of view are possible.

Third-Person Omniscient. Omniscient means all-knowing. An omniscient narrator can tell us what characters are thinking, show us scenes that only the characters are party to, make judgments about characters and events, and even tell us how to respond. By convention, omniscient narrators are to be trusted implicitly because they are all-knowing. Any attitude that such a narrator expresses, whether directly or indirectly (for example, by choice of adjectives and adverbs), is prime information meant to be accepted. Some omniscient narrators, to be sure, give us much less information than others, and some even tell us things that might be misleading. For instance, think of mysteries, whose narrators try to throw us off the track. Actually, though, we are given all of the information we need to solve the mystery. We just miss (as we are meant to miss) the clues. All the information we need, however much or little, is what all omniscient narrators provide. The omniscient point of view is so common that you are probably familiar with it already, but if you are not, look at the first paragraph of H. H. Munro's "Sredni Vashtar" (page 222) for a typical example.

Third-Person Subjective. Also called "limited omniscient narration," third-person subjective narration is omniscient, but only with respect to certain characters rather than to all. The main function of subjective narrators is to voice characters' feelings and states of mind. Usually, the subjective narrator conveys the view of a major character; but this kind of narrator can tell a story from the vantage point of a minor character or even of one and then of another character in turn. Chekhov's "The Lottery Ticket" (pages 98–102) provides an example. Here the narrator tells the story almost entirely through the outlook of a disgruntled husband. At a critical moment in the story, however, we get a passage narrated from the wife's position. This changes everything. If you're wondering why a writer would choose third-person subjective rather than first-person narration, there are at least two answers. First, the author might wish to shift perspectives, as does Chekhov. Or the character through whose eyes events are seen may not be able to render an account, perhaps because the character is inarticulate, confused, or otherwise unable to relate a story. In all such cases, third-person subjective narration is ideal.

Third-Person Objective. Omniscient and third-person subjective narrators show us things through lenses tinted to one degree or another. The objective narrator is impartial, recording scenes and characters through, or so it seems, a clear lens. That is, objective narrators express no attitudes, whether their own or those of characters, and do not predispose the reader toward any attitude. They tell their stories from the outside, as it were, noting external details but not telling us anything about what characters are thinking or feeling and not swaying us in any way as to our judgments of characters. Zoshchenko's "A Confession" (pages 219-20) is a good example. Here we are introduced to two characters without being told much of anything about either. We must judge entirely for ourselves. This type of story demands maximum attention on the readers's part; it offers as reward maximum involvement.

NARRATOR, AUTHOR, AND STORY

It is important to realize that often the meaning of a story depends on our judgment of the type of narrator *the author devised* to tell it. Again, narrators should not be confused with authors. The writer's attitude is expressed through the story as a whole, not through just one of its components. A story narrated by a child, for instance, is not to be taken as a story written by that child. The adult author has chosen such a narrator for the purpose at hand, and that purpose is what must be attended to. In other words, the attitude of the narrator does not necessarily coincide with the attitude expressed by a story as a whole. Especially in stories with first-person or third-person subjective narration, the distinction is often crucial. If you remember to keep questioning narrators until you are sure of the kind of narrator a story is spoken by, you will not fall into the trap of confusing the point of a story with that of its narrator if the two diverge.

SUMMARY SUGGESTIONS: UNDERSTANDING NARRATION

1. Separate in your mind author and narrator. Remember that the point of a story might be quite different from any point the narrator makes.

2. Determine as quickly as possible what kind of narrator you're dealing with. You can distinguish between first-person and third-person narration almost immediately. The finer distinctions—especially between credible and unreliable narration—will have to be tested as you continue reading.

3. If you think that you have an unreliable narrator, keep questioning what the narrator says. Does the narrator make statements that contradict each other? Does the narrator say something that you know not to be true? What do other characters have to say about the narrator? All these are considerations that aid in judging narrators.

4. If you think you have a third-person subjective narrator, remember that this type of narrator expresses the outlook of one or another character. Therefore, what this narrator says must be questioned no less than what any other character says.

5. Finally, relate a story's narration to its theme. Because the mode of narration the author has chosen helps to shape the reader's responses, it is closely connected to the theme. This is true even of stories with unreliable narrators, though here the relationship between theme and narrator will probably be ironic.

WRITING ON NARRATORS AND NARRATION

Narrators and narration can be great fun to write on. The first-person credible narrator, for instance, is usually likable, so writing about such a narrator can hold the same pleasure as talking about a friend. Or take the unreliable narrator. The recognition that a narrator is limited or completely unreliable may change the meaning of a story entirely. To treat such a narrator, then, is not only to get at the meaning of a story but to do so with subtlety, which offers the delight of exercising and displaying one's mental agility. Third-person subjective narration is equally interesting, especially if the perspective shifts between characters. Whatever one's focus, narration of any type is so basic to what fiction is that to write on it is to be at the very heart of both fiction's means and its purpose.

The easiest and often most interesting narrator to write about is the first-person narrator. Is the narrator credible or not? How does the author persuade us of this? What kind of a person is the narrator? Why did the author choose to have this type of person narrate the story? How does the narrator shape our attitudes toward other characters? In what way does the narrator help us to understand the point of the story overall? As you think about a story, these are some of the questions to ask of its narrator. Your answers will provide any number of topics on which you could write an engaging paper. Take Maugham's story "The Ant and the Grasshopper" (pages 288–91), in which the narrative point of view is pivotal. We see George, the story's protagonist, through the narrator's eyes and so see him quite differently from the way he sees himself. What Maugham accomplishes by having us see George as we do could be the basis of a fine paper on the story. Here one would want to discuss the character of the narrator and then move to consider how we are swayed to laugh at George because of our acceptance of the narrator's credibility.

If a story's narrator is unreliable, as exemplified by Williams's "The Buffalos" (pages 256–59), this unreliability is also rich in possibilities for writing. How do we come to judge the narrator as unreliable? What difference does the judgment make in our reading of the story? What is the narrator like? Why did the author choose unreliable narration? Given that the narrator is unreliable, what, then, is the point of the story? To answer questions of this sort is to be well on the way to an interesting piece of writing. For example, your perception that the narrator of "The Buffalos" is a rampant sexist, among other things, might lead you to reject his explanations entirely, a judgment that would affect your interpretation of the story. A paper explaining how you arrived at such a judgment and therefore how you interpret the story could be compelling.

The possibilities are less obvious for writing on third-person narration. Nevertheless, third-person narration offers a number of topics if we look for them. For instance, the way in which the third-person subjective narrator reflects the attitudes of one or more characters can be a rewarding topic. The narration of Chekhov's "The Lottery Ticket" (pages 98–102) is a case in point. By shifting from the husband's to the wife's perspective, the narrator reveals a conflict that affects our understanding of the story's meaning. To take a further example, the short essay on Cynthia Ozick's "The Shawl" in chapter 1 (pages 25–28) points to narration when imputing to Rosa a belief in magic. Recognizing the story's narrator to be third-person subjective, the writer of the essay realized that it is Rosa's attitude that the narrator expresses. Even though Rosa herself is not the narrator of the story (for obvious reasons—she has gone mad by the end of the story and is probably soon to die), we see through her eyes from beginning to end.

In considering a story narrated from the third-person objective point of view, one could write a stimulating paper focused on the effect of the contrast between the impersonal tone of the narrator and the highly personal struggles of the characters. Zoshchenko's "A Confession" could be explored in this way. Indeed, the tone of any narrator, if the specific tone can be related to the story's meaning, can be a good subject for writing. We saw as much when discussing "The Shawl" in chapter 1. The omniscient point of view provides many other possible topics. Why, for instance, since the omniscient narrator knows all, are we told only certain things and not others? Often, too, we may be given information that appears to have no real bearing on the story. Why? A paper could address what the reasons for the narrator's giving us such information might be. Another interesting topic is how omniscient narration leads the reader to adopt a particular attitude, whether toward a character, an event, or some other element or aspect of a story. In this regard, "Sredni Vashtar" (pages 222–26) might be intriguing to write on: specifically, how the reader is moved by the narrator to accept the boy's outlook could be an excellent topic. One final thing to be aware of with respect to the narrative points of view we've just considered (objective and omniscient) is that, no matter what aspect of a story you may be writing on, anything said from these points of view can be used as reliable evidence to support your argument.

Whatever you do when it comes to writing on stories, don't forget that how a story gets told and by whom is usually crucial to interpreting it. Therefore, narration is always a consideration and always a possible source of support as well as of thesis.

GENERAL WRITING ASSIGNMENTS

1. (a) In a paragraph or two recount an imaginary event from the point of view of an unreliable narrator. That is, invent a speaker clearly not yourself (for example, if you're a male, choose a female; if a female, choose a male). Something in the piece must suggest that your speaker is not to be trusted.

    (b) Now write a paragraph analyzing your narrator. In what way is the narrator unreliable? How does the reader come to grasp that the narrator is not to be taken at face value? What details in your story lead to this conclusion?

2. Most of us know something about our family history as passed down from generation to generation. Narrate some bit of your family history that you find particularly significant. Determine beforehand what kind of narrative voice you wish to project (for example, warm and loving, cool and objective, ironic) and keep to that voice throughout.

3. If you are a movie buff, write an essay on cinematic point of view. How are audiences swayed by one type of shot versus another? How do filters and the like change perspective? How do directors use cameras to get across their points? Make general statements about these matters but refer to specific movies for examples. You might conclude with a statement about point of view applicable to stories and novels as well as to movies.

4. Probably, at some time in your life, someone told you a story about a mutual acquaintance that you didn't believe. You concluded that the person was lying. What led you to this conclusion? Write a paragraph analyzing how in such a situation you might come to judge a person to be lying and the story untrue.

You Were Perfectly Fine

Dorothy Parker

The pale young man eased himself carefully into the low chair, and rolled his head to the side, so that the cool chintz comforted his cheek and temple.

"Oh, dear," he said. "Oh, dear, oh, dear, oh, dear. Oh."

The clear-eyed girl, sitting light and erect on the couch, smiled brightly at him.

"Not feeling so well today?" she said.

"Oh, I'm great," he said. "Corking, I am. Know what time I got up? Four o'clock this afternoon, sharp. I kept trying to make it, and every time I took my head off the pillow, it would roll under the bed. This isn't my head I've got on now. I think this is something that used to belong to Walt Whitman. Oh, dear, oh, dear, oh, dear."

"Do you think maybe a drink would make you feel better?" she said.

"The hair of the mastiff that bit me?" he said. "Oh, no, thank you. Please never speak of anything like that again. I'm through. I'm all, all through. Look at that hand; steady as a humming-bird. Tell me, was I very terrible last night?"

"Oh, goodness," she said, "everybody was feeling pretty high. You were all right."

"Yeah," he said. "I must have been dandy. Is everybody sore at me?"

"Good heavens, no," she said. "Everyone thought you were terribly funny. Of course, Jim Pierson was a little stuffy, there for a minute at dinner. But people sort of held him back in his chair, and got him calmed down. I don't think anybody at the other tables noticed it at all. Hardly anybody."

"He was going to sock me?" he said. "Oh, Lord. What did I do to him?"

"Why, you didn't do a thing," she said. "You were perfectly fine. But you know how silly Jim gets, when he thinks anybody is making too much fuss over Elinor."

"Was I making a pass at Elinor?" he said. "Did I do that?"

"Of course you didn't," she said. "You were only fooling, that's all. She thought you were awfully amusing. She was having a marvelous time. She only got a little tiny bit annoyed just once, when you poured the clam-juice down her back."

"My God," he said. "Clam-juice down that back. And every vertebra a little Cabot. Dear God. What'll I ever do?"

"Oh, she'll be all right," she said. "Just send her some flowers, or something. Don't worry about it. It isn't anything."

"No, I won't worry," he said. "I haven't got a care in the world. I'm sitting pretty. Oh, dear, oh, dear. Did I do any other fascinating tricks at dinner?"

"You were fine," she said. "Don't be so foolish about it. Everybody was crazy about you. The maître d'hôtel was a little worried because you wouldn't stop singing, but he really didn't mind. All he said was, he was afraid they'd close the place again, if there was so much noise. But he didn't care a bit, himself. I think he loved seeing you have such a good time. Oh, you were just singing away, there, for about an hour. It wasn't so terribly loud, at all."

"So I sang," he said. "That must have been a treat. I sang."

"Don't you remember?" she said. "You just sang one song after another. Everybody in the place was listening. They loved it. Only you kept insisting that you wanted to sing some song about some kind of fusiliers or other, and everybody kept shushing you, and you'd keep trying to start it again. You were wonderful. We were all trying to make you stop singing for a minute, and eat something, but you wouldn't hear of it. My, you were funny."

"Didn't I eat any dinner?" he said.

"Oh, not a thing," she said. "Every time the waiter would offer you something, you'd give it right back to him, because you said that he was your long-lost brother, changed in the cradle by a gypsy band, and that anything you had was his. You had him simply roaring at you."

"I bet I did," he said. "I bet I was comical. Society's Pet, I must have been. And what happened then, after my overwhelming success with the waiter?"

"Why, nothing much," she said. "You took a sort of dislike to some old man with white hair, sitting across the room, because you didn't like his necktie and you wanted to tell him about it. But we got you out, before he got really mad."

"Oh, we got out," he said. "Did I walk?"

"Walk? Of course you did," she said. "You were absolutely all right. There was that nasty stretch of ice on the sidewalk, and you did sit down awfully hard, you poor dear. But good heavens, that might have happened to anybody."

"Oh, surely," he said. "Mrs. Hoover or anybody. So I fell down on the sidewalk. That would explain what's the matter with my— Yes. I see. And then what, if you don't mind?"

"Ah, now, Peter!" she said. "You can't sit there and say you don't remember what happened after that! I did think that maybe you were just a little tight at dinner—oh, you were perfectly all right, and all that, but I did know you were feeling pretty gay. But you were so serious, from the time you fell down—I never knew you to be that way. Don't you know, how you told me I had never seen your real self before? Oh, Peter, I just couldn't bear it, if you didn't remember that lovely long ride we took together in the taxi! Please, you do remember that, don't you? I think it would simply kill me, if you didn't."

"Oh, yes," he said. "Riding in the taxi. Oh, yes, sure. Pretty long ride, hmm?"

"Round and round and round the park," she said. "Oh, and the trees were shining so in the moonlight. And you said you never knew before that you really had a soul."

"Yes," he said. "I said that. That was me."

"You said such lovely, lovely things," she said. "And I'd never known, all this time, how you had been feeling about me, and I'd never dared to let you see how I felt about you. And then last night—oh, Peter dear, I think that taxi ride was the most important thing that ever happened to us in our lives."

"Yes," he said. "I guess it must have been."

"And we're going to be so happy," she said. "Oh, I just want to tell everybody! But I don't know—I think maybe it would be sweeter to keep it all to ourselves."

"I think it would be," he said.

"Isn't it lovely?" she said.

"Yes," he said. "Great."

"Lovely!" she said.

"Look here," he said, "do you mind if I have a drink? I mean, just medicinally, you know. I'm off the stuff for life, so help me. But I think I feel a collaspe coming on."

"Oh, I think it would do you good," she said. "You poor boy, it's a shame you feel so awful. I'll go make you a highball."

"Honestly," he said, "I don't see how you could ever want to speak to me again, after I made such a fool of myself, last night. I think I'd better go join a monastery in Tibet."

"You crazy idiot!" she said. "As if I could ever let you go away now! Stop talking like that. You were perfectly fine."

She jumped up from the couch, kissed him quickly on the forehead, and ran out of the room.

The pale young man looked after her and shook his head long and slowly, then dropped it in his damp and trembling hands.

"Oh, dear," he said. "Oh, dear, oh, dear, oh, dear."

[1929–U.S.A.]

QUESTIONS

1. What kind of characters—flat, round, or stock—do we find engaged in dialogue here? In what way might Parker's female be thought of as stock?
2. What is the female up to in this story? Why does Peter want a drink toward the end?
3. Though slight, the story dramatizes a theme of some social significance, at least with respect to the time in which it was written. What is that theme?
4. What are the limitations of a dialogue format that you can detect from this story?
5. Some stories seem relevant though written hundreds and even thousands of years ago. Others, even of relatively recent origin, do not. Has "You Were Perfectly Fine" aged well, or does it now seem a period piece? Why do some works endure and others become dated?

WRITING SUGGESTIONS

1. In a paragraph or two, write a critique of this story in which you judge its merits as story along with its relevance to a contemporary audience. Is it simply dated, or does it still have something to say about the relationship of men and women in our culture?
2. Write an essay in which you suggest why some works endure and others become dated. Use other stories you've read as examples, as well as "You Were Perfectly Fine."

A Confession*

Mikhail Zoshchenko

During the final week of Lent, Fekla threw caution to the winds, spent a goodly portion of her savings on a twenty-kopeck candle, and placed it before one of the saints.

With the utmost care and deliberation, Fekla arranged the candle close by the image. When she'd adjusted it, she stepped back a bit and, admiring her handiwork, set about her prayers, requesting various absolutions and graces as recompense for her expenditure of twenty kopecks.

Fekla prayed at length, mumbling her petitions under her breath; and then, having pressed her brow to the dirty stone floor, went to confession with much sighing and groaning.

Confession was administered at the altar behind a screen.

Fekla took her place in line behind a very old woman and fussily began crossing herself and muttering. They didn't detain a person long behind the screen.

The confessors would go in and, after a moment, with a sigh and a hushed cough, they'd return and make their obeisances before the saints.

"The priest's hurrying things along," thought Fekla. "What's the rush? He's not going to a fire."

Fekla went behind the screen, bowed low before the priest, and kissed his hand.

"What is your name?" the priest asked, giving his blessing.

"They call me Fekla."

* Translated by John W. Strahan and Rosalind Zoglin.

"Now then, tell me, Fekla," said the priest, "what are your transgressions? Wherein have you sinned? Have you given vain utterance to evil thoughts? Haven't you been coming before your God rather rarely?"

"Indeed, Father, I am a sinner," said Fekla, bowing.

"God will pardon," said the priest, covering Fekla with his stole. "You *do* however believe in God? You don't harbor any doubts?"

"I most certainly do believe in God," said Fekla. "My son, though, just take him for example . . . he gives out with his opinions and, if I dare say a word or two, does do some criticizing . . . But I believe."

"That's good, Mother," said the priest. "Don't be an easy prey to temptation. By the way, tell me, what does your boy say? In what way does he criticize?"

"Oh, he's a faultfinder," said Fekla. "'It's all fiddle-faddle—their faith,' he says. 'No,' he says, 'there is no God. Even if you explored the entire sky and the clouds . . .'"

"There is a God," the priest said severely. "Don't fall for that . . . And do you remember anything else that your son said?"

"Yes—he's been saying many of the same kind of things—various things."

"The same kind of various things!" the priest said angrily. "And whence came all that surrounds us? Whence the planets, stars, moon, if there is no God? Your son didn't by any chance say where all that surrounds us came from, did he? It couldn't by any chance be just plain chemistry."

"He didn't say."

"Maybe it *is* just chemistry," said the priest, pondering. "It is of course possible, my little Mother, that if there isn't a God, that the whole answer lies in . . . chemistry . . ."

Fekla looked at the priest in terror. But he placed his stole on her head and began muttering the words of a prayer.

"Well, be off now, my good woman, be off," the priest said dismally. Don't detain the faithful."

Fekla, rather frightened, looked once again at the priest and left, sighing and coughing meekly. Then she went up to her saint, examined the candle, straightened the burnt wick, and left the church.

[1923–U.S.S.R.]

QUESTIONS

1. Do we learn anything about the narrator here? Does the narrator predispose us in any way as to our reception of the story's characters? What kind of narration, then, do we have in "A Confession"?

2. What kind of character is Fekla (flat, round, stock)? And the priest? Whose story is it, finally?
3. Why might the priest have been "hurrying things along"? Comment on the ironic nature of the title.
4. Given the story's date of publication as well as its country of origin (what was happening in the U.S.S.R. in 1923?), what large theme does it touch on despite its limited compass?

WRITING SUGGESTIONS

1. In a paragraph or more, discuss the conflicts felt by the priest and their cause.
2. In a paragraph, classify the type of narration that "A Confession" exhibits and discuss the effect of the disparity between the impersonal tone of the narration and the inner turmoil and terror we witness in Zoshchenko's characters.

Sredni Vashtar

H. H. Munro

Conradin was ten years old, and the doctor had pronounced his professional opinion that the boy would not live another five years. The doctor was silky and effete, and counted for little, but his opinion was endorsed by Mrs. de Ropp, who counted for nearly everything. Mrs. de Ropp was Conradin's cousin and guardian, and in his eyes she represented those three-fifths of the world that are necessary and disagreeable and real; the other two-fifths, in perpetual antagonism to the foregoing, were summed up in himself and his imagination. One of these days Conradin supposed he would succumb to the mastering pressure of wearisome necessary things—such as illnesses and coddling restrictions and drawn-out dullness. Without his imagination, which was rampant under the spur of loneliness, he would have succumbed long ago.

Mrs. de Ropp would never, in her honestest moments, have confessed to herself that she disliked Conradin, though she might have been dimly aware that thwarting him "for his good" was a duty which she did not find particularly irksome. Conradin hated her with a desperate sincerity which he was perfectly able to mask. Such few pleasures as he could contrive for himself gained an added relish from the likelihood that they would be displeasing to his guardian, and from the realm of his imagination she was locked out—an unclean thing, which should find no entrance.

In the dull, cheerless garden, overlooked by so many windows that were ready to open with a message not to do this or that, or a reminder that medicines were due, he found little attraction. The few fruit-trees that it contained were set jealously apart from his plucking, as though they were rare specimens of their kind blooming in an arid waste; it would probably have been difficult to find a market-gardener who would have offered ten shillings for their entire yearly produce. In a forgotten corner, however, almost hidden behind a dismal shrubbery, was a disused tool-shed of respectable proportions, and within its walls Conradin found a haven, something that took on the varying aspects of a playroom and a cathedral. He had peopled it with a legion of familiar phantoms, evoked partly from fragments of history and partly from his own brain, but it also boasted two inmates of flesh and blood. In one corner lived a ragged-plumaged Houdan hen, on which the boy lavished an affection that had scarcely another outlet. Further back in the gloom stood a large hutch, divided into two compartments, one of which was fronted with close iron bars. This was the abode of a large polecat-ferret, which a friendly butcher-boy had once smuggled, cage and all, into its present quarters, in exchange for a long-secreted hoard of small silver. Conradin was dreadfully afraid of the lithe, sharp-fanged beast, but it was his most treasured possession. Its very presence in the tool-shed was a secret and fearful joy, to be kept scrupulously from the knowledge of the Woman, as he privately dubbed his cousin. And one day, out of Heaven knows what material, he spun the beast a wonderful name, and from that moment it grew into a god and a religion. The Woman indulged in religion once a week at a church near by, and took Conradin with her, but to him the church service was an alien rite in the House of Rimmon. Every Thursday, in the dim and musty silence of the tool-shed, he worshipped with mystic and elaborate ceremonial before the wooden hutch where dwelt Sredni Vashtar, the great ferret. Red flowers in their season and scarlet berries in the winter-time were offered at his shrine, for he was a god who laid some special stress on the fierce impatient side of things, as opposed to the Woman's religion, which, as far as Conradin could observe, went to great lengths in the contrary direction. And on great festivals powdered nutmeg was strewn in front of his hutch, an important feature of the offering being that the nutmeg had to be stolen. These festivals were of irregular occurrence, and were chiefly appointed to celebrate some passing event. On one occasion, when Mrs. de Ropp suffered from acute toothache for three days, Conradin kept up the festival during the entire three days, and almost succeeded in persuading himself that Sredni Vashtar was personally responsible for the toothache. If the malady had lasted for another day the supply of nutmeg would have given out.

The Houdan hen was never drawn into the cult of Sredni Vashtar. Conradin had long ago settled that she was an Anabaptist. He did not pretend to have the remotest knowledge as to what an Anabaptist was, but he privately hoped that it was dashing and not very respectable. Mrs. de

Ropp was the ground plan on which he based and detested all respectability.

After a while Conradin's absorption in the tool-shed began to attract the notice of his guardian. "It is not good for him to be pottering down there in all weathers." She promptly decided, and at breakfast one morning she announced that the Houdan hen had been sold and taken away overnight. With her short-sighted eyes she peered at Conradin, waiting for an outbreak of rage and sorrow, which she was ready to rebuke with a flow of excellent precepts and reasoning. But Conradin said nothing: there was nothing to be said. Something perhaps in his white set face gave her a momentary qualm, for at tea that afternoon there was toast on the table, a delicacy which she usually banned on the ground that it was bad for him; also because the making of it "gave trouble," a deadly offence in the middle-class feminine eye.

"I thought you liked toast," she exclaimed, with an injured air, observing that he did not touch it.

"Sometimes," said Conradin.

In the shed that evening there was an innovation in the worship of the hutch-god. Conradin had been wont to chant his praises, tonight he asked a boon.

"Do one thing for me, Sredni Vashtar."

The thing was not specified. As Sredni Vashtar was a god he must be supposed to know. And choking back a sob as he looked at that other empty corner, Conradin went back to the world he so hated.

And every night, in the welcome darkness of his bedroom, and every evening in the dusk of the tool-shed, Conradin's bitter litany went up: "Do one thing for me, Sredni Vashtar."

Mrs. de Ropp noticed that the visits to the shed did not cease, and one day she made a further journey of inspection.

"What are you keeping in that locked hutch?" she asked. "I believe it's guinea-pigs. I'll have them all cleared away."

Conradin shut his lips tight, but the Woman ransacked his bedroom till she found the carefully hidden key, and forthwith marched down to the shed to complete her discovery. It was a cold afternoon, and Conradin had been bidden to keep to the house. From the furthest window of the dining-room the door of the shed could just be seen beyond the corner of the shrubbery, and there Conradin stationed himself. He saw the Woman enter, and then he imagined her opening the door of the sacred hutch and peering down with her short-sighted eyes into the thick straw bed where his god lay hidden. Perhaps she would prod at the straw in her clumsy impatience. And Conradin fervently breathed his prayer for the last time.

But he knew as he prayed that he did not believe. He knew that the Woman would come out presently with that pursed smile he loathed so well on her face, and that in an hour or two the gardener would carry away his wonderful god, a god no longer, but a simple brown ferret in a hutch. And he knew that the Woman would triumph always as she triumphed now, and that he would grow ever more sickly under her pestering and domineering and superior wisdom, till one day nothing would matter much more with him, and the doctor would be proved right. And in the sting and misery of his defeat, he began to chant loudly and defiantly the hymn of his threatened idol:

> Sredni Vashtar went forth,
> His thoughts were red thoughts and his teeth were white.
> His enemies called for peace, but he brought them death.
> Sredni Vashtar the Beautiful.

And then of a sudden he stopped his chanting and drew closer to the windowpane. The door of the shed still stood ajar as it had been left, and the minutes were slipping by. They were long minutes, but they slipped by nevertheless. He watched the starlings running and flying in little parties across the lawn; he counted them over and over again, with one eye always on that swinging door. A sour-faced maid came in to lay the table for tea, and still Conradin stood and waited and watched. Hope had crept by inches into his heart, and now a look of triumph began to blaze in his eyes that had only known the wistful patience of defeat. Under his breath, with a furtive exultation, he began once again the paean of victory and devastation. And presently his eyes were rewarded: out through that doorway came a long, low, yellow-and-brown beast, with eyes a-blink at the waning daylight, and dark wet stains around the fur of jaws and throat. Conradin dropped on his knees. The great polecat-ferret made its way down to a small brook at the foot of the garden, drank for a moment, then crossed a little plank bridge and was lost to sight in the bushes. Such was the passing of Sredni Vashtar.

"Tea is ready," said the sour-faced maid; "where is the mistress?"

"She went down to the shed some time ago," said Conradin.

And while the maid went to summon her mistress to tea, Conradin fished a toasting-fork out of the sideboard drawer and proceeded to toast himself a piece of bread. And during the toasting of it and the buttering of it with much butter and the slow enjoyment of eating it, Conradin listened to the noises and silences which fell in quick spasms beyond the dining-room door. The loud foolish screaming of the maid, the answering chorus of wondering ejaculations from the kitchen region, the scuttering footsteps and hurried embassies for outside help, and then, after a lull, the scared sobbings and the shuffling tread of those who bore a heavy burden into the house.

"Whoever will break it to the poor child? I couldn't for the life of me!" exclaimed a shrill voice. And while they debated the matter among themselves, Conradin made himself another piece of toast.

[1927–Great Britain]

QUESTIONS

1. What is the narrative point of view of this story? Does the narrator sway the reader in judging Mrs. de Ropp and Conradin?
2. What contrasting values do Mrs. de Ropp and Conradin have and perhaps even represent? Which values would the story move us to affirm? What is the theme of the story?
3. Is there anything symbolic about Mrs. de Ropp's shortsightedness? What is ironic about the last paragraph?
4. Some critics have found Munro to be sentimental and superficial. Judge this story in that regard, pointing to specifics.
5. Whatever your answer to the preceding question, "Sredni Vashtar" certainly shows the power that plot can have. How so?

WRITING SUGGESTIONS

1. Write a paragraph in which you contrast the values of Mrs. de Ropp and Conradin. Consider which of the two characters and value systems the story would sway us to accept, and state the theme of the story in light of that consideration.
2. In a short essay, contrast "Sredni Vashtar" and "A Confession" as to their narration. In doing so be sure to discuss exactly how Munro's narrator moves the reader toward one outlook and away from another.
3. Write a short review of "Sredni Vashtar" in which you judge the worth of the story with respect to how it is put together, its effect on the readers, and what it says. Whatever your judgment, support it with evidence from the story. Assume an audience not familiar with the story.

Mr. Andrews

E. M. Forster

The souls of the dead were ascending towards the Judgment Seat and the Gate of Heaven. The world soul pressed them on every side, just as the atmosphere presses upon rising bubbles, striving to vanquish them, to break their thin envelope of personality, to mingle their virtue with its own. But they resisted, remembering their glorious individual life on earth, and hoping for an individual life to come.

Among them ascended the soul of a Mr. Andrews who, after a beneficent and honourable life, had recently deceased at his house in town. He knew himself to be kind, upright and religious, and though he approached his trial with all humility, he could not be doubtful of its result. God was not now a jealous God. He would not deny salvation merely because it was expected. A righteous soul may reasonably be conscious of its own righteousness and Mr. Andrews was conscious of his.

"The way is long," said a voice, "but by pleasant converse the way becomes shorter. Might I travel in your company?"

"Willingly," said Mr. Andrews. He held out his hand, and the two souls floated upward together.

"I was slain fighting the infidel," said the other exultantly, "and I go straight to those joys of which the Prophet speaks."

"Are you not a Christian?" asked Mr. Andrews gravely.

"No, I am a Believer. But you are a Moslem, surely?"

"I am not," said Mr. Andrews. "I am a Believer."

The two souls floated upward in silence, but did not release each other's hands. "I am broad church," he added gently. The word "broad" quavered strangely amid the interspaces.

"Relate to me your career," said the Turk at last.

"I was born of a decent middle-class family, and had my education at Winchester and Oxford. I thought of becoming a missionary, but was offered a post in the Board of Trade, which I accepted. At thirty-two I married, and had four children, two of whom have died. My wife survives me. If I had lived a little longer I should have been knighted."

"Now I will relate my career. I was never sure of my father, and my mother does not signify. I grew up in the slums of Salonika. Then I joined a band and we plundered the villages of the infidel. I prospered and had three wives, all of whom survive me. Had I lived a little longer I should have had a band of my own."

"A son of mine was killed travelling in Macedonia. Perhaps you killed him."

"It is very possible."

The two souls floated upward, hand in hand. Mr. Andrews did not speak again, for he was filled with horror at the approaching tragedy. This man, so godless, so lawless, so cruel, so lustful, believed that he would be admitted into Heaven. And into what a heaven—a place full of the crude pleasures of a ruffian's life on earth! But Mr. Andrews felt neither disgust nor moral indignation. He was only conscious of an immense pity, and his own virtues confronted him not at all. He longed to save the man whose hand he held more tightly, who, he thought, was now holding more tightly on to him. And when he reached the Gate of Heaven, instead of saying, "Can I enter?" as he had intended, he cried out, "Cannot *he* enter?"

And at the same moment the Turk uttered the same cry. For the same spirit was working in each of them.

From the gateway a voice replied, "Both can enter." They were filled with joy and pressed forward together.

Then the voice said, "In what clothes will you enter?"

"In my best clothes," shouted the Turk, "the ones I stole." And he clad himself in a splendid turban and a waistcoat embroidered with silver, and baggy trousers, and a great belt in which were stuck pipes and pistols and knives.

"And in what clothes will you enter?" said the voice to Mr. Andrews.

Mr. Andrews thought of his best clothes, but he had no wish to wear them again. At last he remembered and said, "Robes."

"Of what colour and fashion?" asked the voice.

Mr. Andrews had never thought about the matter much. He replied, in hesitating tones, "Whites, I suppose, of some flowing material," and he was immediately given a garment such as he had described. "Do I wear it rightly?" he asked.

"Wear it as it pleases you," replied the voice. "What else do you desire?"

"A harp," suggested Mr. Andrews. "A small one."

A small gold harp was placed in his hand.

"And a palm—no, I cannot have a palm, for it is the reward of martyrdom; my life has been tranquil and happy."

"You can have a palm if you desire it."

But Mr. Andrews refused the palm, and hurried in his white robes after the Turk, who had already entered Heaven. As he passed in at the open gate, a man, dressed like himself, passed out with gestures of despair.

"Why is he not happy?" he asked.

The voice did not reply.

"And who are all those figures, seated inside on thrones and mountains? Why are some of them terrible, and sad, and ugly?"

There was no answer. Mr. Andrews entered, and then he saw that those seated figures were all the gods who were then being worshipped on the earth. A group of souls stood around each, singing his praises. But the gods paid no heed, for they were listening to the prayers of living men, which alone brought them nourishment. Sometimes a faith would grow weak, and then the god of that faith also drooped and dwindled and fainted for his daily portion of incense. And sometimes, owing to a revivalist movement, or to a great commemoration, or to some other cause, a faith would grow strong, and the god of that faith grow strong also. And, more frequently still, a faith would alter, so that the features of its god altered and became contradictory, and passed from ecstasy to respectability, or from mildness and universal love to the ferocity of battle. And at times a god would divide into two gods, or three, or more, each with his own ritual and precarious supply of prayer.

Mr. Andrews saw Buddha, and Vishnu, and Allah, and Jehovah, and the Elohim. He saw little ugly determined gods who were worshipped by a few savages in the same way. He saw the vast shadowy outlines of the neo-pagan Zeus. There were cruel gods, and coarse gods, and tortured gods, and, worse still, there were gods who were peevish, or deceitful, or vulgar. No aspiration of humanity was unfulfilled. There was even an intermediate state for those who wished it, and for the Christian Scientists a place where they could demonstrate that they had not died.

He did not play his harp for long, but hunted vainly for one of his dead friends. And though souls were continually entering Heaven, it still seemed curiously empty. Though he had all that he expected, he was conscious of no great happiness, no mystic contemplation of beauty, no mystic union with good. There was nothing to compare with that moment outside the gate, when he prayed that the Turk might enter and heard the Turk uttering the same prayer for him. And when at last he saw his companion, he hailed him with a cry of human joy.

The Turk was seated in thought, and round him, by sevens, sat the virgins who are promised in the Koran.

"Oh, my dear friend!" he called out. "Come here, and we will never be parted, and such as my pleasures are, they shall be yours also. Where are my other friends? Where are the men whom I love, or whom I have killed?"

"I, too, have only found you," said Mr. Andrews. He sat down by the Turk, and the virgins, who were all exactly alike, ogled them with coal black eyes.

"Though I have all that I expected," said the Turk, "I am conscious of no great happiness. There is nothing to compare with that moment outside the gate when I prayed that you might enter, and heard you uttering the same prayer for me. These virgins are as beautiful and good as I had fashioned, yet I could wish that they were better."

As he wished, the forms of the virgins became more rounded, and their eyes grew larger and blacker than before. And Mr. Andrews, by a wish similar in kind, increased the purity and softness of his garment and the glitter of his harp. For in that place their expectations were fulfilled, but not their hopes.

"I am going," said Mr. Andrews at last. "We desire infinity and we cannot imagine it. How can we expect it to be granted? I have never imagined anything infinitely good or beautiful excepting .in my dreams."

"I am going with you," said the other.

Together they sought the entrance gate, and the Turk parted with his virgins and his best clothes, and Mr. Andrews cast away his robes and his harp.

"Can we depart?" they asked.

"You can both depart if you wish," said the voice, "but remember what lies outside."

As soon as they passed the gate, they felt again the pressure of the world soul. For a moment they stood hand in hand resisting it. Then they suffered it to break in upon them, and they, and all the experience they had gained, and all the love and wisdom they had generated, passed into it, and made it better.

[1928–Great Britain]

QUESTIONS

1. What kind of narrator narrates "Mr. Andrews"? Are there any points where the narration changes to another narrative point of view?
2. Describe Mr. Andrews and the Turk. What kind of characters are they? Are their differences as important as their likenesses? If not, why not?
3. What does the story suggest about human conceptions in general and human conceptions of heaven in particular?
4. In what way does the story's theme concern individualism?
5. Overall, how does the narrative voice of "Mr. Andrews" strike you (for instance, is it aloof or warm, austere or friendly)? Is the narrative voice in keeping with the story's theme?

WRITING SUGGESTIONS

1. In a paragraph, define the narrative voice of "Mr. Andrews." What kind of tone do you hear when reading the story? How is this tone established? How does it condition your response and how is it right for the story overall?
2. In a paragraph, compare and contrast Mr. Andrews and the Turk. Begin with their dissimilarities and move to their similarities. With regard to the story's theme, why are their likenesses more important than their differences?

Six Years After

Katherine Mansfield

It was not the afternoon to be on deck—on the contrary. It was exactly the afternoon when there is no snugger place than a warm cabin, a warm bunk. Tucked up with a rug, a hot-water bottle and a piping hot cup of tea she would not have minded the weather in the least. But he—hated cabins, hated to be inside anywhere more than was absolutely necessary. He had a passion for keeping, as he called it, above board, especially when he was travelling. And it wasn't surprising, considering the enormous amount of time he spent cooped up in the office. So, when he rushed away from her as soon as they got on board and came back five minutes later to say he had secured two deck chairs on the lee side and the steward was undoing the rugs, her voice through the high sealskin collar murmured "Good"; and because he was looking at her, she smiled with bright eyes and blinked quickly, as if to say, "Yes, perfectly all right—absolutely," and she meant it.

"Then we'd better—" said he, and he tucked her hand inside his arm and began to rush her off to where the two chairs stood. But she just had time to breathe, "Not so fast, Daddy, please," when he remembered too and slowed down.

Strange! They had been married twenty-eight years, and it was still an effort to him, each time, to adapt his pace to hers.

"Not cold, are you?" he asked, glancing sideways at her. Her little nose, geranium pink above the dark fur, was answer enough. But she thrust her free hand into the velvet pocket of her jacket and murmured gaily, "I shall be glad of my rug."

232

He pressed her tighter to his side—a quick, nervous pressure. He knew, of course, that she ought to be down in the cabin; he knew that it was no afternoon for her to be sitting on deck, in this cold and raw mist, lee side or no lee side, rugs or no rugs, and he realized how she must be hating it. But he had come to believe that it really was easier for her to make these sacrifices than it was for him. Take their present case, for instance. If he had gone down to the cabin with her, he would have been miserable the whole time, and he couldn't have helped showing it. Any any rate, she would have found him out. Whereas, having made up her mind to fall in with his ideas, he would have betted anybody she would even go so far as to enjoy the experience. Not because she was without personality of her own. Good Lord! She was absolutely brimming with it. But because . . . but here his thoughts always stopped. Here they always felt the need of a cigar, as it were. And, looking at the cigar-tip, his fine blue eyes narrowed. It was a law of marriage, he supposed. . . . All the same, he always felt guilty when he asked these sacrifices of her. That was what the quick pressure meant. His being said to her being: "You do understand, don't you?" and there was an answering tremor of her fingers. "I *understand*."

Certainly, the steward—good little chap—had done all in his power to make them comfortable. He had put up their chairs in whatever warmth there was and out of the smell. She did hope he would be tipped adequately. It was on occasions like these (and her life seemed to be full of such occasions) that she wished it was the woman who controlled the purse.

"Thank you, steward. That will do beautifully."

"Why are stewards so often delicate-looking?" she wondered, as her feet were tucked under. "This poor little chap looks as though he'd got a chest, and yet one would have thought . . . the sea air. . . ."

The button of the pigskin purse was undone. The tray was tilted. She saw sixpences, shillings, half-crowns.

"I should give him five shillings," she decided, "and tell him to buy himself a good nourishing—"

He was given a shilling, and he touched his cap and seemed genuinely grateful.

Well, it might have been worse. It might have been sixpence. It might, indeed. For at that moment Father turned towards her and said, half-apologetically, stuffing the purse back, "I gave him a shilling. I think it was worth it, don't you?"

"Oh, quite! Every bit!" said she.

It is extraordinary how peaceful it feels on a little steamer once the bustle of leaving port is over. In a quarter of an hour one might have been at sea for days. There is something almost touching, childish, in the way people submit themselves to the new conditions. They go to bed in the early afternoon, they shut their eyes and "it's night" like little children who turn the table upside down and cover themselves with the table-cloth. And those who remain on deck—they seem to be always the same, those few hardened men travellers—pause, light their pipes, stamp softly, gaze out to sea, and their voices are subdued as they walk up and down. The long-legged little girl chases after the red-cheeked boy, but soon both are captured; and the old sailor, swinging an unlighted lantern, passes and disappears. . . .

He lay back, the rug up to his chin and she saw he was breathing deeply. Sea air! If anyone believed in sea air, it was he. He had the strongest faith in its tonic qualities. But the great thing was, according to him, to fill the lungs with it the moment you came on board. Otherwise, the sheer strength of it was enough to give you a chill. . . .

She gave a small chuckle, and he turned to her quickly. "What is it?"

"It's your cap," she said. "I never can get used to you in a cap. You look such a thorough burglar."

"Well, what the deuce am I to wear?" He shot up one grey eyebrow and wrinkled his nose. "It's very good cap, too. Very fine specimen of its kind. It's got a very rich white satin lining." He paused. He declaimed, as he had hundreds of times before at this stage, "Rich and rare were the gems she wore."

But she was thinking he really was childishly proud of the white satin lining. He would like to have taken off his cap and made her feel it. "Feel the quality!" How often had she rubbed between finger and thumb his coat, his shirt cuff, tie, sock, linen handkerchief, while he said that.

She slipped down more deeply into her chair.

And the little steamer pressed on, pitching gently, over the grey, unbroken, gently-moving water, that was veiled with slanting rain.

Far out, as though idly, listlessly, gulls were flying. Now they settled on the waves, now they beat up into the rainy air, and shone against the pale sky like the lights within the pearl. They looked cold and lonely. How lonely it will be when we have passed by, she thought. There will be nothing but the waves and those birds and rain falling.

She gazed through the rust-spotted railing along which big drops trembled, until suddenly she shut her lips. It was as if a warning voice inside her had said, "Don't look!"

"No, I won't," she decided. "It's too depressing, much too depressing."

But immediately, she opened her eyes and looked again. Lonely birds, water lifting, white pale sky—how were they changed?

And it seemed to her there was a presence far out there, between the sky and the water; someone very desolate and longing watched them pass and cried as if to stop them—but cried to her alone.

"Mother!"

"Don't leave me," sounded the cry. "Don't forget me! You are forgetting me, you know you are!" And it was as though from her own breast there came the sound of childish weeping.

"My son—my precious child—it isn't true!"

Sh! How was it possible that she was sitting there on that quiet steamer beside Father and at the same time she was hushing and holding a little slender boy—so pale—who had just waked out of a dreadful dream?

"I dreamed I was in a wood—somewhere far away from everybody,—and I was lying down and a great blackberry vine grew over me. And I called and called to you—and you wouldn't come—you wouldn't come—so I had to lie there for ever."

What a terrible dream! He had always had terrible dreams. How often, years ago, when he was small, she had made some excuse and escaped from their friends in the dining-room or the drawing-room to come to the foot of the stairs and listen. "Mother!" And when he was asleep, his dream had journeyed with her back into the circle of lamplight; it had taken its place there like a ghost. And now—

Far more often—at all times—in all places—like now, for instance—she never settled down, she was never off her guard for a moment but she heard him. He wanted her. "I am coming as fast as I can! As fast as I can!" But the dark stairs have no ending, and the worst dream of all—the one that is always the same—goes for ever and ever uncomforted.

This is anguish! How is it to be borne? Still, it is not the idea of her suffering which is unbearable—it is his. Can one do nothing for the dead? And for a long time the answer had been—Nothing!

. . . But softly without a sound the dark curtain has rolled down. There is no more to come. That is the end of the play. But it can't end like that—so suddenly. There must be more. No, it's cold, it's still. There is nothing to be gained by waiting.

But—did he go back again? Or, when the war was over, did he come home for good? Surely, he will marry—later on—not for several years. Surely, one day I shall remember his wedding and my first grandchild—a beautiful dark-haired boy born in the early morning—a lovely morning—spring!

"Oh, Mother, it's not fair to me to put these ideas into my head! Stop, Mother, stop! When I think of all I have missed, I can't bear it."

"I can't bear it!" She sits up breathing the words and tosses the dark rug away. It is colder than ever, and now the dusk is falling, falling like ash upon the pallid water.

And the little steamer, growing determined, throbbed on, pressed on, as if at the end of the journey there waited. . . .

[1923–Great Britain]

QUESTIONS

1. We see through the eyes of both characters in "Six Years After." Where do we see through the husband's eyes? Where through the wife's?
2. Contrast the husband and wife of Mansfield's delicate story. What character type is each: stock, flat, or round? Similarly, contrast the story's beginning and concluding paragraphs. What do the former serve to do with respect to the latter?
3. The wife's "toss[ing] the dark rug away" at the end of the story could be taken as symbolic. What could it mean?

WRITING SUGGESTION

1. Write a paragraph examining the type of narration found in "Six Years After." Evaluate the effectiveness of Mansfield's treatment of narration as it helps the reader to understand the characters.
2. In a paragraph or more contrast the states of mind of the story's two main characters. In light of this contrast, what might be the theme of the story?
3. Is it really possible to make ethical judgments when it comes to the different ways people respond to death? Write a paper on the subject using "Six Years After" for examples, as well as anything in your own experience that has relevance.

The Sin of Jesus*

Isaac Babel

Arina was a servant at the hotel. She lived next to the main staircase, while Seryoga, the janitor's helper, lived over the back stairs. Between them there was shame. On Palm Sunday Arina gave Seryoga a present— twins. Water flows, stars shine, a man lusts, and soon Arina was big again, her sixth month was rolling by—they're slippery, a woman's months. And now Seryoga must go into the army. There's a mess for you!

So Arina goes and says: "No sense, Seryoga. There's no sense in my waiting for you. For four years we'll be parted, and in four years, whichever way you look at it, I'll be sure to bring two or three more into this world. It's like walking around with your skirt turned up, working at the hotel. Whoever stops here, he's your master, let him be a Jew, let him be anybody at all. By the time you come home, my insides will be no good any more. I'll be a used-up woman, no match for you."

"That's so," Seryoga nodded.

"There's many that want me. Trofimych the contractor—but he's no gentleman. And Isai Abramych, the warden of Nikolo-Svyatsky Church, a feeble old man, but anyway I'm sick to the stomach of your murderous strength. I tell you this now, and I say it like I would at confession, I've got the wind plain knocked out of me. I'll spill my load in three months, then I'll take the baby to the orphanage and marry the old man."

When Seryoga heard this, he took off his belt and beat her like a hero, right on the belly.

"Look out there," Arina says to him, "go soft on the belly. It's your stuffing, no one else's."

* Translated by Walter Morison

237

There was no end to the beating, no end to the man's tears and the woman's blood, but that is neither here nor there.

Then the woman came to Jesus Christ.

"So on and so forth," she says, "Lord Jesus, I am the woman from the Hotel Madrid and Louvre, the one on Tverskaya Street. Working at the hotel, it's just like going around with your skirt up. Just let a man stop there, and he's your lord and master, let him be a Jew, let him be anyone at all. There is another slave of yours walking the earth, the janitor's helper, Seryoga. Last year on Palm Sunday I bore him twins."

And so she described it all to the Lord.

"And what if Seryoga were not to go into the army after all? the Saviour suggested.

"Try and get away with it—not with the policeman around. He'll drag him off as sure as daylight."

"Oh yes, the policeman," the Lord bowed His head, "I've never thought of him. Then perhaps you ought to live in purity for a while?"

"For four years?" the woman cried. "To hear you talk, all people should deny their animal nature. That's just your old ways all over again. And where will the increase come from? No, you'd better give me some sensible advice."

The Lord's cheeks turned scarlet, the woman's words had touched a tender spot. But He said nothing. You cannot kiss your own ear—even God knows that.

"I'll tell you what, God's servant, glorious sinner, maiden Arina," the Lord proclaimed in all His glory, "I have a little angel here in heaven, hanging around uselessly. His name is Alfred. Lately he's gotten out of hand altogether, keeps crying and nagging all the time: 'What have you done to me, Lord? Why do you turn me into an angel in my twentieth year, and me a hale young fellow?' So I'll give you Alfred the angel as a husband for four years. He'll be your prayer, he'll be your protection and he'll be your solace. And as for offspring, you've nothing to worry about—you can't bear a duckling from him, let alone a baby, for there's a lot of fun in him, but no seriousness."

"That's just what I need," the maid Arina wept gratefully. "Their seriousness takes me to the doorstep of the grave three times every two years."

"You'll have a sweet respite, God's child Arina. May your prayer be light as a song. Amen."

And so it was decided. Alfred was brought in—a frail young fellow, delicate, two wings fluttering behind his pale-blue shoulders, rippling with rosy light like two doves playing in heaven. Arina threw her hefty arms about him, weeping out of tenderness, out of her woman's soft heart.

"Alfred, my soul, my consolation, my bridegroom . . ."

In parting, the Lord gave her strict instructions to take off the angel's wings every night before he went to bed. His wings were attached to hinges, like a door, and every night she was to take them and wrap them in a clean sheet, because they were brittle, his wings, and could snap as he tossed in bed—for what were they made of but the sighs of babes, no more than that.

For the last time the Lord blessed the union, while the choir of bishops, called in for the occasion, rendered thunderous praises. No food was served, not a crumb—that wasn't the style in heaven—and then Arina and Alfred, their arms about each other, ran down a silken ladder, straight back to earth. They came to Petrovka, the street where nothing but the best is sold. The woman would do right by her Alfred for he, if one might say so, not only lacked socks, but was altogether as natural as when his mother bore him. And she bought him patent-leather half-boots, checked jersey trousers, a fine hunting jacket, and an electric-blue vest.

"The rest," she says, "we'll find at home."

That day Arina begged off from work. Seryoga came and raised a fuss, but she did not even come out to him, only said from behind her locked door:

"Sergey Nifantyich, I am at present a-washing my feet and beg you to retire without further noise."

He went away without a word—the angel's power was already beginning to manifest itself!

In the evening Arina set out a supper fit for a merchant—the woman had devilish vanity! A half-pint of vodka, wine on the side, Danube herring with potatoes, a samovar of tea. When Alfred had partaken of all these earthly blessings, he keeled over in a dead sleep. Quick as wink, Arina lifted off his wings from the hinges, packed them away, and carried him to bed in her arms.

There it lies, the snowy wonder on the eiderdown pillow of her tattered, sinful bed, sending forth a heavenly radiance: moon-sliver shafts of light pass and repass, alternate with red ones, float across the floor, sway over his shining feet. Arina weeps and rejoices, sings and prays. Arina, thou hast been granted a happiness unheard of on this battered earth. Blessed art thou among women!.

They had drunk the vodka to the last drop, and now it took effect. As soon as they fell asleep, she went and rolled over on top of Alfred with her hot, six-months-belly. Not enough for her to sleep with an angel, not enough that nobody beside her spat at the wall, snored and snorted—that wasn't enough for the clumsy, ravening slut. No, she had to warm her belly too, her burning belly big with Seryoga's lust. And so she smothered

him in her fuddled sleep, smothered him like a week-old babe in the midst
of her rejoicing, crushed him under her bloated weight, and he gave up the
ghost, and his wings, wrapped in her sheet, wept pale tears.

Dawn came—and all the trees bowed low to the ground. In distant
northern forests each fir tree turned into a priest, each fir tree bent its knees
in silent worship.

Once more the woman stands before the Lord's throne. She is broad
in the shoulders, mighty, the young corpse drooping in her huge red arms.

"Behold, Lord . . ."

But here the gentle heart of Jesus could endure no more, and He
cursed the woman in His anger:

"As it is on earth, so shall it be with you, Arina, from this day on."

"How is it then, Lord?" the woman replied in a scarcely audible voice.
"Was it I who made my body heavy, was it I that brewed vodka on earth,
was it I that created a woman's soul, stupid and lonely?"

"I don't wish to be bothered with you," exclaimed the Lord Jesus.
"You've smothered my angel, you filthy scum."

And Arina was thrown back to earth on a putrid wind, straight down to
Tverskaya Street, to the Hotel Madrid and Louvre, where she was doomed
to spend her days. And once there, the sky was the limit. Seryoga was
carousing,, drinking away his last days, seeing as he was a recruit. The
contractor Trofimych, just come from Kolomna, took one look at Arina,
hefty and red-cheeked: "Oh, you cute little belly," he said, and so on and
so forth.

Isai Abramych, the old codger, heard about this cute little belly, and
he was right there too, wheezing toothlessly:

"I cannot wed you lawfully," he said, "after all that happened.
However, I can lie with you the same as anyone."

The old man ought to be lying in cold mother earth instead of
thinking of such things, but no, he too must take his turn at spitting into
her soul. It was as though they had all slipped the chain—kitchen-boys,
merchants, foreigners. A fellow in trade—he likes to have his fun.

And that is the end of my tale.

Before she was laid up, for three months had rolled by in the
meantime, Arina went out into the back yard, behind the janitor's rooms,
raised her monstrous belly to the silken sky, and said stupidly:

"See, Lord, what a belly! They hammer at it like peas falling in a
colander. And what sense there's in it I just can't see. But I've had
enough."

With His tears Jesus loved Arina when He heard these words. The
Saviour fell on His knees before her.

"Forgive me, little Arina. Forgive your sinful God for all He has done to you . . ."

But Arina shook her head and would not listen.

"There's no forgiveness for you, Jesus Christ," she said. "No forgiveness, and never will be."

[1922–U.S.S.R.]

QUESTIONS

1. Babel's story proper ends when the narrator says, "And that is the end of my tale." Who narrates what follows, which forms a kind of epilogue or afterword?
2. After having gone over the story carefully, analyze the mentality of the narrator. Are his views profound or merely traditional? Are his judgments compelling or merely conventional? For whom does the narrator speak? What kind of narrator is he?
3. In what ways has the narrator deliberately been made to contrast with Arina? What is the point of the contrast?
4. How is Arina's moral authority established? What is the nature of her complaint against Jesus? What is the meaning of Jesus's assent?
5. The author can be thought of as a kind of puppeteer, managing all of a story's elements from behind the scenes. This story demonstrates the point. How so?

WRITING SUGGESTIONS

1. (a) In a paragraph or two, draw a portrait of Babel's narrator, suggesting what kind of narrator he is and whose views he expresses. Why is this important to understand with respect to our reception of Arina?

   (b) In a separate paragraph state your response to "The Sin of Jesus" and discuss what it is about the story that leads you to respond thus.
2. Write a short paper analyzing Arina's complaint against Jesus. Is it rational? Does it make emotional sense? What underlying conflicts of the Christian world view does it expose?

Señor Payroll

William E. Barrett

Larry and I were Junior Engineers in the gas plant, which means that we were clerks. Anything that could be classified as paper work came to the flat double desk across which we faced each other. The Main Office downtown sent us a bewildering array of orders and rules that were to be put into effect.

Junior Engineers were beneath the notice of everyone except the Mexican laborers at the plant. To them we were the visible form of a distant, unknowable paymaster. We were Señor Payroll.

Those Mexicans were great workmen; the aristocrats among them were the stokers, big men who worked Herculean eight-hour shifts in the fierce heat of the retorts. They scooped coal with huge shovels and hurled it with uncanny aim at tiny doors. The coal streamed out from the shovels like black water from a high-pressure nozzle, and never missed the narrow opening. The strokers worked stripped to the waist, and there was pride and dignity in them. Few men could do such work, and they were the few.

The Company paid its men only twice a month, on the fifth and on the twentieth. To a Mexican, this was absurd. What man with money will make it last fifteen days? If he hoarded money beyond the spending of three days, he was a miser—and when, Señor, did the blood of Spain flow in the veins of misers? Hence, it was the custom for our strokers to appear every third or fourth day to draw the money due to them.

There was a certain elasticity in the Company rules, and Larry and I sent the necessary forms to the Main Office and received an "advance" against a man's pay check. Then, one day, Downtown favored us with a memorandum:

"There have been too many abuses of the advance-against-wages privilege. Hereafter, no advance against wages will be made to any employee except in a case of genuine emergency."

We had no sooner posted the notice when in came stoker Juan Garcia. He asked for an advance. I pointed to the notice. He spelled it through slowly, then said, "What does this mean, this 'genuine emergency'?"

I explained to him patiently that the Company was kind and sympathetic, but that it was a great nuisance to have pay wages every few days. If someone was ill or if money was urgently needed for some other good reason, then the Company would make an exception to the rule.

Juan Garcia turned his hat over and over slowly in his big hands. "I do not get my money?"

"Next payday, Juan. On the Twentieth."

He went out silently and I felt a little ashamed of myself. I looked across the desk at Larry. He avoided my eyes.

In the next hour two other stokers came in, looked at the notice, had it explained and walked solemnly out; then no more came. What we did not know was that Juan Garcia, Pete Mendoza, and Francisco Gonzalez had spread the word, and that every Mexican in the plant was explaining the order to every other Mexican. "To get money now, the wife must be sick. There must be medicine for the baby."

The next morning Juan Garcia's wife was practically dying, Pete Mendoza's mother would hardly last the day, there was a veritable epidemic among children, and, just for variety, there was one sick father. We always suspected that the old man was really sick; no Mexican would otherwise have thought of him. At any rate, nobody paid Larry and me to examine private lives; we made out our forms with an added line describing the "genuine emergency." Our people got paid.

That went on for a week. Then came a new order, curt and to the point: "Hereafter, employees will be paid ONLY on the fifth and the twentieth of the month. No exceptions will be made except in the cases of employees leaving the service of the Company."

The notice went up on the board, and we explained its significance gravely. "No, Juan Garcia, we cannot advance your wages. It is too bad about your wife and your cousins and your aunts, but there is a new rule."

Juan Garcia went out and thought it over. He thought out loud with Mendoza and Gonzales and Ayala, then, in the morning, he was back. "I am quitting this company for different job. You pay me now?"

We argued that it was a good company and that it loved its employees like children, but in the end we paid off, because Juan Garcia quit. And so did Gonzalez, Mendoza, Obregon, Ayala and Ortez, the best stokers, men who could not be replaced.

Larry and I looked at each other; we knew what was coming in about three days. One of our duties was to sit on the hiring line early each morning, engaging transient workers for the handy gangs. Any man was accepted who could walk up and ask for a job without falling down. Never before had we been called upon to hire such skilled virtuosos as stokers for handy-gang work, but we were called upon to hire them now.

The day foreman was wringing his hands and asking the Almighty if he was personally supposed to shovel this condemned coal, while there in a stolid, patient line were skilled men—Garcia, Mendoza, and others—waiting to be hired. We hired them, of course. There was nothing else to do.

Every day we had a line of resigning stokers, and another line of stokers seeking work. Our paper work became very complicated. At the main Office they were jumping up and down. The procession of forms showing Juan Garcia's resigning and being hired over and over again was too much for them. Sometimes Downtown had Garcia on the payroll twice at the same time when someone down there was slow in entering a resignation. Our phone rang early and often.

Tolerantly and patiently we explained. "There's nothing we can do if a man wants to quit, and if there are stokers available when the plant needs stokers, we hire them."

Out of chaos, Downtown issued another order. I read it and whistled. Larry looked at it and said, "It is going to be very quiet around here."

The order read: "Hereafter, no employee who resigns may be rehired within a period of 30 days."

Juan Garcia was due for another resignation, and when he came in we showed him the order and explained that standing in line the next day would do him no good if he resigned today. "Thirty days is a long time, Juan."

It was a grave matter and he took time to reflect on it. So did Gonzalez, Mendoza, Ayala and Ortez. Ultimately, however, they were all back—and all resigned.

We did our best to dissuade them and we were sad about the parting. This time it was for keeps and they shook hands with us solemnly. It was very nice knowing us. Larry and I looked at each other when they were gone and we both knew that neither of us had been pulling for Downtown to win the duel. It was a blue day.

In the morning, however, they were all back in line. With the utmost gravity, Juan Garcia informed me that he was a stoker looking for a job. "No dice, Juan," I said. "Come back in thirty days. I warned you." His eyes looked straight into mine without a flicker. "There is some mistake, Señor," he said. "I am Manuel Hernández. I work a the stoker in Pueblo, in Santa Fe, in many places."

I stared back at him, remembering the sick wife and the babies without medicine, the mother-in-law in the hospital, the many resignations and the rehirings. I knew that there was a gas plant in Pueblo, and that there wasn't any in Santa Fe; but who was I to argue with a man about his own name? A stoker is a stoker.

So I hired him. I hired Gonzalez, too, who swore that his name was Carrera, and Ayala, who had shamelessly become Smith.

Three days later the resigning started.

Within a week our payroll read like a history of Latin America. Everyone was on it: Lopez and Obregon, Villa, Diaz, Batista, Gomez, and even San Martín and Bolívar. Finally Larry and I, growing weary of staring at familiar faces and writing unfamiliar names, went to the Superintendent and told him the whole story. He tried not to grin, and said, "Damned nonsense!"

The next day the orders were taken down. We called our most prominent stokers into the office and pointed to the board. No rules any more.

"The next time we hire you hombres," Larry said grimly, "come in under the names you like best, because that's the way you are going to stay on the books."

They looked at us and they looked at the board; then for the first time in the long duel, their teeth flashed white. "Si. Señores," they said.

And so it was.

[1943–U.S.A.]

QUESTIONS

1. Can we believe the narrator we have here? What kind of narrator is he?
2. Describe the narrator and comment on how he is characterized.
3. Summarize the scheme of the Mexican workers. What are they up against? What are the narrator's feelings about the whole affair? Whose side is the story on?
4. What is the general meaning of this realistic story? What does it say about conflict between classes or types of people?

WRITING SUGGESTIONS

1. In a paragraph, classify Barrett's narrator and discuss how we come to determine the type of narrator he is, as well as how our reception of him affects our understanding of the story as a whole.
2. Write a short paper on "Señor Payroll" in which you address the fact that people are often kept apart by their differing ways of looking at things. In doing so, contrast the values of the Mexican workers and those of their "downtown" bosses. How do the values and views of both the workers and the bosses keep them from understanding each other?

Personal Letter

William March

Hamburg, Germany,
December 17th, 1932

DEAR MR. TYLER:

I wrote you a long, official letter last week and forwarded same via the S.S. *Manhattan*. That letter, which should be in your hands by the time you receive this, contained information you wanted regarding berthing facilities, pilotage in and out, tug hire, stevedoring costs, etc., etc. If I failed to cover any point that you had in mind, or if any part of my report is not detailed enough, please let me know, and I'll remedy the situation promptly.

As you will remember, you also asked me to drop a line under private cover regarding my personal impression of this country, and that is what I would like to do in this letter. I have thought a good deal about the best way to accomplish this, and have come to the conclusion that the easiest way to do it is to simply recount a little incident which happened the other night in a cafe.

First, let me say again that the agents you have in mind for representing us here are very efficient and have co-operated with me at all times. Herr Voelker, director of the agency, has been especially helpful. He is an intelligent and highly educated man. A few nights ago, he asked me to have dinner with him and attend the opera later, which I did. After that, he suggested we take in a beer cafe that he knew of, and so we went there, too. This place was pretty well filled up when we arrived, mostly with men in storm trooper uniforms. I won't explain who they are, as I covered that point in my first letter under the heading of Political Situation and Future Outlook, to which I refer you.

247

Well, Herr Voelker and I went to the basement bar and ordered our drinks, talking together all the time. We were speaking in English and discussing business matters and things in general, and at first I didn't notice that a group of these storm troopers had closed around us, shutting us off from the others at the bar.

To make a long story short, the leader of the group touched me on the shoulder and told me that I was in Germany now, and that while I was in Germany I would speak German or nothing at all. Most of these North Germans speak English very well indeed, since they have eights years of it in school, and so, naturally, this fellow spoke English, too.

I twisted around and looked these boys over, but they only held their backs stiffer, threw out their chests and frowned, just like something out of the opera I'd just seen. I still couldn't believe I'd heard correctly, and so I said, "Were you speaking to me?" And this leader answered in a voice which trembled with anger, "I repeat for the last time. When you are in Germany, you are to speak German. If you cannot speak German, you are to remain silent. Is that clear? We will endure no further insults from foreigners."

By that time I was sure it was some sort of a gag which Herr Voelker and his boys had cooked up for me. You know the sort of thing I mean, don't you? Like the time at the Traffic Association dinner when they played that joke on Oscar Wilcoxon. If you remember now, a girl with a baby in her arms burst into the dining-room just before the speeches began. She asked if there was a man present named Oscar Wilcoxon, and when the master of ceremonies said that there was, she demanded that he marry her, like he had promised to do, and give a name to his child.

Everybody was in on the stunt except Oscar himself, and it got a lot of laughs. Oscar kept trying to explain that somebody else must have been using his name illegally, because he'd never seen the young lady before in his life; but this girl had been carefully coached in her part, and the more Oscar tried to explain matters, the worse things got. I kept thinking to myself at the time that if anybody pulled a trick like that on me, I'd fall right in with the gag and say yes, I was the father of the baby all right, but I couldn't be sure about the mother because it was always so dark in the alley back of the pickle works where we met.

Well, when the storm trooper said what he did about not speaking English in Germany, I wanted to laugh, it struck me as comical, but I didn't. I'd already decided to play it their way and pretend to take the whole thing seriously. So I kept a straight face and said, "You gentlemen would like others to believe that you are real Germans, but you are not real

Germans at all. If a real German heard what you have just said, he'd cover his face with shame."

I waited a moment and then added, "If you were real Germans, like you pretend to be, you'd realize that since I'm not a German, but an American, that I'm not as bright as you are. You'd know that Americans haven't got your culture, and that we haven't had your natural advantages. Americans think slowly," I said. "They don't master languages the way you do." Then I sighed and turned back to Herr Voelker, as if the subject was ended, as far as I was concerned.

The storm troopers seemed nonplused at my attitude, and they went into a huddle at one end of the bar. My German isn't the best in the world, but I could understand most of what they said without any trouble. The gist of it was that I was right, and that they were wrong; that even though I was a foreigner, I had the true philosophy. Well, I let them talk it over for a while, and then suddenly I wheeled around and gave them the other barrel. "A true German doesn't expect the same perfection from inferior people that he expects from himself," I said. "I thought that was something everybody knew by this time."

I said all this in a quick, stern voice, Mr. Tyler, and the troopers straightened up and stood at attention while I gave them a thorough dressing down. At the end of my speech, I said, "So you see? If you were true Germans, and believed in your mission, you wouldn't humiliate me before my friends. Oh, no, you wouldn't do that at all! Instead, you'd come to me as a teacher and say, 'Let me instruct you in our beautiful language! Let me explain to you our wonderful way of life!'" I waited a moment and then said sadly, "No. No, you are not true Germans. You only pretend to be. And now go away please before I lose the last of my illusions."

I nudged Herr Voelker with my elbow and winked behind my hand, but he only raised his eyes and stared at me over the edge of his glass. By that time there were tears in the eyes of the leader of the troopers. He wanted to buy me a drink, to prove that everything was all right, but I thought I'd keep the thing going a little longer, and played hard to butter up. Finally, I did let him buy me a drink, and then I bought him one in return. I thought, then, that the joke would break, and the laughter and the explanations come, but that didn't happen, and I began to feel a little uneasy.

Not long afterwards, Herr Voelker and I got up to leave. When we were outside, Herr Voelker said he was sorry such an unpleasant incident had occurred, and that he would have prevented it if he had been able to do so. He said he thought I had acted with rare presence of mind in being frank and aboveboard with the storm troopers, instead of trying to lie my way out of the situation. I was so astonished that I stood still on the pavement and said, "Did you think I meant what I said? An intelligent, educated man like yourself? Did you really believe I was in earnest?"

And, before God, Mr. Tyler, Herr Voelker drew himself up haughtily and said, "Why shouldn't I think you meant it? Every point you made was logical and entirely true."

Mr. Tyler, I've often read in books about an icy hand which clutched at somebody-or-other's heart. I never before took the words seriously, thinking it was just a phrase that writers used, but now I know that it's a true expression. That's exactly the way I felt as I walked along with Herr Voelker until we reached the taxi rank on the corner, and I got into a cab alone, and went back to my hotel.

Now, maybe there isn't anything important in the incident, but I think there is. There's something going on beneath the surface here as sure as you're a foot high. I don't quite know what it is so far, but I do know that it's something horrible.

This turned out to be a long letter, didn't it? I suppose you'll be receiving it during the Christmas holidays, so let me take this opportunity of wishing you a happy Christmas and a prosperous New Year. People here celebrate Christmas in a big way. They gather together in groups, sing songs about the Christ child, and weep over the loved ones who are far away. It is the season of love, goodwill, and the renewal of old affections, or so Herr Voelker tells me. He invited me, as a special compliment, to spend the day in the bosom of his own family, so I could see first hand what a German Christmas is really like; but I expressed my regrets, and said that business obligations made it necessary for me to be in Paris on that day. To tell you the truth, Mr Tyler, everybody here frightens me a little—they are all so full of sentiment and fury.

With best regards, and again wishing you the compliments of the season, I remain,

Sincerely yours,

ROBERT B. McINTOSH.

[1945–U.S.A.]

QUESTIONS

1. What kind of a person is Mr. McIntosh? How does what he says serve to characterize him? How are we to judge the narrative point of view here?
2. Because we have witnessed the outcome of the historical event that McIntosh is

witnessing at the outset, we know more that he. What is the effect of this disparity?

3. In what way does this story reach beyond its particular historical situation to express a pattern that has often repeated itself in human history?

4. How is Herr Voelker characterized toward the beginning of the story? In what way is the story's second climax (about Herr Voelker) more significant than its first (about the storm troopers)? Why doesn't McIntosh accept Voelker's Christmas invitation? With respect to Herr Voelker, what is the point of the story?

5. In the story's second paragraph, the letter writer states the method he has chosen for his report. What method is it? How is the method central to fiction generally?

WRITING SUGGESTIONS

1. Write a paragraph on the disparity referred to in question 2 above and the effect of this disparity. In what way does the disparity heighten the story's impact?

2. In a paragraph, analyze the means by which McIntosh is characterized. Consider his values as well as his personal traits and how, indeed, his values shape those traits.

3. Write a letter about some contemporary movement or trend like McIntosh's letter on the rise of Nazi Germany. Proceed in the same manner, that is, by way of example. Your example, like McIntosh's, should embody your attitude toward your subject.

At Sea*
A Sailor's Story

Anton Chekhov

Only the dimming lights of the receding harbor were visible in an ink-black sky. We could feel the heavy storm clouds overhead about to burst into rain, and it was suffocating, in spite of the wind and cold.

Crowded together in the crew's quarters we, the sailors, were casting lots. Loud, drunken laughter filled the air. One of our comrades was playfully crowing like a cock. A slight shiver ran through me from the back of my heels, as if cold small shot were pouring down my naked body from a hole in the back of my head. I was shivering both from the cold and certain other causes, which I wish to describe.

In my opinion, man is, as a rule, foul; and the sailor can sometimes be the foulest of all the creatures of the earth—fouler than the lowest beast, which has, at least, the excuse of obeying his instincts. It is possible that I may be mistaken, since I do not know life, but it appears to me that a sailor has more occasion than anyone else to despise and curse himself. A man who at any moment may fall headlong from a mast to be forever hidden beneath a wave, a man who may drown, God alone knows when, has need of nothing, and one on dry land feels pity for him. We sailors drink a lot of vodka and are dissolute because we do not know what one needs virtue for at sea. However, I shall continue.

We were casting lots. There were twenty-two of us who, having stood watch, were now at liberty. Out of this number only two were to have the luck of enjoying a rare spectacle. On this particular night the honeymoon cabin was occupied, but the wall of the cabin had only two holes at our

---

* Translated by Ann Dunnigan.

disposal. One of them I myself had made with a fine saw, after boring through with a corkscrew; the other had been cut out with a knife by one of my comrades. We had worked at it for more than a week.

"You got one hole!"

"Who?"

They pointed to me. "Who got the other?"

"Your father."

My father, a humpbacked old sailor with a face like a baked apple, came up to me and clapped me on the back. "Today, my boy, we're lucky!" he said. "Do you hear, boy? Luck came to us both at the same time. That means something." Impatiently he asked the time; it was only eleven o'clock.

I went up on deck, lit my pipe and gazed out to sea. It was dark, but it can be assumed that my eyes reflected what was taking place in my soul, as I made out images on the background of the night, visualizing what was so lacking in my own still young but already ruined life. . . .

At midnight I walked past the saloon and glanced in at the door. The bridegroom, a young pastor with a handsome blond head, sat at a table holding the Gospels in his hands. He was explaining something to a tall, gaunt Englishwoman. The bride, a very beautiful, shapely young woman, sat at her husband's side with her light blue eyes fixed on him. A tall, plump, elderly Englishman, a banker, with a repulsive red face, paced up and down the saloon. He was the husband of the middle-aged lady to whom the pastor was talking.

"Pastors have a habit of talking for hours," I thought. "He won't finish before morning." At one o'clock my father came to me, pulled me by the sleeve and said: "It's time. They've left the saloon."

In the twinkling of an eye I flew down the companionway and approached the familiar wall. Between this wall and the side of the ship there was a space where soot, water, and rats collected. I soon heard the heavy tread of the old man, my father. He cursed as he stumbled over a mat-sack and some kerosene cans. I felt for the hole in the wall and pulled out the square piece of wood I had so painstakingly sawed. I was looking at a thin, transparent muslin through which penetrated a soft, rosy light. Together with the light, my burning face was caressed by a delightful, sultry fragrance; this, no doubt, was the smell of an aristocratic bedroom. In order to see the room it was necessary to draw aside the muslin with two fingers, which I hastened to do. I saw bronze, velvet, lace, all bathed in a pink glow. About ten feet from my face stood the bed.

"Let me have your place," said my father, impatiently pushing me aside. "I can see better here." I did not answer him. "Your eyes are better than mine, boy, and it makes no difference to you if you look from far or near."

"Be quiet," I said, "they might hear us."

The bride sat on the side of the bed, dangling her little feet in a foot muff. She was staring at the floor. Before her stood her husband, the young pastor. He was telling her something, what I do not know; the noise of the steamer made it impossible for me to hear. He spoke passionately, with gestures, his eyes flashing. She listened and shook her head in refusal.

"The devil!" my father muttered. "A rat bit me!"

I pressed my chest to the wall, as if fearing my heart would jump out. My head was burning.

The bride and groom talked at great length. At last he sank to his knees and held out his arms, imploring her. She shook her head in refusal. He leaped to his feet, crossed the cabin, and from the expression on his face and the movements of his arms I surmised that he was threatening her. The young wife rose and went slowly towards the wall where I was standing. She stopped near the opening and stood motionless in thought. I devoured her face with my eyes. It seemed to me that she was suffering, struggling with herself, not knowing what to do; but at the same time her features expressed anger. I did not understand it.

We continued to stand there face to face for above five minutes, then she moved slowly away and, pausing in the middle of the cabin, nodded to the pastor—a sign of consent, undoubtedly. He smiled happily, kissed her hand and went out.

Within three minutes the door opened and the pastor reentered followed by the tall, plump Englishman whom I mentioned above. The Englishman went over to the bed and asked the beautiful woman a question. Pale, not looking at him, she nodded her head affirmatively. The banker then took out of his pocket a packet of some sort—evidently bank notes—and handed it to the pastor, who examined it, counted it, bowed and went out. The elderly Englishman locked the door after him.

I sprang away from the wall as if I had been stung. I was frightened. It seemed to me the wind was tearing our ship to pieces, that we were going down. My father, that drunken, debauched old man, took me by the arm and said: "Let's go away from here! You shouldn't see that. You're still a boy."

He was hardly able to stand. I carried him up the steep winding stairs. Above an autumn rain had begun to fall.

[1884–Russia]

QUESTIONS

1. What do we as well as the two sailors believe to be happening in the cabin as the new bride argues with her husband? Why do we assume what we do?
2. What does the story say about the relation of convention and reality?
3. Characterize the narrator. What kind of narrator is he? Is he really base? If not, why does he think of himself as such? Why are we inclined to accept what he tells us?
4. What other elements of fiction does Chekhov work with here? Comment especially on the plot and setting (the crawl space as opposed to the bridal cabin).
5. What is the overall effect of the story? In what way does the story demonstrate dramatically that we are all bound by conventional views?

WRITING SUGGESTIONS

1. In a paragraph or two, analyze the story with regard to its narrative point of view. What clues are we given well before the end as to the type of narrator we're dealing with? What might keep us from picking up on these clues until a second reading?
2. Convention is a powerful force, as Chekhov's story brings home. Write an essay on some incident, perhaps from your own life, that illustrates how we tend to see things through the prism of convention and how seeing thus restricts our understanding of reality.

The Buffalos

William Carlos Williams

Once I had a beautiful friend whom I loved and who loved me. It was not easy for us to see each other, every moment that we could spend together having to be stolen. So that it was only at great cost of trouble and invention that we succeeded in our small enterprises. Even then, it was sometimes months together before we could meet at all.

Thus our moments were very precious and for a long time we enjoyed them to the full. What did we do? Is it necessary to say, for who would believe it, either way? We were happy together and we were young enough to have illusions so that the time passed pleasantly uphill and downhill as it does under such circumstances.

But the lady, whom I shall call Francie, had one defect— or habit, rather, which at first amused me. She was a great talker for woman's rights.

All this happened in those days when Mrs. Pankhurst in England and the others here would be parading the streets with banners demanding equal rights with men. Votes for Women was their slogan which they put forward on every occasion.

This might be well enough for the run of those who with seamed faces and angry looks talked from platforms and even upon street corners but it was nothing for the lovely woman with whom I rushed so eagerly to spend my hardly won minutes.

Often such matters did not come into our talk but we would sway as one person in thought and word during an entire afternoon.

But at other times, whether it was the moon or what we had eaten that day or how we had slept the night before or what, things would at once on my arrival start to run away. And the invariable twist which the conversation would take would be toward politics and woman's rights.

I objected. It wasted our time. But this only inflamed the spirit of the lady to such a point that I found I was getting nowhere. Of course it was important, she objected, for women to have the vote. What did I mean?

I meant, I tried to explain, that the important thing for us to do when we were together was to enjoy each other and not to run off on something which concerned us not at all.

No, she almost snorted, it does not concern us. It does not concern you, you mean. You have the vote, what do you care? But we who are the mothers of the nation are not supposed to have the brains for it. No, we haven't the brains of a street cleaner.

But that isn't it, I tried to say. I acknowledge that you women are perhaps far more suited to rule than we men are but why bother about such a trifle. I would gladly give you my vote, I said, if I could. But you, my dear, are beautiful, do you not understand?

Rot, she retorted. You are trying to treat me like a child. If you haven't the manhood to treasure the vote, your prerogative as a citizen of the United States, I must say I thought more of you. President Roosevelt . . .

Oh, my God, I couldn't help crying.

Yes, Roosevelt, she repeated. And I must explain that the lady always pronounced the former president's name as though it had an a in the middle. Roosavelt is for us and with his help, I tell you, it will go through. But you are a Democrat, she ended haughtily.

Don't imagine that she was fooling when she said these things. Not on your life. And that is what gave me my first idea. I could have pretended to be won over or I might perhaps have diverted the flood of conversation with a gift or a loving gesture of some startling sort. But one day when Francie was in the middle of one of her suffragist tirades I noted how beautiful she was in the heat of her excitement and I resolved then and there that I was luckier than I thought.

I took it as my pleasure from that time forward for almost a month to be greatly interested in what she had to say, raising objection after objection to torment her. Meanwhile I drank in the fiery looks of her scornful eyes, the lovely curl of her lips. I watched the glow mount in her cheeks. All her features would brighten, take a form and a fire that was delectable to me. I had found a way to enjoy this bad habit from which I could not break her.

Occasionally at the very height of her railing at me I would quietly take her in my arms. And if she did not grow at once furiously angry she would say no more and the time for my departure would rush upon like a storm.

But the woman was really obsessed with this idea. I grew tired of my pastime of inciting her to display her plumage, so to speak. It really was too much. What in the world could she mean? Was it a form of shyness, of dull wit? an attempt to upset my too tranquil pleasure in her till it became something more biting? Was she not really trying to defend herself, to break down my guard—to have me take her—more seriously than I desired? I thought of all the reasons but decided finally that I didn't give a damn for them anyway. Beautiful as she was—and often a passionate mistress—I was growing bored.

So one day when she had started again on her favorite theme I halted her rather abruptly. Let me tell you a story, I said.

She made no reply but sat up a little straighter, her full lips pressed firmly together, and looked me square in the eye.

I have been down in the meadows on an inspection trip today, I told her, and while I was there one of the foremen of our ditching gang pointed out a hut to me. It is his own but he has rented it to three men who live there the year round, except in the cold of winter, when they board in Jersey City, he told me.

There are three of them, young fellows who earn their living there in that desolate spot, can you imagine how? In the late fall they begin to gather the down from the dry cattails which they pack into bags and sells as stuffing for cheap furniture. Later they trap muskrats. There are many of these rodents still in the swamps, and do you know what a muskrat skin brings? A dollar and a half for a good one sometimes. And in the spring and summer they pick blueberries.

But what has this to do with me? Francie asked.

Do you not see? answered I. The men earn their living that way, they are independent, self-supporting. The three work together; when two are out the third prepares the meals. They even have a few dollars over sometimes for small pleasures. Then the three go off together, to Jersey City, to Hoboken or wherever it might be.

Yes, I suppose they go to a saloon and get drunk.

Oh, I suppose so, but at least they manage it very well together and have done so for several years.

Now this gave me an idea, I continued. What is it that causes all the trouble in this world? Property, of course. It is what we own, the thing that gives us our importance—as it seems—the thing that has been largely the monopoly of the male down through the centuries, the thing finally that has governed the vote. And the thing for which we go to war, the thing for which we fight, even to quarrels between lovers.

And my idea is this. Let the men get rid of their property. If the women want the vote, give it to them, give them all the votes there are to be had, give them the votes the men have had also. And at the same time give them all the property of the world. They are the ones who biologically need it most, they are the ones economically, reasonably who should have it. You have convinced me by your suffragist arguments that you are right.

Francie looked at me hard but said nothing, perhaps she already sensed my waning affections.

And then, I said, we should have a society something like this: The women, possessing all the land, all the means for acquiring industrial wealth, would live in cities scattered over the country, walled cities defended by whatever weapons or armaments happened to be the fashion and from which all men should be excluded.

Meanwhile the men would gather in herds about the woods and plains, like the buffalo who used to be seen from the train windows on the great plains in the middle of the last century. Divided into tribes the men would spend their time hunting, fishing and fighting as men used to do—with fists, with stones, clubs as they may desire—and no doubt they would be far happier than now.

Then once a year, at the proper times certain women of the cities would send out chosen emissaries, eunuchs perhaps, to trade with the tribes—then in the pink of condition, trained, hardened by their rigorous life out of doors—and those most able, most vigorous, most desirable would be admitted for the breeding.

At this Francie jumped to her feet, fire in her eyes and turning her back on me left the room. I quietly took up my hat, took out a cigarette and lit it and jumping into my roadster before the door turned quietly down the driveway and went my way. Perhaps as I went I saw a curtain slightly rustled in a window of the second floor, perhaps it was only my vanity that made me believe this.

[1932–U.S.A.]

QUESTIONS

1. "You are trying to treat me like a child," Francie is reported to have said to Williams's narrator. What evidence is there in the story that she was right?
2. What was the narrator's attitude toward Francie when he visited her? What do we learn of her through him? Did he truly love her, as he says he did?
3. What else can we say about the narrator here? Does he contradict himself anywhere? Is he serious in his discourse on the separation of men into herds? What do you make of his last sentence? What kind of narrator is he?

4. What does the title imply? What is the point of the story (as opposed to the point of its narrator)?

WRITING SUGGESTIONS

1. In a paragraph, argue that the narrator is right or that he is wrong in his judgments of Francie. Use evidence from the story for support, and explain what attitude the story sways the reader to take?
2. Write an essay describing the narrator of "The Buffalos." Define his mentality in some detail, support your judgment point by point, and draw a conclusion as to the story's theme from what you say about its narrator.
3. Write a diary entry on the last visit of the narrator of "The Buffalos" from Francie's outlook (it is her diary). Try to be true to whatever you learn about her in the story (for instances, if you think she is refined, then don't have her rant and rave). What might she think about the man and the end of their relationship?

Stories and Texts for Nothing, 4

Samuel Beckett

Where would I go, if I could go, who would I be, if I could be, what would I say, if I had a voice, who says this, saying it's me? Answer simply, someone answer simply. It's the same old stranger as ever, for whom alone accusative I exist, in the pit of my inexistence, of his, of ours, there's a simple answer. It's not with thinking he'll find me, but what is he to do, living and bewildered, yes, living, say what he may. Forget me, know me not, yes, that would be the wisest, none better able than he. Why this sudden affability after such desertion, it's easy to understand, that's what he says, but he doesn't understand. I'm not in his head, nowhere in his old body, and yet I'm there, for him I'm there, with him, hence all the confusion. That should have been enough for him, to have found me absent, but it's not, he wants me there, with a form and a world, like him, in spite of him, me who am everything, like him who is nothing. And when he feels me void of existence it's of his he would have me void, and vice versa, mad, mad, he's mad. The truth is he's looking for me to kill me, to have me dead like him, dead like the living. He knows all that, but it's no help his knowing it, I don't know it, I know nothing. He protests he doesn't reason and does nothing but reason, crooked, as if that could improve matters. He thinks words fail him, he thinks because words fail him he's on his way to my speechlessness, to being speechless with my speechlessness, he would like it to be my fault that words fail him, of course words fail him. He tells his story every five minutes, saying it is not his, there's cleverness for you. He would like it to be my fault that he has no story, of course he has no story, that's no reason for trying to foist one on me. That's how he reasons, wide of the mark, but wide of what mark, answer us that. He has me say things saying it's not me, there's profundity for you, he has me who say nothing say it's not me. All that is truly crass. If at least he would dignify me with the third person, like his other figments, not he, he'll be satisfied with nothing less than me, for his me. When he had me, when he was me, he couldn't get rid of me quick enough, I didn't exist, he couldn't have that, that was no kind of life, of course I didn't exist, any more than he did, of course it was no kind of life, now he has it, his kind of life, let him lose it, if he wants to be in peace, with a bit of luck. His life, what a mine, what a life, he can't have that, you can't fool him, ergo it's not his, it's not him, what a thought, treat him like that, like a vulgar Molloy, a common Malone, those mere mortals, happy mortals, have a heart, land him in that shit, who never stirred, who is none but me, all things considered, and what things, and how considered, he had only to keep out of it. That's how he speaks, this evening, how he has me speak, how he speaks to himself, how I speak, there is only me, this evening, here, on earth, and a voice that makes no sound because it goes towards none, and a head strewn with arms laid down and corpses fighting fresh, and a body, I nearly forgot. This evening, I say this evening, perhaps it's morning. And all these things, what things, all about me, I won't deny them any more, there's no sense in that any more. If it's nature perhaps it's trees and birds, they go together, water and air, so that all may go on, I don't need to know the details, perhaps I'm sitting under a palm. Or it's a room, with furniture, all that's required to make life comfortable, dark, because of the wall outside the window. What am I doing, talking, having my figments talk, it can only be me. Spells of silence too, when I listen, and hear the local sounds, the world sounds, see what an effort I make, to be reasonable. There's my life, why not, it is one, if you like, if you must, I don't say no, this evening. There has to be one, it seems, once there is a speech, no need of a story, a story is not compulsory, just a life, that's the mistake I made, one of the mistakes, to have wanted a story for myself, whereas life alone is enough. I'm making progress, it was time, I'll learn to keep my foul mouth shut before I'm done, if nothing foreseen crops up. But he who somehow comes and goes, unaided from place to place, even though nothing happens to him, true, what of him? I stay here, sitting, if I'm sitting, often I feel sitting, sometimes standing, it's one or the other, or lying down, there's another possibility, often I feel lying down, it's one of the three, or kneeling. What counts is to be in the world, the posture is immaterial, so long as one is on earth. To breathe is all that is required, there is no obligation to ramble, or receive company, you may even believe yourself dead on condition you make no bones about it, what more liberal regimen could be imagined, I don't know, I don't imagine. No point under such circumstances in saying I am somewhere else, someone else, such as I am I have all I need to hand, for to do what, I don't know, all I have to do, there I am on my own again at last, what a relief that must be. Yes, there are moments, like this moment, when I seem almost restored to the feasible. Then it goes, all goes, and I'm far again, with a far story again, I wait for me afar for my story to begin, to end, and again this voice cannot be mine. That's where I'd go, if I could go, that's who I'd be, if I could be.

[1958–Ireland]

QUESTIONS

1. Who narrates this piece? What is the narrator's fundamental problem?
2. This monologue exemplifies a narrative technique called stream-of-consciousness, which renders the thoughts of a character, with all the jumps and inconsistencies that mark actual thought, as a character thinks them. What conclusions can we draw about the self that is doing the thinking in this story?
3. The narrator realizes that "life alone is enough." Why can't he rest with this knowledge?
4. Putting the story aside, what is your impression of it overall? What can you say about its narrator that might suggest its meaning?

WRITING SUGGESTIONS

1. Write a paragraph explaining the effect on the reader of the special type of narration Beckett employs (see question 2 above), and the suitability of this technique to the subject matter of Beckett's story.
2. Write a bit of stream-of-consciousness yourself. Focus on some topic and let your mind wander all around it as you write. See to what extent you can be fluid as Beckett in handling the stream of the mind thinking intensely.

Frankie the Newspaperman

William Carlos Williams

She's one of the funniest women I have ever known. Everything amuses her.

What's her name?

Mrs. Weber. She has a son named Frankie and she's always talking about Frankie. He must be a fairly bright boy at that because he's a senior in high school at seventeen. That's not bad around here. Frankie is always in trouble.

She's your washerwoman, you say?

Yes, just this morning she was down on her knees scrubbing floor and laughing to herself when I came in from downtown. What is it, Margaret? I said to her. What's so funny now?

My son Frankie, she says. He's in trouble again.

What's so funny about that?

They won't let him graduate from the school this year because he don't have enough algebra.

As a matter of fact Frankie wants to be a newspaperman. That's what he likes but they insist on his taking algebra and he doesn't want to do it.

Well? I said. Is that all?

No. But you know he has an English teacher who has a very flat chest and the children all make fun of her.

That's not nice, I said.

No. But anyhow they do. So yesterday they had some kind of sentences they had to make and she made Frankie stand up for her. They had to give a sentence, they had to make it up. And then when they had given the sentence they had to give an answer to it.

264

Some sort of exercise, I suppose.

Yes, that's it. So she asked Frankie to make a sentence and to give an answer to it afterward to tell why he had thought of it. So he says, I think we should ask everybody to chip in a dollar and take up a collection for the teacher.

So then she asks him why. Why should they take up a collection for the teacher? You see he had to give a good answer.

And what did he say?

Well, he says that all the pupils should chip in a dollar each—because she is so flat busted!

What? What? What? I said. No wonder she disciplined him.

But Margaret was laughing fit to kill as she grabbed the brush and started vigorously scrubbing the floor again.

[1950–U.S.A.]

QUESTIONS

1. Describe Frankie's mother and the story's narrator in turn. How do they differ?
2. How many narrators do we have in this story? What kinds are they? How would you describe Williams's narrative mode overall?
3. In what way is narration itself a possible theme here?

WRITING SUGGESTIONS

1. In a paragraph, contrast Frankie's mother (herself a narrator) and the narrator of the story overall. How does this contrast help shape our attitude toward the narrator and so condition our reception of his or her general outlook?
2. Write a short paper addressed to question 3 above. Consider such issues as these: How many narrators are there in Williams's story? What type of narrator is each? How do we come to judge each narrator? What is the point of the story with respect to narration?

The Vicar of Lynch

Logan Pearsall Smith

When I heard through country gossip of the strange happening at
Lynch which had caused so great a scandal, and had led to the
disappearance of the deaf old Vicar of that remote village, I collected all
the reports I could about it, for I felt that at the centre of this
uncomprehending talk and wild anecdote, there was something with more
meaning than a mere sudden outbreak of blasphemy and madness.

It appeared that the old Vicar, after some years spent in the quiet
discharge of his parochial duties, had been noticed to become more and
more odd in his appearance and behaviour; and it was also said that he had
gradually introduced certain alterations into the Church services. These
had been vaguely supposed at the time to be of a High Church character,
but afterward they were put down to a growing mental derangement,
which had finally culminated at that infamous Harvest Festival, when his
career as a clergyman of the Church of England had ended. On this
painful occasion the old man had come into church outlandishly dressed,
and had gone through a service with chanted gibberish and unaccustomed
gestures, and prayers which were unfamiliar to his congregation. There
was also talk of a woman's figure on the altar, which the Vicar had
unveiled at a solemn moment in this performance; and I also heard echo of
other gossip—gossip that was, however, authoritatively contradicted and
suppressed as much as possible—about the use of certain other symbols of
a most unsuitable kind. Then a few days after the old man had
disappeared—some of the neighbours believed that he was dead; some,
that he was now shut up in an asylum for the insane.

Such was the fantastic and almost incredible talk I listened to, but in which, as I say, I found more meaning than my neighbours. For one thing, although they knew that the Vicar had come from Oxford to this remote College living, they knew nothing of his work and scholarly reputation in that University, and none of them had probably ever heard of—much less read—an important book which he had written, and which was the standard work on his special subject. To them he was simply a deaf, eccentric, and solitary clergyman; and I think I was the only person in the neighbourhood who had conversed with him on the subject concerning which he was the greatest living authority in England.

For I had seen the old man once—curiously enough at the time of a Harvest Festival, though it was some years before the one which had led to his disappearance. Bicycling one day over the hills, I had ridden down into a valley of cornfields, and then, passing along an unfenced road that ran across a wide expanse of stubble, I came, after getting off to open three or four gates, upon a group of thatched cottages, with a little, unrestored Norman church standing among great elms. I left my bicycle and walked through the churchyard, and as I went into the church, through its deeply-recessed Norman doorway, a surprisingly pretty sight met my eyes. The dim, cool, little interior was set out and richly adorned with an abundance of fruit and vegetables, yellow gourds, apples and plums and golden wheat-sheaves, great loaves of bread, and garlands of September flowers. A shabby-looking old clergyman was standing on the top of a step-ladder, finishing the decorations, when I entered. As soon as he saw me he came down, and I spoke to him, praising the decorations, and raising my voice a little, for I noticed that he was deaf. We spoke of the Harvest Festival; and as I soon perceived that I was talking with a man of books and University education, I ventured to hint at what had vividly impressed me in that old, gaudily-decorated church—its pagan character, as if it were a rude archaic temple in some corner of the antique world, which had been adorned, two thousand years ago, by pious country folk for some local festival. The old clergyman was not in the least shocked by my remark; it seemed indeed rather to please him; there was, he agreed, something of a pagan character in the modern Harvest Festival—it was no doubt a bit of the old primitive Vegetation Ritual, the old Religion of the soil; a Festival which, like so many others, had not been destroyed by Christianity, but absorbed into it, and given a new meaning. "Indeed," he added, talking on as if the subject interested him, and expressing himself with a certain donnish carefulness of speech that I found pleasant to listen to, "the Harvest Festival is undoubtedly a survival of the prehistoric worship of that Corn Goddess who, in classical times, was called Demeter and Ioulo and Ceres, but whose cult as an Earth-Mother and Corn-Spirit is of much greater antiquity. For there is no doubt that this Vegetation Spirit has been worshipped from the earliest times by agricultural peoples; the wheat fields and ripe harvest being naturally suggestive of the presence amid the corn of a kindly Being, who, in return for due rites and offerings, will vouchsafe nourishing rains and golden harvest." He mentioned the references in Virgil, and the description in Theocritus of a Sicilian Harvest Festival—these were no doubt familiar to me; but if I was interested in the subject, I should find, he said, much more information collected in a book which he had written, but of which I had probably never heard, about the Vegetation Deities in Greek Religion. I knew the book, and felt now much interested in my chance meeting with its author; and after expressing this as best I could, I rode off, promising to visit him again. This promise I was never able to fulfil; but when afterward, on my return to the neighbour-hood, I heard of that unhappy scandal, my memory of this meeting and our talk enabled me to form a theory as to what had really happened.

It seemed plain to me that the change had been too violent for this elderly student, taken from his books and college rooms and set down in the solitude of this remote valley, amid the richness and living sap of Nature. The gay spectacle, right under his old eyes, of growing shoots and budding foliage, of blossoming and flowering, and the ripening of fruits and crops, the pairing of birds and the mating of cattle, had little by little (such was my theory) unhinged his brains. More and more his thoughts had come to dwell, not on the doctrines of the Church in which he had long ago taken orders, but on the pagan rites which had formed his life-long study, and which had been the expression of ways not unlike the agricultural life amid which he now found himself living. So as his derangement grew upon him in his isolation, he had gradually trans-formed, with a holy cunning, the Christian services, and led his little congregation, all unknown to themselves, back toward their ancestral worship of the Corn-Goddess. At last he had thrown away all disguise, and had appeared as a hierophant of Demeter, dressed in a fawn skin, with a crown of poplar leaves, and pedantically carrying the mystic basket and the winnowing fan appropriate to these mysteries. The wheaten posset he offered the shocked communicants belonged to these also, and the figure of a woman on the altar was of course the holy Wheatsheaf, whose unveiling was the culminating point in that famous ritual.

It is much to be regretted that I could not recover full and more exact details of that celebration, in which this great scholar had probably embodied his mature knowledge concerning a subject which has puzzled generations of students. But what powers of careful observation could one expect from a group of labourers and small farmers? Some of the things that reached my ears I refused to believe—the mention of pig's blood, for instance, and especially the talk of certain ithyphallic symbols, which the choir boys, it was whispered, had carried in their hands about the church in ceremonious procession. Village people have strange imaginations; and to this event, growing more and more monstrous as they talked it over, they must themselves have added this grotesque detail. However, I have written to consult an Oxford authority on this interesting point, and he has been kind enough to explain at length that although at the *Haloa*, or winter festival of the Corn-Goddess, and also at the *Chloeia*, or festival in early spring, some symbolization of the reproductive powers of Nature would be proper and appropriate, such ritualism would have been quite out of place at the Thalysia, or autumn festival of thanksgiving. I feel certain that a solecism of this nature—the introduction into a particular rite of features not sanctioned by the texts—would have seemed a shocking thing to one who had always been so accurate a scholar.

[1917–U.S.A.]

QUESTIONS

1. The narrator of this story is learned, snobbish, observant, strongly rational, articulate, proper, staid, and passionless. What details in the text support this statement?
2. In the last paragraph, the narrator's reasoning is spurious. How so? Also, why should he accept some of the gossip he has heard but reject the more extreme stories as unfounded? Does he have an ax to grind?
3. Compare and contrast the Vicar and the narrator, especially as to the fervor of their spirituality. What light does their difference shed on the narrator's motives and judgments?
4. In part, "The Vicar of Lynch" is a mystery waiting to be solved by the reader. Playing the role of detective, try to solve the riddles the story presents us with: Was the Vicar really mad or did he have a purpose in his actions that the personality of the narrator keeps him (the narrator) from seeing? What is the narrator's motive in defending the Vicar as he does? What became of the Vicar? Relate your answer to this last question to your conception of the story's theme.

WRITING SUGGESTIONS

1. In a paragraph argue that the Vicar was perfectly sane, motivated only by a desire to show his parishioners something about the substance as well as the form of their religion.

2. Write a paragraph assessing the narrator's credibility and showing how you arrive at your assessment.

3. Without meaning to, Smith's narrator demonstrates the limits of rationality. Write an essay discussing these limits, drawing on "The Vicar of Lynch" and your own experience for examples.

4. Write a paragraph or short essay arguing that Smith's narrator confuses form and substance, and that this is why he cannot understand the Vicar's intentions.

5. In a paragraph or more, construct a plausible explanation of what became of the Vicar (you might consider the story's title in this regard). In light of your explanation, what is the story's theme?

·6·

MOOD/IRONY/STYLE

INTERPRETING MOOD

Applied to fiction, "mood" means what it means in our everyday conversation when we speak of feeling happy, gloomy, angry, and so forth. Described by such adjectives as "lighthearted," "nostalgic," "humorous," "sad," or "tragic," mood, then, is the emotional state that a story produces in the reader. Every story creates a mood of some sort, and some stories arouse several different moods. Of course, no one tells us how we should feel as we read a story, just as no one tells us what kind of a narrator we have, or what is ironic, or what symbols a story contains and what they mean. These things we must judge for ourselves. As to mood specifically, in order to interpret the mood of a story, what is most important is for you to be aware of your own feelings. Does a story make you feel sad, or happy, or nostalgic, or angry? Although one can respond inappropriately to a story just as one can to an event in real life, the chances are good that what you feel as you read is what you should feel. If you are aware of your own feelings, that is, you will most likely be in touch with the mood of the given story. And if you are aware of its mood, you will be close to its theme, for mood and theme are intimately linked. To feel that one story is comic and another tragic is in each case to infer attitude; and attitude, as we've discussed, is often equivalent to theme.

Notice that I said "your own feelings." Here we must make another crucial distinction, like the one between author and narrator. When reading, you must clearly distinguish between the moods of characters within a story—including its narrator—and the mood or moods created in

271

you by the story overall. Quickly look back at Thurber's "The Unicorn in the Garden" in this regard (pages 47–48). To us, the wife's being carted off to the "booby hatch" is funny; Thurber has characterized her in such a way as to curtail any sympathy we might have. We're glad to see her dragged off protesting all the way, though we realize that *she* does not feel happy about the turn of events. A character in a story, then, might feel sad, yet the story itself be comic; so *we* don't feel sad. The story overall makes us laugh; so its mood is humorous, however sad a particular character might feel. To be sure, in many stories the mood of one character or another does coincide with that of the story. Stories of this sort are so constructed as to make us sympathize with these characters and thus to assume their moods ourselves. But this is not true of all pieces of fiction. If you always make the distinction between the moods of characters and the mood of the story overall, you'll be prepared to deal with stories in which the two diverge; stories in which the two coincide will take care of themselves.

One more point about mood should be stressed: mood is created entirely by other elements. When analyzing the mood of a story, therefore, one must look at the other elements that go into its making in order to demonstrate its mood. We've just seen that characterization can be an agent of mood; so can setting. For example, the setting of the typical horror story (lightning, thunder, rain, an old castle, a wolf howling) very much creates mood. In analyzing the mood of such a story, then, one would need to consider setting. Plot, too, especially if it builds suspense or takes an ironic turn, can give rise to mood. Style is also important in establishing mood, as we'll see shortly. In sum, you must take into account all of the elements found in a story when focusing on its mood and how that mood is aroused in you, the reader.

INCONGRUITY: LIFE AND FICTION

I have mentioned irony already several times in passing, for, though irony is not a mood as such, the recognition of irony always establishes mood. Spanning both the tragic and the comic, the satiric and the pathetic, irony inevitably involves a sense of discrepancy. Rationality aside, human existence is a mass of incongruities. We know that appearances can deceive, that language can be used to conceal as well as reveal, that expectations and realizations can and do often diverge. The very texture of human life seems in good measure to be ironic. It is no wonder, then, that irony should be prevalent in literature, for literary irony simply reflects and acts as a comment upon the ironies of everyday existence. The doubleness of irony allows an author to capture concisely the complexity of human awareness in the face of life's contradictions, incongruities, discrepancies. Most important, irony in a text immediately governs our understanding. But we must be able to spot irony when irony is present. To do so it is useful to know the three primary types of irony: verbal, circumstantial, and dramatic.

Verbal Irony

The simplest type of irony, this type entails saying the opposite of what is meant. The discrepancy lies between what has been said and what is known to be true. So you might say, "What a beautiful day," when it's really rotten out; or "Boy, are you smart," when what is meant is "stupid." (The latter, with its mocking tone, is an example of sarcasm, which is a subtype of verbal irony.) But how is such irony recognized? The answer is *by the context*. Take "What a beautiful day," meaning "unutterably horrible." The speaker would signal an ironic intent by facial expression, gesture, and tone of voice (perhaps by giving the word "beautiful" a special twist); but our recognition of an ironic possibility in the first place comes from our knowledge that it is not a beautiful day. Unless we had reason to think the speaker mad, we would grasp the ironic nature of the statement because it would be at odds with the facts. In fiction, context is all. We must weigh every statement of every character (including the narrator) against the known facts as established in a story. If there is a discrepancy, then the character is either lying or being ironic. The function of verbal irony in fiction is the same as its function in ordinary discourse: whenever it is found, verbal irony is a rhetorical device that helps drive home a point with concision and with force.

Circumstantial Irony

The discrepancy of this type of irony (also called "situational irony") lies in the difference between what seems (or is expected) to be and what actually is; or between what is expected (or intended) to happen and what does happen. It is ironic, for instance, that the pastor in Chekhov's "At Sea" (pages 252–54) turns out to be entirely different from what he seems and what we expect; it is equally ironic that Tom, in Maugham's "The Ant and the Grasshopper" (pages 288–91), should unexpectedly, and through no effort of his own, wind up rich. Guy de Maupassant's "The Venus of Branzia" (pages 294–96) provides another example of circumstantial irony. In this story a man finds himself trapped by his own beliefs. Unwittingly, he helped to create that very trap by teaching some of those beliefs to his wife. He is thus "hoisted by his own petard" (that is, blown up by his own bomb).

Dramatic Irony

Here the discrepancy lies between what is believed by a character (or characters) and what the reader knows to be true. A character might be blind to something, or believe something about another character, or even about himself or herself, that isn't true. The reader, however, knows better and so is in a position to assess the character's judgments and beliefs. In Maugham's "The Ant and the Grasshopper" (pages 288–91), for instance, we come to know a good deal more about George than George himself knows. He believes that he is suffering because of his brother, Tom; we know that he suffers because of his own bad character as well as his childish notion of fairness. A sense of irony results from the divergence of understanding, his and ours, and in this case enables us to laugh at George at the end. Irony here very much helps to create a comic mood.

The hallmark of irony, whatever the type, is a sense of discrepancy or incongruity, a sense to which you should try to be alert and responsive. For irony always helps to shape the reader's attitude without intervening explanation (and thus helps the writer to dramatize and to gain compression). That is, to say that the mood of a story entails tragic irony, or sardonic irony, or comic irony, is to suggest the attitude we are to take toward the material at hand. Irony can make us laugh, or move us to tears, or instill horror or wonder or both. It touches us because we recognize it in some deep truth.

STYLE: THE MEDIUM AND THE MESSAGE

In everyday life we convey meaning as much by the various tones we project when speaking as by the meanings of our words and sentences. The same is true of fiction. Consider the following passage from Virginia Woolf's *Mrs. Dalloway:*

> Sir William Bradshaw stopped at the door to look at a picture. He looked in the corner for the engraver's name. His wife looked too. Sir William Bradshaw was so interested in art.

Was he, really? No, for the tone of the passage is mockingly ironic. Note the childish sentence pattern, as banal as judging a work of art by the name in the corner. Note the repetition of the name "Sir William Bradshaw" and how the repetition lends an air of pomposity. Note especially the single word "so," which serves to undercut the literal sense of the last sentence entirely. Much can be inferred from this passage: that Sir William's interest is in money and not art; that his wife shares that interest; that both are probably snobs. All of this we sense from the tone of voice of the narrator, and that tone is created by the author's style in the passage.

Style, then, is instrumental in establishing meaning. To borrow Marshall McLuhan's phrase, we might say that "the medium is the message." Certainly, how something is said greatly affects what is said. "I believe you are in error," for instance, is not the same statement as "You're wrong," and both are quite different from "You're full of it." A matter of style, the difference in the choice of words here is responsible for the radically different tones. Style refers to the words used (diction) and the sentence patterns they form (syntax), as well as to the effect gained by the choice of words and sentence patterns.

Diction means the selection of words, or the kind of words selected, in a given passage. It can be abstract or concrete ("a meal" vs. "a juicy steak"); literal or metaphorical ("the surface of the sea" vs. "the breast of the sea"); denotative or connotative ("domicile" vs. "home"). Is the language of a given passage flat or lyrical? Is the author's use of adjectives and adverbs copious or spare? Is the vocabulary primarily that of standard English, or is it marked by slang or perhaps by technical jargon? Even the sounds of words should be considered: some passages gain their effect by purposefully chosen patterns of sound, harsh and grating or liquid and soothing.

Syntax covers that aspect of verbal style having to do with how words and phrases are put together into sentences. Certainly, a story written in long, involved sentences will have an effect quite different from a story written in short, simple sentences, just as a story whose vocabulary tends to be literal and denotative will have a different effect from a story whose vocabulary is predominantely metaphorical and connotative. Sentences can be loose or periodic, with the main information coming either at the head or at the end; simple or complex, marked by much coordination or by much subordination; recurrent in pattern, with one type of pattern repeating, or varied. And all the choices an author makes as to syntax go into the making of the rhythm of a passage or a story overall, prose rhythm being a subtle contributor to the way in which fiction affects us.

Particular stylistic choices tend to be characteristic of particular writers. One writer is characteristically metaphorical and prefers complex sentences; another writes story after story in which syntax is simple and diction is slangy. Hemingway's style, for instance, is generally simple and Faulkner's is complex; and the two styles have vastly different effects on the reader, effects closely related to meaning. This does not mean, however, that the style of a story is uniform. The writer adjusts style to particular characters and circumstances. Therefore, we can often tell as much about characters from the ways in which they speak as we can about real people. Character contrast, too, is facilitated by an author's fashioning of different manners of speech for characters of different backgrounds and capacities.

Writers must make many choices about language in order to maintain control over their stories. In our turn, we as readers need to develop sensitivity to the intricate relationship between style and meaning, the medium and the message. To know an author well is to understand that author's characteristic choices; to grasp a particular story well is to understand how all aspects of its style contribute to its meaning. The more one reads, of course, the more precisely one can make determinations of this sort.

SUMMARY SUGGESTIONS: UNDERSTANDING MOOD/IRONY/STYLE

1. As you read, be aware of what you're feeling. What you feel has probably been engineered by the writer, so your feeling is a guide to meaning.

2. Be sure to distinguish the mood of a story overall from the mood or moods of individual characters. The two do not necessarily coincide.

3. Look for discrepancies between what is said and what is meant, or between what is expected and what happens, or between what a character believes and what you as the reader know to be true. Such discrepancies generally signal an ironic intent.

4. Hear the voices as you read and try to catch their various tones. Don't forget how much our tones of voice condition the meaning of what we say to each other. No less is true of the written language.

5. Determine the main stylistic features of the text at hand—long or short sentences, figurative or literal language, recurring patterns of verbal constructions. Though style will work its ends whether we know why or not, some attention to the language used in a story is always rewarding.

6. Most of all, take the crucial step from mood, tone, and style to meaning. That is, relate these qualities of a story to what you think it is about. Or perhaps I should put this the other way round: test what you think the theme of a story is against your perception of its mood, tone, and style overall. If the two judgments fit, the story is yours.

WRITING ON MOOD/IRONY/STYLE

Though mood, irony, and style are intimately linked, the best way to proceed in our discussion of writing on these topics is to take each up in turn. So, mood first. Should you choose or be asked to write about the mood of a story, you will be writing about what it makes you feel and why (not, note, what you feel *about* it, which is a different matter). As usual, the *why* will be the substance of what you write. That is, you must explain what it is about the story that creates in you the mood you feel when reading it. To support your thesis you will need to consider characterization, descriptive details, plot, and the like—whatever contributes to the mood. How does this or that character affect the way you feel? Does the plot take a surprising turn, thereby affecting you in some special way? Or perhaps the kind of language used touches you and makes you feel joyous, or angry, or reflective. Certainly you would also want to consider the theme of the story in so far as mood helps to establish the theme. Finally, you should always consider irony when writing on mood, for irony when present is instrumental in creating mood.

But if a story is ironic to the core, as is Chekhov's "At Sea" (pages 252–54), then irony itself can be taken as the basis of a paper. In writing on "At Sea," you might argue that the story is thematically or structurally ironic (your thesis); demonstrate how this is so by considering what discrepancy the theme itself involves and how this discrepancy is enacted in the story; and consider how the story entraps the reader in its irony in order to drive home its point.

Another way of dealing with irony is to classify the type of irony a given story exhibits and then to discuss the story in terms of that classification. Circumstantial and dramatic irony are especially well suited to use in this way. To suggest that a story is built on circumstantial or dramatic irony is to have a thesis immediately. What is left to do is to demonstrate how the story establishes the one or the other and how its type of irony goes into the making of its mood and theme. Maugham's "Appointment in Samarra" (page 292) would be an excellent story to treat in this way. Exemplifying both circumstantial and dramatic irony, the story creates a sense of divergence between what the servant believes and what the reader knows will happen (here would be your thesis); it does so by plot especially, which is structured so that the story's ironic revelation comes in its last sentence (support); the discrepancy produces a chill in the reader (mood, which points to the story's fatalistic theme) and allows the reader both to judge the servant's expectations and to see his circumstance as representative of how, finally, we are all trapped by fate (theme). For a paper, this outline would have to be expanded. But by classifying the type of irony found in Maugham's story, you have a thesis that could easily lead to a paper and that clearly directs what must be done.

One of the most interesting things to do with style is to compare authors as to style. Another is to consider several stories by the same author in order to define the author's characteristic style. To be sure, the general style of an author is perhaps the most challenging topic one can write on. For though omnipresent, style is elusive, and the stylistic habits of an author must be clearly distinguished from styles created for characters, including narrators. Nevertheless, fine pieces of writing have been done on Hemingway's terseness, Woolf's liquid rhythms, Faulkner's figurative language, and so forth. In pieces of this sort, the writer first specifies some general stylistic trait or traits of the author (thesis) and then exemplifies in detail from at least several works by that author (support). What is difficult about writing on style is not so much how to proceed as what evidence to use. If you are adventuresome and decide to write on style, you will need to take into account all that has been said about style in this chapter. Diction, imagery, figurative language, rhythm, and so forth—these will be your concerns.

Style in fiction, though a complex subject, is one of the most rewarding you can choose. Tackle it and do the best you can. With time and practice in analyzing style, you should find that your understanding of language and what it can do has deepened and, very possibly, that your own writing has improved. It is necessary to examine many types of style and to see the language used well in various ways before one can ever use it truly well oneself. But if you pursue the subject, then you will perhaps develop a style of your own.

GENERAL WRITING ASSIGNMENTS

1. (a) Write a dialogue between two people of very different backgrounds, places or origin, classes, or whatever. For example, you could confront a corporate president with a disgruntled stockboy; an authoritarian teacher with a recalcitrant student; a society lady with a bag lady. Whatever the case, the differing styles of speech of your characters should reflect their differing backgrounds, classes, and so one.

(b) Now write an analytic paragraph in which you compare and contrast the linguistic styles of your characters and point out what their styles suggest about them.

2. You probably know someone whose habitual tone of voice drives you mad. If so, write a paragraph on this person's usual tone. Describe it, analyze what makes for this type of tone (diction? sentence patterns? pacing? other things?), and try to get at why this tone of voice affects you as it does.

3. Briefly describe a horror movie you were frightened by, explaining what specifically it made you feel (that is, its mood). Then analyze how the mood was established. For example, what film techniques were used (camera angles, types of shot, et cetera)? Did plot or characterization come into play? What conventional devices, if any, were used (a stormy night, a wolf howling)? What other aspects of the setting contributed?

4. Recount something that happened to you that seemed ironic. Then analyze and discuss the irony. What type of irony was displayed by the incident? What was the discrepancy? What did your realization of the irony make you feel? Did your recognition of irony change your interpretation of the incident? If so, how?

5. Write a paragraph or essay on irony in everyday life. Address in particular verbal irony as a common rhetorical habit of speech. Most of us use verbal irony frequently. Why? What do we gain from such irony? You could also address the other types of irony. What circumstantial or dramatic ironies might you perceive as you move through a typical day? In what ways, if any, does the recognition of irony help you cope with your experience?

The Blue Bouquet*

Octavio Paz

I woke covered with sweat. Hot steam rose from the newly sprayed, red-brick pavement. A gray-winged butterfly, dazzled, circled the yellow light. I jumped from my hammock and crossed the room barefoot, careful not to step on some scorpion leaving his hideout for a bit of fresh air. I went to the little window and inhaled the country air. One could hear the breathing of the night, feminine, enormous. I returned to the center of the room, emptied water from a jar into a pewter basin, and wet my towel. I rubbed my chest and legs with the soaked cloth, dried myself a little, and, making sure that no bugs were hidden in the folds of my clothes, got dressed. I ran down the green stairway. At the door of the boardinghouse I bumped into the owner, a one-eyed taciturn fellow. Sitting on a wicker stool, he smoked, his eye half closed. In a hoarse voice, he asked:

"Where are you going?"

"To take a walk. It's too hot."

"Hmmm—everything's closed. And no streetlights around here. You'd better stay put."

I shrugged my shoulders, muttered "back soon" and plunged into the darkness. At first I couldn't see anything. I fumbled along the cobblestone street. I lit a cigarette. Suddenly the moon appeared from behind a black cloud, lighting a white wall that was crumbled in places. I stopped, blinded by such whiteness. Wind whistled slightly. I breathed the air of the tamarinds. The night hummed, full of leaves and insects. Crickets bivouacked in the tall grass. I raised my head: up there the stars too had set up camp. I thought that the universe was a vast system of signs, a conversation between giant beings. My actions, the cricket's saw, the star's

* Translated by Eliot Weinberger.

blink, were nothing but pauses and syllables, scattered phrases from that dialogue. What word could it be, of which I saw only a syllable? Who speaks the word? To whom is it spoken? I threw my cigarette down on the sidewalk. Falling, it drew a shining curve, shooting out brief sparks like a tiny comet.

I walked a long time, slowly. I felt free, secure between the lips that were at that moment speaking me with such happiness. The night was a garden of eyes. As I crossed the street, I heard someone come out of a doorway. I turned around, but could not distinguish anything. I hurried on. A few moments later I heard the dull shuffle of sandals on the hot stone. I didn't want to turn around, although I felt the shadow getting closer with every step. I tried to run. I couldn't. Suddenly I stopped short. Before I could defend myself, I felt the point of a knife in my back, and a sweet voice:

"Don't move, mister, or I'll stick it in."

Without turning, I asked:

"What do you want?"

"Your eyes, mister," answered the soft, almost painful voice.

"My eyes? What do you want with my eyes? Look, I've got some money. Not much, but it's something. I'll give you everything I have if you let me go. Don't kill me."

"Don't be afraid, mister. I won't kill you. I'm only going to take your eyes."

"But why do you want my eyes?" I asked again.

"My girlfriend has this whim. She wants a bouquet of blue eyes. And around here they're hard to find."

"My eyes won't help you. They're brown, not blue."

"Don't try to fool me, mister. I know very well that yours are blue."

"Don't take the eyes of a fellow man. I'll give you something else."

"Don't play saint with me," he said harshly. "Turn around."

I turned. He was small and fragile. His palm sombrero covered half his face. In his right hand he held a country machete that shone in the moonlight.

"Let me see your face."

I struck a match and put it close to my face. The brightness made me squint. He opened my eyelids with a firm hand. He couldn't see very well. Standing on tiptoe, he stared at me intensely. The flame burned my fingers. I dropped it. A silent moment passed.

"Are you convinced now? They're not blue."

"Pretty clever, aren't you?" he answered. "Let's see. Light another one."

I struck another match, and put it near my eyes. Grabbing my sleeve, he ordered:

"Kneel down."

I knelt. With one hand he grabbed me by the hair, pulling my head back. He bent over me, curious and tense, while his machete slowly dropped until it grazed my eyelids. I closed my eyes.

"Keep them open," he ordered.

I opened my eyes. The flame burned my lashes. All of the sudden, he let me go.

"All right, they're not blue. Beat it."

He vanished. I leaned against the wall, my head in my hands. I pulled myself together. Stumbling, falling, trying to get up again. I ran for an hour through the deserted town. When I got to the plaza, I saw the owner of the boardinghouse, still sitting in front of the door. I went in without saying a word. The next day I left town.

[1969–Mexico]

QUESTIONS

1. The first paragraph of this story sets a somewhat foreboding mood. How?
2. Shortly before the central incident, the narrator says, "I thought the universe was a vast system of signs." Is that view borne out as the story proceeds?
3. In his momentary happiness the narrator declares, "The night was a garden of eyes." In light of what happens, what is ironic here?
4. Why is the beginning of the sixth paragraph ("I walked a long time") ironic with respect to what follows? Who, finally, "speaks the word," a purposeful God or blind chance?
5. What is the mood of this story overall? How is it established?

WRITING SUGGESTIONS

1. (a) Write a paragraph in answer to question 5 above. In doing so, consider how plot and irony are agents of mood.

   (b) In discussing the story's mood, you were stating what the story makes you feel. Now, in a separate paragraph, discuss what you feel *about* the story. That is, what is your response, and what in "The Blue Bouquet" accounts for that response?

2. In a paragraph or more, discuss the discrepancy between the narrator's mood upon setting out and the terror that follows. How does this ironic contrast heighten the mood of the story overall? What theme does the contrast help to establish?

3. In a short paper, establish the theme of Paz's story and, using examples, discuss how this somewhat abstract theme is made concrete.

Innocence

Sean O'Faolain

All this month the nuns have been preparing my little boy for his first Confession. In a few days he will go in a crocodile from the school to the parish church; enter the strange-looking cabinet in the corner of the aisle and see in the dusk of this secretive box an old priest's face behind a grille. He will acknowledge his wickedness to this pale, crisis-crossed face. He will be a little frightened but he will enjoy it too, because he does not really believe any of it—for him it is a kind of game that the nuns and the priest are playing between them.

How could he believe it? The nuns tell him that the Infant Jesus is sad when he is wicked. But he is never wicked, so what can it matter? If they told him instead of the sorrow he causes the Weasel, or Two Toes, or the Robin in the Cow's Ear, all of which live in the fields below our house, he would believe it in just the same way. To be sure he tells lies, he is a terrible liar, and when he plays Rummy with me he cheats as often as he can, and when he is slow and I flurry him he flies into furious rages and his eyes swim with tears and he dashes the cards down and calls me A Pig. For this I love him so much that I hug him, because it is so transparent and innocent; and at night if I remember his tears I want to go into his room and hold his fat, sweaty hand that lies on the coverlet clutching some such treasure as an empty reel. How, then, can he believe that God could be angry with him because he tells lies or calls his daddy A Pig?

Yet, I hate to see him being prepared for his first Confession because one day he will really do something wicked, and I know the fear that will come over him on that day—and I cannot prevent it.

I have never forgotten the first time I knew that I had committed sin. I had been going to Confession for years, ever since I was seven, as he is now, telling the same things time after time just as he will do. "Father, I told a lie . . . Father, I forgot to say my morning prayers . . . Father, I was disobedient to my parents . . . And that is all, Father." It was always quite true: I had done these things; but, as with him, it was only true as a fable or a mock-battle is true since none of these things were any more sinful than childish lies and rages. Until, one dim, wintry afternoon, not long after Christmas, when I went as usual to Confession in an old, dark, windy church called Saint Augustine's, down a side-lane, away from the city's traffic, a place as cold and damp and smelly as a tomb. It has since been pulled down and if they had not pulled it down it must soon have fallen down. It was the sort of church where there was always a beggar or two sheltering from the weather in the porch or in the dusky part under the back gallery; and always some poor shawled woman sighing her prayers in a corner like the wind fluttering in the slates. The paint was always clean and fresh, but the floor and the benches and the woodwork were battered and worn by the generations. The priests dressed in the usual black Augustinian garment with a cowl and a leather cincture. Altogether, a stranger would have found it a gloomy place. But I was familiar with it ever since my mother brought me there to dedicate me to Saint Monica, the mother of Augustine, and I loved the bright candles before her picture, and the dark nooks under the galleries, and the painted tondos on the ceiling, and the stuffy confessional boxes with their heavy purple curtains, underneath which the heels of the penitents stuck out when they knelt to the grille.

There I was, glad to be out of the January cold, kneeling before Saint Monica, brilliant with the candles of her mendicants. I was reading down through the lists of sins in my penny prayer-book, heeding the ones I knew, passing over the ones I didn't know, when I suddenly stopped at the name of a sin that I had hitherto passed by as having nothing to do with me.

As I write down these words I again feel the terror that crept into me like a snake as I realized that I knew that sin. I knew it well. No criminal who feels the sudden grip of a policeman on his arm can have felt more fear than I did as I stared at the horrible words . . .

I joined the long silent queue of penitents seated against the wall. I went, at last, into the dark confessional. I told my usual innocent litany. I whispered the sin.

Now, the old priest inside the confessional was a very aged man. He was so old and feeble that the community rarely allowed him to do anything but say Mass and hear Confessions. Whenever they let him preach he would ramble on and on for an hour; people would get up and go away; the sacristan would peep out in despair through the sacristy door; and in the end an altar-boy would be sent out to ring the great gong on the altar-steps to make him stop. I have seen the boy come out three times to the gong before the old man could be lured down from the pulpit.

When this old priest heard what I said to him he gave a groan that must have been heard in the farthest corner of the church. He leaned his face against the wire and called me his "child," as all priests in the confessional call every penitent. Then he began to question me about the details. I had not counted on this. I had thought that I would say my sin and be forgiven: for up to this every priest had merely told me that I was a very good little boy and asked me to pray for him as if I were a little angel whose prayers had a special efficacy, and then I would be dismissed jumping with joy.

To his questions I replied tremulously that it had happened "more than once"—How soon we begin to evade the truth!—and, I said, "Yes, Father, it was with another." At this he let out another groan so that I wanted to beg him to be quiet or the people outside would hear him. Then he asked me a question that made my clasped hands sweat and shake on the ledge of the grille. He asked me if any harm had been done to me. At first I didn't know what he meant. Then horrible shapes of understanding came creeping towards me along the dark road of my ignorance, as, in some indistinct manner, I recognized that he was mistaking me for a girl! I cried out that nothing at all had happened, Father. Nothing! Nothing! Nothing! But he only sighed like the south wind and said:

"Ah, my poor child, you won't know for several months."

I now had no desire but to escape. I was ready to tell him any story, any lie, if he would only stop his questions. What I did say I don't know but in some fashion I must have made the old man understand that I was a male sinner. For his next question, which utterly broke me, was:

"I see, I see. Well, tell me, my poor child. Was she married or unmarried?"

I need hardly say that as I remember this now I laugh at it for an absurd misadventure, and I have sometimes made my friends laugh at his questions and his groans, and at me with my two skinny heels sticking out under the curtains and knocking like castanets, and the next penitents wondering what on earth was going on inside the box. But, then, I was like a pup caught in a bramble bush, recanting and retracting and trying to get to the point where he would say the blessed words "*Absolvo te. . .*" and tell me what my penance would be.

What I said I cannot recall. All I remember distinctly is how I emerged under the eyes of the queue, walked up the aisle, as far away as I could get from the brightness of Saint Monica into the darkest corner under the gallery where the poorest of the poor crowd on Sundays. I saw everything through smoke. The scarlet eye of the sanctuary lamp—the only illumination apart from the candles before the shrine—stared at me. The shawled woman sighed at me. The wind under my bare knees crept away from me. A beggar in a corner, picking his nose and scratching himself, was Purity itself compared to me.

In the streets the building stood dark and wet against the after-Christmas pallor of the sky. High up over the city there was one tiny star. It was as bright and remote as lost innocence. The blank windows that held the winter sky were sullen. The wet cement walls were black. I walked around for hours. When I crept in home my mother demanded angrily where I had been all these hours and I told her lies that *were* lies, because I wanted to deceive her, and I knew that from this on I would always be deceiving everybody because I had something inside me that nobody must ever know. I was afraid of the dark night before me. And I still had to face another Confession when I would have to confess all these fresh lies that I had just told the old priest and my mother.

It's forty years ago, now: something long since put in its unimportant place. Yet, somehow, when I look across at this small kid clutching his penny prayer-book in his sweaty hands and wrinkling up his nose at the hard words—I cannot laugh. It does not even comfort me when I think of that second Confession, after I had carefully examined those lists of sins for the proper name of my sin. For, what I said to the next priest was: "Father, I committed adultery." With infinite tenderness he assured me that I was mistaken, and that I would not know anything about that sin for many years to come, indeed, that I would have to be married before I could commit it—and then asked me to pray for him, and said I was a very good little boy and sent me away jumping with joy. When I think of that and look at this small Adam he becomes like that indescribably remote and tender star, and I sigh like that old, dead priest, and it does not help to know that he is playing a fable of—"Father, I told lies . . . Father, I forgot to say my morning prayers. . . . Father, I called my daddy A Pig."

[1946–Ireland]

QUESTIONS

1. What kind of narrator do we have here?
2. Why is the flashback an appropriate technique for this story?
3. What are the various moods to be felt in "Innocence" as they spring from the

narrator's shifting perspectives on his own childhood and then on that of his son?

4. What does the story overall make you feel? What theme does its final mood (as manifested in its last paragraph) suggest?

WRITING SUGGESTIONS

1. There are four distinct moods felt by O'Faolain's narrator as he thinks about his own past and about his son. Write a short paper in which you name each of these moods and provide quotations to show where each is felt. Specify what accounts for the shifts in mood.

2. In a paragraph or more, describe an incident from your own childhood that you can laugh at now but that then was painful. Explain how this doubleness of perspective—your feelings then and now—sheds light on O'Faolain's "Innocence."

The Ant and the Grasshopper

Somerset Maugham

When I was a very small boy I was made to learn by heart certain of the fables of La Fontaine, and the moral of each was carefully explained to me. Among those I learnt was *The Ant and The Grasshopper*, which is devised to bring home to the young the useful lesson that in an imperfect world industry is rewarded and giddiness punished. In this admirable fable (I apologize for telling something which everyone is politely, but inexactly, supposed to know) the ant spends a laborious summer gathering its winter store, while the grasshopper sits on a blade of grass singing to the sun. Winter comes and the ant is comfortably provided for, but the grasshopper has an empty larder: he goes to the ant and begs for a little food. Then the ant gives him her classic answer:

"What were you doing in the summer time?"

"Saving your presence, I sang, I sang all day, all night."

"You sang. Why, then go and dance."

I do not ascribe it to perversity on my part, but rather to the inconsequence of childhood, which is deficient in moral sense, that I could never quite reconcile myself to the lesson. My sympathies were with the grasshopper and for some time I never saw an ant without putting my foot on it. In this summary (and as I have discovered since, entirely human) fashion I sought to express my disapproval of prudence and common sense.

I could not help thinking of this fable when the other day I saw George Ramsay lunching by himself in a restaurant. I never saw anyone wear an expression of such deep gloom. He was staring into space. He looked as though the burden of the whole world sat on his shoulders. I was sorry for him: I suspected at once that his unfortunate brother had been causing trouble again. I went up to him and held out my hand.

"How are you?" I asked.

"I'm not in hilarious spirits," he answered.

"Is it Tom again?"

He sighed.

"Yes, it's Tom again."

"Why don't you chuck him? You've done everything in the world for him. You must know by now that he's quite hopeless."

I suppose every family has a black sheep. Tom had been a sore trial to his for twenty years. He had begun life decently enough: he went into business, married, and had two children. The Ramsays were perfectly respectable people and there was every reason to suppose that Tom Ramsay would have a useful and honourable career. But one day, without warning, he announced that he didn't like work and that he wasn't suited for marriage. He wanted to enjoy himself. He would listen to no expostulations. He left his wife and his office. He had a little money and he spent two happy years in the various capitals of Europe. Rumours of his doings reached his relations from time to time and they were profoundly shocked. He certainly had a very good time. They shook their heads and asked what would happen when his money was spent. They soon found out: he borrowed. He was charming and unscrupulous. I have never met anyone to whom it was more difficult to refuse a loan. He made a steady income from his friends and he made friends easily. But he always said that the money you spent on necessities was boring; the money that was amusing to spend was the money you spent on luxuries. For this he depended on his brother George. He did not waste his charm on him. George was a serious man and insensible to such enticements. George was respectable. Once or twice he fell to Tom's promises of amendment and gave him considerable sums in order that he might make a fresh start. On these Tom bought a motor-car and some very nice jewellery. But when circumstances forced George to realize that his brother would never settle down and he washed his hands of him, Tom, without a qualm, began to blackmail him. It was not very nice for a respectable lawyer to find his brother shaking cocktails behind the bar of his favourite restaurant or to see him waiting on the box-seat of a taxi outside his club. Tom said that to serve in a bar or to drive a taxi was a perfectly decent occupation, but if George could oblige him with a couple of hundred pounds he didn't mind for the honour of the family giving it up. George paid.

Once Tom nearly went to prison. George was terribly upset. He went into the whole discreditable affair. Really Tom had gone too far. He had been wild, thoughtless, and selfish, but he had never before done anything dishonest, by which George meant illegal; and if he were prosecuted he would assuredly be convicted. But you cannot allow your only brother to go to gaol. The man Tom had cheated, a man called Cronshaw, was vindictive. He was determined to take the matter into court; he said Tom was a scoundrel and should be punished. It cost George an infinite deal of trouble and five hundred pounds to settle the affair. I have never seen him in such a rage as when he heard that Tom and Cronshaw had gone off together to Monte Carlo the moment they cashed the cheque. They spent a happy month there.

For twenty years Tom raced and gambled, philandered with the prettiest girls, danced, ate in the most expensive restaurants, and dressed beautifully. He always looked as if he had just stepped out of a bandbox. Though he was forty-six you would never have taken him for more than thirty-five. He was a most amusing companion and though you knew he was perfectly worthless you could not but enjoy his society. He had high spirits, an unfailing gaiety, and incredible charm. I never grudged the contributions he regularly levied on me for the necessities of his existence. I never lent him fifty pounds without feeling that I was in his debt. Tom Ramsay knew everyone and everyone knew Tom Ramsay. You could not approve of him, but you could not help liking him.

Poor George, only a year older than his scapegrace brother, looked sixty. He had never taken more than a fortnight's holiday in the year for a quarter of a century. He was in his office every morning at nine-thirty and never left it till six. He was honest, industrious, and worthy. He had a good wife, to whom he had never been unfaithful even in thought, and four daughters to whom he was the best of fathers. He made a point of saving a third of his income and his plan was to retire at fifty-five to a little house in the country where he proposed to cultivate his garden and play golf. His life was blameless. He was glad that he was growing old because Tom was growing old too. He rubbed his hands and said:

"It was all very well when Tom was young and good-looking, but he's only a year younger than I am. In four years he'll be fifty. He won't find life so easy then. I shall have thirty thousand pounds by the time I'm fifty. For twenty-five years I've said that Tom would end in the gutter. And we shall see how he likes that. We shall see if it really pays best to work or be idle."

Poor George! I sympathized with him. I wondered now as I sat down beside him what infamous thing Tom had done. George was evidently very much upset.

"Do you know what's happened now?" he asked me.

I was prepared for the worst. I wondered if Tom had got into the hands of the police at last. George could hardly bring himself to speak.

"You're not going to deny that all my life I've been hardworking, decent, respectable, and straightforward. After a life of industry and thrift I can look forward to retiring on a small income in gilt-edged securities. I've always done my duty in that state of life in which it has pleased Providence to place me."

"True."

"And you can't deny that Tom has been an idle, worthless, dissolute, and dishonourable rogue. If there were any justice he'd be in the workhouse."

"True."

George grew red in the face.

"A few weeks ago he became engaged to a woman old enough to be his mother. And now she's died and left him everything she had. Half a million pounds, a yacht, a house in London, and a house in the country."

George Ramsay beat his clenched fist on the table.

"It's not fair, I tell you, it's not fair. Damn it, it's not fair."

I could not help it. I burst into a shout of laughter as I looked at George's wrathful face, I rolled in my chair, I very nearly fell on the floor. George never forgave me. But Tom often asks me to excellent dinners in his charming house in Mayfair, and if he occasionally borrows a trifle from me, that is merely from force of habit. It is never more than a sovereign.

[1924–Great Britain]

QUESTIONS

1. Characterize the narrator of this story. Are we to accept his judgments or are we to side with George?
2. Characterize George and Tom, the fabled ant and grasshopper come to life. Which of the two is preferable as a human being and why?
3. In what way is the story ironic when read in light of the fable for which it is named? What does "The Ant and the Grasshopper" suggest about fables? What is its theme?
4. In what ways do plot, narration, and characterization all go into the making here of a comic mood?
5. Whose mood are we to share at the end, George's or the narrator's? Why?

WRITING SUGGESTIONS

1. Write a paper in which you first contrast George and Tom, and then contrast both with the narrator. Discuss how each contributes to the comic mood of the story.
2. In a paragraph or short paper, classify the type of irony Maugham incorporates, and then explain how irony helps to shape mood and to establish theme.

Appointment in Samarra

Somerset Maugham

There was a merchant in Bagdad who sent his servant to market to buy provisions, and in a little while the servant came back, white and trembling, and said, "Master, just now when I was in the market-place I was jostled by a woman in the crowd and when I turned I saw it was Death that jostled me. She looked at me and made a threatening gesture; now, lend me your horse, and I will ride away from this city and avoid my fate. I will go to Samarra and there Death will not find me." The merchant lent him his horse, and the servant mounted it, and he dug his spurs in its flanks and as fast as the horse could gallop he went. Then the merchant went down to the market-place and he saw Death standing in the crowd and he came to Death and said, "Why did you make a threatening gesture to my servant when you saw him this morning?" "That was not a threatening gesture," Death said. "It was only a start of surprise. I was astonished to see him in Bagdad, for I had an appointment with him tonight in Samarra."

[1933–Great Britain]

QUESTIONS

1. What is ironic here? What kind of irony marks Maugham's story?
2. The theme of this miniature has something to do with fate. What?
3. What is the mood of this piece? How is its mood related to its view of human existence?

WRITING SUGGESTIONS

1. Write a paragraph in which you first classify the type of irony that this story exhibits and then discuss the story in terms of that classification. In other words, use Maugham's tale to exemplify the type of irony it embodies.
2. In a paragraph, describe and account for the mood of this miniature. You might conclude by suggesting how mood here is theme.

The Venus of Braniza*

Guy de Maupassant

Some years ago there lived in Braniza a celebrated Talmudist, renowned no less on account of his beautiful wife, than for his wisdom, his learning, and his fear of God. The Venus of Braniza deserved that name thoroughly; she deserved it for herself, on account of her singular beauty, and even more as the wife of a man deeply versed in the Talmud, for the wives of the Jewish philosophers are, as a rule, ugly or possess some bodily defect.

The Talmud explains this in the following manner: It is well known that marriages are made in heaven, and at the birth of a boy a divine voice calls out the name of his future wife, and *vice versâ*. But just as a good father tries to get rid of his good wares out of doors, and only uses the damaged stuff at home for his children, so God bestows on the Talmudists those women whom other men would not care to have.

Well, God made an exception in the case of our Talmudist, and had bestowed a Venus on him, perhaps only in order to confirm the rule by means of this exception, and to make it appear less hard. This philosoher's wife was a woman who would have done honor to any king's throne, or to a pedestal in any sculpture gallery. Tall, and with a wonderfully voluptuous figure, she carried a strikingly beautiful head, surmounted by thick, black plaits, on her proud shoulders. Two large, dark eyes languished and glowed beneath long lashes, and her beautiful hands looked as if they were carved out of ivory.

This glorious woman, who seemed to have been designed by nature to

---

* Translated by M. Walter Dunne.

rule, to see slaves at her feet, to provide occupation for the painter's brush, the sculptor's chisel, and the poet's pen, lived the life of a rare and beautiful flower shut up in a hothouse. She would sit the whole day long wrapped up in her costly furs looking down dreamily into the street.

She had no children; her husband, the philosopher, studied and prayed and studied again from early morning until late at night; his mistress was "the Veiled Beauty," as the Talmudists call the Kabbalah. She paid no attention to her house, for she was rich, and everything went of its own accord like a clock which has only to be wound up once a week; nobody came to see her, and she never went out of the house; she sat and dreamed and brooded and—yawned.

*   *   *

One day when a terrible storm of thunder and lightning had spent its fury over the town, and all windows had been opened in order to let the Messias in, the Jewish Venus was sitting as usual in her comfortable easy-chair, shivering in spite of her furs, and thinking. Suddenly she fixed her glowing eyes on her husband who was sitting before the Talmud, swaying his body backward and forward, and said suddenly:

"Just tell me, when will Messias, the son of David, come?"

"He will come," the philosopher replied, "when all the Jews have become either altogether virtuous or altogether vicious, says the Talmud."

"Do you believe that all the Jews will ever become virtuous?" the Venus continued.

"How am I to believe that?"

"So Messias will come when all the Jews have become vicious?"

The philosopher shrugged his shoulders, and lost himself again in the labyrinth of the Talmud, out of which, so it is said, only one man returned in perfect sanity. The beautiful woman at the window again looked dreamily out into the heavy rain, while her white fingers played unconsciously with the dark furs of her splendid robe.

*   *   *

One day the Jewish philosopher had gone to a neighboring town, where an important question of ritual was to be decided. Thanks to his learning, the question was settled sooner than he had expected, and instead of returning the next morning, as he had intended, he came back the same evening with a friend who was no less learned than himself. He got out of the carriage at his friend's house and went home on foot. He was not a little surprised when he saw his windows brilliantly illuminated, and found an officer's servant comfortably smoking his pipe in front of his house.

"What are you doing here?" he asked in a friendly manner, but with some curiosity, nevertheless.

"I am on guard, lest the husband of the beautiful Jewess should come home unexpectedly."

"Indeed? Well, mind and keep a good lookout."

Saying this, the philosopher pretended to go away, but went into the house through the garden entrance at the back. When he got into the first room, he found a table laid for two, which had evidently only been left a short time previously. His wife was sitting as usual at her bedroom window wrapped in her furs, but her cheeks were suspiciously red, and her dark eyes had not their usual languishing look, but now rested on her husband with a gaze which expressed at the same time satisfaction and mockery. At that moment his foot stuck against an object on the floor, which gave out a strange sound. He picked it up and examined it in the light. It was a pair of spurs.

"Who has been here with you?" asked the Talmudist.

The Jewish Venus shrugged her shoulders contemptuously, but did not reply.

"Shall I tell you? The Captain of Hussars has been with you."

"And why should he not have been here with me?" she said, smoothing the fur on her jacket with her white hand.

"Woman! are you out of your mind?"

"I am in full possession of my senses," she replied, and a knowing smile hovered round her red voluptuous lips. "But must I not also do my part, in order that Messias may come and redeem us poor Jews?"

[1884–France]

QUESTIONS

1. What type of character is Maupassant working with in his "Venus"? Why is this type appropriate given the mood of the story?
2. What is the mood? What is the relation of mood to ironic effect?
3. What, exactly, is ironic here? What type of irony is exemplified?
4. The philosopher's mood at the end is clearly not the mood of the story overall. Elaborate.

WRITING SUGGESTIONS

1. In a paragraph or two, classify the type of irony found in "The Venus of Braniza," establish the defining characteristics of the class, and apply those characteristics point by point to Maupassant's tale.
2. In a short paper, analyze the mood of this story. Having stated what the mood is, point as specifically as possible to the elements (for instance, characterization) that establish it.

The Eclipse*

Augusto Monterroso

When Brother Bartolome Arrazola felt lost he accepted that nothing could save him anymore. The powerful Guatemalan jungle had trapped him inexorably and definitively. Before his topographical ignorance he sat quietly awaiting death. He wanted to die there, hopelessly and alone, with his thoughts fixed on far-away Spain, particularly on the Los Abrojos convent where Charles the Fifth had once condescended to lessen his prominence and tell him that he trusted the religious zeal of his redemptive work.

Upon awakening he found himself surrounded by a group of indifferent natives who were getting ready to sacrifice him in front of an altar, an altar that to Bartolome seemed to be the place in which he would finally rest from his fears, his destiny, from himself.

Three years in the land had given him a fair knowledge of the native tongues. He tried something. He said a few words which were understood.

He then had an idea he considered worthy of his talent, universal culture and steep knowledge of Aristotle. He remembered that a total eclipse of the sun was expected on that day and in his innermost thoughts he decided to use that knowledge to deceive his oppressors and save his life.

"If you kill me"—he told them, "I can darken the sun in its heights."

The natives looked at him fixedly and Bartolome caught the incredulity in their eyes. He saw that a small counsel was set up and waited confidently, not without some disdain.

---

* Translated by Wilfrido H. Corral.

Two hours later Brother Bartolome Arrazola's heart spilled its fiery blood on the sacrificial stone (brilliant under the opaque light of an eclipsed sun), while one of the natives recited without raising his voice, unhurriedly, one by one, the infinite dates in which there would be solar and lunar eclipses, that the astronomers of the Mayan community had foreseen and written on their codices without Aristotle's valuable help.

[1952–Mexico]

QUESTIONS

1. What type of irony marks Monterroso's story?
2. If we take Brother Bartolome as a representative of European civilization, what does the story suggest about the West's historical attitude toward non-Western cultures?
3. What is the mood of the story overall?

WRITING SUGGESTIONS

1. In a paragraph, address question 2 above. Be sure to state the story's theme somewhere in your paragraph.
2. In a paragraph, define what is ironic about what happens in "The Eclipse." Consider the discrepancy between the reader's knowledge and Brother Bartolome's and how this discrepancy shapes our feelings as we follow Bartolome to his end.

The Jewels of M. Lantin*

Guy de Maupassant

M. Lantin, having met this young lady at a party given by his immediate superior, was literally enmeshed by love.

She was the daughter of a provincial tax collector who had died a few years previously. With her mother, she had come to Paris. Her mother became friendly with several middle-class families of the neighborhood in hopes of marrying off the young lady. Mother and daughter were poor, honorable, quiet, and gentle. The girl seemed to be the typical dream woman into whose hands any young man would yearn to entrust his entire life. Her modest beauty had an angelic quality, and the imperceptible smile which constantly graced her lips, seemed a reflection of her heart.

Everyone sang her praises; everyone who knew her repeated incessantly: "It will be a lucky fellow who wins her. You couldn't find a better catch!"

M. Lantin, now chief clerk of the Minister of the Interior, at a salary of 3500 francs, asked and received her hand in marriage.

He was unbelievably happy. She managed the house with such skill that their life was one of luxury. There was no delicacy, no whim of her husband's which she did not secure and satisfy; and her personal charm was such that, six years after their first meeting, he loved her even more than he had initially.

He begrudged her only two traits—her love of the theater and her passion for artificial jewels.

Her friends (she knew the wives of several minor functionaries) were

---

* Translated by Roger B. Goodman.

299

always getting her seats for the fashionable plays, sometimes even for first nights; and she dragged her poor husband, willy-nilly, to these entertainments which completely wore him out, tired as he was after a hard day's work. He begged her to agree to go to the theater with some lady friend of hers who would accompany her home. She took a long time to decide, claiming this a most inconvenient arrangement. At last, however, she agreed, and he was profoundly grateful to her.

Now, this taste for the theater naturally stirred in her the need to primp. Her toilette remained simple, to be sure—always modest but in good taste; and her gentle grace, her irresistible, humble, smiling grace seemed to acquire a new savor from the simplicity of her dress, but she became accustomed to wearing two huge rhinestone earrings, which looked like diamonds, and she had strings of artificial pearls around her neck, and wore bracelets of similar gems.

Her husband, who somewhat scorned this love of garish display, said, "Dearest, when you haven't the means to wear real jewelry, you should show yourself adorned only with your own grace and beauty; these are the true pearls."

But she, smiling quietly, would insist, "Can I help it? I love it so. This is my vice, I know, my dear, how absolutely right you are; but I can't really remake myself, can I? I think I would just idolize real jewelry."

And she would roll the pearls in her fingers. "See how perfect," she'd say. "You'd swear they were real."

Sometimes, during the evening, while they sat before the fire, she would bring out her jewel chest, put it on the tea table, and commence to examine the contents with passionate attention, as though there were some subtle and profound secret delight in this pursuit. She persisted in draping strings of pearls around her husband's neck; then she would laugh merrily, crying, "How silly you look, my darling!" And she would throw herself into his arms and kiss him wildly.

One wintry evening, when she had been at the opera, she came home shivering with cold. The next day she was coughing wretchedly. A week later she died.

Lantin nearly followed her into the tomb. His despair was such that, in a month's time, his hair turned completely white. He wept incessantly, his very soul seared by unbearable suffering, haunted by the memory, the smile, the voice—by the overwhelming beauty of his deceased wife.

Even the passage of time failed to stem his grief. Frequently, at his office, while his colleagues were chatting idly, his cheeks would tremble and his eyes would fill with tears; he would grimace horribly and commence to sob.

He kept his wife's room intact, and sealed himself in every day to meditate. All her furniture and even her dresses remained just where they had been on the fatal day.

Living became difficult for him. His income which, under his wife's management, amply supplied the needs of both, now became insufficient for him alone. Dazed, he wondered how she had been able to purchase the superb wines and delicacies which he could no longer afford.

He fell into debt and began to scurry around for money as does anyone suddenly plunged into poverty. One fine morning, finding himself penniless a full week before payday, he thought about selling something. Suddenly the idea swept over him of taking a look at his wife's treasure trove, because, if the truth be told, he had always harbored some resentment towards this store of brilliants. The mere sight of them slightly tarnished the memory of his beloved.

It was a difficult business, searching throught the case of jewels, because, even up to the very last days of her life, his wife had shopped stubbornly, bringing home some new bauble practically every night. He finally chose the magnificent necklace she seemed to have preferred, which, he figured, was worth six or seven francs, because, for artificial gems, it was really a masterpiece of craftsmanship.

With the jewels in his pocket he walked towards the Ministry, looking for a reliable jeweler.

Spotting a store, he entered—somewhat chagrined to be making this public display of his poverty and ashamed at attempting to sell so worthless an object.

He approached the merchant. "Excuse me. I wonder what value you would place on this piece."

The man took the necklace, examined it, turned it over, weighed it, called to his partner, talked to him in low tones, placed the necklace on the counter and scrutinized it carefully from a distance as though judging the effect.

M. Lantin, overwhelmed by this process, opened his mouth to protest: "Oh! I know that piece isn't worth anything," but just at that moment the storekeeper said:

"Monsieur, this piece is worth between twelve and fifteen thousand francs, but I cannot buy it until I learn exactly how you came into possession of it."

Lantin stared, wide-eyed, silent—uncomprehending. He finally stammered, "What? You are absolutely sure?"

The gentleman seemed offended by his attitude, and said wryly, "You may go elsewhere if you think you can do better. To me that is worth fifteen thousand at the very most. If you find no better offer, you may come back here."

M. Lantin, stupefied, took the necklace and left, feeling a curious urge to be alone and undisturbed.

But, before he had gone far, he was seized with an impulse to laugh, and he thought, "Imbecile! What a fool! What if I had taken him at his word! What a jeweler—not to know the difference between real gems and fakes!"

And he entered another jewelry store on the Rue de la Paix. As soon as he saw the jewel, the dealer cried, "Of course! I know this necklace well; I sold it!"

Deeply disturbed, M. Lantin asked, "How much is it worth?"

"Sir—I sold it for twenty-five thousand francs. I'm ready to take it back for eighteen thousand, if you will tell me—the law, you know—how you happened to receive it."

This time Lantin sat paralyzed with astonishment. He stuttered, "But—but—examine it very closely, sir. I have always thought it was—artificial."

The jeweler asked, "Would you please tell me your name, sir?"

"Of course. I'm Lantin. I work at the Ministry of the Interior, and I live at 16 Rue des Martyrs."

The merchant opened his ledger, looked through it, and said, "This necklace was sent to Mme. Lantin, 16 Rue des Martyrs, on the twentieth of July, 1876."

And the two men stared at each other, the clerk dumbfounded; the jeweler scenting a robber.

The merchant said, "Would you mind letting me have this for a day? Naturally, I'll give you a receipt."

M. Lantin blurted out, "Of course!" And he left, folding the paper into his pocket.

Then he crossed the street, went back, saw that he had gone out of his way, returned past the Tuileries, saw again he had made a mistake, crossed the Seine, went back to the Champs-Elysées without a single clear notion in his head. He forced himself to think. His wife could not possibly have purchased such valuable jewelry. Absolutely not! Well then? A present? A present! From whom? For what?

He was brought up short, and he stood stock still—there in the middle of the street. A horrible thought flashed across his mind. She? But all those other jewels were also gifts! He felt the earth shiver; a tree just before him seemed to crush him. He threw out his arms and fell, senseless, to the ground.

He regained consciousness in a nearby pharmacy to which passers-by had carried him. He asked that he be taken home, and he locked himself in.

He wept bitterly until nightfall—stuffing a handkerchief into his mouth to stifle his cries. Then he staggered to bed, wrung out with fatigue and chagrin, and he slept heavily.

A ray of sunshine woke him, and he got up slowly to go to his office. After such a blow, it would he hard to carry on with his work. He felt that he could be excused, and he wrote his superior a note. Then he thought that he ought to go back to the jeweler; and he crimsoned with shame. He could not possibly leave the necklace with that man. He dressed hurriedly and went out.

As he walked along, Lantin said to himself, "How easy it is to be happy when you're rich! With money you can even shake off your sorrows; you can go or stay as you please! You can travel and amuse yourself. If only I were really rich!"

Then he became aware of that fact that he was hungry, not having eaten since the previous evening. But his pockets were empty, and he reminded himself of the necklace. Eighteen thousand francs! Eighteen thousand francs! What a fortune!

He reached the Rue de la Paix, and he began pacing up and down opposite the shop. Eighteen thousand francs! More than twenty times he started to enter; but shame always halted him.

He was still hungry—famished—and without a sou. He finally made up his mind, raced across the street so as not to give himself time to think, and burst into the store.

As soon as he saw him, the merchant greeted him royally, offered him a chair with smiling courtesy. The partners then came in and sat down near Lantin, happiness beaming from their eyes and their lips.

The jeweler declared, "I am satisfied, Monsieur, and if you feel as you did yesterday, I am ready to pay you the sum agreed upon."

"Certainly," stammered Lantin.

The merchant took eighteen large notes from a drawer, counted them, gave them to Lantin, who signed a receipt and, with trembling hand, stuffed the money into his pocket.

Then, just as he was going out, he turned back towards the grinning shopkeeper, and, lowering his eyes, murmured, "I—I have some other gems—which came to me in the same way. Would you be willing to buy those from me?"

The jeweler nodded, "Of course, Monsieur."

One of the partners barely stifled a laugh, while the other was forced to leave the room to hide his mirth.

Lantin, impassive and stern, said, "I'll bring them to you."

When he returned to the store, an hour later, he had still not eaten. They set about examining the jewels piece by piece, assessing each one. Then they all went back to Lantin's house.

Now Lantin entered into the spirit of the business, arguing, insisting that they show him the bills of sale, and getting more and more excited as the values rose.

The magnificent earrings were worth twenty thousand francs; the bracelets, thirty-five thousand. The brooches, pins and medallions, sixteen thousand. The whole collection was valued at one hundred ninety-six thousand francs.

The merchant boomed out in a jolly voice, "That's what happens when you put your money into jewelry."

Lantin said solemnly, "That's one way to invest your money!" Then he left, after having agreed with the purchaser to have a second expert appraisal the following day.

When he was out in the street, he looked up at the Vendôme Column. He felt like leaping up to the top. He felt light enough to play leapfrog with the statue of the Emperor perched up there in the clouds.

He went into an elegant restaurant to eat, and he drank wine at twenty francs a bottle.

Then he took a cab and rode around the Bois de Boulogne. He looked at the gleaming carriages, suppressing a desire to cry out, "I'm rich, too! I have two hundred thousand francs!"

He thought of his office. He drove up, entered his Chief's office solemnly, and announced, "Sir—I'm tendering my resignation! I've just inherited three hundred thousand francs!" He went around shaking hands with his colleagues, and telling them all about his plans for the future. Then he went out to dinner at the Café Anglais.

Finding himself seated alongside a distinguished-looking gentleman, he couldn't resist whispering to him, a little archly, that he had just inherited four hundred thousand francs.

For the first time in his life he enjoyed the theater and he spent the night carousing.

Six months later he remarried. His second wife was a most worthy woman, but rather difficult. She made his life unbearable.

[1883–France]

QUESTIONS

1. What kind of narrator narrates M. Lantin's story?
2. What kind of irony does the end of the story involve? Explain.

3. How does this irony help establish the story's theme?
4. Does M. Lantin deserve his fate as spelled out in the story's last paragraph? What, then, is the mood here?

WRITING SUGGESTIONS

1. What is the mood of this story overall? Write a paragraph or short paper on its mood—what it is and how it is created. What role does narration play here? How does irony affect mood? Be sure to distinguish between the mood of the story and that of M. Lantin.
2. "The Jewels of M. Lantin" is a satire on bourgeois morals and mentality. Write a paper on the story as satire. What does it expose and poke fun at about conventional morality? How does laughter serve Maupassant's purpose?
3. "This story exhibits both circumstantial and dramatic irony. Write a short paper in which you delineate each, pointing to specifics.

The Use of Force

William Carlos Williams

They were new patients to me, all I had was the name, Olson. Please come down as soon as you can, my daughter is very sick.

When I arrived I was met by the mother, a big startled looking woman, very clean and apologetic who merely said, Is this the doctor? and let me in. In the back, she added. You must excuse us, doctor, we have her in the kitchen where it is warm. It is very damp here sometimes.

The child was fully dressed and sitting on her father's lap near the kitchen table. He tried to get up, but I motioned for him not to bother, took off my overcoat and started to look things over. I could see that they were all very nervous, eyeing me up and down distrustfully. As often, in such cases, they weren't telling me more than they had to, it was up to me to tell them; that's why they were spending three dollars on me.

The child was fairly eating me up with her cold, steady eyes, and no expression to her face whatever. She did not move and seemed, inwardly, quiet; an unusually attractive little thing, and as strong as a heifer in appearance. But her face was flushed, she was breathing rapidly, and I realized that she had a high fever. She had magnificent blonde hair, in profusion. One of those picture children often reproduced in advertising leaflets and the photogravure sections of the Sunday papers.

She's had a fever for three days, began the father and we don't know what it comes from. My wife has given her things, you know, like people do, but it don't do no good. And there's been a lot of sickness around. So we tho't you'd better look her over and tell us what is the matter.

As doctors often do I took a trial shot at it as a point of departure. Has she had a sore throat?

306

Both parents answered me together, No . . . No, she says her throat don't hurt her.

Does your throat hurt you? added the mother to the child. But the little girl's expression didn't change nor did she move her eyes from my face.

Have you looked?

I tried to, said the mother, but I couldn't see.

As it happens we had been having a number of cases of diphtheria in the school to which this child went during that month and we were all, quite apparently, thinking of that, though no one had as yet spoken of the thing.

Well, I said, suppose we take a look at the throat first. I smiled in my best professional manner and asking for the child's first name I said, come on, Mathilda, open your mouth and let's take a look at your throat.

Nothing doing.

Aw, come on, I coaxed, just open your mouth wide and let me take a look. Look, I said opening both hands wide, I haven't anything in my hands. Just open up and let me see.

Such a nice man, put in the mother. Look how kind he is to you. Come on, do what he tells you to. He won't hurt you.

At that I ground my teeth in disgust. If only they wouldn't use the word "hurt" I might be able to get somewhere. But I did not allow myself to be hurried or disturbed but speaking quietly and slowly I approached the child again.

As I moved my chair a little nearer suddenly with one catlike movement both her hands clawed instinctively for my eyes and she almost reached them too. In fact she knocked my glasses flying and they fell, though unbroken, several feet away from me on the kitchen floor.

Both the mother and father almost turned themselves inside out in embarrassment and apology. You bad girl, said the mother, taking her and shaking her by one arm. Look what you've done. The nice man . . .

For heaven's sake, I broke in. Don't call me a nice man to her. I'm here to look at her throat on the chance that she might have diphtheria and possibly die of it. But that's nothing to her. Look here, I said to the child, we're going to look at your throat. You're old enough to understand what I'm saying. Will you open it now by yourself or shall we have to open it for you?

Not a move. Even her expression hadn't changed. Her breaths however were coming faster and faster. Then the battle began. I had to do it. I had to have a throat culture for her own protection. But first I told the parents that it was entirely up to them. I explained the danger but said that

I would not insist on a throat examination so long as they would take the responsibility.

If you don't do what the doctor says you'll have to go to the hospital, the mother admonished her severely.

Oh yeah? I had to smile to myself. After all, I had already fallen in love with the savage brat, the parents were contemptible to me. In the ensuing struggle they grew more and more abject, crushed, exhausted while she surely rose to magnificent heights of insane fury of effort bred of her terror of me.

The father tried his best, and he was a big man but the fact that she was his daughter, his shame at her behavior and his dread of hurting her made him release her just at the critical moment several times when I had almost achieved success, till I wanted to kill him. But his dread also that she might have diphtheria made him tell me to go on, go on though he himself was almost fainting, while the mother moved back and forth behind us raising and lowering her hands in an agony of apprehension.

Put her in front of you on your lap, I ordered, and hold both her wrists.

But as soon as he did the child let out a scream. Don't you're hurting me. Let go of my hands. Let them go I tell you. Then she shrieked terrifyingly, hysterically. Stop it! Stop it! You're killing me!

Do you think she can stand it, doctor! said the mother.

You get out, said the husband to his wife. Do you want her to die of diphtheria?

Come on now, hold her, I said.

Then I grasped the child's head with my left hand and tried to get the wooden tongue depressor between her teeth. She fought, with clenched teeth, desperately! But now I also had grown furious—at a child. I tried to hold myself down but I couldn't. I know how to expose a throat for inspection. And I did my best. When finally I got the wooden spatula behind the last teeth and just the point of it into the mouth cavity, she opened up for an instant but before I could see anything she came down again and gripping the wooden blade between her molars she reduced it to splinters before I could get it out again.

Aren't you ashamed, the mother yelled at her. Aren't you ashamed to act like that in front of the doctor?

Get me a smooth-handled spoon of some sort, I told the mother. We're going through with this. The child's mouth was already bleeding. Her tongue was cut and she was screaming in wild hysterical shrieks. Perhaps I should have desisted and come back in an hour or more. No doubt it would have been better. But I have seen at least two children lying dead in bed of neglect in such cases, and feeling that I must get a diagnosis now or never I went at it again. But the worst of it was that I too had got beyond reason. I could have torn the child apart in my own fury and enjoyed it. It was a pleasure to attack her. My face was burning with it.

The damned little brat must be protected against her own idiocy, one says to one's self at such times. Others must be protected against her. It is social necessity. And all these things are true. But a blind fury, a feeling of adult shame, bred of a longing for muscular release are the operatives. One goes on to the end.

In a final unreasoning assault I overpowered the child's neck and jaws. I forced the heavy silver spoon back of her teeth and down her throat till she gagged. And there it was—both tonsils covered with membrane. She had fought valiantly to keep me from knowing her secret. She had been hiding that sore throat for three days at least and lying to her parents in order to escape just such an outcome as this.

Now truly she *was* furious. She had been on the defensive before but now she attacked. Tried to get off her father's lap and fly at me while tears of defeat blinded her eyes.

[1938–U.S.A.]

QUESTIONS

1. Focusing on the conflict between the doctor and the parents as well as between the doctor and the girl, summarize the plot of "The Use of Force."
2. What kind of narration do we have here? Characterize the narrator as thoroughly as you can. Consider in particular his self-knowledge and his motivation.
3. What does the style of the story reveal about its narrator?
4. The doctor talks of the need to protect others from the girl and her from herself. "And all these things are true," he adds. However, this statement would be mere rationalization if he chose to probe no further. How so?
5. The title of this story points directly to its theme. What does the story dramatize about the use of force?
6. Had the girl turned out not to have diphtheria, the story would be ironic. But Williams was careful to keep out any major irony. Why? But do you find any irony in passing?

WRITING SUGGESTIONS

1. Write a short essay on how "The Use of Force" compels us to keep the doctor's act and his motives distinct in order to understand the story.

2. How would the story be different if the girl turned out not to have diphtheria? Write a paragraph answering this question.
3. At two crucial points toward the end of his story, Williams could have made it ironic: he could have had the doctor be blind to his own motives, and he could have had the girl show no sign of diphtheria. In both cases Williams chose against irony. Write an essay in which you analyze the importance of these choices to William's theme. In order to do this, note, you must first verbalize the story's theme with care and precision.

Tales of the Swedish Army

Donald Barthelme

Suddenly, turning a corner, I ran into a unit of the Swedish Army. Their vehicles were parked in orderly rows and filled the street, mostly six-by-sixes and jeeps, an occasional A.P.C., all painted a sand color quite different from the American Army's dark green. To the left of the vehicles, on a big school playground, they had set up two-man tents of the same sand color, and the soldiers, blond red-faced men, lounged about among the tents, making not much noise. It was strange to see them there. I assumed they were on their way to some sort of joint maneuvers with our own troops. But it was strange to see them there.

I began talking to a lieutenant, a young, pleasant man; he showed me a portable chess clock he'd made himself, which was for some reason covered in matchstick bamboo, painted purple. I told him I was building an addition to the rear of my house, as a matter of fact I had with me a carpenter's level I'd just bought, and I showed him that. He said he had some free time, and asked if I needed help. I suggested that probably his unit would be moving out fairly soon, but he waved a hand to indicate that their departure was not imminent. He seemed genuinely interested in assisting me, so I accepted.

His name was Bengt and he was from Uppsala. I'd been there so we talked about Uppsala, then about Stockholm and Bornholm and Malmö. I asked him if he knew the work of the Swedish poet Bodil Malmsten; he didn't. My house (not really mine, my sister's, but I lived there and paid rent) wasn't far away. We stood in the garden looking up at the rear windows on the parlor floor; I was putting new ones in. So I climbed the ladder and he began handing me up one of the rather heavy prefab window

311

frames, and my hammer slid from the top of the ladder and fell and smashed into his chess clock, which he'd carefully placed on the ground, against the wall.

I apologized profusely, and Bengt told me not to worry, it didn't matter, but he kept shaking the chess clock and turning it over in his hands, trying to bring it to life. I rushed down the ladder and apologized again, and looked at it myself. Both dials were shattered and part of the purple matchstick casing had come off. He said again not to worry, he could fix it, and that we should get on with the job.

After a while, Bengt was up on the ladder tacking the new frames to the two-by-fours with sixteen-penny nails. He was very skillful and the work was going quickly; I was standing in the garden steadying the ladder as he was sometimes required to lean out rather far. He slipped and tried to recover, and bashed his face against the wall and broke his nose.

He stood in the garden holding his nose with both hands, the hands clasped as if in prayer over his nose. I apologized profusely. I ran into the house and got some ice cubes and paper towels and told him I'd take him to the hospital right away but he shook his head and said no, they had doctors of their own. I wanted to do something for him so I took him in and sat him down and cooked him some of my fried chicken, which is rather well known although the secret isn't much of a secret—just lots of lemon-pepper marinade and then squeezing fresh lemon juice over it just before serving. I could see he was really very discouraged about his nose and I had to keep giving him fresh paper towels but he complimented me very highly on the chicken and gave me a Swedish recipe for chicken stuffed with parsley and butter and stewed, which I wrote down.

Then Bengt told me various things about the Swedish Army. He said that it was a tough army and a sober one, but small; that everybody in the Army pretty well knew everybody else, and that they kept their Saab jets in deep caves that had been dug in the mountains, so that if there was a war nothing could happen to them. He said that the part I'd seen was just his company; there were two more, plus a heavy-weapons company, bivouacking at various spots in the city, making up a full battalion. He said the soldiers were mostly Lutherans, with a few Baptists and Pentecostals, and that drugs were not a problem but that people sometimes overslept, driving the sergeants crazy. He said that the Swedish Army was thought to have the best weapons in the world, and that they kept them very clean. He said that he probably didn't have to name their principal potential enemy, because I knew it already, and that the Army-wide favorite musical group was ABBA, which could sometimes be seen on American television late at night.

By now the table was full of bloody paper towels and some blood had gotten on his camouflage suit, which was in three shades of green and brown. Abruptly, with a manly gesture, Bengt informed me that he had fallen in love with my sister. I said that was very curious, in that he had never met her. "That is no difficulty," he said. "I can see by looking around this house what kind of a woman she must be. Very tall, is she not? And red hair, is that not true?" He went on describing my sister, whose name is Catherine, with a disturbing accuracy and increasing enthusiasm, correctly identifying her as a teacher and furthermore a teacher of painting. "These are hers," he said, "they must be," and rose to inspect some oils in Kulicke frames on the walls. "I knew it. From these, dear friend, a great deal can be known of the temperament of the painter, his or her essential spirit. I will divorce my wife immediately," he said, "and marry Catherine as soon as it is legally possible." "You're already married?" I said, and he hung his head and admitted yes, that it was so. But in Sweden, he said, many people were married to each other who, for one reason or another, no longer loved each other. I said that happened in our own country too, many cases personally known to me, and that if he wished to marry Catherine I would not stand in his way but would, on the contrary, do everything in my power to further the project. At this moment the bell rang; I answered it and Catherine entered and introduced us to her new husband, Richard.

(But difficulties often enhance one's perception of the place in which one encounters them. . . .)

I took Bengt back to his unit in a cab, one hand clutching his nose, the other his chest, the remains of his chess clock in his lap. We got there just in time, a review was in progress, the King of Sweden was present—a handsome young man in dress uniform with a silver sword, surrounded by aides similarly clad. A crowd had gathered and Bengt's company paraded by, looking vastly trim and efficient in their polished boots and red berets, and a very pretty little girl came out of the crowd and shyly handed the King a small bouquet of flowers. He bent graciously to accept them, beautiful small yellow roses, and a Rocky Mountain-spotted-fever tick leaped from a rose and bit him on the cheek. I was horrified, and the King slapped his cheek and swore that the Swedish Army would never visit us again.

[1977–U.S.A.]

QUESTIONS

1. The style of this story is about as nonchalant as it could be. What is the effect of Barthelme's coupling of this kind of style with surrealistic imagery?
2. Describe the tone of the story.

3. Here, tone is theme. That is, it is mainly through tone that Barthelme conveys his view of things. How so?

WRITING SUGGESTIONS

1. Write a critique of this story in which you judge its literary merits and its relevance to our historical moment. Will it survive our moment? Or will it pass into obscurity as circumstances and attitudes change?
2. In a paragraph, describe and analyze the general tone of "Tales of the Swedish Army," and consider how tone is equivalent to theme.

Story for the Slicks

Elinor Goulding Smith

Carol Saunders brushed her thick mop of chestnut hair off her forehead with long, nervous white fingers. *How am I going to tell Jim?* she thought. *How can I tell him?* She thought of Jim's long, lean jaw, his dark tousled hair, and his crooked grin. *Oh, Jim, Jim*—(Opening paragraph plunges you right into the story with all its intense passion and suspense.)

But I mustn't think about that now. I'm so tired, she thought wearily, and the thin fingers twined nervously in the thick hair. She stood up suddenly and went into the bathroom, and she noticed dully that the faucet was still dripping. *I'll have to get Jim to fix it*, she thought automatically. (The homey touch.)

Determinedly, she turned on the cold water full force and let its clean sparkling freshness flow over her thin white wrists, and then she leaned over and dipped up the water with her slim hands and felt the sharp cold on her hot face. She dipped pads of absorbent cotton in the water and bathed her burning eyes, and she brushed out her hair with long, soothing, rhythmic strokes, away from her forehead. (Beauty hints.)

She surveyed herself in the mirror. She saw the white, pointed face and the hair that seemed almost too heavy for the slim neck. It hung round her shoulders in a thick mass. "It's as soft to touch as a spaniel's ears," Jim always said. The lashes around the wide gray eyes were stuck together in dark points with little beads of the cold water still clinging to them. And the lower lip of the full crimson mouth was quivering. (Important that heroine be described, but not too specifically. Sprinkle liberally with "slim" wherever possible. Helpful if heroine can be made to whip in and out of tight sweaters.)

315

Tomorrow, she thought wearily, twisting and untwisting the long, nervous fingers. *Let tomorrow be time enough to tell him. I'm so tired today.* (There has to be at least one sentence starting with "let.")

She moved swiftly, with the easy flowing walk that Jim loved, and stood awkwardly for a moment in the living room. The late afternoon sun made a brilliant, warm golden splash on the center of the soft green carpet. *It's so quiet*, she thought, *and it seems almost strange to be here, in this house, now.* (This doesn't mean a thing, but it almost sounds as though it does, doesn't it?)

She thought suddenly that it was getting late, and Jim would be home soon. She went into the kitchen and leaned on the cool enamel table. The kitchen was bright and sunny with yellow walls and crisp curtains with appliquéd tulips. (Interior decorating hints are absolutely necessary.)

She caught herself humming a tune—"Star Dust," she realized suddenly. Their song. *Oh, Jim, Jim*, she thought, *remember how it was that night on the top of the bus, and it was so cold and clear, and I could feel the roughness of your coat against my cheek!* (Stir in a little nostalgia.)

And you were laughing because the clean cold wind kept whipping my hair across your face. Ah, we had fun. (Always change paragraphs at every possible opportunity, regardless of the meaning. Be sure heroine talks and thinks like a heroine, as opposed to a human being.)

And suddenly the small white face was down on the cold enamel table and bitter sobs shook the slim shoulders. (Got another "slim" in. Good!)

Then she straightened up with determination. *That's enough of that. Carol Saunders*, she thought, and she threw back the slim shoulders and lifted the little pointed chin. (A little pointed chin is always good too—tears at the heartstrings.)

I think I'll make some blueberry torte, she decided, and she glanced at the clock to see if there would be enough time before dinner. There would be, and she started working swiftly; she thought happily, *Jim always loves blueberry torte.* (Always be specific about food. A good recipe never hurts either).

She deftly creamed a quarter of a cup of rich yellow butter and a tablespoon of sugar in the blue bowl, and added one egg yolk and a little salt and flour. (This is the most complicated recipe I could find in the Settlement Cook Book—it ought to be a killer.) She patted and pressed the dough in the shining greased pan (or spring form) with her slim quick fingers till it was a quarter of an inch thick, and placed it in the gleaming refrigerator overnight. Then she filled it with any desired Fruit Mixture, and baked.

Then, still humming to herself, having lined the bottom and sides of a spring form with Muerbe Teig No.1, page 377, she sprinkled it with bread crumbs, added one quart of blueberries (*How ripe the berries are!* she thought, and she ate one, slowly savoring its sweetness), sprinkled it with one quarter of a cup of sugar (*How white the sugar is!* she thought unexpectedly), and cinnamon and two tablespoons of lemon juice. Over all she dripped the yolk of an egg beaten with three tablespoons of rich yellow cream. She baked it in the hot oven for fifteen minutes, then reduced the heat to three hundred and twenty-five degrees Fahrenheit.

This time she baked it till the crust was golden brown. *Jim loves it with the crust nice and brown,* she thought.

She sniffed the heavenly smell of the Muerbe Teig No.1, page 377, and her face was flushed from the heat of the stove and her eyes were shining. She beat four egg whites until they were stiff and stood up in little white crusty peaks, and added powered sugar. When the torte was ready, crust nicely browned, she spread the beaten eggs and sugar over it, returned it quickly to the oven, and baked it fifteen minutes more at three hundred degrees Fahrenheit. (I wonder if anybody ever tried this.)

While she was waiting for it to be ready, she realized suddenly that she was famished, and she thought, *I'll make pickled herring with lots of sour cream, just the way Jim loves it, and chicken soup with matzos balls, and creplach. And pot roast with potato latkes.* (Always give menus. Memo: Remember to get other cook book. Feel certain this is not the right cook book for magazine fiction writer.)

Carol didn't hear Jim's key turning in the lock, and he strode in and stood for a moment in the kitchen doorway, looking at her. Her face was flushed, and one tendril of hair had separated from the chestnut mass and curled over one cheek. (A loose tendril is always good.)

Suddenly she felt his presence, and she turned quickly. He was standing there, grinning that crooked grin that always made her heart turn over. (Crooked grin absolutely essential.) He was at her side with one step, and then he was crushing her to him, and her little white face was pressed tight against the warm roughness of his tweed shoulder. He buried his hands in the thick mass of her hair, and then he lifted her face up to kiss her. *She's so little,* he thought. He was always surprised at how little she was. (This establishes that he is of the necessary height and breadth for a proper hero.)

"Jim, darling," Carol said, "let me get my breath," (*He mustn't suspect,* she thought. *I'll tell him tomorrow.*) "And darling," she said, "you'd better hurry and wash—dinner's ready."

When they sat down to dinner, she was quite composed again. The tall glasses sparkled against the deep blue linen table mats that she had made from that old blue linen dress, and trimmed with the oyster-white cotton fringe that made a happy design against the polished mahogany. (More housekeeping hints.) The lovely old silver that she had got from Grandmother Stanford on her wedding day gleamed softly. She kept the silver polished with reverent care, and its soft sheen never failed to remind her of Grandmother Stanford's shining white hair that she had carried bravely, like a banner. (Bravely, like a banner—isn't that *good?*) If only she could be as brave, if only she could have the strength that Grandmother had had.

Not that Carol Saunders hadn't been brave. She'd been brave the day that Jim had come home from the Army induction center, rejected. She had been strong then. She remembered how he had come home that day, his shoulders bent, his gray eyes smouldering with helpless rage. "Its no good," he had said, "they won't have me—that ankle—" Carol had known about his ankle—that time it had been broken, but he'd fought on to make his touchdown before he collapsed and was carried from the field. That ankle would never be right—she had known that. And she had been strong. (Naturally, there has to be a football injury.)

But this—this was different.

They finished dinner, and Jim helped her to clear away the dishes.

"Darling," she said, blinking back the tears, "I don't feel like washing the dishes tonight—let's just stack them in the sink, and I'll do them in the morning." She pushed her hair back from her forehead with the funny little gesture that Jim loved.

"Sure, honey," he said, "if you say so. It's certainly no hardship for me."

Carol laughed uncertainly. And then suddenly she knew that she had to tell him. Now.

"Come in the living room," she said. Her heart pounded painfully, and she could feel the pulse beating in the soft part of her neck. "I want to talk to you."

Jim looked puzzled, but he followed Carol into the living room. He sank down on the big soft couch covered with deep red frieze and trimmed with a looped woolen fringe of the palest gray. Carol came and sat close to him. She linked her thin fingers, and sat there a moment, looking down at her hands. *I have to tell him now,* she thought. But still she sat there, silently, twining and untwining the long, thin fingers.

Jim sat as still as death, waiting. Suddenly he leaned forward and caught both her hands in his big ones. "What is it, Carol?" he said, his deep voice vibrant with sympathy. "What is it?" he said again. "Darling," he added softly, "remember that I love you."

Carol looked up gratefully, and her wide gray eyes filled with tears. She felt fear, like a cold hand laid across her heart.

And then suddenly she thought of Grandmother Stanford. And she knew then, deep within her, that she could be strong too. She held her little head high, and the gray eyes were shining.

"Jim," she said, "I'm going to tell you straight. I—I—" Her voice broke, but she swallowed and went on bravely in a clear voice. (Now, I believe, if I have learned the method properly, we are at the crux of the story. It just so happens I don't have a good crux on hand at the moment, but I can think one up later. It hardly matters, for the denouement is the same in any case.)

Jim stared at her a moment, unbelief in his honest eyes, his long jaw rigid. She saw a tiny muscle quivering in his temple. The room was very still, and somewhere off in the distance they heard the plaintive cry of a train rushing through the night.

Finally Jim spoke. "Carol," he said, and his voice shook a little. "Carol—we'll be all right. We'll start over, you and I, together."

"Jim!" Carol cried. "Oh, Jim!" She started to cry, and he wrapped her in his strong arms till she was quiet again. "Oh, darling," she said then. "Darling."

Suddenly she sat up straight. "Jim," she said. "Let's wash the dishes *now*."

[1945–U.S.A.]

QUESTIONS

1. What magazines are the slicks, in which we find stories like the story projected here? Who composes the audience for such stories?
2. Characterize the narrator not only from what she says in her parenthetical comments but also from her own natural style as it shows itself in those comments.
3. Compare and contrast the style of the narrator's draft story with that of her parenthetical comments. Notice as you do the profusion of adjectives and adverbs in the former. Why this profusion? Why doesn't the narrator write her story in her natural voice?

WRITING SUGGESTIONS

1. Try your hand at writing in the style of the slicks. From Smith's story determine what the typical stylistic features of a "slick" story are; then write a paragraph in this style.
2. Address question 3 above in a short essay. Define the contrasting styles and then establish what makes for the difference (epithets or the lack thereof, diction, syntax, and so forth). Consider as well the effects, especially on tone, of each style.

Abstraction of the Ball
That Fell in the River*

Peter Handke

As children we often sat at the edge of the river Sunday afternoons watching the soccer game from where we sat at the midfield line. Whenever the ball fell in the water near where we were sitting we ran alongside the river and with long poles fished the ball out of the water. We could take our time doing this since each time the ball fell in the water another ball that was kept in reserve was put into play from the sideline. We ran as fast as the ball was carried along by the river until we fished it out always just before it reached the wall of the weir. As a rule, the river flowed slowly enough so all we had to do was walk alongside the ball. But once when the river was swollen we had to run.

At the edge of a soccer field, which is situated by a river, a number of children are in the habit of having fun running alongside the ball whenever if falls into the river during the course of play; that is, they run alongside the ball from the midfield line to the end of the field and fish it out of the water only there. Once when the river was swollen, the children had to run very quickly.

Children walk alongside the ball each time it falls in the river at midfield.

* Translated by Michael Roloff.

They fish the ball out of the water only at the end of the field. When the river is swollen the children run very quickly.

Persons walk from the midfield line of a soccer field to the end of the field alongside an object that is driftling in the river at the edge of the field. At the moment when they reach the end of the field the referee whistles half-time. When the river is swollen and the persons have to run they come to a stop alongside the object at the end of the field shortly before the half-time whistle blows.

Someone is walking along the edge of a soccer field next to an object that has fallen in the river. He gets under way 30 seconds before the last minute of the first half of the game. At the very moment he has reached the end of the field and stands next to the object the referee blows the half-time whistle. When the river is swollen he reaches the end of the field together with the object precisely one second before the whistle blows and after he has gotten under way simultaneouusly with the object 10 seconds before the referee blows his whistle.

In order to traverse half the length of a playing field (playing field length = 90 meters) someone requires 1 minute, 30 seconds. When he has to run he requires for the same distance only 9 seconds.

It takes someone 90 seconds to traverse 45 meters. Running it takes him 9 seconds.

---

90 sec ——— 45 m
 1 sec ——— speed x m

 9 sec ——— 45 m
 1 sec ——— speed y m

$$90 \ x = 45$$
$$9 \ y = 45$$
$$x = \frac{45}{90}$$
$$y = \frac{45}{9}$$
$$x = \frac{1}{2}$$
$$y = 5$$

As children we walked on Sunday afternoons at a speed of one half meter per second alongside the soccer ball when it was kicked from the playing field into the river. But when the river was swollen we had to run alongside the ball at a speed of five meters per second to fish the ball out of the water before it would be washed over the wall of the weir.

[1972–Germany]

QUESTIONS

1. What types of narration does this experimental piece exhibit? Name the type of narrator of each paragraph. Is there any pattern or progression with respect to narration?
2. Trace the gradual movement in this story from the concrete to the abstract. How is this movement brought about?
3. This story is about style. How so?

WRITING SUGGESTIONS

1. In a paragraph or so, discuss the differing effects of the types of narration found here. Consider as well the implications as to narration of the strictly scientific passages.
2. Compare and contrast Handke's first paragraph with each succeeding section as to style and effect. In your essay, move to a consideration of what Handke is saying about the language of literature as opposed to the language of science through his multiple versions of the same subject.

An Innocent at Rinkside

William Faulkner

The vacant ice looked tired though it shouldn't have. They told him it had been put down only a few minutes ago following a basketball game and after the hockey match it would be taken up again to make room for something else. But it looked out expectant but resigned, like the mirror simulating ice in the Christmas store window, not before the miniature fir trees and reindeer and cosy lamplit cottage were arranged upon it, but after they had been dismantled and cleared away.

Then it was filled with motion, speed. To the innocent, who had never seen it before, it seemed discorded and inconsequent, bizarre and paradoxical like the frantic darting of the weightless bugs which run on the surface of stagnant pools. Then it would break, coalesce through a kind of kaleidoscopic whirl like a child's toy, into a pattern, a design almost beautiful, as if an inspired choreographer had drilled a willing and patient and hard-working troupe of dancers—a pattern, design which was trying to tell him something, say something to him urgent and important and true in that second before, already bulging with the motion and the speed, it began to disintegrate and dissolve.

Then he learned to find the puck and follow it. Then the individual players would emerge. They would not emerge like the sweating bare-handed behemoths from the troglodyte mass of football, but instead as fluid and fast and effortless as rapier thrusts of lightning—Richard with something of the passionate glittering fatal alien quality of snakes, Geoffrion like an agile ruthless precocious boy who maybe couldn't do anything else but then he didn't need to; and others—the veteran Laprade,

324

still with the know-how and the grace. But he had time too now, or rather time had him, and what remained was no longer expendable that recklessly, heedlessly, successfully; not enough of it left now to buy fresh passion and fresh triumph with.

Excitement: men in rapid, hard, close physical conflict, not just with bare hands, but armed with the knife blades of skates and the hard, fast, deft sticks which break bones when used right. He had noticed how many women were among the spectators, and for just a moment he thought that perhaps this was why—that here actual male blood could flow, not from the crude impact of a heavier fist but from the rapid and delicate stroke of weapons, which, like the European rapier or the frontier pistol, reduced mere size and brawn to its proper perspective to the passion and the will. But only for a moment because he, the innocent, didn't like that idea either. It was the excitement of speed and grace, with the puck for catalyst, to give it reason, meaning.

He watched it—the figure-darted glare of ice, the concentric tiers rising in sections stipulated by the hand-lettered names of the individual fan-club idols, vanishing upward into the pall of tobacco smoke trapped by the roof—the roof which stopped and trapped all that intent and tense watching, and concentrated it downward upon the glare of ice frantic and frenetic with motion; until the byproduct of the speed and the motion— their violence—had no chance to exhaust itself upward into space and so leave on the ice only the swift glittering changing pattern. And he thought how perhaps something is happening to sport in America (assuming that by definition sport is something you do yourself, in solitude or not, because it is fun), and that something is the roof we are putting over it and them. Skating, basketball, tennis, track meets and even steeplechasing have moved indoors; football and baseball function beneath covers of arc lights and in time will be rain and coldproofed too. There still remain the proper working of a fly over trout water or the taking of a rise of birds in front of a dog or the right placing of a bullet in a deer or even a bigger animal which will hurt you if you don't. But not for long: in time that will be indoors too beneath lights and the trapped pall of spectator tobacco, the concentric sections bearing the name and device of the lion or the fish as well as that of the Richard or Geoffrion of the scoped rifle or four-ounce rod.

But (to repeat) not for long, because the innocent did not quite believe that either. We—Americans—like to watch, we like the adrenalic discharge of vicarious excitement or triumph or success. But we like to do also: the discharge of the personal excitement of the triumph and the fear to be had from actually setting the horse at the stone wall or pointing the overcanvased sloop or finding by actual test if you can line up two sights and one buffalo in time. There must have been little boys in that throng too, frantic with the slow excruciating passage of time, panting for the hour when they would be Richard or Geoffrion or Laprade—the same little Negro boys whom the innocent has seen shadowboxing in front of a photograph of Joe Louis in his own Mississippi town, the same little Norwegian boys he watched staring up the snowless slope of the Holmen-kollen jump one July day in the hills above Oslo.

Only he (the innocent) did wonder just what a professional hockey-match, whose purpose is to make a decent and reasonable profit for its owners, had to do with our National Anthem. What are we afraid of? Is it our national character of which we are so in doubt, so fearful that it might not hold up in the clutch, that we not only dare not open a professional athletic contest or a beauty-pageant or a real-estate auction, but we must even use a Chamber of Commerce race for Miss Sewage Disposal or a wildcat land-sale, to remind us that liberty gained without honor and sacrifice and held without constant vigilance and undiminished honor and complete willingness to sacrifice again at need, was not worth having to begin with? Or, by blaring or chanting it at ourselves every time ten or twelve or eighteen or twenty-two young men engage formally for the possession of a puck or a ball, or just one young woman walks across a lighted platform in a bathing-suit, do we hope to so dull and eviscerate the words and tune with repetition, that when we do hear it we will not be disturbed from that dream-like state in which "honor" is a break and "truth" an angle?

[1955–U.S.A]

QUESTIONS

1. What kind of narrator tells us of the innocent here? Characterize the innocent. Whom do we know more about by the end of this piece, the boy or the narrator?
2. Is this piece a story or an essay with fictional trappings? Defend your judgment.
3. Compare and contrast "An Innocent at Rinkside" and Hemingway's "A Clean, Well-Lighted Place" (which follows) as to sentence length and complexity. What are the differing effects of each style?
4. Jot down a few of Faulkner's many metaphors and analyze their effect in context.

WRITING SUGGESTIONS

1. Consider question 2 above and write a paragraph stating and defending your judgment.
2. Assuming a reader not familiar with the story, write a review of "An Innocent at Rinkside." Try to persuade your reader of the rightness of your assessment by backing it up with evidence from the story itself.
3. Whether a story or not, "An Innocent at Rinkside" displays Faulkner's unique way of putting words together. In a paragraph, analyze the attributes of Faulkner's style as seen here. Then weigh its merits and judge its effectiveness.

A Clean, Well-Lighted Place

Ernest Hemingway

It was late and every one had left the café except an old man who sat in the shadow the leaves of the tree made against the electric light. In the day time the street was dusty, but at night the dew settled the dust and the old man liked to sit late because he was deaf and now at night it was quiet and he felt the difference. The two waiters inside the café knew that the old man was a little drunk, and while he was a good client they knew that if he became too drunk he would leave without paying, so they kept watch on him.

"Last week he tried to commit suicide," one waiter said.

"Why?"

"He was in despair."

"What about?"

"Nothing."

"How do you know it was nothing?"

"He has plenty of money."

They sat together at a table that was close against the wall near the door of the café and looked at the terrace where the tables were all empty except where the old man sat in the shadow of the leaves of the tree that moved slightly in the wind. A girl and a soldier went by in the street. The street light shone on the brass number on his collar. The girl wore no head covering and hurried beside him.

"The guard will pick him up," one waiter said.

"What does it matter if he gets what he's after?"

"He had better get off the street now. The guard will get him. They went by five minutes ago."

The old man sitting in the shadow rapped on his saucer with his glass. The younger waiter went over to him.

"What do you want?"

The old man looked at him. "Another brandy," he said.

"You'll be drunk," the waiter said. The old man looked at him. The waiter went away.

"He'll stay all night," he said to his colleague. "I'm sleepy now. I never get into bed before three o'clock. He should have killed himself last week."

The waiter took the brandy bottle and another saucer from the counter inside the café and marched out to the old man's table. He put down the saucer and poured the glass full of brandy.

"You should have killed yourself last week," he said to the deaf man. The old man motioned with his finger. "A little more," he said. The waiter poured on into the glass so that the brandy slopped over and ran down the stem into the top saucer of the pile. "Thank you," the old man said. The waiter took the bottle back inside the café. He sat down at the table with his colleague again.

"He's drunk now," he said.

"He's drunk every night."

"What did he want to kill himself for?"

"How should I know."

"How did he do it?"

"He hung himself with a rope."

"Who cut him down?"

"His niece."

"Why did they do it?

"Fear for his soul."

"How much money has he got?"

"He's got plenty."

"He must be eighty years old."

"Anyway I should say he was eighty."

"I wish he would go home. I never get to bed before three o'clock. What kind of hour is that to go to bed?"

"He stays up because he likes it."

"He's lonely. I'm not lonely. I have a wife waiting in bed for me."

"He had a wife once too."

"A wife would be no good to him now."

"You can't tell. He might be better with a wife."

"His niece looks after him."

"I know. You said she cut him down."

"I wouldn't want to be that old. An old man is a nasty thing."

"Not always. This old man is clean. He drinks without spilling. Even now, drunk. Look at him."

"I don't want to look at him. I wish he would go home. He has no regard for those who must work."

The old man looked from his glass across the square, then over at the waiters.

"Another brandy," he said, pointing to his glass. The waiter who was in a hurry came over.

"Finished," he said, speaking with that omission of syntax stupid people employ when talking to drunk people or foreigners. "No more tonight. Close now."

"Another," said the old man.

"No. Finished." The waiter wiped the edge of the table with a towel and shook his head.

The old man stood up, slowly counted the saucers, took a leather coin purse from his pocket and paid for the drinks, leaving half a peseta tip.

The waiter watched him go down the street. a very old man walking unsteadily but with dignity.

"Why didn't you let him stay and drink?" the unhurried waiter asked. They were putting up the shutters. "It is not half-past two."

"I want to go home to bed."

"What is an hour?"

"More to me than to him."

"An hour is the same."

"You talk like an old man yourself. He can buy a bottle and drink at home."

"It's not the same."

"No, it is not," agreed the waiter with a wife. He did not wish to be unjust. He was only in a hurry.

"And you? You have no fear of going home before your usual hour?"

"Are you trying to insult me?"

"No, hombre, only to make a joke."

"No," the waiter who was in hurry said, rising from pulling down the metal shutters. "I have confidence. I am all confidence."

"You have youth, confidence, and a job," the older waiter said. "You have everything."

"And what do you lack?"

"Everything but work."

"You have everything I have."

"No. I have never had confidence and I am not young."

"Come on. Stop talking nonsense and lock up."

"I am of those who like to stay late at the café," the older waiter said. "With all those who do not want to go to bed. With all those who need a light for the night."

"I want to go home and into bed."

"We are of two different kinds," the older waiter said. He was now dressed to go home. "It is not only a question of youth and confidence although those things are very beautiful. Each night I am reluctant to close up because there may be some one who needs the café."

"Hombre, there are bodegas open all night long."

"You do not understand. This is a clean and pleasant café. It is well lighted. The light is very good and also, now, there are shadows of the leaves."

"Good night," said the younger waiter.

"Good night," the other said. Turning off the electric light he continued the conversation with himself. It is the light of course but it is necessary that the place be clean and pleasant. You do not want music. Certainly you do not want music. Nor can you stand before a bar with dignity although that is all that is provided for these hours. What did he fear? It was not fear or dread. It was nothing that he knew too well. It was all a nothing and a man was nothing too. It was only that and light was all it needed and a certain cleanness and order. Some lived in it and never felt it but he knew it all was nada y pues nada y nada y pues nada. Our nada who art in nada, nada be thy name thy kingdom nada thy will be nada in nada as it is in nada. Give us this nada our daily nada and nada us our nada as we nada our nadas and nada us not into nada but deliver us from nada; pues nada. Hail nothing full of nothing, nothing is with thee. He smiled and stood before a bar with a shining steam pressure coffee machine.

"What's yours? asked the barman.

"Nada."

"Otro loco mas," said the barman and turned away.

"A little cup," said the waiter.

The barman poured it for him.

"The light is very bright and pleasant but the bar is unpolished," the waiter said.

The barman looked at him but did not answer. It was too late at night for conversation.

"You want another copita?" the barman asked.

"No, thank you," said the waiter and went out. He disliked bars and bodegas. A clean, well-lighted café was a very different thing. Now, without thinking further, he would go home to his room. He would lie in the bed and finally, with daylight, he would go to sleep. After all, he said to himself, it is probably only insomnia. Many must have it.

[1933–U.S.A.]

QUESTIONS

1. Contrast the two waiters, whose characterization emphasizes their differences. With which of the two do you sympathize? Why?
2. Why does the older waiter sympathize with the old man? Why does the younger waiter not understand him?
3. In light of the story as it unfolds, the use of the word "nothing" (or "nada") is ironic. How so?
4. Light, primarily, and cleanliness and order, secondarily, are symbolic here. What do they symbolize?
5. Why is the older waiter's final thought a rationalization only, especially in light of his answer, "Otro loco mas" (another more crazy)? What theme does this story explore?
6. Analyze Hemingway's style. Take into account sentence length and structure; repetition of sentence patterns and the rhythm that results; diction; and the use of adjectives and adverbs. How is the story's style appropriate to its theme? Compare the effects of Hemingway's style and Faulkner's ("An Innocent at Rinkside"), and Hemingway's and Woolf's ("A Haunted House"—which follows).

WRITING SUGGESTIONS

1. Determine the main features of Hemingway's style as seen in the present story. Then write a short dialogue or paragraph in this style. Try to be aware of the stylistic choices you are making as you make them.
2. In a paragraph or two, compare and contrast Hemingway's style and that of William Carlos Williams as seen in "The Use of Force" (pages 306–09). There are many similarities, yet the overall effect is quite different. Define the similarities and try to account for the difference in effect.
3. In a paragraph or more, discuss the relationship of Hemingway's style to his theme in "A Clean, Well-Lighted Place." Establish what his theme is and identify the special qualities of Hemingway's style that seem in accord with his theme.
4. In a short essay, contrast Hemingway's story and Faulkner's "An Innocent at Rinkside" as to style. Establish the main features of the style of each author, and analyze the difference between the two styles and their effects.

A Haunted House

Virginia Woolf

Whatever hour you woke there was a door shutting. From room to room they went, hand in hand, lifting here, opening there, making sure—a ghostly couple.

"Here we left it," she said. And he added, "Oh, but here too!" "It's upstairs," she murmured. "And in the garden," he whispered. "Quietly," they said, "or we shall wake them."

But it wasn't that you woke us. Oh, no. "They're looking for it; they're drawing the curtain," one might say, and so read on a page or two. "Now they've found it," one would be certain, stopping the pencil on the margin. And then, tired of reading, one might rise and see for oneself, the house all empty, the doors standing open, only the wood pigeons bubbling with content and the hum of the threshing machine sounding from the farm. "What did I come in here for? What did I want to find?" My hands were empty. "Perhaps it's upstairs then?" The apples were in the loft. And so down again, the garden still as ever, only the book had slipped into the grass.

But they had found it in the drawing-room. Not that one could ever see them. The window panes reflected apples, reflected roses; all the leaves were green in the glass. If they moved in the drawing-room, the apple only turned its yellow side. Yet, the moment after, if the door was opened, spread about the floor, hung upon the walls, pendant from the ceiling— what? My hands were empty. The shadow of a thrush crossed the carpet; from the deepest wells of silence the wood pigeon drew its bubble of sound. "Safe, safe, safe," the pulse of the house beat softly. "The treasure buried; the room . . ." the pulse stopped short. Oh, was that the buried treasure?

A moment later the light had faded. Out in the garden then? But the trees spun darkness for a wandering beam of sun. So fine, so rare, coolly sunk beneath the surface the beam I sought always burnt behind the glass. Death was the glass; death was between us; coming to the woman first, hundreds of years ago, leaving the house, sealing all the windows; the rooms were darkened. He left it, left her, went North, went East, saw the stars turned in the Southern sky; sought the house, found it dropped beneath the Downs. "Safe, safe, safe," the pulse of the house beat gladly. "The Treasure yours."

The wind roars up the avenue. Trees stoop and bend this way and that. Moonbeams splash and spill wildly in the rain. But the beam of the lamp falls straight from the window. The candle burns stiff and still. Wandering through the house, opening the windows, whispering not to wake us, the ghostly couple seek their joy.

"Here we slept," she says. And he adds, "Kisses without number." "Waking in the morning—" "Silver between the trees—" "Upstairs—" "In the garden—" "When summer came—" "In winter snowtime—" The doors go shutting far in the distance, gently knocking like the pulse of a heart.

Nearer they come; cease at the doorway. The wind falls, the rain slides silver down the glass. Our eyes darken; we hear no steps beside us; we see no lady spread her ghostly cloak. His hands shield the lantern. "Look," he breathes. "Sound asleep. Love upon their lips."

Stooping, holding their silver lamp above us, long they look and deeply. Long they pause. The wind drives straightly; the flame stoops slightly. Wild beams of moonlight cross both floor and wall, and, meeting, stain the faces bent; the faces pondering; the faces that search the sleepers and seek their hidden joy.

"Safe, safe, safe," the heart of the house beats proudly. "Long years—" he sighs. "Again you found me." "Here," she murmurs, "sleeping; in the garden reading; laughing, rolling apples in the loft. Here we left our treasure—" Stooping, their light lifts the lids upon my eyes. "Safe! safe! safe!" the pulse of the house beats wildly. Waking, I cry "Oh, is this *your* buried treasure? The light in the heart."

[1921–Great Britain]

QUESTIONS

1. Read aloud a passage from each of the last three stories. In general, how do they differ tonally and rhythmically? In what ways are the special qualities of each appropriate to each?
2. This first-person monologue concerns all older houses (thus "a" rather than "the" in the title) with new occupants. How so?
3. Describe the narrator's mood, which here coincides with that of the story. How does Woolf's style contribute to the mood overall?

WRITING SUGGESTIONS

1. Woolf's narrator engages in a daydream. Write a paragraph on how the style of the story helps to create the mood and feel of daydreaming.
2. In an essay, compare and contrast the styles of Faulkner, Hemingway, and Woolf. Because Woolf's style is similar in one way or another to both Faulkner's and Hemingway's, hers might be the best to focus on in getting at the likenesses and differences.

The Story of an Hour

Kate Chopin

Knowing that Mrs. Mallard was afflicted with a heart trouble, great care was taken to break to her as gently as possible the news of her husband's death.

It was her sister Josephine who told her, in broken sentences, veiled hints that revealed in half concealing. Her husband's friend Richards was there, too, near her. It was he who had been in the newspaper office when intelligence of the railroad disaster was received, with Brently Mallard's name leading the list of "killed." He had only taken the time to assure himself of its truth by a second telegram, and had hastened to forestall any less careful, less tender friend in bearing the sad message.

She did not hear the story as many women have heard the same, with a paralyzed inability to accept its significance. She wept at once, with sudden, wild abandonment, in her sister's arms. When the storm of grief had spent itself she went away to her room alone. She would have no one follow her.

There stood, facing the open window, a comfortable, roomy arm-chair. Into this she sank, pressed down by a physical exhaustion that haunted her body and seemed to reach into her soul.

She could see in the open square before her house the tops of trees that were all aquiver with the new spring life. The delicious breath of rain was in the air. In the street below a peddler was crying his wares. The notes of a distant song which some one was singing reached her faintly, and countless sparrows were twittering in the eaves.

There were patches of blue sky showing here and there through the clouds that had met and piled above the other in the west facing her window.

She sat with her head thrown back upon the cushion of the chair quite motionless, except when a sob came up into her throat and shook her, as a child who has cried itself to sleep continues to sob in its dreams.

She was young, with a fair, calm face, whose lines bespoke repression and even a certain strength. But now there was a dull stare in her eyes, whose gaze was fixed away off yonder on one of those patches of blue sky. It was not a glance of reflection, but rather indicated a suspension of intelligent thought.

There was something coming to her and she was waiting for it, fearfully. What was it? She did not know; it was too subtle and elusive to name. But she felt it, creeping out of the sky, reaching toward her through the sounds, the scents, the color that filled the air.

Now her bosom rose and fell tumultuously. She was beginning to recognize this thing that was approaching to posses her, and she was striving to beat it back with her will—as powerless as her two white slender hands would have been.

When she abandoned herself a little whispered word escaped her slightly parted lips. She said it over and over under her breath: "Free, free, free!" The vacant stare and the look of terror that had followed it went from her eyes. They stayed keen and bright. Her pulses beat fast, and the coursing blood warmed and relaxed every inch of her body.

She did not stop to ask if it were not a monstrous joy that held her. A clear and exalted perception enabled her to dismiss the suggestion as trivial.

She knew that she would weep again when she saw the kind, tender hands folded in death: the face that had never looked save with love upon her, fixed and gray and dead. But she saw beyond that bitter moment a long procession of years to come that would belong to her absolutely. And she opened and spread her arms out to them in welcome.

There would be no one to live for during those coming years; she would live for herself. There would be no powerful will bending her in that blind persistence with which men and women believe they have a right to impose a private will upon a fellow-creature. A kind intention or a cruel intention made the act seem no less a crime as she looked upon it in that brief moment of illumination.

And yet she had loved him—sometimes. Often she had not. What did it matter! What could love, the unsolved mystery, count for in face of this possession of self-assertion which she suddenly recognized as the strongest impulse of her being!

"Free! Body and soul free!" she kept whispering.

Josephine was kneeling before the closed door with her lips to the keyhole, imploring for admission. "Louise, open the door! I beg; open the door—you will make yourself ill. What are you doing, Louise? For heaven's sake open the door."

"Go away. I am not making myself ill." No; she was drinking in a very elixir of life through that open window.

Her fancy was running riot along those days ahead of her. Spring days, and summer days, and all sort of days that would be her own. She breathed a quick prayer that life might be long. It was only yesterday she had thought with a shudder that life might be long.

She arose at length and opened the door to her sister's importunities. There was a feverish triumph in her eyes, and she carried herself unwittingly like a goddess of Victory. She clasped her sister's waist, and together they descended the stairs. Richards stood waiting for them at the bottom.

Some one was opening the front door with a latchkey. It was Brently Mallard who entered, a little travel-stained, composedly carrying his grip-sack and umbrella. He had been far from the scene of accident, and did not even know there had been one. He stood amazed at Josephine's piercing cry; at Richards' quick motion to screen him from the view of his wife.

But Richards was too late.

When the doctors came they said she had died of heart disease—of joy that kills.

[1894–U.S.A.]

QUESTIONS

1. Summarize Chopin's plot. What is ironic about it? What other ironies are to be found in the story?
2. Plot here creates irony, which in turn goes into the making of mood. What is the overall mood of "The Story of an Hour"?
3. Does Louise hate her husband? Has he been dreadful to her? Has her life with him been terrible? Does she feel grief at his supposed death? Choosing freely, would Louise choose this man again? Why, then, does she feel what she feels? What do her feelings tell us about the author's view of the social codes governing women at the time?
4. What is Chopin's theme, and how does mood help to establish it?
5. Compare the fifth and sixth paragraphs (beginning "She could see in the open square . . .) with the third to last paragraph (beginning "Some one was opening

the front door . . .) as to style. How do they differ and how are their differing effects achieved? (Consider diction, sound, rhythm, and imagery.) What is intimated by the calculated stylistic difference between these passages?

WRITING SUGGESTIONS

1. (a) In a paragraph, discuss the mood of the "The Story of an Hour" in connection with its irony. What is its mood and how does irony help to create it?

   (b) In a separate paragraph, discuss your response to this story and detail why you so respond.
2. In an essay, address question 5 above. Compare such stylistic traits as diction, sound, rhythm, and imagery. Also, define the differing effects of the passages in question.
3. To what extent does this story remain relevant today? In a short paper, argue that it is or is not relevant to the contemporary situation of women. Whatever your judgment, consider also what it is about "The Story of an Hour" that makes it compelling still, or that keeps it from seeming dated.

· 7 ·

SETTING/SYMBOL

OF TIME AND PLACE

The word *setting* refers to all of a story's details that go into the making in our minds of a specific physical locale, whether real or imagined, and a specific cultural environment. Every story has a setting of some sort, though, to be sure, in many stories setting isn't of great importance; it is present only as backdrop, mentioned only in passing and only because people do not exist except in specific times and places. But in many other stories setting is essential to the meaning. For example, should we fail to realize that Graham Greene's "I Spy" (pages 358–60) is set during wartime (World War I), we would have no hope of grasping the story.

This doesn't mean that a setting has to be especially emphasized to function in a story. If anything, the setting of "I Spy" is underplayed; yet it is primarily its wartime setting that activates the story's plot. Setting, then, can inform and drive a plot. It can also be an agent of mood. Times and places often have special atmospheric qualities about them. By exploiting these qualities, or by evoking the feelings people generally associate with distinct times and places, writers can create and guide mood overall. A story set in Italy during the Renaissance will certainly be quite different in mood from a story set in Antarctica at present. Or take horror and ghost stories, with their howling storms and haunted houses. Setting is usually a key agent of mood in fictions of this type. Setting may even contribute directly to our perception of theme. The theme of "An Episode of War" (pages 372–75), for instance, has much to do with Crane's description of landscape coupled with his description of war; and the place in Heming-

340

way's "A Clean, Well-Lighted Place" (pages 328–31) is central with respect to the theme of the story.

Especially, setting can contribute to characterization. As I suggested when speaking of characterization, one can usually tell much about a person from that person's home region, as one can from a person's cultural background (both matters of location in place and time). Moreover, people express themselves through their personal effects, their homes, their modes of dress. We judge one person tasteful and another a boor, one well adjusted and another neurotic on the basis of their possessions, their habitual ways of dressing, the condition of where they live. In fiction, these various aspects of setting reveal no less than they do in life. The historical context in many stories can also help to reveal something of the inner lives of characters, as can the geographical locale (the sea, a desert, and so on). Setting can inform us, as well, about what has shaped a character and determined the character's way of seeing. For example, the Dublin of Joyce's two stories "Eveline" and "Araby" (pages 381–85 and 386–90 respectively) becomes of special importance in our understanding of the protagonists of each and their psychological disabilities.

That a setting may manifest psychological traits of characters further suggests that setting can provide a writer with a rich source of symbols, and so it can. In a story depicting a fugitive riding across a wide, deserted plain, for example, description of the plain would probably be a token of the loneliness of the fugitive. That is, the story's setting would become symbolic, conveying meaning over and above its relevance as literal backdrop. Psychological traits and emotional states are intangible. How can they be depicted dramatically without the incursion of direct comment? This is a question that every writer faces with respect to the inner lives of characters. Of course, a narrator can simply describe the traits and states of characters. But undramatic, lengthy description is a bore; and the shorter a story is, the less room there is for protracted description. How much better to make details serve double duty, as they are made to serve in Sean O'Faolain's "The Trout" (pages 393–96). Here, a tunnel of trees and a pool with a trout in it function literally, but they also objectify the inner state of the story's young protagonist. By functioning symbolically as well as literally, the setting helps to create the general revelation the story entails.

THE LITERARY IMPULSE

I have just defined, in effect, what I conceive to be the fundamental literary impulse: to make every detail in a work take its place in a chain of details each of which finally contributes to some general revelation. No word is wasted; no detail that does not further a story's progress toward meaning can be allowed in. Given this impulse toward unity, writers naturally tend to choose details that serve multiple functions—not only to set the scene but also to establish character; not only to further plot but also to enhance mood. The symbol is our case in point.

From one vantage point, everything in human life is symbolic: every gesture and facial expression carries special significance; every word stands in for whatever the word denotes; every image we conjure up represents some aspect of the self. From this outlook, every story, too, is a symbol—the embodiment of an idea or the concrete expression of a general insight. But this view is too broad to be of much help when it comes to dealing with specific symbols. For the purposes of literary analysis, we usually restrict the word "symbol" to anything that in its context suggests meaning over and above its literal significance. Dreams are full of symbols in this sense. You dream that you're walking down a street when suddenly a steamroller heads right at you; you try to escape, but the more you run, the closer the steamroller gets. Though a literal agent of the action of the dream, the steamroller is also symbolic, embodying a wealth of meaning from the felt experience of the dreamer. That many pages would probably be required to spell out that meaning in full points to why writers use symbols. The beauty of the symbol is its compactness. Like irony, symbolism allows for compression (much said in few words) as well as for dramatic presentation. That is, the symbol is a means of expressing attitudes, feelings, and ideas concretely through objects, actions, situations, or whatever. The "dust" mentioned in "Eveline" (pages 381–85), for example, is literal dust, an aspect of the story's setting and an atmospheric detail. Yet during the course of the story it comes to mean more. Indeed, by the end of "Eveline" one feels that its meaning can almost be summed up by the one word "dust." Because of the context, this descriptive detail becomes a symbol, helping to embody and reinforce the story's theme.

Again, the symbol is a means of expressing attitudes, feelings, ideas through objects, actions, situations, or whatever. We've just seen that an object—dust—can become a symbol. A familiar example of the object-as-symbol is the hats worn in classical Hollywood Westerns. The hats are literal hats, but they also signify by way of their colors (white or black) the moral qualities of their wearers, good or bad. Names, too, can be symbolic. In life, names tell us little except perhaps for nationality. And when a name does seem to have a symbolic ring to it, we're struck by a sense of irony because we don't expect names to be symbolic: I've heard of a judge named "Fix," a welfare supervisor named "Overcash," and a sewer commissioner named "Drainoff." Pseudonyms are a different matter. Chosen by their bearers, many are pointedly symbolic: "Lenin," meaning "man of iron"; "Stalin," meaning "man of steel"; the first names of a good number of Hollywood actors ("Rip," "Rock," and so forth), suggesting virility. We sometimes find names like these in fiction: Dickens's "M'Choakumchild," for a brutal Scottish teacher; Galsworthy's "Forsyte," for a practical lawyer; "Darth Vader," evocative in associations and sound alike. All are literal names of characters, yet all carry meaning over and above their literal significance as names.

Titles of stories may be symbolic as well, which is yet another reason why it is good to pay attention to titles. Alan Paton's title "The Waste Land" (pages 362–64), for instance, points not only to the setting of his story but also to the state of mind of its protagonist, objectified by that setting; and Hemingway's title "A Clean, Well-Lighted Place" (pages 328–31) poignantly captures the human yearning for order and stability to which the story as a whole gives voice. Finally, as we have noted, situations and actions may have symbolic weight. For example, the situation in Graham Greene's "I Spy" (pages 358–60) seems particularly meaningful: the boy's spying on his father proves an ironic prelude to the father's being arrested as a spy. Here, too, there is symbolic action—the boy's smoking of a cigarette. This action signifies the boy's movement to adulthood, which is what the story is about. Or take the girl's refusal to open her mouth in Williams's "The Use of Force" (pages 306–09). Aside from being a token of her fierce independence, her refusal suggests the unconscious mechanism of denial and repression that the doctor who must open her mouth fights off in himself.

But how does one recognize symbols in the first place and interpret them once recognized? Here are some guidelines, first for recognition and then for interpretation.

Recognizing Symbols

Broadly speaking, symbols can be divided into two types: conventional and created. Conventional symbols are a matter of general knowledge. The flag, the cross, and "mom and apple pie" are examples of conventional cultural symbols in the West, "mom and apple pie" being further restricted to American culture. In fiction as in life, conventional symbols are apparent because we've grown up with them. If one is attuned to one's culture, conventional symbols by and large take care of themselves. (Older literature, however, and literature of other cultures usually require some groundwork in order for one to recognize specific conventional symbols.) Created symbols, on the other hand, are more or less unique to their contexts. It is the created symbol that requires special attention to spot and interpret.

Anything that becomes symbolic by virtue of its context alone is a created symbol. Most dream symbols are of this sort. What draws our attention to the possibility that an object, an action, a situation is symbolic is the context. With respect to fiction, this means that a story *itself* must signal that one or another of its details is symbolic. It can do so by way of repetition, elaboration, and placement. For example, both repetition and placement suggest that dust in "Eveline" is symbolic as well as literal: Joyce tells of the dustiness of Eveline's home four times, once in the first paragraph (beginnings and endings are of special importance). Why? Or why should an author elaborate upon a detail if it is nothing more than part of the descriptive background? The answer in both cases is that the element is not merely descriptive. Repetition, elaboration, and placement usually indicate that more is going on. Therefore, if something is repeated, elaborated, or placed in a significant spot, we have reason to think that it might be symbolic.

Sometimes, too, the question "If not symbolic, what?" will lead to immediate recognition of symbolic intent. When I remember a dream, the main reason I have for taking its various features as symbols is that they don't make a great deal of sense taken literally. There are stories like this. For example, Nigel Dennis's "The Pukey" (pages 351–55) is a story that does not present much of a literal level at all. In that we know that there is no such thing as a pukey, we must conclude that the story is either crazy or thoroughly symbolic.

Finally, some details will show themselves to be symbolic if we ask the question "Why this rather than that?" In "Eveline," for instance, the city of Buenos Aires is mentioned twice as the place to which Eveline's sailor would take her. Why Buenos Aires rather than Paris, or Madrid, or New York? The story suggests an answer. Therefore, Joyce's chosen city is not only a literal place but also symbolic, conveying meaning different from its meaning as literal referent.

Interpreting Symbols

Conventional symbols in fiction are understood according to their cultural associations. For instance, in Katherine Anne Porter's story "The Grave" (pages 397–402), a silver dove and a gold ring figure prominently.

Both are conventional symbols, the dove of peace, the ring of unity and completion. And both have these meanings within the story. Once we recognize dove and ring to be symbols, we still have to come to an understanding of their functions in the fictional context; but by bringing to the story a general awareness of our culture's conventional symbolism, we have already access to the primary symbolic meanings of both dove and ring and, as a consequence, at least partial access to the story as it unfolds.

Whereas we find the meaning of a conventional symbol in our culture, we must think our way into the meaning of a created symbol. That is, we must construct the symbolic meaning by carefully considering both the attributes of the thing (or place, person, action) itself and its associations in the particular story. In Sean O'Faolain's "The Trout" (pages 393–96), for instance, there is a dark walk of trees forming a tunnel. This passageway is frightening to Julia, the story's protagonist, who is on the verge of adolescence. In the context of the story, the dark walkway suggests—both by virtue of what it is literally (a passageway) and by virtue of the associations of apprehensiveness or even fear that it evokes—the passage that is adolescence and all of its attendant fears. Symbolic meanings must differ from literal meanings, of course, or there could be no symbols in the first place. Still, they are usually closely related.

Conventional or created, every symbol must be taken in context. Even conventional symbols must be seen in the given context for their functions to be understood. And created symbols have only their specific contexts to lead us to see them as symbols and to guide and validate interpretation. We considered a while back that the girl's refusal to open her mouth in "The Use of Force" (pages 306–09) could be taken as symbolic of denial and repression generally, which is something over and above its literal meaning in the story. But we have to add, *"in this context."* For the suggestion makes sense only in light of the fact that the story itself brings to consciousness the usually unconscious mechanism of denial and repression, which its protagonist fights off in himself. In other words, we're not just conjuring up meaning out of nowhere. We take our cue from the context, and in turn we must relate everything we have to say about symbols to the context.

Before concluding, we should note that most stories are literal by and large. What symbols they contain are reinforcing—that is, they don't control our understanding of a story but rather serve to buttress its literal meaning. The symbols in "Eveline" (pages 381–85) are of this sort. One can miss them entirely yet still grasp the import of the story. It is best, therefore, not to become a symbol hunter, looking for symbolic significance in every detail. To do so would be to distort the average story.

Remember, a story itself must somehow give indication as to whether a detail has symbolic weight.

In some stories, however, symbols carry or control so much of the meaning that the stories cannot be understood unless we grasp their symbolic structure. Porter's "The Grave" (pages 397–402) and Kafka's "First Sorrow" (406–08) are both of this type, though they are quite different in effect. "The Grave" is like a dream: it has a literal level, but its literal aspect seems somewhat inconsequential. Like a dream, the story is centrally symbolic and cannot be comprehended without an understanding of its symbols in relationship to one another. Even then, the story refuses to be neatly translated. Its symbols are multidimensional, dense and rich in emotional resonance. As the novelist Henry James said of symbols of this sort, they "cast long shadows." "First Sorrow" is also centrally symbolic, having virtually no literal level. In contrast to "The Grave," however, the symbolic elements of "First Sorrow" resolve themselves into neat equivalents (this equals that). The reason for this difference is that "First Sorrow" is an allegory, that is, a work in which characters and events enact the ideas they stand for.

Stories in which symbols are essential to the meaning are easy enough to spot: they quickly give rise to the question "If not symbolic, what?" If a story doesn't force this question, then whatever symbols it contains are most likely reinforcing and not controlling. They enrich, they deepen, but they do not direct. To be sure, we're not always conscious of symbols and their reverberations as we encounter them in daily life or in fiction. To become fully responsive readers, though, we need to be sensitive to the symbols writers use and the possible meanings of those symbols in context.

SUMMARY SUGGESTIONS: UNDERSTANDING SETTING AND SYMBOL

1. When considering the setting of a story, ask if the story could be set in another time or place. If it could, then setting is of little consequence, nothing more than a backdrop. If it could not, then setting is probably one of the elements in the story that go into the making of the story's meaning. Just as narration is (usually) a controlling element, directing us toward attitude and theme, so setting may control, governing mood, for instance, and thereby helping to establish theme. We must make that determination as we read. If setting is only backdrop, it can be pushed to the back of the mind. If it is more, it must be attended to.

2. Remember that setting is often a means of characterization, suggesting various qualities of the characters. Therefore, though setting

may sometimes be pushed to the back of the mind, it should not be pushed out entirely. Even in stories in which setting is little more than backdrop, it frequently tells us something about characters. Therefore, it should always be considered at least briefly with respect to characterization.

3. Remember, too, that certain aspects of a setting may be symbolic. It is usually rewarding to consider this possibility if a certain detail of a setting calls attention to itself.

4. As to symbols, almost anything in a story can be symbolic—a setting, an object, an action, a situation. What makes something symbolic, remember, is that it conveys meaning different from (though related to) its literal meaning. Don't forget, too, that the meaning you feel a symbol to have must be tested as to relevance against the general context. And the context must itself suggest that a detail is more than literal. Context is all.

5. Don't be a symbol hunter. However, do try to be open to symbolic possibilities as they present themselves. Be alert to such matters of structure as repetition, elaboration, and placement, all of which can signal special significance. Writers gain emphasis by way of structure. We, in our turn, must learn to respond appropriately to the clues given. The writer's job is to create a story that contains its own meaning; our job as readers is to live through that meaning and make it our own.

WRITING ON SYMBOLS AND SYMBOLISM

Once one has grasped a few symbols in a text, or perhaps seen that its very structure springs from symbolic details, the question is how to use these insights. What can be done with symbols and symbolism when it comes to writing? Our consideration earlier of the interpretation of symbols gives us a clue. Both reinforcing symbols and controlling symbols can provide material for writing, though in somewhat different ways.

The analysis of a single reinforcing symbol could give rise to an interesting paragraph or short essay. Such a paper might examine how a given detail in a story is established as a symbol and how its meaning— which you would want to specify—relates to that of the story overall. The image of dust in "Eveline" would be ideal for this kind of exploration. Here you could point to the repetition of the image as the means by which it is established as a symbol, suggest its possible symbolic meanings by detailing its associations, and demonstrate the relevance of these meanings to the story at large, especially to the life of its protagonist as we leave her.

The opening of Joyce's "Araby" (pages 386–90) contains three fascinating images, used in connection with setting, that one might explore: some books of a dead priest, a wild garden with a central apple tree, and a rusty bicycle pump. Why did Joyce choose these specific things, one must ask, and why did he place them prominently at the beginning of the story? The answer to the second question is that they are symbols; the answer to the first involves their meaning in context, which would be the subject of your paper. In a number of ways, the three images, together with the reference to a dead priest, sum up the meaning of the story as a whole. Here would be a good thesis. You could proceed to argue it by discussing the story scene by scene and relating the associations of the imagery found in its opening paragraphs to the emotional import of each scene. By so doing, you would wind up with an interpretation of the symbols derived from their associations and their relevance in context and, in turn, a deeper understanding of the story overall.

When writing about a story whose symbols are controlling, you are working near the heart of the story, engaged directly with the story's meaning. All of the meaning of "The Grave," for instance, is housed in its images of dove, ring, and rabbit. Although you could discuss other things about the story—characterization, say, in which case reference to the story's individual symbols could be used as support—to get at its theme you would ultimately have to tackle its symbolism head on. You would need to name its controlling symbols and discuss how they are established; analyze their conventional meanings and then carry over those meanings to the story, examining their relevance in the context the author provides; and relate the story's symbolism to its theme.

Writing on symbolism, note, requires a measure of deftness and flexibility on the part of the writer. For symbols are usually multi-dimensional. Thus, you must be prepared to interpret a symbol in different lights. Porter's dove, for instance, means different things to her two characters. To explicate its meaning fully, therefore, one would have to discuss what those different meanings are and how they are related to the dove as conventional symbol rather than forcing a single meaning to prevail.

Symbolism is especially challenging to write on. But it can also be especially rewarding. Stories in which symbolism is prominent require time for thought, a maximum of intellectual agility, and a stretching of one's verbal capacities to articulate the meaning of their symbolism. Yet it is by taking up challenges like this that we grow. If you give yourself over to the task, writing on symbolism will help you become more subtle in your thought and more expressive in your writing generally.

GENERAL WRITING ASSIGNMENTS

1. (a) Write a paragraph in which you convey something significant about a person entirely through a description of his or her effects (clothing, room or apartment, car). Allow no comments into your paragraph. In other words, at least some of the objects you choose to describe should come to symbolize the traits you mean your reader to see.

    (b) Now write a paragraph analyzing the symbolism of your description. What objects in your piece are symbolic? What do they reveal about the person you had in mind? How do they come to mean what they do in your context? How would a reader come to recognize the symbolic possibility in the first place? Your analysis should address questions of this sort.

2. Write a paragraph on the typical setting of a horror movie or television show. Describe the setting in detail and then explain how it helps to create mood: What do we feel when exposed to such a setting? How does mood as established by setting affect our reception of the movie or show overall? How is it that we understand the symbolic aspects of a setting of this sort?

3. We are all conditioned by time and place. Write a paragraph or an essay on yourself in this regard. What in yourself do you see as a product of the era into which you were born and the specific locale in which you grew up? How have your values and general outlook been shaped by these accidents of birth? What might a stranger be able to tell about you simply by knowing where and when you grew up? Consider these questions as you write.

4. If you did the first question under "General Writing Assignments" in chapter 2 (page 43), dig it out and write a paragraph interpreting the dream's symbolism. All dreams are symbolic. What of yours? What are its symbols and what could they mean? If you did not do the assignment, you may wish to do it now and follow it up with the paragraph just outlined.

5. Symbolism is hardly unique to literature. We are bombarded with symbols everywhere we turn. Write an essay on some aspect of symbolism in everyday life. For instance, you could discuss symbolism and sports (every sport is symbol-laden) or symbolism and advertising, which feeds on symbols and mass-produces them for the purposes of persuasion.

6. Clothing is often symbolic: we express ourselves through what we choose to wear and sometimes we even express specific views (political, for instance) through the way we dress. Write an essay on the symbolism of clothing. Your thesis will be that clothing is symbolic; your support will consist of analyzed examples.

7. Every family has its in jokes and turns of phrase that no one outside of the family understands. Similarly, people within a family share an understanding of family symbols. A certain bottle that a grandmother brought over with her when she came to this country radiates for her family a sense of family history; a wedding ring passed down for generations speaks of family continuity; or

perhaps a certain gesture originally associated with an uncle comes to symbolize to one side of a family all that it dislikes about another side. Can you think of any symbols—whether objects, gestures, turns of phrase, or whatever—understood in your family? If so, write an essay about your family symbolism. What do the symbols mean to you? How did they become symbols in the first place? What do they serve to do with respect to the family unit? Conclude by considering in what ways they are like literary symbols as to both what they mean and what they serve to do.

The Pukey

Nigel Dennis

Mr. Troy's refusal to have a pukey in the house had caused enormous trouble in the family. "Pukeys are nasty, degenerate things," he said: "they make filthy messes all over the floor, they corrupt the young, they interrupt homework and sap the nation, and we have nowhere to put one." His wife would answer: "Well, well, we are getting distinguished, aren't we? It seems we're the Duke of Devonshire. Let me tell you that Blanche and Mabel both have pukeys in their drawing-rooms, and far from being corrupted, they are happier." Young Miss Troy appealed to her father's sense of status, saying: "Everywhere I go, Father, it's always: 'What did your pukey do last night?' I have to admit we haven't got one." "Oh, all right," said Mr. Troy, after a couple of years, "I'll let the pukey-man come and give a demonstration."

A few days later, the man arrived with the pukey and put its box against the wall opposite the fireplace. When Mrs. Troy asked: "Won't it catch the draught there?" the pukey-man only laughed and said: "The point about a pukey, madam, is that it's bred to be insensible." "But it is *alive*, isn't it?" asked Mrs. Troy quickly, "because we'd never pay for something dead. And if it's alive, won't the dog resent it?" "Both dog and budgie will be unconscious of it, madam," said the pukey-man, "a pukey speaks only to a human brain." "Well, cut the brainy cackle and open the box," said Mr. Troy roughly.

Let us admit at once that the first impression the pukey made on Mr. Troy was a good one. Even lying stupefied on the carpet, its eyes had a wondering gaze that fell hardly short of sweetness. "It's not just going to flopdown like that all the time, is it?" asked Mr. Troy, to hide the fact that

351

he liked it so far. "Give it a minute, my dear sir!" begged the pukey-man, "it's hardly got its bearings." "Pay him no attention!" exclaimed Mrs. Troy, "he's been picking on pukeys for years." "Oh, what shall we *call* it?" said Miss Troy.

She had hardly spoken when the pukey shuddered from snout to stern and let its muzzle fall right open, showing six rows of vivid pink gums and bubbles of sparkling saliva: "No teeth; that's curious!" muttered Mr. Troy. Then, with no warning, it vomited all over the carpet—a perfectly-filthy, greenish-yellow mess—causing Mrs. Troy to cry spontaneously: "Oh, the filthy little beast!" and Miss Troy to say: "Oh, Mum, don't *fuss!*" and Mr. Troy to say: "I told you it would foul everything up. Take the little brute away!" "An ounce of patience, if you please," asked the pukey-man, "or how can it grow on you?" "I'm sure that's true—and I don't mean I don't like it," said Mrs. Troy, rallying. "Isn't it actually *good* for the carpet?" Miss Troy asked the pukey-man, "I know the Vicar said, reasonably used, it was." "That is perfectly correct, Miss Troy," said the pukey-man, "it's not the vomit but the abuse of it." "Now, there's a remark I always like to hear," said Mr. Troy.

At that moment the pukey, which had been staring at its own emission in a rather vague, contented way, changed its expression entirely. A sort of pathetic anguish came over its whole face: it held its snout sideways and looked at Miss Troy in a pleading, tender way. "Oh, *look!*" cried Mrs. Troy, "it's trying to say it didn't mean bad." They were all wrenched by the pukey's fawning expression, and when it slobbered and grovelled and brownish tears dripped from the corners of its eyes, Mrs. Troy could have hugged it. "Damned sentimental, hypocritical brute!" said Mr. Troy, "I still reserve my judgement." But he was the first to jump in his seat when the pukey, suddenly throwing-up on to the carpet a clot of gritty mucus, followed this up with a string of shrieks and groans. Everyone was deafened except Miss Troy, who sensed at once that the pukey was illustrating the dilemma of girls of her own age in search of happiness. "Why, bless my soul!" said Mrs. Troy soon, "it's trying to have *sex*, that's what it is"—and sure enough, the pukey was now twisting its hind-parts in the most indecent way and rubbing its flanks in its own vomit. "I'll not have that in *my* house," said Mrs. Troy, pursing her lips, "it's just plain filth, and showing-off." "My dear madam, it never actually *gets* there," said the pukey-man: "nothing ever really *happens*." "Oh, Mother, you and Father make everything seem obscene!" said Miss Troy, "even love." "Well, as long as it only suggests but can't actually do it, I don't mind," said Mrs. Troy, watching the pukey with a new curiosity. "My mind is still unmade up," said Mr. Troy.

Worn out, it seemed, by sexual frustration, the pukey lay still for a moment. Then, suddenly fixing its eye on Mrs. Troy, it gave her such a glare of horrible malignancy that she reached for her husband's arm. Next minute, there was a dreadful spectacle: throwing itself into a spasm of rage, the pukey began tearing and biting at its own body, like a thing bent on suicide. "Stop it! Stop it! Put the lid on!" screamed Mrs. Troy, "it's cruel, and drawing blood." "Frankly, you'll have to adjust to that madam," said the pukey-man, "because it fights more than anything else." "Oh, then, that's decisive for me," said Mr. Troy, "because I love to see a good scrap." "It *is* the men who like that best," agreed the pukey-man, as the pukey went through the motions of winding its entrails round the throat of an enemy and jumping on his face. "I don't *mind* its fighting," Mrs. Troy said grudgingly, "but I'll put its lid on if it overdoes it. I like *beautiful* things best." The words, alas, were hardly out of her mouth when the pukey, sighting backwards over its spine like a mounted cowboy firing at his pursuers, shot her full in the face with an outrageous report. "Now, no grumbling, Mother!" screamed poor Miss Troy, knowing her mother's readiness to take affront. "But it's *not* nice!" protested Mrs. Troy, fanning herself with an evening paper. "Oh, Mother, can't you see it *means* nothing?" cried Miss Troy, "it's not like *us*, with our standards." "Standards or no," said Mrs. Troy, "I never saw Mabel's pukey do that to *her*." "Ah, but this is an improved model, madam," said the pukey-man.

"Am I correct in supposing," asked Mr. Troy, "that nothing substantial ever comes out of its rear end anyway?" "That is correct, sir," answered the pukey-man, "all secretion and excretion are purely visual and oral. The vent is hot air at most: hence, no sand-box." "Yet it has a belly on it," said Mr. Troy, "I know because I can see one." "You can see a belly, sir," answered the pukey-man, "but you can't see any guts, can you?" They all laughed at this, because it was so true.

After throwing-up another couple of times ("Mercy, what a messy little perisher it is!" said kind Mrs. Troy), the pukey became inordinately grave and a whole rash of wettish pimples spread over its face. "Well, you are in luck!" said the pukey-man, jumping up as if genuinely interested, "it never does this more than once a week at most. Can you guess what it is?" They all racked their brains, guessing everything from sewage farming to guitar-playing, and still couldn't imagine; until Miss Troy, who was the quickest of the family, screamed: "I know! It's *thinking!*" "*Mes compliments*, young lady," said the pukey-man, bowing.

They all watched the pukey thinking because it was so unexpected; but none of them really liked it. "When it vomits, it only makes me laugh," said Mr. Troy, "but when it thinks, *I* feel like vomiting." "I just feel nervous and embarrassed, like it was something you'd seen and shouldn't," said Mrs. Troy, and even Miss Troy for once agreed with her mother, saying, "You feel it's only doing it as a change from being sick, but it's the same really." "Don't judge it too hardly," said the pukey-man, "surely the wonder is that with no brains it can think at all." "Has it really no brains?" asked Mr. Troy, curious. "No, sir," said the pukey-man: "that's *why* its thinking makes you sick." "Funny sort of animal, I must say," said Mr. Troy, "thinks without brains, bites without teeth, throws-up with no guts, and screws without sex." "Oh, *please* stop it thinking!" begged Mrs. Troy. "I had an experience once that smelt like that." At which words, the pukey's pimples disappeared completely and, lying prone with its paws out, it gave Mrs. Troy a smug, complacent look, showing all its gums in a pleading whimpering. "Oh, the little angel! It wants to be congratulated for having thought!" cried Mrs. Troy: "then we *will*—yes! we *will*, you smelly little darling—you little, stinking, clever, mother's thing!" "I find that touching, too," said Mr. Troy, "no wonder there's so much nicker in pukeys." "It's for love and culture, too, Dad," Miss Troy reminded. "Thank you, Miss Troy," said the pukey-man, "we breeders tell ourselves that too."

During the next hour the pukey did all manner of things—such as marching like the Coldstream Guards, dancing and balancing on one paw like Pavlova, folding its arms like a Member of Parliament, singing the national anthem, plucking away at its parts mysteriously, fighting like mad, and making such vulgar explosive noises at both ends that the Troys were all left speechless with wonder. What charmed them as much as anything was feeling that the pukey made no distinction about what it did: whether it was fawning or screeching, or thinking or puking, it made it all like the same, because it loved each thing equally and looked at you always so proudly for it. "I can only say you breeders must be jolly highly-skilled," summed-up Mr. Troy, "to root out all the natural organs and still poison the air." "It's more a sixth sense than a skill," said the pukey-man modestly, "and one which your wife, I may say, seems to have instinctively." This was the first compliment Mrs. Troy had had since she gave birth to Miss Troy, and to cover her natural embarrassment she said sharply, "Well, put its lid on again now and take it away. We'll come and fill out the Never-never forms tomorrow."

With the pukey gone, it wasn't like the same home. The walls seemed to have been sprayed with a dribble the colour of maple-syrup, and dead flies kept dropping from the ceiling. The state of the carpet was beyond description, although the last thing the pukey had done before the lid closed was puff a sort of scented detergent powder over the stinking mess it had made. But the Troys were much too impressed to worry about the room: they could only think of buying the pukey and doing this every night. "It baffles me," said Mr. Troy, as they went to bed: "it's not human, it's not mechanical, it's not like any animal I've ever known." "What it leaves on the carpet is human through-and-through," said Mrs. Troy, and they all laughed at this because it was so true.

[1957–Great Britain]

QUESTIONS

1. "The Pukey" demonstrates the nature and process of thinking in analogies. What is the pukey analogous to? In answering, consider the cultural context as well as the fictional context.
2. Test your initial guess about what the pukey is analogous to against the gathering details of the story as it unfolds. Everything we are told about the pukey must apply as well to what the pukey stands in for. If anything isn't accounted for, then either your initial guess is wrong or you haven't felt out the analogy fully.
3. Now, what is the point of the analogy? Why didn't Dennis just come right out with what he had to say?

WRITING SUGGESTIONS

1. (a) Write a paragraph in which you explain what the pukey stands in for. Show how at least three attributes of this imaginary creature satirize what it represents.

   (b) What is your response to this story? In a separate paragraph state your response and analyze your reasons for responding thus.
2. What is the point of Dennis's analogy? In an essay, consider what Dennis achieves by way of the pukey, focusing especially on how the story is a satire.

Oberfest

James Stevenson

Through scenery of surpassing loveliness, we descend into the tranquil valley, and make our way to the ancient, fortified town of Oberfest. The origin of the old town is veiled in the poetic darkness of tradition. For many centuries, it has ruled itself, and coined its own monies. As one enters the square, the Town Hall is admirably brought before the eye. It is the very embodiment of grandeur and sublimity: a colossal, many-towered, complex structure, aspiring toward heaven, with countless gables and spires, turrets, and gilded cupolas. One is compelled to venerate the simple townsfolk whose stern virtue and zeal have enabled them to oppose the incursions of those who would conquer, yet have made of their town a repository of all that is grand in antiquity, and ceaselessly striven to beautify and adorn, to elevate and refine. . . . Rising above the sunlit pinnacles of the Hall loom mountains of extraordinary steepness, and awesome, savage magnificence. In winter, it is said, fearful avalanches roll down from these heights.

—"A Traveller in Europe," by G. Brown, F.B.S., with Numerous Wood Engravings by the Best Artists, 1871.

On a morning in early spring, 1873, the people of Oberfest left their houses and took refuge in the town hall. No one knows why, precisely. A number of rumors had raced through the town during recent weeks, and there was a profound uneasiness among the people. Idle talk and gossip were passed on and converted to news; predictions became certainties. On this particular morning, fear turned into terror, and people rushed through the narrow streets, carrying their most precious possessions, pulling their children, and dashed into the great hall. The first to arrive occupied the largest rooms; the others found space in smaller rooms, in hallways, on stairs, in the towers. The doors were nailed shut, and men took turns watching out the windows. Two days passed. Order was maintained. The unruly, the sick, and the unstable were consigned to the cellars; the cellar stairs were guarded. When no disaster came, the fear grew worse, because

356

the people began to suspect that the danger was already within the hall, locked inside. No one spoke to anybody else; people watched each other, looking for signs. It was the children who rang the great bell in the first bell tower—a small band of bored children, unable to bear the silence and having run through all the halls, slid down all the bannisters, climbed all the turrets. They found the bell rope and swung on it—set the bell clanging. This was the traditional signal of alarm, and in a moment the elders were dashing in panic to all the other bell towers and ringing the bells. For nearly an hour, the valley reverberated with the wild clangor— and then, a thousand feet above, the snow began to crack, and the avalanche began; a massive cataract of ice and snow thundered down and buried the town, silencing the bells. There is no trace of Oberfest today, not even a spire, because the snow is so deep; and, in the shadow of the mountains, it is very cold.

[1971–U.S.A.]

QUESTIONS

1. How is what happens in this story a direct result of its Alpine setting, or a result of the effect this setting has on the story's characters?
2. We're told in the epigraph, "One is compelled to venerate the simple townsfolk whose stern virtue and zeal have enabled them to oppose the incursions of those who would conquer." What is ironic about this statement when read in connection with the story that follows? What is the prime irony upon which "Oberfest" turns?
3. "The danger was already within the hall, locked inside." In light of this statement, what is the story's theme?
4. Compare the lengthy epigraph and the story. What is the difference in focus and point between the two? Why is one a piece of exposition and the other a story? Comment on their stylistic differences.

WRITING SUGGESTIONS

1. In a paragraph, address question 2 above. Remember that irony entails discrepancy. What is the discrepancy implied here?
2. Focusing on the differences between the epigraph and the story proper, discuss in a paragraph or short paper what makes one a piece of exposition and the other a piece of fiction.
3. In "Oberfest," the setting instigates the plot and together both lead to the theme. In a short paper, argue that the statement just made accurately describes the story. Consider, too, how irony shapes the mood and therefore, along with setting and plot, contributes to the theme.

I Spy

Graham Greene

Charlie Stowe waited until he heard his mother snore before he got out of bed. Even then he moved with caution and tiptoed to the window. The front of the house was irregular, so that it was possible to see a light burning in his mother's room. But now all the windows were dark. A searchlight passed across the sky, lighting the banks of cloud and probing the dark deep spaces between, seeking enemy airships. The wind blew from the sea, and Charlie Stowe could hear behind his mother's snores the beating of the waves. A draught through the cracks in the window-frame stirred his nightshirt. Charlie Stowe was frightened.

But the thought of the tobacconist's shop which his father kept down a dozen wooden stairs drew him on. He was twelve years old, and already boys at the County School mocked him because he had never smoked a cigarette. The packets were piled twelve deep below, Gold Flake and Players, De Reszke, Abdulla, Woodbines, and the little shop lay under a thin haze of stale smoke which would completely disguise his crime. That it was a crime to steal some of his father's stock Charlie Stowe had no doubt, but he did not love his father; his father was unreal to him, a wraith, pale, thin, and indefinite, who noticed him only spasmodically and left even punishment to his mother. For his mother he felt a passionate demonstrative love; her large boisterous presence and her noisy charity filled the world for him; from her speech he judged her the friend of everyone, from the rector's wife to the "dear Queen," except the "Huns," the monsters who lurked in Zeppelins in the clouds. But his father's affection and dislike were as indefinite as his movements. Tonight he had said he would be in Norwich, and yet you never knew. Charlie Stowe had no sense of safety as he crept down the wooden stairs. When they creaked he clenched his fingers on the collar of his nightshirt.

At the bottom of the stairs he came out quite suddenly into the little shop. It was too dark to see his way, and he did not dare touch the switch. For half a minute he sat in despair on the bottom step with his chin cupped in his hands. Then the regular movement of the searchlight was reflected through an upper window and the boy had time to fix in memory the pile of cigarettes, the counter, and the small hole under it. The footsteps of a policeman on the pavement made him grab the first packet to his hand and dive for the hole. A light shone along the floor and a hand tried the door, then the footsteps passed on, and Charlie cowered in the darkness.

At last he got his courage back by telling himself in his curiously adult way that if he were caught now there was nothing to be done about it, and he might as well have his smoke. He put a cigarette in his mouth and then remembered that he had no matches. For a while he dared not move. Three times the searchlight lit the shop, while he muttered taunts and encouragements. "May as well be hung for a sheep," "Cowardy, cowardy custard," grown-up and childish exhortations oddly mixed.

But as he moved he heard footfalls in the street, the sound of several men walking rapidly. Charlie Stowe was old enough to feel surprise that anybody was about. The footsteps came nearer, stopped; a key was turned in the shop door, a voice said, "Let him in," and then he heard his father, "If you wouldn't mind being quiet, gentlemen. I don't want to wake up the family." There was a note unfamiliar to Charlie in the undecided voice. A torch flashed and the electric globe burst into blue light. The boy held his breath; he wondered whether his father would hear his heart beating, and he clutched his nightshirt tightly and prayed, "O God, don't let me be caught." Through a crack in the counter he could see his father where he stood, one hand held to his high stiff collar, between two men in bowler hats and belted mackintoshes. They were strangers.

"Have a cigarette," his father said in a voice dry as a biscuit. One of the men shook his head. "It wouldn't do, not when we are on duty. Thank you all the same." He spoke gently, but without kindness; Charlie Stowe thought his father must be ill.

"Mind if I put a few in my pocket?" Mr. Stowe asked, and when the man nodded he lifted a pile of Gold Flake and Players from a shelf and caressed the packets with the tips of his fingers.

"Well," he said, "there's nothing to be done about it, and I may as well have my smokes." For a moment Charlie Stowe feared discovery, his father stared round the shop so thoroughly; he might have been seeing it for the first time. "It's a good little business," he said, "for those that like it. The wife will sell out, I suppose. Else the neighbours'll be wrecking it. Well, you want to be off. A stitch in time. I'll get my coat."

"One of us'll come with you, if you don't mind," said the stranger gently.

"You needn't trouble. It's on the peg here. There, I'm all ready."

The other man said in an embarrassed way: "Don't you want to speak to your wife?" The thin voice was decided. "Not me. Never do today what you can put off till tomorrow. She'll have her chance later, won't she?"

"Yes, yes," one of the strangers said and he became very cheerful and encouraging. "Don't you worry too much. While there's life . . ." And suddenly his father tried to laugh.

When the door had closed Charlie Stowe tiptoed upstairs and got into bed. He wondered why his father had left the house again so late at night and who the strangers were. Surprise and awe kept him for a little while awake. It was as if a familiar photograph had stepped from the frame to reproach him with neglect. He remembered how his father had held tight to his collar and fortified himself with proverbs, and he thought for the first time that, while his mother was boisterous and kindly, his father was very like himself, doing things in the dark which frightened him. It would have pleased him to go down to his father and tell him that he loved him, but he could hear through the window the quick steps going away. He was alone in the house with his mother, and he fell asleep.

[1930–Great Britain]

QUESTIONS

1. In what period of time is this story set? What details tell us of its time frame? Why is the temporal setting significant?
2. What kind of a narrator tells this story? Why this kind?
3. What is ironic about the story's title?
4. The boy's smoking is symbolic. What kind of a symbol is this act? What does it signify?
5. A mystery of sorts, "I Spy" leaves us to figure out what the boy is still too young to understand: why and by whom the father is taken away. How do you answer these questions?
6. In terms of general theme, this story is akin to a number of others in this book, for example, "My First Goose," "Innocence," "The Trout," and "Araby." How so? What is its theme in full? In answering, consider the story's mood.

WRITING SUGGESTIONS

1. The wartime setting of "I Spy" is crucial. Write a paragraph on when the story is set, how we come to recognize its time frame, and how our knowledge of its setting in time allows us to grasp the gravity of what we witness along with the boy.
2. In a paragraph, enumerate the passing symbols found in "I Spy" and suggest the meaning of each. Consider, for example, the boy's smoking and the "belted mackintoshes" worn by the strangers. What kind of symbols are these? How are they significant to our understanding of the story as it proceeds?
3. Write an essay comparing and contrasting "I Spy" with any of the stories referred to in question 6 above. Consider both similarity of theme and the differences in the ways theme is treated. Note especially irony and mood as you weigh "I Spy" against the other story you choose.
4. What were you blind to when young but now understand? How did coming to that understanding help move you from a childish mentality to a more adult awareness of things? Write a short essay detailing your experience and the difference between your perception when you were a child and your perception now.

The Waste Land

Alan Paton

The moment that the bus moved on he knew he was in danger, for by the lights of it he saw the figures of the young men waiting under the tree. That was the thing feared by all, to be waited for by the young men. It was a thing he had talked about, now he was to see it for himself.

It was too late to run after the bus; it went down the dark street like an island of safety in a sea of perils. Though he had known of his danger only for a second, his mouth was already dry, his heart was pounding in his breast, something within him was crying out in protest against the coming event.

His wages were in his purse, he could feel them weighing heavily against his thigh. That was what they wanted from him. Nothing counted against that. His wife could be made a widow, his children made fatherless, nothing counted against that. Mercy was the unknown word.

While he stood there irresolute he heard the young men walking towards him, not only from the side where he had seen them, but from the other also. They did not speak, their intention was unspeakable. The sound of their feet came on the wind to him. The place was well chosen, for behind him was the high wall of the Convent, and the barred door that would not open before a man was dead. On the other side of the road was the waste land, full of wire and iron and the bodies of old cars. It was his only hope, and he moved towards it; as he did so he knew from the whistle that the young men were there too.

His fear was great and instant, and the smell of it went from his body to his nostrils. At that very moment one of them spoke, giving directions. So trapped was he that he was filled suddenly with strength and anger, and

362

he ran towards the waste land swinging his heavy stick. In the darkness a form loomed up at him, and he swung the stick at it, and heard it give a cry of pain. Then he plunged blindly into the wilderness of wire and iron and the bodies of old cars.

Something caught him by the leg, and he brought his stick crashing down on it, but it was no man, only some knife-edged piece of iron. He was sobbing and out of breath, but he pushed on into the waste, while behind him they pushed on also, knocking against the old iron bodies and kicking against tins and buckets. He fell into some grotesque shape of wire; it was barbed and tore at his clothes and flesh. Then it held him, so that it seemed to him that death must be near, and having no other hope, he cried out, "Help me, help me!" in what should have been a great voice but was voiceless and gasping. He tore at the wire, and it tore at him too, ripping his face and his hands.

Then suddenly he was free. He saw the bus returning, and he cried out again in the great voiceless voice, "Help me, help me!" Against the lights of it he could plainly see the form of one of the young men. Death was near him, and for a moment he was filled with the injustice of life, that could end thus for one who had always been hardworking and law-abiding. He lifted the heavy stick and brought it down on the head of his pursuer, so that the man crumpled to the ground, moaning and groaning as though life had been unjust to him also.

Then he turned and began to run again, but ran head first into the side of an old lorry which sent him reeling. He lay there for a moment expecting the blow that would end him, but even then his wits came back to him, and he turned over twice and was under the lorry. His very entrails seemed to be coming into his mouth, and his lips could taste sweat and blood. His heart was like a wild thing in his breast, and seemed to lift his whole body each time that it beat. He tried to calm it down, thinking it might be heard, and tried to control the noise of his gasping breath, but he could not do either of these things.

Then suddenly against the dark sky he saw two of the young men. He thought they must hear him; but they themselves were gasping like drowning men, and their speech came by fits and starts.

Then one of them said, "Do you hear?"

They were silent except for their grasping, listening. And he listened also, but could hear nothing but his own exhausted heart.

"I heard a man . . . running . . . on the road," said one. "He's got away . . . let's go."

Then some more of the young men came up, gasping and cursing the man who had got away.

"Freddy," said one, "your father's got away."

But there was no reply.

"Where's Freddy?" one asked.

One said "Quiet!" Then he called in a loud voice, "Freddy."

But still there was no reply.

"Let's go," he said.

They moved off slowly and carefully, then one of them stopped.

"We are saved," he said, "here is the man."

He knelt down on the ground, and then fell to cursing.

"There's no money here," he said.

One of them lit a match, and in the small light of it the man under the lorry saw him fall back.

"It's Freddy," one said, "he's dead."

Then the one who had said "Quiet" spoke again.

"Lift him up," he said. "Put him under the lorry."

The man under the lorry heard them struggling with the body of the dead young man, and he turned once, twice, deeper into his hiding-place. The young men lifted the body and swung it under the lorry so that it touched him. Then he heard them moving away, not speaking, slowly and quietly, making an occasional sound against some obstruction in the waste.

He turned on his side, so that he would not need to touch the body of the young man. He buried his face in his arms, and said to himself in the idiom of his own language, "People, arise! The world is dead." Then he arose himself, and went heavily out of the waste land.

[1955–South Africa]

QUESTIONS

1. Though the specifics of its waste-land locale are vivid, this story's setting is not particularized as to country and city. We don't even know in what language its characters speak (thus the phrase "in the idiom of his own language"). What is Paton's purpose in keeping his setting general?

2. The setting here functions symbolically as well as literally. What does it symbolize? In answering, take into account the nature of any junkyard in and of itself.

3. Has the man killed his own son? What is the cause of conflict here— economic, generational, racial, class? What is the effect of the story's ambiguities on these matters?

4. Could this text possibly be read as an allegory? If so, what do its components stand for?

WRITING SUGGESTIONS

1. Write a paragraph in answer to question 2 above. Be sure to keep in mind what junkyards are (literally) as you interpret Paton's symbolism.
2. Is "The Waste Land" an allegory? In a paragraph or more, consider the possibility that the story's protagonist, the boys, and the junkyard are all allegorical figures representing and enacting Paton's view of the modern world.
3. Write a critique of this story. Judge both its effectiveness as a story and the relevance and insightfulness of the vision it embodies. To do the former, you will have to consider the kind of story "The Waste Land" is. To do the latter, you will have to bring to bear your own understanding of the world we live in. (Note: even should you reject Paton's theme, the story might still have merit as story.)

At Sea*

Guy de Maupassant

The following item recently appeared in the papers under the dateline "Boulogne-sur-Mer, January 22":

> A frightful disaster has caused consternation among our coastal population, which has already been so hard-hit during the last two years. A fishing trawler commanded by Captain Javel was carried westward off its course as it was entering port and thrown against the breakwater.
>
> Despite the efforts of the lifeboat and the life lines thrown to them, four men and a boy were lost.
>
> The bad weather continues and fresh disasters are feared.

Who was Captain Javel? Could it be the brother of one-armed Javel?

Was the poor man swept away by the waves, or perhaps dead under the debris of his wrecked ship, the Javel I'm thinking of? If so, he had once before witnessed a tragedy at sea, terrible and simple as are all great tragedies of the deep.

It happened eighteen years ago. The elder Javel was then master of a smack, which is an ideal fishing boat. Sturdy, fearing no weather, round-bellied, constantly bobbing on the waves like a cork, always out at sea, forever whipped by the biting, salty winds of the Channel, it plows the billows tirelessly—its sails ballooning, trailing at its side a great net that sweeps over the ocean bottom, grabbing and tearing loose all the sleeping creatures of the rocks: the flat fish that hug the sands, the heavy crabs with their hooked claws, and the lobsters with their pointed whiskers. When the

---

* Translated by Andrew R. MacAndrew

breeze is fresh and the waves are short and choppy, the smack begins to trawl. The net is tied to a long, iron-sheathed wooden bar that is lowered by means of two cables running through two blocks rigged one at each end of the boat. And so the smack, drifting with the wind and the current, drags along this rig which ravages and robs the sea floor.

Javel's crew consisted of his younger brother, four other men, and a boy. They set out from Boulogne on a clear day, hoping to trawl. But when they were out, the wind rose and a squall chased the smack. They reached the English coast, but the stormy seas smashing against the cliffs made it impossible to enter a port. The smack then turned back to sea and returned toward the coast of France. The storm was still so violent that the breakwaters could not be negotiated, and the harbor entrances were wrapped in froth, din, and danger. The little smack turned away once more. The waves tossed it around, shook it, and battered it; but it took all this pluckily, accustomed as it was to rough weather that had sometimes forced it to wander for five or six days between the two neighboring countries without being able to put into a port on either side.

Finally, while the craft was out in the open sea, the storm subsided somewhat, and although the waves were still quite big, the skipper ordered the trawl lowered.

The heavy net was passed overboard and two men forward and two aft began to pay out the cables that held it through the blocks. But when the trawl touched the bottom, a large wave tipped the boat; and the younger Javel, who was on the forward block directing the maneuver, slipped and got his arm caught between the ship's side and the rope that had been slackened for a second when the net had reached the bottom and then had tightened again when the boat was lifted by the waves. He made a desperate effort to loosen the rope with his free hand, but by now it was taut and wouldn't budge.

Shaken by pain, he called for help. They all rushed to him. His brother abandoned the wheel and also joined them. They all took hold of the rope and pulled, trying to slacken it and free the arm that it was crushing. It was all in vain.

"Must be cut," a seaman said, and he produced a big, sharp jackknife that in two slashes could have saved the younger Javel's arm.

But of course, cutting the rope meant losing the trawl net and that meant losing money, a great deal of money—fifteen hundred francs—and it was the property of the elder Javel who hated to let go of what he had. So, his heart filled with agony, he shouted:

"Wait, don't cut it! I'll try to luff. . . ." And he rushed to the wheel and tried to bring the boat closer to the wind. But the smack hardly responded because the net made it unmaneuverable; in addition, it was drifting with the wind and current.

The younger Javel slipped down to his knees, his teeth clenched, his eyes haggard. He said nothing. His brother came back, still worried about the jackknife.

"Wait, wait, don't cut it yet. We'll anchor. . . ."

The anchor was dropped, the chain paid out. Then they tried to wind the cables around the capstan to slacken the ropes that held the trawl. Finally they got enough slack and released the lifeless arm in its blood-stained, woolen sleeve.

The younger Javel's face was blank. They removed his jacket and saw a horrible mass of flesh with blood gushing from it in many streams, as if someone were pumping it out. The man looked at his arm and said: "I've had it!"

As the blood formed a river on the deck, a seaman shouted: "Why, he'll empty himself like that. We must tie it off."

So they got a rope, a dark, tarred piece of rope, turned it around the arm above the wound, and tied it as tight as they could. The jets of blood diminished gradually and finally the bleeding stopped completely.

The younger Javel got up, his arm hanging at his side. He took it in his other hand, lifted it, turned it, and shook it. It was quite loose. The bones were broken and only the tendons held it to the rest of his body. He looked at it gloomily, thinking something over. Then he sat down on a folded sail and the others advised him to keep wetting his injured arm with brine to prevent the "black rot."

They placed a bucket of water next to him and every minute or so, he would dip a glass into it and pour a thin, transparent stream over his horrible wound.

"You'd be better off down below," his brother said, and he went down. But within an hour he was back on deck, for he hadn't felt too good down there all by himself. Besides, he preferred to be out in the fresh air. So he sat down on the folded sail and started bathing his arm again.

The fishing was good. Big, white-bellied fish lay next to him, jerking in their death agony, and he watched them as he poured the seawater on his wounded limb.

When they were about to return to Boulogne, a new squall came up and the little fishing boat resumed its mad rush back and forth between the French and English coasts, jouncing, shaking, and rolling the gloomy wounded man.

Night came and the sea remained rough until dawn. As the sun rose, the English coast was once more in sight. But then the weather improved a bit, and they turned back toward France, beating into the wind.

Toward evening the wounded man called his shipmates and showed them some black stains on his arm—the sinister marks of rot on the loose part of the limb.

The sailors examined it and voiced their opinions.

"It could very well be the Black One," one man mused.

"You must keep it in the brine," another seaman advised.

They brought a bucket of seawater and poured it on the arm. The injured man turned livid, his teeth gnashed, his body twisted slightly. But he didn't cry out. And when the scorching pain caused by the salt water had subsided a bit, he said to his brother:

"Give me your knife," and when the other handed it to him, he said: "Hold my arm up straight. That's right, now pull."

His brother did as he was told.

Then the younger Javel began to cut off his own arm. He cut it slowly, thoughtfully, snapping off the remaining tendons with the razor-sharp blade of the jackknife, and soon he had nothing but a stump left. He gave a deep sigh and said: "Had to do it. I'd had it, otherwise."

He seemed relieved, took a deep breath, then began again to pour water on what was left of his arm.

The night that followed was again too rough to enter port.

When it was day again, the younger Javel picked up his severed arm and examined it at length. The rot was now easily visible. His shipmates came and looked at it too, and it passed from hand to hand, all of them poking and smelling it.

The older brother said:

"Seeing the state it's in, it's best to throw it overboard."

But now the younger brother lost his temper.

"Oh no! No, sir! I don't want it tossed overboard and it's not going to be, since it's my arm!" And he took it back and put it between his knees.

"Still, you can't stop it from rotting," his brother said.

Then the wounded man got an idea: when they stayed at sea for a long time, they preserved their fish in barrels of brine. So he said:

"I guess it'd keep in brine, though?"

"It ought to," the others agreed.

They emptied a barrel which was already full of fish they had caught on an earlier day and put the arm at the bottom of it. They poured brine in over it and then replaced the fish, one by one.

One of the seaman cracked a joke on this occasion:

"Hope we don't sell it in the market by mistake!"

And all except the two Javels laughed.

The wind was still blowing and they had to beat to windward again; they didn't come within sight of Boulogne until ten o'clock. The wounded man kept tirelessly throwing water over his wound. From time to time he would get up and walk from one end of the boat to the other. His brother, who was at the wheel, followed him with his eyes, shaking his head.

Finally they put into Boulogne.

A doctor examined the wound and declared it to be in good shape. He dressed it and prescribed rest for the patient. But Javel wouldn't lie down until he had recovered his arm. He rushed back to port, went on board his brother's smack, and found the barrel that he had marked with a cross in chalk. They emptied it while he watched, then he picked up his limb, which had been very nicely preserved in the brine. It looked rather fresher than before, although it was strangely wrinkled. He wrapped it in a napkin that he had brought with him for the purpose and returned home.

His wife and children examined this piece of their father at length, touching the fingers and removing the traces of salt from under the nails. Then they called the carpenter and asked him to make a little coffin.

The following day, the full crew of the smack followed the funeral of their shipmate's severed limb. The two brothers, side by side, led the procession. The parish sexton carried the little corpse under his arm.

The younger Javel didn't go back to sea. He got a job in the port; and later, when he would speak of the incident, he would confide to his listener in a low voice:

"If my brother had been willing to cut loose his trawl, I'd still have my arm, no doubt about that. . . . But he sure didn't like to part with his goods, my brother."

[1883–France]

QUESTIONS

1. "The fault, dear Brutus, is not in our stars,/But in ourselves," says Cassius in Shakespeare's *Julius Caesar* (Act I, Scene ii). Restated slightly, such is the theme of Maupassant's "At Sea." How so? In answering, consider the difference between the view of things implied in the last sentence of the news report that begins the story and the view suggested by the story as a whole.

2. If the Captain Javel referred to in the news report was indeed the "brother of the one-armed Javel," why did the ship probably go down? Before answering, consider the characterization of the two brothers.

3. Consider the rather macabre business having to do with the brother's saving of

the arm. What is the function of this business with respect to the story's theme?

4. Given the theme, we might expect two elements of fiction to be prominent here: characterization and setting. And so they are. Why these two? In what ways is setting symbolic in this story?

WRITING SUGGESTIONS

1. We considered the difference between news reports and fiction in chapter 2. Maupassant's "At Sea" further demonstrates that difference. In a paragraph, identify the essential differences between the report that opens "At Sea" and the story proper.

2. In a paragraph or more, discuss this story in terms of irony. What, for instance, is ironic about the juxtaposition of the news report and the story proper, or what irony emerges from this juxtaposition? In what way is the brother's saving of the arm ironic? How does irony reinforce the story's theme?

3. Write a paper taking off from question 4 above. Your focus will be on character and setting, including the possible symbolism of the setting, and why these elements are prominent given the story's theme.

An Episode of War

Stephen Crane

The lieutenant's rubber blanket lay on the ground, and upon it he had poured the company's supply of coffee. Corporals and other representatives of the grimy and hot-throated men who lined the breastwork had come for each squad's portion.

The lieutenant was frowning and serious at this task of division. His lips pursed as he drew with his sword various crevices in the heap until brown squares of coffee, astoundingly equal in size, appeared on the blanket. He was on the verge of a great triumph in mathematics and the corporals were thronging forward, each to reap a little square, when suddenly the lieutenant cried out and looked quickly at a man near him as if he suspected it was a case of personal assault. The others cried out also when they saw blood upon the lieutenant's sleeve.

He had winced like a man stung, swayed dangerously, and then straightened. The sound of his hoarse breathing was plainly audible. He looked sadly, mystically, over the breastwork at the green face of a wood where now were many little puffs of white smoke. During this moment, the men about him gazed statue-like and silent, astonished and awed by this catastrophe which had happened when catastrophes were not expected—when they had leisure to observe it.

As the lieutenant stared at the wood, they too swung their heads so that for another moment all hands, still silent, contemplated the distant forest as if their minds were fixed upon the mystery of a bullet's journey.

The officer had, of course, been compelled to take his sword at once into his left hand. He did not hold it by the hilt. He gripped it at the middle of the blade, awkwardly. Turning his eyes from the hostile wood, he looked at the sword as he held it there, and seemed puzzled as to what to do with it, where to put it. In short this weapon had of a sudden become a strange thing to him. He looked at it in a kind of stupefaction, as if he had been miraculously endowed with a trident, a sceptre, or a spade.

Finally, he tried to sheath it. To sheath a sword held by the left hand, at the middle of the blade, in a scabbard hung at the left hip, is a feat worthy of a sawdust ring. This wounded officer engaged in a desperate struggle with the sword and the wobbling scabbard, and during the time of it, he breathed like a wrestler.

But at this instant the men, the spectators, awoke from their stone-like poses and crowded forward sympathetically. The orderly-sergeant took the sword and tenderly placed it in the scabbard. At the time, he leaned nervously backward, and did not allow even his finger to brush the body of the lieutenant. A wound gives strange dignity to him who bears it. Well men shy from this new and terrible majesty. It is as if the wounded man's hand is upon the curtain which hangs before the revelations of all existence, the meaning of ants, potentates, wars, cities, sunshine, snow, a feather dropped from a bird's wing, and the power of it sheds radiance upon a bloody form, and makes the other men understand sometimes that they are little. His comrades look at him with large eyes thoughtfully. Moreover, they fear vaguely that the weight of a finger upon him might send him headlong, precipitate the tragedy, hurl him at once into the dim grey unknown. And so the orderly-sergeant while sheathing the sword leaned nervously backward.

There were others who proffered assistance. One timidly presented his shoulder and asked the lieutenant if he cared to lean upon it, but the latter waved them away mournfully. He wore the look of one who knows he is the victim of a terrible disease and understands his helplessness. He again stared over the breastwork at the forest, and then turning went slowly rearward. He held his right wrist tenderly in his left hand, as if the wounded arm was made of very brittle glass.

And the men in silence stared at the wood, then at the departing lieutenant—then at the wood, then at the lieutenant.

As the wounded officer passed from the line of battle, he was enabled to see many things which as a participant in the fight were unknown to him. He saw a general on a black horse gazing over the lines of blue infantry at the green woods which veiled his problems. An aide galloped furiously, dragged his horse suddenly to a halt, saluted, and presented a paper. It was, for a wonder, precisely like an historical painting.

To the rear of the general and his staff, a group, composed of a bugler, two or three orderlies, and the bearer of the corps standard, all upon maniacal horses, were working like slaves to hold their ground, preserve their respectful interval, while the shells bloomed in the air about them, and caused their chargers to make furious quivering leaps.

A battery, a tumultuous and shining mass, was swirling toward the right. The wild thud of hoofs, the cries of the riders shouting blame and praise, menace and encouragement, and, last, the roar of the wheels, the slant of the glistening guns, brought the lieutenant to an intent pause. The battery swept in curves that stirred the heart; it made halts as dramatic as the crash of a wave on the rocks, and when it fled onward, this aggregation of wheels, levers, motors, had a beautiful unity, as if it were a missile. The sound of it was a war-chorus that reached into the depths of man's emotion.

The lieutenant, still holding his arm as if it were of glass, stood watching this battery until all detail of it was lost, save the figures of the riders, which rose and fell and waved lashes over the black mass.

Later he turned his eyes toward the battle where the shooting sometimes crackled like bush-fires, sometimes sputtered with exasperating irregularity, and sometimes reverberated like the thunder. He saw the smoke rolling upward and saw crowds of men who ran and cheered, or stood and blazed away at the inscrutable distance.

He came upon some stragglers and they told him how to find the field hospital. They described its exact location. In fact these men, no longer having part in the battle, knew more of it than others. They told the performance of every corps, every division, the opinion of every general. The lieutenant, carrying his wounded arm rearward, looked upon them with wonder.

At the roadside a brigade was making coffee and buzzing with talk like a girls' boarding-school. Several officers came out to him and inquired concerning things of which he knew nothing. One, seeing his arm, began to scold. "Why, man, that's no way to do. You want to fix that thing." He appropriated the lieutenant and the lieutenant's wound. He cut the sleeve and laid bare the arm, every nerve of which softly fluttered under his touch. He bound his handkerchief over the wound, scolding away in the meantime. His tone allowed one to think that he was in the habit of being wounded every day. The lieutenant hung his head, feeling, in this presence, that he did not know how to be correctly wounded.

The low white tents of the hospital were grouped around an old school-house. There was here a singular commotion. In the foreground two ambulances interlocked wheels in the deep mud. The drivers were tossing the blame of it back and forth, gesticulating and berating, while from the ambulances, both crammed with wounded, there came an occasional groan. An interminable crowd of bandaged men were coming and going. Great numbers sat under the trees nursing heads or arms or legs. There was a dispute of some kind raging on the steps of the school-house. Sitting with his back against a tree a man with a face as grey as a new army blanket was serenely smoking a corn-cob pipe. The lieutenant wished to rush forward and inform him that he was dying.

A busy surgeon was passing near the lieutenant. "Good morning," he said with a friendly smile. Then he caught sight of the lieutenant's arm and his face at once changed. "Well, let's have a look at it." He seemed possessed suddenly of a great contempt for the lieutenant. This wound evidently placed the latter on a very low social plane. The doctor cried out impatiently. What mutton-head had tied it up that way anyhow. The lieutenant answered: "Oh, a man."

When the wound was disclosed the doctor fingered it disdainfully. "Humph," he said. "You come along with me and I'll tend to you." His voice contained the same scorn as if he were saying: "You will have to go to jail."

The lieutenant had been very meek but now his face flushed, and he looked into the doctor's eyes. "I guess I won't have it amputated," he said.

"Nonsense, man! nonsense! nonsense!" cried the doctor. "Come along, now. I won't amputate it. Come along. Don't be a baby."

"Let go of me," said the lieutenant, holding back wrathfully. His glance fixed upon the door of the old school-house, as sinister to him as the portals of death.

And this is the story of how the lieutenant lost his arm. When he reached home his sisters, his mother, his wife, sobbed for a long time at the sight of the flat sleeve. "Oh, well," he said, standing shamefaced amid these tears, "I don't suppose it matters so much as all that."

[1899–U.S.A.]

QUESTIONS

1. The narration here is objective, the style cool and uninvolved. Why? In a similar vein, is there any significance to the fact that the lieutenant isn't named?
2. Neither plot nor characterization figures much in this story. How is the absence of these elements significant?
3. Crane lingers over the setting in this story. Why? If we can't quite call the setting symbolic, what is its function?
4. "An Episode of War" is fundamentally ironic. What are its ironies?
5. What is the mood of the story? How is the mood related to the theme?

6. Most of all, this story concerns perspective—the double perspective that we human beings can take with respect to ourselves on the one hand and the universe on the other. Explain.

WRITING SUGGESTIONS

1. In a paragraph or two, discuss the wounded lieutenant's perspective on the lot of humanity in the kind of universe the story presents. In doing so, consider why setting is a major element in this story and how it is treated.
2. "An Episode of War" is notable for its lack of certain elements: plot, characterization, and symbolism. In a short paper, discuss the theme of the story in terms of these absences. What does the lack of plot and significant characterization suggest about human beings and their place in the universe? What does the pointed lack of symbolism suggest about the universe at large?
3. Consider this brief poem by Crane:

> A man said to the universe:
> "Sir, I exist!"
> "However," replied the universe,
> "The fact has not created in me
> A sense of obligation."

In a paragraph, compare this poem with "An Episode of War" as to mood and theme. In what way or ways does the poem shed light on the story? What do the two together reveal about Crane's characteristic stance?
4. What is your view of things—human life, the universe, and so forth? Write a paper arguing that Crane is right on target or that he misses the truth of things. Articulate and bring to bear your beliefs as you argue for or against Crane's.

Danse Pseudomacabre

William Carlos Williams

That which is possible is inevitable. I defend the normality of every distortion to which the flesh is susceptible, every disease, every amputation. I challenge anyone who thinks to discomfit my intelligence by limiting the import of what I say to the expounding of a shallow morbidity, to prove that health alone is inevitable. Until he can do that his attack upon me will be imbecilic.

Allons! Commençons la danse.

The telephone is ringing. I have awakened sitting erect in bed, unsurprised, almost uninterested, but with an overwhelming sense of death pressing my chest together as if I had come reluctant from the grave to which a distorted homesickness continued to drag me, a sense as of the end of everything. My wife lies asleep, curled against her pillow. Christ, Christ! how can I ever bear to be separated from this my boon companion, to be annihilated, to have her annihilated? How can a man live in the face of this daily uncertainty? How can a man not go mad with grief, with apprehension?

I wonder what time it is. There is a taxi just leaving the club. Tang, tang, tang. Finality. Three o'clock.

The moon is low, its silent flame almost level among the trees, across the budding rose garden, upon the grass.

The streets are illumined with the moon and the useless flares of the purple and yellow street lamps hanging from the dark each above its little circular garden of flowers.

Hurry, hurry, hurry! Upstairs! He's dying! Oh my God! my God, what will I do without him? I won't live! I won't—I won't—

What a face! Erysipelas. Doesn't look so bad—in a few days the moon will be full.

Quick! Witness this signature— It's his will— A great blubber of a thirty-year-old male seated, hanging, floating erect in the center of the sagging double-bed spring, his long hair in a mild mass, his body wrapped in a downy brown wool dressing gown, a cord around the belly, a great pudding face, the whole right side of it a dirty purple, swollen, covered with watery blebs, the right eye swollen shut. He is trembling, wildly excited—a paper on his unsteady knees, a fountain pen in his hand. Witness this signature! Will it be legal? Yes, of course. He signs. I sign after him. When the Scotch go crazy they are worse than a Latin. The nose uninvolved. What a small nose.

My God, I'm done for.

Oh my God, what will I do without him?

Kindly be quiet, madam. What sort of way is that to talk in a sickroom? Do you want to kill him? Give him a chance, if you please.

Is he going to die, doctor? He's only been sick a few days. His eye started to close yesterday. He's never been sick in his life. He has no one but his father and me. Oh, I won't live without him.

Of course when a man as full-blooded as he is has erysipelas—

Do you think it's erysipelas?

How much does he weigh?

Two hundred and forty pounds.

Temperature 102. That's not bad.

He won't die? Are you kidding me, doctor?

What for? The moon has sunk. Almost no more at all. Only the Scotch have such small noses. Follow these directions. I have written down what you are to do.

Again the moon. Again. And why not again? It is a dance. Everything that varies a hair's breadth from another is an invitation to the dance. Either dance or annihilation. There can be only the dance or ONE. So, the next night, I enter another house. And so I repeat the trouble of writing that which I have already written, and so drag another human being from oblivion to serve my music.

It is a baby. There is a light at the end of a broken corridor. A man in a pointed beard leads the way. Strong foreign accent. Holland Dutch. We walk through the corridor to the back of the house. The kitchen. In the kitchen turn to the right. Someone is sitting back of the bedroom door. A nose, an eye emerge, sniffing and staring, a wrinkled nose, a cavernous eye. Turn again to the right through another door and walk toward the front of the house. We are in a sickroom. A bed has been backed against the corridor entry making this detour necessary.

Oh, here you are, doctor. British. The nurse I suppose.

The baby is in a smother of sheets and crumpled blankets, its head on a pillow. The child's left eye closed, its right partly opened, It emits a soft whinning cry continuously at every breath. It can't be more than a few weeks old.

Do you think it is unconscious, doctor?

Yes.

Will it live? It is the mother. A great tender-eyed blonde. Great full breasts. A soft gentle-minded woman of no mean beauty. A blue cotton house wrapper, shoulder to ankle.

If it lives it will be an idiot perhaps. Or it will be paralysed—or both. It is better for it to die.

There it goes now! The whining has stopped. The lips are blue. The mouth puckers as for some diabolic kiss. It twitches, twitches faster and faster, up and down. The body slowly grows rigid and begins to fold itself like a flower folding again. The left eye opens slowly, the eyeball is turned so the pupil is lost in the angle of the nose. The right eye remains open and fixed staring forward. Meningitis. Acute. The arms are slowly raised more and more from the sides as if in the deliberate attitude before a mad dance, hands clenched, wrists flexed. The arms now lie upon each other crossed at the wrists. The knees are drawn up as if the child were squatting. The body holds this posture, the child's belly rumbling with a huge contortion. Breath has stopped. The body is stiff, blue. Slowly it relaxes, the whimpering cry begins again. The left eye falls closed.

It began with that eye. It was a lovely baby. Normal in every way. Breast fed. I have not taken it anywhere. It is only six weeks old. How can he get it?

The pointed beard approaches. It is infection, is it not, doctor?

Yes.

But I took him nowhere. How could he get it?

He must have gotten it from someone who carries it, maybe from one of you.

Will he die?

Yes, I think so.

Oh, I pray God to take him.

Have you any other children?

One girl five, and this boy.

Well, one must wait.

Again the night. The beard has followed me to the door. He closes the door carefully. We are alone in the night.

It is an infection?

Yes.

My wife is Catholic—not I. She had him for baptism. They pour water from a can on his head, so. It runs down in front of him, there where they baptize all kinds of babies, into his eye perhaps. It is a funny thing.

[1938–U.S.A.]

QUESTIONS

1. Characterize this story's narrator. What kind of a narrator is he? Does he resolve his perplexities by the end of his story or does he remain ambivalent?
2. Summarize Williams's plot. What is ironic about it?
3. Are there any details here that are repeated? What symbols do you find and how might they be interpreted? Is the story centrally symbolic (that is, a story in which symbols carry and control the meaning), or are its symbols reinforcing (meaning being conveyed primarily by narration, plot, and so forth)?
4. What do you make of the final paragraph? What is the story's theme?

WRITING SUGGESTIONS

1. Write a short paper on the symbolism of this story. Name what is symbolic, and classify Williams's symbols as to type (conventional or created; reinforcing or controlling). Then analyze the story's symbols in the context of the story overall.
2. In an essay, compare and contrast "Danse Pseudomacabre" (take note of the title) and "An Episode of War" as to their views of the universe and the place of human beings in it. The outlooks that Crane and Williams project are similar, yet there are telling differences between the stories. Analyzing the mood of each story might help you in getting at the latter.

Eveline

James Joyce

She sat at the window watching the evening invade the avenue. Her head was leaned against the window curtains and in her nostrils was the odour of dusty cretonne. She was tired.

Few people passed. The man out of the last house passed on his way home; she heard his footsteps clacking along the concrete pavement and afterwards crunching on the cinder path before the new red houses. One time there used to be a field there in which they used to play every evening with other people's children. Then a man from Belfast bought the field and built houses in it—not like their little brown houses but bright brick houses with shining roofs. The children of the avenue used to play together in that field—the Devines, the Waters, the Dunns, little Keogh the cripple, she and her brothers and sisters. Ernest, however, never played: he was too grown up. Her father used often to hunt them in out of the field with his blackthorn stick; but usually little Keogh used to keep *nix* and call out when he saw her father coming. Still they seemed to have been rather happy then. Her father was not so bad then; and besides, her mother was alive. That was a long time ago; she and her brothers and sisters were all grown up; her mother was dead. Tizzie Dunn was dead, too, and the Waters had gone back to England. Everything changes. Now she was going to go away like the others, to leave her home.

Home! She looked round the room, reviewing all its familiar objects which she had dusted once a week for so many years, wondering where on earth all the dust came from. Perhaps she would never see again those familiar objects from which she had never dreamed of being divided. And yet during all those years she had never found out the name of the priest whose yellowing photograph hung on the wall above the broken harmonium beside the coloured print of the promises made to Blessed Margaret Mary Alacoque. He had been a school friend of her father. Whenever he showed the photograph to a visitor her father used to pass it with a casual word:

"He is in Melbourne now."

She had consented to go away, to leave her home. Was that wise? She tried to weigh each side of the question. In her home anyway she had shelter and food; she had those whom she had known all her life about her. Of course she had to work hard, both in the house and at business. What would they say of her in the Stores when they found out that she had run away with a fellow? Say she was a fool, perhaps; and her place would be filled up by advertisement. Miss Gavan would be glad. She had always had an edge on her, especially whenever there were people listening.

"Miss Hill, don't you see these ladies are waiting?"

"Look lively, Miss Hill, please."

She would not cry many tears at leaving the Stores.

But in her new home, in a distant unknown country, it would not be like that. Then she would be married—she, Eveline. People would treat her with respect then. She would not be treated as her mother had been. Even now, though she was over nineteen, she sometimes felt herself in danger of her father's violence. She knew it was that that had given her the palpitations. When they were growing up he had never gone for her, like he used to go for Harry and Ernest, because she was a girl; but latterly he had begun to threaten her and say what he would do to her only for her dead mother's sake. And now she had nobody to protect her. Ernest was dead and Harry, who was in the church decorating business, was nearly always down somewhere in the country. Besides, the invariable squabble for money on Saturday nights had begun to weary her unspeakably. She always gave her entire wages—seven shillings—and Harry always sent up what he could but the trouble was to get any money from her father. He said she used to squander the money, that she had no head, that he wasn't going to give her his hard-earned money to throw about the streets, and much more, for he was usually fairly bad on Saturday night. In the end he would give her the money and ask her had she any intention of buying Sunday's dinner. Then she had to rush out as quickly as she could and do her marketing, holding her black leather purse tightly in her hand as she elbowed her way through the crowds and returning home late under her load of provisions. She had hard work to keep the house together and to see that the two young children who had been left to her charge went to school regularly and got their meals regularly. It was hard work—a hard life—but now that she was about to leave it she did not find it a wholly undesirable life.

She was about to explore another life with Frank. Frank was very kind, manly, open-hearted. She was to go away with him by the night-boat to be his wife and to live with him in Buenos Ayres where he had a home waiting for her. How well she remembered the first time she had seen him; he was lodging in a house on the main road where she used to visit. It seemed a few weeks ago. He was standing at the gate, his peaked cap pushed back on his head and his hair tumbled forward over a face of bronze. Then they had come to know each other. He used to meet her outside the Stores every evening and see her home. He took her to see *The Bohemian Girl* and she felt elated as she sat in an unaccustomed part of the theatre with him. He was awfully fond of music and sang a little. People knew that they were courting and, when he sang about the lass that loves a sailor, she always felt pleasantly confused. He used to call her Poppens out of fun. First of all it had been an excitement for her to have a fellow and then she had begun to like him. He had tales of distant countries. He had started as a deck boy at a pound a month on a ship of the Allan Line going out to Canada. He told her the names of the ships he had been on and the names of the different services. He had sailed through the Straits of Magellan and he told her stories of the terrible Patagonians. He had fallen on his feet in Buenos Ayres, he said, and had come over to the old country just for a holiday. Of course, her father had found out the affair and had forbidden her to have anything to say to him.

"I know these sailor chaps," he said.

One day he had quarrelled with Frank and after that she had to meet her lover secretly.

The evening deepened in the avenue. The white of the two letters in her lap grew indistinct. One was to Harry; the other was to her father. Ernest had been her favourite but she liked Harry too. Her father was becoming old lately, she noticed; he would miss her. Sometimes he could be very nice. Not long before, when she had been laid up for a day, he had read her out a ghost story and made toast for her at the fire. Another day, when their mother was alive, they had all gone for a picnic to the Hill of Howth. She remembered her father putting on her mother's bonnet to make the children laugh.

Her time was running out but she continued to sit by the window, leaning her head against the window curtain, inhaling the odour of dusty cretonne. Down far in the avenue she could hear a street organ playing.

She knew the air. Strange that it should come that very night to remind her of the promise to her mother, her promise to keep the home together as long as she could. She remembered the last night of her mother's illness; she was again in the close dark room at the other side of the hall and outside she heard a melancholy air of Italy. The organ-player had been ordered to go away and given sixpence. She remembered her father strutting back into the sickroom saying:

"Damned Italians! coming over here!"

As she mused the pitiful vision of her mother's life laid its spell on the very quick of her being—that life of commonplace sacrifices closing in final craziness. She trembled as she heard again her mother's voice saying constantly with foolish insistence:

"Derevaun Seraun! Derevaun Seraun!"

She stood up in a sudden impulse of terror. Escape! She must escape! Frank would save her. He would give her life, perhaps love, too. But she wanted to live. Why should she be unhappy? She had a right to happiness. Frank would take her in his arms, fold her in his arms. He would save her.

.   .   .

She stood among the swaying crowd in the station at the North Wall. He held her hand and she knew that he was speaking to her, saying something about the passage over and over again. The station was full of soldiers with brown baggages. Through the wide doors of the sheds she caught a glimpse of the black mass of the boat, lying in beside the quay wall, with illumined portholes. She answered nothing. She felt her cheek pale and cold and, out of a maze of distress, she prayed to God to direct her, to show her what was her duty. The boat blew a long mournful whistle into the mist. If she went, tomorrow she would be on the sea with Frank, steaming towards Buenos Ayres. Their passage had been booked. Could she still draw back after all he had done for her? Her distress awoke a nausea in her body and she kept moving her lips in silent fervent prayer.

A bell clanged upon her heart. She felt him seize her hand:

"Come!"

All the seas of the world tumbled about her heart. He was drawing her into them: he would drown her. She gripped with both hands at the iron railing.

"Come!"

No! No! No! It was impossible. Her hands clutched the iron in frenzy. Amid the seas she sent a cry of anguish.

"Eveline! Evvy!"

He rushed beyond the barrier and called to her to follow. He was shouted at to go on but he still called to her. She set her white face to him, passive, like a helpless animal. Her eyes gave him no sign of love or farewell or recognition.

[1905–Ireland]

QUESTIONS

1. Characterize Eveline. What does the description of her house and neighborhood tell us about her?
2. The two primary reinforcing symbols in this text are "dust" and "Buenos Ayres." What symbolic weight do these symbols carry in connection with each other?
3. Do any other details in the story have symbolic overtones? Which ones? What meanings other than the literal do they suggest?
4. Consider the end of the story carefully. What is suggested by Eveline's clutching the iron railing? Why doesn't she go with Frank? What symbolic meaning could Joyce's water imagery have?
5. *Dubliners*, the book in which "Eveline" appears, ends with a long story called "The Dead." What light might this information shed on "Eveline"?

WRITING SUGGESTIONS

1. Write a paragraph or two on the symbolism of the closing images of "Eveline"—specifically, "All the seas of the world" and "She gripped with both hands the iron railing." Discuss how the water imagery embodies Eveline's fear and her reasons for not going, and how the image of her gripping the railing concretizes her state of mind and being as we leave her.
2. Write a letter from Eveline to Frank explaining why she could not leave. Try to make the tone and diction of the letter appropriate to Eveline as you come to understand her in the story; try as well to keep the letter in line with what we know about her psychology. Don't, for instance, have her engage in extensive self-analysis. If possible, imply her deeper reasons by way of a few significant details that symbolically suggest her true reasons for not going.
3. Anything that Joyce wrote has prompted a wealth of critical interpretation. Do some research (read at least three interpretations of "Eveline"), and then write a research paper on the story. Don't just summarize what other critics have said. Rather, get a thesis of your own and use your research to support that thesis. Of course, quote and cite appropriately.

Araby

James Joyce

North Richmond Street, being blind, was a quiet street except at the hour when the Christian Brothers School set the boys free. An uninhabited house of two storeys stood at the blind end, detached from its neighbours in a square ground. The other houses of the street, conscious of decent lives within them, gazed at one another with brown imperturbable faces.

The former tenant of our house, a priest, had died in the back drawing-room. Air, musty from having been long enclosed, hung in all the rooms, and the waste room behind the kitchen was littered with old useless papers. Among these I found a few paper-covered books, the pages of which were curled and damp: *The Abbott*, By Walter Scott, *The Devout Communicant* and *The Memoirs of Vidocq*. I liked the last best because its leaves were yellow. The wild garden behind the house contained a central apple-tree and a few straggling bushes under one of which I found the late tenant's rusty bicycle-pump. He had been a very charitable priest; in his will he had left all his money to institutions and the furniture of his house to his sister.

When the short days of winter came dusk fell before we had well eaten our dinners. When we met in the street the houses had grown sombre. The space of sky above us was the colour of ever-changing violet and towards it the lamps of the street lifted their feeble lanterns. The cold air stung us and we played till our bodies glowed. Our shouts echoed in the silent street. The career of our play brought us through the dark muddy lanes behind the houses where we ran the gauntlet of the rough tribes from the cottages, to the back doors of the dark dripping gardens where odours arose from the ashpits, to the dark odorous stables where a coachman smoothed and combed the horse or shook music from the buckled harness. When we returned to the street light from the kitchen windows had filled the areas. If my uncle was seen turning the corner we hid in the shadow until we had seen him safely housed. Or if Mangan's sister came out on the doorstep to call her brother in to his tea we watched her from our shadow peer up and down the street. We waited to see whether she would remain or go in and, if she remained, we left our shadow and walked up to Mangan's steps resignedly. She was waiting for us, her figure defined by the light from the half-opened door. Her brother always teased her before he obeyed and I stood by the railings looking at her. Her dress swung as she moved her body and the soft rope of her hair tossed from side to side.

Every morning I lay on the floor in the front parlour watching her door. The blind was pulled down to within an inch of the sash so that I could not be seen. When she came out on the doorstep my heart leaped. I ran to the hall, seized my books and followed her. I kept her brown figure always in my eye and, when we came near the point at which our ways diverged, I quickened my pace and passed her. This happened morning after morning. I had never spoken to her, except for a few casual words, and yet her name was like a summons to all my foolish blood.

Her image accompanied me even in places the most hostile to romance. On Saturday evenings when my aunt went marketing I had to go to carry some of the parcels. We walked through the flaring streets, jostled by drunken men and bargaining women, amid the curses of labourers, the shrill litanies of shop-boys who stood on guard by the barrels of pigs' cheeks, the nasal chanting of street-singers, who sang a *come-all-you* about O'Donovan Rossa, or a ballad about the troubles in our native land. These noises converged in a single sensation of life for me: I imagined that I bore my chalice safely through a throng of foes. Her name sprang to my lips at moments in strange prayers and praises which I myself did not understand. My eyes were often full of tears (I could not tell why) and at times a flood from my heart seemed to pour itself out into my bosom. I thought little of the future. I did not know whether I would ever speak to her or not or, if I spoke to her, how I could tell her of my confused adoration. But my body was like a harp and her words and gestures were like fingers running upon the wires.

One evening I went into the back drawing-room in which the priest had died. It was a dark rainy evening and there was no sound in the house. Through one of the broken panes I heard the rain impinge upon the earth, the fine incessant needles of water playing in the sodden beds. Some distant lamp or lighted window gleamed below me. I was thankful that I could see so little. All my senses seemed to desire to veil themselves and, feeling that I was about to slip from them, I pressed the palms of my hands together until they trembled, murmuring: "*O Love! O Love!*" many times.

At last she spoke to me. When she addressed the first words to me I was so confused that I did not know what to answer. She asked me was I going to *Araby*. I forgot whether I answered yes or no. It would be a splendid bazaar, she said she would love to go.

"And why can't you?" I asked.

While she spoke she turned a silver bracelet round and round her wrist. She could not go, she said, because there would be a retreat that week in her convent. Her brother and two other boys were fighting for their caps and I was alone at the railings. She held one of the spikes, bowing her . head towards me. The light from the lamp opposite our door caught the white curve of her neck, lit up her hair that rested there and, falling, lit up the hand upon the railing. It fell over one side of her dress and caught the white border of a petticoat, just visible as she stood at ease.

"It's well for you," she said.

"If I go," I said, "I will bring you something."

What innumerable follies laid waste my waking and sleeping thoughts after that evening! I wished to annihilate the tedious intervening days. I chafed against the work of school. At night in my bedroom and by day in the classroom her image came between me and the page I strove to read. The syllables of the word *Araby* were called to me through the silence in which my soul luxuriated and cast an Eastern enchantment over me. I asked for leave to go to the bazaar on Saturday night. My aunt was surprised and hoped it was not some Freemason affair. I answered few questions in class. I watched my master's face pass from amiability to sternness; he hoped I was not beginning to idle. I could not call my wandering thoughts together. I had hardly any patience with the serious work of life which, now that it stood between me and my desire, seemed to me child's play, ugly monotonous child's play.

On Saturday morning I reminded my uncle that I wished to go to the bazaar in the evening. He was fussing at the hallstand, looking for the hat-brush, and answered me curtly:

"Yes, boy, I know."

As he was in the hall I could not go into the front parlour and lie at the window. I felt the house in bad humour and walked slowly towards the school. The air was pitilessly raw and already my heart misgave me.

When I came home to dinner my uncle had not yet been home. Still it was early. I sat staring at the clock for some time and, when its ticking began to irritate me, I left the room. I mounted the staircase and gained the upper part of the house. The high cold empty gloomy rooms liberated me and I went from room to room singing. From the front window I saw my companions playing below in the street. Their cries reached me weakened and indistinct and, leaning my forehead against the cool glass, I looked over at the dark house where she lived. I may have stood there for an hour, seeing nothing but the brown-clad figure cast by my imagination, touched discreetly by the lamplight at the curved neck, at the hand upon the railings and at the border below the dress.

When I came downstairs again I found Mrs. Mercer sitting at the fire. She was an old garrulous woman, a pawnbroker's widow, who collected used stamps for some pious purpose. I had to endure the gossip of the tea-table. The meal was prolonged beyond an hour and still my uncle did not come. Mrs. Mercer stood up to go: she was sorry she couln't wait any longer, but it was after eight o'clock and she did not like to be out late, as the night air was bad for her. When she had gone I began to walk up and down the room, clenching my fists. My aunt said:

"I'm afraid you may put off your bazaar for this night of Our Lord."

At nine o'clock I heard my uncle's latchkey in the halldoor. I heard him talking to himself and heard the hallstand rocking when it had received the weight of his overcoat. I could interpret these signs. When he was midway through his dinner I asked him to give me the money to go to the bazaar. He had forgotten.

"The people are in bed and after their first sleep now," he said.

I did not smile. My aunt said to him energetically:

"Can't you give him the money and let him go? You've kept him late enough as it is."

My uncle said he was very sorry he had forgotten. He said he believed in the old saying: "All work and no play makes Jack a dull boy." He asked me where I was going and, when I had told him a second time he asked me did I know *The Arab's Farewell to his Steed*. When I left the kitchen he was about to recite the opening lines of the piece to my aunt.

I held a florin tightly in my hand as I strode down Buckingham Street towards the station. The sight of the streets thronged with buyers and glaring with gas recalled to me the purpose of my journey. I took my seat in a third-class carriage of a deserted train. After an intolerable delay the train moved out of the station slowly. It crept onward among ruinous houses and over the twinkling river. At Westland Row Station a crowd of people pressed to the carriage doors; but the porters moved them back, saying that it was a special train for the bazaar. I remained alone in the bare carriage. In few minutes the train drew up beside an improvised wooden platform. I passed out on to the road and saw by the lighted dial of a clock that it was ten minutes to ten. In front of me was a large building which displayed the magical name.

I could not find any sixpenny entrance and, fearing that the bazaar would be closed, I passed in quickly through a turnstile, handing a shilling to a weary-looking man. I found myself in a big hall girdled at half its height by a gallery. Nearly all the stalls were closed and the greater part of the hall was in darkness. I recognised a silence like that which pervades a church after a service. I walked into the centre of the bazaar timidly. A few people were gathered about the stalls which were still open. Before a curtain, over which the words *Café Chantant* were written in coloured lamps, two men were counting money on a salver. I listened to the fall of the coins.

Remembering with difficulty why I had come I went over to one of the stalls and examined porecelain vases and flowered tea-sets. At the door of the stall a young lady was talking and laughing with two young gentlemen. I remarked their English accents and listened vaguely to their conversation.

"O, I never said such a thing!"

"O, but you did!"

"O, but I didn't!"

"Didn't she say that?"

"Yes. I heard her."

"O, there's a . . . fib!"

Observing me the young lady came over and asked me did I wish to buy anything. The tone of her voice was not encouraging; she seemed to have spoken to me out of a sense of duty. I looked humbly at the great jars that stood like eastern guards at either side of the dark entrance to the stall and murmured:

"No, thank you."

The young lady changed the position of one of the vases and went back to the two young men. They began to talk of the same subject. Once or twice the young lady glanced at me over her shoulder.

I lingered before her stall, though I knew my stay was useless, to make my interest in her wares seem the more real. Then I turned away slowly and walked down the middle of the bazaar. I allowed the two pennies to fall against the sixpence in my pocket. I heard a voice call from one end of the gallery that the light was out. The upper part of the hall was now completely dark.

Gazing up into the darkness I saw myself as a creature driven and derided by vanity; and my eyes burned with anguish and anger.

[1905–Ireland]

QUESTIONS

1. From the story's sentence structure, vocabulary, imagery, and distanced narrative point of view, what can we conclude about its narrator? What difference does that conclusion make to our understanding of his story?
2. Look at the story's first two paragraphs carefully. What mood do they establish? What symbolic images do they contain? What do these images suggest taken together?
3. What do we learn about the boy from his house and neighborhood? What do we learn about him and his culture from the dead priest's books of chivalry and devotion?
4. Given the kind of man the uncle is, his recitation of *The Arab's Farewell to his Steed* is ironic. How so? What might this irony suggest about Joyce's view of Irish culture generally?
5. What implications are there in the fact that Mangan's sister is not named? Mangan's sister has been interpreted as an allegorical figure of Ireland. Play with this possibility and see if it can be related to the more realistic aspects of the text.
6. A case could be made that the symbolic elements of this story are reinforcing. It could also be argued, however, that they are controlling. Which description do you think best suits the text? Why?

WRITING SUGGESTIONS

1. In a paragraph, characterize the narrator of "Araby." How old is he, roughly? Is he uneducated or highly educated? Is he a laborer or an intellectual? Is he mundane or poetic in sensibility? How do we know? Enumerate the attributes of the narrator that can be gleaned from the story, and in each case state how you inferred that attribute.
2. Most of the symbolic details of "Araby" suggest that the culture of Ireland in Joyce's day was, at least as viewed by Joyce, cheap, tawdry, and decayed. Choose three or four such details and, in a paragraph or more, discuss how we recognize them as symbols and how in context they come to embody Joyce's view of the country he exiled himself from.
3. One of the story's most telling symbols is the almost sadistic uncle's recitation from *The Arab's Farewell.* Write a paragraph on the irony of this recitation and what it symbolizes with respect to Irish idealism as Joyce viewed the idealism of the Irish of his day.
4. Once we reach adulthood, we all need to examine ourselves and our ideas, and expunge whatever in us is no longer appropriate to who we are or want to be. So the narrator of "Araby." But what of you in this regard? Write a paragraph or short essay on what attitudes, views, or feelings you acquired in childhood but have consciously shed or are in the process now of leaving behind.
5. Is "Araby" a naturalistic tale with reinforcing symbols or is it all allegory, its symbolism controlling? Both views have been held by critics. Write a paper arguing one or the other possibility. If you choose the second, then you must be

rigorous in your treatment of the story's symbolism. If you choose the first, you should establish what the main reinforcing symbols are, but your focus should be primarily on plot, character, and the like.

6. Go to the library and read three or four critical studies of "Araby" (look in the Joyce section). Then do one of the following:

(a) Write a summary of the main points of each, noting any points of disagreement. Which view seems most accurate to you? Discuss why.

(b) Write a research paper on "Araby" in which you make some point of your own. Use your research as research should be used: to help stimulate your mind into ideas of its own and to provide support for your thesis. Cite your sources appropriately.

The Trout

Sean O'Faolain

One of the first places Julia always ran to when they arrived in G— was The Dark Walk. It is a laurel walk, very cold; almost gone wild, a lofty midnight tunnel of smooth, sinewy branches. Underfoot the tough brown leaves are never dry enough to crackle: there is always a suggestion of damp and cool trickle.

She raced right into it. For the first few yards she always had the memory of the sun behind her, then she felt the dusk closing swiftly down on her so that she screamed with pleasure and raced on to reach the light at the far end; and it was always just a little too long in coming so that she emerged gasping, clasping her hands, laughing, drinking in the sun. When she was filled with the heat and glare she would turn and consider the ordeal again.

This year she had the extra joy of showing it to her small brother, and of terrifying him as well as herself. And for him the fear lasted longer because his legs were so short and she had gone out at the far end while he was still screaming and racing.

When they had done this many times they came back to the house to tell everybody that they had done it. He boasted. She mocked. They squabbled.

"Cry babby!"

"You were afraid yourself, so there!"

"I won't take you anymore."

"You're a big pig."

"I hate you."

Tears were threatening so somebody said, "Did you see the well?" She opened her eyes at that and held up her long lovely neck suspiciously and decided to be incredulous. She was twelve and at that age little girls are beginning to suspect most stories: they have already found out too many, from Santa Claus to the Stork. How could there be a well! In The Dark Walk? That she had visited year after year? Haughtily she said, "Nonsense."

But she went back, pretending to be going somewhere else, and she found a hole scooped in the rock at the side of the walk, choked with damp leaves, so shrouded by ferns that she only uncovered it after much searching. At the back of this little cavern there was about a quart of water. In the water she suddenly perceived a panting trout. She rushed for Stephen and dragged him to see, and they were both so excited that they were no longer afraid of the darkness as they hunched down and peered in at the fish panting in his tiny prison, his silver stomach going up and down like an engine.

Nobody knew how the trout got there. Even old Martin in the kitchen-garden laughed and refused to believe that it was there, or pretended not to believe, until she forced him to come down and see. Kneeling and pushing back his tattered old cap he peered in.

"Be cripes, you're right. How the divil in hell did that fella get there?"

She stared at him suspiciously.

"You knew?" she accused; but he said, "The divil a know"; and reached down to lift it out. Convinced she hauled him back. If she had found it then it was her trout.

Her mother suggested that a bird had carried the spawn. Her father thought that in the winter a small streamlet might have carried it down there as a baby, and it had been safe until the summer came and the water began to dry up. She said, "I see," and went back to look again and consider the matter in private. Her brother remained behind, wanting to hear the whole story of the trout, not really interested in the actual trout but much interested in the story which his mummy began to make up for him on the lines of, "So one day Daddy Trout and Mammy trout . . ." When he retailed it to her she said, "Pooh."

It troubled her that the trout was always in the same position; he had no room to turn; all the time the silver belly went up and down; otherwise he was motionless. She wondered what he ate and in between visits to Joey Pony, and the boat and a bathe to get cool, she thought of his hunger. She brought him down bits of dough; once she brought him a worm. He ignored the food. He just went on panting. Hunched over him she thought how, all the winter, while she was at school he had been in there. All the winter, in The Dark Walk, all day, all night, floating around alone. She drew the leaf of her hat down around her ears and chin and stared. She was still thinking of it as she lay in bed.

It was late June, the longest days of the year. The sun had sat still for a week, burning up the world. Although it was after ten o'clock it was still bright and still hot. She lay on her back under a single sheet, with her long legs spread, trying to keep cool. She could see the D of the moon through the fir-tree—they slept on the ground floor. Before they went to bed her mummy had told Stephen the story of the trout again, and she, in her bed, had resolutely presented her back to them and read her book. But she kept one ear cocked.

"And so, in the end, this naughty fish who would not stay at home got bigger and bigger and bigger, and the water got smaller and smaller . . ."

Passionately she had whirled and cried, "Mummy, don't make it a horrible old moral story!" Her mummy had brought in a Fairy Godmother, then, who sent lots of rain, and filled the well, and a stream poured out and the trout floated away down to the river below. Staring at the moon she knew that there are no such things as Fairy Godmothers and that the trout, down in The Dark Walk, was panting like an engine. She heard somebody unwind a fishing-reel. Would the *beasts* fish him out!

She sat up. Stephen was a hot lump of sleep, lazy thing. The Dark Walk would be full of little scraps of moon. She leaped up and looked out the window, and somehow it was not so lightsome now that she saw the dim mountains far away and the black firs against the breathing land and heard a dog say, bark-bark. Quietly she lifted the ewer of water, and climbed out the window and scuttled along the cool but cruel gravel down to the maw of the tunnel. Her pyjamas were very short so that when she splashed water it wet her ankles. She peered into the tunnel. Something alive rustled inside there. She raced in, and up and down she raced, and flurried, and cried aloud, "Oh, Gosh, I can't find it," and then at last she did. Kneeling down in the damp she put her hand into the slimy hole. When the body lashed they were both mad with fright. But she gripped him and shoved him into the ewer and raced, with her teeth ground, out to the other end of the tunnel and down the steep paths to the river's edge.

All the time she could feel him lashing his tail against the side of the ewer. She was afraid he would jump right out. The gravel cut into her soles until she came to the cool ooze of the river's bank where the moon-mice on the water crept into her feet. She poured out watching until he plopped. For a second he was visible in the water. She hoped he was not dizzy. Then all she saw was the glimmer of the moon in the silent-flowing river, the dark firs, the dim mountains, and the radiant pointed face laughing down at her out of the empty sky.

She scuttled up the hill, in the window, plonked down the ewer and flew through the air like a bird into bed. The dog said bark-bark. She heard the fishing-reel whirring. She hugged herself and giggled. Like a river of joy her holiday spread before her.

In the morning Stephen rushed to her, shouting that "he" was gone, and asking "where" and "how." Lifting her nose in the air she said superciliously, "Fairy Godmother, I suppose?" and strolled away patting the palms of her hands.

[1945–Ireland]

QUESTIONS

1. Though there is a literal level here, it doesn't amount to much. This story exists primarily at the symbolic level. What, then, are its major symbols? (To answer, consider prominence, placement, and repetition.)
2. Think into these symbolic images. What do they suggest by virtue of what they are in themselves? How does what they suggest function in the literary context?
3. Characterize Julia. What stage in life is she going through? What do the story's symbols reveal about her?
4. Two great sources of pleasure to be derived from literature are recognition of the known and confrontation with the unknown. Which of these does the pleasure one feels in reading "The Trout" spring from? Elaborate.

WRITING SUGGESTIONS

1. (a) In a paragraph, address question 3 above. Be sure to discuss how we come to understand what we do about Julia (that is, what serves to characterize her in the story).

   (b) In a separate paragraph, discuss your response to the story—what that respone is and why you so respond.
2. Write a short paper on the symbolism of "The Trout." Isolate the main symbols, think into them (see question 2 above), and determine their significance in context. In your paper, state what the story's symbols are, suggest how they are recognized to be symbols, and analyze their meaning in relation to Julia and the moment in life she is going through.

The Grave

Katherine Anne Porter

The grandfather, dead for more than thirty years, had been twice disturbed in his long repose by the constancy and possessiveness of his widow. She removed his bones first to Louisiana and then to Texas as if she had set out to find her own burial place, knowing well she would never return to the places she had left. In Texas she set up a small cemetery in a corner of her first farm, and as the family connection grew, and oddments of relations came over from Kentucky to settle, it contained at last about twenty graves. After the grandmother's death, part of her land was to be sold for the benefit of certain of her children, and the cemetery happened to lie in the part set aside for sale. It was necessary to take up the bodies and bury them again in the family plot in the big new public cemetery, where the grandmother had been buried. At last her husband was to lie beside her for eternity, as she had planned.

The family cemetery had been a pleasant small neglected garden of tangled rose bushes and ragged cedar trees and cypress, the simple flat stones rising out of uncropped sweet-smelling wild grass. The graves were lying open and empty one burning day when Miranda and her brother Paul, who often went together to hunt rabbits and doves, propped their twenty-two Winchester rifles carefully against the rail fence, climbed over and explored among the graves. She was nine years old and he was twelve.

They peered into the pits all shaped alike with such purposeful accuracy, and looking at each other with pleased adventurous eyes, they said in solemn tones: "These were graves!" trying by words to shape a special, suitable emotion in their minds, but they felt nothing except an agreeable thrill of wonder: they were seeing a new sight, doing something they had not done before. In them both there was also a small disappointment at the entire commonplaceness of the actual spectacle. Even if it had once contained a coffin for years upon years, when the coffin was gone a grave was just a hole in the ground. Miranda leaped into the pit that had held her grandfather's bones. Scratching around aimlessly and pleasurably as any young animal, she scooped up a lump of earth and weighed it in her palm. It had a pleasantly sweet, corrupt smell, being mixed with cedar needles and small leaves, and as the crumbs fell apart, she saw a silver dove no larger than a hazel nut, with spread wings and a neat fan-shaped tail. The breast had a deep round hollow in it. Turning it up to the fierce sunlight, she saw that the inside of the hollow was cut in little whorls. She scrambled out, over the pile of loose earth that had fallen back into one end of the grave, calling to Paul that she had found something, he must guess what . . . His head appeared smiling over the rim of another grave. He waved a closed hand at her. "I've got something too!" They ran to compare treasures, making a game of it, so many guesses each, all wrong, and a final showdown with opened palms. Paul had found a thin wide gold ring carved with intricate flowers and leaves. Miranda was smitten at sight of the ring and wished to have it. Paul seemed more impressed by the dove. They made a trade, with some little bickering. After he had got the dove in his hand, Paul said, "Don't you know what this is? This is a screw head for a *coffin*! . . . I'll bet nobody else in the world has one like this!"

Miranda glanced at it without covetousness. She had the gold ring on her thumb; it fitted perfectly. "Maybe we ought to go now," she said, "maybe one of the niggers'll see us and tell somebody." They knew the land had been sold, the cemetery was no longer theirs, and they felt like trespassers. They climbed back over the fence, slung their rifles loosely under their arms—they had been shooting at targets with various kinds of firearms since they were seven years old—and set out to look for the rabbits and doves or whatever small game might happen along. On these expeditions Miranda always followed at Paul's heels along the path, obeying instructions about handling her gun when going through fences; learning how to stand it up properly so it would not slip and fire unexpectedly; how to wait her time for a shot and not just bang away in the air without looking, spoiling shots for Paul, who really could hit things if given a chance. Now and then, in her excitement at seeing birds whizz up suddenly before her face, or a rabbit leap across her very toes, she lost her head, and almost without sighting she flung her rifle up and pulled the trigger. She hardly ever hit any sort of mark. She had no proper sense of hunting at all. Her brother would be often completely disgusted with her. "You don't care whether you get your bird or not," he said. "That's no way to hunt." Miranda could not understand his indignation. She had seen him smash his hat and yell with fury when he had missed his aim. "What I like about shooting," said Miranda, with exasperating inconsequence, "is pulling the trigger and hearing the noise."

"Then, by golly," said Paul, "whyn't you go back to the range and shoot at bulls-eyes?"

"I'd just as soon," said Miranda, "only like this, we walk around more."

"Well, you just stay behind and stop spoiling my shots," said Paul, who, when he made a kill, wanted to be certain he had made it. Miranda, who alone brought down a bird once in twenty rounds, always claimed as her own any game they got when they fired at the same moment. It was tiresome and unfair and her brother was sick of it.

"Now, the first dove we see, or the first rabbit, is mine," he told her. "And the next will be yours. Remember that and don't get smarty."

"What about snakes?" asked Miranda idly. "Can I have the first snake?"

Waving her thumb gently and watching her gold ring glitter, Miranda lost interest in shooting. She was wearing her summer roughing outfit: dark blue overalls, a light blue shirt, a hired-man's straw hat, and thick brown sandals. Her brother had the same outfit except his was a sober hickory-nut color. Ordinarily Miranda preferred her overalls to any other dress, though it was making rather a scandal in the countryside, for the year was 1903, and in the back country the law of female decorum had teeth in it. Her father had been criticized for letting his girls dress like boys and go careering around astride barebacked horses. Big sister Maria, the really independent and fearless one, in spite of her rather affected ways, rode at a dead run with only a rope knotted around her horse's nose. It was said the motherless family was running down, with the Grandmother no longer there to hold it together. It was known that she had discriminated against her son Harry in her will, and that he was in straits about money. Some of his old neighbors reflected with vicious satisfaction that now he would probably not be so stiffnecked, nor have any more high-stepping horses either. Miranda knew this, though she could not say how. She had met along the road old women of the kind who smoked corn-cob pipes, who had treated her grandmother with most sincere respect. They slanted their gummy old eyes side-ways at the granddaughter and said, "Ain't you ashamed of yoself, Missy? It's against the Scriptures to dress like that. Whut yo Pappy thinkin about?" Miranda, with her powerful social sense, which was like a fine set of antennae radiating from every pore of her skin, would feel ashamed because she knew well it was rude and ill-bred to shock anybody, even bad-tempered old crones, though she had faith in her father's judgment and was perfectly comfortable in the clothes. Her father had said, "They're just what you need, and they'll save your dresses for school . . ." This sounded quite simple and natural to her. She had been brought up in rigorous economy. Wastefulness was vulgar. It was also a sin. These were truths; she had heard them repeated many times and never once disputed.

Now the ring, shining with the serene purity of fine gold on her rather grubby thumb, turned her feelings against her overalls and sockless feet, toes sticking through the thick brown leather straps. She wanted to go back to the farmhouse, take a good cold bath, dust herself with plenty of Maria's violet talcum powder—provided Maria was not present to object, of course—put on the thinnest, most becoming dress she owned, with a big sash, and sit in a wicker chair under the trees . . . These things were not all she wanted, of course; she had vague stirrings of desire for luxury and a grand way of living which could not take precise form in her imagination but were founded on family legend of past wealth and leisure. These immediate comforts were what she could have, and she wanted them at once. She lagged rather far behind Paul, and once she thought of just turning back without a word and going home. She stopped, thinking that Paul would never do that to her, and so she would have to tell him. When a rabbit leaped, she let Paul have it without dispute. He killed it with one shot.

When she came up with him, he was already kneeling, examining the wound, the rabbit trailing from his hands. "Right through the head," he said complacently, as if he had aimed for it. He took out his sharp, competent bowie knife and started to skin the body. He did it very cleanly and quickly. Uncle Jimbilly knew how to prepare the skins so that Miranda always had fur coats for her dolls, for though she never cared much for her dolls she liked seeing them in fur coats. The children knelt facing each other over the dead animal. Miranda watched admiringly while her brother stripped the skin away as if he were taking off a glove. The flayed flesh emerged dark scarlet, sleek, firm; Miranda with thumb and finger felt the long fine muscles with the silvery flat strips binding them to the joints. Brother lifted the oddly bloated belly. "Look," he said, in a low amazed voice. "It was going to have young ones."

Very carefully he slit the thin flesh from the center ribs to the flanks, and a scarlet bag appeared. He slit again and pulled the bag open, and there lay a bundle of tiny rabbits, each wrapped in a thin scarlet veil. The brother pulled these off and there they were, dark gray, their sleek wet down lying in minute even ripples, like a baby's head just washed, their unbelievably small delicate ears folded close, their little blind faces almost featureless.

Miranda said, "Oh, I want to *see*," under her breath. She looked and looked—excited but not frightened, for she was accustomed to the sight of animals killed in hunting—filled with pity and astonishment and a kind of shocked delight in the wonderful little creatures for their own sakes, they were so pretty. She touched one of them ever so carefully, "Ah, there's blood running over them" she said and began to tremble without knowing why. Yet she wanted most deeply to see and to know. Having seen, she felt at once as if she had known all along. The very memory of her former ignorance faded, she had always known just this. No one had ever told her anything outright, she had been rather unobservant of the animal life around her because she was so accustomed to animals. They seemed simply disorderly and unaccountably rude in their habits, but altogether natural and not very interesting. Her brother had spoken as if he had known about everything all along. He may have seen all this before. He had never said a word to her, but she knew now a part at least of what he knew. She understood a little of the secret formless intuitions in her own mind and body, which had been clearing up, taking form, so gradually and so steadily she had not realized that she was learning what she had to know. Paul said cautiously, as if he were talking about something forbidden: "They were just about ready to be born." His voice dropped on the last word. "I know," said Miranda, "like kittens. I know, like babies." She was quietly and terribly agitated, standing again with her rifle under her arm, looking down at the bloody heap. "I don't want the skin," she said, "I won't have it." Paul buried the young rabbits again in their mother's body, wrapped the skin around her, carried her to a clump of sage bushes, and hid her away. He came out again at once and said to Miranda, with an eager friendliness, a confidential tone quite unusual in him, as if he were taking her into an important secret on equal terms: "Listen now. Now you listen to me, and don't ever forget. Don't you ever tell a living soul that you saw this. Don't tell a soul. Don't tell Dad because I'll get into trouble. He'll say I'm leading you into things you ought not to do. He's always saying that. So now don't you go and forget and blab out sometime the way you're always doing . . . Now, that's a secret. Don't you tell."

Miranda never told, she did not even wish to tell anybody. She thought about the whole worrisome affair with confused unhappiness for a few days. Then it sank quietly into her mind and was heaped over by accumulated thousands of impressions, for nearly twenty years. One day she was picking her path among the puddles and crushed refuse of a market street in a strange city of a strange country, when without warning, plain and clear in its true colors as if she looked through a frame upon a scene that had not stirred nor changed since the moment it happened, the episode of that far-off day leaped from its burial place before her mind's eye. She was so reasonlessly horrified she halted suddenly staring, the scene before her eyes dimmed by the vision back of them. An Indian vendor had held up before her a tray of dyed sugar sweets, in the shapes of all kinds of small creatures: birds, baby chicks, baby rabbits, lambs, baby pigs. They were in gay colors and smelled of vanilla, maybe. . . . It was a very hot day and the smell in the market, with its piles of raw flesh and wilting flowers, was like the mingled sweetness and corruption she had smelled that other day in the empty cemetery at home: the day she had remembered always until now vaguely as the time she and her brother had found treasure in the opened graves. Instantly upon this thought the dreadful vision faded, and she saw clearly her brother, whose childhood face she had forgotten, standing again in the blazing sunshine, again twelve years old, a pleased sober smile in his eyes, turning the silver dove over and over in his hands.

[1934–U.S.A.]

QUESTIONS

1. What do dove, ring, and rabbits symbolize in our culture?
2. Describe the specific ring that Paul finds. Why does Miranda want the ring? What does it mean to her and reveal about her? What of the rabbit with its young in this regard?
3. Why the title, with its definite article? Dove, ring, and rabbits, as well as the children and Miranda's memory of that day they killed the rabbit ("the episode of that far-off day leaped from its burial place before her mind's eye"), are all associated with graves. What is the symbolic significance of these linked associations? Why, incidentally, the word "leaped" in the passage just quoted?
4. How does the story's final scene derive from and bring to a climax its opening scene in the graveyard and its central scene with the rabbits?
5. What does the story say, finally, about the relationship of childhood and maturity, of past and present, and most especially of life and death?
6. Porter's symbolism accomplishes what Paul and Miranda can't in mere words—"to shape a special, suitable emotion in their minds." Explain.

WRITING SUGGESTIONS

1. In a short paper, compare and contrast "The Grave" and "The Trout" (the story before this) with respect to symbolism. What kinds of symbol does each contain

(conventional or created)? Is the symbolism of each reinforcing or controlling? How do their symbols announce themselves and how are their symbols related to their themes?

2. Consider the three prime symbols of this story—dove, ring, and rabbit. Write a paper on these symbols as used by Porter. Classify them and discuss what they symbolize in our culture at large. How does what they symbolize carry over to "The Grave" and how does Porter adapt their symbolic meanings to the specific purposes of her story? In answering the latter part of this question, consider the facts that both dove and ring are found in a grave and that the rabbit becomes a kind of grave with respect to her young.

3. Write a research paper on "The Grave." First find out what its critics have to say. Then write an analysis of the story using your research to support *your* interpretation. That is, your interpretation should be your own, though you will want to refer to what others have had to say to support your argument as you go.

The Flowers

Alice Walker

It seemed to Myop as she skipped lightly from hen house to pigpen to smokehouse that the days had never been as beautiful as these. The air held a keenness that made her nose twitch. The harvesting of the corn and cotton, peanuts and squash, made each day a golden surprise that caused excited little tremors to run up her jaws.

Myop carried a short, knobby stick. She struck out at random at chickens she liked, and worked out the beat of a song on the fence around the pigpen. She felt light and good in the warm sun. She was ten, and nothing existed for her but her song, the stick clutched in her dark brown hand, and the tat-de-ta-ta-ta of accompaniment.

Turning her back on the rusty boards of her family's sharecropper cabin, Myop walked along the fence till it ran into the stream made by the spring. Around the spring, where the family got drinking water, silver ferns and wildflowers grew. Along the shallow banks pigs rooted. Myop watched the tiny white bubbles disrupt the thin black scale of soil and the water that silently rose and slid away down the stream.

She had explored the woods behind the house many times. Often, in late autumn, her mother took her to gather nuts among the fallen leaves. Today she made her own path, bouncing this way and that way, vaguely keeping an eye out for snakes. She found, in addition to various common but pretty ferns and leaves, an armful of strange blue flowers with velvety ridges and a sweetsuds bush full of the brown, fragrant buds.

By twelve o'clock, her arms laden with sprigs of her findings, she was a mile or more from home. She had often been as far before, but the strangeness of the land made it not as pleasant as her usual haunts. It seemed gloomy in the little cove in which she found herself. The air was damp, the silence close and deep.

Myop began to circle back to the house, back to the peacefulness of the morning. It was then she stepped smack into his eyes. Her heel became lodged in the broken ridge between brow and nose, and she reached down quickly, unafraid, to free herself. It was only when she saw his naked grin that she gave a little yelp of surprise.

He had been a tall man. From feet to neck covered a long space. His head lay beside him. When she pushed back the leaves and layers of earth and debris Myop saw that he'd had large white teeth, all of them cracked or broken, long fingers, and very big bones. All his clothes had rotted away except some threads of blue denim from his overalls. The buckles of the overalls had turned green.

Myop gazed around the spot with interest. Very near where she'd stepped into the head was a wild pink rose. As she picked it to add to her bundle she noticed a raised mound, a ring, around the rose's root. It was the rotted remains of a noose, a bit of shredding plowline, now blending benignly into the soil. Around an overhanging limb of a great spreading oak clung another piece. Frayed, rotted, bleached, and frazzled—barely there—but spinning restlessly in the breeze. Myop laid down her flowers.

And the summer was over.

[1967–U.S.A.]

QUESTIONS

1. The plot of "The Flowers" turns on a shocking past event. What is it?
2. What is the function of the mood of the first five paragraphs with respect to the rest of the story?
3. What can we infer about Myop's world from her lack of terror? Does her lack of terror seem plausible? Why or why not?
4. If we don't take Myop's lack of terror literally, what could be made of it? Might the story be an allegory? Comment on Myop's name and her laying down of her flowers in this regard.

WRITING SUGGESTIONS

1. Write an essay explaining how Myop's lack of terror is pivotal in interpreting "The Flowers." Consider how the implausibility of her response suggests that we should look at the story as something other than a realistic accounting of an incident in the life of one little girl.
2. A rewarding comparison could be made between Walker's story and Lewis Allan's lyric "Strange Fruit," made famous by Billie Holiday and widely reprinted in anthologies of black poetry. Find Allan's poem and write a short essay comparing the two works. In particular, what do both reveal about black consciousness with respect to black history in America?

First Sorrow*

Franz Kafka

A trapeze artist—this art, practiced high in the vaulted domes of the great variety theaters, is admittedly one of the most difficult humanity can achieve—had so arranged his life that, as long as he kept working in the same building, he never came down from his trapeze by night or day, at first only from a desire to perfect his skill, but later because custom was too strong for him. All his needs, very modest needs at that, were supplied by relays of attendants who watched from below and sent up and hauled down again in specially constructed containers whatever he required. This way of living caused no particular inconvenience to the theatrical people, except that, when other turns were on the stage, his being still up aloft, which could not be dissembled, proved somewhat distracting, as also the fact that, although at such times he mostly kept very still, he drew a stray glance here and there from the public. Yet the management overlooked this, because he was an extraordinary and unique artist. And of course they recognized that this mode of life was no mere prank, and that only in this way could he really keep himself in constant practice and his art at the pitch of its perfection.

Besides, it was quite healthful up there, and when in the warmer seasons of the year the side windows all around the dome of the theater were thrown open and sun and fresh air came pouring irresistibly into the dusky vault, it was even beautiful. True, his social life was somewhat limited, only sometimes a fellow acrobat swarmed up the ladder to him, and then they both sat on the trapeze, leaning left and right against the supporting ropes, and chatted, or builders' workmen repairing the roof

* Translated by Willa and Edwin Muir.

exchanged a few words with him through an open window, or the fireman, inspecting the emergency lighting in the top gallery, called over to him something that sounded respectful but could hardly be made out. Otherwise nothing disturbed his seclusion; occasionally, perhaps, some theater hand straying through the empty theater of an afternoon gazed thoughtfully up into the great height of the roof, almost beyond eyeshot, where the trapeze artist, unaware that he was being observed, practiced his art or rested.

The trapeze artist could have gone on living peacefully like that, had it not been for the inevitable journeys from place to place, which he found extremely trying. Of course his manager saw to it that his sufferings were not prolonged one moment more than necessary; for town travel, racing automobiles were used, which whirled him, by night if possible or in the earliest hours of the morning, through the empty streets at breakneck speed, too slow all the same for the trapeze artist's impatience; for railway journeys, a whole compartment was reserved, in which the trapeze artist, as a possible though wretched alternative to his usual way of living, could pass the time up on the luggage rack; in the next town on their circuit, long before he arrived, the trapeze was already slung up in the theater and all the doors leading to the stage were flung wide open, all corridors kept free—yet the manager never knew a happy moment until the trapeze artist set his foot on the rope ladder and in a twinkling, at long last, hung aloft on his trapeze.

Despite so many journeys having been successfully arranged by the manager, each new one embarrassed him again, for the journeys, apart from everything else, got on the nerves of the artist a great deal.

Once when they were again traveling together, the trapeze artist lying on the luggage rack dreaming, the manager leaning back in the opposite window seat reading a book, the trapeze artist addressed his companion in a low voice. The manager was immediately all attention. The trapeze artist, biting his lips, said that he must always in future have two trapezes for his performance instead of only one, two trapezes opposite each other. The manager at once agreed. But the trapeze artist, as if to show that the manager's consent counted for as little as his refusal, said that never again would he perform on only one trapeze, in no circumstances whatever. The very idea that it might happen at all seemed to make him shudder. The manager, watchfully feeling his way, once more emphasized his entire agreement, two trapezes were better than one, besides it would be an advantage to have a second bar, more variety could be introduced into the performance. At that the trapeze artist suddenly burst into tears. Deeply distressed, the manager sprang to his feet and asked what was the matter, then getting no answer climbed up on the seat and caressed him, cheek to cheek, so that his own face was bedabbled by the trapeze artist's tears. Yet it took much questioning and soothing endearment until the trapeze artist sobbed: "Only the one bar in my hands—how can I go on living!" That made it somewhat easier for the manager to comfort him; he promised to wire from the very next station for a second trapeze to be installed in the first town on their circuit; reproached himself for having let the artist work so long on only one trapeze; and thanked and praised him warmly for having at last brought the mistake to his notice. And so he succeeded in reassuring the trapeze artist, little by little, and was able to go back to his corner. But he himself was far from reassured, with deep uneasiness he kept glancing secretly at the trapeze artist over the top of his book. Once such ideas began to torment him, would they ever quite leave him alone? Would they not rather increase in urgency? Would they not threaten his very existence? And indeed the manager believed he could see, during the apparently peaceful sleep which had succeeded the fit of tears, the first furrows of care engraving themselves upon the trapeze artist's smooth, childlike forehead.

[1922–Austria]

QUESTIONS

1. Taking Kafka's "trapeze artist" as a synecdoche (a part that stands for the whole—in this case, one type of artist standing for all artists), consider this story as an allegory. Whom does the manager stand for? What does it mean that the artist wishes to stay in his trapeze and never come down? What does the train ride represent?
2. What is Kafka saying about the lives of writers, painters, and so forth by way of his little allegory?
3. Why does the artist wish for a second trapeze? Will this solve his problem? What is his problem?
4. In light of the story's end, what does its title imply?
5. Is Kafka's conception of the artist valid? Whether your answer is positive or negative, why?

WRITING SUGGESTIONS

1. In a short essay, state how "First Sorrow" is an allegory and examine its meaning.
2. Assuming an audience not familiar with this story, write a review of it. In doing so, consider the conception of the artist as embodied in Kafka's man on the trapeze. Is the conception meaningful or merely conventional? Is it applicable to all historical periods, our own included, or is it historically localized and perhaps dated? Try to persuade a reader of the rightness of your judgment.

Signs and Symbols

Vladimir Nabokov

1

For the fourth time in as many years they were confronted with the problem of what birthday present to bring a young man who was incurably deranged in his mind. He had no desires. Man-made objects were to him either hives of evil, vibrant with a malignant activity that he alone could perceive, or gross comforts for which no use could be found in his abstract world. After eliminating a number of articles that might offend him or frighten him (anything in the gadget line for instance was taboo), his parents chose a dainty and innocent trifle: a basket with ten different fruit jellies in ten little jars.

At the time of his birth they had been married already for a long time; a score of years had elapsed, and now they were quite old. Her drab gray hair was done anyhow. She wore cheap black dresses. Unlike other women of her age (such as Mrs. Sol, their next-door neighbor, whose face was all pink and mauve with paint and whose hat was a cluster of brookside flowers), she presented a naked white countenance to the faultfinding light of spring days. Her husband, who in the old country had been a fairly successful businessman, was now wholly dependent on his brother Isaac, a real American of almost forty years standing. They seldom saw him and had nicknamed him "the Prince."

That Friday everything went wrong. The underground train lost its life current between two stations, and for a quarter of an hour one could hear nothing but the dutiful beating of one's heart and the rustling of newspapers. The bus they had to take next kept them waiting for ages; and when it did come, it was crammed with garrulous high-school children. It was raining hard as they walked up the brown path leading to the sanitarium. There they waited again; and instead of their boy shuffling into the room as he usually did (his poor face blotched with acne, ill-shaven, sullen, and confused), a nurse they knew, and did not care for, appeared at last and brightly explained that he had again attempted to take his life. He was all right, she said, but a visit might disturb him. The place was so miserably understaffed, and things got mislaid or mixed up so easily, that they decided not to leave their present in the office but to bring it to him next time they came.

She waited for her husband to open his umbrella and then took his arm. He kept clearing his throat in a special resonant way he had when he was upset. They reached the bus-stop shelter on the other side of the street and he closed his umbrella. A few feet away, under a swaying and dripping tree, a tiny half-dead unfledged bird was helplessly twitching in a puddle.

During the long ride to the subway station, she and her husband did not exchange a word; and every time she glanced at his old hands (swollen veins, brown-spotted skin), clasped and twitching upon the handle of his umbrella, she felt the mounting pressure of tears. As she looked around trying to hook her mind onto something, it gave her a kind of soft shock, a mixture of compassion and wonder, to notice that one of the passengers, a girl with dark hair and grubby red toenails, was weeping on the shoulder of an older woman. Whom did that woman resemble? She resembled Rebecca Borisovna, whose daughter had married one of the Soloveichiks—in Minsk, years ago.

The last time he had tried to do it, his method had been, in the doctor's words, a masterpiece of inventiveness; he would have succeeded, had not an envious fellow patient thought he was learning to fly—and stopped him. What he really wanted to do was to tear a hole in this world and escape.

The system of his delusions had been the subject of an elaborate paper in a scientific monthly, but long before that she and her husband had puzzled it out for themselves. "Referential mania," Herman Brink had called it. In these very rare cases the patient imagines that everything happening around him is a veiled reference to his personality and existence. He excludes real people from the conspiracy—because he considers himself to be so much more intelligent than other men. Phenomenal nature shadows him wherever he goes. Clouds in the staring sky transmit to one another, by means of slow signs, incredibly detailed information regarding him. His inmost thoughts are discussed at nightfall, in manual alphabet, by darkly gesticulating trees. Pebbles or stains or sun flecks form patterns representing in some awful way messages which he must intercept. Everything is a cipher and of everything he is the theme.

Some of the spies are detached observers, such as glass surfaces and still pools; others, such as coats in store windows, are prejudiced witnesses, lynchers at heart; others again (running water, storms) are hysterical to the point of insanity, have a distorted opinion of him and grotesquely misinterpret his actions. He must be always on his guard and devote every minute and module of life to the decoding of the undulation of things. The very air he exhales is indexed and filed away. If only the interest he provokes were limited to his immediate surroundings—but alas it is not! With distance the torrents of wild scandal increase in volume and volubility. The silhouettes of his blood corpuscles, magnified a million times, flit over vast plains; and still farther, great mountains of unbearable solidity and height sum up in terms of granite and groaning firs the ultimate truth of his being.

2

When they emerged from the thunder and foul air of the subway, the last dregs of the day were mixed with the street lights. She wanted to buy some fish for supper, so she handed him the basket of jelly bars, telling him to go home. He walked up to the third landing and then remembered he had given her his keys earlier in the day.

In silence he sat down on the steps and in silence rose when some ten minutes later she came, heavily trudging upstairs, wanly smiling, shaking her head in deprecation of her silliness. They entered their two-room flat and he at once went to the mirror. Straining the corners of his mouth apart by means of his thumbs, with a horrible masklike grimace, he removed his new hopelessly uncomfortable dental plate and severed the long tusks of saliva connecting him to it. He read his Russian-language newspaper while she laid the table. Still reading, he ate the pale victuals that needed no teeth. She knew his moods and was also silent.

When he had gone to bed, she remained in the living room with her pack of soiled cards and her old albums. Across the narrow yard where the rain tinkled in the dark against some battered ash cans, windows were blandly alight and in one of them a black-trousered man with his bare elbows raised could be seen lying supine on an untidy bed. She pulled the blind down and examined the photographs. As a baby he looked more surprised than most babies. From a fold in the album, a German maid they had had in Leipzig and her fat-faced fiancé fell out. Minsk, the Revolution, Leipzig, Berlin, Leipzig, a slanting house front badly out of focus. Four years old, in a park: moodily, shyly, with puckered forehead, looking away from an eager squirrel as he would from any other stranger.

Aunt Rosa, a fussy, angular, wild-eyed old lady, who had lived in a tremulous world of bad news, bankruptcies, train accidents, cancerous growths—until the Germans put her to death, together with all the people she had worried about. Age six—that was when he drew wonderful birds with human hands and feet, and suffered from insomnia like a grown-up man. His cousin, now a famous chess player. He again, aged about eight, already difficult to understand, afraid of the wallpaper in the passage, afraid of a certain picture in a book which merely showed an idyllic landscape with rocks on a hillside and an old cart wheel hanging from the branch of a leafless tree. Aged ten: the year they left Europe. The shame, the pity, the humiliating difficulties, the ugly, vicious, backward children he was with in that special school. And then came a time in his life, coinciding with a long convalescence after pneumonia, when those little phobias of his which his parents had stubbornly regarded as the eccentricities of a prodigiously gifted child hardened as it were into a dense tangle of logically interacting illusions, making him totally inaccessible to normal minds.

This, and much more, she accepted—for after all living did mean accepting the loss of one joy after another, not even joys in her case—mere possibilities of improvement. She thought of the endless waves of pain that for some reason or other she and her husband had to endure; of the invisible giants hurting her boy in some unimaginable fashion; of the incalculable amount of tenderness contained in the world; of the fate of this tenderness, which is either crushed, or wasted, or transformed into madness; of neglected children humming to themselves in unswept corners; of beautiful weeds that cannot hide from the farmer and helplessly have to watch the shadow of his simian stoop leave mangled flowers in its wake, as the monstrous darkness approaches.

3

It was past midnight when from the living room she heard her husband moan; and presently he staggered in, wearing over his nightgown the old overcoat with astrakhan collar which he much preferred to the nice blue bathrobe he had.

"I can't sleep," he cried.

"Why," she asked, "why can't you sleep? You were so tired."

"I can't sleep because I am dying," he said and lay down on the couch.

"Is it your stomach? Do you want me to call Dr. Solov?"

"No doctors, no doctors," he moaned. "To the devil with doctors! We must get him out of there quick. Otherwise we'll be responsible. Responsible!" he repeated and hurled himself into a sitting position, both feet on the floor, thumping his forehead with his clenched fist.

"All right," she said quietly, "we shall bring him home tomorrow morning."

"I would like some tea," said her husband and retired to the bathroom.

Bending with difficulty, she retrieved some playing cards and a photograph or two that had slipped from the couch to the floor: knave of hearts, nine of spades, ace of spades, Elsa and her bestial beau.

He returned in high spirits, saying in a loud voice: "I have it all figured out. We will give him the bedroom. Each of us will spend part of the night near him and the other part on this couch. By turns. We will have the doctor see him at least twice a week. It does not matter what the Prince says. He won't have to say much anyway because it will come out cheaper."

The telephone rang. It was an unusual hour for their telephone to ring. His left slipper had come off and he groped for it with his heel and toe as he stood in the middle of the room, and childishly, toothlessly, gaped at his wife. Having more English that he did, it was she who attended to calls.

"Can I speak to Charlie," said a girl's dull little voice.

"What number you want? No. That is not the right number."

The receiver was gently cradled. Her hand went to her old tired heart.

"It frightened me," she said.

He smiled a quick smile and immediately resumed his excited monologue. They would fetch him as soon as it was day. Knives would have to be kept in a locked drawer. Even at his worst he presented no danger to other people.

The telephone rang a second time. The same toneless anxious young voice asked for Charlie.

"You have the incorrect number. I will tell you what you are doing: you are turning the letter O instead of the zero."

They sat down to their unexpected festive midnight tea. The birthday present stood on the table. He sipped noisily; his face was flushed; every now and then he imparted a circular motion to his raised glass so as to make the sugar dissolve more thoroughly. The vein on the side of his bald head where there was a large birthmark stood out conspicuously and, although he had shaved that morning, a silvery bristle showed on his chin. While she poured him another glass of tea, he put on his spectacles and re-examined with pleasure the luminous yellow, green, red little jars. His clumsy moist lips spelled out their eloquent labels: apricot, grape, beech plum, quince. He had got to crab apple, when the telephone rang again.

[1948–U.S.A.]

QUESTIONS

1. Kafka's symbols translate rather neatly into what they stand for. In what way or ways is Nabokov's symbolism different?
2. What in "Signs and Symbols" seems symbolic? What might each symbol mean?
3. Can meaning be easily assigned here? What does the story show us about signs and symbols?
4. As well as concerning signs and symbols, Nabokov's story concerns the nature of the artist and artistic creation. How is the son like the artist? Yet how do they differ? What does the story in its own structure reveal about the nature of artistic creation?

WRITING SUGGESTIONS

1. In a paragraph or more, contrast "First Sorrow" and "Signs and Symbols" as to their symbolism. What conclusion can be drawn from these two stories about symbolism?
2. In a short paper, discuss what might be symbolic in "Signs and Symbols," how its potential symbols are recognized, and what they might mean. Use at least three examples.
3. The creative artist transforms reality by making it meaningful in every detail. Write an essay in which you show that this is what Nabokov accomplishes in the present story.

·8·

SOME LONGER STORIES
FOR FURTHER READING

Good Country People

Flannery O'Connor

Besides the neutral expression that she wore when she was alone, Mrs. Freeman had two others, forward and reverse, that she used for all her human dealings. Her forward expression was steady and driving like the advance of a heavy truck. Her eyes never swerved to left or right but turned as the story turned as if they followed a yellow line down the center of it. She seldom used the other expression because it was not often necessary for her to retract a statement, but when she did, her face came to a complete stop, there was an almost imperceptible movement of her black eyes, during which they seemed to be receding, and then the observer would see that Mrs. Freeman, though she might stand there as real as several grain sacks thrown on top of each other, was no longer there in spirit. As for getting anything across to her when this was the case, Mrs. Hopewell had given it up. She might talk her head off. Mrs. Freeman could never be brought to admit herself wrong on any point. She would stand there and if she could be brought to say anything, it was something like, "Well, I wouldn't of said it was and I wouldn't of said it wasn't," or letting her gaze range over the top kitchen shelf where there was an assortment of dusty bottles, she might remark, "I see you ain't ate many of them figs you put up last summer."

They carried on their most important business in the kitchen at breakfast. Every morning Mrs. Hopewell got up at seven o'clock and lit her gas heater and Joy's. Joy was her daughter, a large blonde girl who had an artificial leg. Mrs. Hopewell thought of her as a child though she was thirty-two years old and highly educated. Joy would get up while her mother was eating and lumber into the bathroom and slam the door, and before long, Mrs. Freeman would arrive at the back door. Joy would hear her mother call, "Come on in," and then they would talk for a while in low voices that were indistinguishable in the bathroom. By the time Joy came in, they had usually finished the weather report and were on one or the other of Mrs. Freeman's daughters, Glynese or Carramae. Joy called them Glycerin and Caramel. Glynese, a redhead, was eighteen and had many admirers; Carramae, a blonde, was only fifteen but already married and pregnant. She could not keep anything on her stomach. Every morning Mrs. Freeman told Mrs. Hopewell how many times she had vomited since the last report.

Mrs. Hopewell liked to tell people that Glynese and Carramae were two of the finest girls she knew and that Mrs. Freeman was a *lady* and that she was never ashamed to take her anywhere or introduce her to anybody they might meet. Then she would tell how she had happened to hire the Freemans in the first place and how they were a godsend to her and how she had had them four years. The reason for her keeping them so long was that they were not trash. They were good country people. She had telephoned the man whose name they had given as a reference and he had told her that Mr. Freeman was a good farmer but that his wife was the nosiest woman ever to walk the earth. "She's got to be into everything," the man said. "If she don't get there before the dust settles, you can bet she's dead, that's all. She'll want to know all your business. I can stand him real good," he had said, "but me nor my wife neither could have stood that woman one more minute on this place." That had put Mrs. Hopewell off for a few days.

She had hired them in the end because there were no other applicants but she had made up her mind beforehand exactly how she would handle the woman. Since she was the type who had to be into everything, then, Mrs. Hopewell had decided, she would not only let her be into everything, she would *see to it* that she was into everything—she would give her the responsibility of everything, she would put her in charge. Mrs. Hopewell had no bad qualities of her own but she was able to use other people's in such a constructive way that she never felt the lack. She had hired the Freemans and she had kept them four years.

Nothing is perfect. This was one of Mrs. Hopewell's favorite sayings. Another was: that is life! And still another, the most important, was: well, other people have their opinions too. She would make these statements, usually at the table, in a tone of gentle insistence as if no one held them but her, and the large hulking Joy, whose constant outrage had obliterated every expression from her face, would stare just a little to the side of her, her eyes icy blue, with the look of someone who has achieved blindness by an act of will and means to keep it.

When Mrs. Hopewell said to Mrs. Freeman that life was like that, Mrs. Freeman would say, "I always said so myself." Nothing had been arrived at by anyone that had not first been arrived at by her. She was quicker than Mr. Freeman. When Mrs. Hopewell said to her after they had been on the place a while, "You know, you're the wheel behind the wheel," and winked, Mrs. Freeman had said, "I know it. I've always been quick. It's some that are quicker than others."

"Everybody is different," Mrs. Hopewell said.

"Yes, most people is," Mrs. Freeman said.

"It takes all kinds to make the world."

"I always said it did myself."

The girl was used to this kind of dialogue for breakfast and more of it for dinner; sometimes they had if for supper too. When they had no guest they ate in the kitchen because that was easier. Mrs. Freeman always managed to arrive at some point during the meal and to watch them finish it. She would stand in the doorway if it were summer but in the winter she would stand with one elbow on top of the refrigerator and look down on them, or she would stand by the gas heater, lifting the back of her skirt slightly. Occasionally she would stand against the wall and roll her head from side to side. At no time was she in any hurry to leave. All this was very trying on Mrs. Hopewell but she was a woman of great patience. She realized that nothing is perfect and that in the Freemans she had good country people and that if, in this day and age, you get good country people, you had better hang onto them.

She had had plenty of experience with trash. Before the Freemans she had averaged one tenant family a year. The wives of these farmers were not the kind you would want to be around you for very long. Mrs. Hopewell, who had divorced her husband long ago, needed someone to walk over the fields with her; and when Joy had to be impressed for these services, her remarks were usually so ugly and her face so glum that Mrs. Hopewell would say, "If you can't come pleasantly, I don't want you at all," to which the girl, standing square and rigid-shouldered with her neck thrust slightly forward, would reply, "If you want me, here I am—LIKE I AM."

Mrs. Hopewell excused this attitude because of the leg (which had been shot off in a hunting accident when Joy was ten). It was hard for Mrs. Hopewell to realize that her child was thirty-two now and that for more than twenty years she had had only one leg. She thought of her still as a child because it tore her heart to think instead of the poor stout girl in her thirties who had never danced a step or had any *normal* good times. Her name was really Joy but as soon as she was twenty-one and away from home, she had had it legally changed. Mrs. Hopewell was certain that she had thought and thought until she had hit upon the ugliest name in any language. Then she had gone and had the beautiful name, Joy, changed without telling her mother until after she had done it. Her legal name was Hulga.

When Mrs. Hopewell thought the name, Hulga, she thought of the broad blank hull of a battleship. She would not use it. She continued to call her Joy to which the girl responded but in a purely mechanical way.

Hulga had learned to tolerate Mrs. Freeman, who saved her from taking walks with her mother. Even Glynese and Carramae were useful when they occupied attention that might otherwise have been directed at her. At first she had thought she could not stand Mrs. Freeman for she had found that it was not possible to be rude to her. Mrs. Freeman would take on strange resentments and for days together she would be sullen but the source of her displeasure was always obscure; a direct attack, a positive leer, blatant ugliness to her face—these never touched her. And without warning one day, she began calling her Hulga.

She did not call her that in front of Mrs. Hopewell who would have been incensed but when she and the girl happened to be out of the house together, she would say something and add the name Hulga to the end of it, and the big spectacled Joy-Hulga would scowl and redden as if her privacy had been intruded upon. She considered the name her personal affair. She had arrived at it first purely on the basis of its ugly sound and then the full genius of its fitness had struck her. She had a vision of the name working like the ugly sweating Vulcan who stayed in the furnace and to whom, presumably, the goddess had to come when called. She saw it as the name of her highest creative act. One of her major triumphs was that her mother had not been able to turn her dust into Joy, but the greater one was that she had been able to turn it herself into Hulga. However, Mrs. Freeman's relish for using the name only irritated her. It was as if Mrs. Freeman's beady steel-pointed eyes had penetrated far enough behind her face to reach some secret fact. Something about her seemed to fascinate Mrs. Freeman and then one day Hulga realized that it was the artificial leg. Mrs. Freeman had a special fondness for the details of secret infections, hidden deformities, assaults upon children. Of diseases, she preferred the lingering or incurable. Hulga had heard Mrs. Hopewell give her the details of the hunting accident, how the leg had been literally blasted off, how she had never lost consciousness. Mrs. Freeman could listen to it any time as if it had happened an hour ago.

When Hulga stumped into the kitchen in the morning (she could walk without making the awful noise but she made it—Mrs. Hopewell was certain—because it was ugly-sounding), she glanced at them and did not speak. Mrs. Hopewell would be in her red kimono with her hair tied around her head in rags. She would be sitting at the table, finishing her breakfast and Mrs. Freeman would be hanging by her elbow outward from the refrigerator, looking down at the table. Hulga always put her eggs on the stove to boil and then stood over them with her arms folded, and Mrs. Hopewell would look at her—a kind of indirect gaze divided between her and Mrs. Freeman—and would think that if she would only keep herself up a little, she wouldn't be so bad looking. There was nothing wrong with her face that a pleasant expression wouldn't help. Mrs. Hopewell said that people who looked on the bright side of things would be beautiful even if they were not.

Whenever she looked at Joy this way, she could not help but feel that it would have been better if the child had not taken the Ph.D. It had certainly not brought her out any and now that she had it, there was no more excuse for her to go to school again. Mrs. Hopewell thought it was nice for girls to go to school to have a good time but Joy had "gone through." Anyhow, she would not have been strong enough to go again. The doctors had told Mrs. Hopewell that with the best of care, Joy might see forty-five. She had a weak heart. Joy had made it plain that if it had not been for this condition, she would be far from these red hills and good country people. She would be in a university lecturing to people who knew what she was talking about. And Mrs. Hopewell could very well picture her there, looking like a scarecrow and lecturing to more of the same. Here she went about all day in a six-year-old skirt and a yellow sweat shirt with a faded cowboy on a horse embossed on it. She thought this was funny; Mrs Hopewell thought it was idiotic and showed simply that she was still a child. She was brilliant but she didn't have a grain of sense. It seemed to Mrs. Hopewell that every year she grew less like other people and more like herself—bloated, rude, and squint-eyed. And she said such strange things! To her own mother she had said—without warning, without excuse, standing up in the middle of a meal with her face purple and her mouth half full—"Woman! do you ever look inside? Do you ever look inside and see what you are *not*? God!" she had cried sinking down again and staring at her plate, "Malebranche was right: we are not our own light. We are not our own light!" Mrs. Hopewell had no idea to this day what brought that on. She had only made the remark, hoping Joy would take it in, that a smile never hurt anyone.

The girl had taken the Ph.D in philosophy and this left Mrs. Hopewell at a complete loss. You could say, "My daughter is a nurse," or "My daughter is a school teacher," or even, "My daughter is a chemical engineer." You could not say, "My daughter is a philosopher." That was something that had ended with the Greeks and Romans. All day Joy sat on her neck in a deep chair, reading. Sometimes she went for walks but she didn't like dogs or cats or birds or flowers or nature or nice young men. She looked at nice young men as if she could smell their stupidity.

One day Mrs. Hopewell had picked up one of the books the girl had just put down and opening it at random, she read, "Science, on the other hand, has to assert its soberness and seriousness afresh and declare that it is concerned solely with what-is. Nothing—how can it be for science anything but a horror and a phantasm? If science is right, then one thing stands firm; science wishes to know nothing of nothing. Such is after all the strictly scientific approach to Nothing. We know it by wishing to know nothing of Nothing." These words had been underlined with a blue pencil and they worked on Mrs. Hopewell like some evil incantation in gibberish. She shut the book quickly and went out of the room as if she were having a chill.

This morning when the girl came in, Mrs. Freeman was on Carramae. "She thrown up four times after supper," she said, "and was up twict in the night after three o'clock. Yesterday she didn't do nothing but ramble in the bureau drawer. All she did. Stand up there and see what she could run up on."

"She's got to eat," Mrs. Hopewell muttered, sipping her coffee, while she watched Joy's back at the stove. She was wondering what the child had said to the Bible salesman. She could not imagine what kind of a conversation she could possibly have had with him.

He was a tall gaunt hatless youth who had called yesterday to sell them a Bible. He had appeared at the door, carrying a large black suitcase that weighted him so heavily on one side that he had to brace himself against the door facing. He seemed on the point of collapse but he said in a cheerful voice, "Good morning, Mrs. Cedars!" and set the suitcase down on the mat. He was not a bad-looking young man though he had on a bright blue suit and yellow socks that were not pulled up far enough. He had prominent face bones and a streak of sticky-looking brown hair falling across his forehead.

"I'm Mrs. Hopewell," she said.

"Oh!" he said, pretending to look puzzled but with his eyes sparkling, "I saw it said 'The Cedars,' on the mailbox so I thought you was Mrs. Cedars!" and he burst out in a pleasant laugh. He picked up the satchel and under cover of a pant, he fell forward into her hall. It was rather as if the suitcase had moved first, jerking him after it. "Mrs. Hopewell!" he said and grabbed her hand. "I hope you are well!"

and he laughed again and then all at once his face sobered completely. He paused and gave her a straight earnest look and said, "Lady, I've come to speak of serious things."

"Well, come in," she muttered, none too pleased because her dinner was almost ready. He came into the parlor and sat down on the edge of a straight chair and put the suitcase between his feet and glanced around the room as if he were sizing her up by it. Her silver gleamed on the two sideboards; she decided he had never been in a room as elegant as this.

"Mrs. Hopewell," he began, using her name in a way that sounded almost intimate, "I know you believe in Chrustian service."

"Well yes," she murmured.

"I know," he said and paused, looking very wise with his head cocked on one side, "that you're a good woman. Friends have told me."

Mrs. Hopewell never liked to be taken for a fool. "What are you selling?" she asked.

"Bibles," the young man said and his eye raced around the room before he added, "I see you have no family Bible in your parlor, I see that is the one lack you got!"

Mrs. Hopewell could not say, "My daughter is an atheist and won't let me keep the Bible in the parlor." She said, stiffening slightly, "I keep my Bible by my bedside." This was not the truth. It was in the attic somewhere.

"Lady," he said, "the word of God ought to be in the parlor."

"Well, I think that's a matter of taste," she began. "I think . . ."

"Lady," he said, "for a Chrustian, the word of God ought to be in every room in the house besides in his heart. I know you're a Chrustian because I can see it in every line of your face."

She stood up and said, "Well, young man, I don't want to buy a Bible and I smell my dinner burning."

He didn't get up. He began to twist his hands and looking down at them, he said softly, "Well lady, I'll tell you the truth—not many people want to buy one nowadays and besides, I know I'm real simple. I don't know how to say a thing but to say it. I'm just a country boy." He glanced up into her unfriendly face. "People like you don't like to fool with country people like me!"

"Why!" she cried, "good country people are the salt of the earth! Besides, we all have different ways of doing, it takes all kinds to make the world go 'round. That's life!"

"You said a mouthful," he said.

"Why, I think there aren't enough good country people in the world!" she said, stirred. "I think that's what's wrong with it!"

His face had brightened. "I didn't inraduce myself," he said. "I'm Manley Pointer from out in the country around Willohobie, not even from a place, just from near a place."

"You wait a minute," she said. "I have to see about my dinner." She went out to the kitchen and found Joy standing near the door where she had been listening.

"Get rid of the salt of the earth," she said, "and let's eat."

Mrs. Hopewell gave her a pained look and turned the heat down under the vegetables. "I can't be rude to anybody," she murmured and went back into the parlor.

He had opened the suitcase and was sitting with a Bible on each knee. "You might as well put those up," she told him. "I don't want one."

"I appreciate your honesty," he said. "You don't see any more real honest people unless you go way out in the country."

"I know," she said, "real genuine folks!" Through the crack in the door she heard a groan.

"I guess a lot of boys come telling you they're working their way through college," he said, "but I'm not going to tell you that. Somehow," he said, "I don't want to go to college. I want to devote my life to Christian service. See," he said, lowering his voice, "I got this heart condition. I may not live long. When you know it's something wrong with you and you may not live long, well then, lady . . ." He paused, with his mouth open, and stared at her.

He and Joy had the same condition! She knew that her eyes were filling with tears but she collected herself quickly and murmured, "Won't you stay for dinner? We'd love to have you!" and was sorry the instant she heard herself say it.

"Yes mam," he said in an abashed voice, "I would sher love to do that!"

Joy had given him one look on being introduced to him and then throughout the meal had not glanced at him again. He had addressed several remarks to her, which she had pretended not to hear. Mrs. Hopewell could not understand deliberate rudeness, although she lived with it, and she felt she had always to overflow with hospitality to make up for Joy's lack of courtesy. She urged him to talk about himself and he did. He said he was the seventh child of twelve and that his father had been crushed under a tree when he himself was eight year old. He had been crushed very badly, in fact, almost cut in two and was practically not recognizable. His mother had got along the best she could by hard working and she had always seen that her children went to Sunday School and that they read the Bible every evening. He was now nineteen year old and he had been selling Bibles for four months. In that time he had sold seventy-seven Bibles and had the promise of two more sales. He wanted to become a missionary because he thought that was the way you could do most for people. "He who losest his life shall find it," he said simply and he was so sincere, so genuine and earnest that Mrs. Hopewell would not for the world have smiled. He prevented his peas from sliding onto the table by blocking them with a piece of bread which he later cleaned his plate with. She could see Joy observing sidewise how he handled his knife and fork and she saw too that every few minutes, the boy would dart a keen appraising glance at the girl as if he were trying to attract her attention.

After dinner Joy cleared the dishes off the table and disappeared and Mrs. Hopewell was left to talk with him. He told her again about his childhood and his father's accident and about various things that had happened to him. Every five minutes or so she would stifle a yawn. He sat for two hours until finally she told him she must go because she had an appointment in town. He packed his Bibles and thanked her and prepared to leave, but in the doorway he stopped and wrung her hand and said that not on any of his trips had he met a lady as nice as her and he asked if he could come again. She had said she would always be happy to see him.

Joy had been standing in the road, apparently looking at something in the distance, when he came down the steps toward her, bent to the side with his heavy valise. He stopped where she was standing and confronted her directly. Mrs. Hopewell could not hear what he said but she trembled to think what Joy would say to him. She could see that after a minute Joy said something and that then the boy began to speak again, making an excited gesture with his free hand. After a minute Joy said something else at which the boy began to speak once more. Then to her amazement, Mrs. Hopewell saw the two of them walk off together, toward the gate. Joy had walked all the way to the gate with him and Mrs. Hopewell could not imagine what they had said to each other, and she had not yet dared to ask.

Mrs. Freeman was insisting upon her attention. She had moved from the refrigerator to the heater so that Mrs. Hopewell had to turn and face her in order to seem to be listening. "Glynese gone out with Harvey Hill again last night," she said. "She had this sty."

"Hill," Mrs. Hopewell said absently, "is that the one who works in the garage?"

"Nome, he's the one that goes to chiropracter school," Mrs. Freeman said. "She had this sty. Been had it two days. So she says when he brought her in the other night he says, 'Lemme get rid of that sty for you,' and she says, 'How?' and he says, 'You just lay yourself down acorst the seat of that car and I'll show you.' So she done it and he popped her neck. Kept on a-popping it several times until she made him quit. This morning," Mrs. Freeman said, "she ain't got no sty. She ain't got no traces of a sty."

"I never heard of that before," Mrs. Hopewell said.

"He ast her to marry him before the Ordinary," Mrs. Freeman went on, "and she told him she wasn't going to be married in no *office*."

"Well, Glynese is a fine girl," Mrs. Hopewell said, "Glynese and Carramae are both fine girls."

"Carramae said when her and Lyman was married Lyman said it sure felt sacred to him. She said he said he wouldn't take five hundred dollars for being married by a preacher."

"How much would he take?" the girl asked from the stove.

"He said he wouldn't take five hundred dollars," Mrs. Freeman repeated.

"Well we all have work to do," Mrs. Hopewell said.

"Lyman said it just felt more sacred to him," Mrs. Freeman said. "The doctor wants Carramae to eat prunes. Says instead of medicine. Says them cramps is coming from pressure. You know where I think it is?"

"She'll be better in a few weeks," Mrs. Hopewell said.

"In the tube," Mrs. Freeman said. "Else she wouldn't be as sick as she is."

Hulga had cracked her two eggs into a saucer and was bringing them to the table along with a cup of coffee that she had filled too full. She sat down carefully and began to eat, meaning to keep Mrs. Freeman there by questions if for any reason she showed an inclination to leave. She could perceive her mother's eye on her. The first roundabout question would be about the Bible salesman and she did not wish to bring it on. "How did he pop her neck?" she asked.

Mrs. Freeman went into a description of how he had popped her neck. She said he owned a '55 Mercury but that Glynese said she would rather marry a man with only a '36 Plymouth who would be married by a preacher. The girl asked what if he had a '32 Plymouth and Mrs. Freeman said what Glynese had said was a '36 Plymouth.

Mrs. Hopewell said there were not many girls with Glynese's common sense. She said what she admired in those girls was their common sense. She said that reminded her that they had a nice visitor yesterday, a young man selling Bibles. "Lord," she said, "he bored me to death but he was so sincere and genuine I couldn't be rude to him. He was just good country people, you know," she said, "—just the salt of the earth."

"I seen him walk up," Mrs. Freeman said, "and then later—I seen him walk off," and Hulga could feel the slight shift in her voice, the slight insinuation, that he had not walked off alone, had he? Her face remained expressionless but the color rose into her neck and she seemed to swallow it down with the next spoonful of egg. Mrs. Freeman was looking at her as if they had a secret together.

"Well, it takes all kinds of people to make the world go 'round," Mrs. Hopewell said. "It's very good we aren't all alike."

"Some people are more alike than others," Mrs. Freeman said.

Hulga got up and stumped, with about twice the noise that was necessary, into her room and locked the door. She was to meet the Bible salesman at ten o'clock at the gate. She had thought about it half the night. She had started thinking of it as a great joke and then she had begun to see profound implications in it. She had lain in bed imagining dialogues for them that were insane on the surface but that reached below to depths that no Bible salesman would be aware of. Their conversation yesterday had been of this kind.

He had stopped in front of her and had simply stood there. His face was bony and sweaty and bright, with a little pointed nose in the center of it, and his look was different from what it had been at the dinner table. He was gazing at her with open curiosity, with fascination, like a child watching a new fantastic animal at the zoo, and he was breathing as if he had run a great distance to reach her. His gaze seemed somehow familiar but she could not think where she had been regarded with it before. For almost a minute he didn't say anything. Then on what seemed an insuck of breath, he whispered, "You ever ate a chicken that was two days old?"

The girl looked at him stonily. He might have just put this question up for consideration at the meeting of a philosophical association. "Yes," she presently replied as if she had considered it from all angles.

"It must have been mighty small!" he said triumphantly and shook all over with little nervous giggles, getting very red in the face, and subsiding finally into his gaze of complete admiration, while the girl's expression remained exactly the same.

"How old are you?" he asked softly.

She waited some time before she answered. Then in a flat voice she said, "Seventeen."

His smiles came in succession like waves breaking on the surface of a little lake. "I see you got a wooden leg," he said. "I think you're real brave. I think you're real sweet."

The girl stood blank and solid and silent.

"Walk to the gate with me," he said. "You're a brave sweet little thing and I liked you the minute I seen you walk in the door."

Hulga began to move forward.

"What's your name?" he asked, smiling down on the top of her head.

"Hulga," she said.

"Hulga," he murmured, "Hulga. Hulga. I never heard of anybody name Hulga before. You're shy, aren't you, Hulga?" he asked.

She nodded, watching his large red hand on the handle of the giant valise.

"I like girls that wear glasses," he said. "I think a lot. I'm not like these people that a serious thought don't ever enter their heads. It's because I may die."

"I may die too," she said suddenly and looked up at him. His eyes were very small and brown, glittering feverishly.

"Listen," he said, "don't you think some people was meant to meet on account of what all they got in common and all? Like they both think serious thoughts and all?" He shifted the valise to his other hand so that the hand nearest her was free. He caught hold of her elbow and shook it a little. "I don't work on Saturday," he said. "I like to walk in the woods and see what Mother Nature is wearing. O'er the hills and far away. Pic-nics and things. Couldn't we go on a pic-nic tomorrow? Say yes, Hulga," he said and gave her a dying look as if he felt his insides about to drop out of him. He had even seemed to sway slightly toward her.

During the night she had imagined that she seduced him. She imagined that the two of them walked on the place until they came to the storage barn beyond the two back fields and there, she imagined, that things came to such a pass that she very easily seduced him and that then, of course, she had to reckon with his remorse. True genius can get an idea across even to an inferior mind. She imagined that she took his remorse in hand and changed in into a deeper understanding of life. She took all his shame way and turned it into something useful.

She set off for the gate at exactly ten o'clock, escaping without drawing Mrs. Hopewell's attention. She didn't take anything to eat, forgetting that food is usually taken on a picnic. She wore a pair of slacks and a dirty white shirt, and as an afterthought, she had put some Vapex on the collar of it since she did not own any perfume. When she reached the gate no one was there.

She looked up and down the empty highway and had the furious feeling that she had been tricked, that he had only meant to make her walk to the gate after the idea of him. Then suddenly he stood up, very tall, from behind a bush on the opposite embankment. Smiling, he lifted his hat which was new and wide-brimmed. He had not worn it yesterday and she wondered if he had bought it for the occasion. It was toast-colored with a red and white band around it and was slightly too large for him. He stepped from behind the bush still carrying the black valise. He had on the same suit and the same yellow socks sucked down in his shoes from walking. He crossed the highway and said, "I knew you'd come!"

The girl wondered acidly how he had known this. She pointed to the valise and asked, "Why did you bring your Bibles?"

He took her elbow, smiling down on her as if he could not stop. "You can never tell when you'll need the word of God, Hulga," he said. She had a moment in which she doubted that this was actually happening and then they began to climb the embankment. They went down into the pasture toward the woods. The boy walked lightly by her side, bouncing on his toes. The valise did not seem to be heavy today; he even swung it. They crossed half the pasture without saying anything and then, putting his hand easily on the small of her back, he asked softly, "Where does your wooden leg join on?"

She turned an ugly red and glared at him and for an instant the boy looked abashed. "I didn't mean you no harm," he said. "I only meant you're so brave and all. I guess God takes care of you."

"No," she said, looking forward and walking fast, "I don't believe in God."

At this he stopped and whistled. "No!" he exclaimed as if he were too astonished to say anything else.

She walked on and in a second he was bouncing at her side, fanning with his hat. "That's very unusual for a girl," he remarked, watching her out of the corner of his eye. When they reached the edge of the wood, he put his hand on her back again and drew her against him without a word and kissed her heavily.

The kiss, which had more pressure than feeling behind it, produced that extra surge of adrenalin in the girl that enables one to carry a packed trunk out of a burning house, but in her, the power went at once to the brain. Even before he released her, her mind, clear and detached and ironic anyway, was regarding him from a great distance, with amusement but with pity. She had never been kissed before and she was pleased to discover that it was an unexceptional experience and all a matter of the mind's control. Some people might enjoy drain water if they were told it was vodka. When the boy, looking expectant but uncertain, pushed her gently away, she turned and walked on, saying nothing as if such business, for her, were common enough.

He came along panting at her side, trying to help her when he saw a root that she might trip over. He caught and held back the long swaying blades of thorn vine until she had passed beyond them. She led the way and he came breathing heavily behind her. Then they came out on a sunlit hillside, sloping softly into another one a little smaller. Beyond, they could see the rusted top of the old barn where the extra hay was stored.

The hill was sprinkled with small pink weeds. "Then you ain't saved?" he asked suddenly, stopping.

The girl smiled. It was the first time she had smiled at him at all. "In my economy," she said, "I'm saved and you are damned but I told you I didn't believe in God."

Nothing seemed to destroy the boy's look of admiration. He gazed at her now as if the fantastic animal at the zoo had put its paw through the bars and given him a loving poke. She thought he looked as if he wanted to kiss her again and she walked on before he had the chance.

"Ain't there somewheres we can sit down sometime?" he murmured, his voice softening toward the end of the sentence.

"In that barn," she said.

They made for it rapidly as if it might slide away like a train. It was a large two-story barn, cool and dark inside. The boy pointed up the ladder that led into the loft and said, "It's too bad we can't go up there."

"Why can't we?" she asked.

"Yer leg," he said reverently.

The girl gave him a contemptuous look and putting both hands on the ladder, she climbed it while he stood below, apparently awestruck. She pulled herself expertly through the opening and then looked down at him and said, "Well, come on if you're coming," and he began to climb the ladder, awkwardly bringing the suitcase with him.

"We won't need the Bible," she observed.

"You never can tell," he said, panting. After he had got into the loft, he was a few seconds catching his breath. She had sat down in a pile of straw. A wide sheath of sunlight, filled with dust particles, slanted over her. She lay back against a bale, her face turned away, looking out the front opening of the barn where hay was thrown from a wagon into the loft. The two pink-speckled hill sides lay against a dark ridge of woods. The sky was cloudless and cold blue. The boy dropped down by her side and put one arm under her and the other over her and began methodically kissing her face, making little noises like a fish. He did not remove his hat but it was pushed far enough back not to interfere. When her glasses got in his way, he took them off of her and slipped them into his pocket.

The girl at first did not return any of the kisses but presently she began to and after she had put several on his cheek, she reached his lips and remained there, kissing him again and again as if she were trying to draw all the breath out of him. His breath was clear and sweet like a child's and the kisses were sticky like a child's. He mumbled about loving her and about knowing when he first seen her that he loved her, but the mumbling was like the sleepy fretting of a child being put to sleep by his mother. Her mind, throughout this, never stopped or lost itself for a second to her feelings. "You ain't said you love me none," he whispered finally, pulling back from her. "You got to say that."

She looked away from him off into the hollow sky and then down at a black ridge and then down farther into what appeared to be two green swelling lakes. She didn't realize he had taken her glasses but this landscape could not seem exceptional to her for she seldom paid any close attention to her surroundings.

"You got to say it," he repeated. "You got to say you love me."

She was always careful how she committed herself. "In a sense," she began, "if you use the word loosely, you might say that. But it's not a word I use. I don't have illusions. I'm one of those people who see *through* to nothing."

The boy was frowning. "You got to say it. I said it and you got to say it," he said.

The girl looked at him almost tenderly. "You poor baby," she murmured. "It's just as well you don't understand," and she pulled him by the neck, face down, against her. "We are all damned," she said, "but some of us have taken off our blindfolds and see that there's nothing to see. It's a kind of salvation."

The boy's astonished eyes looked blanky through the ends of her hair. "Okay," he almost whined, "but do you love me or don'tcher?"

"Yes," she said and added, "in a sense. But I must tell you something. There mustn't be anything dishonest between us." She lifted his head and looked him in the eye. "I am thirty years old," she said. "I have a number of degrees."

The boy's look was irritated but dogged. "I don't care," he said. "I don't care a thing about what all you done. I just want to know if you love me or don'tcher?" and he caught her to him and wildly planted her face with kisses until she said, "Yes, yes."

"Okay then," he said, letting her go. "Prove it."

She smiled, looking dreamily out on the shifty landscape. She had seduced him without even making up her mind to try. "How?" she asked, feeling that he should be delayed a little.

He leaned over and put his lips to her ear. "Show me where your wooden leg joins on," he whispered.

The girl uttered a sharp little cry and her face instantly drained of color. The obscenity of the suggestion was not what shocked her. As a child she had sometimes been subject to feelings of shame but education had removed the last traces of that as a good surgeon scrapes for cancer; she would no more have felt it over what he was asking than she would have believed in his Bible. But she was as sensitive about the artificial leg as a peacock about his tail. No one ever touched it but her. She took care of it as someone else would his soul, in private and almost with her own eyes turned away. "No," she said.

"I known it," he muttered, sitting up. "You're just playing me for a sucker."

"Oh no no!" she cried. "It joins on at the knee. Only at the knee. Why do you want to see it?"

The boy gave her a long penetrating look. "Because," he said, "it's what makes you different. You ain't like anybody else."

She sat staring at him. There was nothing about her face on her round freezing blue eyes to indicate that this had moved her; but she felt as if her heart had stopped and left her mind to pump her blood. She decided that for the first time in her life she was face to face with real innocence. This boy, with an instinct that came from beyond wisdom, had touched the truth about her. When after a minute, she said in a hoarse high voice, "All right," it was like surrendering to him completely. It was like losing her own life and finding it again, miraculously, in his.

Very gently he began to roll the slack leg up. The artificial limb, in a white sock and brown flat shoe, was bound in a heavy material like canvas and ended in an ugly jointure where it was attached to the stump. The boy's face and his voice were entirely reverent as he uncovered it and said, "Now show me how to take it off and on."

She took it off for him and put it back on again and then he took it off himself, handling it as tenderly as if it were a real one, "See!" he said with a delighted child's face. "Now I can do it myself!"

"Put it back on," she said. She was thinking that she would run away with him and that every night he would take the leg off and every morning put it back on again. "Put it back on," she said.

"Not yet," he murmured, setting it on its foot out of her reach. "Leave if off for a while. You got me instead."

She gave a little cry of alarm but he pushed her down and began to kiss her again. Without the leg she felt entirely dependent on him. Her brain seemed to have stopped thinking altogether and to be about some other function that it was not very good at. Different expressions raced back and forth over her face. Every now and then the boy, his eyes like two steel spikes, would glance behind him where the leg stood. Finally she pushed him off and said, "Put it back on me now."

"Wait," he said. He leaned the other way and pulled the valise toward him and opened it. It had a pale blue spotted lining and there were only two Bibles in it. He took one of these out and opened the cover of it. It was hollow and contained a pocket flask of whiskey, a pack of cards, and a small blue box with printing on it. He laid these out in front of her one at a time in an evenly spaced row, like one presenting offerings at the shrine of a goddess. He put the blue box in her hand. THIS PRODUCT TO BE USED ONLY FOR THE PREVENTION OF DISEASE, she read, and dropped it. The boy was unscrewing the top of the flask. He stopped and pointed, with a smile, to the deck of cards. It was not an ordinary deck but one with an obscene picture on the back of each card. "Take a swig," he said, offering her the bottle first. He held it in front of her, but like one mesmerized, she did not move.

Her voice when she spoke had an almost pleading sound. "Aren't you," she murmured, "aren't you just good country people?"

The boy cocked his head. He looked as if he were just beginning to understand that she might be trying to insult him. "Yeah," he said, curling his lip slightly, "but it ain't held me back none. I'm as good as you any day in the week."

"Give me my leg," she said.

He pushed it farther away with his foot. "Come on now, let's begin to have us a good time," he said coaxingly. "We ain't got to know one another good yet."

"Give me my leg!" she screamed and tried to lunge for it but he pushed her down easily.

"What's the matter with you all of a sudden?" he asked, frowning as he screwed the top on the flask and put it quickly back inside the Bible. "You just a while ago said you didn't believe in nothing. I thought you was some girl!"

Her face was almost purple. "You're a Christian!" she hissed. "You're a fine Christian! You're just like them all—say one thing and do another. You're a perfect Christian, you're . . ."

The boy's mouth was set angrily. "I hope you don't think," he said in a lofty indignant tone, "that I believe in that crap! I may sell Bibles but I know which end is up and I wasn't born yesterday and I know where I'm going!"

"Give me my leg!" she screeched. He jumped up so quickly that she barely saw him sweep the cards and the blue box back into the Bible and throw the Bible into the valise. She saw him grab the leg and then she saw it for an instant slanted forlornly across the inside of the suitcase with a Bible at either side of its opposite ends. He slammed the lid shut and snatched up the valise and swung it down the hole and then stepped through himself.

When all of him had passed but his head, he turned and regarded her with a look that no longer had any admiration in it. "I've gotten a lot of interesting things," he said. "One time I got a woman's glass eye this way. And you needn't to think you'll catch me because Pointer ain't really my name. I use a different name at every house I call at and don't stay nowhere long. And I'll tell you another thing, Hulga," he said, using the name as if he didn't think much of it, "you ain't so smart. I been believing in nothing ever since I was born!" and then the toast-colored hat disappeared down the hole and the girl was left, sitting on the straw in the dusty sunlight. When she turned her churning face toward the opening, she saw his blue figure struggling successfully over the green speckled lake.

Mrs. Hopewell and Mrs. Freeman, who were in the back pasture, digging up onions, saw him emerge a little later from the woods and head across the meadow toward the highway. "Why, that looks like that nice dull young man that tried to sell me a Bible yesterday," Mrs. Hopewell said, squinting. "He must have been selling them to the Negroes back in there. He was so simple," she said, "but I guess the world would be better off if we were all that simple."

Mrs. Freeman's gaze drove forward and just touched him before he disappeared under the hill. Then she returned her attention to the evil-smelling onion shoot she was lifting from the ground. "Some can't be that simple," she said. "I know I never could."

[1950–U.S.A.]

QUESTIONS

1. What values does O'Connor's title bring to mind? What, then, is ironic about it in the context of the story it names?
2. What types of character are Mrs. Hopewell, Mrs. Freeman, and Manley Pointer? What do their names suggest about them? Compare Mrs. Hopewell and Mrs. Freeman. Their approach to things differs, but at heart they are the same. How so?
3. What type of character is Hulga? To what is she blind? Why is she open to the type of fantasy she has the night before her date with Manley? What does her question to Manley about "good country people" reveal?
4. Manley and Hulga share in the story's central irony. With respect to both, what is that irony? What does it tell us about people in general that Mrs. Hopewell, say, could never recognize?
5. "Good Country People" is a satire. What does it satirize? Katherine Anne Porter described Eudora Welty's satiric story "Petrified Man" as one of a "just cruelty." Could the same be said of "Good Country People"? Or is its laughter of a different order?

WRITING SUGGESTIONS

1. In a paragraph or more, analyze Hulga. Be sure to discuss the difference between how she wishes to be seen (and sees herself) and what she really is. What is the reason for and the significance of this disparity?
2. Write a short paper addressed to question 4 above. Be sure to consider what happens at the end of the story and to specify what is ironic about what happens. Consider, as well, what the irony here says about people in general.
3. Read Eudora Welty's "Petrified Man" (pages 463–74) with "Good Country People" in mind. Now write a paper comparing and contrasting the two. When contrasting, consider such questions as these: Which is more remorseless? Is O'Connor as just as Welty in her comic cruelty? In what ways does the laughter of each story differ, if at all? You might conclude with a judgment of the two stories when held side by side.

The Man Who Was Almost a Man

Richard Wright

Dave struck out across the fields, looking homeward through paling light. Whut's the use talkin wid em niggers in the field? Anyhow, his mother was putting supper on the table. Them niggers can't understan nothing. One of these days he was going to get a gun and practice shooting, then they couldn't talk to him as though he were a little boy. He slowed, looking at the ground. Shucks, Ah ain scareda them even ef they are biggern me! Aw, Ah know whut Ahma do. Ahm going by ol Joe's sto n git that Sears Roebuck catlog n look at them guns. Mebbe Ma will lemme buy one when she gits mah pay from ol man Hawkins. Ahma beg her t gimme some money. Ahm ol ernough to hava gun. Ahm seventeen. Almost a man. He strode, feeling his long loose-jointed limbs. Shunks, a man oughta hava little gun aftah he done worked hard all day.

He came in sight of Joe's store. A yellow lantern glowed on the front porch. He mounted steps and went through the screen door, hearing it bang behind him. There was a strong smell of coal oil and mackerel fish. He felt very confident until he saw fat Joe walk in through the rear door, then his courage began to ooze.

"Howdy, Dave! Whutcha want?"

"How yuh, Mistah Joe? Aw, Ah don wanna buy nothing. Ah jus wanted t see ef yuhd lemme look at tha catlog erwhile."

"Sure! You wanna see it here?"

"Nawsuh. Ah wants t take it home wid me. Ah'll bring it back termorrow when Ah come in from the fiels."

435

"You plannin on buying something?"

"Yessuh."

"Your ma lettin you have your own money now?"

"Shucks. Mistah Joe, Ahm gittin t be a man like anybody else!"

Joe laughed and wiped his greasy white face with a red bandanna.

"What you plannin on buyin?"

Dave looked at the floor, scratched his head, scratched his thigh, and smiled. Then he looked up shyly.

"Ah'll tell yuh, Mistah Joe, ef yuh promise yuh won't tell."

"I promise."

"Waal, Ahma buy a gun."

"A gun? What you want with a gun?"

"Ah wanna keep it."

"You ain't nothing but a boy. You don't need a gun."

"Aw, lemme have the catlog, Mistah Joe. Ah'll bring it back."

Joe walked through the rear door. Dave was elated. He looked around at barrels of sugar and flour. He heard Joe coming back. He craned his neck to see if he were bringing the book. Yeah, he's got it. Gawddog, he's got it!

"Here, but be sure you bring it back. It's the only one I got."

"Sho, Mistah Joe."

"Say, if you wanna buy a gun, why don't you buy one from me? I gotta gun to sell."

"Will it shoot?"

"Sure it'll shoot."

"Whut kind is it?"

"Oh, it's kinda old . . . a left-hand Wheeler. A pistol. A big one."

"Is it got bullets in it?"

"It's loaded."

"Kin Ah see it?"

"Where's your money?"

"What yuh wan fer it?"

"I'll let you have it for two dollars."

"Just two dollahs? Shucks, Ah could buy tha when Ah git mah pay."

"I'll have it here when you want it."

"Awright, suh. Ah be in fer it."

He went through the door, hearing it slam again behind him. Ahma git some money from Ma n buy me a gun! Only two dollahs! He tucked the thick catalogue under his arm and hurried.

"Where yuh been, boy?" His mother held a steaming dish of black-eyed peas.

"Aw, Ma, Ah just stopped down the road t talk wid the boys."

"Yuh know bettah t keep suppah waiting."

He sat down, resting the catalogue on the edge of the table.

"Yuh git up from there and git to the well n wash yosef! Ah ain feedin no hogs in mah house!"

She grabbed his shoulder and pushed him. He stumbled out of the room, then came back to get the catalogue.

"Whut this?"

"Aw, Ma, it's jusa catlog."

"Who yuh git it from?"

"From Joe, down at the sto."

"Waal, thas good. We kin use it in the outhouse."

"Naw, Ma." He grabbed for it. "Gimme ma catlog, Ma."

She held onto it and glared at him.

"Quit hollerin at me! Whut's wrong wid yuh? Yuh crazy?"

"But Ma, please. It ain't mine! It's Joe's! He tol me t bring it back t im termorrow."

She gave up the book. He stumbled down the back steps, hugging the thick book under his arm. When he had splashed water on his face and hands, he groped back to the kitchen and fumbled in a corner for the towel. He bumped into a chair; it clattered to the floor. The catalogue sprawled at his feet. When he dried his eyes he snatched up the book and held it again under his arms. His mother stood watching him.

"Now, ef yuh gonna act a fool over that ol book, Ah'll take it n burn it up."

"Naw, Ma, please."

"Waal, set down n be still!"

He sat down and drew the oil lamp close. He thumbed page after page, unaware of the food his mother set on the table. His father came in. Then his small brother.

"Whutcha got there, Dave?" his father asked.

"Jusa catlog," he answered, not looking up.

"Yeah, here they is!" His eyes glowed at blue-and-black revolvers. He glanced up, feeling sudden guilt. His father was watching him. He eased the book under the table and rested it on his knees. After the blessing was asked, he ate. He scooped up peas and swallowed fat meat without chewing. Buttermilk helped to wash it down. He did not want to mention money before his father. He would do much better by cornering his mother when she was alone. He looked at his father uneasily out of the edge of his eye.

"Boy, how come yuh don quit foolin wid tha book n eat yo suppah?"

"Yessuh."

"How you n ol man Hawkins gitten erlong?"

"Suh?"

"Can't yuh hear? Why don yuh listen? Ah ast yu how wuz yuh n ol man Hawkins gittin erlong?"

"Oh, swell, Pa. Ah plows mo lan than anybody over there."

"Waal, yuh oughta keep your mind on whut yuh doing."

"Yessuh."

He poured his plate full of molasses and sopped it up slowly with a chunk of cornbread. When his father and brother had left the kitchen, he still sat and looked again at the guns in the catalogue, longing to muster courage enough to present his case to his mother. Lawd, ef Ah only had tha pretty one! He could almost feel the slickness of the weapon with his fingers. If he had a gun like that he would polish it and keep it shining so it would never rust. N Ah'd keep it loaded, by Gawd!

"Ma?" His voice was hesitant.

"Hunh?"

"Ol man Hawkins give yuh mah money yit?"

"Yeah, but ain no usa yuh thinking about throwin nona it erway. Ahm keepin tha money sos yuh kin have cloes t go to school this winter."

He rose and went to her side with the open catalogue in his palms. She was washing dishes, her head bent low over a pan. Shyly he raised the book. When he spoke, his voice was husky, faint.

"Ma, Gawd knows Ah wans one of these."

"One of whut?" she asked, not raising her eyes.

"One of these," he said again, not daring even to point. She glanced up at the page, then at him with wild eyes.

"Nigger, is yuh gone plumb crazy?"

"Aw, Ma—"

"Git outta here! Don yuh talk t me bout no gun! Yuh a fool!"

"Ma, Ah kin buy one fer two dollahs."

"Not ef Ah knows it, yuh ain!"

"But yuh promised me one—"

"Ah don care what Ah promised! Yuh ain nothing but a boy yit!"

"Ma ef yuh lemme buy one Ah'll *never* ast yuh fer nothing no mo."

"Ah tol yuh t git outa here! Yuh ain gonna touch a penny of tha money fer no gun! Thas how come Ah has Mistah Hawkins t pay yu wages t me, cause Ah knows yuh ain got no sense."

"But, Ma, we needa gun. Pa ain got no gun. We needa gun in the house. Yuh kin never tell whut might happen."

"Now don yuh try to maka fool outta me, boy! Ef we did hava gun, yuh wouldn't have it!"

He laid the catalogue down and slipped his arm around her waist.

"Aw, Ma, Ah done worked hard alla summer n ain ast yuh fer nothing, is Ah, now?

"Thas whut yuh spose t do!"

"But Ma, Ah wans a gun. Yuh kin lemme have two dollahs outta mah money. Please, Ma. I kin give it to Pa . . . Please, Ma! Ah loves yuh, Ma."

When she spoke her voice came soft and low.

"What yu wan wida gun, Dave? Yuh don need no gun. Yuh'll git in trouble. N ef yo pa jus thought Ah let yuh have money t buy a gun he'd hava fit."

"Ah'll hide it, Ma. It ain but two dollahs."

"Lawd, chil, whut's wrong wid yuh?"

"Ain nothin wrong, Ma. Ahm almos a man now. Ah wans a gun."

"Who gonna sell yuh a gun?"

"Ol Joe at the sto."

"N it don cos but two dollahs?"

"Thas all, Ma. Just two dollahs. Please, Ma."

She was stacking the plates away; her hands moved slowly, reflectively. Dave kept an anxious silence. Finally, she turned to him.

"Ah'll let yuh git tha gun ef yuh promise me one thing."

"Whut's tha, Ma."

"Yuh bring it straight back t me, yuh hear? It be fer Pa."

"Yessum! Lemme go now, Ma."

She stooped, turned slightly to one side, raised the hem of her dress, rolled down the top of her stocking, and came up with a slender wad of bills.

"Here," she said. "Lawd knows yuh don need no gun. But yer pa does. Yuh bring it right back t me, yuh hear? Ahma put it up. Now ef yuh don, Ahma have yuh pa lick yuh so hard yuh won fergit it."

"Yessum."

He took the money, ran down the steps, and across the yard.

"Dave! Yuuuuu Daaaaave!"

He heard, but he was not going to stop now. "Naw, Lawd!'

The first movement he made the following morning was to reach under his pillow for the gun. In the gray light of dawn he held it loosely, feeling a sense of power. Could kill a man with a gun like this. Kill anybody, black or white. And if he were holding his gun in his hand, nobody could run over him; they would have to respect him. It was a big gun, with a long barrel and a heavy handle. He raised and lowered it in his hand, marveling at its weight.

He had not come straight home with it as his mother had asked; instead he had stayed out in the fields, holding the weapon in his hand, aiming it now and then at some imaginary foe. But he had not fired it; he had been afraid that his father might hear. Also he was not sure he knew how to fire it.

To avoid surrendering the pistol he had not come into the house until he knew that they were all asleep. When his mother had tiptoed to his bedside late that night and demanded the gun, he had first played possum; then he had told her that the gun was hidden outdoors, that he would bring it to her in the morning. Now he lay turning it slowly in his hands. He broke it, took out the catridges, felt them, and then put them back.

He slid out of bed, got a long strip of old flannel from a trunk, wrapped the gun in it, and tied it to his naked thigh while it was still loaded. He did not go in to breakfast. Even though it was not yet daylight, he started for Jim Hawkins' plantation. Just as the sun was rising he reached the barns where the mules and plows were kept.

"Hey! That you, Dave?"

He turned. Jim Hawkins stood eying him suspiciously.

"What're yuh doing here so early?"

"Ah didn't know Ah wuz gittin up so early, Mistah Hawkins. Ah was fixin t hitch up ol Jenny n take her t the fiels."

"Good. Since you're so early, how about plowing that stretch down by the woods?"

"Suits me, Mistah Hawkins."

"O.K. Go to it!" '

He hitched Jenny to a plow and started across the fields. Hot dog! This was just what he wanted. If he could get down by the woods, he could shoot his gun and nobody would hear. He walked behind the plow, hearing the traces creaking, feeling the gun tied tight to his thigh.

When he reached the woods, he plowed two whole rows before he decided to take out the gun. Finally, he stopped, looked in all directions, then untied the gun and held it in his hand. He turned to the mule and smiled.

"Know whut this is, Jenny? Naw, yuh wouldn't know! Yuhs jusa ol mule! Anyhow, this is a gun, n it kin shoot, by Gawd!"

He held the gun at arm's length. Whut t hell, Ahma shoot this thing! He looked at Jenny again.

"Lissen here, Jenny! When Ah pull this ol trigger, Ah don wan yuh to run n acka fool now?

Jenny stood with head down, her short ears pricked straight. Dave walked off about twenty feet, held the gun far out from him at arm's length, and turned his head. Hell, he told himself, Ah ain afraid. The gun felt loose in his fingers; he waved it wildly for a moment. Then he shut his eyes and tightened his forefinger. Bloom! A report half deafened him and he thought his right hand was torn from his arm. He heard Jenny whinnying and galloping over the field, and he found himself on his knees, squeezing his fingers hard between his legs. His hand was numb; he jammed it into his mouth, trying to warm it, trying to stop the pain. The gun lay at his feet. He did not quite know what had happened. He stood up and stared at the gun as though it were a living thing. He gritted his teeth and kicked the gun. Yuh almos broke mah arm! He turned to look for Jenny; she was far over the fields, tossing her head and kicking wildly.

"Hol on there, ol mule!"

When he caught up with her she stood trembling, walling her big white eyes at him. The plow was far away; the traces had broken. Then Dave stopped short, looking, not believing. Jenny was bleeding. Her left side was red and wet with blood. He went closer, Lawd, have mercy! Wondah did Ah shoot this mule? He grabbed for Jenny's mane. She flinched, snorted, whirled, tossing her head.

"Hol on now! Hol on."

Then he saw the hole in Jenny's side, right between the ribs. It was round, wet, red. A crimson stream streaked down the front leg, flowing fast. Good Gawd! Ah wuzn't shootin at tha mule. He felt panic. He knew he had to stop that blood, or Jenny would bleed to death. He had never seen so much blood in all his life. He chased the mule for half a mile, trying to catch her. Finally she stopped, breathing hard, stumpy tail half arched. He caught her mane and led her back to where the plow and gun lay. Then he stooped and grabbed handfuls of damp black earth and tried to plug the bullet hole. Jenny shuddered, whinnied, and broke from him.

"Hol on! Hol on now!"

He tried to plug it again, but blood came anyhow. His fingers were hot and sticky. He rubbed dirt into his palms, trying to dry them. Then again he attempted to plug the bullet hole, but Jenny shied away, kicking her heels high. He stood helpless. He had to do something. He ran at Jenny; she dodged him. He watched a red stream of blood flow down Jenny's leg and form a bright pool at her feet.

"Jenny . . . Jenny," he called weakly.

His lips trembled. She's bleeding t death! He looked in the direction of home, wanting to go back, wanting to get help. But he saw the pistol lying in the damp black clay. He had a queer feeling that if he only did something, this would not be; Jenny would not be there bleeding to death.

When he went to her this time, she did not move. She stood with sleepy, dreamy eyes; and when he touched her she gave a low-pitched whinny and knelt to the ground, her front knees slopping in blood.

"Jenny . . . Jenny . . ." he whispered.

For a long time she held her neck erect; then her head sank, slowly. Her ribs swelled with a mighty heave and she went over.

Dave's stomach felt empty, very empty. He picked up the gun and held it gingerly between his thumb and forefinger. He buried it at the foot of a tree. He took a stick and tried to cover the pool of blood with dirt—but what was the use? There was Jenny lying with her mouth open and her eyes walled and glassy. He could not tell Jim Hawkins he had shot his mule. But he had to tell something. Yeah, Ah'll tell em Jenny started gittin' wil n fell on the joint of the plow. . . . But that would hardly happen to a mule. He walked across the field slowly, head down.

It was sunset. Two of Jim Hawkins' men were over near the edge of the woods digging a hole in which to bury Jenny. Dave was surrounded by a knot of people, all of whom were looking down at the dead mule.

"I don't see how in the world it happened," said Jim Hawkins for the tenth time.

The crowd parted and Dave's mother, father, and small brother pushed into the centre.

"Where Dave?" his mother called.

"There he is," said Jim Hawkins.

His mother grabbed him.

"Whut happened, Dave? Whut yuh done?"

"Nothin."

"C'mon, boy, talk," his father said.

Dave took a deep breath and told the story he knew nobody believed.

"Waal," he drawled. "Ah brung ol Jenny down here sos Ah could do mah plowin. Ah plowed bout two rows, just like yuh see." He stopped and pointed at the long rows of upturned earth. "Then somethin musta been wrong wid ol Jenny. She wouldn ack right a-tall. She started snortin n kickin her heels. Ah tried t hol her, but she pulled erway, rearin n goin in. Then when the point of the plow was stickin up in the air, she swung erroun n twisted herself back on it . . . She stuck herself n started t bleed. N fo Ah could do anything, she wuz dead."

"Did you ever hear of anything like that in all your life?" asked Jim Hawkins.

There were white and black standing in the crowd. They murmured. Dave's mother came close to him and looked hard into his face. "Tell the truth, Dave," she said.

"Looks like a bullet hole to me," said one man.

"Dave, whut yuh do wid tha gun?" his mother asked.

The crowd surged in, looking at him. He jammed his hands into his pockets, shook his head slowly from left to right, and backed away. His eyes were wide and painful.

"Did he hava gun?" asked Jim Hawkins.

"By Gawd, Ah tol yuh tha wuz a gun wound," said a man, slapping his thigh.

His father caught his shoulders and shook him till his teeth rattled.

"Tell whut happened, yuh rascal! Tell whut . . ."

Dave looked at Jenny's stiff legs and began to cry.

"Whut yuh do wid tha gun?" his mother asked.

"Whut wuz he doin wida gun?" his father asked.

"Come on and tell the truth," said Hawkins. "Ain't nobody going to hurt you . . ."

His mother crowded close to him.

"Did yuh shoot tha mule, Dave?"

Dave cried, seening blurred white and black faces.

"Ahh ddinn gggo tt sshooot hher. . . Ah sswear tt Gawd Ahh ddin. . . . Ah wuz a-tryin t sssee ef the gggun would sshoot—"

"Where yuh git the gun from?" his father asked.

"Ah got if from Joe, at the sto."

"Where yuh git the money?"

"Ma give it t me."

"He kept worryin me, Bod. Ah had t. Ah tol im t bring the gun right back t me . . . It was fer yuh, the gun."

"But how yuh happen to shoot that mule?" asked Jim Hawkins.

"Ah wuzn shootin at the mule, Mistah Hawkins! The gun jumped when Ah pulled the trigger . . . N fo Ah knowed anythin Jenny was there a-bleedin."

Somebody in the crowd laughed. Jim Hawkins walked close to Dave and looked into his face.

"Well, looks like you have bought you a mule, Dave."

"Ah swear fo Gawd. Ah didn go t kill the mule, Mistah Hawkins!"

"But you killed her!"

All the crowd was laughing now. They stood on tiptoe and poked heads over one another's shoulders.

"Well, boy, looks like yuh done bought a dead mule! Hahaha!"

"Ain tha ershame."

"Hohohohoho."

Dave stood, head down, twisting his feet in the dirt.

"Well, you needn't worry about it, Bob," said Jim Hawkins to Dave's father. "Just let the boy keep on working and pay me two dollars a month."

"Whut yuh wan fer yo mule, Mistah Hawkins?"

Jim Hawkins screwed up his eyes.

"Fifty dollars."

"Whut yuh do wid tha gun?" Dave's father demanded.

Dave said nothing."

"Yuh wan me t take a tree n beat yuh till yuh talk!"

"Nawsuh!"

"Whut yuh do wid it?"

"Ah throwed it erway."

"Where?"

"Ah . . . Ah throwed it in the creek."

"Waal, c mon home. N firs thing in the mawnin git to tha creek n fin tha gun."

"Yessuh."

"Whut yuh pay fer it?"

"Two dollahs."

"Take tha gun n git yo money back n carry it t Mistah Hawkins, yuh hear? N don fergit Ahma lam you black bottom good fer this! Now march yoself on home, suh!"

Dave turned and walked slowly. He heard people laughin. Dave glared, his eyes welling with tears. Hot anger bubbled in him. Then he swallowed and stumbled on.

That night Dave did not sleep. He was glad that he had gotten out of killing the mule so easily, but he was hurt. Something hot seemed to turn over inside him each time he remembered how they had laughed. He tossed on his bed, feeling his hard pillow. N Pa says he's gonna beat me . . . He remembered other beatings, and his back quivered. Naw, naw, Ah sho don wan im t beat me tha way no mo. Dam em all! Nobody ever gave him anything. All he did was work. They treat me like a mule, n then they beat me. He gritted his teeth. N Ma had t tell on me.

Well, if he had to, he would take old man Hawkins that two dollars. But that meant selling the gun. And he wanted to keep the gun. Fifty dollars for a dead mule.

He turned over, thinking how he had fired the gun. He had an itch to fire it again. Ef other men kin shoota gun, by Gawd, Ah kin! He was still, listening. Mebbe they all sleepin now. The house was still. He heard the soft breathing of his brother. Yes, now! He would go down and get that gun and see if he could fire it! He eased out of bed and slipped into overalls.

The moon was bright. He ran almost all the way to the edge of the woods. He stumbled over the ground, looking for the spot where he had buried the gun. Yeah, here it is. Like a hungry dog scratching for a bone, he pawed it up. He puffed his black cheeks and blew dirt from the trigger and barrel. He broke it and found four cartridges unshot. He looked around; the fields were filled with silence and moonlight. He clutched the gun stiff and hard in his fingers. But, as soon as he wanted to pull the trigger, he shut his eyes and turned his head. Naw, Ah can't shoot wid mah eyes closed n mah head turned. With effort he held his eyes open; then he squeezed. *Blooooom!* He was stiff, not breathing. The gun was still in his hands. Dammit, he'd done it! He fired again. *Blooooom!* He smiled. *Blooooom! Blooooom! Click, click.* There! It was empty. If anybody could shoot a gun, he could. He put the gun into his hip pocket and started across the fields.

When he reached the top of a ridge he stood straight and proud in the moonlight, looking at Jim Hawkins' big white house, feeling the gun sagging in his pocket. Lawd, ef Ah had just one mo bullet Ah'd taka shot at tha house. Ah'd like t scare ol man Hawkins jusa little . . . Jusa enough t let im know Dave Saunders is a man.

To his left the road curved, running to the tracks of the Illinois Central. He jerked his head, listening. From far off came a faint hoooof-hoooof; hoooof-hoooof . . . He stood rigid. Two dollahs a mont. Les see now . . . Tha means it'll take bout two years. Shucks! Ah'll be dam! He started down the road, toward the tracks. Yeah, here she comes! He stood beside the track and held himself stiffly. Here she comes, erroun the ben . . . C mon, yuh slow poke! C mon! He had his hand on his gun; something quivered in his stomach. Then the train thundered past, the gray and brown box cars rumbling and clinking. He gripped the gun tightly; then he jerked his hand out of his pocket. Ah betcha Bill wouldn't do it! Ah betcha . . . The cars slid past, steel grinding upon steel. Ahm ridin yuh ternight, so help me Gawd! He was hot all over. He hesitated just a moment; then he grabbed, pulled atop of a car, and lay flat. He felt his pocket; the gun was still there. Ahead the long rails were glinting in the moonlight, stretching away, away to somewhere, somewhere where he could be a man . . .

[1940–U.S.A.]

QUESTIONS

1. How does the setting function in Wright's story? How do both the physical and the social backdrops help us to understand Dave?

2. "The Man Who Was Almost a Man" has been said to deal with an "essentially American rite of passage." How so? What does the gun symbolize to Dave? Why?

3. In order to clarify the structure of the story, summarize its plot. How does plot here help to create the mood? Is the story tragic, comic, or something else?

4. What is the symbolic significance of the end of the story? Given Dave's burning desire to be a "man," what irony does this ending entail?

5. Generally speaking, "The Man Who Was Almost a Man" concerns initiation into adult life. Formulate its theme in more specific terms. How does the story's title relate to its specific theme?

WRITING SUGGESTIONS

1. Write a paragraph or a short essay in which you first describe who Dave is (for instance, his personality traits) and then analyze why he is the way he is. Would he be different had he been born in a different time and place? How does his physical and especially his social setting help condition his definitions and desires?

2. Compare and contrast Dave and the narrator of "I Want to Know Why" (pages 476–83). You might structure your paper (four or five paragraphs at least) so that it moves from differences to an underlying similarity; or you could take up similarities first and move to some fundamental difference. Your choice should depend upon your thesis.

That Evening Sun

William Faulkner

1

Monday is no different from any other weekday in Jefferson now. The streets are paved now, and the telephone and electric companies are cutting down more and more of the shade trees—the water oaks, the maples and locusts and elms—to make room for iron poles bearing clusters of bloated and ghostly and bloodless grapes, and we have a city laundry which makes the rounds on Monday morning, gathering the bundles of clothes into bright-colored, specially made motorcars: the soiled wearing of a whole week now flees apparitionlike behind alert and irritable electric horns, with a long diminishing noise of rubber and asphalt like tearing silk, and even the Negro women who still take in white people's washing after the old custom, fetch and deliver it in automobiles.

But fifteen years ago, on Monday morning the quiet, dusty shady streets would be full of Negro women with, balanced on their steady, turbaned heads, bundles of clothes tied up in sheets, almost as large as cotton bales, carried so without touch of hand between the kitchen door of the white house and the blackened washpot beside a cabin door in Negro Hollow.

Nancy would set her bundle on top of her head, then upon the bundle in turn she would set the black straw sailor hat which she wore winter and summer. She was tall, with a high, sad face sunken a little where her teeth were missing. Sometimes we would go a part of the way down the lane and across the pasture with her, to watch the balanced bundle and the hat that never bobbed or wavered, even when she walked down into the ditch and up the other side and stooped through the fence. She would go down on her hands and knees and crawl through the gap, her head rigid, uptilted, the bundle steady as a rock or a balloon, and rise to her feet again and go on.

Sometimes the husbands of the washing women would fetch and deliver the clothes, but Jesus never did that for Nancy, even before Father told him to stay away from our house, even when Dilsey was sick and Nancy would come to cook for us.

And then about half the time we'd have to go down the lane to Nancy's cabin and tell her to come on and cook breakfast. We would stop at the ditch, because Father told us to not have anything to do with Jesus—he was a short black man, with a razor scar down his face—and we would throw rocks at Nancy's house until she came to the door, leaning her head around it without any clothes on.

"What yawl mean, chunking my house?" Nancy said. "What you little devils mean?"

"Father says for you to come on and get breakfast," Caddy said. "Father says it's over a half an hour now, and you've got to come this minute."

"I ain't studying no breakfast," Nancy said. "I going to get my sleep out."

"I bet you're drunk," Jason said. "Father says you're drunk. Are you drunk, Nancy?"

"Who says I is?" Nancy said. "I got to get my sleep out. I ain't studying no breakfast."

So after a while we quit chunking the cabin and went back home. When she finally came, it was too late for me to go to school. So we thought it was whiskey until that day they arrested her again and they were taking her to jail and they passed Mr. Stovall. He was the cashier in the bank and a deacon in the Baptist church, and Nancy began to say:

"When you going to pay me, white man? When you going to pay me, white man? It's been three times now since you paid me a cent—" Mr. Stovall knocked her down, but she kept on saying, "When you going to pay me, white man? It's been three times now since—" until Mr. Stovall kicked her in the mouth with his heel and the marshal caught Mr. Stovall back, and Nancy lying in the street, laughing. She turned her head and spat out some blood and teeth and said, "It's been three times now since he paid me a cent."

That was how she lost her teeth, and all that day they told about Nancy and Mr. Stovall, and all that night the ones that passed the jail could hear Nancy singing and yelling. They could see her hands holding to the window bars, and a lot of them stopped along the fence, listening to her and the jailer trying to make her stop. She didn't shut up until almost daylight, when the jailer began to hear a bumping and scraping upstairs and he went up there and found Nancy hanging from the window bar. He said that it was cocaine and not whiskey, because no nigger would try to commit suicide unless he was full of cocaine, because a nigger full of cocaine wasn't a nigger any longer.

The jailer cut her down and revived her; then he beat her, whipped her. She had hung herself with her dress. She had fixed it all right, but when they arrested her she didn't have on anything except a dress and so she didn't have anything to tie her hands with and she couldn't make her hands let go of the window ledge. So the jailer heard the noise and ran up there and found Nancy hanging from the window, stark naked, her belly already swelling out a little, like a little balloon.

When Dilsey was sick in her cabin and Nancy was cooking for us, we could see her apron swelling out; that was before Father told Jesus to stay away from the house. Jesus was in the kitchen, sitting behind the stove, with his razor scar on his black face like a piece of dirty string. He said it was a watermelon that Nancy had under her dress.

"It never come off of your vine, though," Nancy said.

"Off of what vine?" Caddy said.

"I can cut down the vine it did come off of," Jesus said.

"What makes you want to talk like that before these chillen?" Nancy said. "Whyn't you go on to work? You done et. You want Mr. Jason to catch you hanging around his kitchen, talking that way before these chillen?"

"Talking what way?" Caddy said. "What vine?"

"I can't hang around white man's kitchen," Jesus said. "But white man can hang around mine. White man can come in my house, but I can't stop him. When white man want to come in my house, I ain't got no house. I can't stop him, but he can't kick me outen it. He can't do that."

Dilsey was still sick in her cabin. Father told Jesus to stay off our place. Dilsey was still sick. It was a long time. We were in the library after supper.

"Isn't Nancy through in the kitchen yet?" Mother said. "It seems to me that she has had plenty of time to have finished the dishes."

"Let Quentin go and see," Father said. "Go and see if Nancy is through, Quentin. Tell her she can go on home."

I went to the kitchen. Nancy was through. The dishes were put away and the fire was out. Nancy was sitting in a chair, close to the cold stove. She looked at me.

"Mother wants to know if you are through," I said.

"Yes," Nancy said. She looked at me. "I done finished." She looked at me.

"What is it?" I said. "What is it?"

"I ain't nothing but a nigger," Nancy said. "It ain't none of my fault."

She looked at me, sitting in the chair before the cold stove, the sailor hat on her head. I went back to the library. It was the cold stove and all, when you think of a kitchen being warm and busy and cheerful. And with a cold stove and the dishes all put away, and nobody wanting to eat at that hour.

"Is she through?" Mother said.

"Yessum," I said.

"What is she doing?" Mother said.

"She's not doing anything. She's through."

"I'll go and see," Father said.

"Maybe she's waiting for Jesus to come and take her home," Caddy said.

"Jesus is gone," I said. Nancy told us how one morning she woke up and Jesus was gone.

"He quit me," Nancy said. "Done gone to Memphis, I reckon. Dodging them city po-lice for a while, I reckon."

"And a good riddance," Father said. "I hope he stays there."

"Nancy's scaired of the dark," Jason said.

"So are you," Caddy said.

"I'm not," Jason said.

"Scairy cat," Caddy said.

"I'm not," Jason said.

"You, Candace!" Mother said. Father came back.

"I am going to walk down the lane with Nancy," he said. "She says that Jesus is back."

"Has she seen him?" Mother said.

"No. Some Negro sent her word that he was back in town. I won't be long."

"You'll leave me alone, to take Nancy home?" Mother said. "Is her safety more precious to you than mine?"

"I won't be long," Father said.

"You'll leave these children unprotected, with that Negro about?"

"I'm going, too," Caddy said. "Let me go, Father."

"What would he do with them, if he were unfortunate enough to have them?" Father said.

"I want to go, too," Jason said.

"Jason!" Mother said. She was speaking to Father. You could tell that by the way she said the name. Like she believed that all day Father had been trying to think of doing the thing she wouldn't like the most, and that she knew all the time that after a while he would think of it. I stayed quiet, because Father and I both knew that Mother would want him to make me stay with her if she just thought of it in time. So Father didn't look at me. I was the oldest. I was nine and Caddy was seven and Jason was five.

"Nonsense," Father said. "We won't be long."

Nancy had her hat on. We came to the lane. "Jesus always been good to me," Nancy said. "Whenever he had two dollars, one of them was mine." We walked in the lane. "If I can just get through the lane," Nancy said, "I be all right then."

The lane was always dark. "This is where Jason got scaired on Halloween," Caddy said.

"I didn't," Jason said.

"Can't Aunt Rachel do anything with him?" Father said. Aunt Rachel was old. She lived in a cabin beyond Nancy's by herself. She had white hair and she smoked a pipe in the door, all day long; she didn't work any more. They said she was Jesus' mother. Sometimes she said she was and sometimes she said she wasn't any kin to Jesus.

"Yes you did," Caddy said. "You were scairder than Frony. You were scairder than T. P. even. Scairder than niggers."

"Can't nobody do nothing with him," Nancy said. "He say I done woke up the devil in him and ain't but one thing going to lay it down again."

"Well, he's gone now," Father said. "There's nothing for you to be afraid of now. And if you'd just let white men alone."

"Let white men alone?" Caddy said. "How let them alone?"

"He ain't gone nowhere," Nancy said. "I can feel him. I can feel him now, in this lane. He hearing us talk, every word, hid somewhere, waiting. I ain't seen him, and I ain't going to see him again but once more, with that razor in his mouth. That razor on that string down his back, inside his shirt. And then I ain't going to be even surprised."

"I wasn't scaired," Jason said.

"If you'd behave yourself, you'd have kept out of this," Father said. "But it's all right now. He's probably in Saint Louis now. Probably got another wife by now and forgot all about you."

"If he has, I better not find out about it," Nancy said. "I'd stand there right over them, and every time he wropped her, I'd cut that arm off. I'd cut his head off and I'd slit her belly and I'd shove—"

"Hush," Father said.

"Slit whose belly, Nancy?" Caddy said.

"I wasn't scaired," Jason said. "I'd walk right down this lane by myself."

"Yah," Caddy said. "You wouldn't dare to put your foot down in it if we were not here too."

2

Dilsey was still sick, so we took Nancy home every night until Mother said, "How much longer is this going on? I to be left alone in this big house while you take home a frightened Negro?"

We fixed a pallet in the kitchen for Nancy. One night we waked up, hearing the sound. It was not singing and it was not crying, coming up the dark stairs. There was a light in Mother's room and we heard Father going down the hall, down the back stairs, and Caddy and I went into the hall. The floor was cold. Our toes curled away from it while we listened to the sound. It was like singing and it wasn't like singing, like the sound that Negroes make.

Then it stopped and we heard Father going down the back stairs, and we went to the head of the stairs. Then the sound began again, in the stairway, not loud, and we could see Nancy's eyes halfway up the stairs, against the wall. They looked like cat's eyes do, like a big cat against the wall, watching us. When we came down the steps to where she was, she quit making the sound again, and we stood there until Father came back up from the kitchen, with his pistol in his hand. He went back down with Nancy and they came back with Nancy's pallet.

We spread the pallet in our room. After the light in Mother's room went off, we could see Nancy's eyes again. "Nancy," Caddy whispered, "are you asleep, Nancy?"

Nancy whispered something. It was oh or no, I don't know which. Like nobody had made it, like it came from nowhere and went nowhere, until it was like Nancy was not there at all; that I had looked so hard at her eyes on the stairs that they had got printed on my eyeballs, like the sun does when you have closed your eyes and there is no sun. "Jesus," Nancy whispered. "Jesus."

"Was it Jesus?" Caddy said. "Did he try to come into the kitchen?"

"Jesus," Nancy said. Like this: Jeeeeeeeeeeeeeesus, until the sound went out, like a match or a candle does.

"It's the other Jesus she means," I said.

"Can you see us, Nancy?" Caddy whispered. "Can you see our eyes too?"

"I ain't nothing but a nigger," Nancy said. "God knows. God knows."

"What did you see down there in the kitchen?" Caddy whispered. "What tried to get in?"

"God knows," Nancy said. We could see her eyes. "God knows."

Dilsey got well. She cooked dinner. "You'd better stay in bed a day or two longer," Father said.

"What for?" Dilsey said. "If I had been a day later, this place would be to rack and ruin. Get on out of here now, and let me get my kitchen straight again."

Dilsey cooked supper too. And that night, just before dark, Nancy came into the kitchen.

"How do you know he's back?" Dilsey said. "You ain't seen him."

"Jesus is a nigger," Jason said.

"I can feel him," Nancy said. "I can feel him laying yonder in the ditch."

"Tonight?" Dilsey said. "Is he there tonight?"

"Dilsey's a nigger too," Jason said.

"You try to eat something," Dilsey said.

"I don't want nothing," Nancy said.

"I ain't a nigger," Jason said.

"Drink some coffee," Dilsey said. She poured a cup of coffee for Nancy. "Do you know he's out there tonight? How come you know it's tonight?"

"I know," Nancy said. "He's there, waiting. I know. I done lived with him too long. I know what he is fixing to do fore he know it himself."

"Drink some coffee," Dilsey said. Nancy held the cup to her mouth and blew into the cup. Her mouth pursed out like a spreading adder's, like a rubber mouth, like she had blown all the color out of her lips with blowing the coffee.

"I ain't a nigger," Jason said. "Are you a nigger, Nancy?"

"I hellborn, child," Nancy said. "I won't be nothing soon. I going back where I come from soon."

3

She began to drink the coffee. While she was drinking, holding the cup in both hands, she began to make the sound again. She made the sound into the cup and the coffee sploshed out onto her hands and her dress. her eyes looked at us and she sat there, her elbows on her knees, holding the cup in both hands, looking at us across the wet cup, making the sound.

"Look at Nancy," Jason said. "Nancy can't cook for us now. Dilsey's got well now."

"You hush up," Dilsey said. Nancy held the cup in both hands, looking at us, making the sound, like there were two of them: one looking at us and the other making the sound. "Whyn't you let Mr. Jason telefoam the marshal?" Dilsey said. Nancy stopped then, holding the cup in her long brown hands. She tried to drink some coffee again, but it slposhed out of the cup, onto her hands and her ddress, and she put the cup down. Jason watcher her.

"I can't swallow it," Nancy said. "I swallows but it won't go down me."

"You go down to the cabin," Dilsey said. "Frony will fix you a pallet and I'll be there soon."

"Won't no nigger stop him," Nancy said.

"I ain't a nigger," Jason said. "Am I, Dilsey?"

"I reckon not," Dilsey said. She looked at Nancy. "I don't reckon so. What you going to do, then?"

Nancy looked at us. Her eyes went fast, like she was afraid there wasn't time to look, without hardly moving at all. She looked at us, at all three of us at one time. "You remember that night I stayed in yawls' room?" she said. She told about how we waked up early the next morning, and played. We had to play quiet, on her pallet, until Father woke up and it was time to get breakfast. "Go and ask your maw to let me stay here tonight," Nancy said. "I won't need no pallet. We can play some more."

Caddy asked Mother. Jason went too. "I can't have Negroes sleeping in the bedrooms," Mother said. Jason cried. He cried until Mother said he couldn't have any dessert for three days if he didn't stop. Then Jason said he would stop if Dilsey would make a chocolate cake. Father was there.

"Why don't you do something about it?" Mother said. "what do we have officers for?"

"Why is Nancy afraid of Jesus?" Caddy said. "Are you afraid of Father, Mother?"

"What could the officers do?" Father said. "If Nancy hasn't seen him, how could the officers find him?"

"Then why is she afraid?" Mother said.

"She says he is there. She says she knows he is there tonight."

"Yet we pay taxes," Mother said. "I must wait here alone in this big house while you take a Negro woman home."

"You know that I am not lying outside with a razor," Father said.

"I'll stop if Dilsey will make a chocolate cake," Jason said. Mother told us to go out and Father said he didn't know if Jason would get a chocolate cake or not, but he knew what Jason was going to get in about a minute. We went back to the kitchen and told Nancy.

"Father said for you to go home and lock the door, and you'll be all right," Caddy said. "All right from what, Nancy? Is Jesus mad at you?" Nancy was holding the coffee cup in her hands again, her elbows on her knees and her hands holding the cup between her knees. She was looking into the cup. "What have you done that made Jesus mad?" Caddy said. Nancy let the cup go. It didn't break on the floor, but the coffee spilled out, and Nancy sat there with her hands still making the shape of the cup. She began to make the sound again, not loud. Not singing and not unsinging. We watched her.

"Here," Dilsey said. "You quit that, now. You get aholt of yourself. You wait here. I going to get Versh to walk home with you." Dilsey went out.

We looked at Nancy. Her shoulders kept shaking, but she quit making the sound. We stood and watched her.

"What's Jesus going to do to you?" Caddy said. "He went away."

Nancy looked at us. "We had fun that night I stayed in yawls' room, didn't we?"

"I didn't," Jason said. "I didn't have any fun."

"You were asleep in Mother's room," Caddy said. "You were not there."

"Let's go down to my house and have some more fun," Nancy said.

"Mother won't let us," I said. "It's too late now."

"Don't bother her," Nancy said. "We can tell her in the morning. She won't mind."

"She wouldn't let us," I said.

"Don't ask her now," Nancy said. "Don't bother her now."

"She didn't say we couldn't go," Caddy said.

"We didn't ask," I said.

"If you go, I'll tell," Jason said.

"We'll have fun," Nancy said. "They won't mind, just to my house. I been working for yawl a long time. They won't mind."

"I'm not afraid to go," Caddy said. "Jason is the one that's afraid. He'll tell."

"I'm not," Jason said.

"Yes, you are," Caddy said. "You'll tell."

"I won't tell," Jason said. "I'm not afraid."

"Jason ain't afraid to go with me," Nancy said. "Is you, Jason?"

"Jason is going to tell," Caddy said. The lane was dark. We passed the pasture gate. "I bet if something was to jump out from behind that gate, Jason would holler."

"I wouldn't," Jason said. We walked down the lane. Nancy was talking loud.

"What are you talking so loud for, Nancy?" Caddy said.

"Who, me?" Nancy said. "Listen at Quentin and Caddy and Jason saying I'm talking loud."

"You talk like there was five of us here," Caddy said. "You talk like Father was here too."

"Who; me talking loud, Mr. Jason?" Nancy said.

"Nancy called Jason 'Mister,'" Caddy said.

"Listen how Caddy and Quentin and Jason talk," Nancy said.

"We're not talking loud," Caddy said. "You're the one that's talking like Father—"

"Hush," Nancy said; "hush, Mr. Jason."

"Nancy called Jason 'Mister' aguh—"

"Hush," Nancy said. She was talking loud when we crossed the ditch and stooped through the fence where she used to stoop through with the clothes on her head. Then we came to her house. We were going fast then. She opened the door. The smell of the house was like the lamp and the smell of Nancy was like the wick, like they were waiting for one another to begin to smell. She lit the lamp and closed the door and put the bar up. Then she quit talking loud, looking at us.

"What're we going to do?" Caddy said.

"What do yawl want to do?" Nancy said.

"You said we would have some fun," Caddy said.

There was something about Nancy's house; something you could smell besides Nancy and the house. Jason smelled it, even. "I don't want to stay here," he said. "I want to go home."

"Go home, then," Caddy said.

"I don't want to go by myself," Jason said.

"We're going to have some fun," Nancy said.

"How?" Caddy said.

Nancy stood by the door. She was looking at us, only it was like she had emptied her eyes, like she had quit using them. "What do you want to do?" she said.

"Tell us a story," Caddy said. "Can you tell a story?"

"Yes," Nancy said.

"Tell it," Caddy said. We looked at Nancy. "You don't know any stories."

"Yes," Nancy said. "Yes I do."

She came and sat in a chair before the hearth. There was a little fire there. Nancy built it up, when it was already hot inside. She built a good blaze. She told a story. She talked like her eyes looked, like her eyes watching us and her voice talking to us did not belong to her. Like she was living somewhere else, waiting somewhere else. She was outside the cabin. Her voice was inside and the shape of her, that Nancy that could stoop under a barbed wire fence with a bundle of clothes balanced on her head as though without weight, like a balloon, was there. But that was all. "And so this here queen come walking up to the ditch, where that bad man was hiding. She was walking up to the ditch, and she say, 'If I can just get past this here ditch,' was what she say . . ."

"What ditch?" Caddy said. "A ditch like that one out there? Why did a queen want to go into a ditch?"

"To get to her house," Nancy said. She looked at us. "She had to cross the ditch to get into her house quick and bar the door."

"Why did she want to go home and bar the door?" Caddy said.

4

Nancy looked at us. She quit talking. She looked at us. Jason's legs stuck straight out of his pants where he sat on Nancy's lap. "I don't think that's a good story," he said. "I want to go home."

"Maybe we had better," Caddy said. She got up from the floor. "I bet they are looking for us right now." She went toward the door.

"No," Nancy said. "Don't open it." She got up quick and passed Caddy. She didn't touch the door, the wooden bar.

"Why not?" Caddy said.

"Come back to the lamp," Nancy said. "We'll have fun. You don't have to go."

"We ought to go," Caddy said. "Unless we have a lot of fun." She and Nancy came back to the fire, the lamp.

"I want to go home," Jason said. "I'm going to tell."

"I know another story," Nancy said. She stood close to the lamp. She looked at Caddy, like when your eyes look up at a stick balanced on your nose. She had to look down to see Caddy, but her eyes looked like that, like when you are balancing a stick.

"I won't listen to it," Jason said. "I'll bang on the door."

"It's a good one," Nancy said. "It's better than the other one."

"What's it about?" Caddy said. Nancy was standing by the lamp. Her hand was on the lamp, against the light, long and brown.

"Your hand is on that hot globe," Caddy said. "Don't it feel hot to your hand?"

Nancy looked at her hand on the lamp chimney. She took her hand away, slow. She stood there, looking at Caddy, wringing her long hand as though it were tied to her wrist with a string.

"Let's do something else," Caddy said.

"I want to go home," Jason said.

"I got some popcorn," Nancy said. She looked at Caddy and then at Jason and then at me and then at Caddy again. "I got some popcorn."

"I don't like popcorn," Jason said. "I'd rather have candy."

Nancy looked at Jason. "You can hold the popper." She was still wringing her hand; it was long and limp and brown.

"All right," Jason said. "I'll stay a while if I can do that. Caddy can't hold it. I'll want to go home again if Caddy holds the popper."

Nancy built up the fire. "Look at Nancy putting her hands in the fire," Caddy said. "What's the matter with you, Nancy?"

"I got popcorn," Nancy said. "I got some." She took the popper from under the bed. It was broken. Jason began to cry.

"Now we can't have any popcorn," he said.

"We ought to go home anyway," Caddy said. "Come on, Quentin."

"Wait," Nancy said; "wait. I can fix it. Don't you want to help me fix it?"

"I don't think I want any," Caddy said. "It's too late now."

"You help me, Jason," Nancy said. "Don't you want to help me?"

"No," Jason said. "I want to go home."

"Hush," Nancy said; "hush. Watch. Watch me. I can fix it so Jason can hold it and pop the corn." She got a piece of wire and fixed the popper.

"It won't hold good," Caddy said.

"Yes it will," Nancy said. "Yawl watch. Yawl help me shell some corn."

The popcorn was under the bed too. We shelled it into the popper and Nancy helped Jason hold the popper over the fire.

"It's not popping," Jason said. "I want to go home."

"You wait," Nancy said. "It'll begin to pop. We'll have fun then."

She was sitting close to the fire. The lamp was turned up so high it was beginning to smoke. "Why don't you turn it down some?" I said.

"It's all right," Nancy said. "I'll clean it. Yawl wait. The popcorn will start in a minute."

"I don't believe it's going to start," Caddy said. "We ought to start home, anyway. They'll be worried."

"No," Nancy said. "It's going to pop. Dilsey will tell um yawl with me. I been working for yawl long time. They won't mind if yawl at my house. You wait, now. It'll start popping any minute now."

Then Jason got some smoke in his eyes and he began to cry. He dropped the popper into the fire. Nancy got a wet rag and wiped Jason's face, but he didn't stop crying.

"Hush," she said. "Hush." He didn't hush. Caddy took the popper out of the fire.

"It's burned up," she said. "You'll have to get some more popcorn, Nancy."

"Did you put all of it in?" Nancy said.

"Yes," Caddy said. Nancy looked at Caddy. Then she took the popper and opened it and poured the cinders into her apron and began to sort the grains, her hands long and brown, and we watched her.

"Haven't you got any more?" Caddy said.

"Yes," Nancy said; "yes. Look. This here ain't burnt. All we need to do is—"

"I want to go home," Jason said. "I'm going to tell."

"Hush," Caddy said. We all listened. Nancy's head was already turned toward the door, her eyes filled with red lamplight. "Somebody is coming," Caddy said.

Then Nancy began to make that sound again, not loud, sitting there above the fire, her long hands dangling between her knees; all of a sudden water began to come out of her face in big drops, running down her face, carrying in each one a little turning ball of firelight like a spark until it dropped off her chin. "She's not crying," I said.

"I ain't crying," Nancy said. Her eyes were closed. "I ain't crying. Who is it?"

"I don't know," Caddy said. She went to the door and looked out. "We've got to go now," she said. "Here comes Father."

"I'm going to tell," Jason said. "Yawl made me come."

The water still ran down Nancy's face. She turned in her chair. "Listen. Tell him. Tell him we going to have fun. Tell him I take good care of yawl until in the morning. Tell him to let me come home with yawl and sleep on the floor. Tell him I won't need no pallet. We'll have fun. You remember last time how we had so much fun?"

"I didn't have fun," Jason said. "You hurt me. You put smoke in my eyes. I'm going to tell."

5

Father came in. He looked at us. Nancy did not get up.

"Tell him," she said.

"Caddy made us come down here," Jason said. "I didn't want to."

Father came to the fire. Nancy looked up at him. "Can't you go to Aunt Rachel's and stay?" he said. Nancy looked up at Father, her hands between her knees. "He's not here," Father said. "I would have seen him. There's not a soul in sight."

"He in the ditch," Nancy said. "He waiting in the ditch yonder."

"Nonsense," Father said. He looked at Nancy. "Do you know he's there?"

"I got the sign," Nancy said.

"What sign?"

"I got it. It was on the table when I came in. It was a hog-bone, with blood meat still on it, laying by the lamp. He's out there. When yawl walk out that door, I gone."

"Gone where, Nancy?" Caddy said.

"I'm not a tattletale," Jason said.

"Nonsense," Father said.

"He out there," Nancy said. "He looking through that window this minute, waiting for yawl to go. Then I gone."

"Nonsense," Father said. "Lock up your house and we'll take you on to Aunt Rachel's."

"'Twon't do no good," Nancy said. She.didn't look at Father now, but he looked down at her, at her long limp, moving hands. "Putting it off won't do no good."

"Then what do you want to do?" Father said.

"I don't know," Nancy said. "I can't do nothing. Just put it off. And that don't do no good. I reckon it belong to me. I reckon what I going to get ain't no more than mine."

"Get what?" Caddy said. "What's yours?"

"Nothing," Father said. "You all must get to bed."

"Caddy made me come," Jason said.

"Go on to Aunt Rachel's," Father said.

"It won't do no good." Nancy said. She sat down before the fire, her elbows on her knees, her long hands between her knees. "When even your own kitchen wouldn't do no good. When even if I was sleeping on the floor in the room with your chillen, and the next morning there I am, and blood—"

"Hush," Father said. "Lock your door and put out the lamp and go to bed."

"I scaired of the dark," Nancy said. "I scaired for it to happen in the dark."

"You mean you're going to sit right here with the lamp lighted?" Father said. Then Nancy began to make the sound again, sitting before the fire, her long hands between her knees. "Ah, damnation," Father said. "Come along, chillen. It's past bedtime."

"When yawl go home, I gone," Nancy said. She talked quieter now, and her face looked quiet, like her hands. "Anyway. I got my coffin money saved up with Mr. Lovelady." Mr. Lovelady was a short, dirty man who collected the Negro insurance, coming around to the cabins or the kitchens every Saturday morning, to collect fifteen cents. He and his wife lived at the hotel. One morning his wife committed suicide. They had a child, a little girl. He and the child went away. After a week or two he came back alone. We would see him going along the lanes and the back streets on Saturday mornings.

"Nonsense," Father said. "You'll be the first thing I'll see in the kitchen tomorrow morning."

"You'll see what you'll see, I reckon," Nancy said. "But it will take the Lord to say what that will be."

6

We left her sitting before the fire.

"Come and put the bar up," Father said. But she didn't move. She didn't look at us again, sitting quietly there between the lamp and the fire. From some distance down the lane we could look back and see her through the open door.

"What, Father?" Caddy said. "What's going to happen?"

"Nothing," Father said. Jason was on Father's back, so Jason was the tallest of all of us. We went down into the ditch. I looked at it, quiet. I couldn't see much where the moonlight and the shadows tangled.

"If Jesus *is* hid here, he can see us, can't he?" Caddy said.

"He's not there," Father said. "He went away a long time ago."

"You made me come," Jason said, high; against the sky it looked like Father had two heads, a little one and a big one. "I didn't want to."

We went up out of the ditch. We could still see Nancy's house and the open door, but we couldn't see Nancy now, sitting before the fire with the door open, because she was tired. "I just done got tired," she said. "I just a nigger. It ain't no fault of mine."

But we could hear her, because she began just after we came up out of the ditch, the sound that was not singing and not unsinging. "Who will do our washing now, Father?" I said.

"I'm not a nigger," Jason said, high and close above Father's head.

"You're worse," Caddy said, "you are a tattletale. If something was to jump out, you'd be scairder than a nigger."

"I wouldn't," Jason said.

"You'd cry," Caddy said.

"Caddy," Father said.
"I wouldn't!" Jason said.
"Scairy cat," Caddy said.
"Candace!" Father said.

[1931–U.S.A.]

QUESTIONS

1. The story contains several contrasting worlds. What are they? What joins them into a unified story? For instance, compare Nancy and the mother as to characterization. Though opposite in most regards, they are alike in at least one. What?
2. Which other characters feel what Nancy and the mother express? What is the origin of this feeling? What does this shared feeling say about human relations in the time and place of "That Evening Sun"?
3. The title of the present story is from W. C. Handy's "St. Louis Blues," a lament on the part of a woman whose man has gone off with a "St. Louis woman." The whole line that the title comes from is "I hate to see that evening sun go down." Given these points of reference, what significance does the title have in the context of Faulkner's story?
4. Is there any special significance in Faulkner's choice of the name "Jesus"? What are the implications of the father's statement "He went away a long time ago"? In sum, what is Faulkner's theme here and how does it help unify the disparate material of his story?
5. What do you make of the way the story ends? Is what the children chatter about at all relevant? And why are we left not knowing whether or not Jesus has come back with the intent of killing Nancy? What light does this shed on her fear?

WRITING SUGGESTIONS

1. Write an essay on Caddy, Jason, and Quentin (who, years later, narrates the story). How is each characterized so that each is a separate personality in our minds? What might they grow up to be like given what we know about them now and their social context as detailed in the story?
2. In a paragraph, name and discuss the various kinds of fear that are to be found in "That Evening Sun" in relation to the social climate evidenced in the story. What is the connection? In what ways does the social climate breed dis-ease in all, black and white?
3. Research what others have had to say about "That Evening Sun." After you have absorbed your research, write a paper expressing your view of the story, though taking into account what others have had to say.

Petrified Man

Eudora Welty

"Reach in my purse and git me a cigarette without no powder in it if you kin, Mrs. Fletcher, honey," said Leota to her ten o'clock shampoo-and-set customer. "I don't like no perfumed cigarettes."

Mrs. Fletcher gladly reached over to the lavender shelf under the lavender-framed mirror, shook a hair net loose from the clasp of the patent-leather bag, and slapped her hand down quickly on a powder puff which burst out when the purse was opened.

"Why, look at the peanuts, Leota!" said Mrs. Fletcher in her marvelling voice.

"Honey, them goobers has been in my purse a week if they's been in it a day. Mrs. Pike bought them peanuts."

"Who's Mrs. Pike?" asked Mrs. Fletcher, settling back. Hidden in this den of curling fluid and henna packs, separated by a lavender swing-door from the other customers, who were being gratified in other booths, she could give her curiosity its freedom. She looked expectantly at the black part in Leota's yellow curls as she bent to light the cigarette.

"Mrs. Pike is this lady from New Orleans," said Leota, puffing, and pressing into Mrs. Fletcher's scalp with strong red-nailed fingers. "A friend, not a customer. You see, like maybe I told you last time, me and Fred and Sal and Joe all had us a fuss, so Sal and Joe up and moved out, so we didn't do a thing but rent out their room. So we rented it to Mrs. Pike. And Mr. Pike." She flicked an ash into the basket of dirty towels. "Mrs. Pike is a very decided blonde. *She* bought me the peanuts."

"She must be cute," said Mrs. Fletcher.

"Honey, 'cute' ain't the word for what she is. I'm tellin' you, Mrs. Pike

463

is attractive. She has her a good time. She's got a sharp eye out, Mrs. Pike has."

She dashed the comb through the air, and paused dramatically as a cloud of Mrs. Fletcher's hennaed hair floated out of the lavender teeth like a small storm-cloud.

"Hair fallin'."

"Aw, Leota."

"Uh-huh, commencin' to fall out," said Leota, combing again, and letting fall another cloud.

"Is it any dandruff in it?" Mrs. Fletcher was frowning, her hair-line eyebrows diving down toward her nose, and her wrinkled, beady-lashed eyelids batting with concentration.

"Nope." She combed again. "Just fallin' out."

"Bet it was the last perm'nent you gave me that did it," Mrs. Fletcher said cruelly. "Remember you cooked me fourteen minutes."

"You had fourteen minutes comin' to you," said Leota with finality.

"Bound to be somethin'," persisted Mrs. Fletcher. "Dandruff, dandruff. I couldn't of caught a thing like that from Mr. Fletcher, could I?"

"Well," Leota answered at last, "you know what I heard in here yestiddy, one of Thelma's ladies was settin' over yonder in Thelma's booth gittin' a machineless, and I don't mean to insist or insinuate or anything, Mrs. Fletcher, but Thelma's lady just was happ'med to throw out—I forgotten what she was talkin' about at the time—that you was p-r-e-g., and lots of times that'll make your hair do awful funny, fall out and God knows what all. It just ain't our fault, is the way I look at it."

There was a pause. The women stared at each other in the mirror.

"Who was it?" demanded Mrs. Fletcher.

"Honey, I really couldn't say," said Leota. "Not that you look it."

"Where's Thelma? I'll get it out of her," said Mrs. Fletcher.

"Now, honey, I wouldn't go and git mad over a little thing like that," Leota said, combing hastily, as though to hold Mrs. Fletcher down by the hair. "I'm sure it was somebody didn't mean no harm in the world. How far gone are you?"

"Just wait," said Mrs. Fletcher, and shrieked for Thelma, who came in and took a drag from Leota's cigarette.

"Thelma, honey, throw your mind back to yestiddy if you kin," said Leota, drenching Mrs. Fletcher's hair with a thick fluid and catching the overflow in a cold wet towel at her neck.

"Well, I got my lady half-wound for a spiral," said Thelma doubtfully.

"This won't take but a minute," said Leota. "Who is it you got in there, old Horse Face? Just cast your mind back and try to remember who your lady was yestiddy who happ'm to mention that my customer was pregnant, that's all. She's dead to know."

Thelma drooped her blood-red lips and looked over Mrs. Fletcher's head into the mirror. "Why, honey, I ain't got the faintest," she breathed. "I really don't recollect the faintest. But I'm sure she meant no harm. I declare, I forgot my hair finally got combed and thought it was a stranger behind me."

"Was it that Mrs. Hutchinson?" Mrs. Fletcher was tensely polite.

"Mrs. Hutchinson? Oh, Mrs. Hutchinson." Thelma batted her eyes. "Naw, precious, she come on Thursday and didn't ev'm mention your name. I doubt if she ev'm knows you're on the way."

"Thelma!" cried Leota staunchly.

"All I know is, whoever it is 'll be sorry some day. Why, I just barely knew it myself!" cried Mrs. Fletcher. "Just let her wait!"

"Why? What're you gonna do to her?"

It was a child's voice, and the women looked down. A little boy was making tents with aluminum wave pinchers on the floor under the sink.

"Billy Boy, hon, mustn't bother nice ladies," Leota smiled. She slapped him brightly and behind her back waved Thelma out of the booth. "Ain't Billy Boy a sight? Only three years old and already just nuts about the beauty-parlor business."

"I never saw him here before," said Mrs. Fletcher, still unmollified.

"He ain't been here before, that's how come," said Leota. "He belongs to Mrs. Pike. She got her a job but it was Fay's Millinery. He oughtn't to try on those ladies' hats, they come down over his eyes like I don't know what. They just git to look ridiculous, that's what, an' of course he's gonna put 'em on: hats. They tole Mrs. Pike they didn't appreciate him hangin' around there. Here, he couldn't hurt a thing."

"Well! I don't like chidren that much," said Mrs. Fletcher.

"Well!" said Leota moodily.

"Well! I'm almost tempted not to have this one," said Mrs. Fletcher. "That Mrs. Hutchinson! Just looks straight through you when she sees you on the street and then spits at you behind your back."

"Mr. Fletcher would beat you on the head if you didn't have it now," said Leota reasonably. "After going this far."

Mrs. Fletcher sat up straight. "Mr. Fletcher can't do a thing with me."

"He can't!" Leota winked at herself in the mirror.

"No, siree, he can't. If he so much as raises his voice against me, he knows good and well I'll have one of my sick headaches, and then I'm just not fit to live with. And if I really look that pregnant already—"

"Well, now, honey, I just want you to know—I habm't told any of my ladies and I ain't goin' to tell 'em—even that you're losin' your hair. You just get you one of those Stork-a-Lure dresses and stop worryin'. What people don't know don't hurt nobody, as Mrs. Pike says."

"Did you tell Mrs. Pike?" asked Mrs. Fletcher sulkily.

"Well, Mrs. Fletcher, look, you ain't ever goin' to lay eyes on Mrs. Pike or her lay eyes on you, so what diffunce does it make in the long run?"

"I knew it!" Mrs. Fletcher deliberately nodded her head so as to destroy a ringlet Leota was working on behind her ear. "Mrs. Pike!"

Leota sighed. "I reckon I might as well tell you. It wasn't any more Thelma's lady tole me you was pregnant than a bat."

"Not Mrs. Hutchinson?"

"Naw, Lord! It was Mrs. Pike."

"Mrs. Pike!" Mrs. Fletcher could only sputter and let curling fluid roll into her ear. "How could Mrs. Pike possibly know I was pregnant or otherwise, when she doesn't even know me? The nerve of some people!"

"Well, here's how it was. Remember Sunday?"

"Yes," said Mrs. Fletcher.

"Sunday, Mrs. Pike an' me was all by ourself. Mr. Pike and Fred had gone over to Eagle Lake, sayin' they was goin' to catch 'em some fish, but they didn't a course. So we was settin' in Mrs. Pike's car, it's a 1939 Dodge—"

"1939, eh," said Mrs. Fletcher.

"—An' we was gettin' us a Jax beer apiece—that's the beer that Mrs. Pike says is made right in N.O., so she won't drink no other kind. So I seen you drive up to the drugstore an' run in for just a secont, leavin' I reckon Mr. Fletcher in the car, an' come runnin' out with looked like a perscription. So I says to Mrs. Pike, just to be makin' talk, 'Right yonder's Mrs. Fletcher, and I reckon that's Mr. Fletcher—she's one of my regular customers,' I says."

"I had on a figured print," said Mrs. Fletcher tentatively.

"You sure did," agreed Leota. "So Mrs. Pike, she give you a good look—she's very observant, a good judge of character, cute as a minute, you know—and she says, 'I bet you another Jax that lady's three months on the way."

"What gall!" said Mrs. Fletcher. "Mrs. Pike!"

"Mrs. Pike ain't goin' to bite you," said Leota. "Mrs. Pike is a lovely girl, you'd be crazy about her, Mrs. Fletcher. But she can't sit still a minute. We went to the travellin' freak show yestiddy after work. I got through early—nine o'clock. In the vacant store next door. What, you ain't been?"

"No, I despise freaks," declared Mrs. Fletcher.

"Aw. Well, honey, talkin' about bein' pregnant an' all, you ought to see those twins in a bottle, you really owe it to yourself."

"What twins?" asked Mrs. Fletcher out of the side of her mouth.

"Well, honey, they got these twins in a bottle, see? Born joined plumb together—dead a course." Leota dropped her voice into a soft lyrical hum. "They was about this long—pardon—must of been full time, all right, wouldn't you say?—an' they had these two heads an' two faces an' four arms an' four legs, all kind of joined *here*. See, this face looked this-a-way, and the other face looked that-a-way, over their shoulder, see. Kinda pathetic."

"Glah!" said Mrs. Fletcher disapprovingly.

"Well, ugly? Honey, I mean to tell you—their parents was first cousins and all like that. Billy Boy, git me a fresh towel from off Teeny's stack—this 'n's wringin' wet—an' quit ticklin' my ankles with that curler. I declare! He don't miss nothin'."

"Me and Mr. Fletcher aren't one speck of kin, or he could never of had me," said Mrs. Fletcher placidly.

"Of course not!" protested Leota. "Neither is me an' Fred, not that we know of. Well, honey, what Mrs. Pike liked was the pygmies. They've got these pygmies down there, too, an' Mrs. Pike was just wild about 'em. You know, the teeniest men in the universe? Well, honey, they can just rest back on their bohunkus an' roll around an' you can't hardly tell if they're sittin' or standin'. That'll give you some idea. They're about forty-two years old. Just suppose it was your husband!"

"Well, Mr. Fletcher is five foot nine and one half," said Mrs. Fletcher quickly.

"Fred's five foot ten," said Leota, "but I tell him he's still a shrimp, account of I'm so tall." She made a deep wave over Mrs. Fletcher's other temple with the comb. "Well, these pygmies are a kind of a dark brown, Mrs. Fletcher. Not bad-lookin' for what they are, you know."

"I wouldn't care for them," said Mrs. Fletcher. "What does that Mrs. Pike see in them?"

"Aw, I don't know," said Leota. "She's just cute, that's all. But they got this man, this petrified man, that ever'thing ever since he was nine years old, when it goes through his digestion, see, somehow Mrs. Pike says it goes to his joints and has been turning to stone."

"How awful!" said Mrs. Fletcher.

"He's forty-two too. That looks like a bad age."

"Who said so, that Mrs. Pike? I bet she's forty-two," said Mrs. Fletcher.

"Naw," said Leota, "Mrs. Pike's thirty-three, born in January, an Aquarian. He could move his head—like this. A course his head and mind ain't a joint, so to speak, and I guess his stomach ain't, either—not yet, anyways. But see—his food, he eats it, and it goes down, see, and then he digests it"—Leota rose on her toes for an instant—"and it goes out to his joints and before you can say 'Jack Robinson,' it's stone—pure stone. He's turning to stone. How'd you like to be married to a guy like that? All he can do, he can move his head just a quarter of an inch. A course he *looks* just *terrible*."

"I should think he would," said Mrs. Fletcher frostily. "Mr. Fletcher takes bending exercises every night of the world. I make him."

"All Fred does is lay around the house like a rug. I wouldn't be surprised if he woke up someday and couldn't move. The petrified man just sat there moving his quarter of an inch though," said Leota reminiscently.

"Did Mrs. Pike like the petrified man?" asked Mrs. Fletcher.

"Not as much as she did the others," said Leota deprecatingly. "And then she likes a man to be a good dresser, and all that."

"Is Mr. Pike a good dresser?" asked Mrs. Fletcher sceptically.

"Oh, well, yeah," said Leota, "but he's twelve or fourteen years older'n her. She ast Lady Evangeline about him."

"Who's Lady Evangeline?" asked Mrs. Fletcher.

"Well, it's this mind reader they got in the freak show," said Leota. "Was real good. Lady Evangeline is her name, and if I had another dollar I wouldn't do a thing but have my other palm read. She had what Mrs. Pike said was the 'sixth mind' but she had the worst manicure I ever saw on a living person."

"What did she tell Mrs. Pike?" asked Mrs. Fletcher.

"She told her Mr. Piike was as true to her as he could be and besides, would come into some money."

"Humph!" said Mrs. Fletcher. "What does he do?"

"I can't tell," said Leota, "because he don't work. Lady Evangeline didn't tell me enough about my nature or anything. And I would like to go back and find out some more about this boy. Used to go with this boy until he got married to this girl. Oh, shoot, that was about three and a half years ago, when you was still goin' to the Robert E. Lee Beauty Shop in Jackson. He married her for her money. Another fortune-teller tole me that at the time. So I'm not in love with him any more, anyway, besides being married to Fred, but Mrs. Pike thought, just for the hell of it, see, to ask Lady Evangeline was he happy."

"Does Mrs. Pike know everything about you already?" asked Mrs. Fletcher unbelievingly. "Mercy!"

"Oh, yeah, I tole her ever'thing about ever'thing, from now on back to I don't know when—to when I first started goin' out," said Leota. "So I ast Lady Evangeline for one of my questions, was he happily married, and she says, just like she was glad I ask her, 'Honey,' she says, 'naw, he idn't. You write down this day, March 8, 1941,' she says, 'and mock it down: three years from today him and her won't be occupyin' the same bed.' There it is, up on the wall with them other dates—see, Mrs. Fletcher? And she says, 'Child, you ought to be glad you didn't git him, because he's so mercenary.' So I'm glad I married Fred. He sure ain't mercenary, money don't mean a thing to him. But I sure would like to go back and have my other palm read."

"Did Mrs. Pike believe in what the fortune-teller said?" asked Mrs. Fletcher in a superior tone of voice.

"Lord, yes, she's from New Orleans. Ever'body in New Orleans believes ever'thing spooky. One of 'em in New Orleans before it was raided says to Mrs. Pike one summer she was goin' to go from State to State and meet some grey-head men, and, sure enough, she says she went on a beautician convention up to Chicago. . . ."

"Oh!" said Mrs. Fletcher. "Oh, is Mrs. Pike a beautician too?"

"Sure she is," protested Leota. "She's a beautician. I'm going to git her in here if I can. Before she married. But it don't leave you. She says sure enough, there was three men who was very large part of making her trip what it was, and they all three had grey in their hair and they went in six States. Got Christmas cards from 'em. Billy Boy, go see if Thelma's got any dry cotton. Look how Mrs. Fletcher's a-drippin'."

"Where did Mrs. Pike meet Mr. Pike?" asked Mrs. Fletcher primly.

"On another train," said Leota.

"I met Mr. Fletcher, or rather he met me, in a rental library," said Mrs. Fletcher with dignity, as she watched the net come down over her head.

"Honey, me an' Fred, we met in a rumble seat eight months ago and we was practically on what you might call the way to the altar inside of half an hour," said Leota in a guttural voice, and bit a bobby pin open. "Course it don't last. Mrs. Pike says nothin' like that ever lasts."

"Mr. Fletcher and myself are as much in love as the day we married," said Mrs. Fletcher belligerently as Leota stuffed cotton into her ears.

"Mrs. Pike says it don't last," repeated Leota in a louder voice. "Now go git under the dryer. You can turn yourself on, can't you? I'll be back to comb you out. Durin' lunch I promised to give Mrs. Pike a facial. You know—free. Her bein' in the business, so to speak."

"I bet she needs one," said Mrs. Fletcher, letting the swing-door fly back against Leota. "Oh, pardon me."

A week later, on time for her appointment, Mrs. Fletcher sank heavily into Leota's chair after first removing a drug-store rental book, called *Life Is Like That*, from the seat. She stared in a discouraged way into the mirror.

"You can tell it when I'm sitting down, all right," she said.

Leota seemed preoccupied and stood shaking out a lavender cloth. She began to pin it around Mrs. Fletcher's neck in silence.

"I said you sure can tell it when I'm sitting straight on and coming at you this way," Mrs. Fletcher said.

"Why, honey, naw you can't," said Leota gloomily. "Why, I'd never know. If somebody was to come up to me on the street and say, 'Mrs. Fletcher is pregnant!' I'd say, 'Heck, she don't look it to me.'"

"If a certain party hadn't found it out and spread it around, it wouldn't be too late even now," said Mrs. Fletcher frostily, but Leota was almost choking her with the cloth, pinning it so tight, and she couldn't speak clearly. She paddled her hands in the air until Leota wearily loosened her.

"Listen, honey, you're just a virgin compared to Mrs. Montjoy," Leota was going on, still absent-minded. She bent Mrs. Fletcher back in the chair and, sighing, tossed liquid from a teacup on to her head and dug both hands into her scalp. "You know Mrs. Montjoy—her husband's that premature-grey-headed fella?"

"She's in the Trojan Garden Club, is all I know," said Mrs. Fletcher.

"Well, honey," said Leota, but in a weary voice, "she come in here not the week before and not the day before she had her baby—she come in here the very selfsame day, I mean to tell you. Child, we was all plumb scared to death. There she was! Come for her shampoo an' set. Why, Mrs. Fletcher, in an hour an' twenty minutes she was layin' up there in the Babtist Hospital with a seb'm-pound son. It was that close a shave. I declare, if I hadn't been so tired I would drank up a bottle of gin that night."

"What gall," said Mrs. Fletcher. "I never knew her at all well."

"See, her husband was waitin' outside in the car, and her bags was all packed an' in the back seat, an' she was all ready, 'cept she wanted her shampoo an' set. An' havin' one pain right after another. Her husband kep' comin' in here, scared-like, but couldn't do nothin' with her a course. She yelled bloody murder, too, but she always yelled her head off when I give her a perm'nent."

"She must of been crazy," said Mrs. Fletcher. "How did she look?"

"Shoot!" said Leota.

"Well, I can guess," said Mrs. Fletcher. "Awful."

"Just wanted to look pretty while she was havin' her baby, is all," said Leota airily. "Course, we was glad to give the lady what she was

after—that's our motto—but I bet a hour later she wasn't payin' no mind
to them little end curls. I bet she wasn't thinkin' about she ought to have
on a net. It wouldn't of done her no good if she had."

"No, I don't suppose it would," said Mrs. Fletcher.

"Yeah man! She was a-yellin'. Just like when I give her perm'nent."

"Her husband ought to make her behave. Don't it seem that way to
you?" asked Mrs. Fletcher. "He ought to put his foot down."

"Ha," said Leota. "A lot he could do. Maybe some women is soft."

"Oh, you mistake me, I don't mean for her to get soft—far from it!
Women have to stand up for themselves, or there's just no telling. But now
you take me—I ask Mr. Fletcher advice now and then, and he appreciates
it, especially on something important, like is it time for a permanent—not
that I've told him about the baby. He says, 'Why, dear, go ahead!' Just ask
their *advice*."

"Huh! If I ever ast Fred's advice we'd be floatin' down the Yazoo River
on a houseboat or somethin' by this time," said Leota. "I'm sick of Fred.
I told him to go over to Vicksburg."

"Is he going?" demanded Mrs. Fletcher.

"Sure. See, the fortune-teller—I went back and had my other palm
read, since we've got to rent the room agin—said my lover was goin' to
work in Vicksburg, so I don't know who she could mean, unless she meant
Fred. And Fred ain't workin' here—that much is so."

"Is he going to work in Vicsburg?" asked Mrs. Fletcher. "And—"

"Sure. Lady Evangeline said so. Said the future is going to be brighter
than the present. He don't want to go, but I ain't gonna put up with nothin'
like that. Lays around the house an' bulls—did bull—with that good-for-
nothin' Mr. Pike. He says if he goes who'll cook, but I says I never get to
eat anyway—not meals. Billy Boy, take Mrs. Grover that *Screen Secrets*
and leg it."

Mrs. Fletcher heard stamping feet go out the door.

"Is that that Mrs. Pike's little boy here again?" she asked, sitting up
gingerly.

"Yeah, that's still him." Leota stuck out her tongue.

Mrs. Fletcher could hardly believe her eyes. "Well! How's Mrs. Pike,
your attractive new friend with the sharp eyes who spreads it around town
that perfect strangers are pregnant?" she asked in a sweetened tone.

"Oh, Mizziz Pike." Leota combed Mrs. Fletcher's hair with heavy
strokes.

"You act like you're tired," said Mrs. Fletcher.

"Tired? Feel like it's four o'clock in the afternoon, already," said
Leota. "I ain't told you the awful luck we had, me and Fred? It's the worst

thing you ever heard of. Maybe *you* think Mrs. Pike's got sharp eyes. Shoot, there's a limit! Well, you know, we rented our room to this Mr. and Mrs. Pike from New Orleans when Sal an' Joe Fentress got mad at us 'cause they drank up some home-brew we had in the closet—Sal an' Joe did. So, a week ago Sat'day Mr. and Mrs. Pike moved in. Well, I kinda fixed up the room, you know—put a sofa pillow on the couch and picked some ragged robbins and put in a vase, but they never did say they appreciated it. Anyway, then I put some old magazines on the table."

"I think that was lovely," said Mrs. Fletcher.

"Wait. So, come night 'fore last, Fred and this Mr. Pike, who Fred just took up with, was back from they said they was fishin', bein' as neither one of 'em has got a job to his name, and we was all settin' around in their room. So Mrs. Pike was settin' there readin' a old *Startling G-Men Tales* that was mine, mind you. I'd bought it myself, and all of a sudden she jumps!—into the air—you'd 'a' thought she'd set on a spider—an' says, 'Canfield'—ain't that silly, that's Mr. Pike—'Canfield, my God A'mighty,' she says, 'honey,' she says, 'we're rich, and you won't have to work.' Not that he turned one hand anyway. Well, me and Fred rushes over to her, and Mr. Pike, too, and there she sets, pointin' her finger at a photo in my copy of *Startling G-Man.* 'See that man?' yells Mrs. Pike. 'Remember him, Canfield?' 'Never forget a face,' says Mr. Pike. 'It's Mr. Petrie, that we stayed with him in the apartment next to ours in Toulouse Street in N.O. for six weeks. Mr. Petrie.' 'Well,' says Mrs. Pike, like she can't hold out one secont longer, 'Mr. Petrie is wanted for five hundred dollars cash, for rapin' four women in California, and I know where he is.' "

"Mercy!" said Mrs. Fletcher. "Where was he?"

At some time Leota had washed her hair and now she yanked her up by the back locks and sat her up.

"Know where he was?"

"I certainly don't," Mrs. Fletcher said. Her scalp hurt all over.

Leota flung a towel around the top of her customer's head. "Nowhere else but in that freak show! I saw him just as plain as Mrs. Pike. *He* was the petrified man!"

"Who would ever have thought that!" cried Mrs. Fletcher sympathetically.

"So Mr. Pike says, 'Well whatta you know about that,' an' he looks real hard at the photo and whistles. And she starts dancin' and singin' about their good luck. She meant our bad luck! I made a point of tellin' that fortune-teller the next time I saw her. I said, 'Listen, that magazine was layin' around the house for a month, and there was the freak show runnin' night an' day, not two steps away from my own beauty parlor, with Mr. Petrie just settin' there waitin'. An' it had to be Mr. and Mrs. Pike, almost perfect strangers.' "

"What gall," said Mrs. Fletcher. She was only sitting there, wrapped in a turban, but she did not mind.

"Fortune-tellers don't care. And Mrs. Pike, she goes around actin' like she thinks she was Mrs. God," said Leota. "So they're goin' to leave tomorrow, Mr. and Mrs. Pike. And in the meantime I got to keep that mean, bad little ole kid here, gettin' under my feet ever' minute of the day an' talkin' back too."

"Have they gotten the five hundred dollars' reward already?" asked Mrs. Fletcher.

"Well," said Leota, "at first Mr. Pike didn't want to do anything about it. Can you feature that? Said he kinda liked that ole bird and said he was real nice to 'em, lent 'em money or somethin'. But Mrs. Pike simply tole him he could just go to hell, and I can see her point. She says, 'you ain't worked a lick in six months, and here I make five hundred dollars in two seconts, and what thanks do I get for it? You go to hell, Canfield,' she says. So," Leota went on in a despondent voice, "they called up the cops and they caught the ole bird, all right, right there in the freak show where I saw him with my own eyes, thinkin' he was petrified. He's the one. Did it under his real name—Mr. Petrie. Four women in California, all in the month of August. So Mrs. Pike gits five hundred dollars. And my magazine, and right next door to my beauty parlor. I cried all night, but Fred said it wasn't a bit of use and to go to sleep, because the whole thing was just a sort of coincidence—you know: can't do nothin' about it. He says it put him clean out of the notion of goin' to Vicksburg for a few days till we rent out the room again—no tellin' who we'll git this time."

"But can you imagine anybody knowing this old man, that's raped four women?" persisted Mrs. Fletcher, and she shuddered audibly. "Did Mrs. Pike *speak* to him when she met him in the freak show?"

Leota had begun to comb Mrs. Fletcher's hair. "I says to her, I says, 'I didn't notice you fallin' on his neck when he was the petrified man—don't tell me you didn't recognize your fine friend?' And she says, 'I didn't recognize him with that white powder all over his face. He just looked familiar.' Mrs. Pike says, 'and lots of people look familiar.' But she says that ole petrified man did put her in mind of somebody. She wondered who it was! Kep' her awake, which man she'd ever knew it reminded her of. So when she seen the photo, it all come to her. Like a flash. Mr. Petrie. The way he'd turn his head and look at her when she took him in his breakfast."

"Took him in his breakfast!" shrieked Mrs. Fletcher. "Listen—don't tell me. I'd a' felt something."

"Four women. I guess those women didn't have the faintest notion at the time they'd be worth a hundred an' twenty-five bucks a piece some day to Mrs. Pike. We ast her how old the fella was then, an' she says he musta had one foot in the grave, at least. Can you beat it?"

"Not really petrified at all, of course," said Mrs. Fletcher meditatively. She drew herself up. "I'd a' felt something," she said proudly.

"Shoot! I did feel somethin'," said Leota. "I tole Fred when I got home I felt so funny. I said, 'Fred, that ole petrified man sure did leave me with a funny feelin.'" He says, 'Funny-haha or funny-peculiar?' and I says, 'Funny-peculiar.'" She pointed her comb into the air emphatically.

"I'll bet you did," said Mrs. Fletcher.

They both heard a crackling noise.

Leota screamed, "Billy Boy! What you doin' in my purse?"

"Aw, I'm just eatin' these ole stale peanuts up," said Billy Boy.

"You come here to me!" screamed Leota, recklessly flinging down the comb, which scattered a whole ashtray full of bobby pins and knocked down a row of Coca-Cola bottles. "This is the last straw!"

"I caught him! I caught him!" giggled Mrs. Fletcher. "I'll hold him on my lap. You bad, bad boy, you! I guess I better learn how to spank little old bad boys," she said.

Leota's eleven o'clock customer pushed open the swing-door upon Leota paddling him heartily with the brush, while he gave angry but belittling screams which penetrated beyond the booth and filled the whole curious beauty parlor. From everywhere ladies began to gather round to watch the paddling. Billy Boy kicked both Leota and Mrs. Fletcher as hard as he could, Mrs. Fletcher with her new fixed smile.

Billy Boy stomped through the group of wildhaired ladies and went out the door, but flung back the words, "If you're so smart, why ain't you rich?"

[1938–U.S.A.]

QUESTIONS

1. What do we learn about Leota and Mrs. Fletcher? What are their emotional lives like? How do they look at things? What generalization can we make about the mental state of each? What, therefore, is our judgment of them to be?
2. What is the mood of the story? In what way does its mood spring from character and help to create the theme?

3. What is the relationship between the story's dialogue and its mood? How does the nature of their dialogue help characterize Leota and Mrs. Fletcher?
4. The state of Leota's purse, the freak show, and the petrified man himself could all be taken as symbols providing mute comment on the intellectual and emotional lives of women before us. How so? In what way does setting also have symbolic value in "Petrified Man"? What do you make of the title in this regard?
5. Katherine Anne Porter described the story at hand as one of "blistering humor and . . . just cruelty." What is Porter pointing to here? What would Welty have us laugh to scorn?

WRITING SUGGESTIONS

1. In a paragraph, briefly describe the intellectual and emotional lives of Leota and Mrs. Fletcher and state how you think we are meant to receive them and what, therefore, the point of the story is.
2. Write a short paper addressed to question 4 above. In order to bring into focus the story's symbolic images, take them for what they are and then look to see the relationship between what each is and the inner lives of Leota and Mrs. Fletcher. In doing so, you will arrive at the symbolic import.

I Want to Know Why

Sherwood Anderson

We got up at four in the morning, that first day in the east. On the evening before we had climbed off a freight train at the edge of town, and with the true instinct of Kentucky boys had found our way across town and to the race track and the stables at once. Then we knew we were all right. Hanley Turner right away found a nigger we knew. It was Bildad Johnson who in the winter works at Ed Becker's livery barn in our home town, Beckersville. Bildad is a good cook as almost all our niggers are and of course he, like everyone in our part of Kentucky who is anyone at all, likes the horses. In the spring Bildad begins to scratch around. A nigger from our country can flatter and wheedle anyone into letting him do most anything he wants. Bildad wheedles the stable men and the trainers from the horse farms in our country around Lexington. The trainers come into town in the evening to stand around and talk and maybe get into a poker game. Bildad gets in with them. He is always doing little favors and telling about things to eat, chicken browned in a pan, and how is the best way to cook sweet potatoes and corn bread. It makes your mouth water to hear him.

When the racing season comes on and the horses go to the races and there is all the talk on the streets in the evenings about the new colts, and everyone says when they are going over to Lexington or to the spring meeting at Churchill Downs or to Latonia, and the horsemen that have been down to New Orleans or maybe at the winter meeting at Havana in Cuba come home to spend a week before they start out again, at such a time when everything talked about in Beckersville is just horses and nothing else and the outfits start out and horse racing is in every breath of air you breathe, Bildad shows up with a job as cook for some outfit. Often when

I think about it, his always going all season to the races and working in
the livery barn in the winter where horses are and where men like to come
and talk about horses, I wish I was a nigger. It's a foolish thing to say, but
that's the way I am about being around horses, just crazy. I can't help it.

Well, I must tell you about what we did and let you in on what I'm
talking about. Four of us boys from Beckersville, all whites and sons of
men who live in Beckersville regular, made up our minds we were going to
the races, not just to Lexington or Louisville, I don't mean, but to the big
eastern track we were always hearing our Beckersville men talk about, to
Saratoga. We were all pretty young then. I was just turned fifteen and I was
the oldest of the four. It was my scheme. I admit that and I talked the
others into trying it. There was Hanley Turner and Henry Rieback and
Tom Tumberton and myself. I had thirty-seven dollars I had earned during
the winter working nights and Saturdays in Enoch Myer's grocery. Henry
Rieback had eleven dollars and the others, Hanley and Tom, had only a
dollar or two each. We fixed it all up and laid low until the Kentucky
spring meetings were over and some of our men, the sportiest ones, the
ones we envied the most, had cut out—then we cut out too.

I won't tell you the trouble we had beating our way on freights and all.
We went through Cleveland and Buffalo and other cities and saw Niagara
Falls. We bought things there, souvenirs and spoons and cards and shells
with pictures of the falls on them for our sisters and mothers, but thought
we had better not send any of the things home. We didn't want to put the
folks on our trail and maybe be nabbed.

We got into Saratoga as I said at night and went to the track. Bildad fed
us up. He showed us a place to sleep in hay over a shed and promised to
keep still. Niggers are all right about things like that. They won't squeal on
you. Often a white man you might meet, when you had run away from
home like that, might appear to be all right and give you a quarter or a
half-dollar or something, and then go right and give you away. White men
will do that, but not a nigger. You can trust them. They are squarer with
kids. I don't know why.

At the Saratoga meeting that year there were a lot of men from home.
Dave Williams and Arthur Mulford and Jerry Myers and others. Then
there was a lot from Louisville and Lexington Henry Rieback knew but I
didn't. They were professional gamblers and Henry Rieback's father is one
too. He is what is called a sheet writer and goes away most of the year to
tracks. In the winter when he is home in Beckersville he don't stay there
much but goes away to cities and deals faro. He is a nice man and
generous, is always sending Henry presents, a bicycle and a gold watch and
a boy scout suit of clothes and things like that.

My own father is a lawyer. He's all right, but don't make much money and can't buy me things and anyway I'm getting so old now I don't expect it. He never said nothing to me against Henry, but Hanley Turner and Tom Tumberton's fathers did. They said to their boys that money so come by is no good and they didn't want their boys brought up to hear gamblers' talk and be thinking about such things and maybe embrace them.

That's all right and I guess the men know what they are talking about, but I don't see what it's got to do with Henry or with horses either. That's what I'm writing this story about. I'm puzzled. I'm getting to be a man and want to think straight and be O.K., and there's something I saw at the race meeting at the eastern track I can't figure out.

I can't help it, I'm crazy about thoroughbred horses. I've always been that way. When I was ten years old and saw I was growing to be big and couldn't be a rider I was so sorry I nearly died. Harry Hellinfinger in Beckersville, whose father is Postmaster, is grown up and too lazy to work, but liked to stand around in the street and get up jokes on boys like sending them to a hardware store for a gimlet to bore square holes and other jokes like that. He played one on me. He told me that if I would eat a half a cigar I would be stunted and not grow any more and maybe could be a rider. I did it. When father wasn't looking I took a cigar out of his pocket and gagged it down some way. It made me awful sick and the doctor had to be sent for, and then it did no good. I kept right on growing. It was a joke. When I told what I had done and why most fathers would have whipped me but mine didn't.

Well, I didn't get stunted and didn't die. It serves Harry Hellinfinger right. Then I made up my mind I would like to be a stable boy, but had to give that up too. Mostly niggers do that work and I knew father wouldn't let me go into it. No use to ask him.

If you've never been crazy about thoroughbreds it's because you've never been around where they are much and don't know any better. They're beautiful. There isn't anything so lovely and clean and full of spunk and honest and everything as some race horses. On the big horse farms that are all around our town Beckersville there are tracks and the horses run in the early morning. More than a thousand times I've got out of bed before daylight and walked two or three miles to the tracks. Mother wouldn't o. et me go but father always says, "Let him alone." So I got some bread out of the bread box and some butter and jam, gobbled it and lit out.

At the tracks you sit on the fence with men, whites and niggers, and they chew tobacco and talk, and then the colts are brought out. It's early and the grass is covered with shiny dew and in another field a man is plowing and they are frying things in a shed where the track niggers sleep, and you know how a nigger can giggle and laugh and say things that make you laugh. A white man can't do it and some niggers can't but a track nigger can every time.

And so the colts are brought out and some are just galloped by stable boys, but almost every morning on a big track owned by a rich man who lives maybe in New York, there are always, nearly every morning, a few colts and some of the old race horses and geldings and mares that are cut loose.

It brings a lump up into my throat when a horse runs. I don't mean all horses but some. I can pick them nearly every time. It's in my blood like in the blood of race track niggers and trainers. Even when they just go slob-jogging along with a little nigger on their backs I can tell a winner. If my throat hurts and it's hard for me to swallow, that's him. He'll run like Sam Hill when you let him out. If he don't win every time it'll be a wonder and because they've got him in a pocket behind another or he was pulled or got off bad at the post or something. If I wanted to be a gambler like Henry Rieback's father I could get rich. I know I could and Henry says so, too. All I would have to do is to wait 'til that hurt comes when I see a horse and then bet every cent. That's what I could do if I wanted to be a gambler, but I don't.

When you're at the tracks in the morning—not the race tracks but the training tracks around Beckersville—you don't see a horse the kind I've been talking about, very often, but it's nice anyway. Any thoroughbred, that is sired right and out of a good mare and trained by a man that knows how, can run. If he couldn't what would he be there for and not pulling a plow?

Well, out of the stables they come and the boys are on their backs and it's lovely to be there. You hunch down on top of the fence and itch inside you. Over in the sheds the niggers giggle and sing. Bacon is being fried and coffee made. Everything smells lovely. Nothing smells better than coffee and manure and horses and niggers and bacon frying and pipes being smoked out of doors on a morning like that. It just gets you, that's what it does.

But about Saratoga. We was there six days and not a soul from home seen us and everything came off just as we wanted it to, fine weather and horses and races and all. We beat our way home and Bildad gave us a basket with fried chicken and bread and other eatables in, and I had eighteen dollars when we got back to Beckersville. Mother jawed and cried but Pop didn't say much. I told everything we done except one thing. I did and saw that alone. That's what I'm writing about. It got me upset. I think about it at night. Here it is.

At Saratoga we laid up nights in the hay in the shed Bildad had showed us and ate with the niggers early and at night when the race people had all gone away. The men from home stayed mostly in the grandstand and betting field, and didn't come out around the places where the horses are kept except to the paddocks just before a race when the horses are saddled. At Saratoga they don't have paddocks under an open shed as at Lexington and Churchill Downs and other tracks down in our country, but saddle the horses right out in an open place under trees on a lawn as smooth and nice as Banker Bohon's front yard here in Beckersville. It's lovely. The horses are sweaty and nervous and shine and the men come out and smoke cigars and look at them and the trainers are there and the owners, and your heart thumps so you can hardly breathe.

Then the bugle blows for post and the boys that ride come running out with their silk clothes on and you run to get a place by the fence with the niggers.

I always am wanting to be a trainer or owner, and at the risk of being seen and caught and sent home I went to the paddocks before every race. The other boys didn't but I did.

We got to Saratoga on a Friday and on Wednesday the next week the big Mullford Handicap was to be run. Middlestride was in it and Sunstreak. The weather was fine and the track fast. I couldn't sleep the night before.

What had happened was that both these horses are the kind it makes my throat hurt to see. Middlestride is long and looks awkward and is a gelding. He belongs to Joe Thompson, a little owner from home who only has a half-dozen horses. The Mullford Handicap is for a mile and Middlestride can't untrack fast. He goes away slow and is always way back at the half, then he begins to run and if the race is a mile and a quarter he'll just eat up everything and get there.

Sunstreak is different. He is a stallion and nervous and belongs on the biggest farm we've got in our country, the Van Riddle place that belongs to Mr. Van Riddle of New York. Sunstreak is like a girl you think about sometimes but never see. He is hard all over and lovely too. When you look at his head you want to kiss him. He is trained by Jerry Tillford who knows me and has been good to me lots of times, lets me walk into a horse's stall to look at him close and other things. There isn't anything as sweet as that horse. He stands at the post quiet and not letting on, but he is just burning up inside. Then when the barrier goes up he is off like his name,

Sunstreak. It makes you ache to see him. It hurts you. He just lays down and runs like a bird dog. There can't anything I ever see run like him except Middlestride when he gets untracked and stretches himself.

Gee! I ached to see that race and those two horses run, ached and dreaded it too. I didn't want to see either of our horses beaten. We had never sent a pair like that to the races before. Old men in Beckersville said so and the niggers said so. It was a fact.

Before the race I went over to the paddocks to see. I looked a last look at Middlestride, who isn't such a much standing in a paddock that way, then I went to see Sunstreak.

It was his day. I knew when I see him. I forgot all about being seen myself and walked right up. All the men from Beckersville were there and no one noticed me except Jerry Tillford. He saw me and something happened. I'll tell you about that.

I was standing looking at that horse and aching. In some way, I can't tell how, I knew just how Sunstreak felt inside. He was quiet and letting the niggers rub his legs and Mr. Van Riddle himself put the saddle on, but he was just a raging torrent inside. He was like the water in the river at Niagara Falls just before it goes plunk down. That horse wasn't thinking about running. He don't have to think about that. He was just thinking about holding himself back 'til the time for the running came. I knew that. I could just in a way see right inside him. He was going to do some awful running and I knew it. He wasn't bragging or letting on much or prancing or making a fuss, but just waiting. I knew it and Jerry Tillford his trainer knew. I looked up and then that man and I looked into each other's eyes. Something happened to me. I guess I loved the man as much as I did the horse because he knew what I knew. Seemed to me there wasn't anything in the world but that man and the horse and me. I cried and Jerry Tillford had a shine in his eyes. Then I came away to the fence to wait for the race. The horse was better than me, more steadier, and now I know better than Jerry. He was the quietest and he had to do the running.

Sunstreak ran first of course and he busted the world's record for a mile. I've seen that if I never see anything more. Everything came out just as I expected. Middlestride got left at the post and was way back and closed up to be second, just as I knew he would. He'll get a world's record too some day. They can't skin the Beckersville country on horses.

I watched the race calm because I knew what would happen. I was sure. Hanley Turner and Henry Rieback and Tom Tumberton were all more excited than me.

A funny thing had happened to me. I was thinking about Jerry Tillford the trainer and how happy he was all through the race. I liked him that afternoon even more than I ever liked my own father. I almost forgot the horses thinking that way about him. It was because of what I had seen in his eyes as he stood in the paddocks beside Sunstreak before the race started. I knew he had been watching and working with Sunstreak since the horse was a baby colt, had taught him to run and be patient and when to let himself out and not to quit, never. I knew that for him it was like a mother seeing her child do something brave or wonderful. It was the first time I ever felt for a man like that.

After the race that night I cut out from Tom and Hanley and Henry. I wanted to be by myself and I wanted to be near Jerry Tillford if I could work it. Here is what happened.

The track in Saratoga is near the edge of town. It is all polished up and trees around, the evergreen kind, and grass and everything painted and nice. If you go past the track you get to a hard road made of asphalt for automobiles, and if you go along this for a few miles there is a road turns off to a little rummy-looking farm house set in a yard.

That night after the race I went along that road because I had seen Jerry and some other men go that way in an automobile. I didn't expect to find them. I walked for a ways and then sat down by a fence to think. It was the direction they went in. I wanted to be as near Jerry as I could. I felt close to him. Pretty soon I went up the side road—I don't know why—and came to the rummy farm house. I was just lonesome to see Jerry, like wanting to see your father at night when you are a young kid. Just then an automobile came along and turned in. Jerry was in it and Henry Rieback's father, and Arthur Bedford from home, and Dave Williams and two other men I didn't know. They got out of the car and went into the house, all but Henry Rieback's father who quarreled with them and said he wouldn't go. It was only about nine o'clock, but they were all drunk and the rummy-looking farm house was a place for bad women to stay in. That's what it was. I crept up along a fence and looked through a window and saw.

It's what give me the fantods. I can't make it out. The women in the house were all ugly mean-looking women, not nice to look at or be near. They were homely too, except one who was tall and looked a little like the gelding Middlestride, but not clean like him, but with a hard ugly mouth. She had red hair. I saw everything plain. I got up by an old rose bush by an open window and looked. The women had on loose dresses and sat around in chairs. The men came in and some sat on the women's laps. The place smelled rotten and there was rotten talk, the kind a kid hears around a livery stable in a town like Beckersville in the winter but don't ever expect to hear talked when there are women around. It was rotten. A nigger wouldn't go into such a place.

I looked at Jerry Tillford. I've told you how I had been feeling about him on account of his knowing what was going on inside of Sunstreak in the minute before he went to the post for the race in which he made a world's record.

Jerry bragged in that bad woman house as I know Sunstreak wouldn't never have bragged. He said that he made that horse, that it was him that won the race and made the record. He lied and bragged like a fool. I never heard such silly talk.

And then, what do you suppose he did! He looked at the woman in there, the one that was lean and hard-mouthed and looked a little like the gelding Middlestride, but not clean like him, and his eyes began to shine just as they did when he looked at me and at Sunstreak in the paddocks at the track in the afternoon. I stood there by the window—gee!—but I wished I hadn't gone away from the tracks, but had stayed with the boys and the niggers and the horses. The tall rotten-looking woman was between us just as Sunstreak was in the paddocks in the afternoon.

Then, all of a sudden, I began to hate that man. I wanted to scream and rush in the room and kill him. I never had such a feeling before. I was so mad clean through that I cried and my fists were doubled up so my finger nails cut my hands.

And Jerry's eyes kept shining and he waved back and forth, and then he went and kissed that woman and I crept away and went back to the tracks and to bed and didn't sleep hardly any, and then next day I got the other kids to start home with me and never told them anything I seen.

I been thinking about it ever since. I can't make it out. Spring has come again and I'm nearly sixteen and go to the tracks mornings same as always, and I see Sunstreak and Middlestride and a new colt named Strident I'll bet will lay them all out, but no one thinks so but me and two or three niggers.

But things are different. At the tracks the air don't taste as good or smell as good. It's because a man like Jerry Tillford, who knows what he does, could see a horse like Sunstreak run, and kiss a woman like that the some day. I can't make it out. Darn him, what did he want to do like that for? I keep thinking about it and it spoils looking at horses and smelling things and hearing niggers laugh and everything. Sometimes I'm so mad about it I want to fight someone. It gives me the fantods. What did he do it for? I want to know why.

[1921–U.S.A.]

QUESTIONS

1. What kind of narration do we have in "I Want to Know Why?" Why is this kind particularly apt for this story?
2. Describe the narrator. By what means is he characterized? Style, certainly, is one. How so? What other means can you point to?
3. How old is the narrator at the time when the story takes place? In what way is his age particularly significant given the story's theme?
4. What is ironic about the story? What kind of irony does it exhibit?
5. What is the general theme of "I Want to Know Why"? In thinking about its theme, consider everything said in the story about the white adult world.

WRITING SUGGESTIONS

1. (a) In a paragraph, discuss and give examples of the main stylistic traits of Anderson's prose in this story: the kinds of sentence used, the many exclamations and digressions, the level of vocabulary. Suggest as well how the story's style is appropriate to its speaker.

   (b) In a separate paragraph, state your response to "I Want to Know Why" and then discuss why you respond as you do.
2. Write a paragraph on yourself at an age when you failed to understand something because of your immaturity. What do you now understand that you didn't then? Has your present understanding changed your outlook in general?
3. In an essay, compare and contrast Anderson's story with Joyce's "Araby" (pages 386–90). Focus on narration and style especially. Try to account for the differences in style by the difference in the ages of the narrators. You might conclude with a judgment as to which story is the more meaningful. If you do, be sure to defend your case.

Bliss

Katherine Mansfield

Although Bertha Young was thirty she still had moments like this when she wanted to run instead of walk, to take dancing steps on and off the pavement, to bowl a hoop, to throw something up in the air and catch it again, or to stand still and laugh at—nothing—at nothing, simply.

What can you do if you are thirty and, turning the corner of your own street, you are overcome, suddenly, by a feeling of bliss—absolute bliss!—as though you'd suddenly swallowed a bright piece of that late afternoon sun and it burned in your bosom, sending out a little shower of sparks into every particle, into every finger and toe? . . .

Oh, is there no way you can express it without being "drunk and disorderly"? How idiotic civilization is! Why be given a body if you have to keep it shut up in a case like a rare, rare fiddle?

"No, that about the fiddle is not quite what I mean," she thought, running up the steps and feeling in her bag for the key—she'd forgotten it, as usual—and rattling the letter-box. "It's not what I mean, because— Thank you, Mary"—she went into the hall. "Is nurse back?"

"Yes, M'm"

"And has the fruit come?"

"Yes, M'm. Everything's come."

"Bring the fruit up to the dining-room, will you? I'll arrange it before I go upstairs."

It was dusky in the dining-room and quite chilly. But all the same Bertha threw off her coat; she could not bear the tight clasp of it another moment, and the cold air fell on her arms.

But in her bosom there was still that bright glowing place—that shower of little sparks coming from it. It was almost unbearable. She hardly dared to breathe for fear of fanning it higher, and yet she breathed deeply, deeply. She hardly dared to look into the cold mirror—but she did look, and it gave her back a woman, radiant, with smiling, trembling lips, with big, dark eyes and an air of listening, waiting for something . . . divine to happen . . . that she knew must happen . . . infallibly.

Mary brought in the fruit on a tray and with it a glass bowl, and a blue dish, very lovely, with a strange sheen on it as though it had been dipped in milk.

"Shall I turn on the light, M'm?"

"No, thank you. I can see quite well."

There were tangerines and apples stained with strawberry pink. Some yellow pears, smooth as silk, some white grapes covered with a silver bloom and a big cluster of purple ones. These last she had bought to tone in with the new dining-room carpet. Yes, that did sound rather far-fetched and absurd, but it was really why she had bought them. She had thought in the shop: "I must have some purple ones to bring the carpet up to the table." And it had seemed quite sense at the time.

When she had finished with them and had made two pyramids of these bright round shapes, she stood away from the table to get the effect—and it really was most curious. For the dark table seemed to melt into the dusky light and the glass dish and the blue bowl to float in the air. This, of course in her present mood, was so incredibly beautiful. . . . She began to laugh.

"No, no. I'm getting hysterical." And she seized her bag and coat and ran upstairs to the nursery.

Nurse sat at a low table giving Little B her supper after her bath. The baby had on a white flannel gown and a blue woollen jacket, and her dark, fine hair was brushed up into a funny little peak. She looked up when she saw her mother and began to jump.

"Now, my lovely, eat it up like a good girl," said Nurse, setting her lips in a way that Bertha knew, and that meant she had come into the nursery at another wrong moment.

"Has she been good, Nanny?"

"She's been a little sweet all the afternoon," whispered Nanny. "We went to the park and I sat down on a chair and took her out of the pram and a big dog came along and put its head on my knee and she clutched its ear, tugged it. Oh, you should have seen her."

Bertha wanted to ask if it wasn't rather dangerous to let her clutch at a strange dog's ear. But she did not dare to. She stood watching them, her hands by her side, like the poor little girl in front of the rich little girl with the doll.

The baby looked up at her again, stared, and then smiled so charmingly that Bertha couldn't help crying:

"Oh, Nanny, do let me finish giving her her supper while you put the bath things away."

"Well, M'm, she oughtn't to be changed hands while she's eating," said Nanny, still whispering. "It unsettles her; it's very likely to upset her."

How absurd it was. Why have a baby if it had to be kept—not in a case like a rare, rare fiddle—but in another woman's arms?

"Oh, I must!" said she.

Very offended, Nanny handed her over.

"Now, don't excite her after her supper. You know you do, M'm. And I have such a time with her after!"

Thank heaven! Nanny went out of the room with the bath towels.

"Now I've got you to myself, my little precious," said Bertha, as the baby leaned against her.

She ate delightfully, holding up her lips for the spoon and then waving her hands. Sometimes she wouldn't let the spoon go; and sometimes, just as Bertha had filled it, she waved it away to the four winds.

When the soup was finished Bertha turned round to the fire.

"You're nice—you're very nice!" said she, kissing her warm baby. "I'm fond of you. I like you."

And, indeed, she loved Little B so much—her neck as she bent forward, her exquisite toes as they shone transparent in the firelight—that all her feeling of bliss came back again, and again she didn't know how to express it—what to do with it.

"You're wanted on the telephone," said Nanny, coming back in triumph and seizing *her* Little B.

Down she flew. It was Harry.

"Oh, is that you, Ber? Look here. I'll be late. I'll take a taxi and come along as quickly as I can, but get dinner put back ten minutes—will you? All right?"

"Yes, perfectly. Oh, Harry!"

"Yes?"

What had she to say? She'd nothing to say. She only wanted to get in touch with him for a moment. She couldn't absurdly cry: "Hasn't it been a divine day!"

"What is it?" rapped out the little voice.

"Nothing. *Entendu*," said Bertha, and hung up the receiver, thinking how more than idiotic civilization was.

They had people coming to dinner. The Norman Knights—a very sound couple—he was about to start a theatre, and she was awfully keen on interior decoration, a young man, Eddie Warren, who had just published a little book of poems and whom everybody was asking to dine, and a "find" of Bertha's called Pearl Fulton. What Miss Fulton did, Bertha didn't know. They had met at the club and Bertha had fallen in love with her, as she always did fall in love with beautiful women who had something strange about them.

The provoking thing was that, though they had been about together and met a number of times and really talked, Bertha couldn't yet make her out. Up to a certain point Miss Fulton was rarely, wonderfully frank, but the certain point was there, and beyond that she would not go.

Was there anything beyond it? Harry said "No." Voted her dullish, and "cold like all blond women, with a touch, perhaps, of anaemia of the brain." But Bertha wouldn't agree with him; not yet, at any rate.

"No, the way she has of sitting with her head a little on one side, and smiling, has something behind it, Harry, and I must find out what that something is."

"Most likely it's a good stomach," answered Harry.

He made a point of catching Bertha's heels with replies of that kind . . . "liver frozen, my dear girl," or "pure flatulence," or "kidney disease," . . . and so on. For some strange reason Bertha liked this, and almost admired it in him very much.

She went into the drawing-room and lighted the fire; then, picking up the cushions, one by one, that Mary had disposed so carefully, she threw them back on to the chairs and the couches. That made all the difference; the room came alive at once. As she was about to throw the last one she surprised herself by suddenly hugging it to her, passionately, passionately. But it did not put out the fire in her bosom. Oh, on the contrary!

The windows of the drawing-room opened on to a balcony overlooking the garden. At the far end, against the wall, there was a tall, slender pear tree in fullest, richest bloom; it stood perfect, as though becalmed against the jade-green sky. Bertha couldn't help feeling, even from this distance, that it had not a single bud or a faded petal. Down below, in the garden beds, the red and yellow tulips, heavy with flowers, seemed to lean upon the dusk. A grey cat, dragging its belly, crept across the lawn, and a black one, its shadow, trailed after. The sight of them, so intent and so quick, gave Bertha a curious shiver.

"What creepy things cats are!" she stammered, and she turned away from the window and began walking up and down. . . .

How strong the jonquils smelled in the warm room. Too strong? Oh, no. And yet, as though overcome, she flung down on a couch and pressed her hands to her eyes.

"I'm too happy—too happy!" she murmured.

And she seemed to see on her eyelids the lovely pear tree with its wide open blossoms as a symbol of her own life.

Really—really—she had everything. She was young. Harry and she were as much in love as ever, and they got on together splendidly and were really good pals. She had an adorable baby. They didn't have to worry about money. They had this absolutely satisfactory house and garden. And friends—modern, thrilling friends, writers and painters and poets or people keen on social questions—just the kind of friends they wanted. And then there were books, and there was music, and she had found a wonderful little dressmaker, and they were going abroad in the summer, and their new cook made the most superb omelettes. . . .

"I'm absurd. Absurd!" She sat up; but she felt quite dizzy, quite drunk. It must have been the spring.

Yes, it was the spring. Now she was so tired she could not drag herself upstairs to dress.

A white dress, a string of jade beads, green shoes and stockings. It wasn't intentional. She had thought of this scheme hours before she stood at the drawing-room window.

Her petals rustled softly into the hall, and she kissed Mrs. Norman Knight, who was taking off the most amusing orange coat with a procession of black monkeys round the hem and up the fronts.

". . . Why! Why! is the middle-class so stodgy—so utterly without a sense of humour! My dear, it's only by a fluke that I am here at all—Norman being the protective fluke. For my darling monkeys so upset the train that it rose to a man and simply ate me with its eyes. Didn't laugh—wasn't amused—that I should have loved. No, just stared—and bored me through and through."

"But the cream of it was," said Norman, pressing a large tortoiseshell-rimmed monocle into his eye, "you don't mind me telling this, Face, do you?" (In their home and among their friends they called each other Face and Mug.) "The cream of it was when she, being full fed, turned to the woman beside her and said: 'Haven't you ever seen a monkey before?'"

"Oh, yes!" Mrs. Norman Knight joined in the laughter. "Wasn't that too absolutely creamy?"

And a funnier thing still was that now her coat was off she did look like a very intelligent monkey—who had even made that yellow silk dress out of scraped banana skins. And her amber ear-rings; they were like little dangling nuts.

"This is a sad, sad fall!" said Mug, pausing in front of Little B's perambulator. "When the perambulator comes into the hall—" and he waved the rest of the quotation away.

The bell rang. It was lean, pale Eddie Warren (as usual) in a state of acute distress.

"It *is* the right house, *isn't* it?" he pleaded.

"Oh, I think so—I hope so," said Bertha brightly.

"I have had such a *dreadful* experience with a taxi-man; he was *most* sinister. I couldn't get him to *stop*. The *more* I knocked and called the *faster* he went. And *in* the moonlight this *bizarre* figure with the *flattened head crouching* over the *lit tle* wheel. . . ."

He shuddered, taking off an immense white silk scarf. Bertha noticed that his socks were white, too—most charming.

"But how dreadful!" she cried.

"Yes, it really was," said Eddie, following her into the drawing-room. "I saw myself *driving* through Eternity in a *timeless* taxi."

He knew the Norman Knights. In fact, he was going to write a play for N. K. when the theatre scheme came off.

"Well, Warren, how's the play?" said Norman Knight, dropping his monocle and giving his eye a moment in which to rise to the surface before it was screwed down again.

And Mrs. Norman Knight: "Oh, Mr. Warren, what happy socks!"

"I *am* so glad you like them," said he, staring at his feet. "They seem to have got so *much* whiter since the moon rose." And he turned his lean sorrowful young face to Bertha. "There *is* a moon, you know."

She wanted to cry: "I am sure there is—often—often!"

He really was a most attractive person. But so was Face, crouched before the fire in her banana skins, and so was Mug, smoking a cigarette and saying as he flicked the ash: "Why doth the bridegroom tarry?"

"There he is, now."

Bang went the front door open and shut. Harry shouted: "Hullo, you people. Down in five minutes." And they heard him swarm up the stairs. Bertha couldn't help smiling; she knew how he loved doing things at high pressure. What, after all, did an extra five minutes matter? But he would pretend to himself that they mattered beyond measure. And then he would make a great point of coming into the drawing-room, extravagantly cool and collected.

Harry had such a zest for life. Oh, how she appreciated it in him. And his passion for fighting—for seeking in everything that came up against him another test of his power and of his courage—that, too, she understood. Even when it made him just occasionally, to other people, who didn't know him well, a little ridiculous perhaps. . . . For there were moments when he rushed into battle where no battle was. . . . She talked and laughed and positively forgot until he had come in (just as she had imagined) that Pearl Fulton had not turned up.

"I wonder if Miss Fulton has forgotten?"

"I expect so," said Harry. "Is she on the 'phone?"

"Ah! There's a taxi, now." And Bertha smiled with that little air of proprietorship that she always assumed while her women finds were new and mysterious. "She lives in taxis."

"She'll run to fat if she does," said Harry coolly, ringing the bell for dinner. "Frightful danger for blond women."

"Harry—don't," warned Bertha, laughing up at him.

Came another tiny moment, while they waited, laughing and talking, just a trifle too much at their ease, a trifle too unaware. And then Miss Fulton, all in silver, with a silver fillet binding her pale blond hair, came in smiling, her head a little on one side.

"Am I late?"

"No, not at all," said Bertha. "Come along." And she took her arm and they moved into the dining-room.

What was there in the touch of that cool arm that could fan—fan—start blazing—blazing—the fire of bliss that Bertha did not know what to do with?

Miss Fulton did not look at her; but then she seldom did look at people directly. Her heavy eyelids lay upon her eyes and the strange half smile came and went upon her lips as though she lived by listening rather than seeing. But Bertha knew, suddenly, as if the longest, most intimate look had passed between them—as if they had said to each other: "You, too?—that Pearl Fulton, stirring the beautiful red soup in the grey plate, was feeling just what she was feeling.

And the others? Face and Mug, Eddie and Harry, their spoons rising and falling—dabbing their lips with their napkins, crumbling bread, fiddling with the forks and glasses and talking.

"I met her at the Alpha show—the weirdest little person. She'd not only cut off her hair, but she seemed to have taken a dreadfully good snip of her legs and arms and her neck and her poor little nose as well."

"Isn't she very *liée* with Michael Oat?"

"The man who wrote *Love in False Teeth?*"

"He wants to write a play for me. One act. One man. Decides to commit suicide. Gives all the reasons why he should and why he shouldn't. And just as he has made up his mind either to do it or not to do it—curtain. Not half a bad idea."

"What's he going to call it—'Stomach Trouble'?"

"I *think* I've come across the *same* idea in a lit-tle French review, *quite* unknown in England."

No, they didn't share it. They were dears—dears—and she loved having them there, at her table, and giving them delicious food and wine. In fact, she longed to tell them how delightful they were, and what a decorative group they made, how they seemed to set one another off and how they reminded her of a play by Tchekof!

Harry was enjoying his dinner. It was part of his—well, not his nature, exactly, and certainly not his pose—his—something or other—to talk about food and to glory in his "shameless passion for the white flesh of the lobster" and "the green of pistachio ices—green and cold like the eyelids of Egyptian dancers."

When he looked up at her and said: "Bertha, this is a very admirable *soufflée!*" She almost could have wept with child-like pleasure.

Oh, why did she feel so tender towards the whole world tonight? Everything was good—was right. All that happened seemed to fill again her brimming cup of bliss.

And still, in the back of her mind, there was the pear tree. It would be silver now, in the light of poor dear Eddie's moon, silver as Miss Fulton, who sat there turning a tangerine in her slender fingers that were so pale a light seemed to come from them.

What she simply couldn't make out—what was miraculous—was how she should have guessed Miss Fulton's mood so exactly and so instantly. For she never doubted for a moment that she was right, and yet what had she to go on? Less than nothing.

"I believe this does happen very, very rarely between women. Never between men," thought Bertha. "But while I am making the coffee in the drawing-room perhaps she will 'give a sign.'"

What she meant by that she did not know, and what would happen after that she could not imagine.

While she thought like this she saw herself talking and laughing. She had to talk because of her desire to laugh.

"I must laugh or die."

But when she noticed Face's funny little habit of tucking something down the front of her bodice—as if she kept a tiny, secret hoard of nuts there, too—Bertha had to dig her nails into her hands—so as not to laugh too much.

It was over at last. And: "Come and see my new coffee machine," said Bertha.

"We only have a new coffee machine once a fortnight," said Harry. Face took her arm this time; Miss Fulton bent her head and followed after.

The fire had died down in the drawing-room to a red, flickering "nest of baby phoenixes," said Face.

"Don't turn up the light for a moment. It is so lovely." And down she crouched by the fire again. She was always cold . . . "without her little red flannel jacket, of course," thought Bertha.

At that moment Miss Fulton "gave the sign."

"Have you a garden?" said the cool, sleepy voice.

This was so exquisite on her part that all Bertha could do was to obey. She crossed the room, pulled the curtains apart, and opened those long windows.

"There!" she breathed.

And the two women stood side by side looking at the slender, flowering tree. Although it was so still it seemed, like the flame of a candle, to stretch up, to point, to quiver in the bright air, to grow taller and taller as they gazed—almost to touch the rim of the round, silver moon.

How long did they stand there? Both, as it were, caught in that circle of unearthly light, understanding each other perfectly, creatures of another world, and wondering what they were to do in this one with all this blissful treasure that burned in their bosoms and dropped, in silver flowers, from their hair and hands?

For ever—for a moment? And did Miss Fulton murmur: "Yes. Just *that*." Or did Bertha dream it?

Then the light was snapped on and Face made the coffee and Harry said: "My dear Mrs. Knight, don't ask me about my baby. I never see her. I shan't feel the slightest interest in her until she has a lover," and Mug took his eye out of the conservatory for a moment and then put it under glass again and Eddie Warren drank his coffee and set down the cup with a face of anguish as though he had drunk and seen the spider.

"What I want to do is to give the young men a show. I believe London is simply teeming with first-chop, unwritten plays. What I want to say to 'em is: 'Here's the theatre. Fire ahead.'"

"You know, my dear, I am going to decorate a room for the Jacob Nathans. Oh, I am so tempted to do a fried-fish scheme, with the backs of the chairs shaped like frying pans and lovely chip potatoes embroidered all over the curtains."

"The trouble with our young writing men is that they are still too romantic. You can't put out to sea without being seasick and wanting a basin. Well, why won't they have the courage of those basins?"

"A *dreadful* poem about a *girl* who was *violated* by a beggar *without* a nose in a lit-tle wood. . . ."

Miss Fulton sank into the lowest, deepest chair and Harry handed round the cigarettes.

From the way he stood in front of her shaking the silver box and saying abruptly: "Egyptian? Virginia? The're all mixed up," Bertha realized that she not only bored him; he really disliked her. And she decided from the way Miss Fulton said: "No, thank you, I won't smoke," that she felt it, too, and was hurt.

"Oh, Harry, don't dislike her. You are quite wrong about her. She's wonderful, wonderful. And besides, how can you feel so differently about someone who means so much to me? I shall try to tell you when we are in bed to-night what has been happening. What she and I have shared."

At those last words something strange and almost terrifying darted into Bertha's mind. And this something blind and smiling whispered to her: "Soon these people will go. The house will be quiet—quiet. The lights will be out. And you and he will be alone together in the dark room—the warm bed. . . ."

She jumped up from her chair and ran over to the piano.

"What a pity someone does not play!" she cried. "What a pity somebody does not play."

For the first time in her life Bertha Young desired her husband.

Oh, she'd loved him—she'd been in love with him, of course, in every other way, but just not in that way. And, equally, of course, she'd understood that he was different. They'd discussed it so often. It had worried her dreadfully at first to find that she was so cold, but after a time it had not seemed to matter. They were so frank with each other—such good pals. That was the best of being modern.

But now—ardently! ardently! The word ached in her ardent body! Was this what that feeling of bliss had been leading up to? But then, then—

"My dear," said Mrs. Norman Knight, "you know our shame. We are the victims of time and train. We live in Hampstead. It's been so nice."

"I'll come with you into the hall," said Bertha. "I loved having you. But you must not miss the last train. That's so awful, isn't it?"

"Have a whisky, Knight, before you go?" called Harry.

"No, thanks, old chap."

Bertha squeezed his hand for that as she shook it.

"Good night, good-bye," she cried from the top step, feeling that this self of hers was taking leave of them for ever.

When she got back into the drawing-room the others were on the move.

". . . Then you can come part of the way in my taxi."

"I shall be *so* thankful *not* to have to face *another* drive *alone* after my *dreadful* experience."

"You can get a taxi at the rank just at the end of the street. You won't have to walk more than a few yards."

"That's a comfort. I'll go and put on my coat."

Miss Fulton moved towards the hall and Bertha was following when Harry almost pushed past.

"Let me help you."

Bertha knew that he was repenting his rudeness—she let him go. What a boy he was in some ways—so impulsive—so—simple.

And Eddie and she were left by the fire.

"I *wonder* if you have seen Bilks' *new* poem called *Table d'Hôte*," said Eddie softly. "It's *so* wonderful. In the last Anthology. Have you got a copy? I'd *so* like to *show* it to you. It begins with an *incredibly* beautiful line: 'Why Must it Always be Tomato Soup?'"

"Yes," said Bertha. And she moved noiselessly to a table opposite the drawing-room door and Eddie glided noiselessly after her. She picked up the little book and gave it to him; they had not made a sound.

While he looked it up she turned her head towards the hall. And she saw . . . Harry with Miss Fulton's coat in his arms and Miss Fulton with her back turned to him and her head bent. He tossed the coat away, put his hands on her shoulders and turned her violently to him. His lips said: "I adore you," and Miss Fulton laid her moonbeam fingers on his cheeks and smiled her sleepy smile. Harry's nostrils quivered; his lips curled back in a hideous grin while he whispered: "To-morrow," and with her eyelids Miss Fulton said: "Yes."

"Here it is," said Eddie. "'Why Must it Always be Tomato Soup?' It's so *deeply* true, don't you feel? Tomato Soup is so *dreadfully* eternal."

"If you prefer," said Harry's voice, very loud, from the hall, "I can phone you a cab to come to the door."

"Oh, no. It's not necessary," said Miss Fulton, and she came up to Bertha and gave her the slender fingers to hold.

"Good-bye. Thank you so much."

"Good-bye," said Bertha.

Miss Fulton held her hand a moment longer.

"Your lovely pear tree!" she murmured.

And then she was gone, with Eddie following, like the black cat following the grey cat.

"I'll shut up shop," said Harry, extravagantly cool and collected.

"Your lovely pear tree—pear tree—pear tree!"

Bertha simply ran over to the long windows.

"Oh, what is going to happen now?" she cried.

But the pear tree was as lovely as ever and as full of flower and as still.

[1917–Great Britain]

QUESTIONS

1. "Bliss" is all atmosphere and mood. How does Mansfield convey the mood pointed to by her title? For instance, what concrete details does she use?
2. How does the style of the story with respect to sentence structure also help in conveying mood? What is the effect of the many short sentences here and the many dashes?
3. What kind of narration does "Bliss" exhibit? Why is this kind particularly suited to the story's aim and focus? Why might first-person narration be less effective?
4. Irony compounds irony at the end of the story. What strikes you as ironic? Why is it ironic that Bertha should find out about her husband's infidelity on this particular day?
5. Both Bertha and Miss Fulton find a focus of feeling in the pear tree. Why? What symbolic value does the tree have for them?
6. Why the "But" of the story's last sentence? How do you take the sentence as a whole? What theme does it suggest having to do with bliss, nature, and human beings?

WRITING SUGGESTIONS

1. In a paragraph or short essay, discuss how Mansfield conveys mood in this story and how its mood is related to the theme.
2. Have you ever felt blissful? If so, write a description of the feeling concretely. Tell where you were and whether you were alone or with others. What did your body feel like, what was the weather like, and so forth? Can you think of any figures of speech that might help communicate the feeling? Perhaps even your

sentence structure could convey feeling. In any event, see what you can do in capturing the feeling on paper. Whether or not you succeed, you should come to a better understanding of the nature and challenge of literary art.

3. There are four shorter stories by Mansfield earlier in the book (check the index under "Mansfield"). Read all four and, keeping "Bliss" in mind, draw some conclusions about Mansfield's style, characteristic subject matter, thematic interests, general view of things, and so forth. Now write an essay in which you state and then support your conclusions point by point.

The Tree of Knowledge

Henry James

1

It was one of the secret opinions, such as we all have, of Peter Brench that his main success in life would have consisted in his never having committed himself about the work, as it was called, of his friend Morgan Mallow. This was a subject on which it was, to the best of his belief, impossible with veracity to quote him, and it was nowhere on record that he had, in the connection, on any occasion and in any embarrassment, either lied or spoken the truth. Such a triumph had its honor even for a man of other triumphs—a man who had reached fifty, who had escaped marriage, who had lived within his means, who had been in love with Mrs. Mallow for years without breathing it, and who, last not least, had judged himself once for all. He had so judged himself in fact that he felt an extreme and general humility to be his proper portion; yet there was nothing that made him think so well of his parts as the course he had steered so often through the shallows just mentioned. It became thus a real wonder that the friends in whom he had most confidence were just those with whom he had most reserves. He couldn't tell Mrs. Mallow—or at least he supposed, excellent man, he couldn't—that she was the one beautiful reason he had never married; any more than he could tell her husband that the sight of the multiplied marbles in that gentleman's studio was an affliction of which even time had never blunted the edge. His victory, however, as I have intimated, in regard to these productions, was not simply in his not having let it out that he deplored them; it was, remarkably, in his not having kept it in by anything else.

The whole situation, among these good people, was verily a marvel, and there was probably not such another for a long way from the spot that engages us—the point at which the soft declivity of Hampstead began at that time to confess in broken accents to Saint John's Wood. He despised Mallow's statues and adored Mallow's wife, and yet was distinctly fond of Mallow, to whom, in turn, he was equally dear. Mrs. Mallow rejoiced in the statues—though she preferred, when pressed, the busts; and if she was visibly attached to Peter Brench it was because of his affection for Morgan. Each loved the other moreover for the love borne in each case to Lancelot, whom the Mallows respectively cherished as their only child and whom the friend of their fireside identified as the third—but decidedly the handsomest—of his godsons. Already in the old years it had come to that—that no one, for such a relation, could possibly have occured to any of them, even to the baby itself, but Peter. There was luckily a certain independence, of the pecuniary sort, all round: the Master could never otherwise have spent his solemn *Wanderjahre* in Florence and Rome, and continued by the Thames as well as by the Arno and the Tiber to add unpurchased group to group and model, for what was too apt to prove in the event mere love, fancy-heads of celebrities either too busy or too buried—too much of the age or too little of it—to sit. Neither could Peter, lounging in almost daily, have found time to keep the whole complicated tradition so alive by his presence. He was massive but mild, the depositary of these mysteries—large and loose and ruddy and curly, with deep tones, deep eyes, deep pockets, to say nothing of the habit of long pipes, soft hats and brownish grayish weather-faded clothes, apparently always the same.

He had "written," it was known, but had never spoken, never spoken in particular of that; and he had the air (since, as was believed, he continued to write) of keeping it up in order to have something more—as if he hadn't at the worst enough—to be silent about. Whatever his air, at any rate, Peter's occasional unmentioned prose and verse were quite truly the result of an impluse to maintain the purity of his taste by establishing still more firmly the right relation of fame to feebleness. The little green door of his domain was in a garden wall on which the discolored stucco made patches, and in the small detached villa behind it everything was old, the furniture, the servants, the books, the prints, the immemorial habits and the new improvements. The Mallows, at Carrara Lodge, were within ten minutes, and the studio there was on their little land, to which they had added, in their happy faith, for building it. This was the good fortune, if it was not the ill, of her having brought him in marriage a portion that put them in a manner at their ease and enabled them thus, on their side, to keep it up. And they did keep it up—they always had—the infatuated sculptor and his wife, for whom nature had refined on the impossible by relieving them of the sense of the difficult. Morgan had at all events everything of the sculptor but the spirit of Phidias—the brown velvet, the becoming *beretto*, the "plastic" presence, the fine fingers, the beautiful accent in Italian and the old Italian factotum. He seemed to make up for everything when he addressed Egidio with the "tu" and waved him to turn one of the rotary pedestals of which the place was full. They were tremendous Italians at Carrara Lodge, and the secret of the part played by this fact in Peter's life was in a large degree that it gave him, sturdy Briton as he was, just the amount of "going abroad" he could bear. The Mallows were all his Italy, but it was in a measure for Italy he liked them. His one worry was that Lance—to which they had shortened his godson—was, in spite of a public school, perhaps a shade too Italian. Morgan meanwhile looked like somebody's flattering idea of somebody's own person as expressed in the great room provided at the Uffizzi Museum for the general illustration of that idea by eminent hands. The Master's sole regret that he hadn't been born rather to the brush than to the chisel sprang from his wish that he might have contributed to that collection.

It appeared with time at any rate to be to the brush that Lance had been born; for Mrs. Mallow, one day when the boy was turning twenty, broke it to their friend, who shared, to the last delicate morsel, their problems and pains, that it seemed as if nothing would really do but that he should embrace the career. It had been impossible longer to remain blind to the fact that he was gaining no glory at Cambridge, where Brench's own college had for a year tempered its tone to him as for Brench's own sake. Therefore why renew the vain form of preparing him for the impossible? The impossible—it had become clear—was that he should be anything but an artist.

"Oh dear, dear!" said poor Peter.

"Don't you believe in it?" asked Mrs. Mallow, who still, at more than forty, had her violet velvet eyes, her creamy satin skin and her silken chestnut hair.

"Believe in what?"

"Why in Lance's passion."

"I don't know what you mean by 'believing in it.' I've never been unaware, certainly, of his disposition, from his earliest time, to daub and draw; but I confess I've hoped it would burn out."

"But why should it," she sweetly smiled, "with his wonderful heredity? Passion is passion—though of course indeed *you*, dear Peter, know nothing of that. Has the Master's ever burned out?'

Peter looked off a little and, in his familiar formless way, kept up for a moment a sound between a smothered whistle and a subdued hum. "Do you think he's going to be another Master?"

She seemed scarce prepared to go that length, yet she had on the whole a marvelous trust. "I know what you mean by that. Will it be a career to incur the jealousies and provoke the machinations that have been at times almost too much for his father? Well—say it may be, since nothing but claptrap, in these dreadful days, *can*, it would seem, make its way, and since, with the curse of refinement and distinction, one may easily find one's self begging one's bread. Put it at the worst—say he has the misfortune to wing his flight further than the vulgar taste of his stupid countrymen can follow. Think, all the same, of the happiness—the same the Master has had. He'll *know*."

Peter looked rueful. "Ah but *what* will he know?"

"Quiet joy!" cried Mrs. Mallow, quite impatient and turning away.

2

He had of course before long to meet the boy himself on it and to hear that practically everything was settled. Lance was not to go up again, but to go instead to Paris where, since the die was cast, he would find the best advantages. Peter had always felt he must be taken as he was, but had never perhaps found him so much of that pattern as on this occasion. "You chuck Cambridge then altogether? Doesn't that seem rather a pity?"

Lance would have been like his father, to his friend's sense, had he had less humor, and like his mother had he had more beauty. Yet it was a good middle way for Peter that, in the modern manner, he was, to the eye, rather the young stockbroker than the young artist. The youth reasoned that it was a question of time—there was such a mill to go through, such an awful lot to learn. He had talked with fellows and had judged. "One has got, today," he said, "don't you see? to know."

His interlocutor, at this, gave a groan. "Oh hang it, *don't* know!"

Lance wondered. "'Don't'? Then what's the use—?"

"The use of what?"

"Why of anything. Don't you think I've talent?"

Peter smoked away for a little in silence; then went on; "It isn't knowledge, it's ignorance that—as we've been beautifully told—is bliss."

"Don't you think I've talent," Lance repeated.

Peter, with his trick of queer kind demonstrations, passed his arm round his godson and held him a moment. "How do I know?"

"Oh," said the boy, "if it's your own ignorance you're defending?—"

Again, for a pause, on the sofa, his godfather smoked. "It isn't. I've the misfortune to be omniscient."

"Oh well," Lance laughed agian, "if you know *too* much—!"

"That's what I do, and it's why I'm so wretched."

Lance's gaiety grew. "Wretched? Come, I say!"

"But I forgot," his companion went on—"you're not to know about that. It would indeed for you too make the too much. Only I'll tell you what I'll do." And Peter got up from the sofa. "If you'll go up again I'll pay your way at Cambridge."

Lance stared, a little rueful in spite of being still more amused. "Oh Peter! You disapprove so of Paris?"

"Well, I'm afraid of it."

"Ah, I see!"

"No, you don't see—yet. But you will—that is you would. And you mustn't."

The young man thought more gravely. "But one's innocence, already—!"

"Is considerably damaged? Ah that won't matter," Peter persisted— "we'll patch it up here."

"Here? Then you want me to stay at home?"

Peter almost confessed to it. "Well, we're so right—we four together—just as we are. We're so safe. Come, don't spoil it."

The boy, who had turned to gravity, turned from this, on the real pressure in his friend's tone, to consternation. "Then what's a fellow to be?"

"My particular care. Come, old man"—and Peter now fairly pleaded—"*I'll* look out for you."

Lance, who had remained on the sofa with his legs out and his hands in his pockets, watched him with eyes that showed suspicion. Then he got up. "You think there's something the matter with me—that I can't make a success."

"Well, what do you call a success?"

Lance thought again. "Why the best sort, I suppose, is to please one's self. Isn't that the sort that, in spite of cabals and things, is—in his own peculiar line—the Master's?

There were so much too many things in this question to be answered at once that they practically checked the discussion, which became particularly difficult in the light of such renewed proof that, though the young man's innocence might, in the course of his studies, as he contended, somewhat have shrunken, the finer essence of it still remained. That was indeed exactly what Peter had assumed and what above all he desired; yet perversely enough it gave him a chill. The boy believed in the cabals and things, believed in the peculiar line, believed, to be brief, in the Master. What happened a month or two later wasn't that he went up again at the expense of his godfather, but that a fortnight after he had got settled in Paris this personage sent him fifty pounds.

He had meanwhile at home, this personage, made up his mind to the worst; and what might be had never yet grown quite so vivid to him as when, on his presenting himself one Sunday night, as he never failed to do, for supper, the mistress of Carrara Lodge met him with an appeal as to—of all things in the world— the wealth of the Canadians. She was earnest, she was even excited. "Are many of them *really* rich?"

He had to confess he knew nothing about them, but he often thought afterwards of that evening. The room in which they sat was adorned with sundry specimens of the Master's genius, which had the merit of being, as Mrs. Mallow herself frequently suggested, of an unusually convenient size. They were indeed of dimensions not customary in the products of the chisel, and they had the singularity that, if the objects and features intended to be small looked too large, the objects and features intended to be large looked too small. The Master's idea, either in respect to this matter or to any other, had in almost any case, even after years, remained undiscoverable to Peter Brench. The creations that so failed to reveal it stood about on pedestals and brackets, on tables and shelves, a little staring white population, heroic, idyllic, allegoric, mythic, symbolic, in which "scale" had so strayed and lost itself that the public square and the chimney piece seemed to have changed places, the monumental being all diminutive and the dimunitive all monumental; branches at any rate, markedly, of a family in which stature was rather oddly irrespective of function, age, and sex. They formed, like the Mallows themselves, poor Brench's own family—having at least to such a degree the note of familiarity. The occasion was one of those he had long ago learned to know and to name—short flickers of the faint flame, soft gusts of a kinder air. Twice a year regularly the Master believed in his fortune, in addition to believing all the year round in his genius. This time it was to be made by a bereaved couple from Toronto, who had given him the handsomest order for a tomb to three lost children, each of whom they desired to see, in the composition, emblematically and characteristically represented.

Such was naturally the moral of Mrs. Mallow's question: if their wealth was to be assumed, it was clear, from the nature of their admiration, as well as from mysterious hints thrown out (they were a little odd!) as to other possibilites for the same mortuary sort, that their further patronage might be; and not less evident that should the Master become at

all known in those climes nothing would be more inevitable than a run of
Canadian custom. Peter had been present before at runs of custom,
colonial and domestic—present at each of those of which the aggregation
had left so few gaps in the marble company round him; but it was his habit
never at these junctures to prick the bubble in advance. The fond illusion,
while it lasted, eased the wound of elections never won, the long ache of
medals and diplomas carried off, on every chance, by everyone but the
Master; it moreover lighted the lamp that would glimmer through the next
eclipse. They lived, however, after all—as it was always beautiful to
see—at a height scarce susceptible to ups and downs. They strained a
point at times charmingly, strained it to admit that the public was here and
there not too bad to buy; but they would have been nowhere without their
attitude that the Master was always too good to sell. They were at all events
deliciously formed, Peter often said to himself, for their fate; the Master
had a vanity, his wife had a loyalty, of which success, depriving these
things of innocence, would have diminished the merit and the grace.
Anyone could be charming under a charm, and as he looked about him
at a world of prosperity more void of proportion even than the Master's
museum he wondered if he knew another pair that so completely escaped
vulgarity.

"What a pity Lance isn't with us to rejoice!" Mrs. Mallow on this
occasion sighed at supper.

"We'll drink to the health of the absent," her husband replied, filling
his friend's glass and his own and giving a drop to their companion; "but
we must hope he's preparing himself for a happiness much less like this of
ours this evening—excusable as I grant it to be!—than like the comfort we
have always (whatever has happened or has not happened) been able to
trust ourselves to enjoy. The comfort," the Master explained, leaning back
in the pleasant lamplight and firelight, holding up his glass and looking
round at his marble family, quartered more or less, a monstrous brood, in
every room—"the comfort of art in itself!"

Peter looked a little shyly at his wine. "Well—I don't care what you
may call it when a fellow doesn't—but Lance must learn to *sell*, you
know. I drink to his acquisition of the secret of a base popularity!"

"Oh, yes, *he* must sell," the boy's mother, who was still more,
however, this seemed to give out, the Master's wife, rather artlessly
allowed.

"Ah," the sculptor after a moment confidently pronounced, "Lance
will. Don't be afraid. He'll have learned."

"Which is exactly what Peter," Mrs. Mallow gaily returned—"why in
the world were you so perverse, Peter?—wouldn't when he told him
hear of."

Peter, when this lady looked at him with accusatory affection—a grace on her part not infrequent—could never find a word; but the Master, who was always all amenity and tact, helped him out now as he had often helped him before. "That's his old idea, you know—on which we've so often differed: his theory that the artist should be all impulse and instinct. *I* go in of course for a certain amount of school. Not too much—but a due proportion. There's where his protest came in," he continued to explain to his wife, "as against what *might*, don't you see? be in question for Lance."

"Ah well"—and Mrs. Mallow turned the violet eyes across the table at the subject of this discourse—"he's sure to have meant of course nothing but good. Only that wouldn't have prevented him, if Lance *had* taken his advice, from being in effect horribly cruel."

They had a sociable way of talking of him to his face as if he had been in the clay or—at most—in the plaster, and the Master was unfailingly generous. He might have been waving Egidio to make him revolve. "Ah but poor Peter wasn't so wrong as to what it may after all come to that he *will* learn."

"Oh but nothing artistically bad," she urged—still, for poor Peter, arch and dewy.

"Why just the little French tricks," said the Master: on which their friend had to pretend to admit, when pressed by Mrs. Mallow, that these aestheic vices had been the objects of his dread.

3

"I know now," Lance said to him the next year, "why you were so much against it." He had come back supposedly for a mere interval and was looking about him at Carrara Lodge, where indeed he had already on two or three occasions since his expatriation briefly reappeared. This had the air of a longer holiday. "Something rather awful has happened to me. It *isn't* so very good to know."

"I'm bound to say high spirits don't show in your face," Peter was rather ruefully forced to confess. "Still, are you very sure you do know?"

"Well, I at least know about as much as I can bear." These remarks were exchanged in Peter's den, and the young man, smoking cigarettes, stood before the fire with his back against the mantel. Something of his bloom seemed really to have left him.

Poor Peter wondered. "You're clear then as to what in particular I wanted you not to go for?"

"In particular?" Lance thought. "It seems to me that in particular there can have been only one thing."

They stood for a little sounding each other. "Are you quite sure?"
"Quite sure I'm a beastly duffer? Quite—by this time."
"Oh!"—and Peter turned away as if almost with relief.
"It's *that* that isn't pleasant to find out."
"Oh I don't care for 'that,'" said Peter, presently coming round again.
"I mean I personally don't."
"Yet I hope you can understand a little that I myself should!"
"Well, what do you mean by it?" Peter skeptically asked.

And so this Lance had to explain—how the upshot of his studies in Paris had inexorably proved a mere deep doubt of his means. These studies had so waked him up that a new light was in his eyes; but what the new light did was really to show him too much. "Do you know what's the matter with me? I'm too horribly intelligent. Paris was really the last place for me. I've learned what I can't do."

Poor Peter stared—it was a staggerer; but even after they had had, on the subject, a longish talk in which the boy brought out to the full the hard truth of his lesson, his friend betrayed less pleasure than usually breaks into a face to the happy tune of "I told you so!" Poor Peter himself made now indeed so little a point of having told him so that Lance broke ground in a different place a day or two after. "What was it then that—before I went—you were afraid I should find out?" This, however, Peter refused to tell him—on the ground that if he hadn't yet guessed perhaps he never would, and that in any case nothing at all for neither of them was to be gained by giving the thing a name. Lance eyed him on this an instant with the bold curiosity of youth—with the air indeed of having in his mind two or three names, of which one or other would be right. Peter nevertheless, turning his back again, offered no encouragement, and when they parted afresh it was with some show of impatience on the side of the boy. Accordingly on their next encounter Peter saw at a glance that he had now, in the interval, divined and that, to sound his note, he was only waiting till they should find themselves alone. This he had soon arranged and he then broken straight out. "Do you know your conundrum has been keeping me awake? But in the watches of the night the answer came over me—so that, upon my honor, I quite laughed out. Had you been supposing I had to go to Paris to learn *that?*" Even now, to see him still so sublimely on his guard, Peter's young friend had to laugh afresh. "You won't give a sign till you're sure? Beautiful old Peter!" But Lance at last produced it. "Why, hang it, the truth about the Master."

It made between them for some minutes a lively passage, full of wonder for each at the wonder of the other. "Then how long have you understood—"

"The true value of his work? I understood it," Lance recalled, "as soon as I began to understand anything. But I didn't begin fully to do that, I admit, till I got là-bas."

"Dear, dear!"—Peter gasped with retrospective dread.

"But for what have you taken me? I'm a hopeless muff—that I *had* to have rubbed in. But I'm not such a muff as the Master!" Lance declared.

"Then why did you never tell me—?"

"That I hadn't, after all"—the boy took him up—"remained such an idiot? Just because I never dreamed *you* knew. But I beg your pardon. I only wanted to spare you. And what I don't now understand is how the deuce then for so long you've managed to keep bottled."

Peter produced his explanation, but only after some delay and with a gravity not void of embarrassment. "It was for your mother."

"Oh!" said Lance.

"And that's the great thing now—since the murder *is* out. I want a promise from you. I mean"—and Peter almost feverishly followed it up—"a vow from you, solemn and such as you owe me here on the spot, that you'll sacrifice anything rather than let her ever guess—"

"That I've guessed?"—Lance took it in. "I see." He evidently after a moment had taken in much. "But what is it you've in mind that I may have a chance to sacrifice?"

"Oh one has always something."

Lance looked at him hard. "Do you mean that *you've* had—?" The look he received back, however, so put the question by that he found soon enough another. "Are you really sure my mother doesn't know?"

Peter, after renewed reflection, was really sure. "If she does she's too wonderful."

"But aren't we all too wonderful?"

"Yes," Peter granted—"but in different ways. The things's so desperately important because your father's little public consists only, as you know then," Peter developed—"well, of how many?"

"First of all," the Master's son risked, "of himself. And last of all too. I don't quite see of whom else."

Peter had an approach to impatience. "Of your mother, I say—*always.*"

Lance cast it all up. "You absolutely feel that?"

"Absolutely."

"Well then with yourself that makes three."

"Oh *me!*"—and Peter, with a wag of his kind old head, modestly excused himself. "The number's at any rate small enough for any individual dropping out to be too dreadfully missed. Therefore, to put it in a nutshell, take care, my boy—that's all—that *you're* not!"

"I've got to keep on humbugging?" Lance wailed.

"It's just to warn you of the danger of your failing of that that I've seized this opportunity."

"And what do you regard in particular," the young man asked, "as the danger?"

"Why this certainty: that the moment your mother, who feels so strongly, should suspect your secret—well," said Peter desperately, "the fat would be on the fire."

Lance for a moment seemed to stare at the blaze. "She'd throw me over?"

"She'd throw *him* over?"

"And come round to us?"

Peter, before he answered, turned away. "Come round to *you*." But he had said enough to indicate—and, as he evidently trusted, to avert—the horrid contingency.

4

Within six months again, none the less, his fear was on more occasions than one all before him. Lance had returned to Paris for another trial; then had reappeared at home and had had, with his father, for the first time in his life, one of the scenes that strike sparks. He described it with much expression to Peter, touching whom (since they had never done so before) it was the sign of a new reserve on the part of the pair at Carrara Lodge that they at present failed, on a matter of intimate interest, to open themselves—if not in joy then in sorrow—to their good friend. This produced perhaps practically between the parties a shade of alienation and a slight intermission of commerce—marked mainly indeed by the fact that to talk at his ease with his old playmate Lance had in general to come to see him. The closest if not quite the gayest relation they had yet known together was thus ushered in. The difficulty for poor Lance was a tension at home—begotten by the fact that his father wished him to be at least the sort of success he himself had been. He hadn't "chucked" Paris— though nothing appeared more vivid to him than that Paris had chucked him: he would go back again because of the fascination in trying, in seeing, in sounding the depths—in learning one's lesson, briefly, even if the lesson were simply that of one's impotence in the presence of one's larger vision. But what did the Master, all aloft in his senseless fluency, know of impotence, and what vision—to be called such—had he in all his blind life ever had? Lance, heated and indignant, frankly appealed to his godparent on this score.

His father, it appeared, had come down on him for having, after so long, nothing to show, and hoped that on his next return this deficiency would be repaired. *The* thing, the Master complacently set forth, was—for any artist, however inferior to himself—at least to "do" something. "What can you do? That's all I ask!" He had certainly done enough, and there was no mistake about what he had to show. Lance had tears in his eyes when it came thus to letting his old friend know how great the strain might be on the "sacrifice" asked of him. It wasn't so easy to continue humbugging—as from son to parent—after feeling one's self despised for not groveling in mediocrity. Yet a noble duplicity was what, as they intimately faced the situation, Peter went on requiring; and it was still for a time what his young friend, bitter and sore, managed loyally to comfort him with. Fifty pounds more than once again, it was true, rewarded both in London and in Paris the young friend's loyalty; none the less sensibly, doubtless, at the moment, that the money was a direct advance on a decent sum for which Peter had long since privately prearranged an ultimate function. Whether by these arts or others, at all events, Lance's just resentment was kept for a season—but only for a season—at bay. The day arrived when he warned his companion that he could hold out—or hold in—no longer. Carrara Lodge had had to listen to another lecture delivered from a great height—an infliction really heavier at last than, without striking back or in some way letting the Master have the truth, flesh and blood could bear.

"And what I don't see is," Lance observed with a certain irritated eye for what was after all, if it came to that, owing to himself too; "what I don't see is, upon my honor, how *you*, as things are going, can keep the game up."

"Oh the game for me is only to hold my tongue," said placid Peter. "And I have my reason."

"Still my mother?"

Peter showed a queer face as he had often shown it before—that is by turning it straight away. "What will you have? I haven't ceased to like her."

"She's beautiful—she's a dear of course," Lance allowed; "but what is she to you, after all, and what is it to you that, as to anything whatever, she should or she shouldn't?"

Peter, who had turned red, hung fire a little. "Well—it's all simply what I make of it."

There was now, however, in his young friend a strange, an adopted insistence. "What are you after all to *her*?"

"Oh nothing. But that's another matter."

"She cares only for my father," said Lance the Parisian.

"Naturally—and that's just why."

"Why you've wished to spare her?"

"Because she cares so tremendously much."

Lance took a turn about the room, but with his eyes still on his host. "How awfully—always—you must have liked her!"

"Awfully. Always," said Peter Brench.

The young man continued for a moment to muse—then stopped again in front of him. "Do you know how much she cares?" Their eyes met on it, as if his own found something new in Lance's, appeared to hesitate, for the first time in an age, to say he did know. "I've only just found out," said Lance. "She came to my room last night, after being present, in silence and only with her eyes on me, at what I had had to take from him: she came—and she was with me an extraordinary hour."

He had paused again, and they had again for a while sounded each other. Then something—and it made him suddenly turn pale—came to Peter. "She *does* know?"

"She does know. She let it all out to me—so as to demand of me no more than 'that', as she said, of which she herself had been capable. She has always, always known," said Lance without pity.

Peter was silent a long time; during which his companion might have heard him gently breathe, and on touching him might have felt within him the vibration of a long low sound suppressed. By the time he spoke at last he had taken everything in. "Then I do see how tremendously much."

"Isn't it wonderful?" Lance asked.

"Wonderful," Peter mused.

"So that if your original effort to keep me from Paris was to keep me from knowledge—!" Lance exclaimed as if with a sufficient indication of this futility.

It might have been at the futility Peter appeared for a little to gaze. "I think it must have been—without my quite at the time knowing it—to keep *me!*" he replied at last as he turned away.

[1900–U.S.A.]

QUESTIONS

1. Look at the last sentence of the first paragraph of section 1. What is remarkable about what is said? Which of its four characters might be narrating the story? Does it make a difference whom we conceive to be its narrator? Whoever the narrator may be, the story is told mainly from Peter's standpoint. Why?

2. Even though more seems to be going on in the internal than the external world in "The Tree of Knowledge," its plot is important. Summarize it. How does it lead inevitably to the story's last scene?

3. What is the effect of James's style? How is it right given his characters—their concerns, their way of life, their refinement?

4. What are the ironic implications of Peter's being the last to know? What is ironic about the last sentence of the story?

5. Leon Edel, an authority on James, says that "The Tree of Knowledge," among other late stories, concerns "the ultimate tragedy—that of helplessly knowing the emptiness of . . . (one's) past." Is Peter, then, a tragic figure? Or could a case be made for his being comic?

6. How does James's title function? What meanings does it suggest? How do these meanings relate to the story? What, then, is the story's theme?

WRITING SUGGESTIONS

1. Write a short paper addressed to question 1 above. Choose one of James's characters as narrator and give reasons for your choice. Also, point out what is gained with respect to the impact of the story as a whole by our thinking of it as being narrated by the character you have chosen.

2. What is the mood of the story, tragic or comic? How does it affect you? After clarifying your own feelings, write a short essay on "The Tree of Knowledge" as tragedy or as comedy. Or if you feel that it is both, or perhaps neither, argue your case accordingly.

3. Go to the library and read James's story "The Beast in the Jungle." As you do, note how it is like and how unlike "The Tree of Knowledge." Then write a paper comparing and contrasting the two stories. The thematic material of the two stories is alike; the treatment of that material, however, or what we are led to feel about it, is . . . But this is for you to determine.

Everyday Use

Alice Walker

I will wait for her in the yard that Maggie and I made so clean and wavy yesterday afternoon. A yard like this is more comfortable than most people know. It is not just a yard. It is like an extended living room. When the hard clay is swept clean as a floor and the fine sand around the edges lined with tiny, irregular grooves anyone can come and sit and look up into the elm tree and wait for the breezes that never come inside the house.

Maggie will be nervous until after her sister goes: she will stand hopelessly in corners homely and ashamed of the burn scars down her arms and legs, eyeing her sister with a mixture of envy and awe. She thinks her sister has held life always in the palm of one hand, that "no" is a word the world never learned to say to her.

You've no doubt seen those TV shows where the child who has "made it" is confronted, as a surprise, by her own mother and father, tottering in weakly from backstage. (A pleasant surprise, of course: What would they do if parent and child came on the show only to curse out and insult each other?) On TV mother and child embrace and smile into each other's faces. Sometimes the mother and father weep, the child wraps them in her arms and leans across the table to tell how she would not have made it without their help. I have seen these programs.

Sometimes I dream a dream in which Dee and I are suddenly brought together on a TV program of this sort. Out of a dark and soft-seated limousine I am ushered into a bright room filled with many people. There I meet a smiling, gray, sporty man like Johnny Carson who shakes my hand and tells me what a fine girl I have. Then we are on the stage and Dee is embracing me with tears in her eyes. She pins on my dress a large orchid, even though she has told me once that she thinks orchids are tacky flowers.

In real life I am a large, big-boned woman with rough, man-working hands. In the winter I wear flannel nightgowns to bed and overalls during the day. I can kill and clean a hog as mercilessly as a man. My fat keeps me hot in zero weather. I can work all day, breaking ice to get water for washing. I can eat pork liver cooked over the open fire minutes after it comes steaming from the hog. One winter I knocked a bull calf straight in the brain between the eyes with a sledge hammer and had the meat hung up to chill before nightfall. But of course all this does not show on television. I am the way my daughter would want me to be: a hundred pounds lighter, my skin like an uncooked barley pancake. My hair glistens in the hot bright lights. Johnny Carson has much to do to keep up with my quick and witty tongue.

But that is a mistake. I know even before I wake up. Who ever knew a Johnson with a quick tongue? Who can even imagine me looking a strange white man in the eye? It seems to me I have talked to them always with one foot raised in flight, with my head turned in whichever way is farthest from them. Dee, though. She would always look anyone in the eye. Hesitation was no part of her nature.

"How do I look, Mama?" Maggie says, showing just enough of her thin body enveloped in pink skirt and red blouse for me to know she's there, almost hidden by the door.

"Come out into the yard," I say.

Have you ever seen a lame animal, perhaps a dog run over by some careless person rich enough to own a car, sidle up to someone who is ignorant enough to be kind to him? That is the way my Maggie walks. She has been like this, chin on chest, eyes on ground, feet in shuffle, ever since the fire that burned the other house to the ground.

Dee is lighter than Maggie, with nicer hair and a fuller figure. She's a woman now, though sometimes I forget. How long ago was it that the other house burned? Ten, twelve years? Sometimes I can still hear the flames and feel Maggie's arm sticking to me, her hair smoking and her dress falling off her in little black papery flakes. Her eyes seemed stretched open, blazed open by the flames reflected in them. And Dee. I see her standing off under the sweet gum tree she used to dig gum out of; a look of concentration on her face as she watched the last dingy gray board of the house fall in toward the red-hot brick chimney. Why don't you do a dance around the ashes? I'd wanted to ask her. She had hated the house that much.

I used to think she hated Maggie, too. But that was before we raised the money, the church and me, to send her to Augusta to school. She used to read to us without pity; forcing words, lies, other folks' habits, whole lives upon us two, sitting trapped and ignorant underneath her voice. She washed us in a river of make-believe, burned us with a lot of knowledge we didn't necessarily need to know. Pressed us to her with the serious way she read, to shove us away at just the moment, like dimwits, we seemed about to understand.

Dee wanted nice things. A yellow organdy dress to wear to her graduation from high school; black pumps to match a green suit she'd made from an old suit somebody gave me. She was determined to stare down any disaster in her efforts. Her eyelids would not flicker for minutes at a time. Often I fought off the temptation to shake her. At sixteen she had a style of her own: and knew what style was.

I never had an education myself. After second grade the school was closed down. Don't ask me why: in 1927 colored asked fewer questions than they do now. Sometimes Maggie reads to me. She stumbles along good-naturedly but can't see well. She knows she is not bright. Like good looks and money, quickness passed her by. She will marry John Thomas (who has mossy teeth in an earnest face) and then I'll be free to sit here and I guess just sing church songs to myself. Although I never was a good singer. Never could carry a tune. I was always better at a man's job. I used to love to milk till I was hoofed in the side in '49. Cows are soothing and slow and don't bother you, unless you try to milk them the wrong way.

I have deliberately turned my back on the house. It is three rooms, just like the one that burned, except the roof is tin; they don't make shingle roofs any more. There are no real windows, just some holes cut in the sides, like the portholes in a ship, but not round and not square, with rawhide holding the shutters up on the outside. This house is in a pasture, too, like the other one. No doubt when Dee sees it she will want to tear it down. She wrote me once that no matter where we "choose" to live, she will manage to come see us. But she will never bring her friends. Maggie and I thought about this and Maggie asked me, "Mama, when did Dee ever *have* any friends?"

She had a few. Furtive boys in pink shirts hanging about on washday after school. Nervous girls who never laughed. Impressed with her they worshiped the well-turned phrase, the cute shape, the scalding humor that erupted like bubbles in lye. She read to them.

When she was courting Jimmy T she didn't have much time to pay to us, but turned all her faultfinding power on him. He *flew* to marry a cheap gal from a family of ignorant flashy people. She hardly had time to recompose herself.

When she comes I will meet—but there they are!

Maggie attempts to make a dash for the house, in her shuffling way, but I stay her with my hand. "Come back here," I say. And she stops and tries to dig a well in the sand with her toe.

It is hard to see them clearly through the strong sun. But even the first glimpse of leg out of the car tells me it is Dee. Her feet were always neat-looking, as if God himself had shaped them with a certain style. From the other side of the car comes a short, stocky man. Hair is all over his head a foot long and hanging from his chin like a kinky mule tail. I hear Maggie suck in her breath. "Uhnnnh," is what is sounds like. Like when you see the wriggling end of a snake just in front of your foot on the road. "Uhnnnh."

Dee next. A dress down to the ground, in this hot weather. A dress so loud it hurts my eyes. There are yellows and oranges enough to throw back the light of the sun. I feel my whole face warming from the heat waves it throws out. Earrings, too, gold and hanging down to her shoulders. Bracelets dangling and making noises when she moves her arm up to shake the folds of the dress out of her armpits. The dress is loose and flows, and as she walks closer, I like it. I hear Maggie go "Uhnnnh" again. It is her sister's hair. It stands straight up like the wool on a sheep. It is black as night and around the edges are two long pigtails that rope about like small lizards disappearing behind her ears.

"Wa-su-zo-Tean-o!" she says, coming on in that gliding way the dress makes her move. The short stocky fellow with the hair to his navel is all grinning and he follows up with "Asalamalakim, my mother and sister!" He moves to hug Maggie but she falls back, right up against the back of my chair. I feel her trembling there and when I look up I see the perspiration falling off her chin.

"Don't get up," says Dee. Since I am stout it takes something of a push. You can see me trying to move a second or two before I make it. She turns, showing white heels through her sandals, and goes back to the car. Out she peeks next with a Polaroid. She stoops down quickly and lines up picture after picture of me sitting there in front of the house with Maggie cowering behind me. She never takes a shot without making sure the house is included. When a cow comes nibbling around the edge of the yard she snaps it and me and Maggie *and* the house. Then she puts the Polaroid in the back seat of the car, and comes up and kisses me on the forehead.

Meanwhile Asalamalakim is going through the motions with Maggie's hand. Maggie's hand is as limp as a fish, and probably as cold, despite the sweat, and she keeps trying to pull it back. It looks like Asalamalakim wants to shake hands but wants to do it fancy. Or maybe he don't know how people shake hands. Anyhow, he soon gives up on Maggie.

"Well," I say. "Dee."

"No, Mama," she says. "Not 'Dee,' Wangero Leewanika Kemanjo!"

"What happened to 'Dee'?" I wanted to know.

"She's dead," Wangero said. "I couldn't bear it any longer being named after the people who oppress me."

"You know as well as me you was named after your aunt Dicie," I said. Dicie is my sister. She named Dee. We called her "Big Dee" after Dee was born.

"But who was *she* named after?" asked Wangero.

"I guess after Grandma Dee," I said.

"And who was she named after?" asked Wangero.

"Her mother," I said, and saw Wangero was getting tired. "That's about as far back as I can trace it," I said. Though, in fact, I probably could have carried it back beyond the Civil War through the branches.

"Well," said Asalamalakim, "there you are."

"Uhnnnh," I heard Maggie say.

"There I was not," I said, "before 'Dicie' cropped up in our family, so why should I try to trace it that far back?"

He just stood there grinning, looking down on me like somebody inspecting a Model A car. Every once in a while he and Wangero sent eye signals over my head.

"How do you pronounce this name?" I asked.

"You don't have to call me by it if you don't want to," said Wangero.

"Why shouldn't I?" I asked. "If that's what you want us to call you, we'll call you."

"I know it might sound awkward at first," said Wangero.

"I'll get used to it," I said. "Ream it out again."

Well, soon we got the name out of the way. Asalamalakim had a name twice as long and three times as hard. After I tripped over it two or three times he told me to just call him Hakim-a-barber. I wanted to ask him was he a barber, but I didn't really think he was, so I didn't ask.

"You must belong to those beef-cattle peoples down the road," I said. They said "Asalamalakim" when they met you, too, but they didn't shake hands. Always too busy: feeding the cattle, fixing the fences, putting up salt-lick shelters, throwing down hay. When the white folks poisoned some of the herd the men stayed up all night with rifles in their hands. I walked a mile and a half just to see the sight.

Hakim-a-barber said, "I accept some of their doctrines, but farming and raising cattle is not my style." (They didn't tell me, and I didn't ask, whether Wangero [Dee] had really gone and married him.)

We sat down to eat and right away he said he didn't eat collards and pork was unclean. Wangero, though, went on through the chitlins and corn bread, the greens and everything else. She talked a blue streak over the sweet potatoes. Everything delighted her. Even the fact that we still used the benches her daddy made for the table when we couldn't afford to buy chairs.

"Oh, Mama!" she cried. Then turned to Hakim-a-barber. "I never knew how lovely these benches are. You can feel the rump prints," she said, running her hands underneath her and along the bench. Then she gave a sigh and her hand closed over Grandma Dee's butter dish. "That's it!" she said. "I knew there was something I wanted to ask you if I could have." She jumped up from the table and went over in the corner where the churn stood, the milk in its clabber by now. She looked at the churn and looked at it.

"This churn top is what I need," she said. "Didn't Uncle Buddy whittle it out of a tree you all used to have?"

"Yes," I said.

"Uh huh," she said happily. "And I want the dasher, too."

"Uncle Buddy whittle that, too?" asked the barber.

Dee (Wangero) looked up at me.

"Aunt Dee's first husband whittled the dash," said Maggie so low you almost couldn't hear her. "His name was Henry, but they called him Stash."

"Maggie's brain is like an elephant's," Wangero said, laughing. "I can use the churn top as a centerpiece for the alcove table," she said, sliding a plate over the churn, "and I'll think of something artistic to do with the dasher."

When she finished wrapping the dasher the handle stuck out. I took it for a moment in my hands. You didn't even have to look close to see where hands pushing the dasher up and down to make butter had left a kind of sink in the wood. In fact, there were a lot of small sinks; you could see where thumbs and fingers had sunk into the wood. It was beautiful light yellow wood, from a tree that grew in the yard where Big Dee and Stash had lived.

After dinner Dee (Wangero) went to the trunk at the foot of my bed and started rifling through it. Maggie hung back in the kitchen over the dishpan. Out came Wangero with two quilts. They had been pieced by Grandma Dee and then Big Dee and me had hung them on the quilt frames on the front porch and quilted them. One was in the Lone Star pattern. The other was Walk Around the Mountain. In both of them were scraps of dresses Grandma Dee had worn fifty and more years ago. Bits and pieces of Grandpa Jarrell's Paisley shirts. And one teeny faded blue piece, about the size of a penny matchbox, that was from Great Grandpa Ezra's uniform that he wore in the Civil War.

"Mama," Wangero said sweet as a bird. "Can I have these old quilts?"

I heard something fall in the kitchen, and a minute later the kitchen door slammed.

"Why don't you take one or two of the others?" I asked. "These old things was just done by me and Big Dee from some tops your grandma pieced before she died."

"No," said Wangero. "I don't want those. They are stitched around the borders by machine."

"That's make them last better," I said.

"That's not the point," said Wangero. "These are all pieces of dresses Grandma used to wear. She did all this stitching by hand. Imagine!" She held the quilts securely in her arms, stroking them.

"Some of the pieces, like those lavender ones, come from old clothes her mother handed down to her," I said, moving up to touch the quilts. Dee (Wangero) moved back just enough so that I couldn't reach the quilts. They already belonged to her.

"Imagine!" she breathed again, clutching them closely to her bosom.

"The truth is," I said, "I promised to give them quilts to Maggie, for when she marries John Thomas."

She gasped like a bee had stung her.

"Maggie can't appreciate these quilts!" she said. "She'd probably be backward enough to put them to everyday use."

"I reckon she would," I said. "God knows I been saving 'em for long enough with nobody using 'em. I hope she will!" I didn't want to bring up how I had offered Dee (Wangero) a quilt when she went away to college. Then she had told me they were old-fashion, out of style.

"But they're *priceless!*" she was saying now, furiously; for she has a temper. "Maggie would put them on the bed and in five years they'd be in rags. Less than that!"

"She can always make some more," I said. "Maggie knows how to quilt."

Dee (Wangero) looked at me with hatred. "You just will not understand. The point is these quilts, *these* quilts!"

"Well," I said, stumped. "What would you do with them?"

"Hang them," she said. As if that was the only thing you could do with quilts.

Maggie by now was standing in the door. I could almost hear the sound her feet made as they scraped over each other.

"She can have them, Mama," she said, like somebody used to never winning anything, or having anything reserved for her. "I can 'member Grandma Dee without the quilts."

I looked at her hard. She had filled her bottom lip with checkerberry snuff and it gave her face a kind of dopey, hangdog look. It was Grandma Dee and Big Dee who taught her how to quilt herself. She stood there with her scarred hands hidden in the folds of her skirt. She looked at her sister with something like fear but she wasn't mad at her. This was Maggie's portion. This was the way she knew God to work.

When I looked at her like that something hit me in the top of my head and ran down to the soles of my feet. Just like when I'm in church and the spirit of God touches me and I get happy and shout. I did something I never had done before: hugged Maggie to me, then dragged her on into the room, snatched the quilts out of Miss Wangero's hands and dumped them into Maggie's lap. Maggie just sat there on my bed with her mouth open.

"Take one or two of the others," I said to Dee.

But she turned without a word and went out to Hakim-a-barber.

"You just don't understand," she said, as Maggie and I came out to the car.

"What don't I understand?" I wanted to know.

"Your heritage," she said. And then she turned to Maggie, kissed her, and said, "You ought to try to make something of yourself, too, Maggie. It's really a new day for us. But from the way you and Mama still live you'd never know it."

She put on some sunglasses that hid everything above the tip of her nose and her chin.

Maggie smiled; maybe at the sunglasses. But a real smile, not scared. After we watched the car dust settle I asked Maggie to bring me a dip of snuff. And then the two of us sat there just enjoying, until it was time to go in the house and go to bed.

[1973–U.S.A.]

QUESTIONS

1. What is the mood overall of "Everyday Use"? In what way does its mood tie in with its theme? Given its mood, what attitude are we directed to take toward Wangero, born Dee?

2. From what narrative point of view is the story told? How does this point of view help establish the theme?
3. Contrast the mother and Wangero as to characterization. How, especially, are the values of each in conflict? Why does the mother take the quilts from Wangero and give them to Maggie?
4. The contrast referred to in question 3 gives rise to the story's central irony. What is it? What function do the story's title and last paragraph have with respect to its ironic core?
5. What, then, is Walker's satiric theme, fully stated? How is the theme itself ironic?

WRITING SUGGESTIONS

1. Write an essay about irony in "Everyday Use" Establish what the story's central irony is and suggest how its irony accounts for its title, for the mother's giving the quilts to Maggie, and for the mood of the last paragraph.
2. The irony at the heart of Walker's story is very much like the ironies of everyday life. Drawing on your own experience, write a paragraph or short essay about something ironic in your life or something ironic about someone you know, someone who sees less about a given situation than you do.

The Rocking-Horse Winner

D. H. Lawrence

There was a woman who was beautiful, who started with all the advantages, yet she had no luck. She married for love, and the love turned to dust. She had bonny children, yet she felt they had been thrust upon her, and she could not love them. They looked at her coldly, as if they were finding fault with her. And hurriedly she felt she must cover up some fault in herself. Yet what it was that she must cover up she never knew. Nevertheless, when her children were present, she always felt the centre of her heart go hard. This troubled her, and in her manner she was all the more gentle and anxious for her children, as if she loved them very much. Only she herself knew that at the centre of her heart was a hard little place that could not feel love, no, not for anybody. Everybody else said of her: "She is such a good mother. She adores her children." Only she herself, and her children themselves, knew it was not so. They read it in each other's eyes.

There were a boy and two little girls. They lived in a pleasant house, with a garden, and they had discreet servants, and felt themselves superior to anyone in the neighbourhood.

Although they lived in style, they felt always an anxiety in the house. There was never enough money. The mother had a small income, and the father had a small income, but not nearly enough for the social position which they had to keep up. The father went into town to some office. But though he had good prospects, these prospects never materialised. There was always the grinding sense of the shortage of money, though the style was always kept up.

At last the mother said: "I will see if I can't make something." But she did not know where to begin. She racked her brains, and tried this thing and the other, but could not find anything successful. The failure made deep lines come into her face. Her children were growing up, they would have to go to school. There must be more money, there must be more money. The father, who was always very handsome and expensive in his tastes, seemed as if he never *would* be able to do anything worth doing. And the mother, who had a great belief in herself, did not succeed any better, and her tastes were just as expensive.

And so the house came to be haunted by the unspoken phrase: *There must be more money! There must be more money!* The children could hear it all the time, though nobody said it aloud. They heard it at Christmas, when the expensive and splendid toys filled the nursery. Behind the shining modern rocking-horse, behind the smart doll's house, a voice would start whispering: "There *must* be more money! There *must* be more money!" And the children would stop playing, to listen for a moment. They would look into each other's eyes, to see if they had all heard. And each one saw in the eyes of the other two that they too had heard. "There *must* be more money! There *must* be more money!"

It came whispering from the springs of the still-swaying rocking-horse, and even the horse, bending his wooden, champing head, heard it. The big doll, sitting so pink and smirking in her new pram, could hear it quite plainly, and seemed to be smirking all the more self-consciously because of it. The foolish puppy, too, that took the place of the teddy-bear, he was looking so extraordinarily foolish for no other reason but that he heard the secret whisper all over the house: "There *must* be more money!"

Yet nobody ever said it aloud. The whisper was everywhere, and therefore no one spoke it. Just as no one ever says: "We are breathing!" in spite of the fact that breath is coming and going all the time.

"Mother," said the boy Paul one day, "why don't we keep a car of our own? Why do we always use uncle's, or else a taxi?"

"Because we're the poor members of the family," said the mother.

"But why are we, mother?"

"Well—I suppose," she said slowly and bitterly, "it's because your father has no luck."

The boy was silent for some time.

"Is luck money, mother?" he asked, rather timidly.

"No, Paul. Not quite. It's what causes you to have money."

"Oh!" said Paul vaguely. "I thought when Uncle Oscar said *filthy lucker*, it meant money."

"*Filthy lucre* does mean money," said the mother. "But it's lucre, not luck."

"Oh!" said the boy. "Then what *is* luck, mother?"

"It's what causes you to have money. If you're lucky you have money. That's why it's better to be born lucky than rich. If you're rich, you may lose your money. But if you're lucky, you will always get more money."

"Oh! Will you? And is father not lucky?"

"Very unlucky, I should say," she said bitterly.

The boy watched her with unsure eyes.

"Why?" he asked.

"I don't know. Nobody ever knows why one person is lucky and another unlucky."

"Don't they? Nobody at all? Does *nobody* know?"

"Perhaps God. But He never tells."

"He ought to, then. And aren't you lucky either, mother?"

"I can't be, if I married an unlucky husband."

"But by yourself, aren't you?"

"I used to think I was, before I married. Now I think I am very unlucky indeed."

"Why?"

"Well—never mind! Perhaps I'm not really," she said.

The child looked at her to see if she meant it. But he saw, by the lines of her mouth, that she was only trying to hide something from him.

"Well, anyhow," he said stoutly, "I'm a lucky person."

"Why?" said his mother, with a sudden laugh.

He stared at her. He didn't know why he had said it.

"God told me," he asserted, brazening it out.

"I hope He did, dear!" she said, again with a laugh, but rather bitter.

"He did, mother!"

"Excellent!" said the mother, using one of her husband's exclamations.

The boy saw she did not believe him; or rather, that she paid no attention to his assertion. This angered him somewhere, and made him want to compel her attention.

He went off by himself, vaguely, in a childish way, seeking for the clue to "luck." Absorbed, taking no heed of other people, he went about with a sort of stealth, seeking inwardly for luck. He wanted luck, he wanted it, he wanted it. When the two girls were playing dolls in the nursery, he would sit on his big rocking-horse, charging madly into space, with a frenzy that made the little girls peer at him uneasily. Wildly the horse careened, the waving dark hair of the boy tossed, his eyes had a strange glare in them. The little girls dared not speak to him.

When he had ridden to the end of his mad little journey, he climbed down and stood in front of his rocking-horse, staring fixedly into its lowered face. Its red mouth was slightly open, its big eye was wide and glassy-bright.

"Now!" he would silently command the snorting steed. "Now, take me to where there is luck! Now take me!"

And he would slash the horse on the neck with the little whip he had asked Uncle Oscar for. He *knew* the horse could take him to where there was luck, if only he forced it. So he would mount again and start on his furious ride, hoping at last to get there. He knew he could get there.

"You'll break your horse, Paul!" said the nurse.

"He's always riding like that! I wish he'd leave off!" said his sister Joan.

But he only glared down on them in silence. Nurse gave him up. She could make nothing of him. Anyhow, he was growing beyond her.

One day his mother and his Uncle Oscar came in when he was on one of his furious rides. He did not speak to them.

"Hallo, you young jockey! Riding a winner?" said his uncle.

"Aren't you growing too big for a rocking-horse? You're not a very little boy any longer, you know," said his mother.

But Paul only gave a blue glare from his big, rather close-set eyes. He would speak to nobody when he was in full tilt. His mother watched him with an anxious expression on her face.

At last he suddenly stopped forcing his horse into the mechanical gallop and slid down.

"Well, I got there!" he announced fiercely, his blue eyes still flaring, and his sturdy long legs straddling apart.

"Where did you get to?" asked his mother.

"Where I wanted to go," he flared back at her.

"That's right, son!" said Uncle Oscar. "Don't you stop till you get there. What's the horse's name?"

"He doesn't have a name," said the boy.

"Gets on without all right?" asked the uncle.

"Well, he has different names. He was called Sansovino last week."

"Sansovino, eh? Won the Ascot. How did you know this name?"

"He always talks about horse-races with Bassett," said Joan.

The uncle was delighted to find that his small nephew was posted with all the racing news. Bassett, the young gardener, who had been wounded in the left foot in the war and had got his present job through Oscar Cresswell, whose batman he had been, was a perfect blade of the "turf.' He lived in the racing events, and the small boy lived with him.

Oscar Cresswell got it all from Bassett.

"Master Paul comes and asks me, so I can't do more than tell him, sir," said Bassett, his face terribly serious, as if he were speaking of religious matters.

"And does he ever put anything on a horse he fancies?"

"Well—I don't want to give him away—he's a young sport, a fine sport, sir. Would you mind asking him himself? He sort of takes a pleasure in it, and perhaps he'd feel I was giving him away, sir, if you don't mind."

Bassett was serious as a church.

The uncle went back to his nephew and took him off for a ride in the car.

"Say, Paul, old man, do you ever put anything on a horse?" the uncle asked.

The boy watched the handsome man closely.

"Why, do you think I oughtn't to?" he parried.

"Not a bit of it! I thought perhaps you might give me a tip for the Lincoln."

The car sped on into the country, going down to Uncle Oscar's place in Hampshire.

"Honour bright?" said the nephew.

"Honour bright, son!" said the uncle.

"Well, then, Daffodil."

"Daffodil! I doubt it, sonny. What about Mirza?"

"I only know the winner," said the boy. "That's Daffodil."

"Daffodil, eh?"

There was a pause. Daffodil was an obscure horse comparatively.

"Uncle!"

"Yes, son?"

"You won't let it go any further, will you? I promised Bassett."

"Bassett be damned, old man! What's he got to do with it?"

"We're partners. We've been partners from the first. Uncle, he lent me my first five shillings, which I lost. I promised him, honour bright, it was only between me and him; only you gave me that ten-shilling note I started winning with, so I thought you were lucky. You won't let it go any further, will you?"

The boy gazed at his uncle from those big, hot, blue eyes, set rather close together. The uncle stirred and laughed uneasily.

"Right you are, son! I'll keep your tip private. Daffodil, eh? How much are you putting on him?"

"All except twenty pounds," said the boy. "I keep that in reserve."

The uncle thought it a good joke.

"You keep twenty pounds in reserve, do you, you young romancer? What are you betting, then?"

"I'm betting three hundred," said the boy gravely. "But it's between you and me, Uncle Oscar! Honour bright?"

The uncle burst into a roar of laughter.

"It's between you and me all right, you young Nat Gould," he said, laughing. "But where's your three hundred?"

"Bassett keeps if for me. We're partners."

"You are, are you! And what is Bassett putting on Daffodil?"

"He won't go quite as high as I do, I expect. Perhaps he'll go a hundred and fifty."

"What, pennies?" laughed the uncle.

"Pounds," said the child, with a surprised look at his uncle. "Bassett keeps a bigger reserve than I do."

Between wonder and amusement Uncle Oscar was silent. He pursued the matter no further, but he determined to take his nephew with him to the Lincoln races.

"Now, son," he said, "I'm putting twenty on Mirza, and I'll put five on for you on any horse you fancy. What's yor pick?"

"Daffodil, uncle."

"No, not the fiver on Daffodil!"

"I should if it was my own fiver," said the child.

"Good! Good! Right you are! A fiver for me and a fiver for you on Daffodil."

The child had never been to a race-meeting before, and his eyes were blue fire. He pursed his mouth tight and watched. A Frenchman just in front had put his money on Lancelot. Wild with excitement, he flayed his arms up and down, yelling "*Lancelot! Lancelot!*" in his French accent.

Daffodil came in first, Lancelot second, Mirza third. The child, flushed and with eyes blazing, was curiously serene. His uncle brought him four five-pound notes, four to one.

"What am I do with these?" he cried, waving them before the boy's eyes.

"I suppose we'll talk to Bassett," said the boy. "I expect I have fifteen hundred now; and twenty in reserve; and this twenty."

His uncle studied him for some moments.

"Look here, son!" he said. "You're not serious about Bassett and that fifteen hundred, are you?"

"Yes, I am. But it's between you and me, uncle. Honour bright?"

"Honour bright all right, son! But I must talk to Bassett."

"If you'd like to be a partner, uncle, with Bassett and me, we could all be partners. Only, you'd have to promise, honour bright, uncle, not to let it go beyond us three. Bassett and I are lucky, and you must be lucky, because it was your ten shillings I started winning with. . . ."

Uncle Oscar took both Bassett and Paul into Richmond Park for an afternoon, and there they talked.

"It's like this, you see, sir," Bassett said. "Master Paul would get me talking about racing events, spinning yarns, you know, sir. And he was always keen on knowing if I'd made or if I'd lost. It's about a year since, now, that I put five shillings on Blush of Dawn for him: and we lost. Then the luck turned, with that ten shillings he had from you: that we put on Singhalese. And since that time, it's been pretty steady, all things considering. What do you say, Master Paul?"

"We're all right when we're sure," said Paul. "It's when we're not quite sure that we go down."

"Oh, but we're careful then," said Bassett.

"But when are you *sure?*" smiled Uncle Oscar.

"It's Master Paul, sir," said Bassett in a secret, religious voice. "It's as if he had it from heaven. Like Daffodil, now, for the Lincoln. That was as sure as eggs."

"Did you put anything on Daffodil?" asked Oscar Cresswell.

"Yes, sir. I made my bit."

"And my nephew?"

Bassett was obstinately silent, looking at Paul.

"I made twelve hundred, didn't I, Bassett? I told uncle I was putting three hundred on Daffodil."

"That's right," said Bassett, nodding.

"But where's the money?" asked the uncle.

"I keep it safe locked up, sir. Master Paul he can have it any minute he likes to ask for it."

"What, fifteen hundred pounds?"

"And twenty! and *forty*, that is, with the twenty he made on the course."

"It's amazing!" said the uncle.

"If Master Paul offers you to be partners, sir, I would, if I were you: if you'll excuse me," said Bassett.

Oscar Cresswell thought about it.

"I'll see the money," he said.

They drove home again, and, sure enough, Bassett came round to the garden-house with fifteen hundred pounds in notes. The twenty pounds reserve was left with Joe Glee, in the Turf Commission deposit.

"You see, it's all right, uncle, when I'm *sure!* Then we go strong, for all we're worth. Don't we, Bassett?"

"We do that, Master Paul."

"And when are you sure?" said the uncle, laughing.

"Oh, well, sometimes I'm *absolutely* sure, like about Daffodil," said the boy; "and sometimes I have an idea; and sometimes I haven't even an idea, have I, Bassett? Then we're careful, because we mostly go down."

"You do, do you! And when you're sure, like about Daffodil, what makes you sure, sonny?"

"Oh, well, I don't know," said the boy uneasily. "I'm sure, you know, uncle; that's all."

"It's as if he had it from heaven, sir," Bassett reiterated.

"I should say so!" said the uncle.

But he became a partner. And when the Leger was coming on Paul was "sure" about Lively Spark, which was a quite inconsiderable horse. The boy insisted on putting a thousand on the horse, Bassett was for five hundred, and Oscar Cresswell two hundred. Lively Spark came in first, and the betting had been ten to one against him. Paul had made ten thousand.

"You see," he said, "I was absolutely sure of him."

Even Oscar Cresswell had cleared two thousand.

"Look here, son," he said, "this sort of thing makes me nervous."

"It needn't, uncle! Perhaps I shan't be sure again for a long time."

"But what are you going to do with your money?" asked the uncle.

"Of course," said the boy, "I started it for mother. She said she had no luck, because father is unlucky, so I thought if I was lucky, it might stop whispering."

"What might stop whispering?"

"Our house. I *hate* our house for whispering."

"What does it whisper?"

"Why—why"—the boy fidgeted—"why, I don't know. But it's always short of money, you know, uncle."

"I know it, son, I know it."

"You know people send mother writs, don't you, uncle?"

"I'm afraid I do," said the uncle.

"And then the house whispers, like people laughing at you behind your back. It's awful, that is! I thought if I was lucky——"

"You might stop it," added the uncle.

The boy watched him with big blue eyes, that had an uncanny cold fire in them, and he said never a word.

"Well, then!" said the uncle. "What are we doing?"

"I shouldn't like mother to know I was lucky," said the boy.

"Why not, son?"

"She'd stop me."

"I don't think she would."

"Oh!"—and the boy writhed in an odd way—"I *don't* want her to know, uncle."

"All right, son! We'll manage it without her knowing."

They managed it very easily. Paul, at the other's suggestion, handed over five thousand pounds to his uncle, who deposited it with the family lawyer, who was then to inform Paul's mother that a relative had put five thousand pounds into his hands, which sum was to be paid a thousand pounds at a time, on the mother's birthday, for the next five years.

"So she'll have a birthday present of a thousand pounds for five successive years," said Uncle Oscar. "I hope it won't make it all the harder for her later."

Paul's mother had her birthday in November. The house had been "whispering" worse than ever lately, and, even in spite of his luck, Paul could not bear up against it. He was very anxious to see the effect of the birthday letter, telling his mother about the thousand pounds.

When there were no visitors, Paul now took his meals with his parents, as he was beyond the nursery control. His mother went into town nearly every day. She had discovered that she had an odd knack of sketching furs and dress materials, so she worked secretly in the studio of a friend who was the chief "artist" for the leading drapers. She drew the figures of ladies in furs and ladies in silk and sequins for the newspaper advertisements. This young woman artist earned several thousand pounds a year, but Paul's mother only made several hundreds, and she was again dissatisfied. She so wanted to be first in something, and she did not succeed, even in making sketches for drapery advertisements.

She was down to breakfast on the morning of her birthday. Paul watched her face as she read her letters. He knew the lawyer's letter. As his mother read it, her face hardened and became more expressionless. Then a cold, determined look came on her mouth. She hid the letter under the pile of others, and said not a word about it.

"Didn't you have anything nice in the post for your birthday, mother?" said Paul.

"Quite moderately nice," she said, her voice cold and absent.

She went away to town without saying more.

But in the afternoon Uncle Oscar appeared. He said Paul's mother had had a long interview with the lawyer, asking if the whole five thousand could not be advanced at once, as she was in debt.

"What do you think, uncle?" said the boy.

"I leave it to you, son."

"Oh, let her have it, then! We can get some more with the other," said the boy.

"A bird in the hand is worth two in the bush, laddie!" said Uncle Oscar.

"But I'm sure to *know* for the Grand National; or the Lincolnshire; or else the Derby. I'm sure to know for *one* of them," said Paul.

So Uncle Oscar signed the agreement, and Paul's mother touched the whole five thousand. Then something very curious happened. The voices in the house suddenly went mad, like a chorus of frogs on a spring evening. There were certain new furnishings, and Paul had a tutor. He was *really* going to Eton, his father's school, in the following autumn. There were flowers in the winter, and a blossoming of the luxury Paul's mother had been used to. And yet the voices in the house, behind the sprays of mimosa and almondblossom, and from under the piles of iridescent cushions, simply trilled and screamed in a sort of ecstasy: "There *must* be more money! Oh-h-h; there *must* be more money. Oh, now, now-w! Now-w-w—there *must* be more money!—more than ever! More than ever!"

It frightened Paul terribly. He studied away at his Latin and Greek with his tutor. But his intense hours were spent with Bassett. The Grand National had gone by: he had not "known," and had lost a hundred pounds. Summer was at hand. He was in agony for the Lincoln. But even for the Lincoln he didn't "know," and he lost fifty pounds. He became wild-eyed and strange, as if something were going to explode in him.

"Let it alone, son! Don't you bother about it!" urged Uncle Oscar. But it was as if the boy couldn't really hear what his uncle was saying.

"I've got to know for the Derby! I've got to know for the Derby!" the child reiterated, his big blue eyes blazing with a sort of madness.

His mother noticed how overwrought he was.

"You'd better go to the seaside. Wouldn't you like to go now to the seaside, instead of waiting? I think you'd better," she said, looking down at him anxiously, her heart curiously heavy because of him.

But the child lifted his uncanny blue eyes.

"I couldn't possibly go before the Derby, mother!" he said, "I couldn't possibly!"

"Why not?" she said, her voice becoming heavy when she was opposed. "Why not? You can still go from the seaside to see the Derby with your Uncle Oscar, if that's what you wish. No need for you to wait here. Besides, I think you care too much about these races. It's a bad sign. My family has been a gambling family, and you won't know till you grow up how much damage it has done. But it had done damage. I shall have to send Bassett away, and ask Uncle Oscar not to talk racing to you, unless you promise to be reasonable about it: go away to the seaside and forget it. You're all nerves!"

"I'll do what you like, mother, so long as you don't send me away till after the Derby," the boy said.

"Send you away from where? Just from this house?"

"Yes," he said, gazing at her.

"Why, you curious child, what makes you care about this house so much, suddenly? I never knew you loved it."

He gazed at her without speaking. He had a secret within a secret, something he had not divulged, even to Bassett or to his Uncle Oscar.

But his mother, after standing undecided and a little bit sullen for some moments, said:

"Very well, then! Don't go to the seaside till after the Derby, if you don't wish it. But promise me you won't let your nerves go to pieces. Promise you won't think so much about horse-racing and *events*, as you call them!"

"Oh no," said the boy casually. "I won't think much about them, mother. You needn't worry. I wouldn't worry, mother, if I were you."

"If you were me and I were you," said his mother, "I wonder what we *should* do!"

"But you know you needn't worry, mother, don't you?" the boy repeated.

"I should be awfully glad to know it," she said wearily.

"Oh, well, you *can*, you know. I mean, you *ought* to know you needn't worry," he insisted.

"Ought I? Then I'll see about it," she said.

Paul's secret of secrets was his wooden horse, that which had no name. Since he was emancipated from a nurse and a nursery-governess, he had had his rocking-horse removed to his own bedroom at the top of the house.

"Surely you're too big for a rocking-horse!" his mother had remonstrated.

"Well, you see, mother, till I can have a *real* horse, I like to have *some* sort of animal about," had been his quaint answer.

"Do you feel he keeps you company?" she laughed.

"Oh yes! He's very good, he always keeps me company, when I'm there," said Paul.

So the horse, rather shabby, stood in an arrested prance in the boy's bedroom.

The Derby was drawing near, and the boy grew more and more tense. He hardly heard what was spoken to him, he was very frail, and his eyes were really uncanny. His mother had sudden strange seizures of uneasiness about him. Sometimes, for half an hour, she would feel a sudden anxiety about him that was almost anguish. She wanted to rush to him at once, and know he was safe.

Two nights before the Derby, she was at a big party in town, when one of her rushes of anxiety about her boy, her first-born, gripped her heart till she could hardly speak. She fought with the feeling, might and main, for she believed in common sense. But it was too strong. She had to leave the dance and go downstairs to telephone to the country. The children's nursery-governess was terribly surprised and startled at being rung up in the night.

"Are the children all right, Miss Wilmot?"

"Oh yes, they are quite all right."

"Master Paul? Is he all right?"

"He went to bed as right as a trivet. Shall I run up and look at him?"

"No," said Paul's mother reluctantly. "No! Don't trouble. It's all right. Don't sit up. We shall be home fairly soon." She did not want her son's privacy intruded upon.

"Very good," said the governess.

It was about one o'clock when Paul's mother and father drove up to their house. All was still. Paul's mother went to her room and slipped off her white fur cloak. She had told her maid not to wait up for her. She heard her husband downstairs, mixing a whisky and soda.

And then, because of the strange anxiety at her heart, she stole upstairs to her son's room. Noiselessly she went along the upper corridor. Was there a faint noise? What was it?

She stood, with arrested muscles, outside his door, listening. There was a strange, heavy, and yet not loud noise. Her heart stood still. It was a soundless noise, yet rushing and powerful. Something huge, in violent, hushed motion. What was it? What in God's name was it? She ought to know. She felt that she knew the noise. She knew what it was.

Yet she could not place it. She couldn't say what it was. And on and on it went, like a madness.

Softly, frozen with anxiety and fear, she turned the doorhandle.

The room was dark. Yet in the space near the window, she heard and saw something plunging to and fro. She gazed in fear and amazement.

Then suddenly she switched on the light, and saw her son, in his green pyjamas, madly surging on the rocking-horse. The blaze of light suddenly lit him up, as he urged the wooden horse, and lit her up, as she stood, blonde, in her dress of pale green and crystal, in the doorway.

"Paul!" she cried. "Whatever are you doing?"

"It's Malabar!" he screamed in a powerful, strange voice. "It's Malabar!"

His eyes blazed at her for one strange and senseless second, as he ceased urging his wooden horse. Then he fell with a crash to the ground, and she, all her tormented motherhood flooding upon her, rushed to gather him up.

But he was unconscious, and unconscious he remained, with some brain-fever. He talked and tossed, and his mother sat stonily by his side.

"Malabar! It's Malabar! Bassett, Bassett, I *know!* It's Malabar!"

So the child cried, trying to get up and urge the rocking-horse that gave him his inspiration.

"What does he mean by Malabar?" asked the heart-frozen mother.

"I don't know," said the father stonily.

"What does he mean by Malabar?" she asked her brother Oscar.

"It's one of the horses running for the Derby," was the answer.

And, in spite of himself, Oscar Cresswell spoke to Bassett, and himself put a thousand on Malabar: at fourteen to one.

The third day of the illness was critical: they were waiting for a change. The boy, with his rather long, curly hair, was tossing ceaselessly on the pillow. He neither slept nor regained consciousness, and his eyes were like blue stones. His mother sat, feeling her heart had gone, turned actually into a stone.

In the evening, Oscar Cresswell did not come, but Bassett sent a message, saying could he come up for one moment, just one moment? Paul's mother was very angry at the intrusion, but on second thoughts she agreed. The boy was the same. Perhaps Bassett might bring him to consciousness.

The gardener, a shortish fellow with a little brown moustache and sharp little brown eyes, tiptoed into the room, touched his imaginary cap to Paul's mother, and stole to the bedside, staring with glittering, smallish eyes at the tossing, dying child.

"Master Paul!" he whispered. "Master Paul! Malabar came in first all right, a clean win. I did as you told me. You've made over seventy thousand pounds, you have; you've got over eighty thousand. Malabar came in all right, Master Paul."

"Malabar! Malabar! Did I say Malabar, mother? Did I say Malabar? Do you think I'm lucky, mother? I knew Malabar, didn't I? Over eighty thousand pounds! I call that lucky, don't you, mother? Over eighty thousand pounds! I knew, didn't I know I knew? Malabar came in all right. If I ride my horse till I'm sure, then I tell you, Bassett, you can go as high as you like. Did you go for all you were worth, Bassett?"

"I went a thousand on it, Master Paul."

"I never told you, mother, that if I can ride my horse, and *get there*, then I'm absolutely sure—oh, absolutely! Mother, did I ever tell you? I *am* lucky!"

"No, you never did," said his mother.

But the boy died in the night.

And even as he lay dead, his mother heard her brother's voice saying to her: "My God, Hester, you're eighty-odd thousand to the good, and a poor devil of a son to the bad. But, poor devil, poor devil, he's best gone out of a life where he rides his rocking-horse to find a winner."

[1933–Great Britain]

QUESTIONS

1. In many ways, "The Rocking-Horse Winner" is like a fairy tale. How so? Consider style, general atmosphere, and characterization in this regard. In what ways are the fairy-tale elements of the story apt?

2. Yet the story is very unlike fairy tales in other ways. How so? Constrast the values in fairy tales with those of the world depicted by Lawrence.

3. Characterize Paul's mother. How is she like and yet unlike fairy-tale stepmothers? Is she really unlucky, as she feels? What confusion of values does she represent? How does Paul also betray such a confusion? Consider here the conversation between mother and son on luck as well as Paul's mistaking of "lucre" and "luck."

4. Why do the voices in the house get worse *after* the mother receives the money from Paul? What is it about Paul's riding of the rocking-horse that parallels the voices' getting worse? What, then, is this "shining modern" rocking-horse a figure of?

5. There is much irony in Lawrence's tale. What are some of its ironies? For example, consider both separately and together the story's beginning and its climax (the death of Paul).

6. What does this story tell us about the modern world, or at least Lawrence's view of it? What, then, is Lawrence's theme? (In considering theme, take into account the uncle's last sentence.)

WRITING SUGGESTIONS

1. In a paragraph or two, discuss the definition of luck that Paul's mother passes on to him. Go on to discuss whether or not this meaning is viable. What would be a better definition? How does the mother's definition affect her life and her son's, and what does it tell us about the modern world generally?

2. In a short essay, address questions 1 and 2 above. State how the story is both like and unlike fairy tales. Consider especially the purpose this contrast serves in the story.

3. If you agree with Lawrence on the economic focus of the modern world and the

life-denying effect of that focus, write an essay on this aspect of our lives with "The Rocking-Horse Winner" used as support. If you disagree, make a case against Lawrence, with the story serving as your point of reference.

4. Much has been written on "The Rocking-Horse Winner." Do some research (three or four articles and/or sections in books); then use your research to write a paper in which you argue a view of your own. You can agree or disagree with the critics you've read. But don't just repeat what they have said. The purpose of a research paper is to allow one to make one's own case fully in light of what others have had to say.

The Open Boat

Stephen Crane

1

None of them knew the colour of the sky. Their eyes glanced level, and were fastened upon the waves that swept toward them. These waves were of the hue of slate, save for the tops, which were of foaming white, and all of the men knew the colours of the sea. The horizon narrowed and widened, and dipped and rose, and at all times its edge was jagged with waves that seemed thrust up in points like rocks.

Many a man ought to have a bathtub larger than the boat which here rode upon the sea. These waves were most wrongfully and barbarously abrupt and tall, and each froth-top was a problem in small-boat navigation.

The cook squatted in the bottom, and looked with both eyes at the six inches of gunwale which separated him from the ocean. His sleeves were rolled over his fat forearms, and the two flaps of his unbottoned vest dangled as he bent to bail out the boat. Often he said, "Gawd! that was a narrow clip." As he remarked it he invariably gazed eastward over the broken sea.

The oiler, steering with one of the two oars in the boat, sometimes raised himself suddenly to keep clear of water that swirled in over the stern. It was a thin little oar, and it seemed often ready to snap.

The correspondent, pulling at the other oar, watched the waves and wondered why he was there.

The injured captain, lying in the bow, was at this time buried in that profound dejection and indifference which comes, temporarily at least, to even the bravest and most enduring when, willy-nilly, the firm fails, the army loses, the ship goes down. The mind of the master of a vessel is rooted deep in the timbers of her, though he command for a day or a decade; and this captain had on him the stern impression of a scene in the greys of dawn of seven turned faces, and later a stump of a topmast with a white ball on it, that slashed to and fro at the waves, went low and lower, and down. Thereafter there was something strange in his voice. Although steady, it was deep with mourning, and of a quality beyond oration or tears.

"Keep'er a little more south, Billie," said he.

"A little more south, sir," said the oiler in the stern.

A seat in his boat was not unlike a seat upon a bucking broncho, and by the same token a broncho is not much smaller. The craft pranced and reared and plunged like an animal. As each wave came, and she rose for it, she seemed like a horse making at a fence outrageously high. The manner of her scramble over these walls of water is a mystic thing, and, moreover, at the top of them were ordinarily these problems in white water, the foam racing down from the summit of each wave requiring a new leap, and a leap from the air. Then, after scornfully bumping a crest, she would slide and race and splash down a long incline, and arrive bobbing and nodding in front of the next menace.

A singular disadvantage of the sea lies in the fact that after successfully surmounting one wave you discover that there is another behind it just as important and just as nervously anxious to do something effective in the way of swamping boats. In a ten-foot dinghy one can get an idea of the resources of the sea in the line of waves that is not probable to the average experience which is never at sea in a dinghy. As each slaty wall of water approached, it shut all else from the view of the men in the boat, and it was not difficult to imagine that this particular wave was the final outburst of the ocean, the last effort of the grim water. There was a terrible grace in the move of the waves, and they came in silence, save for the snarling of the crests.

In the wan light the faces of the men must have been grey. Their eyes must have glinted in strange ways as they gazed steadily astern. Viewed from a balcony, the whole thing would doubtless have been weirdly picturesque. But the men in the boat had no time to see it, and if they had had leisure, there were other things to occupy their minds. The sun swung steadily up the sky, and they knew it was broad day because the colour of the sea changed from slate to emerald green streaked with amber lights, and the foam was like tumbling snow. The process of the breaking day was unknown to them. They were aware only of this effect upon the colour of the waves that rolled toward them.

In disjointed sentences the cook and the correspondent argued as to the difference between a life-saving station and a house of refuge. The cook had said: "There's a house of refuge just north of the Mosquito Inlet Light, and as soon as they see us they'll come off in their boat and pick us up."

"As soon as who see us?" said the correspondent.

"The crew," said the cook.

"Houses of refuge don't have crews," said the correspondent. "As I understand them, they are only places where clothes and grub are stored for the benefit of shipwrecked people. They don't carry crews."

"Oh, yes, they do," said the cook.

"No, they don't," said the correspondent.

"Well, we're not there yet, anyhow," said the oiler, in the stern.

"Well," said the cook, "perhaps it's not a house of refuge that I'm thinking of as being near Mosquito Inlet Light; perhaps it's a life-saving station."

"We're not there yet," said the oiler in the stern.

2

As the boat bounced from the top of each wave the wind tore through the hair of the hatless men, and as the craft plopped her stern down again the spray slashed past them. The crest of each of these waves was a hill, from the top of which the men surveyed for a moment a broad tumultuous expanse, shining and wind-riven. It was probably splendid, it was probably glorious, this play of the free sea, wild with lights of emerald and white and amber.

"Bully good thing it's an on-shore wind," said the cook. "If not, where would we be? Wouldn't have a show."

"That's right," said the respondent.

The busy oiler nodded his assent.

Then the captain, in the bow, chuckled in a way that expressed humour, contempt, tragedy, all in one. "Do you think we've got much of a show now, boys?" said he.

Whereupon the three were silent, save for a trifle of hemming and hawing. To express any particular optimism at this time they felt to be childish and stupid, but they all doubtless possessed this sense of the situation in their minds. A young man thinks doggedly at such times. On the other hand, the ethics of their condition was decidedly against any open suggestion of hopelessness. So they were silent.

"Oh, well," said the captain, soothing his children, "we'll get ashore all right."

But there was that in his tone which made them think; so the oiler quoth, "Yes! if this wind holds."

The cook was bailing, "Yes! if we don't catch hell in the surf."
Canton-flannel gulls flew near and far. Sometimes they sat down on
the sea, near patches of brown seaweed that rolled over the waves with a
movement like carpets on a line in a gale. The birds sat comfortably in
groups, and they were envied by some in the dinghy, for the wrath of the
sea was no more to them than it was to a covey of prairie chickens a
thousand miles inland. Often they came very close and stared at the men
with black bead-like eyes. At these times they were uncanny and sinister in
their unblinking scrutiny, and the men hooted angrily at them, telling
them to be gone. One came, and evidently decided to alight on the top of
the captain's head. The bird flew parallel to the boat and did not circle, but
made short sidelong jumps in the air in chicken-fashion. His black eyes
were wistfully fixed upon the captain's head. "Ugly brute," said the oiler to
the bird. "You look as if you were made with a jackknife." The cook and
the correspondent swore darkly at the creature. The captain naturally
wished to knock it away with the end of the heavy painter, but he did not
dare do it, because anything resembling an emphatic gesture would have
capsized this freighted boat; and so, with his open hand, the captain gently
and carefully waved the gull away. After it had been discouraged from the
pursuit the captain breathed easier on account of his hair, and others
breathed easier because the bird struck their minds at this time as being
somehow gruesome and ominous.

In the meantime the oiler and the correspondent rowed. And also they
rowed. They sat together in the same seat, and each rowed an oar. Then
the oiler took both oars; then the correspondent took both oars; then the
oiler; then the correspondent. They rowed and they rowed. The very
ticklish part of the business was when the time came for the reclining one
in the stern to take his turn at the oars. By the very last star of truth, it is
easier to steal eggs from under a hen than it was to change seats in the
dinghy. First the man in the stern slid his hand along the thwart and
moved with care, as if he were of Sèvres. Then the man in the rowing-seat
slid his hand along the other thwart. It was all done with the most
extraordinary care. As the two sidled past each other, the whole party kept
watchful eyes on the coming wave, and the captain cried: "Look out, now!
Steady, there!"

The brown mats of seaweed that appeared from time to time were like
islands, bits of earth. They were travelling, apparently, neither one way
nor the other. They were, to all intents, stationary. They informed the
men in the boat that it was making progress slowly toward the land.

The captain, rearing cautiously in the bow after the dinghy soared on
a great swell, said that he had seen the lighthouse at Mosquito Inlet.

Presently the cook remarked that he had seen it. The correspondent was at the oars then, and for some reason he too wished to look at the lighthouse; but his back was toward the far shore, and the waves were important, and for some time he could not seize an opportunity to turn his head. But at last there came a wave more gentle than the others, and when at the crest of it he swiftly scoured the western horizon.

"See it?" said the captain.

"No," said the correspondent, slowly; "I didn't see anything."

"Look again," said the captain. He pointed. "It's exactly in that direction."

At the top of another wave the correspondent did as he was bid, and this time his eyes chanced on a small, still thing on the edge of the swaying horizon. It was precisely like the point of a pin. It took an anxious eye to find a lighthouse so tiny.

"Think we'll make it, Captain?"

"If this wind holds and the boat don't swamp, we can't do much else," said the captain.

The little boat, lifted by each towering sea and splashed viciously by the crests, made progress that in the absence of seaweed was not apparent to those in her. She seemed just a wee thing wallowing, miraculously top up, at the mercy of five oceans. Occasionally a great spread of water, like white flames, swarmed into her.

"Bail her, cook," said the captain, serenely.

"All right, Captain," said the cheerful cook.

3

It would be difficult to describe the subtle brotherhood of men that was here established on the seas. No one said that it was so. No one mentioned it. But it dwelt in the boat, and each man felt it warm him. They were a captain, an oiler, a cook, and a correspondent, and they were friends—friends in a more curiously iron-bound degree than may be common. The hurt captain, lying against the water-jar in the bow, spoke always in a low voice and calmly; but he could never command a more ready and swiftly obedient crew than the motley three of the dinghy. It was more than a mere recognition of what was best for the common safety. There was surely in it a quality that was personal and heart-felt. And after this devotion to the commander of the boat, there was this comradeship, that the correspondent, for instance, who had been taught to be cynical of men, knew even at the time was the best experience of his life. But no one said that it was so. No one mentioned it.

"I wish we had a sail," remarked the captain. "We might try my overcoat on the end of an oar, and give you two boys a chance to rest." So the cook and the correspondent held the mast and spread wide the overcoat; the oiler steered; and the little boat made good way with her new rig. Sometimes the oiler had to scull sharply to keep a sea from breaking into the boat, but otherwise sailing was a success.

Meanwhile the lighthouse had been growing slowly larger. It had now almost assumed colour, and appeared like a little grey shadow on the sky. The man at the oars could not be prevented from turning his head rather often to try for a glimpse of this little grey shadow.

At last, from the top of each wave, the men in the tossing boat could see land. Even as the lighthouse was an upright shadow on the sky, this land seemed but a long black shadow on the sea. It certainly was thinner than paper. "We must be about opposite New Smyrna," said the cook, who had coasted this shore often in schooners. "Captain, by the way, I believe they abandoned that life-saving station there about a year ago."

"Did they?" said the captain.

The wind slowly died away. The cook and the correspondent were not now obliged to slave in order to hold high the oar. But the waves continued their old impetuous swooping at the dinghy, and the little craft, no longer under way, struggled woundily over them. The oiler or the correspondent took the oars again.

Shipwrecks are apropos of nothing. If men could only train for them and have them occur when the man had reached pink condition, there would be less drowning at sea. Of the four in the dinghy none had slept any time worth mentioning for two days and two nights previous to embarking in the dinghy, and in the excitement of clambering about the deck of a foundering ship they had also forgotten to eat heartily.

For these reasons, and for others, neither the oiler nor the correspondent was fond of rowing at this time. The correspondent wondered ingenuously how in the name of all that was sane could there be people who thought it amusing to row a boat. It was not an amusement; it was a diabolical punishment and even a genius of mental aberrations could never conclude that it was anything but a horror to the muscles and a crime against the back. He mentioned to the boat in general how the amusement of rowing struck him, and the weary-faced oiler smiled in full sympathy. Previously to the foundering, by the way, the oiler had worked a double watch in the engine-room of the ship.

"Take her easy now, boys," said the captain. "Don't spend yourselves. If we have to run a surf you'll need all your strength, because we'll sure have to swim for it. Take your time."

Slowly the land arose from the sea. From a black line it became a line of black and a line of white—trees and sand. Finally the captain said that he could make out a house on the shore. "That's the house of refuge, sure," said the cook. "They'll see us before long, and come out after us."

The distant lighthouse reared high. "The keeper ought to be able to make us out now, if he's looking through a glass," said the captain. "He'll notify the life-saving people."

"None of those other boats could have got ashore to give word of this wreck," said the oiler, in a low voice, "else the life-boat would be out hunting us."

Slowly and beautifully the land loomed out of the sea. The wind came again. It had veered from the north-east to the south-east. Finally a new sound struck the ears of the men in the boat. It was the low thunder of the surf on the shore. "We'll never be able to make the lighthouse now," said the captain. "Swing her head a little more north, Billie."

"A little more north, sir," said the oiler.

Whereupon the little boat turned her nose once more down the wind, and all but the oarsman watched the shore grow. Under the influence of this expansion doubt and direful apprehension were leaving the minds of the men. The management of the boat was still most absorbing, but it could not prevent a quiet cheerfulness. In a hour, perhaps, they would be ashore.

Their backbones had become thoroughly used to balancing in the boat, and they now rode this wild colt of a dinghy like circus men. The correspondent thought that he had been drenched to the skin, but happening to feel in the top pocket of his coat, he found therein eight cigars. Four of them were soaked with sea-water; four were perfectly scatheless. After a search, somebody produced three dry matches; and thereupon the four waifs rode impudently in their little boat and, with an assurance of an impending rescue shining in their eyes, puffed at the big cigars, and judged well and ill of all men. Everybody took a drink of water.

4

"Cook," remarked the captain, "there don't seem to be any signs of life about your house of refuge."

"No," replied the cook. "Funny they don't see us!"

A broad stretch of lowly coast lay before the eyes of the men. It was of low dunes topped with dark vegetation. The roar of the surf was plain, and sometimes they could see the white lip of a wave as it spun up the beach. A tiny house was blocked out black upon the sky. Southward, the slim lighthouse lifted its little grey length.

Tide, wind, and waves were swinging the dinghy northward. "Funny they don't see us," said the men.

The surf's roar was here dulled, but its tone was nevertheless thunderous and mighty. As the boat swam over the great rollers the men sat listening to this roar. "We'll swamp sure," said everybody.

It is fair to say here that there was not a life-station station within twenty miles in either direction; but the men did not know this fact, and in consequence they made dark and opprobrious remarks concerning the eyesight of the nation's life-savers. Four scowling men sat in the dinghy and surpassed records in the invention of epithets.

"Funny they don't see us."

The light-heartedness of a former time had completely faded. To their sharpened minds it was easy to conjure pictures of all kinds of incompetency and blindness and, indeed, cowardice. There was the shore of the populous land, and it was bitter and bitter to them that from it came no sign.

"Well," said the captain, ultimately, "I suppose we'll have to make a try for ourselves. If we stay out here too long, we'll none of us have strength left to swim after the boat swamps."

And so the oiler, who was at the oars, turned the boat straight for the shore. There was a sudden tightening of muscles. There was some thinking.

"If we don't all get ashore," said the captain—"if we don't all get ashore, I suppose you fellows know where to send news of my finish?"

They then briefly exchanged some addresses and admonitions. As for the reflections of the men, there was a great deal of rage in them. Perchance they might be formulated thus: "If I am going to be drowned—if I am going to be drowned—if I am going to be drowned, why, in the name of the seven mad gods who rule the sea, was I allowed to come thus far and contemplate sand and trees? Was I brought here merely to have my nose dragged away as I was about to nibble the sacred cheese of life? It is preposterous. If this old ninny-woman, Fate, cannot do better than this, she should be deprived of the management of men's fortunes. She is an old hen who knows not her intention. If she has decided to drown me, why did she not do it in the beginning and save me all this trouble? The whole affair is absurd—But no; she cannot mean to drown me. She dare not drown me. She cannot drown me. Not after all this work." Afterward the man might have had an impulse to shake his fist at the clouds. "Just you drown me, now, and then hear what I call you!"

The billows that came at this time were more formidable. They seemed always just about to break and roll over the little boat in a turmoil of foam. There was a preparatory and long growl in the speech of them. No mind unused to the sea would have concluded that the dinghy could ascend these sheer heights in time. The shore was still afar. The oiler was a wily surfman. "Boys," he said swiftly, "she won't live three minutes more, and we're too far out to swim. Shall I take her to sea again, Captain?"

"Yes; go ahead!" said the captain.

This oiler, by a series of quick miracles and fast and steady oarsmanship, turned the boat in the middle of the surf and took her safety to sea again.

There was a considerable silence as the boat bumped over the furrowed sea to deeper water. Then somebody in gloom spoke: "Well, anyhow, they must have seen us from the shore by now."

The gulls went in slanting flight up the wind toward the grey, desolate east. A squall, marked by dingy clouds and clouds brick-red like smoke from a burning building, appeared from the south-east.

"What do you think of those life-saving people? Ain't they peaches?"

"Funny they haven't seen us."

"Maybe they think we're out here for sport! Maybe they think we're fishin'. Maybe they think we're damned fools."

It was a long afternoon. A changed tide tried to force them southward, but wind and wave said northward. Far ahead, where coast-line, sea, and sky formed their mighty angle, there were little dots which seemed to indicate a city on the shore.

"St. Augustine?"

The captain shook his head. "Too near Mosquito Inlet."

And the oiler rowed, and then the correspondent rowed; then the oiler rowed. It was a weary business. The human back can become the seat of more aches and pains than are registered in books for the composite anatomy of a regiment. It is a limited area, but it can become the theatre of innumerable muscular conflicts, tangles, wrenches, knots, and other comforts.

"Did you ever like to row, Billie?" said the correspondent.

"No," said the oiler; "hang it!"

When one exchanged the rowing-seat for a place in the bottom of the boat, he suffered a bodily depression that caused him to be careless of everything save an obligation to wiggle one finger. There were cold sea-water swashing to and fro in the boat, and he lay in it. His head, pillowed on a thwart, was within an inch of the swirl of a wave-crest, and sometimes a particularly obstreperous sea came inboard and drenched him once more. But these matters did not annoy him. It is almost certain that if the boat had capsized he would have tumbled comfortably out upon the ocean as if he felt sure that it was a great soft mattress.

"Look! There's a man on the shore!"

"Where?"

"There! See 'im? See 'im?"

"Yes, sure! He's walking along."

"Now he's stopped. Look! He's facing us!"

"He's waving at us!"

"So he is! By thunder!"

"Ah, now we're all right! Now we're all right! There'll be a boat out here for us in half an hour."

"He's going on. He's running. He's going up to that house there."

The remote beach seemed lower than the sea, and it required a searching glance to discern the little black figure. The captain saw a floating stick, and they rowed to it. A bath towel was by some weird chance in the boat, and, tying this on the stick, the captain waved it. The oarsman did not dare turn his head, so he was obliged to ask questions.

"What's he doing now?"

"He's standing still again. He's looking, I think. —There he goes again—toward the house. —Now he's stopped again."

"Is he waving at us?"

"No, not now; he was, though."

"Look! There comes another man!"

"He's running."

"Look at him go, would you!"

"Why, he's on a bicycle. Now he's met the other man. They're both waving at us. Look!"

"There comes something up the beach."

"What the devil is that thing?"

"Why, it looks like a boat."

"Why, certainly, it's a boat."

"No; it's on wheels."

"Yes, so it is. Well, that must be the life-boat. They drag them along shore on a wagon."

"That's the life-boat, sure."

"No, by God, it's—it's an omnibus."

"I tell you it's a life-boat."

"It is not! It's an omnibus. I can see it plain. See. One of these big hotel omnibuses."

"By thunder, you're right. It's an omnibus, sure as fate. What do you suppose they are doing with an omnibus? Maybe they are going around collecting the life-crew, hey?"

"That's it, likely. Look! There's a fellow waving a little black flag. He's standing on the steps of the omnibus. There come those other two fellows. Now they're all talking together. Look at the fellow with the flag. Maybe he ain't waving it!"

"That ain't a flag, is it? That's his coat. Why, certainly, that's his coat."

"So it is; it's his coat. He's taken it off and is waving it around his head. But would you look at him swing it!"

"Oh, say, there isn't any life-saving station there. That's just a winter-resort hotel omnibus that has brought over some of the boarders to see us drown."

"What's that idiot with the coat mean? What's he signalling, anyhow?"

"It looks as if he were trying to tell us to go north. There must be a life-saving station up there."

"No; he thinks we're fishing. Just giving us a merry hand. See? Ah, there, Willie!"

"Well, I wish I could make something out of those signals. What do you suppose he means?"

"He don't mean anything; he's just playing."

"Well, if he'd just signal us to try the surf again, or to go to sea and wait, or go north, or go south, or go to hell, there would be some reason in it. But look at him! He just stands there and keeps his coat revolving like a wheel. The ass!"

"There come more people."

"Now there's quite a mob. Look! Isn't that a boat?"

"Where? Oh, I see where you mean. No, that's no boat."

"That fellow is still waving his coat."

"He must think we like to see him do that. Why don't he quit it? It don't mean anything."

"I don't know. I think he is trying to make us go north. It must be that there's a life-saving station there somewhere."

"Say, he ain't tired yet. Look at 'im wave!"

"Wonder how long he can keep that up. He's been revolving his coat ever since he caught sight of us. He's an idiot. Why aren't they getting men to bring a boat out? A fishing boat—one of those big yawls—could come out here all right. Why don't he do something?"

"Oh, it's all right now."

"They'll have a boat out here for us in less than no time, now that they've seen us."

A faint yellow tone came into the sky over the low land. The shadows on the sea slowly deepened. The wind bore coldness with it, and the men began to shiver.

"Holy smoke!" said one, allowing his voice to express his impious mood, "if we keep on monkeying out here! If we've got to flounder out here all night!"

"Oh, we'll never have to stay here all night! Don't you worry. They've seen us now, and it won't be long before they'll come chasing out after us."

The shore grew dusky. The man waving a coat blended gradually into this gloom, and it swallowed in the same manner the omnibus and the group of people. The spray, when it dashed uproariously over the side, made the voyagers shrink and swear like men who were being branded.

"I'd like to catch the chump who waved the coat. I feel like socking him one, just for luck."

"Why? What did he do?"

"Oh, nothing, but then he seemed so damned cheerful."

In the meantime the oiler rowed, and then the correspondent rowed, and then the oiler rowed. Grey-faced and bowed forward, they mechanically, turn by turn, plied the leaden oars. The form of the lighthouse had vanished from the southern horizon, but finally a pale star appeared, just lifting from the sea. The streaked saffron in the west passed before the all-merging darkness, and the sea to the east was black. The land had vanished, and was expressed only by the low and drear thunder of the surf.

"If I am going to be drowned—if I am going to be drowned—if I am going to be drowned, why, in the name of the seven mad gods who rule the sea, was I allowed to come thus far and contemplate sand and trees? Was I brought here merely to have my nose dragged away as I was about to nibble the sacred cheese of life?"

The patient captain, drooped over the water-jar, was sometimes obliged to speak to the oarsman.

"Keep her head up! Keep her head up!"

"Keep her head up, sir." The voices were weary and low.

This was surely a quiet evening. All save the oarsman lay heavily and listlessly in the boat's bottom. As for him, his eyes were just capable of noting the tall black waves that swept forward in a most sinister silence, save for an occasional subdued growl of a crest.

The cook's head was on a thwart, and he looked without interest at the water under his nose. He was deep in other scenes. Finally he spoke. "Billie," he murmured, dreamfully, "what kind of pie do you like best?"

5

"Pie!" said the oiler and correspondent, agitatedly. "Don't talk about those things, blast you!"

"Well," said the cook, "I was just thinking about ham sandwiches, and—"

A night on the sea in an open boat is a long night. As darkness settled finally, the shine of the light, lifting from the sea in the south, changed to full gold. On the northern horizon a new light appeared, a small bluish gleam on the edge of the waters. These two lights were the furniture of the world. Otherwise there was nothing but waves.

Two men huddled in the stern, and distances were so magnificent in the dinghy that the rower was enabled to keep his feet partly warm by thrusting them under his companions. Their legs indeed extended far under the rowing-seat until they touched the feet of the captain forward. Sometimes, despite the efforts of the tired oarsman, a wave came piling into the boat, an icy wave of the night, and the chilling water soaked them anew. They would twist their bodies for a moment and groan, and sleep the dead sleep once more, while the water in the boat gurgled about them as the craft rocked.

The plan of the oiler and the correspondent was for one to row until he lost the ability, and then arouse the other from his sea-water couch in the bottom of the boat.

The oiler plied the oars until his head drooped forward and the overpowering sleep blinded him; and he rowed yet afterward. Then he touched a man in the bottom of the boat, and called his name. "Will you spell me for a little while?" he said meekly.

"Sure, Billie," said the correspondent, awakening and dragging himself to a sitting position. They exchanged places carefully, and the oiler, cuddling down in the sea-water at the cook's side, seemed to go to sleep instantly.

The particular violence of the sea had ceased. The waves came without snarling. The obligation of the man at the oars was to keep the boat headed so that the tilt of the rollers would not capsize her, and to preserve her from filling when the crests rushed past. The black waves were silent and hard to be seen in the darkness. Often one was almost upon the boat before the oarsman was aware.

In a low voice the correspondent addressed the captain. He was not sure that the captain was awake, although this iron man seemed to be always awake. "Captain, shall I keep her making for that light north, sir?"

The same steady voice answered him. "Yes. Keep it about two points off the port bow."

The cook had tied a life-belt around himself in order to get even the warmth which this clumsy cork contrivance could donate, and he seemed almost stove-like when a rower, whose teeth invariably chattered wildly as soon as he ceased his labour, dropped down to sleep.

The correspondent, as he rowed, looked down at the two men sleeping underfoot. The cook's arm was around the oiler's shoulders, and, with their fragmentary clothing and haggard faces, they were the babes of the sea—a grotesque rendering of the old babes in the wood.

Later he must have grown stupid at his work, for suddenly there was a growling of water, and a crest came with a roar and a swash into the boat, and it was a wonder that it did not set the cook afloat in his life-belt. The cook continued to sleep, but the oiler sat up, blinking his eyes and shaking with the new cold.

"Oh, I'm awful sorry, Billie," said the correspondent contritely.

"That's all right, old boy," said the oiler, and lay down again and was asleep.

Presently it seemed that even the captain dozed, and the correspondent thought that he was the one man afloat on all the ocean. The wind had a voice as it came over the waves, and it was sadder than the end.

There was a long, loud swishing astern of the boat, and a gleaming trail of phosphorescence, like blue flame, was furrowed on the black waters. It might have been made by a monstrous knife.

Then there came a stillness, while the correspondent breathed with open mouth and looked at the sea.

Suddenly there was another swish and another long flash of bluish light, and this time it was alongside the boat, and might almost have been reached with an oar. The correspondent saw an enormous fin speed like a shadow through the water, hurling the crystalline spray, and leaving the long glowing trail.

The correspondent looked over his shoulder at the captain. His face was hidden, and he seemed to be asleep. He looked at the babes of the sea. They certainly were asleep. So, being bereft of sympathy, he leaned a little way to one side and swore softly into the sea.

But the thing did not then leave the vicinity of the boat. Ahead or astern, on one side or the other, at intervals long or short, fled the long sparkling streak, and there was to be heard the *whirroo* of the dark fin. The speed and power of the thing was greatly to be admired. It cut the water like a gigantic and keen projectile.

The presence of this biding thing did not affect the man with the same horror that it would if he had been a picnicker. He simply looked at the sea dully and swore in an undertone.

Nevertheless, it is true that he did not wish to be alone with the thing. He wished one of his companions to awake by chance and keep him company with it. But the captain hung motionless over the water-jar, and the oiler and the cook in the bottom of the boat were plunged in slumber.

6

"If I am going to be drowned—if I am going to be drowned—if I am going to be drowned, why, in the name of the seven mad gods who rule the sea, was I allowed to come thus far and contemplate sand and trees?" During this dismal night, it may be remarked that a man would conclude that it was really the intention of the seven mad gods to drown him, despite the abominable injustice of it. For it was certainly an abominable injustice to drown a man who had worked so hard, so hard. The man felt it would be a crime most unnatural. Other people had drowned at sea since galleys swarmed with painted sails, but still—

When it occurs to a man that nature does not regard him as important, and that she feels she would not maim the universe by disposing of him, he at first wishes to throw bricks at the temple, and he hates deeply the fact that there are no bricks and no temples. Any visible expression of nature would surely be pelleted with his jeers.

Then, if there be no tangible thing to hoot, he feels, perhaps, the desire to confront a personification and indulge in pleas, bowed to one knee, and with hands supplicant, saying, "Yes, but I love myself."

A high cold star on a winter's night is the word he feels that she says to him. Thereafter he knows the pathos of his situation.

The men in the dinghy had not discussed these matters, but each had, no doubt, reflected upon them in silence and according to his mind. There was seldom any expression upon their faces save the general one of complete weariness. Speech was devoted to the business of the boat.

To chime the notes of his emotion, a verse mysteriously entered the correspondent's head. He had even forgotten that he had forgotten this verse, but it suddenly was in his mind.

A soldier of the Legion lay dying in Algiers;
There was lack of woman's nursing, there was dearth of woman's tears;
But a comrade stood beside him, and he took that comrade's hand,
And he said, "I never more shall see my own, my native land."

In his childhood the correspondent had been made acquainted with the fact that a soldier of the Legion lay dying in Algiers, but he had never regarded the fact as important. Myriads of his school-fellows had informed him of the soldier's plight, but the dinning had naturally ended by making him perfectly indifferent. He had never considered it his affair that a soldier of the Legion lay dying in Algiers, nor had it appeared to him as a matter for sorrow. It was less to him than the breaking of a pencil's point.

Now, however, it quaintly came to him as a human, living thing. It was no longer merely a picture of a few throes in the breast of a poet, meanwhile drinking tea and warming his feet at the grate; it was an actuality—stern, mournful, and fine.

The correspondent plainly saw the soldier. He lay on the sand with his feet out straight and still. While his pale left hand was upon his chest in an attempt to thwart the going of his life, the blood came between his fingers. In the far Algerian distance, a city of low square forms was set against a sky that was faint with the last sunset hues. The correspondent, plying the oars and dreaming of the slow and slower movements of the lips of the soldier, was moved by a profound and perfectly impersonal comprehension. He was sorry for the soldier of the Legion who lay dying in Algiers.

The thing which had followed the boat and waited had evidently grown bored at the delay. There was no longer to be heard the slash of the cutwater, and there was no longer the flame of the long trail. The light in the north still glimmered, but it was apparently no nearer to the boat. Sometimes the boom of the surf rang in the correspondent's ears, and he turned the craft seaward then and rowed harder. Southward, some one had evidently built a watch-fire on the beach. It was too low and too far to be seen, but it made a shimmering, roseate reflection upon the bluff in back of it, and this could be discerned from the boat. The wind came stronger, and sometimes a wave suddenly raged out like a mountain cat, and there was to be seen the sheen and sparkle of a broken crest.

The captain, in the bow, moved on his water-jar and sat erect. "Pretty long night," he observed to the correspondent. He looked at the shore. "Those life-saving people take their time."

"Did you see that shark playing around?"

"Yes, I saw him. He was a big fellow, all right."

"Wish I had known you were awake."

Later the correspondent spoke into the bottom of the boat. "Billie!" There was a slow and gradual disentanglement. "Billie, will you spell me?"

"Sure," said the oiler.

As soon as the correspondent touched the cold, comfortable sea-water in the bottom of the boat and had huddled close to the cook's life-belt he was deep in sleep, despite the fact that his teeth played all the popular airs. This sleep was so good to him that it was but a moment before he heard a voice call his name in a tone that demonstrated the last stages of exhaustion. "Will you spell me?"

"Sure, Billie."

The light in the north had mysteriously vanished, but the correspondent took his course from the wide-awake captain.

Later in the night they took the boat farther out to sea, and the captain directed the cook to take one oar at the stern and keep the boat facing the seas. He was to call out if he should hear the thunder of the surf. This plan enabled the oiler and the correspondent to get respite together. "We'll give those boys a chance to get into shape again," said the captain. They curled down and, after a few preliminary chatterings and trembles, slept once more the dead sleep. Neither knew they had bequeathed to the cook the company of another shark, or perhaps the same shark.

As the boat caroused on the waves, spray occasionally bumped over the side and gave them a fresh soaking, but this had no power to break their repose. The ominous slash of the wind and the water affected them as it would have affected mummies.

"Boys," said the cook, with the notes of every reluctance in his voice, "she's drifted in pretty close. I guess one of you had better take her to sea again." The correspondent, aroused, heard the crash of the toppled crests.

As he was rowing, the captain gave him some whiskey-and-water, and this steadied the chills out of him. "If I ever get ashore and anybody shows me even a photograph of an oar—"

At last there was a short conversation.

"Billie!—Billie, will you spell me?"

"Sure," said the oiler.

7

When the correspondent again opened his eyes, the sea and the sky were each of the grey hue of the dawning. Later, carmine and gold was painted upon the waters. The morning appeared finally, in its splendour, with a sky of pure blue, and the sunlight flamed on the tips of the waves.

On the distant dunes were set many little black cottages, and a tall white windmill reared above them. No man, nor dog, nor bicycle appeared on the beach. The cottages might have formed a deserted village.

The voyagers scanned the shore. A conference was held in the boat. "Well," said the captain, "if no help is coming, we might better try a run through the surf right away. If we stay out here much longer we will be too weak to do anything for ourselves at all." The others silently acquiesced in this reasoning. The boat was headed for the beach. The correspondent wondered if none ever ascended the tall wind-tower, and if then they never looked seaward. This tower was a giant, standing with its back to the plight of the ants. It represented in a degree, to the correspondent, the serenity of nature amid the struggles of the individual—nature in the wind, and nature in the vision of men. She did not seem cruel to him then, nor beneficent, nor treacherous, nor wise. But she was indifferent, flatly indifferent. It is, perhaps, plausible that a man in this situation, impressed with the unconcern of the universe, should see the innumerable flaws of his life, and have them taste wickedly in his mind, and wish for another chance. A distinction between right and wrong seems absurdly clear to him, then, in this new ignorance of the grave-edge, and he understands that if he were given another opportunity he would mend his conduct and his words, and be better and brighter during an introduction or at a tea.

"Now, boys," said the captain, "she is going to swamp sure. All we can do is to work her in as far as possible, and then when she swamps, pile out and scramble for the beach. Keep cool now, and don't jump until she swamps sure."

The oiler took the oars. Over his shoulders he scanned the surf. "Captain," he said, "I think I'd better bring her about and keep her head-on to the seas and back her in."

"All right, Billie," said the captain. "Back her in." The oiler swung the boat then, and, seated in the stern, the cook and the correspondent were obliged to look over their shoulders to contemplate the lonely and indifferent shore.

The monstrous inshore rollers heaved the boat high until the men were again enabled to see the white sheets of water scudding up the slanted beach. "We won't get in very close," said the captain. Each time a man could wrest his attention from the rollers, he turned his glance toward the shore, and in the expression of the eyes during this contemplation there was a singular quality. The correspondent, observing the others, knew that they were not afraid, but the full meaning of their glances was shrouded.

As for himself, he was too tired to grapple fundamentally with the fact. He tried to coerce his mind into thinking of it, but the mind was dominated at this time by the muscles, and they did not care. It merely occurred to him that if he should drown it would be a shame.

There were no hurried words, no pallor, no plain agitation. The men simply looked at the shore. "Now, remember to get well clear of the boat when you jump," said the captain.

Seaward the crest of a roller suddenly fell with a thunderous crash, and the long white comber came roaring down upon the boat.

"Steady now," said the captain. The men were silent. They turned their eyes from the shore to the comber and waited. The boat slid up the incline, leaped at the furious top, bounced over it, and swung down the long back of the wave. Some water had been shipped, and the cook bailed it out.

But the next crest crashed also. The tumbling, boiling flood of white water caught the boat and whirled it almost perpendicular. Water swarmed in from all sides. The correspondent had his hands on the gunwale at this time, and when the water entered at that place he swiftly withdrew his fingers, as if he objected to wetting them.

The little boat, drunken with this weight of water, reeled and snuggled deeper into the sea.

"Bail her out, cook! Bail her out!" said the captain.

"All right, Captain," said the cook.

"Now, boys, the next one will do for us sure," said the oiler. "Mind to jump clear of the boat."

The third wave moved forward, huge, furious, implacable. It fairly swallowed the dinghy, and almost simultaneously the men tumbled into the sea. A piece of life-belt had lain in the bottom of the boat, and as the correspondent went overboard he held this to his chest with his left hand.

The January water was icy, and he reflected immediately that it was colder than he had expected to find it off the coast of Florida. This appeared to his dazed mind as a fact important enough to be noted at the time. The coldness of the water was sad; it was tragic. This fact was somehow mixed and confused with his opinion of his own situation, so that it seemed almost a proper reason for tears. The water was cold.

When he came to the surface he was conscious of little but the noisy water. Afterward he saw his companions in the sea. The oiler was ahead in the race. He was swimming strongly and rapidly. Off to the correspondent's left, the cook's great white and corked back bulged out of the water; and in the rear the captain was hanging with his one good hand to the keep of the overturned dinghy.

There is a certain immovable quality to a shore, and the correspondent wondered at it amid the confusion of the sea.

It seemed also very attractive; but the correspondent knew that it was a long journey, and he paddled leisurely. The piece of life-preserver lay under him, and sometimes he whirled down the incline of a wave as if he were on a hand-sled.

But finally he arrived at a place in the sea where travel was beset with difficulty. He did not pause swimming to inquire what manner of current had caught him, but there his progress ceased. The shore was set before him like a bit of scenery on a stage, and he looked at it and understood with his eyes each detail of it.

As the cook passed, much farther to the left, the captain was calling to him, "Turn over on your back, cook! Turn over on your back and use the oar."

"All right, sir." The cook turned on his back, and paddling with an oar, went ahead as if he were a canoe.

Presently the boat also passed to the left of the correspondent, with the captain clinging with one hand to the keel. He would have appeared like a man raising himself to look over a board fence if it were not for the extraordinary gymnastics of the boat. The correspondent marvelled that the captain could still hold to it.

They passed on nearer to shore—the oiler, the cook, the captain—and following them went the water-jar, bouncing gaily over the seas.

The correspondent remained in the grip of this strange new enemy—a current. The shore, with its white slope of sand and its green bluff topped with little silent cottages, was spread like a picture before him. It was very near to him then, but he was impressed as one who, in a gallery, looks at a scene from Brittany or Algiers.

He thought: "I'm going to drown? Can it be possible? Can it be possible? Can it be possible?" Perhaps an individual must consider his own death to be the final phenomenon of nature.

But later a wave perhaps whirled him out of this small deadly current, for he found suddenly that he could again make progress toward the shore. Later still he was aware that the captain, clinging with one hand to the keel of the dinghy, had his face turned away from the shore and toward him, and was calling his name. "Come to the boat! Come to the boat!"

In his struggle to reach the captain and the boat, he reflected that when one gets properly wearied drowning must really be a comfortable arrangement—a cessation of hostilities accompanied by a large degree of relief; and he was glad of it, for the main thing in his mind for some moments had been horror of the temporary agony. He did not wish to be hurt.

Presently he saw a man running along the shore. He was undressing with most remarkable speed. Coat, trousers, shirt, everything flew magically off him.

"Come to the boat!" called the captain.

"All right, Captain." As the correspondent paddled, he saw the captain let himself down to bottom and leave the boat. Then the correspondent performed his own little marvel of the voyage. A large wave caught him and flung him with ease and supreme speed completely over the boat and far beyond it. It struck him even then as an event in gymnastics and a true miracle of the sea. An overturned boat in the surf is not a plaything to a swimming man.

The correspondent arrived in water that reached only to his waist, but his condition did not enable him to stand for more than a moment. Each wave knocked him into a heap, and the undertow pulled at him.

Then he saw the man who had been running and undressing, and undressing and running, come bounding into the water. He dragged ashore the cook, and then waded toward the captain; but the captain waved him away and sent him to the correspondent. He was naked—naked as a tree in winter; but a halo was about his head, and he shone like a saint. He gave a strong pull, and a long drag, and a bully heave at the correspondent's hand. The correspondent, schooled in the minor formulae, said, "Thanks, old man." But suddenly the man cried, "What's that?" He pointed a swift finger. The correspondent said, "Go."

In the shallows, face downward, lay the oiler. His forehead touched sand that was periodically, between each wave, clear of the sea.

The correspondent did not know all that transpired afterward. When he achieved safe ground he fell, striking the sand with each particular part of his body. It was as if he had dropped from a roof, but the thud was grateful to him.

It seems that instantly the beach was populated with men with blankets, clothes, and flasks, and women with coffee-pots and all the remedies sacred to their minds. The welcome of the land to the men from the sea was warm and generous; but a still and dripping shape was carried slowly up the beach, and the land's welcome for it could only be the different and sinister hospitality of the grave.

When it came night, the white waves paced to and fro in the moonlight, and the wind brought the sound of the great sea's voice to the men on the shore, and they felt that they could then be interpreters.

[1898–U.S.A.]

QUESTIONS

1. Crane's story is based on a real-life event, one which, indeed, Crane reported himself in the *New York Press*. (Crane was a correspondent for the *Press* on his way to Cuba when his ship, the *Commodore*, went down on January 2, 1897.) In many ways Crane's story is like a news report, but the differences are more striking yet. What are the similarities? How does the story differ from a report? In other words, what makes it a piece of fiction as opposed to a piece of reportage? (Consider, for example, pacing, symbolism, and theme.)

2. There is no description of the men in the boat, and only one is named. Why? What does Crane accomplish and perhaps also avoid by his lack of characterization? In the same vein, why the third-person narration? Why is it better in establishing the tone Crane wants than first-person narration would be?

3. "A high cold star on a winter's night is the word he [man] feels she [nature] says to him," we are told in section 6. Here is the theme of the story. What does nature say? What, in Crane's view, is the condition of humankind?

4. Both the boat and the sea in "The Open Boat" are tangible realities, yet they

also seem symbolic. What do they symbolize with respect to the story's general theme?

5. What are the tone and implications of "nibble on the cheese of life" (section 4) and "the plight of ants" (section 7)? How do these phrases relate to Crane's theme?

6. What is the dominant mood of the story? How does its mood go along with and help convey its theme?

WRITING SUGGESTIONS

1. In a paragraph or more, compare and contrast "The Open Boat" and "The Rocking-Horse Winner." They are utterly different, and yet they are both pieces of fiction. You might, then, begin with their dissimilarities and move to their fundamental likeness.

2. Take an incident from your own life and see if you can turn it to fiction. To do so you will need to discover some theme in your material and then shape that material accordingly, as you find what elements of fiction will best serve your purposes.

3. Do you agree with Crane or reject his view of things as embodied in "The Open Boat"? Write a short essay on your view of things using Crane for support (if you agree with him) or as a foil to set off your view (if you disagree).

4. Research Crane's reportage, which appeared in the *New York Press*, January 4, 5, and 7, 1897, and in the *Florida Times-Union*, January 5, 1897. You might be able to locate the original papers, but the material can also be found in a number of books. Now, in a carefully organized essay, analyze the difference between the reports and the story at hand, providing sufficient examples from both to make your analysis meaningful to a reader familiar with the story but not with the background material. As you proceed, consider what your analysis reveals about fiction generally. If appropriate, you might wish to state your thoughts on this matter in your paper.

APPENDIX: A BRIEF GUIDE TO THE USE AND DOCUMENTATION OF SOURCES AND RELATED MATTERS

USING SOURCES

Plagiarism

Plagiarism is the unacknowledged use—whether intentional or not—of another person's words or ideas. What you should know first about the use of source material is that anything not your own in a paper will be considered plagiarized if it is not attributed properly. Every direct quotation must be either put within quotation marks or blocked and indented, and a citation must be given referring to a Works Cited list at the end of your paper. Summaries and paraphrases also call for citations. If you cite your sources appropriately, there will be no problem. If you don't, your theft—for that is what it will be—will most likely be caught. Plagiarism usually shouts its presence, especially if the student has lifted something from a published text. Even if the instructor does not know the source, plagiarism can be recognized on stylistic or ideational grounds alone. And how silly plagiarism is. It insults the intelligence of the reader and shows that the student has completely misunderstood the purpose of research.

When you do research, proudly show the work you've done by your citations. What is impressive is how you use your sources to buttress *your* ideas.

Referring to Titles

The way titles are quoted is simple: as a general rule, the title of something published in a longer work with a title of its own is put within quotation marks; the title of anything published as an independent unit is italicized (underlined in a typed text). For instance, the title of any short story in this book should be put in quotation marks: "Just Lather, That's All" or "Smile" or "The Open Boat." Should you refer to the book as a whole, underline its title: Reading and Writing about Short Fiction. Titles of books, newspapers, and magazines are underlined; the titles of chapters within books, articles in magazines, short stories and lyric poems, and so forth are put in quotation marks. Incidentally, just as quotation marks and italics (underlining) are not used in titles of the works themselves, you should use neither when you place your own title at the head of your paper. However, if your paper title *includes* a story or book title, these should be put in quotation marks or underlined, as appropriate. Here are two examples of paper titles containing titles of published works:

Contagious Fear in "That Evening Sun"

The Use of the Elements as Defined in Reading and Writing

about Short Fiction

Remember that *your whole* title should not have quotation marks around it or be underlined (unless, of course, your title consists of nothing but the title of the work you are writing about—a practice almost always to be discouraged).

Continuous vs. Blocked Quotations

When quoting from a source, you must make a decision depending upon what is being quoted and how much of it. That is, one or two lines of verse and up to four lines of prose should be put in quotation marks and typed so as to be continuous with your text. The following exemplifies this mode of quotation and the way it looks: I began this paragraph by saying, "When quoting from a source, you must make a decision depending upon what is being quoted and how much of it." However, more than four lines of prose (or more than two lines of verse) should be blocked and indented—that is, separated from the lines of your own writing and indented from the left ten spaces. Such quotations are often introduced by a clause ending in a colon, though other punctuation, or even none, may sometimes serve, depending on how the beginning of the quoted text flows grammatically from your own text. The following blocked quotation illustrates these points.

Ursula LeGuin's haunting "The Ones Who Walk Away from Omelas" had its origins in a sentence by William James:

> Or if the hypothesis were offered us of a world
> in which . . . utopias should all be outdone,
> and millions kept permanently happy on the one
> simple condition that a certain lost soul on
> the far-off edge of things should lead a life
> of lonely torment, what except a specifical
> and independent sort of emotion can it be
> which would make us immediately feel, even
> though an impulse arose within us to clutch at
> the happiness so offered, how hideous a thing
> would be its enjoyment when deliberately
> accepted as the fruit of such a bargain?

This is the look of a blocked quotation. (It would be followed by a parenthetical citation, but we'll consider such documentation later in this appendix.) Note that there are no quotation marks around the material blocked; the blocking itself signals quotation. Another note of caution: do not use long quotations to excess. Summarize or paraphrase whenever possible. Use your sources for evidence, not padding.

A quotation within a blocked quotation—that is, something being quoted by the author of your source—is put within normal (double) quotation marks (" "). In continuous quotations, such an interior quotation goes within single quotation marks, as in the following sentences quoted from Thurber's "The Owl Who Was God": " 'Aren't you afraid?' he asked. 'Who?' said the owl calmly, for he could not see the truck." Observe the punctuation here. In American English, periods and commas always go *inside* the closing quotation marks thus: "for he could not see the truck." Semicolons and colons go *outside.* Exclamation points and question marks go inside if they are part of the quotation and outside if they are your own.

Changing Punctuation

There are, then, two minor changes of punctuation that you can and often must make with respect to continuous quotations: (1) if quotation marks are found *within* the material you are quoting, change those quotation marks from double (" ") to single (' ') ones; (2) if necessary to make the quotation fit smoothly into your sentence, use a comma (or ellipsis dots—see the next subsection) within the closing quotation marks even though the original may have had no mark of punctuation there or some other mark, such as a period, that you will be replacing with the comma. Consider, for instance, the punctuation changes we must make if we wish to incorporate Thurber's sentence quoted above as part of the following sentence of our own:

```
When Thurber writes, "'Who?' said the owl calmly, for
he could not see the truck," we can almost feel the
truck bearing inexorably down upon the complacent bird
and his disciples.
```

Here Thurber's double quotation marks around the first word, *Who,* have been changed to single ones. And the period at the end of Thurber's original sentence (after *truck*) has been changed to a comma to make Thurber's sentence fit into the new structure. (You may wish to look at Thurber's original sentence on page 46.)

Ellipsis and Square Brackets

Quotations must be exact, except for the two minor changes of punctuation we've just mentioned in connection with continuing quotations. However, quotations need not be complete. You can quote anything you like, from a paragraph or more down to a phrase or even a word. You can also leave words out of a quotation or add words of your own. The first is accomplished by ellipsis. Consider this sentence from Elizabeth Taylor's "The First Death of Her Life" and then the version of it shortened by ellipsis:

"A little bustle began, quick footsteps along the empty
passages, and for a moment she was left alone with her
dead mother."

"A little bustle began . . . and for a moment she was left
alone with her dead mother."

Not used at the beginning of a quotation (for the reader knows that your quotation is an excerpt), ellipsis entails the use of three spaced dots to show that something from the source has been left out (only three dots, note, except when the ellipsis comes at the end of a sentence, in which case the period is also required).

If you wish to insert words of your own into a quotation for some reason—to make the quotation fit more smoothly with the structure of your sentence as a whole, perhaps, or to comment on something within the quotation—you can do so by the use of square brackets. Here, for example, is how you might add a comment of your own in brackets if you were quoting the sentence by Elizabeth Taylor that we used to illustrate ellipsis above:

"A little bustle began . . . and for a moment [notice
that it is only a moment] she was left alone...."

Fitting Quotations with Contexts

A quotation must be exact, yet—as we've noted—it must also fit smoothly into the context in which you are putting it. Often the context, the quotation, or both must be adjusted to make the necessary accommodation. A quotation can be adjusted by ellipsis, by additions in brackets, and by paraphrase (that is, what does not grammatically fit your context can be restated in your own words and the rest quoted). Your own context can also be adjusted. For instance, if you were quoting from my discussion of "The Shawl" in chapter 1, you would not want to write:

In reconsidering "The Shawl," Proffitt stated that he
"find no reason to alter my initial feelings."

The quotation is exact but, in its new context, ungrammatical and confusing. The problem might be solved in various ways. One way would be to change your own sentence by adding the word *could* (which fits grammatically with the quotation's first word, *find*) and by making a bracketed insertion in the quotation itself to change *my* to *his* (the brackets alert the reader that the word is yours, not in the original source):

In reconsidering "The Shawl," Proffitt stated that he could "find no reason to alter [his] initial feelings."

Introducing Quotations

In your remarks introducing a quotation, you will usually want to incorporate the name of the person being quoted, and in any case you will want to make sure that the reason for your quotation is immediately clear. If the reason may not be clear, introduce the quotation by briefly suggesting why you are using it in the present context. For instance, let's say that in a paper on William Carlos Williams's story "The Use of Force" (pages 306–09) you write:

The opening of the girl's mouth in the story is described in exceptionally concrete terms. We are made aware, however, of a symbolic meaning to the opening of the mouth. "No ideas but in things."

You would need to revise this statement to introduce the quotation "No ideas but in things" (a line from a poem by Williams), for here it just sits, a puzzlement to the reader and so an obstacle to achieving your purpose. Note how, in the following version, the quotation is introduced in a way that clarifies its purpose:

The opening of the girl's mouth in the story is described in exceptionally concrete terms. We are made aware, however, of a symbolic meaning to the opening of the mouth. Something Williams wrote in a poem captures the dual nature of this image: "No ideas but in things."

In both versions, of course, you would need to add a citation to the specific source of the line being quoted—a procedure we will consider shortly.

Quotation, Summary, and Paraphrase

Quotation is not the only way, or always the best way, to present the ideas of another. Often a summary or a paraphrase will prove more effective. A summary is a condensation of someone else's thinking down to the core of that person's idea. For instance, the paragraph headed "Fitting Quotations with Contexts" on page 562 could be summarized as follows: Proffitt emphasizes that quotations must fit smoothly into their new contexts (562). A paraphrase is more elaborate but is still a condensation in that it restates someone else's thought in brief. A paraphrase of the paragraph on context that we just summarized would be something like this: As Proffitt emphasizes, in order to make a quotation fit smoothly into its new context—and it is important for the writer to do so—the context itself can be adjusted by, for instance, the use of paraphrase, and the quotation can be adjusted by ellipsis or by addition in square brackets (562).

Observe that the paraphrase, like the summary, is restricted to the ideas in the source and that the paraphrase follows its sequence of ideas. Be sure to be alert and recognize that you are summarizing or paraphrasing if you are. Then provide the proper citations.

CITING SOURCES

Whether you are quoting directly, summarizing, or paraphrasing, you must provide an appropriate citation in your text. The dual purpose of any citation is to acknowledge your borrowing as smoothly and concisely as possible within the text and to enable your reader to locate full information about your source in a list called *Works Cited*, which is arranged alphabetically by authors' last names at the end of your paper. Thus the key element of a citation within your paper is the author's last name, together with the specific page number(s) on which the cited material appears in the source.

Put the author's last name and the page reference (the page or pages on which the material you are quoting, summarizing, or paraphrasing can be found) in parentheses at the end of the quotation, summary, or paraphrase:

```
"Whether you are quoting directly, summarizing, or para-
phrasing, you must provide an appropriate citation in
your text" (Proffitt 564).
```

```
Quotations must fit smoothly into their new context
(Proffitt 562).
```

Often it is smoother, however, to mention the author's name in introducing the summary, paraphrase, or quotation, in which case you need not repeat the name in the parenthetical citation; the page reference alone is then enough:

```
As Proffitt says, "Whether you are quoting directly,
summarizing, or paraphrasing, you must provide an
appropriate citation in your text" (564).
Proffitt stresses that quotations must fit smoothly in
their new context (562).
```

Parenthetical citation is used for books, stories, articles, and newspapers alike, with more detailed information left for the Works Cited list put at the end of a paper (we shall take up this matter shortly).

Citing Continuous vs. Blocked Quotations

There is one small difference between citations coming after continuous quotations and those coming after blocked quotations. When citations for continuous quotations come at the ends of sentences (as they most often do), the sentence period comes *after* the citation as in the following example: The story reaches its most surreal moment with the image of "a butterfly touching a silver vine" (Ozick 7). With blocked quotations, on the other hand, the period comes at the end of the quotation, and the citation stands alone two spaces to the right of the period. Here, for instance, are the first sentences of the previous subsection as they would appear and be cited in a blocked quotation:

```
             Whether you are quoting directly,
             summarizing, or paraphrasing, you must
             provide an appropriate citation in your text.
             The dual purpose of any citation is to
             acknowledge your borrowing as smoothly and
```

concisely as possible within the text and to
enable your reader to locate full information
about your source in a list called <u>Works
Cited</u>, which is arranged alphabetically by
authors' last names at the end of your paper.
(Proffitt 564)

Three Problem Spots

There are a few other matters concerning citation that you will need to know when doing a properly documented paper. If you have parenthetical citations for two or more works by the same author, then each citation must include not only the author's last name but also a short form of the title of the work (followed, of course, by the page reference). For instance, in a paper that contained the following sentences referring to two different stories by William Carlos Williams in this book, "The Use of Force" and "Frankie the Newspaperman," here is how the citations would be handled:

The most startling moment comes when the doctor says that
he had "fallen in love with the savage brat" (Williams,
"Use" 308).

The mother finds her son's having said "because she is
so flat busted" to be terribly funny (Williams,
"Frankie" 265).

Without the short-title designations in the citations, the reader would not be able to tell which of the two works by Williams was being quoted in each case.

A somewhat similar problem is that of two or more authors having the same last name. In this case, each citation must include a first name or initial, as follows: (Elinor G. Smith 315), (Logan P. Smith 266).

Further, in citing an anonymous work such as a news report, use instead of the author's name the first word or phrase (omitting initial articles A, An, or The) of the title of the piece, followed by the page reference: ("Myth" 112) for a citation to page 112 of an article entitled "Myth and the Mythic Mind" in *The Book of All Mythologies*. The reader will be able to locate the full reference in the Works Cited list because anonymous works are alphabetized by the first word of their titles. Finally, a special case of the anonymous work is an article in an encyclopedia or other reference volume in which the articles are arranged alphabetically. When you cite these articles, no page reference is required because the reader can quickly look the article up in its alphabetical location. In sum, use common sense. The main purpose of parenthetical citation is to allow the reader to use the appended Works Cited list with ease. Everything done should serve this purpose.

THE WORKS CITED LIST

At the end of your paper, on its own page, should be a list called Works Cited containing an entry for each of the sources you have used. As we have seen, the information in the citations within your paper is abbreviated. In Works Cited you list your sources alphabetically by the last name of each author (or the title if there is no author indicated) and give your reader complete information for each source so that the reader can go to the source to confirm its validity or to study the subject further. There are a great many possible kinds of entries and so, naturally, a great many possible complications in getting a Works Cited list into shape. However, for our purposes—and, in fact, for the purposes of most people most of the time—only a few types of entry need be considered. We will examine here the most common types, especially those that will be valuable to you in using this book. A Works Cited list including all the examples discussed in this appendix appears at the conclusion (pages 572–73). The style followed here, as throughout this appendix, is the one most commonly used in literature and composition courses, that of the Modern Language Association of America. (Some other styles are used in other disciplines.) Should you happen to need information beyond what is presented here, consult Joseph Gibaldi and Walter S. Achtert, *MLA Handbook for Writers of Research Papers*, 2nd ed., New York: MLA, 1984, which is sure to be in your college library.

Books and Journal Articles

The works most frequently cited are books and articles. An entry for a book should include the name of the author, last name first (if a work has two or more authors, names of authors after the first are straightforward); the full title of the work, including subtitle (separated from the title by a colon), underlined; the edition, if other than the first edition; and finally the city of publication followed by a colon, a shortened form of the publisher's name, and the date of publication. Here are two examples:

Brooks, Cleanth, R. W. B. Lewis, and Robert Penn Warren.
<u>American Literature: The Makers and the Making</u>.
Shorter ed. New York: St. Martin's, 1974.

Forster, E. M. <u>Aspects of the Novel</u>. New York: Harcourt, 1954.

When a work has more than three authors, give only the first author's name, followed by a comma and the phrase "et al." (not in quotation marks), which is Latin for "and others." For instance, had the first book listed above had four authors rather than three, the author would have been given as follows: Brooks, Cleanth, et al.

For articles, treat the author's name exactly as for a book. Then comes the title of the article in quotation marks; next, the name of the journal, underlined; and finally the volume number, issue number, date of publication, and the inclusive page numbers of the article (not the page reference for your specific citation, which appears in parentheses in the text of your paper). For a daily, weekly, or monthly periodical, however, omit volume and issue numbers and give the specific date instead. Following are two typical entries:

Funey, Sean. "The Aroma of Paterson in Williams's
Stories." <u>Journal of Short Fiction Studies</u> 18.2
(1984): 23–41.

Staggs, Sam. "James Dickey." <u>Publishers Weekly</u> 29 May
1987: 62–63.

In the entry for the Funey article, the volume number of the journal is 18, and the issue number is 2 (with this information, only the year of publication, 1984, is given); the article runs from page 23 to page 41. Because the Staggs entry is for a weekly publication, the specific date replaces the volume and issue number.

Observe the spacing in all four entries above: two spaces are used after each discrete item of information that is followed by a period—after the author's name, for example, and again after the title of the book or article, and still again after the edition, as in the entry for Brooks, Lewis, and Warren. The same would be true of other discrete items of information, such as the name of an editor or translator (as other examples in this appendix will show). Note, too, that the first line of an entry is not indented and the rest of the lines are indented five spaces.

Anthologies

For an anthology, give the editor's name, last name first (as for an author), followed by a comma, a space, and the abbreviation "ed." Then give the title and the rest of the information as for any other book. Such an entry looks like this:

Proffitt, Edward, ed. <u>Reading and Writing about Short Fiction</u>. San Diego: Harcourt, 1988.

In a paper in which, for instance, you compare two stories found in the present text, this would be your main entry. How the individual stories would be entered in the list is covered in the next subsection.

A Work in an Anthology

For a story or other selection found in an anthology for which you have provided a main entry as shown just above, begin with the author of the selection (in the usual way). Next give the selection title, followed by a period, in quotation marks (exception: titles of plays are underlined); if the selection is a translation, next give the translator's name preceded by "Trans."; and finally give the last name of the anthology's editor and the inclusive page numbers of the story or other selection as it appears in the anthology. Here are two examples:

García Márquez, Gabriel. "Bitterness for Three Sleep-walkers." Trans. Gregory Rabassa. Proffitt 144–47.

Williams, William Carlos. "Frankie the Newspaperman." Proffitt 264–65.

This kind of entry, referring to a main entry for the anthology itself (in this case the main entry for Proffitt shown in the preceding subsection), is convenient if you cite more than one selection from the same anthology; it saves you the trouble of repeating all the information about the anthology in the entry for each selection. However, if you refer to only one selection from the anthology, you will find it more efficient simply to use one full entry as follows:

```
Williams, William Carlos.  "The Use of Force."  Reading
    and Writing about Short Fiction.  Ed. Edward Prof-
    fitt.  San Diego: Harcourt, 1988, 306-09.
```

Reference Books and Anonymous Material

Treat a *signed* article in an encyclopedia or other reference book as you would an article or story in a collection, except don't include the name of the editor of the reference work:

```
Edel, Leon.  "Henry James and His Followers."  Encyclo-
    paedia Britannica: Macropaedia.  1974 ed.
```

If the article is not signed or if you are listing a book with no author given, the name of the book or article should appear alphabetically thus:

```
The Times Atlas of the World.  5th ed. New York: New York
    Times, 1975.
"Williams, William Carlos."  The Columbia Encyclo-
    paedia.  1950 ed.
```

Titles beginning with "A," "An," or "The" are alphabetized according to the second word of the title. Note, too, how an edition is indicated, and observe that if the materials within the source volume are arranged alphabetically you may omit volume and page numbers.

A Newspaper Article

To list an article from a newspaper, begin with the writer's name if specified (if not, begin with the title of the article), followed by the title of the article (the major headline) in quotation marks, the name of the paper (excluding initial "A," "An," or "The") underlined, the complete date, the edition if an edition, and the section letter, if the paper is divided into sections, along with the inclusive page numbers if the article is continuous (see first example to follow) or the first page number followed by a plus sign if the article is continued after skipping pages (see second example).

```
Crane, Stephen. "Captain Murphy's Shipwrecked Crew."
     Florida Times Union 5 Jan. 1897: 1-2.
"The Literate and the Damned." Bar Harbour Post
     Dispatch 12 July 1953, late ed.: B17+.
```

In the second entry, the article begins on page 17 of section B and then skips to a page farther back, as often happens in magazines and newspapers. Note, incidentally, that the names of all months except May, June, and July (in other words, all months with names more than four letters long) are abbreviated in Works Cited entries (*Jan.* in the first entry above but *July* in the second).

Two or More Works by the Same Author

For two or more works by the same author, give the author's name for the first work and then, for the other works, use three typed hyphens in place of the author's name (the hyphens are followed by a period, as is the author's name). Arrange the words alphabetically by title.

```
Williams, William Carlos. "Frankie the
     Newspaperman." Proffitt 264-65.
---. Paterson. New York: New Directions, 1946.
---. "The Use of Force." Proffitt 306-09.
```

When different books are involved, a full citation for each is necessary, though the author's name is still indicated by the three typed hyphens for the second and subsequent works in the list.

SAMPLE WORKS CITED LIST AND SAMPLE MANUSCRIPT

On the next page is a typewritten Works Cited list in the proper MLA format, listing all the works referred to in the preceding discussions. Study it carefully and be sure that you understand the entries individually and also the reasons for the order in which they are presented. Following this sample list is the sample essay on Ozick's "The Shawl" from pages 25–28 of this book, now revised (for the purpose of illustration) to incorporate documented sources and typewritten in MLA format so that you can see how margins, spacing, page numbering, and other matters are handled.

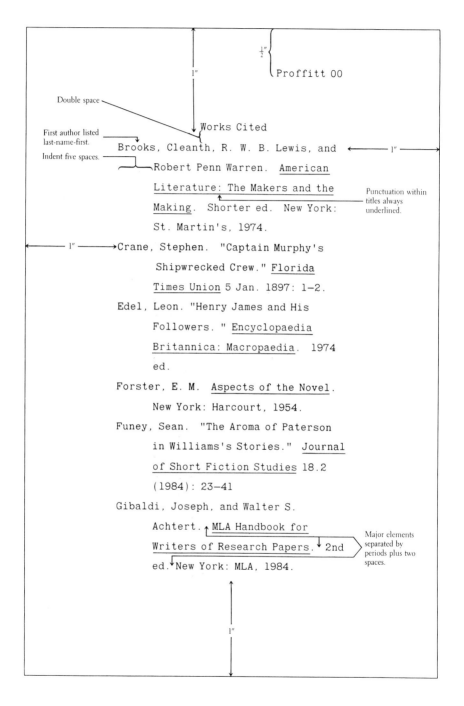

Double space

First author listed last-name-first.

Indent five spaces.

1″

1″

½″

Proffitt 00

Works Cited

Brooks, Cleanth, R. W. B. Lewis, and Robert Penn Warren. American Literature: The Makers and the Making. Shorter ed. New York: St. Martin's, 1974.

Crane, Stephen. "Captain Murphy's Shipwrecked Crew." Florida Times Union 5 Jan. 1897: 1-2.

Edel, Leon. "Henry James and His Followers. " Encyclopaedia Britannica: Macropaedia. 1974 ed.

Forster, E. M. Aspects of the Novel. New York: Harcourt, 1954.

Funey, Sean. "The Aroma of Paterson in Williams's Stories." Journal of Short Fiction Studies 18.2 (1984): 23-41

Gibaldi, Joseph, and Walter S. Achtert. MLA Handbook for Writers of Research Papers. 2nd ed. New York: MLA, 1984.

Punctuation within titles always underlined.

Major elements separated by periods plus two spaces.

½"⎱
⎰

Proffitt 00

Anonymous article alphabetized by title (ignoring "The")

"The Literate and the Damned." <u>Bar</u>

<u>Harbor Post Dispatch</u> 12 July

Article skips pages after beginning on page B17.

1953, late ed.: B17+.

Proffitt, Edward, ed. <u>Reading and</u>

<u>Writing about Short Fiction</u>.

San Diego: Harcourt, 1988.

Staggs, Sam. "James Dickey."

<u>Publishers Weekly</u> 29 May 1987:

62–63.

The Times Atlas of the World. 5th ed.

New York: New York Times, 1975.

Entry for selection, refers to main entry for anthology.

Williams, William Carlos. "Frankie

the Newspaperman." Proffitt

264–65.

Works by same author (Williams)

———. <u>Paterson</u>. New York: New

Directions, 1946.

———. "The Use of Force." Proffitt

306–09.

"Williams, William Carlos." <u>The</u>

<u>Columbia Encyclopedia</u>. 1950 ed. ←

No page numbers required for article in alphabetized reference work.

$\frac{1}{2}''$

1

All pages numbered

1"

Firstname Surname
Professor Wise
English 102, sec. 14
September 11, 1987

Double space

The Meaning of Powerlessness

Two double spaces

Five spaces

For human beings to retain a
sense of integrity, we need some
degree of personal freedom. Stripped ← 1" →
of autonomy entirely, we wither. The
self literally ceases to be itself
because it can have no effect in the
← 1" → external world. Forced into a
condition like that of childhood, we
tend to revert to childish modes of
thought and feeling. Even worse,
powerlessness often leads to madness,
as the psychologist Rollo May
demonstrates in a chapter entitled

Citation: inclusive pages in May

"Madness and Powerlessness"
(19-45). "Power is essential for all

Citations to specific pages where quotations appear

living things" (19). May says, and he

Periods and commas go inside quotation marks *unless* citation intervenes.

1"

Last name
precedes page
number on pages
after the first.

Surname 2

Citations to
specific pages
where quotations
appear

goes on to discuss how "powerlessness

and psychosis" are intimately

related (23). These terrible effects

of powerlessness on the human mind and

spirit can be seen dramatically in

Cynthia Ozick's "The Shawl" through

the deterioration of Rosa, its central

character.

When we first meet Rosa, on the

march, she has become physically

decrepit, but her mind is still

intact. Despite the dislocating

effect of the march itself and the

foul treatment received on it, she is

still capable of logical thought and

rational choice. Thus, she conceives

a plan to give Magda away to someone at

the side of the road; thinking the

plan through, however, she realizes

its impossibility and so rejects it.

Here we have the operation of a

rational mind. How different from

this Rosa is the Rosa we leave at the

end of the story. Her deterioration

proceeds subtly but inevitably.

Surname 3

The first mark of that
deterioration occurs soon after the
incident above. Suddenly we are told
that "It was a magic shawl" (Ozick
5), and this idea is pursued.
Because Ozick's narrator makes us see
through Rosa's eyes, we know that it
is Rosa who has started to believe in
magic. That the shawl is not magic,
of course, is suggested by the story's
title: the shawl is merely a shawl.
Even more, the fact that it doesn't
finally protect Magda but instead is
the cause of her being discovered
evidences its lack of magic
properties. But that Rosa should come
to feel the shawl to be magic quietly
reveals her deterioration, or the
start thereof. A belief in magic, we
might recall, was associated by Freud
both with schizophrenic
hallucinations and with childhood
(83-84).

Rosa's way of seeing as
communicated by some of the story's

Author's name
included here
because not
mentioned in text
leading to this first
citation.

Author's name
(Freud) not needed
here because given
in text leading to
the reference.

Surname 4

images, especially at the end, is
further evidence of her
deterioration. In the context of the
prison camp as described, images like
"jolly light" (6), "a clown out of
Magda's shawl" (6), "light tapped
the helmet and sparkled it into a
goblet" (7), and, most pointedly,
"a butterfly touching a silver vine"
(7) suggest a mind projecting itself
onto the world in order thus to change
reality. P. J. Miller rightly
summarizes the effect of the story's
imagery as having "a surreal quality
... in [the] context, a quality that
imparts a growing sense of madness"
(152).

And Rosa does go mad. At the end
of the story her deterioration is
complete: she has herself become an
infant sucking on and trying to devour
Magda's blanket. With no choice
possible as to external action, she
retreats into herself entirely. But
nothing I can say could communicate

Only page references necessary because author (Ozick) is clear in the context.

Ellipsis signals an intentional omission.

Square brackets show that word not in original source has been added.

Surname 5

the final stage of her deterioration

as well as the last lines of the story

Blocked quotation indented ten spaces.

itself:

Regular double space before (and after) blocked quotation

so she took Magda's shawl

and filled her own mouth

with it, stuffed it in and

stuffed it in, until she was

swallowing up the wolf's

screech and tasting the

cinnamon and almond depth

of Magda's saliva; and Rosa

Citation after blocked quotation *follows* the final period.

drank Magda's shawl until

it dried. (8)

Two spaces

Rosa's steady deterioration to

this point, portrayed subtly and in

depth, communicates vividly the

effects of powerlessness on the mind

and spirit. Every human being needs a

sense of control, however minimal,

over his or her own life. Robbed of

this sense, the mind and spirit

wither. Stripped of autonomy, what

can the self do but, like Rosa, fall

into fantasy and then madness? How

Surname 6

truly terrible powerlessness is, but
especially in a world in which power
and not pity is the dominant force.

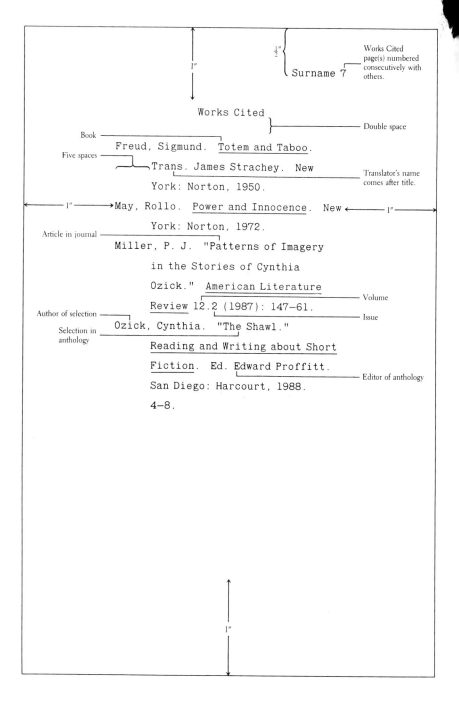

Works Cited page(s) numbered consecutively with others.

½ { Surname 7

1"

Works Cited
}— Double space

Book —
Freud, Sigmund. <u>Totem and Taboo</u>.
Five spaces —
Trans. James Strachey. New
Translator's name comes after title.
York: Norton, 1950.

— 1" — →May, Rollo. <u>Power and Innocence</u>. New ← — 1" —

York: Norton, 1972.

Article in journal —
Miller, P. J. "Patterns of Imagery

in the Stories of Cynthia

Ozick." <u>American Literature</u>
— Volume
Review 12.2 (1987): 147–61.
— Issue

Author of selection —
Ozick, Cynthia. "The Shawl."

Selection in anthology —
<u>Reading and Writing about Short</u>

<u>Fiction</u>. Ed. Edward Proffitt.
— Editor of anthology
San Diego: Harcourt, 1988.

4–8.

1"

Alternate Groupings for Comparison: Theme and Mode

581

Changing Times

Class Conflict

Comedy

The Family

Fantasy/The Surreal

Fate/Chance

Growing

Horror/Detective

Initiation

Insanity

Justice

The Modern World

Nature/Human Nature

Prejudice and Other Social Issues

Sexuality/Marriage

Stories about Stories

Tradition

Glossary of Literary and Writing Terms

Note: Terms printed in bold type have entries of their own to which the reader may wish to refer.

abstraction Any word that denotes a quality, a concept, a classification, or whatever without stimulating in the mind a particular sensation—for example, "edibles." Contrast **concretion**.

allegory A kind of symbolic work in which humans, animals, events, or whatever stand for and enact ideas in a consistent manner. See page 346.

allusion Mention of a figure, place, or other entity in our cultural heritage to evoke a certain meaning or set of associations in the mind of the reader. For example, to say "He is the Babe Ruth of songwriters" would suggest a writer with so many big "hits" as to be legendary.

ambiguity Anything that has two or more possible meanings simultaneously may be said to exhibit ambiguity. Purposeful ambiguity can enrich a text by its addition of another level of meaning. Unintentional ambiguity interferes with clarity.

analogy The explaining or interpreting of something by invoking its similarities to something of a different kind. To proceed by way of analogy (for example, in a thesis paragraph) is to stress likeness in order to lead to the point. **Metaphor** always entails analogy.

analytic prose Prose in which a subject is divided into its component parts or elements and examined accordingly.

authorial attitude The attitude or viewpoint reflected by a story (or other work) *as a whole* rather than through any single feature.

character/characterization "Character" refers to either a personage in a story or the psychological makeup of that personage. Our sense of character in fiction depends on "characterization," which refers to any technique whereby a story communicates the nature of its characters. Broadly, there are three types of literary character: **flat**, **round**, **stock**. For "characterization," see pages 155–157.

chronological organization The organization of a paragraph or an essay according to some time sequence. For instance, a paragraph or paper that moves from "at first" to "later" to "still later" to "at the last" is organized chronologically.

circumstantial irony   Refers to a discrepancy felt by the reader between what seems (or is expected) to be and what actually is, or between what is expected (or intended) to happen and what does happen. See page 273.

coherence   The sense that the relationship of parts in a piece of writing is logical and clear.

comparison and contrast   A prime way of understanding, comparison and contrast is also a tool of analysis. It entails focusing on the likenesses or differences, or both, between two or more things in order to see at least one of them with heightened clarity.

concretion   Any word, phrase, or aspect of a text that has immediate sensory effect. For example, "a juicy steak." Contrast **abstraction**.

conflict   Any struggle, internal or external, on the part of literary characters. If the struggle is external, it usually gives rise to **plot**. See pages 94–95.

connotation/denotation   Denotation is the literal meaning of a word—simply what it refers to. Connotation is what the word suggests or implies (through the associations it evokes in the reader's mind) in addition to what it denotes.

context   The whole passage or work in which a given detail is found and from which it gains meaning. The "cultural context"—the whole set of meanings, associations, and understandings in the heritage out of which the work grows—as well helps to shape the work's meaning and guide interpretation.

controlling element   Any element of fiction in a given text that is of particular importance in guiding the response of the reader. In comedy, for instance, **characterization** is often a controlling element.

conventional symbol   Any symbol that means what it means primarily by virtue of its cultural **context**. "Mom and apple pie," for instance, is a conventional symbol in the context of American culture: over and above its literal meaning, it suggests old-fashioned values, the good life, the American dream. See pages 343–344.

created symbol   Anything that is symbolic primarily by virtue of its literary **context**, which signals symbolic intent and guides and validates interpretation. See page 344.

denotation   See **connotation/denotation**.

denouement   The final outcome of the **conflict** and/or **plot** of a story. Etymologically, "denouement" means "unraveling."

dialogue   Any part of a literary work spoken by characters. See page 207.

diction   The choice of words, or the kind of words chosen, in a given passage or utterance. A few possible distinctions as to diction are: abstract/concrete; denotative/connotative; formal/colloquial; general/specific; technical/common. See page 275.

discourse/discursive   "Discourse" refers to verbal expression in speech or writing. "Discursive" refers specifically to that type of verbal expression that proceeds logically according to the principles and goals of **expository prose**.

discrete paragraph   A paragraph that is self-contained, that stands alone as a short composition in itself.

dramatic   Said of anything that communicates directly (that is, without comment) by virtue of what it is. Contrast **exposition/expository**.

dramatic irony   Refers to a discrepancy between what a character or narrator believes and what the reader knows to be true. See page 274.

enumeration   A way of organizing material that falls into parts. If, for instance, there are three reasons for believing something, then one can proceed by enumeration—first, second, and third.

exposition/expository   Any portion of a piece of fiction in which a narrator explains something is said to be part of the "exposition." **Expository prose** (as distinguished from prose fiction) is called "expository" because its main task is to explain. Contrast **dramatic**.

expository prose   Prose designed to explain or "expose" an idea in a clear, precise manner. The goal of expository prose is the setting forth of what the writer knows or holds to be true about a subject in such a way that the reader will grasp fully the meaning or point of the writer.

fable   A tale designed to illustrate some "moral" regarding human behavior. See pages 39–40.

fiction   A category of literature including such prose works as stories and novels—works that, though they may be based on fact, take their shape in the imagination. See pages 34–37.

figurative language   Any use of words not meant to be taken literally. A metaphor like "He is an ox" is an example. Compare **literal language**.

first-person narration   Narration in which the teller of the story is a character who refers to himself or herself as "I." First-person narrators can be either credible or unreliable. See pages 208–209.

flashback   A passage or episode that breaks the chronology of a work by taking us back to some moment in time earlier than the passage or episode we have been following. See pages 92–93.

flat character   Any character governed by a few characteristics alone, which remain constant over the course of a work. See pages 156–157.

foreshadowing   Said of anything in a text that prepares the reader for something later in that text.

genre   The category into which a literary work falls by virtue of its style, form, and purpose. Tragedy and comedy, for example, are distinct genres, as are poetry and prose fiction.

image/imagery   Images are verbal concretions (words that call up sensations) used to convey feelings as well as states of mind through sense impression. Often, images are used to form metaphors and symbols, which can help reinforce or determine a story's meaning.

informational prose   Prose the purpose of which is to convey information. For example, the consequences on the Jews of anti-Semitism in Nazi Germany could be the subject of an informational essay.

interior monologue   Any passage or story focused solely on a character's thoughts and feelings as revealed by that character in silent introspection.

irony   Refers to a discrepancy or incongruity between what is said and what is meant (verbal irony), between what seems to be and what actually is (circumstantial irony), or between what a character believes and what the reader knows to be true (dramatic irony). The virtue of irony as a literary device lies in its ability to direct attitude without discursive comment. See pages 272–274.

literal language   Any use of words meant to be taken strictly at face value. Contrast **figurative language**.

metaphor   A figure of speech that entails analogy. For example, "He's an ox" is a metaphor. Simile is a type of metaphor that includes an explicit term of comparison such as *like* or *as*: "He's strong as an ox." See also **analogy**.

mood   Describable by such adjectives as "lighthearted," "nostalgic," "humorous," "sad," and "tragic," mood is the feeling or feelings that a story has been designed to arouse in the reader.

motivation   An aspect of characterization involving a character's reasons for doing or thinking what is done or thought.

narration/narrator   "Narration" refers to how a tale is told; "narrator" refers to the teller. Stories are almost always told in the **first person** (with their tellers speaking of themselves as well as others) or the **third person** (with their tellers speaking of others only). The most important point to understand about narrators is that they do not necessarily speak for authors. The **authorial attitude** is expressed through the story as a whole, not through just one or another of its elements. See pages 206–207.

order of climax   The movement of a sentence, paragraph, or paper from less important details or support to more important. Order of climax is so important psychologically that whatever other type of order a paragraph or paper may follow, its parts should also be arranged if possible so that the most salient information comes at the end.

paradox   Any statement that seems to be self-contradictory but, upon analysis, turns out to be valid.

persona   Etymologically meaning "mask," the word "persona" is sometimes used to refer to a literary narrator, emphasizing the distinction between narrator and author.

persuasive prose   Prose designed chiefly to persuade the reader of the rightness of the writer's judgment.

plot   The sequence of events that constitutes the story line of a piece of fiction. Plot always entails causality. See pages 92–93.

point of view   The perspective devised by the author through which a story's characters, actions, setting, and so forth are presented to the reader. The basic narrative points of view are **first person** and **third person**. See pages 206–207.

proofreading   Reading over a piece of writing in order to correct errors in spelling, agreement, punctuation, and so forth. The final proofreading is for typographical errors.

protagonist   The central character in a literary work.

round character   Any character treated in some depth and developed so as to impart a sense of the actual complexity of human beings. See page 156.

sarcasm   A type of **verbal irony** used to show scorn.

satire   Writing, usually comic, that holds a subject up to ridicule.

setting   The location of a story as to place and time. Setting often allows a reader to infer a good deal about characters, and often a setting or a detail of a setting is used symbolically. See pages 340–341.

simile   See **metaphor.**

situation   Stories with little in the way of action or events are said to present a situation rather than a plot. Situational stories concern the inner lives of characters rather than their lives in the external world of action. See page 93.

spatial sequence   The organization of a paragraph or an essay according to the spatial relationship of the parts of the subject being considered. For example, one might describe the motor of a car from top to bottom. If a subject lends itself to spatial treatment, what one must do is to let the reader know how one is going to proceed and then proceed accordingly.

stock character   Any character that exhibits but one dominant trait or that is based on a stereotype. For instance, whether in white or black hats, cowboys in the movies tend to be stock. See page 157.

stream of consciousness   A narrative technique that renders the thoughts of a character, with all the jumps and inconsistencies that mark actual thought, as the character thinks them.

style   The sum of the choices a writer makes as to the selection of words (**diction**) and type of sentence structure (**syntax**). Style tends to be characteristic of a writer, though every writer adjusts style to fit character and circumstance. See pages 274–276.

subordination   The combining of ideas so that one is made grammatically dependent on the other by being put into a phrase or a subordinate clause. The purpose of subordination is to gain coherence as well as to reinforce a sense of unity by making prime information stand out.

support   The material used to exemplify or otherwise demonstrate the validity of a thesis. One can subdivide support material into major and minor, minor support serving to back up major support, which in turn backs up the governing thesis of paragraph or essay.

surreal/surrealistic/surrealism   Used in connection with any work that is dreamlike and that seems to tap the workings of the unconscious.

symbol   Anything in a text that, because of the literary and/or cultural **context**, conveys meaning different from (though usually related to) its literal meaning. The two broad types of symbol are **conventional** and **created**. Most texts contain "reinforcing symbols" (symbols that reflect and enhance the meaning established by characterization, plot, and so forth); in some texts, meaning is conveyed primarily by symbols, in which case the symbolism is "controlling." See pages 342–346.

syntax   The relationship of the position of words in sentences to meaning as well as the way in which words are put together to form various sentence patterns. In English, meaning is primarily determined by position: for example, "Dog bites man" versus "Man bites dog." As to sentence patterns, the two main types are loose (with the main information coming at the head) and periodic (with the main information coming last in the sentence). See page 275.

theme   The controlling attitude, insight, or point of a literary work. Theme should not be confused with a "moral" or a "message" or even a simple idea. It is, rather, what a story in its fullness is about. See pages 37–40.

thesis   The main point of a piece of **expository prose**; that which is being demonstrated, exemplified, discussed, or argued. A thesis, it should be noted, is not the same as a topic. A topic is what a thesis makes a statement about. "Cats" is a topic. "Cats are man's best friend" is a thesis.

third-person narration   Narration in which the teller of the story speaks of others exclusively and therefore stands entirely outside of the story. Third-person narrators can be omniscient, subjective, or objective. See pages 209–211.

tone   The way something is said as that way reveals the feelings or attitude of a narrator, other characters, or—taking the story as a whole—the author. See also **authorial attitude**.

topic   See **thesis**.

transition   Anything in a piece of writing that facilitates the movement from one segment to another.

unity   The sense that everything in a piece of writing relates to one central idea. A lack of unity results from the presence of extraneous material or material that seems unrelated to the central idea because the writer has failed to make the relationship clear.

verbal irony   Refers to any statement in which there is a discrepancy felt between what is said and what is meant. For example, on a rotten day someone might say, "Oh, what a beautiful day!" See page 273.

verisimilitude   Meaning "trueness to life," verisimilitude is a criterion of judgment of any text that is meant to be judged against life. Many texts, of course, are not realistic and so are not to be judged on this ground.

Works Cited

Chapter 1

O'Faolain, Sean. *The Short Story*. New York: Devin-Adair, 1951.

Chapter 3

Forster, E. M. *Aspects of the Novel*. New York: Harcourt, 1954.

Chapter 5

Maugham, Somerset. Preface. *Collected Stories*. Vol. 2. London: Penguin, 1963. 2 vols.

Copyrights and Acknowledgments

Index of Authors and Titles

D
E
F
G   4
H   5
I   6
J   7